STANLEY

·STANLEY·

Sorcerer's apprentice

Frank McLynn

Constable London

First published in Great Britain 1991
by Constable and Company Limited
3 The Lanchesters
162 Fulham Palace Road
London W6 9ER
Copyright © 1991 Frank McLynn
ISBN 0 09 470220 9
Set in Linotron Ehrhardt 11pt by
Rowland Phototypesetting Limited
Bury St Edmunds, Suffolk
Printed in Great Britain by
St Edmundsbury Press Limited
Bury St Edmunds, Suffolk

A CIP catalogue record for this book
is available from the British Library

• CONTENTS •

• ILLUSTRATIONS •

· PREFACE ·

The first volume of this two-volume biography of Henry Morton Stanley ended with his arrival at Boma, on the Lower Congo and within striking distance of the open Atlantic, in August 1877, after his epic journey down the hitherto uncharted Congo River. The moment of his greatest triumph was also a time of despair, for on 6 August he and his party were saved from starvation by a gigantic food hamper, despatched in answer to his distress message by Messrs Da Motta Veiga and Harrison of the trading firm Hatton and Cookson. It is at this point that we recommence the story of Stanley's 'stranger than fiction' life.

My acknowledgements remain the same as in *Stanley: the making of an African explorer*. I feel no further need to expatiate on a project designed to uncover the inner man behind the explorer's mask. To those sympathetic to the aims of psychobiography no apology is necessary. To those hostile no explanation would ever suffice.

Twickenham, February 1990

· 1 ·

Motta Veiga and Harrison, the Hatton and Cookson agents at Boma, were staggered to receive, out of the blue, Stanley's despairing plea for food on 5 August 1877.[1] But once they realised they were dealing with the man who had found Livingstone, and especially when the implications of Stanley's epic 999-day journey across Africa sank in, no expense was too great for them. Yet their hospitality at first met an uncomprehending response. Suffering from profound culture shock on re-emergence in 'civilisation', Stanley on arrival in Boma found himself unable to speak for several minutes as he regarded the sumptuous banquet laid out for him and his followers. He could not adjust to the demeanour and behaviour of white men. When the Dutch and Portuguese in Boma paid homage to him by carrying him in a hammock, he merely remarked coldly that it was an effeminate mode of travel.[2]

But two days of being fêted loosened up the misanthropic explorer, to the point where his hosts found him miraculously transformed from an uncommunicative recluse to a brilliant and witty conversationalist.[3] On 11 August the expedition embarked on the *Kabinda* which took them out on to the broad Atlantic and to the Portuguese port of the same name. The Portuguese housed their distinguished guest in a cottage overlooking the sea and set amid flowered gardens. Here the full force of culture trauma hit Stanley. Like many men who have achieved great things, Stanley discovered that the aftermath of success brought only melancholia and a sense of anti-climax. All seemed pointless and nothing worthwhile. His beloved Dickens now read like rubbish and the finest poetry appeared flat. The *wangwana* too were afflicted by this ennui, depression and *taedium vitae*. Four of them, apparently in good health, died inexplicably at Kabinda.[4]

At Kabinda Stanley met the Portuguese explorer Serpa Pinto, who was on the point of departing eastward for his own crossing of Africa. Serpa Pinto offered him onward transport on the gunboat *Tamega*, so after a stay of eight days that included a fresh round of banqueting, the Anglo-American expedition proceeded on 20 August to Sao Paulo de Loanda. There too they were generously treated; all 114 *wangwana*, including twelve women and some children, were lodged and boarded free until 27 September and the sick were tended in the government hospital. Stanley himself stayed in Serpa Pinto's house, discussing with the Portuguese explorer his projected route to Lake Nyara and Mozambique.[5] The two men had wide-ranging discussions on the slave trade, but when Serpa Pinto tried to get Stanley to sign a document stating that there was no slavery in Portuguese territories, he politely declined. When Stanley later indicted the Portuguese for their role in the trade, the commonest reaction was to brand him as an ingrate in the light of the hospitality he had enjoyed.[6]

Stanley now faced the problem of how he could keep faith with the *wangwana* and take them safely back to Zanzibar. He himself was offered immediate free passage to Lisbon, but he refused to desert his loyal followers. Just when it seemed that the only solution to the conundrum was another trek across the Dark Continent, the Royal Navy took a hand. Captain John Purvis of HMS *Danae* put in at Loanda with a small squadron and at once offered to take the expedition on board HMS *Industry* for the passage to Cape Town. On 27 September the expedition embarked. Once again they were the recipients of the utmost kindness and consideration. On 21 October *Industry* dropped anchor in Simon's Bay.[7]

Stanley's bad luck in making maritime connections was again in evidence. It turned out that they had just missed the eastbound sailing of the Royal Mail steamer *Natal*, so the expedition had to wait in Cape Town for *Industry* to be refitted. Stanley was accommodated at Admiralty House while the authorities wired London for instructions. The *wangwana* were housed in the Sailors' Home.[8]

The fortnight that followed was both interesting and restful. Cape journalists spent a lot of ink on the Victorian lion so unexpectedly in their midst. They found Stanley like Garnett Wolseley in appearance but much more charming and surprisingly gentle in manner and speech.[9] His devotion to his faithful Zanzibari followers was noted. During the day Stanley made sure they were kept interested with sightseeing or attending British Army target practice. When he was the guest of honour at a Chamber of Commerce banquet, attended by the Cape Colony

Prime Minister John Molteno, he insisted that the *wangwana* be brought into the room after dessert and their health drunk.[10] Next day the entire expedition went on an excursion by train to Stellensbosch. Since this was the Zanzibaris' first experience of rail travel, they were as much astonished by the speed of the train as Kalulu had been in France in 1872. Stellensbosch was a glittering social success, marred only by the pointed absence of the pro-Kirk Sir Bartle Frere. But Lady Frere broke rank with her husband by giving the *wangwana* a gift of blankets.[11]

The only cloud over the Cape Town sojourn was the opening ripple of the controversy over his methods in 1874–7 that was to engulf Stanley in England in 1878.[12] The response from London, too, was disappointing. The *Daily Telegraph* and the Admiralty made common cause in urging him to return home immediately, leaving the *wangwana* to be taken home by *Industry*.[13] The real fear in London was that the presence of the loud-mouthed and indiscreet Stanley in Zanzibar might upset delicate British relations with the Sultan. But Stanley was adamant that he had to see his men and women safely home. When *Industry* cleared Simon's Bay on 6 November for Zanzibar, to the accompaniment of fanfares and salutes from the assembled shipping in the harbour, Stanley was on board with his men.[14]

They made slow progress through stormy weather and high seas to Durban (reached on 12 November). *Industry* also put in at Mozambique, where for the first time Stanley learned the unflattering reasons why London did not want him to proceed to Zanzibar.[15] Then the ship beat up the East African coast and made landfall at Zanzibar on 28 November. There was great jubilation in the Zanzibari community at the return of their long-lost brethren; amid the euphoria of returnees and welcomers Stanley's stock rose very high. He further reinforced his reputation by paying off his expedition members meticulously and pursuing back claims for their pay while on the Livingstone expedition.[16]

This involved Stanley in delicate negotiations with his old enemy John Kirk. Kirk made as many difficulties as he could in the way of a swift resolution of the 1872 contracts. While Stanley tried to mend fences with Kirk, Kirk responded with caustic malice. The tenor of relations between the two can be gauged from letters from Stanley to Kirk and from Kirk to the Foreign Office. Here is Stanley on 1 December: 'You are correct in your belief that it will give me pleasure to distribute these medals to the survivors of Dr Livingstone's last journey, but I assure you that it would be a still greater pleasure to be a mere witness while you personally distributed them.'[17] Kirk's response to this was a spiteful despatch to London reporting Stanley's interview with the Sultan: '- Stanley discoursed at length on the many collisions he had had with the native tribes, who seem everywhere to have given way before Snider rifles and repeaters.'[18]

Once aware of the hostility from his old foe, Stanley kept his distance, mixed socially with Augustus Sparhawk and his coterie, and gave advice to the two expeditions that had recently arrived at Zanzibar for the purpose of penetrating East Africa – respectively from the London Missionary Society and Belgium (under the auspices of the Association Internationale Africaine).[19] It soon became clear that the wrangling over the 1872 contracts would take some time to resolve. Stanley therefore availed himself of the stateroom that William Mackinnon had booked for him on the British East India steamer *Pachumba*. After an emotional farewell from the *wangwana* he departed for Aden on 13 December.[20]

On 23 December the ship reached Aden and a week later anchored off Suez. Stanley disembarked and made his way to Cairo, where he was to be received by the Khedive. As ever, he made his base at Shepheard's Hotel.[21] On 4 January he was received in formal audience by Ismail, who awarded him the Egyptian Order of Medjijeh. But next day came a meeting that meant much more to Stanley. Ex-president Ulysses S. Grant, Union commander during Stanley's baptism of fire at Shiloh in 1862, arrived at Alexandria on 5 January 1878, *en route* to Cairo and the Nile. During a three-day sojourn at Alexandria, Grant asked to be introduced to Stanley. The introduction was easily effected, for John Russell Young, managing editor of the *New York Herald*, was accompanying Grant and his wife Julia on a round-the-world tour and Bennett had suggested that Young might meet the returning Stanley somewhere in the Middle East.[22]

Accordingly, on the evening of 5 January Stanley sat down aboard Grant's yacht in Alexandria roads to a dinner of twelve covers. Stanley accounted it one of the proudest moments of his life to be the guest of honour, seated on the right-hand side of America's greatest hero. Grant toasted his fellow-American's achievements in the Dark Continent.[23] A thin and grey-haired Stanley answered with great charm and tact. Next day Young saw him depart for Brindisi and Europe.

At Brindisi Stanley was pressed to make a detour to Marseilles to receive honours that that city proposed to shower on him. The prime mover in this scheme was Alfred Rabaud, president of the Marseilles Geographical Society, a man with business interests in Zanzibar.[24]

Stanley acquiesced and arrived in Marseilles on 13 January. Next day he attended a civic reception in his honour and received three gold medals from local geographical societies. A vast crowd accompanied him next day to the station for a repeat of the rail journey to Paris that had so enthralled Kalulu in 1872.[25] At the Gare de Lyon a vast and enthusiastic crowd greeted him. Throughout 15–22 January he was feted and lionised, the toast of Parisian society.

Stanley was swept unwillingly into a heady social whirl. Banquet followed reception and reception followed soirée. The publisher Edward Marston caught up with him at the Hôtel Meurice, then accompanied him to a reception in the Parc Monceau, where the élite of Paris 'fair women and brave men' had gathered to pay him tribute. Stanley walked down a long avenue of his admirers with great reluctance, looking more like a chained lion at an exhibition than a conquering hero.[26]

There followed honours from all the French geographical societies and a massive reception by the chocolate baron M. Meusnier, which Stanley left early. By the end of the week Marston found him at the end of his tether. He used his boredom and *taedium vitae* to advantage to conclude a favourable agreement on the publication of a book to be called *Through the Dark Continent*. The final reception in the Parisian social round, at the Hôtel du Louvre, found Stanley depressed and suffering from severe feelings of anti-climax and loneliness. He remarked bitterly to Marston: 'What is the good of all this pomp and show? It only makes me more miserable and unhappy.'[27] He was relieved to steal away across the Channel and ensconce himself in London at 30 Sackville Street.[28]

What were the main consequences of Stanley's epic 999-day crossing of Africa? Apart from the personal career consequences to himself, his unique feat of exploration can be considered under three main headings: its impact on Africa, its contribution to geographical knowledge, and its effect on Stanley's reputation.

We have already had occasion to mention the impact of Stanley on individual African societies,[29] but something more needs to be said about the way he affected the general political ecology of Central Africa. Basically, his effect was twofold: he increased European interest in Africa as a possible focus for exploitation; and, albeit unconsciously, he tightened the grip of the slavers on the area.

Stanley's arrival at the court of Mutesa seriously unsettled the balance of power in the Uganda/Equatoria region. Much of Gordon's gubernatorial period in Equatoria in 1876 was taken up with speculation on

Stanley's intentions. He saw Stanley as a rival, someone in the service of the Sultan of Zanzibar, who planned to plant the Zanzibar standard on Lakes Victoria and Albert.[30] Gordon aimed to beat him to the punch by setting up the Egyptian flag there instead. This was the reason for the expedition of Romolo Gessi, who in April 1876 circumnavigated Lake Albert in the teeth of heavy gales. Gessi penetrated Unyoro and raised the Egyptian flag at Magungo.[31] This confirmed Mutesa's worst fears: that his kingdom might be menaced by an alliance of Gordon and Kabba Rega; therein lies the real explanation for his excessive cordiality to Stanley, for he planned to harness the Anglo-American expedition as a counterweight to the putative threat from Bunyoro and Equatoria.[32] Naturally, when Stanley disappeared south as suddenly and mysteriously as he had come, all the political actors in Uganda and its environs were nonplussed, Gordon not least.[33]

But although Stanley was not destined to be a short-term military factor in Central Africa, in the long term his influence was enormous. His spectacular progress from one side of the Dark Continent to the other excited the interest of the most heterogeneous groups: missionaries, speculators, imperial expansionists. Missionaries were drawn to Africa not just by Stanley's explicit call for proselytising in Uganda but by the undreamed-of opportunities revealed by his perilous passage of the Congo in 1877.[34] There was considerable irony here, for Stanley's attitude to missionaries was at best ambivalent and at worst downright hostile.[35]

What Stanley's epic 1874–7 journey *did* show clearly was the enormous fortune to be made from ivory and slaves. Although the first ivory seekers and slave traders from Zanzibar first reached the Upper Congo basin in the late 1860s (there are traces of elephant hunters on the Uele River in 1867)[36], it was Stanley's 'Through the Dark Continent' expedition that truly unlocked the region. In doing so, the expedition also exposed the weakness of potential indigenous resistance. Backward African societies produced only a limited agricultural surplus, so that even a minor impact like that of the Anglo-American expedition produced local inflation and imposed a severe strain on resources. Nor did it escape the notice of ivory hunters and slave traders that the apparent wealth of the invaders often aroused the cupidity of regional warlords. This gave an opportunity for corruption and co-option to the looters. Moreover, as Stanley himself recognised, the demoralising effect of his firepower was such as to make the Congo peoples less inclined to resist the Arab slavers when they appeared on the scene.[37]

While European capitalists were debarred for obvious reasons from benefiting from the slave trade, no such consideration applied to ivory. East African ivory, and later that of the Congo, was soft, ideal for carving, and in great demand in Europe for knife handles, piano keys, billiard balls and to satisfy the Victorian love of ornate décor and furnishing. Ivory inlay work ranged from ivory-handled umbrellas to snuffboxes and chessmen. In Latin countries ivory was used in many articles: fans, fingerboards for Spanish guitars, keys of Italian accordions, carved boudoir articles. There were flourishing ivory-carving centres at Dieppe, St Claude in the Jura, Geislingen in Wurtemberg and Erbach in Hesse, specialising in the production of miniature ornaments, statuettes, crucifixes, mathematical instruments, book covers, combs and serviette rings. Ivory was also used for false teeth until porcelain came in in the latter half of the nineteenth century. In the USA it was particularly favoured for piano and organ keys and especially for billiard and bagatelle balls, to the point where the USA took 80 per cent of the soft ivory exported from Zanzibar in 1894.[38] Because ivory is elastic and flexible and can be cut into almost any shape, nothing was wasted from the tusks. Scraps and even dust could be used for Indian ink and ivory jelly. Not surprisingly, therefore, the opening up of the vast elephant herds in the Congo and Sudan soon led to the near-extinction of the unfortunate animals. By the late 1890s most of the Congo herds had been 'shot out' and Leopold's state had to turn to wild rubber as its principal resource.[39]

The only apparent deterrent to would-be interlopers in Central Africa was the plethora of tales of cannibalism that abounded in Europe. Quite how widespread this practice was in the Congo region and what its effects were is a much disputed question. Some have even claimed that the whole notion of cannibalism was a myth, and that the legend arose from misunderstandings by explorers and missionaries, misunderstandings often actively abetted by local chiefs who tried to discourage Europeans from trading with rival tribes by spreading the canard that they were cannibals.[40] A second source of misunderstanding was the fact that in most of the languages of the area the expression for killing someone by witchcraft was 'eating'; hence statements about witchcraft were often construed as statements about cannibalism.[41] Yet the argument cannot be pushed too far. It is true that stories of cannibalism have to be approached with caution, but the thesis of its absolute non-existence cannot be sustained. Not only is there simply too much evidence from European travellers whose evidence on other aspects of African culture is unimpeachable.[42] More tellingly, modern African research itself confirms the existence of nineteenth-century cannibalism.[43] So the armchair critics who scoffed at Stanley's accounts of *Niama, niama* ('Meat, meat') were being too clever by half.

This brings us to the question of Stanley's geographical discoveries in general during 1874–7. Curiously, although the charting of the unknown Congo was clearly Stanley's greatest achievement, British lack of interest in the Congo led the luminaries of the Royal Geographical Society to assess Stanley as a geographer mainly through the far easier circumnavigation of the great lakes of East Africa. The definitive settling of the Nile issue confirmed Speke's stature as an explorer, to the joy of his confrère James Grant. He described Stanley's circumnavigation of Lake Victoria as 'one of the most important and brilliant that has ever been made in Central Africa or indeed in any other country . . . who amongst us would have had his energy? Who would undertake a cruise in an open boat to absent himself from his camp for fifty-eight days? Who would risk such danger to life and exposure to an African sun in the month of April? Who of us are able to guide, provide for, lead and attend to a little army successfully, and in the midst of all this, take their observations for latitude and longitude?'[44] Sir Rutherford Alcock endorsed the sentiments: 'Mr Stanley had been marvellous as an explorer, but he had now shown that he was still more remarkable as a geographer. They would have to search far in the history of geographical discovery before they could find a man equally successful as an active explorer and as an intelligent observer.'[45] Even the man most adversely affected by Stanley's discoveries, Richard Burton, put a brave face on things and claimed that Stanley's exploration of Lake Victoria vindicated both him *and* Speke, as it demonstrated that the big lake itself was fed by smaller ones.[46]

Yet, inevitably with Stanley, there were critics even in the areas where he was on the strongest ground. Some of this was mere nit-picking, as when Edward Hore criticised Stanley for identifying the otters on Lake Tanganyika as 'water hyenas'.[47] Others were able to query his maps and observations simply because they spent years in a region where Stanley had spent weeks only. Schweinfurth, for instance, thought that his astronomical 'fixes' placed the Congo too far to the north.[48] His maps were found to be impressionistic rather than the work of a precisian.[49] But, as so often, the great African missionary Mackay, who came to know Lake Victoria better than any other white man, had the last word: 'Stanley's charts are wonderful for the short time he had at his disposal, but extremely inaccurate so far as I have been able to test them.'[50]

The truth surely was that all fair-minded explorers were prepared to concede the greatness of Stanley's achievement; Joseph Thomson vindicated his findings on the Lukuga, Harry Johnston on the Lakes and the Congo, and so on.[51] It was generally conceded that the quest for the ultimate source of the Nile was a pursuit of a will o' the wisp or philosopher's stone.[52] It was mainly his sworn enemies who found excessive fault. One can almost sense the smacking of the lips in Kirk's report on Commander Wharton's 1877 exploration of the Rufiji: 'Mr Stanley's description is now found to be exaggerated and inaccurate, nor did he succeed in reaching as far as Captain Elton's crossing at Mpembeno.'[53] The other tactic for Stanley's enemies was to damn with faint praise or to insinuate that anyone equipped with his resources could have done as well. After stating that Stanley's charting of Lake Victoria alone would have entitled him to a very high place among African explorers, Sir Henry Rawlinson drew attention to the munificence of the *Daily Telegraph* and the *New York Herald*: 'such munificence far transcends the efforts of private individuals in the cause of science,' he added archly, in a self-congratulatory reference to the RGS.[54]

But sometimes Stanley was his own worst enemy and deliberately drew the fire of his critics. He was accused of breach of etiquette by Sir Rutherford Alcock because he proposed to rename the Alexandra Nile which had already been explored by Speke and Grant, because he arbitrarily changed some of Speke's nomenclature and failed to carry Speke's *Discovery of the Nile* with him out of arrogant disdain.[55] This, it was alleged, was because Stanley the journalist always needed some 'new discovery' to adorn his latest *Herald* despatch. In retaliation the RGS refused to rename the River Congo the 'Livingstone'[56] Even worse in his enemies' eyes was his lofty contempt for Verney Cameron, whom Stanley charged with leaving the Lualaba question exactly where Livingstone had found it.[57] This drew from Cameron himself the stinging barb that in order to descend the Congo he would have had to connive at Tippu Tip and the slave trade, as Stanley had done.[58]

None of these criticisms made a serious dent in Stanley's reputation as explorer and geographer. It was left to later scholars to point to the flaws in Stanley's account of Central Africa: how he had at once underestimated the area of the Congo basin while overestimating its population.[59] Nor could anyone but the closest student of Stanley appreciate how he had played down the achievements of two other white men. In *Through the Dark Continent* he makes no mention of having met the Swiss trader Philippe Broyon at Mpwapwa, lest any other European appear to share the limelight.[60] And he suppresses the fact that during the march through Bunyoro Frank Pocock claimed to have seen a snow-capped mountain (probably Ruwenzori)[61], lest some other white man later take the credit for what could turn out to be an important discovery.

In 1878 nobody seriously disputed Stanley's claim to be, on paper and in a purely technical sense, the greatest of African explorers. What seemed to contemporaries to vitiate his claim was the appalling brutality he had allegedly visited on the benighted savages of Africa. When it was proposed that the RGS again honour Stanley, all the pent-up fury and resentment towards Stanley in liberal and humanitarian circles, suppressed since 1876, burst out anew.

The *casus belli* between Stanley and his enemies was the attack on Bumbire Island in 1875. Stanley's original stance on this encounter was that the first attack on his party by the islanders justified his later retaliation: 'With such people as the Wanyaturu and Bumbireh what can a man do, for they will listen to no overtures of peace or amity.'[62] But when his account of the slaying of forty-two Bumbire tribesmen was published in the *Daily Telegraph*, the Anti-Slavery and Aborigines Protection Societies jointly protested to the Foreign Office, pointing out that the use of explosive bullets was forbidden in civilised warfare and that Stanley's sole motive was revenge. They wanted a clear statement that the British government did not condone such behaviour.[63] For all that, their own words were hardly the restrained ones of Christianity and civilisation, for they suggested that Stanley be returned to the scene of the crime and hanged there, with the expedition's goods being auctioned off to compensate the inhabitants.[64]

There was little the British government could do. Stanley was (so far as they knew) an American citizen and the alleged atrocities had occurred in unexplored territory. But Kirk took great delight in sending on the Earl of Derby's admonition to Stanley that he had no right to use the British flag to give his actions a cloak of legitimacy.[65] Since Stanley was already launched on the Lualaba by the time this was sent, not surprisingly the message never reached him.[66]

But Stanley's own reports from Bumbire provided his critics with a field day. Burton wrote smugly to Kirk: 'Of course you have seen Stanley who still shoots negroes as if they were monkeys. That young man will be getting into a row – and serve him right. I have, somehow or other, serious doubts how far his assertions are to be believed.'[67] Yet Burton's strictures were mild alongside those of the socialist writer H. M.

Hyndman, who had begun a vehement anti-Stanley crusade in the *Pall Mall Gazette* in December 1875.[68] At an RGS meeting on 13 November 1876 Hyndman tried to introduce a resolution censuring Stanley but was ruled out of order. Seeing the storm clouds gather, Stanley's friends in the Society tried to close ranks. Edwin Arnold stressed that no RGS gold medallist could conceivably be condemned unheard.[69]

On 27 November Hyndman returned to the attack. He read some extracts from the *Daily Telegraph* to an RGS meeting and asked for an opinion on them. Sir Henry Rawlinson again ruled him out of order, on the grounds both that Hyndman was not raising an issue of practical geography – the Society's only remit – and that Stanley was not a member of the RGS nor even a British citizen, but simply a gold medallist.[70] Another gold medallist, Henry Yule, then got to his feet to support Hyndman and chide Rawlinson for hiding behind points of order. The matter was settled when the influential figure of Sir Bartle Frere – no friend to Stanley – arose to request that the RGS move on to its ostensible business of Gordon and the Upper Nile, adding that Hyndman was wrong to raise such a contentious issue.[71] The general feeling was that an honourable draw had resulted: the RGS had not censured Stanley but they had certainly scotched the idea that they gave Stanley unqualified approval.[72] Sir Rutherford Alcock summed up: 'There was not, he thought, two shades of opinion as to the conduct of Mr Stanley. The Earl of Derby had well expressed the opinion of the whole nation when he said that the letters of the explorer had created a most painful feeling throughout the country.'[73]

This criticism of Stanley was grist to the mill of Bennett and the *New York Herald*. Bennett had no fellow-feeling for Stanley, but he hated the British and this campaign against his star reporter gave him an opportunity to whip up the most virulent anti-British American chauvinism and to pour scorn on 'the howling dervishes of civilisation . . . safe in London.'[74] When Stanley arrived at the Atlantic coast in August 1877, the *Herald* commented: 'This will greatly distress the philanthropists of London who will again appeal to the British government to declare him a pirate. Their humane but rather impractical view is that a leader in such a position should permit his men to be slaughtered by the natives and should be slaughtered himself and let discovery go to the dogs, but should never pull a trigger against this species of human vermin that puts its uncompromising savagery in the way of all progress and all increase of knowledge.'[75]

There matters rested until Stanley's return to England in January

1878. To the fury of Hyndman, Yule and the other critics, the RGS proposed to welcome the explorer with open arms, to invite him to speak at the Society without asking for an explanation of his actions at Bumbire.[76] Yule and Hyndman, abetted by Stanley's old enemy Horace Waller, protested bitterly to the Society and threatened to resign if the lecture went ahead.[77] The duo found a receptive home for their anti-Stanley diatribes in the *Pall Mall Gazette* where they lucidly laid out the basis of their charges: for them the issue was not the bloody descent of the Congo, nor whether newspapers should finance African expeditions, nor even the use of explosive bullets or the British flag; it was purely the justifiability of the attack on Bumbire. Yule's indictment was made sharper by his testimony to Stanley's virtues. Stanley, he pointed out, had 'done great deeds and shown great qualities. Mr Stanley's faithful adherence to people who had faithfully served him, till he saw them safe home to Zanzibar is (for example) a rare and noble trait of character.'[78]

In Zanzibar, Kirk, sensing that the time for vengeance had come, launched a full-blooded broadside against his erstwhile tormentor. All of Kirk's correspondents at this time received their share of Stanley-bashing. To the secretary of the RGS he wrote in warning: 'The RGS will make fools of themselves with that fellow once more no doubt . . . he has not wit enough to resist the temptation and learn a lesson that it did not pay before.'[79] To Mackinnon, Stanley's friend, Kirk penned the following 'statesmanlike' lines: 'Stanley is now on his way home. He is the same old man as he was before, pugnacious, conceited and small-minded. He is a fool not to see that he has done enough to be above, and can gain most by dropping, all petty squabbles.'[80] But to Waller, who concurred with him in finding Stanley detestable, Kirk urged caution: 'As to Stanley I see he is the lion of all lions and his position made – I hope now you will do nothing to attack him, you cannot injure him and it will only make him ten times a welcome lion if he has a few detractors.'[81]

But when Stanley swept all his critics before him in England, Kirk changed his tune and forgot his sage advice to Waller. Together with the Revd Farler of the Universities Mission to Central Africa he nagged away at the Zanzibari participants in the expedition until he was able to produce a farrago of slander and downright lies about Stanley.[82] He alleged that the attacks on the Congo descent were gratuitous, that Frank Pocock took a black girl as his mistress and fathered a child on her, that Mutesa presented Stanley with a nubile slave girl as his mistress (anyone who knew Stanley would see the absurdity of that one), that Stanley kicked and beat a man to death and employed a permanent chain gang. The only solid indictment in Kirk's charge sheet was the assault on Bumbire. But Kirk worked himself up into a fine old lather and finished with a flourish: 'If the story of this expedition were known, it would stand unequalled in the annals of African discovery for the reckless use of the power that modern weapons placed in his hands over natives who never before had heard a gun fired . . . the doings of Mr Stanley on this expedition were a disgrace to humanity . . . his proceedings will prove one of the principal obstacles that the future explorers and missionaries will have to meet when following up his track.'[83]

What particularly enraged Kirk was the way Stanley had swept over his enemies at a meeting of the RGS at St James's Hall on 7 February. Despite many protests and resignations from members, Stanley spoke to his own brief and even had the temerity to lash out at his critics.[84] Once again, as in 1872, the intervention of the Royal Family had effectively crushed opposition. The Prince of Wales was present to hear Stanley dilate on his achievements in the Dark Continent.[85] This muzzled would-be objectors, for it was considered unseemly and even indecent for anyone to disrupt the decorum and dignity of such an occasion by interventions from the floor. The press was particularly angered by what it considered a machiavellian RGS ploy to avoid facing the vital issue of whether geographical ends warranted barbarous means.[86]

On 10 February, at a grand dinner given in Willis's Rooms by the assembled Fellows of the RGS, Stanley returned to the fray. Point by point he dealt with the charges against him. He asserted that the attack on Bumbire was essential to protect his flank during the passage to Uganda, and moreover: 'Where I failed to make peace, Livingstone would have failed and where I have made friendships with natives I made firmer and more lasting friendships than even Livingstone himself could have made.'[87] Lord Houghton presiding gently chided Stanley for raising the matter at all and stated airily that the views of a few malcontents did not represent the position of the RGS. But next day the *Pall Mall Gazette* ran a blistering leader, pointing out that in his arrogance Stanley still did not appreciate that he was condemned from his own mouth, that the sole source for the indictment against him was his despatches to the *Daily Telegraph*. The thesis of self-defence would not hold, for 'a European traveller penetrating into a country inhabited by savage tribes is, whatever the services he may be seeking to render civilisation, an intruder. He is not, as so many European philanthropists appear to suppose, the natural lord of the soil in mere virtue of his white skin. Its black possessors have a perfect right to resist his invasion if they choose; and should they do so, we entirely deny that as a "pioneer of civilisation" he is entitled in the name of this mission, to force his way through them by the use of elephant rifles and explosive bullets.'[88]

The controversy rumbled on throughout 1878. Another old enemy, Francis Galton, ingeniously posed the question of the basis in international law for the levying of war by a newspaper correspondent.[89] Stanley's friends and most of his fellow explorers rallied round him. Gordon hit the nail on the head when he said: 'He is to blame for *writing* what he did (as Baker was). These things may be done but not advertised.'[90] Similarly, Baker turned the argument from self-indictment on its head: 'I always declared that the very fact of Mr Stanley's publishing the details of his various encounters with the natives proved that he must have considered them unavoidable – otherwise he would most naturally have concealed them from the public.'[91] Predictably, Stanley was much more intemperate than his friends and allies. The flavour of his various 'apologies' can best be gauged from the following later outburst: 'He only wished he could get every member of Exeter Hall (headquarters of the Evangelical movement) to explore by the same route he had gone from the Atlantic to longitude 23. He would undertake to provide them with seven tons of bibles, any number of surplices, and a church organ into the bargain, and if they reached as far as longitude 23 without chucking some of the bibles at the Negroes' heads, he would . . . '.[92]

How cogent were the criticisms by Stanley's enemies? It was true that he could be found guilty of humbug for the frequent references to Jesus Christ and God while he mowed down Africans with superior firepower.[93] But many of the charges against him were overstated and thus failed to stick. He did not deliberately recruit slaves for his expedition, nor did he encourage his men to loot, as Lugard later alleged.[94] Criticisms of Stanley for brutality during the descent of the Congo are also wide of the mark, as here he was genuinely running the gauntlet. There remains the attack on Bumbire, for which Stanley pleaded military necessity. Unfortunately for him, the argument will not stand up, and we are left with the inescapable conclusion that Stanley attacked the island out of motives of revenge. At one level he had to reassert his power and credibility in the eyes of the *wangwana* and those of Mutesa's lieutenants. But at a deeper level the fountain of unconscious rage from his childhood bubbled over into a murderous assault on those who thwarted him. The 'blind hate' he ascribed to his critics is better laid at his own door.[95]

The most judicious conclusion is that Stanley's critics won the argument on points. At the very best, as his friends and defenders saw, he was guilty of gross insensitivity.[96] Moreover, there was a gaping hole at the very centre of the defences constructed by his apologists. Even if it was conceded that the assault on Bumbire was justified through military exigencies, this in turn raised the question of whether African expeditions themselves were justified at such a price. As the *Saturday Review* ironically put it: 'Perhaps the Geographical Society cannot exist without rivers, and it may be so noble an institution that all the horrors of war must be perpetrated rather than that it should perish.'[97] Moreover, the one organ that could not logically defend Stanley for Bumbire was the *Daily Telegraph*, currently the scourge of the Turks for their atrocities in the Balkans.

The first six months of 1878, while Stanley worked away on the book that would become *Through the Dark Continent*, marked a watershed in his life. He gradually turned away from both England and the United States and towards Europe. England had failed him in 1872 when he returned from finding Livingstone and it failed him again now in the aftermath of his greatest triumph. In his own mind Stanley was the man who had achieved an epic river voyage of 1800 miles from Nyangwe to the sea, fighting thirty-two battles as he went – an 'Odyssey of wandering and an Iliad of combat' as Sir Grant Duff put it.[98] But his enemies concentrated on the cost of the achievement: all his white companions dead, seventy-seven *wangwana* dead and sixty-two desertions. Stanley retorted that Tuckey had lost eighteen Europeans and eleven blacks in three months on the Congo, on the Peddie Niger expedition all the principals lost their lives, while in 1805 the entire Mungo Park force had been wiped out.[99] Moreover, most English attention was in any case focused on Bumbire, not on the Congo River journey.

The attitude to Stanley in England in 1878 was at best ambivalent. True he was laden with honours: a second Royal Medal and Honorary Corresponding Membership from the RGS, the patronage of the Prince of Wales, decorations from the French and even a resolution of thanks from the US Congress.[100] But in liberal circles he was regarded as a man of blood. The split in élite opinion was vividly conveyed at his February address to the RGS. While Sir Edwin Arnold's family stitched together four large sheets to hang in Burlington Hall during Stanley's address, there were 200 vacant seats in the hall, even though the Prince of Wales was present.[101]

The other factor that depressed Stanley was that the Anglo–Saxon world showed no interest whatever in opening up and exploiting the Congo basin. Moreover, his association with James Gordon Bennett was also drawing to a close. Accumulated arrears on his salary from 1 August 1874 to 31 December 1877 provided him with forced savings of £3416 13s 4d. – an almost princely lump sum by the working standards of the day. There was also the prospect of substantial sales from *Through the Dark Continent*, at which he worked assiduously from February to the end of May. In eighty days he averaged over fourteen pages of manuscript a day, producing a total of 1147 pages. The Stanley diary for this period is almost a blank. Consequently he was able to take a much more detached and relaxed view of Bennett's ideas for his future. In the field of discovery Bennett's true love was polar exploration, and in February 1878 he proposed to Stanley that he cap his African exploits by a dash to the North Pole.[102] But when Stanley probed to see exactly what level of financial commitment Bennett was prepared to sanction, he found the old 'Jamie' niggardliness and petty jealousy at work. It was clear that not enough money was being injected to make the polar project a success. Stanley therefore resigned forthwith from Bennett's service.[103]

Bruised by his reception in England, Bennett's attitude, and the blow to his prestige by the public revelation by the *New York Times* of his failure with Alice Pike[104], Stanley entered a limbo period until June 1878, comparable with the similar fallow time in early 1873. In 1873 he had been prised out of his lethargy by the Carlist wars in Spain. In 1878 it was again Europe that prised him from his dogmatic slumbers, this time in the seemingly unlikely guise of King Leopold II of Belgium.

2

A MORE unlikely candidate as standard-bearer of 'civilisation' in the Dark Continent than the Duke of Brabant, Leopold II of the Belgians would be difficult to imagine. Overweight and bearded like an Old Testament patriarch, Leopold was a liar, swindler, lecher and master of machiavellianism. This was the man who was to be the architect of Stanley's fortunes during the last half of his life, yet he as clearly called forth the dark side of Stanley's nature as Livingstone had elicited the good. The only characteristic Leopold shared with Livingstone was that they were both 'heavy grubbers' – Leopold indeed would regularly eat an extra entrée on impulse just after consuming a heavy meal.

Leopold's interest in Africa was evident from the early 1870s but quickened after the meeting of the International Geographical Congress in Paris in August 1875. The Congress's Economic Subcommittee put forward a plan for colonising Africa by regrouping indigenous tribal organisation into communities headed by a handful of Europeans. Each of these European 'cells' could provide a controlling nucleus, leading the benighted Africans by their example and introducing modern production techniques.[1] Leopold was excited by this idea: it involved direct control, not merely 'indirect rule' with a class of native collaborators. He was even more alerted to the possibilities in Central Africa when the French explorer Brazza suggested the establishment of an international organisation to compass the Economic Subcommittee's ends.

The dream of personal empire was born early in Leopold's brain. He knew enough about his own countrymen (with whom he was decidedly unpopular) to realise that they would not rise to some chimerical bait of economic opportunity, so decided to use sentiment against the slave trade to mask his ulterior designs. In May 1876 he crossed to England to consult with Africanists there, including Stanley's friend Baroness

Burdett-Coutts. He encountered no opposition to his 'humanitarian' ideas in élite circles.[2] Apart from high indignation about the slave trade, Leopold found two further encouraging signs during his British talks. One was an inclination to blame the Portuguese for all instances of exploitative behaviour in Africa. The other was a clear British lack of interest in the Congo area. Cameron's 'annexation' of the Katanga area in the name of Queen Victoria had been brutally repudiated by the Foreign Office: one official minuted against the proposal 'not in our generation'.[3] Immediately the King of the Belgians tried to co-opt Verney Cameron. Hearing that the explorer was short of money, he offered to pay his fare back to Europe.[4]

Elated by the discovery of a power vacuum at the very heart of Africa, Leopold next called an international conference in Brussels. This was a triumph of public relations. By brilliant stage-management, dexterous flattery and ego-massaging, Leopold manipulated his guests from each nationality to the point where they were prepared to fall in with his proposals. They acquiesced in his proposal to set up an international body to combat the slave trade and bring light to the Dark Continent. There would be an International Commission under a president and chairman (Leopold, naturally), to direct through an executive committee of four the various national committees, whose task would be to propagandise and fund-raise for the great 'humanitarian' work. The name of the organisation would be the Association Internationale Africaine (AIA) and its first job would be to establish bases at Zanzibar and the Congo mouth, with the aim of working from both coasts of Africa towards the benighted interior.[5]

Immediately Leopold showed his contempt for legal forms. The chairmanship was supposed to rotate annually among the member countries and the International Executive Committee was supposed to be the decision-making body. This committee met just once, in 1877, promptly broke its own rules by re-electing Leopold to the chair and was never heard of again. The putative nexus of International Committee–Executive Committee–National Committees soon became a purely Belgian hierarchy with Leopold at the top. It was already clear that the AIA was a 'spurious exploring and scientific organisation'.[6]

To finance his bogus association's work, Leopold turned to his favourite fund-raising ploy: lotteries. In early 1877 he proposed a lottery of $3,500,000: $2,000,000 for the association's work in Africa, $1,000,000 for the lottery winners and $500,000 for 'expenses'.[7] But by this time Leopold was seriously concerned about British opposition to his designs.

The British government objected to the AIA on the grounds that suppression of the slave trade was a matter for nation-states, not private organisations; that the organisation was not under British control; and that, as in India, commercial activity would inevitably lead to colonisation.[8] As ever, when he was concerned about his failure to sway British public opinion, Leopold addressed himself directly to the Royal Family.[9]

Even at this stage some people saw what Leopold's game really was. Greindl, Belgian Minister in Madrid, correctly analysed the King's crude personal ambitions at an early stage – the giveaway sign was Leopold's frenzied opposition to the suggestion that a non-Belgian could ever be Secretary-General of the AIA.[10] The most Leopold would ever concede privately was that the AIA was a Trojan horse for *Belgian* interests. The real problem for the King was how to divest himself of Belgium so that he could obtain a *personal* African empire. Fortunately for him, there was great opposition in Belgium to the AIA, especially from the Catholic Church, which suspected it of being a front for freemasonry. All that remained, then, for Leopold was to perform a feat of prestidigitation, so that an organisation ostensibly founded to combat the slave trade could be converted into the instrument for acquiring a personal colony in Africa. The wealth extracted from Africa, in turn, would enable him to convert the Belgian monarchy into an independently funded institution, owing nothing to Parliament. This was monarchy as capitalism – what has been termed the 'King Incorporated'.[11] The key to this was continuous confusion, camouflage and obfuscation.

It was at this stage in his grand design that Leopold first began to take an interest in the achievements of Stanley and from June 1877 he watched with caught breath to see whether the explorer would emerge at the Atlantic.[12] When Stanley arrived at Boma in August 1877, Leopold at once sprang into action. He took 'references' on the explorer behind his back, one from James Gordon Bennett, the other from Disraeli, who however replied that he knew no more of Stanley than what he had read in the newspapers.[13] Meanwhile Leopold employed as special emissaries for the Stanley mission both Baron Greindl and Charles Sanford, formerly US Minister to Belgium during the Civil War.[14] If he could recruit Stanley for his service, he would have brought off a considerable coup. Leopold was especially worried by the growing French interest in the Congo area.[15]

Leopold's most extended reflections on Stanley were penned in November 1877 when the explorer was on his way back to Europe via

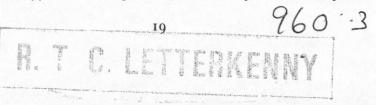

the Cape and Zanzibar. Always a master of timing, the King told his
Minister Solvyns in London that he wanted to interview Stanley as soon
as the period of fêting and lionising had subsided; if he liked the explorer
he would give him money to establish stations along the Congo which
would later be turned into Belgian settlements. Since the British would
prevent him if he tried to use Stanley openly for the purposes of
colonisation, it was important to present the mission as pure exploration.
He added significantly: 'We must be prudent, cunning and ready to act
. . . to procure for ourselves a part of this magnificent cake.'[16]

The consequence was that from Alexandria to London Stanley was
dogged by Leopold's agents, wheedling, insinuating, hinting. They were
under orders not to make a formal offer of employment with the Belgian
King as yet, until things had been cleared with Gordon Bennett. John
Russell Young made the first approach on Leopold's behalf during the
meeting with General Grant on 6 January 1878. When Stanley arrived
at Marseilles, there to meet him were Sanford and Greindl, who again
raised the subject of the work of the AIA.[17] Sanford, an ex-Lincoln
man, resurrected honest Abe's old idea that American blacks might be
persuaded to emigrate *en masse* to a new state – Sanford hinted that
Leopold's Congo state could be the place.[18] Finally, in Paris Greindl
and Sanford made Stanley a formal offer of service with the AIA, but
he responded that for the moment he was still in the service of the *New
York Herald*. But Stanley's indiscretion was notorious and soon the story
of the offer was all over the Belgian press.[19] Leopold took fright and
temporarily ran for cover. It was agreed on all sides that the next overture
to Stanley had better be through Solvyns, the Belgian Minister in
London. Solvyns invited the explorer to lunch and found him not
unwilling, in principle, to work with the AIA. Encouraged by this,
Leopold used Sanford as an intermediary to make a second formal offer
of employment. But at a meeting in London on 13 March Stanley
informed Sanford that he could take no definite decision until he had
completed the writing of *Through the Dark Continent* which he projected
for 15 May.[20]

When 15 May came and there was no sign of the book, Leopold tried
to pressurise Stanley to come to a decision. He sent a message via
Solvyns that if there was any further delay, the King would have to look
for another explorer.[21] Stanley replied that publication date was 10 June.
When, then, could he come to Brussels, Solvyns persisted, since the
King was close to striking a deal with another African explorer? The two
men met for lunch, and Stanley agreed to travel to Brussels on 10 June,

but he made it a point of understanding that he was in no mood to sign another long-term contract so soon after being released from harness with Bennett.[22]

Leopold always combined shrewd manipulation with large slices of luck. When Stanley set out on 10 June for Brussels, he was in sombre mood after the bruising controversies over Bumbire and the refusal of the British to take the Congo seriously.[23] As Sanford reported to Greindl: 'His late escapades in public occasions in England will not have added to his popularity or excited any *enjouement* in his favour for employment on the part of the English, I would suppose.'[24]

On 10 June Stanley and Leopold met for the first time. Both men took to each other. Stanley always liked people who acted rather than talked, and the King's vaulting imagination chimed with his own. Leopold, a shrewd judge of men's weaknesses, perceived that Stanley was just what he wanted. His intelligence had revealed the flaws in Stanley's nature. The mixture of self-pity, ruthlessness and indifference to the sufferings of his European companions made him the ideal agent for the King's Congo dreams. Stanley thought that all men's hands were against him; this would make him impervious to criticisms of his work in Africa, for he would conflate criticism of Leopold and his designs with criticism of himself.[25] Obfuscation was again the key, for if Stanley was criticised, as he would be, he would not think to probe deeply into Leopold's true motives, being too concerned to justify himself. Leopold was a shrewd judge. In the Congo Stanley was to complain plangently and vociferously about his mission but he never criticised its fundamental objectives.

During the discussions at the palace from 10 to 11 June, Stanley made his position clear. He wanted a railway built from Matadi to Stanley Pool to bypass the cataracts and thus open up the Upper Congo. Part philanthropic, part commercial, the Congo railway project should be financed by a Société Internationale de Commerce. Leopold objected that a railway would be immensely costly: he had in mind spending $100,000 over five years, yet a railway would involve at least 12 million francs of 'upfront' money. But the King did not want to be too discouraging. When Stanley mentioned a tramway that would take steamers across the lower falls, Leopold feigned interest.[26] He promised to take soundings among various European capitalists and especially the Rotterdam-based company Afrikaansche Handels Vereeniging, already trading at the mouth of the Congo.

To keep the explorer on ice, Leopold then had Greindl and other members of the Belgian élite wine and dine Stanley for a week before he departed for Paris.[27] He did not reveal that he was proceeding as if Stanley were already netted. Baron Lambermont suggested to the King that the best way further to detach Belgian interests from the AIA was to use the 'international' posts to be set up by Stanley as commercial Belgian stations. Stanley would in effect be serving two masters. The chain of posts on the Congo would be the official AIA business but the parallel business of establishing Belgian trading stations would in the long term place everything in the Congo under Leopold's control. The incompatibility between the ostensible scientific and humanitarian aims of the AIA and the emergent commercial aims of the King was already beginning to worry Belgian statesmen of integrity like Emile Banning.[28]

After Paris Stanley went on to take the waters at Trouville, Deauville and Dieppe before returning to Paris for a round of social engagements: at the Paris Geographical Society, the newly founded Stanley Club, learned societies and expatriate American organisations. He was based at the Hôtel Meurice in the Rue de Rivoli and it was there on 15 July that Leopold cleverly despatched Greindl to make soothing noises about the Congo railway and keep the explorer's interest unflagging.[29] But Stanley seemed both bored and exhausted. A dispute was currently raging between Mason and Gessi on one side and Samuel Baker on the other about the dimensions of Lake Albert. Despite Baker's support for him in February at the RGS, Stanley declined to become involved.[30] At the end of July he quit Paris for a two-week break at the Hôtel de la Paix in Geneva.[31]

He bounded back to Paris refreshed in August, ready for a meeting of the Executive Committee of the AIA, attended by Greindl, Rabaud from Marseilles, Beraud and Lodewijk Pincoffs, chairman of Afrikaansche Handelsvereeniging, whose proceedings Greindl faithfully relayed to Leopold.[32] The Dutch were now inclining towards the idea of a two-tier expedition, one to build a railway to Stanley Pool, the other to exploit the Upper Congo. This made Stanley draw back. When Sanford returned to Paris in September for further consultations, Stanley told him that he would have nothing to do with the Dutch project, as he did not want to be associated with a failure; only a permanent expedition was of any use, and this should be headed by someone who knew Africa intimately.[33] By this time Stanley was clear in his mind what his own terms were. He wanted a contract of £1000 a year for five years, plus 400,000 francs for initial expenditure with 125,000 francs a year thereafter. Sanford managed to beat him down to 318,000 and 115,000 respectively.[34] He also asked for, and obtained, a scheme for nine stations from the Indian Ocean to the Atlantic to be run by eighteen Belgian officers; the cost of this was to be £14,000 initial capital and £9500 thereafter in annual outlay.

On 1 October Stanley paid another visit to Brussels to confer with Leopold. The King put him in the picture about his AIA expedition to the East Coast, led by Ernest Cambier and Ernst Marno. Cambier had founded a naval station at Karema on the eastern shore of Lake Tanganyika.[35] An English employee of the AIA, Frederick Carter, had the idea of importing Indian elephants and mahouts and testing their fitness for African travel by a trek from Zanzibar to Karema; if the experiment was successful, these elephants could be used to train their African counterparts.[36] Stanley told Leopold bluntly that this venture was likely to founder, not least because he was using military personnel on a supposedly commercial endeavour. When the elephant experiment proved a failure and, even worse, when Carter and his British associate Tom Cadenhead later blundered into an African war and were killed by Mirambo's warriors, Stanley's stock with Leopold rose higher and the King largely abandoned the Zanzibar coast and switched resources to the Congo.[37]

Shifting to the subject of the Congo, Stanley now agreed in principle to head an expedition to the basin, provided that its aim was the establishment of permanent posts, and not a purely fact-finding enterprise without any capital investment. He explained to the King that because of the shortage of porters on the Lower Congo the construction of three stations would take three years.[38] The only proviso was that he should be allowed to finish the course of lectures on *Through the Dark Continent* for which he was contracted. Leopold agreed, provided Stanley stuck to his adventures and did not alert his audience to the lucrative possibilities in the Congo.[39] On 6 October from Paris Stanley confirmed the arrangement to Sanford, asked that 25 November be fixed as the date of his contract, and sent on a handful of detailed maps of the Lower Congo based on Tuckey.[40]

On 7 October Stanley left for London and the start of his nationwide lecturing tour. He went north first, vainly trying in Manchester and the other large industrial cities to whip up interest in the Congo.[41] But the financial crisis in Egypt and the gathering stormclouds in Zululand made both public and financial communities wary of further African involvement. Only sublime oratory could have made a difference, and public rhetoric was never Stanley's strong point. After a brief rest with the Webbs at Newstead Abbey, he returned to London and Brighton, then headed north again for more lectures.[42] Stanley was in sententious mood, as the following extract shows: 'How was Texas first peopled by Americans? How came Mackay to dare the long journey of Speke and Grant? What induced that young bank clerk lately to lure a small yacht to dare the ocean? What sent a man like Nicol Fleming to Spain recently? Fear of justice and fear in many forms drove the Egyptians to look beyond Libya and Nubia.'[43] But in general the lecture tour was a dispiriting experience. After reading *Through the Dark Continent* Mark Twain declared: 'Stanley is almost the only man alive today whose name and work will be familiar one hundred years hence.'[44] Although the book sold well, few other contemporaries agreed with Twain. Almost the only pleasing experience for Stanley was being able to salute the coming marriage of Alexander Bruce to Livingstone's daughter Agnes.[45]

Meanwhile in Brussels a syndicate was finally formed to develop a railway and commerce on the Upper Congo. A dozen subscribers put in 450,000 francs: Leopold contributed 133,000, Afrikaansche Handelsvereeniging 100,000.[46] This was followed by Stanley's signing a five-year contract with Leopold. He would receive £1000 a year in salary, and in return would not publish anything nor make any public statement without Leopold's consent. For the expedition itself he would receive £20,000 for the first year, and £5000 p.a. for the second and third years.[47]

When his lecture tour was over, Stanley hastened to Brussels to be present for the formation of a new body to be called Le Comité d'Etudes du Haut Congo (CEHC) – an allegedly philanthropic and scientific organisation with a capital of a million francs and fourteen subscribers. Flesh was put on the bare bones of the October syndicate. The Belgian banker Léon Lambert, the Afrikaansche Handelsvereeniging and the English businessmen William Mackinnon and William Hutton together raised 742,500 francs' worth of the 500-franc shares; Lambert additionally purchased 265,000 francs' worth as Leopold's proxy. But the question no one raised was whether the executive of the AIA had given permission for the formation of the CEHC.[48] The answer was no – both in the sense that Leopold had engineered the demise of the Executive Committee and that he did not inform the AIA national committees. Seeing the blatant chicanery Leopold had exercised in this matter, Stanley impudently requested, and received, a total of £4000 paid in advance for the following two years. This represented his salary as the

King's personal agent and his quite separate salary from the CEHC, for which the contract was not signed until 9 December 1878.[49]

Another underhand development that afforded Stanley wry amusement was that Greindl had been replaced by Colonel Strauch, first as Secretary-General of the AIA, then as chairman of the CEHC. Greindl, a man of too much integrity for Leopold's taste, was packed off in disgrace as Belgian Minister to Mexico.[50] The monocled Strauch, 'a man of exquisite suavity and a thorough gentleman', was more engaging than Greindl but Stanley found him not remotely in the same class for intellectual and moral fibre. Stanley had his doubts about Strauch from the very beginning: he was 'nervous and fidgety – and too amiable in fact – and in an excessive amiability there is often weakness.'[51]

On paper now the situation was that Stanley had a dual contract, with the King and the CEHC, and his task was to build three stations on the Lower Congo and meanwhile explore the commercial possibilities of the Upper Congo. If these proved satisfactory, two companies would be set up, one to construct a link between upper and lower rivers, the other to exploit the Upper Congo. But the suspicious Stanley already intuited that there was something odd about the whole set-up. He was therefore on the alert when the first meeting of the new CEHC took place on 9 December 1878.

His suspicions were borne out, though hardly from the quarter he expected. At the Brussels meeting on 9 December, adjourned from 7 Rue du Luxembourg to the Royal Palace, it was Pincoffs, head of the Dutch company, who made the difficulties. He proceeded to read extracts from pamphlets, including one from a Dr Peschuel-Loesche who had been on the recent German expedition to Loango, purporting to show that any Congo venture was doomed to failure. After a quarter of an hour of this, Stanley's patience snapped. He passed a note to Colonel Strauch to ask what the point of it all was. Strauch shook his head and passed the note round the table. All other members shook their heads, but all seemed to be in awe of Leopold and not to wish to break silence.[52]

Ever the plain-spoken advocate of bluntness, Stanley interrupted Pincoffs' flow of statistics to ask what the purpose of this recital was. Pincoffs replied that it was necessary for the committee to hear the other side of the story, not just the rosy picture of the Congo Stanley painted. How so, retorted Stanley, since it is I not you who will be going to Africa? Let us hear some accounts from people who have succeeded in Africa, not those who have failed. Pincoffs bridled and said it might be Stanley's skin at risk in Africa but it was *their* money. Very well, Stanley bristled, I resign here and now.

At this point Leopold made a hasty intervention. It would be better if Pincoffs read his statistics at anoher time, he suggested. Now in full flight, Stanley refused to be mollified and said his resignation stood unless Pincoffs revealed the true reason for this display of negative thinking. Leopold quickly adjourned the meeting for lunch. In private conversation Stanley then accused Pincoffs of having ulterior motives – possibly he intended to withdraw from the syndicate. Pincoffs protested that he had nothing to hide and invited Stanley to visit his offices in Rotterdam to view his operation for himself.

In the afternoon it was agreed that Stanley would prepare estimates and submit them to a further CEHC meeting on 2 January.[53] At the conclusion of business Stanley accompanied Pincoffs to Rotterdam. All the trappings of an important merchant were on display there, including a Dickensian partner, M. Kerdyks, who reminded Stanley of the Cheerybles. Pincoffs showed Stanley full documentation for the £8000 he had committed to the Congo enterprise. In that case, Stanley pointed out abrasively, your conduct at Brussels is even more inexplicable. Pincoffs' eyes flashed angrily at this and he declared that for two pins he would throw Stanley out for the insult. This was the wrong tone to take with the pugnacious Welsh streetfighter. 'Take care what you say, sir,' he replied coldly, 'or in the wink of an eye I will give you something which will require you to muster your establishment for that purpose.'[54] For a moment both partners showed signs of going through with their threat; then the mood changed, all was smiles and they took their rambunctious guest to dinner. Stanley, however, retracted none of his accusations.

On 2 January 1879 the CEHC definitely accepted all Stanley's plans and estimates and confirmed him as chief of the Congo expedition. The readiness with which they did so may seem surprising, but Stanley's detailed budgeting revealed him for the first time as an administrative talent of a very high order. He had thought through the implications of everything and had overlooked no detail, down to the smallest machine part. His estimates contained provision for three river-steamers, a steam launch, steel lighters, wooden houses in sections, haulage wagons, furniture, utensils and a plethora of tools: jacks, hammers, crowbars, lengths of rope, drills, etc. The hiring of personnel was more difficult, since the British government had vetoed the recruiting of labour in British West Africa. Stanley had at first thought of hiring Liberians, but

Pincoffs advised him they would be impossible to obtain, so he fell back on his old faithfuls, the men of Zanzibar.[55] As back-up he intended to ask the Dutch agent at Banana Point at the mouth of the Congo to recruit up to forty Kabindas for domestic work at the stations and between 75 and 130 of the élite West African labourers, the 'Kruboys' to stiffen the Zanzibari work-force.[56]

Senior personnel were even more dificult to obtain. Sanford originally proposed the employment of fifteen American blacks in this capacity and Stanley seemed to accept. Later he changed his mind and asked Sanford to find him three US whites at a salary of $1000-1500 a year plus passage money and medical expenses.[57] In addition, remembering the Pococks, Stanley took on two young Englishmen named Kirkbright and Moore, neither of whom had ever been out of England before. The final act in the initial preparations was to charter the steamer *Albion* out of Leith for the voyage to and from Zanzibar.[58]

On 3 February Stanley made his final farewells in London and crossed to Brussels for the beginning of an enterprise that would eventually result in the Belgian Congo. On the evening of the 4th he dined privately with Leopold and found him charming, amiable and statesmanlike. No greater contrast could be imagined than that between the 6 foot 5 inches tall monarch with his bushy brown beard and immense wealth and the diminutive Welshman born into dire poverty with an almost fetishistic concern about being clean-shaven. But the two got on famously, each doubtless responding to the ruthlessness in the other. Leopold usually made no concessions to any man but he was so impressed by Stanley that he was on best behaviour. Instead of the usual gourmandising, he ate temperately. The bevy of houris was nowhere in sight; instead Leopold made a virtue of his love of exercise and Stanley remarked with wonder that the King seemed oblivious to the most freezing temperatures.[59]

As yet, however, Stanley had not taken the measure of Leopold's cunning. He found the Belgians innocent and naïve, for at the office of the CEHC there was a huge map of the Congo with all the intended stations marked in red squares. Since there had been such stress on secrecy, Stanley found this odd, and in any case the number of foreigners employed in the enterprise meant that it was surely known to Belgium's rivals in the area, especially France.[60] In fact Leopold's intention was to draw attention to a 'secret' so that no one would fathom the *real* secret of his true future ambitions.

Stanley now received his orders for Zanzibar. He was to recruit upwards of sixty men there, find out what had happened to the Cambier expedition, and investigate the possibilities of a Belgian trade concession. There was a rumour afoot that the Sultan was prepared to lease his country for an annual rent to a trading organisation that would have a monopoly.[61] Hearing that the *Albion* had reached Gibraltar, Stanley set out for Paris on 10 February with Pincoffs and Lambert. All three put up at the Hôtel Meurice while they bought presents of gold for the Sultan of Zanzibar. On the 13th Pincoffs saw Stanley off at the Gare de Lyon, bound for Marseilles. The explorer was in sour mood. Complaints about Sanford's grammar and syntax alternated with animadversions on his travelling companion, a thirty-year-old Belgian army lieutenant, a man who lacked the intelligence to benefit even from careful coaching: 'as simple in all things outside his military duties as a schoolboy.'[62]

Stanley was travelling incognito under the name of 'M. Henri' so when he boarded ship for Alexandria on 20 February he was disconcerted to find Laurence Oliphant among the passengers. Oliphant, a friend of Speke's, had attacked Stanley bitterly in the *Cornhill Magazine* during the 1874–7 expedition and Stanley was afraid he would recognise him. Fortunately a strong gale confined Oliphant below for the first three days of the voyage. Instead he listened to the fulminations of a Scottish Presbyterian minister against the royal princes of England: 'a very wicked pair'.[63]

When the gale subsided, off Naples, Oliphant reappeared and sat down at table opposite Stanley, without betraying the least scintilla of recognition. He boasted of his travels in the East and mounted a vigorous defence of Burton as *the* African traveller, far superior to Baker. For the next few days Stanley engaged him in conversation and found him knowledgeable and witty. Suspecting that Oliphant might be playing the same trick on him and that he really did know who he was, Stanley set Dutalis up to bring up the subject of H. M. Stanley. Speaking in French, Oliphant denounced the explorer as nothing but a '*vaurien*', a murderer and '*mauvais sujet*'. He added with consummate scorn: 'His mother is in a lazaretto in England.' In that case, probed Dutalis, how did he do so well that Queen Victoria give him a diamond snuff box? Oh, said Oliphant, there was no denying his courage and intelligence but he was still a '*vaurien*'.[64]

Arrived at Alexandria, Stanley had trouble with the Customs because of the amount of gold and jewellery he was taking to Zanzibar. At Suez he found the *Albion* waiting for him and at once proceeded into the Red Sea. He was at Aden on 8 March where, true to custom, he engaged a 'slim young Somali boy' called Dualla, who had learned English as a cabin boy on an American ship. Ten days took them to Zanzibar on 18 March.[65]

Stanley expected to have a fight on his hands in Zanzibar to recruit men for the Congo project. His old enemy Sir John Kirk had kept the cauldron of enmity simmering ever since Stanley's departure from the island in December 1877. Stanley had learned some of the details from Augustus Sparhawk in 1878[66] but now he learned the full unsavoury story. Kirk had made trouble on two fronts. First, he had plugged away at the stories of 'atrocities' and sexual peccadilloes during the 1874–7 expedition, not hesitating to put words into the mouths of the *wangwana*.[67] Then he had dragged his feet over paying the claims for back-pay and compensation by the men who accompanied Livingstone in 1873, even after Kirk's superiors pointedly advised him to settle quickly to avoid bad publicity – for Stanley was threatening to open an appeal fund in England.[68]

In an attempt to anticipate Kirk's blocking of his request for manpower, Stanley made a point of visiting the Sultan on the day after his arrival. The Sultan was delighted with his lavish presents but startled Stanley by announcing that he was holding one of the 'old faithfuls', Uledi, prisoner because he had allegedly caused mutiny among the bearers of the Abbé Debaize. At Stanley's intercession, Uledi was eventually released into his personal recognisance.[69]

Stanley also handed the Sultan a letter from Leopold, requesting assistance in an important endeavour. Kirk, who had his spies everywhere, had learned from one of the *Albion*'s sailors that the steamer was scheduled to call at a number of African ports and inferred from this that Stanley's purpose was to return to the Lufiji River for further exploration.[70] Leopold's own note to Kirk spoke merely of the training of Dutalis in African exploration. But after Stanley's second interview on 23 April with Barghash, the cat was out of the bag. It was clear now that Stanley's presence in Zanzibar was to do with recruitment, but for whom and what? Mackinnon? Leopold? Both? East Africa? The Congo?[71] Since all of Kirk's intelligence network could give him no clear line on this, he reported to London that Stanley was influencing the Sultan against British interests. He was alleged to have told Barghash that he was surprised to find him still in place, since the British intended to depose him for their own ends.[72]

The task of recruiting men for an unstated task was clearly not going to be the work of a few days. On the other hand, the dreadful state of relations with Kirk denied Stanley access to all congenial members of the British community on the island.[73] So while Kirk elaborated fantasies on what Stanley was doing in Zanzibar, Stanley crossed to the mainland to reconnoitre the Wami River, in hopes that it might provide a short-cut to the interior, bypassing the Makata swamp. On 3 April he ascended the river in his steam launch and tried out the eighteen-oar whaleboat. A week later it became clear that the Wami did not answer his hopes, so Stanley put about and made for Bagamoyo where he visited old friends. On 13 April he was back in Zanzibar.[74]

On the island he advised Lt. Cambier on suitable sites for posts on Lake Tanganyika. On 17 May Stanley and W. H. Hathorne, the American consul, had another interview with the Sultan, to the apparent satisfaction of both sides. Stanley got formal permission to recruit free men (but not slaves) in Zanzibar. Barghash for his part received a stern warning not to sell an inch of land to the British but to cleave to the USA for protection.[75] The Sultan was so affected by this warning that when Stanley asked for a minor concession for Mackinnon's trading company it was refused.[76]

Still Kirk fussed and fumed away about the real reason for his enemy's presence on the island. An attempt to suborn Dutalis failed when the lieutenant pleaded ignorance of his ultimate destination and suggested the Red Sea or the Juba. French intelligence was in no better case, although the consul made an inspired guess that Leopold intended to place steamers on the Lualaba and build a railway on the Lower Congo.[77] Kirk was deeply resentful and suspicious of Leopold. *He* wanted to be the great power on the east coast and resented the Belgians' 'intrusion'. Leopold repaid his mistrust in kind and made sure that Kirk knew nothing even of his Tanganyika activities.[78]

Pending final resolution of the hiring of manpower, Stanley took the *Albion* on a cruise to Mafia Island and the mouth of the Lufiji, then re-explored the delta in a whaleboat.[79] It was 30 May before he finally cleared from Mombasa for Aden. His visit to Zanzibar had produced mixed results. On the one hand he had recruited sixty men for the Congo, put a spoke in Kirk's wheel and tilted the Sultan in favour of Leopold and against the British. He also bore away with him to the Congo as chief station manager Augustus Sparhawk whom he had known since 1871.[80] Finally, he had been reunited with Kamadi, whom he had last seen in 1877 at Kibonda when he left him a prisoner with the Lower Congo tribes for lack of means to ransom him. After two months of slavery Kamadi escaped to the southern shore of the Congo, thence to the ocean, where he made his case known to the US consul, and finally to Zanzibar via Madeira and the Cape. He arrived on the island just two weeks before the *Albion* docked and promptly re-enlisted with Stanley.[81]

But on the debit side the news of the Belgian expedition to Tanganyika was not good. Dutalis, whom he left at Zanzibar, would do nothing until the more energetic Popelin arrived, and Stanley was frankly sceptical about Carter's elephant scheme[82]. Greffuls, a representative of the Marseilles house Roux de Frassinet, was supposed to be the AIA's commercial anchor man in Zanzibar but was patently not putting his back into the work, through jealousy of the Belgians.[83] And still there was the insidious bile and spite of Kirk, working away through the Sultan against ultimate success for Leopold; his latest ploy was to insinuate that the men hired for the Congo work were all slaves.[84]

As the *Albion* beat up towards Aden, Stanley had time to reflect on the financial composition of the CEHC. The original subscribers had put up 652,500 francs and the rest had come from new subscribers, including his friend Baroness Burdett-Coutts whom he had personally persuaded to contribute £2000.[85] Hutton of Manchester had put in £800 and John Slagg, president of the Manchester Chamber of Commerce, £500. There seemed every prospect of an increasing British shareholding in the enterprise, which might achieve for Stanley by other means his dream of a British Congo. It still rankled with him that his reward for trying to interest the British in the Congo was to be called a mere 'penny-a-liner'. It had even been thrown up at him that he was not British himself, but Stanley dared not take out British naturalisation papers for fear of divulging the secret of his origins.[86]

But when he reached Aden Stanley heard news that destroyed his dreams for ever. The Dutch company headed by Pincoffs and Hendryck had failed, leaving debts of £450,000. The explanation for Pincoffs' odd conduct at Brussels the previous December was now clear. He had had no money and feared that on Stanley's arrival at the Committee he would be asked to produce the pledged £8000.[87] A question-mark hung over the entire Congo project. But what was disappointment to Stanley was serendipity to the devious Leopold. He saw an opportunity to take personal charge of the whole operation. On 17 November 1879, unknown to Stanley, the CEHC ceased to exist. At the AGM on that day shocked shareholders learned that three-quarters of the initial capital had already been spent and the rest was needed to liquidate contracts already signed. Then Leopold made his pitch. Using M. Lambert of Rothschilds as a front, he proposed to shareholders that if they were prepared to dissolve the CEHC, Leopold would return their original investment to them, pay 5 per cent profit to them out of future income, accept any loss himself and take over personal control himself. A new organisation, the Association Internationale du Congo (AIC), was formed. Leopold was a step nearer his personal empire in Central Africa.[88]

The failure of the Dutch company also had immediate consequences for Stanley's expedition. Leopold pretended that he could not really afford to send Stanley on but that he was afraid that if Stanley proceeded to Africa with diminished resources and later failed, he would claim it was the King's fault.[89] Keeping up the charade of being sucked unwillingly into the Congo scheme, Leopold secretly summoned Stanley to Brussels for new orders, which would reveal for the first time something of his true ambitions. The message reached the explorer at Suez. It suggested that Stanley disembark at once, speed to Brussels for new orders and then rejoin the ship at Malaga. The *Albion* would meanwhile steam in a slow circle round the Mediterranean coast, so that no suspicions were aroused.[90]

Stanley brusquely turned the suggestion down. It was too risky to leave his Zanzibaris on the ship: not only were bloody fights likely without his restraining hand, but a drunken indiscretion at any of the Mediterranean ports would blow the secret of the Congo enterprise. Instead he suggested a meeting with a member of the CEHC at Gibraltar. To Stanley's irritation Leopold sent Strauch.[91]

At the Hotel Royal in Gibraltar on 8 July Colonel Strauch and M. Gazelot, representing King and Committee, briefed Stanley on the new situation caused by the collapse of the Dutch company. Pincoffs was reported to be working in Brooklyn as a cab driver.[92] Strauch divulged to Stanley in a private meeting that Leopold's aims now went beyond the mere establishment of three river stations. He wanted a territorial concession in the Congo and looked forward also to a 'new Liberia' – a powerful black confederation; the black president would reside in Europe and hold his powers from the Belgian king. Real power would be in the hands of Leopold's agents in the Congo. Leopold claimed to be influenced both by the *'noyau dirigeant'* idea from the 1875 Paris Congress and by the writings of Schweinfurth.[93] Stanley was sceptical. Cession of land could only come after years of trading with the chiefs; as for a Liberia, that was beyond his abilities or those of any white man. But he promised to do his best, consistent with the original aims contained in his contract of employment; Liberias were matters for the future, and he must first confine himself to the immediate objective of the river stations.[94]

Now for the first time Stanley began to appreciate the way the King's mind was working. He was prepared to fall in with Leopold's ambitions for a colony, especially now that the British had so signally rejected his pleas for a Congo under the Union Jack. The one thing Stanley did not grasp was that Leopold intended the Congo to be a *personal* fief, not a Belgian colony. 'The King is a clever statesman. He is supremely clever, but I have not had thirty opportunities of conversing with him without penetrating his motives. He has been more open with me than he would have been had I appeared as a British subject. Still he has not been so frank as to tell me outright what we are to strive for. Nevertheless it has been pretty evident that under the guise of an International Association he hopes to make a Belgian dependency of the Congo.'[95]

The *Albion* continued on its way, surviving a fire in the Straits. Off Goree there was further damage to the ship's furnace, so they put into Sierra Leone. Here the confidential nature of the Congo mission was exploded. At every port they touched, Stanley remained below, incognito. His cover story was that he was ill with fever.[96] But the unknown white man with a cargo of blacks inevitably excited suspicion of being a slave-ship, especially since Stanley's front-man Swinburne seemed too young to be the ship's real charterer. At Sierra Leone there was a suggestion that the ship might be detained. Then Stanley learned from Swinburne that the governor was the same Dr Rowe he had met with Captain Glover's forces on the Volta in December 1873. He sent Rowe a message, revealing who he was and asking Rowe to expedite matters, since he wished to remain incognito. Once the matter was settled he consented to dine with the governor and accompany him on a picnic on his steam-launch. His story to Rowe was that he was on a philanthropic and scientific mission to the Congo on behalf of King Leopold.[97]

On 10 August they were at Anno Bom Island, where Stanley purchased fresh fruit and vegetables for his Zanzibaris. They were now very near landfall. 'While yet a full day's steaming from our destination, we observed that the ocean became stained; the blue changed to a muddy green, which in a few hours changed to a pale brown, while weeds and forest debris languidly rose and fell on the low, broad rollers.'[98] On 15 August he was off Banana Point. There he found the *Barga* which had left Antwerp in June with the immediately essential *matériel*: four river steamers, wooden houses and the tools for the expedition.[99] Augustus Sparhawk had almost finished unloading everything from the *Barga*.

With him were the expedition's personnel: two Englishmen, Kirkbright and Moore; two Danes, Albert Christopherson and Martin Martinson; and five Belgians, Losewitz, Van Schendel, Gerard, Petit and the carpenter Jansens.[100]

Stanley was now ready to begin the great work on the Congo that was to occupy the next five years of his life. He felt committed to Leopold, for the King had shown greater trust in him than he (Stanley) would have been prepared to extend to another man: 'His faith in me is very great and that in itself indicates a great heart.'[101] But he had still not got the measure of the duplicitous Leopold. Even while the King purred emolliently in Stanley's direction, he was attempting to spread his bets. In August 1879, when Stanley was arriving at Banana Point, Leopold was entertaining the French explorers Brazza and Noel Ballay in Brussels, trying to persuade them to enter his employment.[102] When this bid failed and Brazza used his intelligence on the Stanley mission to get a French expedition launched (Brazza himself left for Central Africa in December 1879), Leopold failed to inform Stanley that there was a rival in the field.[103] Leopold also tried to recruit Gordon to work for his new AIA at the end of the year; the idea was that he would start working inland from the east coast. But Gordon turned the offer down. The lack of an international status for the AIA meant that he would have had to work under the Sultan of Zanzibar's flag and thus appear to countenance slavery.[104] Stanley, who was always jealous of Gordon's reputation, was indignant at this flirtation. 'It is useless to cite Gordon to me,' he exploded. 'Gordon had all Egypt and the Sudan to draw men from and the Egyptian treasury to back him up. I have only £12,000 a year for three years.'[105] The Gordon incident was to be but the first in a long line of incidents that eventually made Stanley regret having taken service with this severest of all taskmasters, whose ambitions increased daily but whose supply of money did not.

3

THE first few days at the Congo mouth were spent in putting the flotilla on the water.[1] The *Albion* was to go with them as far as Hatton and Cookson's at Boma, where Stanley had arrived exhausted almost exactly two years earlier. Accompanying her was a motley assortment of craft. First was the paddle-boat *En Avant*, made of steel with side wheels, 6 metric tons in weight and 43 feet in length. When the Congo became unnavigable, three wagons would be needed to transport it. Then there was the *Royal*, 30 feet long and 5 metric tons, a wooden steam-launch with screw propellers; the *Belgique*, a twin-screw steel steamer, 25 metric tons and 54 feet long; the *Esperance*, 6 metric tons, 42 feet long, a screw-propeller steam-launch; the *Jeune Afrique*, a smaller screw-launch; two steel lighters of 12 and 16 metric tons respectively; and a wooden whaleboat of 3 metric tons.[2] After a few days of sumptuous Dutch hospitality at the Banana factory, this imposing flotilla made its way up the Congo mouth to Boma. On board the ships were 116 working men, as well as the whites. Sparhawk had managed to recruit thirty-seven West African Krumaners and eighteen Kabindas to supplement Stanley's sixty-one Zanzibaris[3] The expedition also possessed 2000 cases of tools and equipment, weighing 80 metric tons.

From Boma Stanley took some of his party upriver to Mussoko for a reconnaissance in the *Royal*. Then he ordered the full flotilla up to Vivi, 110 miles inland from the Atlantic, where he intended to construct his first station. At Vivi a hundred men set to work with machetes, hoes, picks, shovels, crowbars and sledgehammers: 'At a signal we saluted the dawn of a new era with the inspiring sound of striking picks, ringing hoes, metallic strokes of crowbars, and dull thudding of sledgehammers, which rang out on the morning of the first of October 1879, brisk and busy betokening the manner and spirit in which we intended to prosecute the first great enterprise up the Congo.'[4] Stanley appealed to the local chief to help him, but without any great hopes of success. To his surprise, the chief provided sixty-five labourers. Morale was high. Stanley's men cleared the summit of Vivi hill of scrub bush, rough stones and ant mounds, and laid the foundations for houses. Gangs of men with crowbars and sledgehammers prised large boulders over a precipice; smaller ones were pulverised. It was on such an occasion, when they saw him wielding a sledgehammer, that the locals first dubbed Stanley 'Bula Matari' – 'the smasher of rocks'.[5]

Stanley's genius for organisation was everywhere in evidence. Alluvial soil was brought to Vivi from the Nkusu valley. One of the *wangwana* acted as policeman and checked the load to make sure the locals were not defrauding them on the weight of earth. The next stage was to construct a vegetable garden with a palisade around it and sow seeds: carrots, onions, lettuce, turnips, cabbage, beets, tomatoes. Every day except Sunday they toiled from 6 a.m. to 11 a.m., then again from 1 p.m. to 6 p.m. After three months and twenty-four days, although they had started in the hot season when Europeans were wont to drop like flies, Vivi station was completely constructed by 7 January 1880; painting and decorating lasted until 24 January. The first station stood gleaming on Vivi hill, 340 feet above the river, looking to Stanley like the Acropolis itself.[6] Augustus Sparhawk was made the first station chief. His duties were to receive goods and correspondence from Europe, despatch them to the various camps, and organise caravans of porters.

The next station was to be at Isangila, 50 miles farther up-river, past an unnavigable stretch of falls and rapids. 50 miles of river meant a mileage of 520 for the expedition, for they had first to construct a road, then return to Vivi to haul the *Royal* overland with its boiler and machinery return to Vivi again to haul *En Avant* and then make the final round-trip to Vivi with thirteen wagons to convey the remaining boats and heavy impedimenta.

Finally they descended the Lulu valley to Ngoma village, then climbed half-way up the humpy mass of Ngoma mountain, finishing the push to the summit next morning. On the peak of Ngoma they could command a panoramic view of the river all the way to their target at Isangila. On 18 March 1880 work began, inauspiciously, with just 106 effective roadmakers. True, his white staff had received reinforcements, so that he now had fourteen of them either as officers, station administrators or sailors. But the Krumaners were proving disappointing; as soon as any serious work was demanded of them, they threatened to desert.[7]

The work gang began by tracing the line of the road by means of flagstaffs bearing white cloth streamers. Stanley provided a tall stepladder to guide the bearers of a half-mile cord and reel through 10-foot high elephant grass. Such was his ingenuity and woodcraft that he actually made use of the tracks left by buffalo and hippopotami, indicating a flat surface ahead. Stanley had acquired a fund of knowledge about the hippo 'who, short, stout and asthmatic, is very apt to reject any great steepness if he can.'[8]

They cleared stretches of road 15 feet wide and 2500 feet long in a single day. The fecundity of the tall grass was remarkable: between July and September it was invariably consumed by forest fires but by the following March was already as tall as a young forest. By recruiting more men from each settlement they came to, Stanley's men built 15 miles of road by 15 April, good enough progress to make their leader feel he could afford time off for a side trip to Yellala falls.[9]

On 22 April Stanley's men completed the first 22½ mile stretch from Vivi to the Congo, skirting the Livingstone cataracts. On 4 May they hauled the *Royal* over the mountains to camp on the Loa. Thereafter they were engaged in the predicted toing and froing from Vivi, bringing up steamers, boilers and machinery. Stanley was out of action in early June, stricken with billious fever, but by the end of the month he was back in Vivi on the seemingly never-ending shuttle. On 10 July he recorded that since leaving Vivi to reconnoitre Isangila in February, he had clocked up 966 miles, all to achieve a position just 22 miles upriver![10]

By September they confronted the 350-foot high obstacle of Nyongena hill; they mounted *En Avant* on a large steel wagon, ready for a one-in-four ascent. It was laboriously hauled to the top with block and tackle on 2 November, then the same process was repeated with *Royal*; next day they did the same with the boilers, machinery and other impedimenta. Now they lay in camp, commanding a view of Ngoma mountain, weary with their sisyphean labours and aware that Ngoma would be an even greater obstacle.[11]

Suddenly word was brought that a white man was approaching. To Stanley's astonishment, this turned out to be none other than the famous French explorer, Pierre Savorgnan de Brazza. It seemed that Strauch and the other anxiety-ridden members of the CEHC were right after all and France had stolen a march on Leopold. For ever since Brazza left Liverpool for West Africa and the upper Ogowe River on 27 December 1879, Leopold and his acolytes had been deluging Stanley with warnings that the French might get to the Congo ahead of him.[12] Irked by the implicit aspersion on his achievement so far, Stanley replied irritatedly to Strauch in February 1880: 'Relative to your information about the French expedition going over from the Ogowe river to Stanley Pool, or the missionaries going there, I beg leave to say that I am not a party to a race for Stanley Pool, as I have already been in that locality just two and a half years ago, and I do not intend to visit it again until I can arrive with my fifty tons of goods, boats and other property, and after finishing the second station. If my mission simply consisted in marching for Stanley Pool, I might reach it in fifteen days, but what would be the benefit of it for the expedition, or the mission that I have undertaken?'[13]

Who was this man who burst so inopportunely on to the scene of Stanley's labours? Like Stanley, he was an 'outsider' in terms of the foreign power he represented. Italian by birth (in 1852), Brazza began his career in the French navy and from 1871 was in service off the coast of Gabon. In 1875 he set out on his first great African expedition, with the aim of discovering the source of the Ogowe.[14] For three years he charted the Ogowe and Alima Rivers meticulously. On his return to France in December 1878 he read *Through the Dark Continent* and realised for the first time that the Alima was a tributary of the Congo, and that if he had pressed on for another five days he could have planted the French flag on that mighty river.

Brazza was intensely jealous of Stanley's achievements and also resentful that Stanley's battle-strewn passage down the Congo had had unfavourable implications for himself, as when he told his hosts he was in search of his white brother and they, thinking he meant Stanley, turned on him and forced him to flee for his life.[15] Ever afterwards Brazza tried to present himself as a man of peace and a friend of the black man, in contrast to the negrophobic man of force Stanley, though this portrait was severely overdone.[16] It was true that Brazza probably was a man of greater moral courage and had more genuine sympathy for the African. Success was not his *only* yardstick; moreover, he genuinely liked life in the wilds of Africa. Both men revered Livingstone, but if Stanley was to emulate, and outdo, his mentor's achievements in exploration, he never approached his moral stature. Brazza, a lesser explorer, was a worthier *moral* successor to Livingstone. But he was no angel. Like Stanley, he was devious, unfair to rivals and thought that he alone understood Africa.[17]

In 1880 Brazza evidently decided that his slow, careful progress in 1875–8 and his solicitude for the sick was the wrong way to proceed if he was to beat Stanley in the race for the Congo. Ironically, his model was the 1874–7 Stanley expedition, the very model Stanley himself had abandoned in his new manifestation of colony-builder. In this new endeavour Brazza had the wholehearted backing of French Prime Minister Gambetta and Foreign Minister Jules Ferry. This time he followed the Ogowe and the Alima on to the Congo, raised the French flag at Stanley Pool, then began to descend the river to the Atlantic coast. He won the respect of local chiefs both by 'burying war' – flinging his cartridges in a hole and covering them with earth – and by leaving them a tangible memory of his coming.[18] At Dakar on his way to the coast he had hired ten Senegalese, including a Sergeant Malamine Kamara, whom he had left at Stanley Pool as the French stakeholder. Malamine quickly gained great status in the eyes of the chiefs around Stanley Pool through his prowess as a hunter; he had brought with him the latest Winchester repeating rifle.[19]

History records many instances of pairs of great explorers operating in the same time and space (Drake and Quiros, Cook and La Pérouse) and often in direct competition (Scott and Amundsen, Peary and Cooke, Byrd and Amundsen). It was in this category that Stanley and Brazza fitted, although Stanley was incomparably the greater explorer.[20] The traveller Delcommune described their meeting as an encounter of contrasts, the North against the South, the saturnine against the phlegmatic, the snow and ice against the sunshine. Stanley was tenacious, cold, energetic, hard, shrewd, observant, egotistical.[21] It was not surprising then that both men were wary or that Brazza approached the meeting with circumspection.

Brazza came into camp with fifteen Gabonese sailors armed with Winchester repeaters. He was tall, wore a helmet and a naval blue coat, and his feet were swathed in brown leather bandages.[22] Stanley, as always a stickler for sartorial matters, found Brazza's dress sense closer to that of Livingstone at Ujiji than anything else: 'Genius is often distinguished by some eccentricity. De Brazza's is for ragged clothes and going about the country without walking boots.'[23] Stanley found Brazza of a very dark complexion: he could have been Italian, Portuguese or Andalucian. What impressed Stanley was his energy and 'uncontrollable vivacity'.[24] Stanley welcomed him and ordered breakfast prepared, then sat with him all afternoon and evening discussing Africa, though conversation was difficult, as neither spoke much of the other's language. They discoursed on the Ambanghi tribesmen whom both had had trouble with in 1877, Stanley at the confluence of the Mpaka, Brazza on the Alima.[25] Brazza confided that he hated to travel with white companions, as they impeded progress by their timidity and irresolution. As they talked, Stanley took closer stock. The Frenchman reminded him in full face of Winwood Reade and in profile of Serpa Pinto. He was a great romancer, prone to hyperbole and exaggeration, completely out of kilter with the current taste for scientific, factual exponents of African exploration; Stanley remarked scathingly that if Brazza's printed stories were anything like the ones he told over the camp fire, 'African travellers will envy him his reputation and become so many Munchausens or Jules Vernes.'[26]

Stanley was more attracted to Brazza than Brazza to him. The Frenchman wounded him by saying that it would take him six months to get past Ngoma mountain and four years to reach Stanley Pool. Moreover, he was far from straight with Stanley. Later he sneeringly contrasted his own superior methods to Stanley's. Stanley's men, he pointed out, were fed on rice and his mules on hay and oats, all imported from Europe; all his work-force was imported too.[27] By contrast, he, Brazza, could not afford such prodigal expenditure, so used the locals on the Ogowe to good effect. Worst of all, he did not reveal to Stanley that even as he sat there yarning with him he had in his pocket a treaty, dated 3 October 1880, from 'Makoko' of Stanley Pool, ceding him territorial rights on the north bank of the Congo at the Pool.[28] When he later learned this, Stanley was aghast at Brazza's duplicity: 'That's impossible!' he cried in disappointment.[29]

Part of the disappointment came from Stanley's own fantasy that Brazza might be the true male comrade he had sought in vain since Livingstone's death. That he was drawn to the young Frenchman is evident from his diary entry for 7 November 1880.

> I sat hours with him this afternoon and evening and find my ordinary measurements unable to follow his illimitableness, and my senses are somewhat confused by the cataract of illusions. My eyes were fastened intently upon a kind of rapture that came and went with wonderful rapidity. What eyes he has, so reckless, glancing and flashing! And the store of ideas and clouds of figures which he flung upon my dazed senses as he represented the intrinsic value of the Congo to that nation which first asserted its right to it.[30]

When Brazza left for Vivi on the morning of 9 November Stanley suspected from his laughing mocking spirit that he was concealing something. As yet, however, Stanley could report just three solid things about the Frenchman to the CEHC: one, he was a great yarn-spinner, in terms of both the number of elephants he was supposed to have shot and the number of chiefs won over; two, he had learned all of Leopold's most secret plans after his visit to Brussels; three, Brazza echoed his oft-spoken sentiments about the desirability of importing Chinese coolies. Of course, this cost money but as Brazza said: 'Who thinks of money in such a scheme as this? The Livingstone [sic] river is worth forty milliards to that company that opens it.'[31] When Brazza departed, Stanley made sure by letter that Sparhawk at Vivi and all his other contacts on the coast would treat the French party as honoured guests.[32]

Then he turned to the obstacle of Ngoma mountain, determined to prove Brazza wrong. On 24 November he gave Lt. Valcke the task of blasting a road through the side of the 1500-foot mountain wall of quartz and sandstone, using dynamite. The ear-splitting success of this exploit confirmed his nickname of 'Bula Matari' with Africans.[33] Next, by feeding selective titbits from his conversations with Brazza, Stanley was able both to browbeat the CEHC, in Brussels and to energise his own workers. Taunting the Committee with having been systematically hoodwinked by Brazza, who winkled out all their secrets when in Brussels, he praised Brazza's 'brilliant conception' of opening up a trade route to the Congo via the Ogowe and called him a Bismarck in diplomacy and a Moltke on the battlefield. He quoted Brazza's words as an implicit reproach to the Committee: 'You need five hundred men not one hundred. Your task is out of proportion to your numbers. You're in the position I was in on the Ogowe expedition when I could not build roads for lack of wagons.'[34] This was Stanley at his dialectical best. Humiliated by Brazza's advent at Stanley Pool, when he, Stanley, had assured Brussels this was an impossibility, he turned the tables on the CEHC by insinuating that it was their parsimony that had brought about the débâcle. Moreover, Brazza had arrived under the open auspices of the French government – and open Belgian involvement on Stanley's behalf was exactly what Leopold's duplicity and secretiveness ruled out.

Next Stanley turned to his work-force. Brazza had boasted that he was able to travel so much faster than Stanley this time because he brought sailors from French stations in Senegal and Gabon and used the tribesmen of Ogowe as porters. Stanley retorted that Brazza had had 600 porters and fifty canoes, whereas all Stanley had was his sixty-seven *wangwana*. When Susi (of Livingstone fame) heard this, he felt so ashamed for his compatriots that he got them all to volunteer to carry in ten days what had taken Brazza's porters fifteen.[35]

At the end of December the expedition finally got to Isangila, after the most painful stretch of road-building any of them could imagine. They had built three bridges, surveyed mountains, filled several ravines and gorges with earth, and man-hauled all the boats. During the rainy season, the first bridge, near Vivi – two weeks in the making – had been swept away by the swollen torrent.[36] The construction of Isangila station was entrusted to the two army engineers, Lt. Janssen and Lt. Orban, who had just arrived from Europe. Finally, on 21 February 1881, the expedition was ready to move on from Isangila. A year after leaving Vivi, at a cost of 2300 miles' marching, with six Europeans and twenty-two Africans dead and a further thirteen Europeans prostrate with fever, living on a Spartan diet of beans, goat-meat and bananas, they had circumvented the worst of the Lower Congo rapids. Stanley prepared for the advance on Manyanga, leaving Lt. Valcke in charge at Isangila.[37]

On 21 February he launched the *Royal* and *En Avant* on the Congo. Straining every sinew, they squeezed through the rapids at Kunzu; passage would have been easy if the ships had been capable of just an extra 2 knots of speed.

On 28 April Stanley took the whaleboat as far as Manyanga cataract. Manyanga he found a depressing place; moreover, the cataract barred the way and once again they would have to haul the ships overland for the journey to Stanley Pool. Next day Stanley negotiated with the local headman, who was at first unwilling to grant the land for the building of a station but finally grudgingly consented after a lavish gift of cloth and beads.[38] Gloomily Stanley surveyed his achievements so far. In the previous seventy days he had covered 2464 miles in coming 88 miles upriver. Since first leaving Vivi they had spent 436 days on road-making, with a force of sixty-eight Zanzibaris and an equal number of local recruits and West Coast Krumaners, just to get 140 miles from Vivi, and still there were 95 miles to go to Stanley Pool.[39]

But on 5 May Stanley, who had survived 200 fevers already, was attacked by the most powerful one yet. Despite dosing himself with 60 grains of quinine, he lost weight rapidly and soon hovered on the edge of death. For a whole week, from 13 May, he was unconscious. When he came to on 20 May, he was convinced that the end was not far off, so made his farewells to his comrades. But twenty-four hours of sleep took him past the crisis. By 30 May he was out of danger and by the beginning of June he was strong enough to sit in a chair under the awning of his tent. Yet ever afterwards he remembered the horrors of the worst fever of his life, when his head drummed and throbbed more insistently than the Congo tribes in 1877:

The mind drifted away and carried me to a world whose atmosphere was crowded with the most hideously wriggling things imaginable. When these became too hideous to be borne and swarmed about my face and seemed about to enter my nostrils – I made an effort to recover myself and they fled . . . presently I am at the entrance of a very lengthy tunnel, and a light as of a twinkling star is seen an immeasurable length away. There is a sensible increase in the glow, the twinkling ceases, it has become an incandescent globe. It grows large and it advances and I fancy I hear the distant roar. It is a train and it is approaching and the sound of its rush is appalling – and the light grows blinding. It is no more a star, nor a globe but a wide expanding circle of dazzling flames, and the roar is now so overwhelming that I fear I shall be caught in the tunnel – and in this fear I wake up again to hear once more the increasing loud drumming in the head. It is the drumming and the wriggling creatures in the atmosphere of the strange world – and that glowing light and appalling roar that will revert to my memory when I think of this fever.[40]

Recovery was accompanied by good news. The German Otto Lindner had arrived at Isangila with new recruits: there were twenty-four at Isangila and forty-six at Vivi. Cheered by these tidings, the skeletal Stanley (reduced in weight to 100 pounds) put Lt. Harou in charge at Manyanga and ordered a road constructed around the cataract so that he could bring up more boats. He took Valcke, Braconnier and Mahoney and seventy men overland with him for the final difficult stretch to Stanley Pool.[41]

Stanley showed his awareness of the difficulties to come by crossing the river to the south bank for the last stage of the journey to Stanley Pool. The newly-arrived missionaries crossed with him, thus abandoning the original attempt by the Protestant missions to work towards the Pool in echelon on both banks (the LIM were already on the south bank).[42] Had Stanley simply been building a line of stations, as he consistently asserted in his book *The Congo and the Founding of its Free State*, such a manoeuvre would have been unnecessary. It was the hidden part of his work for Leopold, the trade in ivory, that made this necessary[43]

Stanley first reached Stanley Pool in June 1881 but it was the end of that year before his position there was consolidated. Not only was he caught up in tribal middleman politics between the Babwende and the Bakongo, but Malamine, Brazza's deputy, menaced him from the opposite shore of the Pool and threatened to subvert the local chiefs, so that they repudiated any territorial concessions signed with Stanley. This period of Stanley's Congo mission is of byzantine complexity. Much of it hinged on rivalries between and within tribes, particularly the alleged paramountcy of a chief called Makoko and the attempts to wrest his crown by a thirty-four-year-old old banditti chief called Ngalyema, who specialised in the ivory and slave trade. It was December 1881 before Stanley had his final showdown with this ruffian, and the occasion provided him with one of his favourite after-dinner stories.

Stanley suspected that, after many weeks of probing, Ngalyema's next action would be sleight of hand or treachery rather than a frontal assault on his camp. So, while asking Makoko to call a grand council to announce to all the chiefs of the Pool the concession he had made to 'Bula Matari', he made appropriate preparations. Makoko's edict had sensational re-sults. Ngalyema's attempts to rally his neighbours against the white man failed dismally. He was turned down by his neighbours Mpila and Kimbe while another, Ngamberengi, asked him what he meant by taking up arms against his blood brother.[44] Infuriated by this, Ngalyema decided to take the bull by the horns. With a small bodyguard he strode into Stanley's camp. Stanley tried to browbeat him by insisting on his right to enter Kintamo; Ngalyema angrily denied this right. When the chief seemed likely to lose his temper, Stanley sounded a gong and his *wangwana* surrounded Ngalyema's party and forced them ignominiously from camp.[45]

It was typical of Stanley's penchant for fantasy that he later rewrote this incident as a moral tale demonstrating both the superiority of the civilised white man over the benighted black savage and his own Promethean omniscience. Stanley's fantasy version was that he had lured Ngalyema into an elaborate charade. When Ngalyema came into camp, Stanley had hidden the *wangwana*, armed to the teeth, in a nearby thicket. The encampment appeared deserted and Stanley sat yawning in his chair, apparently bored and listless. By his side was a huge gong. When the discussions with Ngalyema petered out into acrimony, Stanley made a point of asking the chief not to touch the gong as it was powerful 'fetish'. After a lengthy period of being tantalised, the foolish Ngalyema could no longer resist the temptation of summoning the spirit of the gong. He beat it and to his consternation a swarm of armed men suddenly came running at the double. Thus was Ngalyema convinced of the superiority of Bula Matari's magic.[46]

By now more than a hundred new recruits had arrived at Vivi, including the first woman, a focus of great interest by the Africans. At Stanley Pool

Stanley himself had 153 blacks, including 117 workers. They set to work to construct the new station at Leopoldville. First they cut down 125 large trees – teak, redwood and plane – plus nearly 3000 small trees to build the blockhouse, terrace, gardens and village. By 10 January 1882 the frame of the blockhouse was almost complete and by the end of the month the whole project was well advanced. When the last nail was in place on the house, on 25 February, work began on an artificial cove, to permit steamers and other boats to enter the harbour safely at high tide. By the beginning of March the village was complete. The vegetable garden was already thriving and on 9 March trading commenced. Stanley inaugurated proceedings by buying two pounds of ivory for the price of six handkerchiefs.[47]

Leopoldville station was a level earthwork cut away from the hillside, 300 yards long. Here stood the blockhouse. On the ground floor was a long clay magazine containing stores, where cloth and a variety of articles were bartered with the tribes for brass rods or *mitakos*. On the first floor was Stanley's apartment. Higher up the hill was a building for European staff, divided into seven bedrooms plus an eighth communal room for meals. The post dominated the lakelike extension of the Congo called Stanley Pool, a circular basin 250 miles in extent.[48]

Yet if the physical basis of Stanley's work was proceeding well, his presence at the Pool for the first three months of 1882 was necessary to prevent civil war as the chiefs at first feared that Stanley would ally himself with one of them to the detriment of the others. Ngalyema seemed well and truly cowed: Stanley reported him as being interested in obtaining wood for a coffin, almost as though he wished to concretise the death of his larger ambitions.[49] And when he received his trade goods in return for the deed of land, he was described as like a child with a toy.[50] But his son Ngeli, who had reproached Ngalyema for failure to cleave the oaths of blood-brotherhood, bade fair to outstrip his father as a troublemaker. Stanley had to address a stiff formal note in March about Ngeli's fourfold insolence and impertinence to 'Bula Matari'.[51] Not until 9 April 1882 did Stanley formally renew his ties of blood-brotherhood with Ngalyema and then not until Ngalyema had concluded a big ivory deal.[52]

The other problem was the French. When Malamine first saw Stanley firmly ensconced at the Pool, he was inclined to take a hard line and delivered a letter from Brazza, dated August 1881, 'to whom it might concern', protesting against the intended occupation of the north side of the Pool by any other European.[53] But when he saw how masterfully

Stanley had his hands on the levers of power in the Pool area, Malamine decided on the better part of valour. A visit to Kinshassa to show off the first steamer on the Upper Congo found Malamine among the friendly crowds who gathered to greet *En Avant*.[54] Any further fire-eating tendencies on the part of the Senegalese sergeant were terminated abruptly when Leon Guiral arrived as his replacement.[55]

By 19 April Stanley felt confident enough both about the impregnability of the Leopoldville post to tribal attack and of French intentions to continue upriver and found a further station. He set off with *En Avant*, the whaleboat and two canoes, making heavy weather for 'the powers of the little paddle-steamer were taxed to the utmost, towing the two canoes.'[56] It took them an unconscionable time to get clear of Stanley Pool. First a rainstorm wet their fuel on the 20th and delayed their start from Bamu Island, a 14-mile long sliver of land teeming with elephant, hippos and buffalo. Next, they were hampered by the straining of the boilers, the excessive heat and the necessarily cramped posture of the passengers. The sole consolation was the staggering beauty of the scenery between Stanley Pool and Mswata. Stanley confessed he could never understand the contemporary passion for Scottish lochs, but he could appreciate any conceivable rhapsody on the Congo, whose splendours dimmed anything he had seen in the Americas from Belize to Omaha.[57]

During the rest of April-May 1882 Stanley alternated between administration at Leopoldville and further forays into the regions of the Upper Congo in the hinterland of Stanley Pool. But on one of these expeditions, he went down with another serious attack of fever. He lost consciousness and remembered nothing until he found himself back in Leopoldville. He was not out of danger until 27 June, but even when on his feet again found himself suffering from chronic gastritis and incipient dropsy.[58]

He took a decision. After three years' hard toil in the Congo, it was time to recuperate in Europe on a home leave. He had achieved his principal objectives and more: he had constructed a line of stations from the ocean to Stanley Pool and, most importantly, by his treaties with Ngalyema and other chiefs like Ngobila, he had circumvented the French and set Brazza's earlier opportunistic feat at nought. The initiative now lay firmly with Leopold and the AIA. Stanley turned his face towards Vivi, the Atlantic and Europe.

4

STANLEY's mood as he came downriver for his convalescent leave was sour. Apart from his serious illness, he was cast down by how little had been achieved at Manyanga, saw little to cheer him at Isangila, and on 8 July 1882 at Vivi received his worst jolt yet. There had been yet another twist in Leopold's complex skein. Finally heeding Stanley's pleas that Otto Lindner's administrative skills were too good to squander on the Loango expedition, Leopold had sent another German, the naturalist Dr Peschuel-Loesche to head up the Loango probe. Peschuel-Loesche and Lindner were old comrades, having been together on the abortive Von Falkenstein expedition into the Loango in 1873–5 when, as Stanley contemptuoously noted, the Germans spent £9000 to advance just 140 miles into the interior.[1] Mysteriously, on arrival at Vivi, Peschuel-Loesche made no move to go up the Loango. The reason became clear when Stanley arrived at Vivi to announce that he was going to Europe on sick leave. It turned out that Peschuel-Loesche had all the time had an order in his pocket from Leopold, nominating him as Stanley's successor in the event of sickness or resignation. As Stanley cynically observed: 'No wonder the man never stirred but has waited to step into my shoes. He has remained here doing nothing since March of this year.'[2]

By now inured to Leopold's secretiveness and duplicity, Stanley was not especially surprised that the King had not consulted him on this appointment, even after he had freely conceded Stanley's right to nominate his own successor.[3] But as he briefed Peschuel-Loesche and was in turn put in the picture by the German on the monarch's latest thinking, it was clear that Leopold still imagined he could advance a number of Congo projects in echelon, despite Stanley's warning. The King still hankered after the opening of a second trade route that could not conceivably be disputed by the French. The Loango mission was de-

47

signed to outflank Brazza and was regarded by Leopold as even more important than the unlocking of the Upper Congo.[4] In addition Peschuel-Loesche was instructed to gain exploitation rights to all mines, forests, vegetable and mineral assets.[5] But most of all, Leopold advanced his most full-blooded colonisation conception yet. Peschuel-Loesche was explicitly admonished to regard the British North Borneo treaties with the Sultans of Brunei and Sulu as models for the treaties he should make with the Congo chiefs; it was territorial concessions alone that would allow Belgian influence to survive on the Congo. In a word, Peschuel-Loesche had been ordered to implement the very plan that Stanley rejected as impracticable at Gibraltar in 1879.[6]

Stanley was too ill to argue the point. A new era for the expedition seemed to be dawning anyway. New personnel had arrived in the form of Von Dankelman and Van de Velde. Valcke had just come in with the fresh force of 200 Zanzibaris. The *wangwana* whose three-year contract was up would be escorted back home by a roundabout route taking in St Helena by Gillis and Albert Christopherson, also departing after three years' service.[7] As a first stage Gillis intended to accompany Stanley to St Paul de Loanda and see the invalid leader on to the first Europe-bound steamer. At this stage Stanley was thinking of convalescing in Madeira prior to coming to a final decision about his future.[8]

At Boma on 15 July Stanley was met by Mgr. Augouard who thanked him for all his help. The meeting was cordial and prolonged.[9] The missionaries of all denominations owed a lot to Stanley, but not all of them acknowledged it. Whereas the Baptist Mission paid tribute to his achievements and poured scorn on the canard that Stanley was invariably a man of force, the Livingstone Inland Mission made common cause with his critics in Europe.[10] This was all part of a differential strategy whereby the BMS preferred to co-operate with Leopold, whereas the LIM set its face against the King and all his works. They alleged, truthfully, that Stanley and the Belgians merely used the missions for their own cynical ends. This ostensible generosity was all part of a general strategy dictated from Brussels of preventing the missions from getting their own land by a veiled threat that if misssions tried to own their own territory, it would all be alienated to the Catholic missionaries.[11]

Transferring from the *Belgique* (on to which he had been carried, so ill was he), Stanley boarded the steamer *Heron* for the journey to Ambriz, where he arrived on 17 July. Once again he experienced his usual bad luck with maritime connections, missing the mail steamer by hours. He pressed on to St Paul de Loanda for an enforced stay of a month. He was put up by Herr Niemann, agent of the Dutch House, and treated by a Dr Olivera for the dropsical swelling in the legs, the result of the latest bout of haematuric fever. After three severe bouts (27–30 April 1880, 5–21 May 1881 and 31 May – 9 July 1882), even Stanley's iron frame was beginning to buckle: 'another one like this would kill the best constitution unless there was a period of recuperation in Europe between.'[12]

As he slowly recovered in the Portuguese port, Stanley could allow his mind to wander to the few occasions on the Congo when he had been able to bask in the luxury of an inner life. He continued to brood about the bad press he enjoyed in England. In 1880 in the House of Commons Robert Fowler and Dr Cameron had bracketed him with the missionaries of Lake Nyasa as a perpetrator of 'outrages' in Africa. Stanley was adamant that he never fought except in self-defence and that the *locus classicus* of his 'atrocities' – Bumbire – had been necessary for the 'credibility' of the white man. He continued to ponder the absurdity of the charges brought against him: to whom was he supposed to look for arbitration when attacked by the tribes of Ituru or Bumbire? Was he supposed to give up more than 300 lives 'without benefit of priest or prayer, at the first demand of a rabble of unreasoning savages who had obtained the land they lived in by force of arms? . . . the sharp lesson we were obliged to inflict on the impudent Wasuma was just what a spirited Englishman would try to give a lot of burglars whom he found in his house, boasting of their exploit and holding their plunder to view.'[13]

His only fault, he concluded, was that his early training as a journalist had taught him to set down the truth as he experienced it. The British public did not want truth – it wanted homiletic parables to disguise its own humbug. In his mind he ran through all the examples he knew of shooting incidents involving Englishmen, including some well-known Africa hands: Verney Cameron and Mackay of Uganda. Then the *pièce de résistance*, aimed at an old enemy: 'The British Consul-General of Zanzibar Dr John Kirk lately shot an Arab on that island. Neither accidentally or wilfully have I done anything of that kind.'[14]

Yet in other respects the three years on the Congo provided evidence of a certain mellowing in Stanley. The award of a doctorate from a German university for 'services to civilisation' helped: 'I have had so much dispraise since 1872 that honours of this kind serve to keep up one's spirit.'[15] It is hard to imagine the old Stanley lending a helping hand to an old adversary. yet when he heard that Pincoffs of the

Afrikaanishche Vereeneging – his opponent at the acrimonious Brussels Committee meeting on 9 December 1878 – had fled to the USA to avoid arrest, Stanley sent him £50; he did, however, draw the line at helping him to get a job as there was something far from creditable and straightforward about the collapse of the Dutch company.[16]

His fascination with the African continued undiminished. As part of his theory that one could match physiognomy with temperaments he had made a detailed physical study of Dualla, who was now accompanying him to Europe. His fascination with the nude African figure is more the sensuous delight of the artist than the lubricity of a homoerotic sensibility.[17] Eyes above all fascinated him. He had used his own steel-grey orbs to stare out and face down some of the greatest chiefs in Africa, so was more than normally disposed to see them as the mirrors of the soul. He claimed to be able to read any man like a book by gazing into his eyes. 'Not even de Brazza could completely hide what moved least. The laughing devil stood in his eyes like a mischievous imp, toyed with the firm lines around them, lowered and raised the eyelids, stepped out with freedom in the iris, or contracted himself into a pinpoint far behind. He was there all the same, joyous and tricky.'[18]

But perhaps the most impressive evidence of the mellowing process in Stanley was in his response to children. In November 1881, while awaiting the final showdown with Ngalyema, he noted the following: 'All this day small children have made themselves at home in my camp – and have gambolled for hours before my tent door. I have never seen such touching confidence displayed before in all my African experience. The sight of these tender naked little beings following my camp into the wilderness, and laughing in my face, and hugging my knees, just thrilled me.'[19]

On 17 August after a month of inactivity and reflection, Stanley boarded the mail-steamer *China* for Lisbon. Its track lay through St Thomas Island, Prince's Island, Bulama, St Jago, St Vincent (Cape Verde Islands) and Madeira – twenty-six days' steaming on a very slow boat. If the human side of Stanley had been triggered by his enforced rest at St Paul de Loanda, exposure to actual human beings at once turned him sour again. He deplored the lack of discipline on the *China* and the failure to enforce the rules on the second-class passengers. 'These, permitted to leave their own quarters, and invade on the narrow (first-class) deck, expectorated, smoked, and sprawled in the most social-istic manner.'[20] Another irritant was the insolent and offhand behaviour of the stewards and the failure of the Portuguese officers to do anything about it: 'An American or a British captain, with a few iron belaying-pins within easy reach, would have restored order in the most peremptory manner.'[21]

By the time the *China* reached Madeira (17 September), which impressed him favourably, Stanley could walk a few paces. Four days later they were steaming up the Tagus and from Lisbon he proceeded to Paris overland (arrived 28 September). By the end of the month he was in Brussels, ready to talk business with Strauch and Leopold.[22] He caught the Comité largely unprepared, for they had assumed that he would return to the Congo from Madeira before taking European leave.

In his first interview with Strauch Stanley made it clear that his return to the Congo was unlikely. As he understood it, his contract with the CEHC had expired, and he had in fact provided the Comité with an extra eight months as a bonus. This was not the way Strauch saw it. He insisted that the explorer's personal contract with the King took precedence. This was still in being, therefore Stanley must return to the Congo at the earliest possible moment. The Belgians intended to find a replacement, but it had to be the right man; such things could not be done in a trice.[23]

Stanley was mightily cast down by this interpretation of the contracts but, after all, Leopold had inserted a clause allowing him the option of renewal after the initial three years. The question was whether Stanley's health could stand up to another tour: 'I had intended to bid adieu to Africa for a few years at least.'[24] When he went to see the King, Stanley was still undecided about whether to yield to the monarch's importunities; one of his physicians had advised him that a return to Africa was tantamount to signing a suicide pact. Leopold, who had so bitterly criticised Stanley behind his back and secretly negotiated to get Gordon as his successor, suddenly realised how vital the finder of Livingstone was to his long-term plans. To Stanley's face he was all honeyed charm: 'Surely, Mr Stanley, you cannot think of leaving me just when I need you?' After much cajolery, Stanley reluctantly agreed to resume his burden in the Congo on or about 1 November 1882, but on certain unambiguous conditions. First, there had to be a better understanding in Brussels of the true state of affairs in the Congo. Secondly, if his letters were bluntly expressed, this should not be resented in the AIA offices or attributed to malice – he must be free to speak as he found.[25]

Warming to his theme now that he realised how badly Leopold needed him, he poured withering scorn on Strauch's tripartite orders (territorial acquisitions, ivory purchases and penetration of the Upper Congo). He could no longer tolerate contradictory orders, sometimes a dozen at a time 'as though I had qualified agents without number fit to perform them simultaneously.' He took the King through his Congo personnel one by one and underlined their shortcomings before reverting to the tripartite instructions from Strauch and rubbing the monarch's nose in it: 'Your bureau should have known that there was only myself capable of doing any one of these things.'[26]

Next he rapped Leopold for having subsumed the CEHC in the AIC without informing him until 1881: 'When I started in 1879 I had one order, which was to build three stations and land *En Avant* on the Upper Congo. That was simplicity itself. But now we have developed into a political power, a commercial company and also an exploring and pioneering expedition.' That being so, it was imperative that there should be someone capable left in charge at Leopoldville when he ventured on to the Upper Congo; perhaps this could be Gordon or Captain Thys, Strauch's assistant. Leopold nodded sagely at each point Stanley made, however roughly, said that all would be done to the explorer's suggestion and proposed an adjournment.[27]

In one compartment of his mind, Stanley knew well enough that Leopold was manipulating him into a return to the Congo. But he found it impossible not to admire the devious old reprobate. After dealing with so many African potentates, he confessed he was no longer much taken in by royal pomp and majesty, but for all that he admitted that there was something different about Leopold; the Prince of Wales was the only other royal personage who could put one completely at ease, and it was providential that it was Leopold, not one of the Rothschilds, say, who was opening up Africa:

He is now in his forty-seventh year in the prime of life. His long flowing beard is quite brown. There is not a wrinkle on his face ... [He possessed] the inimitable courtesy and graciousness of a truly royal gentleman ... While coming down the Congo [in 1877] I dreamed of some young Rothschild undertaking the civilisation of the Congo basin and entrusting me with the task like that imagined Prince in Thomas Carlyle's *Shooting Niagara* saying 'There is the money you need. Go and fulfill your writ.'[28]

On 3 October Stanley put the King out of his suspense by agreeing to return to Africa, against the advice of his physicians. Leopold again promised to fulfil all Stanley's conditions, reiterated that the British

Borneo Company was *the* crucial precedent for the Congo, then passed him on to Strauch. In a no-holds-barred heart-to-heart with Strauch, Stanley finally learned the reason for much of the mysterious behaviour by his employees in the Congo. It turned out that the volunteers had insisted on contracts specifying service to the Comité rather than to a named chief of expedition. Lindner and Peschuel-Loesche, it now transpired, had expressly stipulated that they were not to be part of Stanley's staff. Strauch tried to sugar this pill by saying that he was sure there was no objection to Stanley personally, it was just that they wanted to be explorers in their own right. Stanley put his own gloss on the prima donna-ish behaviour of the personnel on the Congo: they all wanted to loaf about doing nothing while drawing huge salaries and writing articles for newspapers betimes. What sort of example was this? 'No black man will work unless he is supervised, and the white man also is a master in the art of shirking when left to his own will.'[29]

On 4 October Stanley lunched with Leopold and sketched out his ideas for the second part of the Congo enterprise. An ancillary expedition should be sent into the Kwilu-Niari basin to outflank the French. Secondly, Stanley would select the men he wanted to serve with him but his name would be kept out of the contracts. Signatories would have to take an oath of loyalty to the expedition chief personally, rather than the Executive Committee in Brussels; only when they were on board ship at Cadiz would it be revealed to them that they had taken a personal pledge of allegiance to Stanley. Finally, the way to knock out Brazza and the French was to maintain the sort of secrecy that had been conspicuously absent in 1879. A steamer would be chartered, loaded with trade goods, and taken from Antwerp to Cadiz. Stanley meanwhile would board an express and speed down to southern Spain while Brazza thought he was still in Paris. This would provide him with the three months' head start on the French he needed for putting everything on a proper footing on the Lower Congo. He could then take a flotilla on to the Upper Congo in full confidence that his rear was secure.[30]

Before he left for London on 5 October, Stanley twitted Leopold for having contributed £1600 to the French branch of the International Association, which meant that the King had in fact financially staked his rival. But Stanley had still not got the full measure of his master's two-facedness. Two weeks before Stanley arrived in Brussels, Leopold had again entertained his rival Brazza at the royal palace, naïvely hoping to 'turn' the Frenchman to work for him.[31] Nothing came of these talks, except that Brazza's suspicions of Leopold's ultimate designs were deepened. Brazza threw in the additional thought that Stanley's true allegiance was to the British and the Americans, that he hoped ultimately to make the Congo an Anglo-Saxon enclave. Moreover, he insinuated that Stanley's return to Europe was mysterious. This chimed in with Leopold's own conviction that Stanley's 'illness' was bogus and that the real motive for his sudden return to Europe was to cross swords with Brazza.[32]

These allegations were later to bear fruit, though there was not a shred of truth in them. Stanley had offered the Congo to the British on a plate in 1878 and they had turned him down. His activities on behalf of Leopold were generally perceived to be diametrically opposed to British interests in the region. This was a line assiduously peddled by the old enemy Kirk. As early as 1880 he warned Salisbury that the Popelin expedition, if successful in cutting a route through to Stanley Falls, would ensure that all the ivory of Central Africa would be taken down to the Atlantic coast; the east-coast ivory trade would become a backnumber.[33] He repeated this advice frequently during Lord Granville's incumbency as Foreign Secretary, stressing that British interests required the extension of the Sultan's territories ever westward to block Belgian expansionism.[34] When challenged on his intentions, Leopold assured the British that his stations were being set up solely for the interests of commerce and civilisation, that he had no political aims or ambitions.[35]

Even a blind man could have seen that Leopold was lying. His assurances were worthless. Every time the King approached the Sultan of Zanzibar for permission to hire more men on the island, he assured him this was positively his last recruitment request. Then he would shamelessly break his word and wheedle around the Sultan again.[36] Leopold indeed sat long hours with Strauch working out exactly how they could hoodwink the hapless Barghash.[37] But he was deeply worried about the British. Already calls had begun to be heard from Stanley's friends, like Hutton in the Manchester Chamber of Commerce, for a treaty guaranteeing the neutrality of the Congo.[38] This underlines the fact that Stanley and Leopold always had conflicting aims for the Congo. While Leopold was trying to manipulate entrepreneurs like Hutton (and through him the British government) for his own ends, Stanley genuinely wanted the British involved, in the hope that the Congo could yet become part of the Empire.

These irreconcilable interests might have had explosive force in late 1882 but for the intervention of England's old enemy France. Until 1882

Leopold had been lucky. The Eastern question, problems with Afghans and Zulus, and finally the collapse of Dual Control in Egypt had preoccupied the minds of British statesmen, so that Leopold was in effect given free rein in the Congo. Yet the very fact of British triumph over Arabi Pasha in Egypt, which edged out the former French partners, made France determined not to be outmanoeuvred on the Congo.[39]

This determination coincided with the return of Brazza from Brussels – a Brazza armed with new insights into Leopold's true ambitions. The King was right to fear that if Brazza's view prevailed in Paris, his own schemes for 'humanity' (i.e. exploitation) in the Congo would be destroyed, as European conflicts were projected out into Africa; this would mean that he would be put to the unwanted expense of political colonisation.[40] Although Brazza's official superiors in the French Navy Department were not keen on African colonisation, the Ministry of Foreign Affairs, in one of its periodic fits of anger against 'perfidious Albion', decided to publish the 'Makoko' treaties and present them for ratification.[41] Some historians have seen the French ratification of the Makoko treaties as the true origin of the 'scramble for Africa'. But there can be no question about their immediate causality. Even Kirk admitted that jealousy of England was the motive for French ratification of these 'ridiculous' treaties.[42]

The French action played into Leopold's hands in one sense. It allowed him to claim that he now had no option but to obtain sovereign territorial rights in the Congo to protect 'free trade' against French protectionism;[43] in a word France gave him the excuse to do openly what he had all along been attempting surreptitiously. On 16 October the King told Strauch he was not satisfied with the terms of the treaties Stanley had made with the chiefs; an article must be added, ceding to Brussels sovereign rights over their territories.[44]

The new French bearing also plunged Stanley personally into the maelstrom. Back in London Stanley was working on schemes for possible new senior recruits for the Congo, including the traveller Archibald Colquhoun and Verney Cameron (against whom, however, there was a question mark on the grounds that he drank).[45] Suddenly there came an invitation from the Stanley Club in Paris to speak at a banquet. Stanley saw a chance to tarnish the image of Brazza. He was irritated by the way Brazza contrasted himself as the man of peace as against Stanley the man of war, the gentle Latin saving Africa from the brutal Anglo-Saxon.[46] Despite advice from Leopold not to go, Stanley hastened to his old watering hole at the Hôtel Meurice in the Rue de Rivoli.

According to the usual version, Stanley bumped into Brazza on a Paris street and warned him that he was going to attack him in a speech at the Stanley Club banquet.[47] But the true story emerges from Stanley's diaries. Brazza called on him at the Hôtel Meurice and Stanley advised him that he intended to deliver the *coup mortel* that night at the Hôtel Continental. Brazza asked if *he* could attend. Stanley replied that he could promise nothing since he was merely a guest himself. The two evidently parted on good terms: 'We had a good deal of talk of an amiable kind, because personally he is unexceptionable, has lots of good humour and is a gay raconteur.'[48]

The banquet that night turned out to be a much grander affair than Stanley had expected. The cream of Anglo-Saxon Society in Paris was there. For once Stanley indulged himself in champagne, so that when the time came for his address after the toasts, by his own admission it went on too long. He then pitched into Brazza in no uncertain manner. Brazza, he said, was a combination of Lally, Machiavelli and Pizarro. His so-called treaty with the Bateke 'Makoko' was a thing of farce. His Makoko was not paramount chief of the area, so had no right to make the concessions he made. And what kind of behaviour was it to gull an illiterate into signing a treaty in triplicate, then giving Malamine, who could not read, a document requiring him to afford every hospitality to any white man who came to Stanley Pool while verbally instructing him to the contrary? This was machiavellianism in anybody's language; it was the introduction of 'an immoral diplomacy into a virgin continent'. It would have been far better if Brazza had worked under AIA auspices instead of fomenting the narrow nationalism symbolised by the French tricolour. He wound up by saying that he could not join in the paeans of praise for Brazza. So far from bringing morality to Africa, Brazza was the serpent in Eden.[49]

As Stanley worked up towards his peroration, Brazza handed in his card at the door and asked to be admitted. Stanley acceded to the request The US Minister introduced Brazza, in full dinner dress, and had him sit down next to Stanley. A toast was called for and when Brazza stood up to reply there was a roar of approval from the fifty Frenchmen present.[50] Brazza's riposte to Stanley gained from its restraint and its astringent wit. He could have pointed out that the references to the AIA were humbug, since this had been superseded by the CEHC and then by the AIC, of whose very existence Stanley was unaware until 1881.[51] So much for internationalism. He chose instead to ignore the 'international' dimension, as if it did not exist, and proceeded as if Belgian/French rivalries were a fact of life. The contrast between Stanley the conquistador and Brazza the peace-lover was drawn by sly innuendo. He ended his speech by ironically calling for the very international co-operation that Stanley had presumed in his remarks. Proposing a toast to international solidarity, each country under its own flag working together, he threw out the broadest possible intimation that Leopold's 'internationalist' pretensions were spurious. The verbal duel was generally considered a win on points for Brazza.[52]

Stanley did not see it that way at all. He was so convinced that he had had the better of the encounter that he pooh-poohed the idea that it was 'bad form' for Brazza to come to the banquet uninvited and attempt to steal Stanley's thunder; not at all, he replied: the rivalry between the two helped him as it publicised his work in Africa as the successor to Livingstone.[53] But next day he was taken aback by the ferocity of press atttacks on 'Stanley, Albion's Trojan horse': 'What a vocabulary of abuse this polite nation has!'[54] He had not realised that by coming to France at this particularly delicate time he had walked straight into the cannon's mouth. It was no exaggeration to point out, as the London *Times* did, that the French government was launching itself irresponsibly into the unknown in Africa on a wave of crazed public opinion and perfervid patriotism.[55]

Stanley bounced back next day with customary buoyancy. He gave a breakfast at the Hôtel Meurice for thirty guests, including Brazza, Edward King and John Hay, author of the Pike County ballads: 'We had a good time and de Brazza and I laughed uproariously at the consternation of some of the gentlemen at the Continental to whom his presence was unsuspected.'[56] But Stanley was underestimating the fear and hatred entertained towards him by the French, who saw him as Britain's stalking horse, even as he pretended to work for Leopold.[57] Ever afterwards Stanley was a particular *bête noire* in French Foreign Ministry circles.[58]

The rivalry between Brazza and Stanley itself was soon transmogrified as a living symbol of the struggle between Britain and France, even though on paper the two explorers represented the French and *Belgians* respectively.[59] To Brazza's discredit, his smiling countenance at breakfast at the Hôtel Meurice did not reveal his true feelings either about Stanley personally or his intentions. Later he was to underline the canard that Stanley was acting as a kind of British fifth column in the Congo.[60] He also described Stanley's outflanking of him in 1883–4 as a personal vendetta and stated that Stanley was no gentleman.[61] Naturally his intrinsic dislike would have been accentuated by the Welshman's decisive upstaging of him on the Upper Congo in 1883. The barbed remarks at the banquet, which later found their way into print, did not help matters either.[62]

On 22 October Stanley crossed the Channel back to England to find himself once again a target for begging letters and leeching relatives. With a mixture of resignation and bitterness he recorded in his diary:

> People have come to impute to me great riches. Nothing can persuade my poor relations and those who think they have a claim on me but that I am rolling in wealth. By the urgency of their appeals they affect to know my financial condition better than I know it myself. They began as early as 1872 when all my worldly wealth was carried in my pocket but the numbers of believers in my riches are now considerably increased. I was indeed in 1872 rich in health and spirits . . . I am now somewhat richer in experience, with less health and spirits – and as regards money – of what avail is it to think of it when one has very little chance of enjoying any of it. If I did not think each time I was about to enter Africa that there were too many chances against my returning to England, I might indulge in the belief that I need not fear starvation but I am not half so rich as these begging letter writers affect to believe.[63]

For a week he toiled away on the plans for phase two of the Congo operation. He sent a number of men to Brussels for Leopold to look over, among them Captain Grant-Elliott whom he docketed as 'one to note'. Colquhoun turned down his offer of a senior appointment. Verney Cameron, who was not as hostile to Stanley as might have been supposed, and wrote five times to him between 1872 and 1884, likewise declined to serve, eliciting from Stanley the waspish conclusion 'Cameron is of course impossible, not but what he is intelligent enough, but he is not of the stuff to work.'[64]

The end of October saw him back in Brussels, suffering from triple-headed malady. His cardiac arrhythmia had returned, he was suffering from bronchitis and his teeth required urgent work.[65] While he consulted physicians and dentists, he received a set of amended instructions, dated 30 October and 1 November. These clarified the contractual position of Lindner and Peschuel-Loesche *vis-à-vis* the main expedition, explicitly gave him the right to nominate his successor, and contained detailed orders on the push into the Upper Congo; particular target areas for the acquisition of territorial concessions were the stretch between Leopoldville and Ikalemba and between the Bangala and Stanley Falls. There was also a sealed letter to the captain of the *Harkaway*, a charter ship at Cadiz, which informed him that landfall would be advised by the expedition leader once they were at sea.[66] Stanley then prepared for a leisurely journey to Cadiz via Paris or, as he put it to Edward Marston, 'to busy myself in southern Spain, in a genial climate, and get rid of bronchial affections and the misery of chest uneasiness.'[67]

On 12 November he dined at the Hôtel de Londres with his friends Mr and Mrs French Sheldon. He was planning to take the 8 p.m. express from Paris to Madrid that evening. Over soup Stanley sustained a violent attack of the mysterious stomach bug that had first appeared at Manyanga. The attack was so severe that he could scarcely breathe. Stanley felt that if the pain had lasted a minute longer, he would have expired on the spot. A doctor was sent for and, after injecting morphine, debated with French Sheldon as to the aetiology of the illness. Sheldon was certain it was contraction of the pylorus, but the physician diagnosed acute inflammation of the stomach. Stanley's own interpretation (consistent with his tendency to paranoid delusions) was that he had been poisoned, but by whom? The French, Portuguese and Dutch were all plausible candidates, perhaps especially the Dutch, from whose house at Banana he had already received one anonymous death threat.[68]

Though in intermittent agony, Stanley resolved not to stay in Paris but to press on; if he was to die, he preferred it to be in Madrid or on the *Harkaway*. He begged a syringe and vial of black morphine from the doctor, and was driven off to the station in a drowsy state. He boarded the Madrid train, but within minutes the effects of the drugs began to wear off and the dreadful pain returned. He wanted to shriek out in agony but, in true Anglo-Saxon stiff-upper-lip fashion, was afraid of making a scene. Yet in the end an inadvertent groan escaped his lips. A Spanish *marquesa*, who was sharing the compartment, asked Stanley's servant what was the matter. When it was explained, she came over and wiped his face and bathed it in some perfumed water 'and ministered to me with such feminine grace and assiduity that filled me with devout gratitude.'[69] However, she could do nothing about the pain; Stanley's new manservant Illingworth had to spend the next thirty-six hours to Madrid intermittently injecting his master with morphine.

Once in Madrid the *marquesa* saw him to a carriage, which bore him to a suite at the Hotel Russie. Here for seven days he remained under the care of a doctor, occasionally rising from hs sick-bed to fire off a telegram to Strauch about Brazza, the new employees in the Congo and even on one occasion, such was his attention to detail, concerning the measurements for planks of teak wood![70] But on the afternoon of the seventh day, to the Spanish physician's horror, he asked for his bill and made as though to depart. The doctor warned Illingworth that he was putting his master's life at risk. From the mulatto colour on Stanley's face, the physician inferred that he had picked up some unknown tropical strain, which he had then exacerbated by overdosing with drugs to combat it. He prescribed a milk diet for the explorer and warned him to keep off further medication if he valued his life.[71]

Stanley swept out of the hotel, caught the express to Cadiz, arrived next afternoon on board *Harkaway* and ordered an immediate sailing. The captain just had time to obtain his papers. Then, at 11 a.m. on 23 November, the ship cleared for the Congo.

5

STANLEY arrived back in the Congo on 14 December 1882 to find all was chaos and confusion. The two German 'supremos' sent out by Leopold, Lindner and Peschuel-Loesche, had already decamped, leaving behind them an administrative shambles. For two months Stanley struggled manfully to pull the demoralised expedition together. Meanwhile he sent Lt. Van de Velde to take possession of the mouth of the Kwilu and the adjoining coastline. Van de Velde moved very quickly, and by February 1883 had secured a territory on both sides of the river mouth and set up a station called Rudolphstadt. Striking upriver in hopes of meeting another party under Captain Elliott, he signed treaties with the chiefs *en route*, then founded yet another station, Baudoinville, at the confluence of the Kwilu and Lumani.[1] By this time he was out of supplies and returned to the coast just in time to forestall a French gunboat which on Brazza's advice had been sent to take possession of the Kwilu estuary. On the coast there were rumours of a white man sick upstream. Van de Velde went upriver, found Elliott, nursed him through convalescence, then returned with him to Rudolph-stadt. From here Elliott set out again to establish a further station (Grantville) midway between the Kwilu and the Loango. This effectively severed all outlets between the Ogowe, the Congo and the Atlantic; only Loango, claimed by the roving French gunboat, was excluded from the Association's sphere of influence.[2]

Stanley put the final nail in the French coffin by sending Hannsens to set up a line of communication between the Congo and the Niari, so as to link up with the Elliott route. Starting from Manyanga in February 1883, Hannsens reached the upper Niari by the end of April and founded Philippeville. By these three brilliant operations Stanley completely turned the tables on Brazza. Not only was the Kwilu Niari route several times shorter than that by the Ogowe; without control of this valley, along which a railway could be built to Stanley Pool, the French post at the Pool itself lost much of its value.[3]

Thus did Stanley refute all the simple-minded criticisms by Leopold's more intemperate officials. His patient, long-term strategy had paid off spectacular dividends. Late 1882 and early 1883 saw the neurotic fusspots of the Comité in Brussels working themselves into a lather about what would happen when Brazza returned to the Congo. What was his exact route? How could the Comité compete with the credit of 1,275,000 francs voted by the French Assembly for Brazza's work after the ratification of the Makoko treaties? Might not France be contemplating a military occupation of Vivi?[4] All these fears were groundless. When Brazza arrived in Central Africa in February 1883 he at once saw that Stanley had beaten him. He proceeded to Stanley Pool, invoked the now useless and superseded Makoko treaties and reinforced French claims on the left bank of the Congo against the day they might be exchanged for the Niari–Kwilu valley. He then proceeded to write screeds of complaint to France for transmission to Leopold about Stanley's '- underhandedness'. Leopold and Stanley concurred in concluding that this revealed Brazza as a mere opportunist, devoid of real talent; a genuine 'man of Africa' would attempt to challenge Stanley on the Upper Congo.[5]

After dispatching the three Kwilu-Niari expeditions, Stanley wanted to press on upriver at once. But his departure was delayed by an untoward event when Fontaine, Gillis's agent, shot Masala, the interpreter at Vivi station and a key local figure. Fortunately the wound was not mortal, but the local chiefs converged on Vivi to demand reparations and see how the great Bula Matari dispensed justice. They began by demanding a hefty fine of £430 worth of trade goods. When the alarmed Fontaine told Stanley he could not pay, patient negotiation was required from Bula Matari to get a satisfactory resolution. The fine was reduced to £24, the offending revolver was ceremonially broken into small pieces, and Fontaine himself banished for ever.[6]

At last, on 22 January, Stanley was able to get under way. He departed Vivi with a train of ninety-five *wangwana*, ten Kabindas and thirteen locals. He was at Isangila on 31 January and arrived at Manyanga on 4 February. On the 7th the *Royal* was mounted on a steam-launch for transport overland to Leopoldville. Having got as far as the river Inkissi on 27 February, Stanley was dumbfounded to receive the news that Leopoldville station was desperately short of food. To him this made no sense, as all the way on the road to Stanley Pool he encountered nothing but abundant food and friendliness from the tribes. But his stupefaction was complete when he eventually reached Leopoldville after an overland march to find, instead of a prospering agricultural settlement, a station overgrown with grass.[7] Everywhere he discovered evidence of grotesque ineptitude and incompetence. The scale of his officers' failure was breathtaking. The near-starvation had resulted from a total breakdown in communication between the white officers of the Association and the local black chiefs. Stanley reported to Strauch that the scale of decay at Leopoldville beggared description.[8]

When he reflected that the station chief, Braconnier, had been vacationing at Vivi (and even thinking of 'going sick' to Europe into the bargain) while all this was going on, the magma of Stanley's volcanic wrath finally cracked its casing. Braconnier had not helped his own cause by calmly telling Stanley, as if it were an event on Mars, that in his absence most of the Kinshassa chiefs had declared for France.[9] On 31 March Stanley peremptorily dismissed him as station chief and offered him a lesser position. When the Belgian denied his superior authority, Stanley dismissed him. Braconnier then added insolence to injury by claiming that Stanley had no power to dismiss him, that Strauch had given him an absolute and indefeasible power at Leopoldville and a promise that no civilian or military authority could displace him. Stanley reiterated that he was sacked and that he would use main force to keep him off Association premises.[10]

Next he wrote a blistering letter to Strauch to explain the sacking. After all the complaints he had made about Belgian officers with their private contracts (literal privilege), here was the most signal instance yet of Strauch's utter folly in making stupid and vain promises behind the back of the expedition leader. He rehearsed the tortuous history of his relations with Braconnier and pointed out that he had already dismissed Braconnier once, in 1881, and then reinstated him at the Comité's wish. His (Stanley's) very credibility was now at stake; Brussels had to choose between him and Braconnier without further prevarication: 'I would rather beg my bread around the world than be a passive spectator of indolence and incapacity, coolly sitting down uninterested in this drama on the Congo.'[11] In a further private letter to Leopold Stanley protested at the preposterous pledge Braconnier claimed to have from Strauch; one would have to go back to the 'old Jesuits' to find such an idea. He put the King firmly on the spot, as only Stanley could: 'Sire, I had either to discharge Braconnier or to discharge myself. If I have done wrong, Your Majesty will be pleased to reinstate M. Braconnier and also to recall me.' It is not difficult to guess which option Leopold elected.[12]

Stanley's main aim on his second tour was the unlocking of the Upper Congo. He had settled Brazza and the French. But before he could proceed upriver he had also to square the troublesome Leopoldville missionaries and, most important of all, put the Association on a good footing with the Stanley Pool chiefs, Ngalyema especially. Relations with Ngalyema had reached an all-time low in Stanley's absence. On 8 April, when all the Kintamo chiefs called on Bula Matari for a conclave, Ngalyema complained bitterly and vociferously about the haughty and arrogant treatment meted out to him by Braconnier and the other Belgian officers at Leopoldville.[13] But behind this tale of personal slight lurked a story of hard-headed political calculation. After the foundation of Mswata, Ngalyema feared that his position as an intermediary in the Congo ivory market was under threat. When he learned in January 1883 of the good relations between Opontaba and the Association he had tried to stymie expansion upriver by a food blockade which, however, was an ignominious failure.[14] Until Stanley's arrival Ngalyema and Ntsuula teetered on the brink of open warfare. Also, chief Bankwa of Ndolo opposed the signing of a general treaty with the Association.[15]

At first Stanley too beat in vain against the rock of Bankwa, who persuaded Ntsuulu against a general treaty. But his formidable advocacy, the sheer awe in which he was held by the chiefs, and his overpowering mixture of charm and power (aided not inconsiderably by his new European machine guns) turned the tide. A general treaty was signed, vesting sovereignty in the AIC over all regions west and south of Stanley Pool.[16] Harry Johnston, who met up with Stanley again at Leopoldville, accompanied him (with Vangele and eleven Zanzibaris) to Kinshassa for the final showdown with Bankwa and left a detailed description of Stanley's methods at the 'pow-wow'. Stanley, 'looking his most chief-like, with his resolute face and grey hair and sword of state at his side', dealt diplomatically with the chiefs. He announced that it was entirely for them to decide whether to allow 'their son' to build there. Dualla, the interpreter, 'argued and cajoled the black brothers of the "Stone-Breaking" chief into concordance with his wishes.'[17] Eventually Stanley decided it would be impolitic to build at Kinshassa for the moment, because of Bankwa's hostility. But the treaty he secured more than made up for the disappointment.

The treaty had a knock-on effect farther up the river, for Opontaba concluded his agreement with Janssen after visiting Mpila and seeing that Ngobila (on the channel) and Ngalyema (on the Pool) had established a commercial lead over their rivals Ngantsu and Ntsuulu.[18] But Stanley as yet could still buy ivory only from the Tio, principally Ngalyema. His one great advantage as compared with a year before was that his men had opened a second caravan route from Matadi to Kinshassa, supplementing the original 1880–81 road, and had signed further treaties with chiefs and built more way stations.[19]

On 9 May 1883 Stanley's flotilla set out for the Upper Congo, carrying a party of seven whites and seventy-three blacks. Stanley penetrated into the areas he had first charted in 1877 – the lands of the Irebu and Bolobo – founding new stations as he went, at Bolobo, Mswata and Equator. After establishing Equator station – 757 miles from the Atlantic and 412 miles above Leopoldville – he returned to Leopoldville to consolidate affairs there. News that the local tribes had attacked and gutted Bolobo station sent him steaming hard up the Congo once more. He brought the Bolobo tribes to heel with a display of awesome power from his new Krupps gun, and returned to Equator station after an absence of a hundred days.

In October he made peace with his old enemies the Bangala and left his most promising assistant, the Belgian Lt. Camille Coquilhat, in charge of the station there. Resuming his journey, Stanley came at last to the confluence of the Congo and the Aruwimi, where the massive war flotilla of the Soko had fought him in January 1877. As with the Bangala, Stanley was able to conciliate his erstwhile foes, but in so doing made an alarming discovery. His epic descent of the Congo in 1877 had given fresh heart to Tippu Tip's Arabs, who by 1883 had broken through the physical barrier of Stanley Falls and established themselves on the Upper Congo. Near Stanley Falls he ran into the Arab slave traders. A caravan of some 600 persons was arranged as a primitive concentration camp. Faced with the Arabs' inhumanity and brutality, Stanley confessed he had to fight hard against an impulse to open fire. 'What a pity I did not bring up one of the Krupps! I could then have annihilated the camp,' he wrote regretfully.[20]

Instead he settled for cool civilities and took his departure as soon as normal politeness allowed. In December he completed his targets on the Upper Congo by founding a station at Stanley Falls itself. The return journey found the travellers back in the Bangala territory by Christmas Day 1883, whence they proceeded to Leopoldville, arriving 20 January 1884.

On arrival at Leopoldville Stanley at once went down with a fever that lasted a week. He came round at the end of January to find the familiar catalogue of personal problems and queries from Brussels awaiting resolution. He was full of his usual grumbles. 'If Strauch knew anything about figures, I should not have to descend to these minute details, but whenever he has to touch upon numbers, I am under the impression that there is confusion in Brussels.'[21] At the end of the month he wrote a doleful letter to Leopold, lamenting the strain on him caused by finite financial resources and maladministration from Brussels.

Not for the fortune of a Rothschild would I undertake to go through the same experiences I underwent in 1880–81–82. I perceive them looming up again in 1884 – gigantic work, endless contradictory orders – with insufficient means in my sixth year of service to haul a 30-ton steamer with two hundred men while the garrisons of thirty stations are crying out for food! . . . It may be that ill-health makes me write so despondently. It is certain I am not the man I was in 1879 when I began the Congo work.[22]

On 21 March 1884, after licking Leopoldville into shape and making further treaties with the chiefs of Stanley Pool, Stanley set off for Vivi, hoping to hear news of his successor. Visits to the stations at Manyanga and Isangila left him disappointed with their poor progress and decrepit state. It was difficult for him not to make pointed contrasts between the vigour of men like Vangele and Coquilhat on the Upper Congo and the lacklustre performance of his personnel on the lower river.[23]

On 22 April he reached Vivi. His anger spilled over when he saw that things were no better here and that, in the vacuum without a proper leader, the young officers had simply had a good time and allowed the station to go to rack and ruin. There was further correspondence from Leopold. He had tried various possibilities for Stanley's replacement. At one time General Gordon was a strong candidate, but he had to drop out when the British wanted him for service in the Sudan. Finally Leopold signed a contract with Sir Francis de Winton, formerly an administrator in Canada (also a friend of Garnett Wolseley and a protégé of the Royal Family), making him Stanley's successor.[24] De Winton was to arrive at Banana at the beginning of May; Stanley was requested to stay on until then to effect a smooth transition.

During his last month at Vivi, Stanley was able to catch up with the ever more complex international politics and diplomacy that were to make Leopold's Congo venture the trigger for a general 'scramble for Africa'. For by late 1883 the Congo had become the cockpit for a ferocious four-way struggle between Leopold's AIC, France, Britain and the Portuguese that threatened to suck in all the other great powers as well.

Even while Leopold and the French braced themselves at the end of 1882 for a final decisive round in the Stanley–Brazza bout, Portugal decided to take a hand in the Congo; it laid claim to the area on the basis of ancient explorations by the captains of Prince Henry the Navigator and their successors. This claim found many backers. The British attitude was that the best future for the Congo lay in a slow colonisation by Portugal.[25] Paradoxically, the French had concluded that Stanley was really a secret agent for the British, that Britain's aim was annexation of the Congo, that therefore *they* would do best to endorse the Portuguese claim.[26] France was aware that the British had begun to push Portuguese claims in order to checkmate Brazza, and indeed the point was scarcely denied among the power-brokers of the day.[27]

Stanley, meanwhile, after defeating the French in the race for Stanley Pool, was now coming to see Portugal – always for him the hub of slave trading on the African west coast – as the main threat to Leopold's work in the Congo.[28] The great impediment to a meeting of minds between Stanley and Harry Johnston was the latter's partiality for the Portuguese.[29] For Johnston, the French were the real enemy and Portugal a useful bulwark against their African ambitions. The Portuguese in turn responded by accusing Stanley of inciting the Africans against them.[30]

What of Leopold and the AIC in all this? Leopold's difficulty was that he could not simply throw a Belgian hat into the ring by making an overt bid for a colony, for he had all along portrayed his activities in Africa as 'philanthropic', 'international' and 'commercial'. The plain fact was that the AIC was simply Leopold and his own personal moneys. Its capital was provided out of a fortune amassed by clever speculation, possibly in Suez Canal stock. For years now he had cleverly maintained his Chinese box structure of obfuscating fictions: AIA, CEHC, AIC – with the added element of mystification that many people confused the AIA with the AIC; naturally Leopold did nothing to enlighten them. Once Brazza spotted what Leopold's game was he encouraged Jules Ferry to flush the King out of cover by the ratification of the Makoko treaties. At a stroke the AIC's blue flag with golden star, that had fluttered over more than 300 tribal villages by now when treaties with the Association had been signed, would have to be hauled down. For how could a sovereign power be opposed by a mere trading company? Come to that, how could the said company, whose flag was recognised internationally for trading purposes only, make binding treaties?

Leopold had wrestled with this conundrum in international law for a long time, which accounts for his obsessive interest in the Dent/Overbeck treaties with the Sultan of North Borneo and those of early settlers in North America with the aboriginal Indians. He had even hired two tame academics to find favourable precedents for him. The chosen duo, Sir Travers Twiss at Oxford and Professor Arntz of Brussels, cited the practices of the Teutonic knights and the Maltese Knights of St John.[31]

But in early 1883 Leopold feared that all this logic-chopping was in vain, that the Anglo–Portuguese accord, which already seemed to place Vivi and Isangila inside a recognised Portuguese sphere of influence, might be supplemented by a Franco–Portuguese treaty that would return the north bank of the Congo and the Kwilu–Niari territories to France in return for a recognition of Portugal's sovereignty on the south bank.[32] Further alarm bells rang when his agents informed him that Britain was thinking of recognising Portuguese sovereignty on *both* banks as a protest against the Makoko treaties. The King's first step was obviously to nip this in the bud. He organised a campaign through his friends in England, stressing the slavery aspects of Portugal to one group, its protectionism to another. There was an outcry against the proposal to recognise Portuguese sovereignty, both from free-trading business men like Hutton and Mackinnon, alarmed at the thought of Customs barriers, and from humanitarians appalled at slavery. Leopold even enlisted the Prince of Wales on his side.[33] The campaign was successful. Following a passionate denunciation in the Commons by John Bright, the government was defeated on the issue and dropped the proposed Portuguese treaty in April 1883.[34] An attempt by the Portuguese lobby to counterattack by portraying Stanley as Leopold's man of blood failed when Lords Fitzmaurice and Derby (who had been secretly won over by Leopold) feigned ignorance of the relationship between Stanley and the Belgian King.[35]

It was at this point that Harry Johnston seriously disturbed the tenor of Stanley's relations with Brussels. Both men wanted the British to establish a political protectorate over the Congo, but disagreed on the agency, Stanley favouring an alliance with Leopold, Johnston opting for the 'traditional' Anglo–Portuguese friendship.[36] On his return to England Johnston visited the Foreign Office and lobbied for consular posts on the Congo. The officials in turn quizzed him about his talks with Stanley in the Congo and his (Johnston's) later interviews with Leopold in Brussels. Johnston revealed Stanley's enthusiasm for a British Congo; as for Leopold, Johnstone opined that he was either 'marvellously simple or marvellously deep'.[37] But when Johnston's overtures proved unavailing, he tried a more public, and more indiscreet, tack. In a letter of July 1883 Stanley expressed forcibly his view that to deliver the Congo to the Portuguese was to make over the Congolese peoples to slavery.[38] Since Johnston emphatically disagreed with this, he sought a public platform to air his dissent from the views of Africa's greatest explorer.

The opportunity came at the Southport meeting of the British Association for the Advancement of Science on 24 September 1883. The secretary of the Geological Section praised Stanley as the man who was opening up 'the great road across Africa'. Johnston then got to his feet and read out extracts from Stanley's personal letter dated 23 July. This made it abundantly clear that Stanley wanted a British protectorate in the Congo.[39] Stanley's point was that *someone* would sooner or later take the Congo into its sphere of influence, and he wanted that someone to be Britain. At present, either Portugal or France with fifty men was stronger than the Association with 1000, for the international law issue of whether the AIC could resist a nation-state by force had not yet been cleared up.[40]

The reaction to this in Brussels was a stupefied horror that Stanley in person now seemed prepared to enter publicly the domain of international politics. Leopold wrote to Stanley to gag him, reminding him that according to the terms of his 1878 personal five-year contract he had promised not to publish anything or give any information about his work in the Congo. It was therefore imperative for Stanley to request his friends not to publish any of his letters to them.[41] The King's tone was that of gentle chiding, and Stanley replied in injured innocence that it had never crossed his mind that Johnston might reveal the contents of a personal letter.[42] But Strauch chose to put a more sinister interpretation on Stanley's actions. Years later he alleged that Stanley's 'treason' almost cost Belgium the Congo, and that the situation was retrieved only because the Anglo-Saxon nation turned down the gift that Stanley handed them on a plate.[43]

What is the truth of this? Once again the true villain of the piece turns out to be Leopold. By not revealing the full scope of his ambitions and insisting that his interest in the Congo was purely commercial, he cut the ground from under any serious indictment of Stanley. Stanley's action was perfectly consistent with Leopold's interests as he saw them and, more to the point, as he had been advised of them by the King himself. Stanley wanted a free trade area in the Congo of which British merchants would be the main beneficiaries. This was why his friends Hutton and Mackinnon supported Leopold in the Congo. They knew well enough that Portuguese or French rule meant protectionism and tariffs and they hoped for better from the King. Stanley was in effect calling in the power of England to protect Leopold's Congo against France and Portugal. It was not open for Leopold to claim that Stanley had cut across *his* political purposes since he had never told his 'agent in Chief' what they were, or even that he had any.[44]

Leopold indeed had every reason to be grateful to Stanley, for he used his fame as an 'American' in his successful bid to shore up his stake in the Congo with US help. He also used the argument, calculated to appeal to the descendants of President Monroe, that the Congo would be a second Liberia, another home of the free black man. General Sanford, who detested the Portuguese, was again a useful go-between in the process of winning over President Arthur.[45] Arthur announced his support for Leopold in his annual message to Congress on 4 December 1883. He seemed confused about the difference between the AIA and the AIC but then he was scarcely alone in being mystified about that.

Leopold's instinct that another storm was brewing was shrewd. On 24 February 1884 Portugal triumphantly struck back with the signature of a new Anglo–Portuguese treaty acknowledging Congo sovereignty.[46] Once again Leopold mobilised his friends in Europe, but this time the Foreign Office had had enough of his hypocrisy. The head of the Africa desk, Sir Percy Anderson, recommended that Leopold's real objectives be revealed to the world by the publication of the treaties he had made with the Congo tribes in which he acquired political sovereignty. This would expose to the anti-Portuguese 'bleeding hearts' that Leopold's entire operation was just a mask for a barefaced commercial monopoly.[47] Granville took the bait and wrote a polite but firm note to Leopold, threatening to divulge his secret manoeuvres. But by this time Leopold could not be budged, since he had learned from other channels that France feared Britain was about to absorb the AIC so would oppose the treaty with Portugal.[48]

Leopold went from strength to strength in his adroit playing of the French card. He offered Jules Ferry a 'special' deal in the Congo. The Strauch–Ferry statement of 23 April 1884 stated that the AIC would not cede any territory in the Congo but that if circumstances changed, France would get 'first refusal'. In return France would respect the Association's stations and territories in the Congo.[49] Here Leopold was playing an elaborate game. France thought that Leopold did not have the military and financial resources to hold on to the Congo and that it would soon be French. This was also the British conclusion, so Leopold hastened to assure them that the *droit de préférence* was purely theoretical.[50] As the shrewdest modern student of the Belgian King has pointed out, Ferry had allowed himself to be gulled. If the territories of the AIC could not be ceded, then the French first option was meaningless. And because the other powers were prepared to guarantee the neutrality of the Congo *against* France, France had been guaranteed a right which she could never use.[51]

There was thus a wealth of international news for Stanley to chew on as he sat disconsolately at Vivi waiting for his successor de Winton to arrive. He knew he was already a marked man in Portuguese eyes, though he was unaware that from the very earliest days Leopold secretly felt he could use Stanley's indiscretion about a British protectorate to turn the screws on the French.[52] The Strauch–Ferry accord was the triumphant culmination of this tactic.

On 11 May de Winton finally arrived at Vivi. The two men got on well though the friendship was always more marked on de Winton's side. Ever afterwards if Stanley felt de Winton received undue praise for his work in the Congo, he would 'redress the balance' with a little well-primed character assassination.[53] But in the month that remained before Stanley returned to Europe, de Winton was suitably deferential to the great explorer and listened attentively to his advice (dispassionate?) not to venture on to the Upper Congo but to base himself at Vivi, with occasional forays to Leopoldville.[54] Stanley asserted his superiority over his successor by heading a gang of construction workers on their morning shift from 6 a.m. to 11 a.m. while de Winton slowly acclimatised. One morning he returned to find de Winton and his friend Dr Leslie resting under the verandah with novels in their hands, looking downstream and positioned so as to receive the Atlantic breezes. Stanley warned de Winton that they were sitting in the deadliest spot in Vivi, but de Winton simply smiled incredulously. This was a mortification to Stanley, who always hated to have his opinions questioned, but he soon got his revenge: 'The two gentlemen came in to lunch and laughed at my warning, but when dinner time came, neither of them was at table and the next day they had their first bout of severe fever.'[55]

On 6 June, after a decent handing-over period, Stanley made his farewells and, accompanied by de Winton, made his way to Banana Point via Boma. On 10 June he embarked on the British steamer *Kinsembo*. There was a day's stopover at Loango, another at Gabon, and on 20 June the ship put in at Fernando Po, from which Cameroon was visible, 40 miles away. Here the ship needed to be refitted, so Stanley benefited from the week's delay by crossing to Calabar on the mainland and going on a three-day excursion upriver; he found it just like being on the Upper Congo.[56] Re-embarking at Fernando Po, he was at Bonny on 28 June (where he picked up various scabrous anecdotes about Burton and Verney Cameron) and in the roadstead of the Bight of Benin on 2 July. On the 5th they reached Lagos and on the 6th Quettah, where Stanley's sense of European superiority and his taste for flagellation both received a jolt: 'The local news at Quettah is that a white man has been sentenced to eight months' imprisonment for whipping a negro!'[57]

12 July found the *Kinsembo* at Sierra Leone, after which the ship made good speed to arrive at Tenerife on the 20th. Here Stanley got into a furious argument with an Anglophobe French chauvinist, whose distorted view of 'perfidious Albion' Stanley likened to the English view of Americans. But the verbal passage of arms prompted some interesting reflections on the English from a Welsh 'outsider'.

I have noticed that they would rather not say they were religious, or confess to saying their prayers at night. They would prefer not to say who were their parents or where they were born (!!!), or that they did not take cold baths, or that they are poor, or of mean origin, or that they have no acquaintance among the aristocracy, or that they do not agree with the wild opinion of the masses, or their press is licentious and intolerant. They fear ridicule, of *[sic]* being pointed out by their neighbours, of being mocked by sinners, and disdained by the worldly and slighted by public opinion. They would rather affect to be what others wish them to be in manners, dress, habits, but against the contempt of other nations they affect superb indifference and cold reserve, but we cannot tell Frenchmen our faults.[58]

On 23 July Stanley arrived at Madeira to find a telegram from Leopold requesting the earliest possible meeting in Brussels.[59] It was time for him to reflect on what he had achieved in the Congo in five years and to prepare an analysis of the remaining problems.

At a personal level Stanley had achieved something that was to be momentous in its consequences: the foundation of what was later to be the Belgian Congo. He told Puleston in 1887: 'The AIA was the happiest time of my life and the opening of the Lower Congo was the most interesting.'[60] Despite having notched up his African fever by 1884 and despite the carping of envious Germans who alleged that Stanley was a mere explorer who lacked the ability to organise a state[61], this is exactly what he had done. He had laid bare for greedy Europe to see the potential riches of the Congo: palm oil, used especially for cattle feed, gum copal for varnishes, vegetable oils for medicine and cooking, orchilla moss, iron and copper and, above all, ivory.[62] Stanley had already alerted the West to the fortunes to be made from ivory on the east-coast route: $2 a pound in Zanzibar, $1.10 in Unyanyembe and one cent in Manyema, where it was so commonplace that it was used for doorposts and eave stanchions.[63] Stanley compared the lust for ivory to the Australian and Californian gold rushes, the mining boom in Colorado, Idaho and Montana and the diamond fever of Cape Colony, but he neglected to point out that it was his colourful journalism and passionate advocacy that was stoking up the lust.[64]

In fairness to Stanley, it must be pointed out that he sometimes realised the Pandora's box he had unleashed on the poor elephants by his portrait of the Congo as a land flowing with milk and honey. In September 1884 he wrote to de Winton to approve his ban on elephant hunting by the Association, which de Winton had imposed so as not to alienate the tribes with 'sportsmen' shooting out the herds: 'Stop the shooting of the elephants, do not murder any more for the sheer pity of the noble beasts. Let the ground of the Association be sacred to the elephants. We do not yet know, but we may have use for them.'[65]

In military terms he had laid the foundations for Leopold's later bloody and barbarous colony, though he can in no sense be faulted for these later developments. By the end of 1883 he had at his disposal one hundred white men, 600 blacks, eight steamers, twelve Krupps guns, four machine guns, 1000 rapid-firing rifles and over two million cartridges. For once Lady Stanley, usually a purblind hagiographer, hit the nail on the head when she summed up her husband's achievement in the *Autobiography*:

The founding of the Congo Free State was the greatest single enter-prise of Stanley's life. Perhaps nothing else so called out and displayed his essential qualities. Its ultimate fruit cannot be so clearly measured as the search for Livingstone, or the first exploration of the Congo, of those enterprises he was himself the Alpha and the Omega; each was a task for a single man, and the achievement was measured by the man's personality. But the founding of the Free State was a multiple task, involving a host of workers. He had not made the selection of his helpers, except the rank and file, and the rank and file did not fail him. It was his lieutenants, selected by others, among whom the perilous defect was found. Further, his undertaking, in its essential nature, involved dangers which it was doubtless well he did not wholly foresee, for they might have daunted even *his* spirit.[66]

Yet Stanley's achievement should not be exaggerated. He was far from having solved all the problems he wrestled with in his five years. In October 1883 Augouard wrote depreciatingly about his own countrymen: 'As for this precious French territory of which so much fuss is being made in the papers, it is simply a joke and before the vote [sc. to ratify the Makoko treaties] was taken all the deputies and senators should have been sent out to Stanley Pool for a month to live on roots and water.'[67] But by the time of Stanley's departure, the French were striking back hard. Ballay settled at Ngantsu's in November 1883 and established a French station there.[68] Paramount chief Iloo, with French help, compelled homage from Opontaba, Ngalioo and Ngantsu in April 1884.[69] The struggle for mastery in the Stanley Pool area continued after the going of Bula Matari, with Opontaba playing a key role.[70]

The one area where Stanley seemed to have decisively eclipsed the French was on the Upper Congo; with the expedition seemingly becoming more English all the time in French eyes (exactly what Leopold wanted the world to think, hence the recruitment of Gordon, Goldsmid, de Winton, etc.), the enemies of France appeared to have a stranglehold on trade coming down the river.[71] Yet even here Stanley's commercial success was limited. Indigenous ivory traders could only be dealt a death blow by the advent of a railway. As late as 1889 Europeans still bought only five-eighths of the ivory at Stanley Pool, while the traditional caravans accounted for the rest.[72] Moreover, since rubber did not become an important state activity in the Congo until 1889, Tio caravans largely continued to enjoy their monopoly on the sale of rubber.[73]

The great plus Stanley enjoyed on the Upper Congo was the calibre of his officers, especially Coquilhat and Vangele, whom he later identified as the two finest aides he had ever worked with.[74] Yet even a good officer did not guarantee ultimate success. Since Glave's station at Lukolela did not try to control trade or buy ivory, it was notably popular with the indigenous tribes. Yet the Belgians abandoned both Lukolela and Bolobo in 1885–6 since the 1885 Berlin treaty deprived the posts of much of their *raison d'être*[75]

The real 'shirt of Nessus' (to use a favourite Stanley metaphor) that the great explorer left behind him was the post at Stanley Falls. This brought closer the inevitable conflict between Tippu Tip's Arabs and the Belgians that was resolved only by full-scale warfare in the 1890s. The leader of the Arab caravan whom Stanley had met near the falls in late November 1883, Obed-ben-Salim, told Barghash of his encounter with Stanley and asked for further instructions: should he have opposed the building of the fort; was he culpable in neglecting the Sultan's interest by letting Europeans siphon away ivory by the western route?[76] But he was really addressing the wrong person. Tippu Tip, while paying token fealty to Zanzibar, was the real power in the area and he soon made his presence felt. Late in 1884 he came in person to the post at Stanley Falls to teach the Belgians the facts of life in Central Africa. He told Arnid Wester (who replaced Bennie in July 1884) that he intended to pass Stanley Falls and proceed downriver despite the Belgian interdict on interlopers.[77] Wester did not have the military force to stop him, so Tippu Tip openly tweaked Leopold's nose by selling slaves in the Congo state. The nominal suzerainty of Zanzibar was maintained for a while by the combination of Arab strength and Belgian weakness.[78]

The situation continued tense. In 1885 Vangele and Tippu Tip had a firm but friendly confrontation over respective spheres of influence. Tippu Tip insisted that the whole of Africa from Zanzibar to Banana belonged to the Sultan. Vangele rebutted this by pointing out that Stanley claimed the Congo for Leopold by being the first to chart it, rubbing salt in Tippu's wound, for the Arab had told Stanley in 1876 that the descent was impossible. Tippu said his methods were Stanley's: if he needed food, he took it by force. Vangele replied that Stanley at least never pillaged ivory or burned villages to the ground and took slaves.[79] Vangele clearly won the dialectical contest, but this solved nothing as Tippu Tip had the power. By late 1885 the missionary Grenfell found the Arab chief dug in and unprepared to alter his methods one whit.[80] When Wester was replaced by Captain Deane, the Belgian attitude shifted from realism to aggression. This was folly, since for the moment Leopold could do nothing but fume over Tippu's flouting of his authority, But the thorn in his side particularly rankled, as he had already confided in Stanley that it was his ambition to extend the boundaries of the new state as far as Bahr-el-Ghazal to the west of the Upper Nile. The opportunity to score off an old enemy was too good for Stanley to miss. After pointing out that the Arabs on 'Belgian' territory had uplifted 1300 slaves and a million francs' worth of ivory on a single raid, he insinuated that the Arabs were being manipulated from Zanzibar: 'Kirk reflects this faithfully. The stoppage of enlistment of Zanzibaris is due to him, the instructions to the Arabs of Nyangwe and Tippu Tip by the Sultan are also due to him.'[81] The British seemed to be threatening the Congo from both ends, supporting the Portuguese at the Atlantic and the Arabs at Stanley Falls; Tippu Tip remained the wild card, the maverick, the unknown quantity. The 'King Incorporated' now had so many balls in the air simultaneously that even for an expert juggler like him the game was becoming supremely perilous.

6

ON 27 July 1884, by special dispensation of the owners, the *Kinsembo* put in to Plymouth to land Stanley on English soil. In Plymouth Sound a *Times* reporter boarded the steamer for an 'exclusive' with the reporter on his views on Gordon and Khartoum. Stanley declared himself against an expedition to relieve Khartoum – Gordon could get out any time he wanted to – but with the proviso that only the British government knew the full facts.[1] Privately he poured scorn on the press for expecting miracles from Gordon and foresaw the tragedy that was to overtake Khartoum the following January: 'Nothing else could be expected from one who was supposed to come out to help me in my Congo work and wrote about killing slave traders in their haunts. Great piety is not always inconsistent with good sense, but I fear in Gordon's case he is more pious than sensible.'[2]

From Plymouth he caught the train to London, where he found further requests from Leopold to come to Belgium with all speed. On 2 August he met the King at Ostend. There, at the Hotel de la Fontaine, he was Leopold's guest for five days; a special cook was even employed to see that Stanley received the traditional English breakfast every morning. Each day Stanley had two long sessions with the monarch, including a detailed debriefing after dinner.[3] The pace was such that Stanley was forced to telegram Sanford: 'Can find no time to write. Visitors, interviewers, business continually. Am so sorry. Thanks for your welcome.'[4]

The talks ranged far and wide over the international implications of a Congo state, for even while Stanley was on the high seas, the story had moved on a chapter. Leopold had one solid achievement to his credit. His lobbying of the USA, making out the Congo to be a new Liberia, had paid off. President Chester Arthur was impressed by the trading potential of the Congo and thought it significant that the Association's chief executive officer was an 'American'.[5] This was exactly what Leopold had hoped for. US recognition of the AIC followed on 22 April 1884 and there was enthusiastic support for Leopold's idea of a chain of stations from Zanzibar to the Atlantic.[6]

But Britain, thinking that Leopold was in league with France, had set its face against the Association.[7] Even more worrying was that Bismarck had now entered the African arena. On the one hand, he refused to ratify the Anglo–Portuguese treaty, which was therefore still-born.[8] This was part of a process whereby the German Chancellor picked a quarrel with Britain in mid-1884 as a means of signalling to France that he wanted friendly relations; there was also the desire to call 'the Reich in danger' at the forthcoming Reichstag elections and to cripple the Anglophile liberalism of the Crown Prince.[9] So far so good, as far as Leopold was concerned. But on the other hand the 'Iron Chancellor' soon sniffed out the Belgian King's duplicity and low cunning. When Leopold sent him his 'humanitarian' proposals to move into the Sudan so as to snuff out the slave trade, Bismarck at once saw right through him and scrawled '*Schwindel!*' in the margin against the humbug about slavery. His remarks on Leopold reveal him as one of the few contemporaries fully to have taken his measure: 'His Majesty displays the naïve, pretentious egoism of an Italian who assumes as a law of nature that everything will be done for him for the sake of his *beaux yeux* and nothing of equal value asked of him in return.'[10]

The German banker Gerson von Bleichroder, one of Leopold's business associates, warned him that he was alienating Bismarck by his duplicity; Germany wanted a proper trade guarantee in the event of recognition of the AIC as well as modest, realistic boundaries for a Congo state.[11] This news arrived on Stanley's very last day in Ostend. He was on the point of departure when the King asked him to delay for a few hours to draw up a map with reasonable frontiers which would satisfy the Chancellor's insistence that the proposed independent state be forced back on to Congo littoral boundaries.[12] This sort of thing was Stanley's forte. The map he prepared was so thorough and professional that Bismarck was at once won round. He informed the French ambassador in Berlin that there was now nothing to be lost by German recognition of the Congo state.[13] At the beginning of September Bismarck sent Leopold an eight-page handwritten letter to confirm this decision.[14]

But most of the Stanley–Leopold discussions in Ostend in early August had focused on the putative enemy: Portugal and France. The King reassured Stanley that the Johnston gaffe at the British Association had been forgotten; indeed Johnston had performed a useful service by coming straight to Brussels on his return to Europe and giving a clear *tour d'horizon* of the situation in the Congo (Stanley's need for Chinese coolies and so on). Moreover, he had applauded the way Johnston defended Stanley in the European press after he had been accused of subduing the Congo with a horde of savage, murderous *wangwana*. For once the King was giving a true account of his own reactions at the time.[15]

Leopold was reasonably relaxed about the threat from Portugal now that Bismarck had given Lisbon the thumbs-down. Brazza was another matter. The King agreed with Stanley that Brazza could only be knocked out decisively when the AIC had international recognition. Until that time the situation remained as Stanley had described it for Mackinnon from Vivi in May:

> So long as we have not a character recognised by European nations, de Brazza with his walking stick, a French flag and a few words in pursuit of the whites of Leopoldville is really stronger than Stanley with his Krupps and all material of war, faithful adherents, aid of natives, etc. We could easily defeat him and lay him gently down on the soil of his beloved Brazzaville. But what then? The affair is not settled. It has only assumed a greater importance and gravity. France might shriek out: What? – this unrecognised filibuster Stanley has laid hands upon the emissary of the French government and then the *Sagittaire* coolly steams up the Congo and seizes all our boats and shells us out of Vivi and blockades us, and of course then comes the deluge.[16]

Since Leopold and Stanley saw eye to eye on all these matters, it was not surprising that he was able to relate that he had received an ovation at the end of his time in Ostend, 'though not in the noisy manner peculiar to England'.[17] From Ostend he sped to Paris, to put up at his beloved Hôtel Meurice in the Rue de Rivoli, while he pondered his next move. During his brief stop in London on 30 July he had been given the impression that his old quarters at 30 Sackville Street would no longer be available as the premises had changed hands. But so far he had been unable to find suitable apartments in London.[18] Yet at the end of ten days word came through that his old domicile was after all available. He crossed to London, missing Sanford who had set out for the Continent to meet him.[19]

His first task was to lobby Lord Granville to recognise the Association as political 'overseer' on the Congo. But Granville was non-committal. Though generally sympathetic, he had no wish to involve Britain in a war with France over a notionally important territory in Central Africa.[20] So Stanley decided to appeal over the heads of the Foreign Office directly to public opinion. He sat down to prepare a series of lectures arguing for recognition of a new independent Congo state with no Customs barriers. Leopold pledged himself to support the lectures by getting the widest possible coverage in the English press, while cautioning Stanley not to 'over-sell' the Congo just yet.[21]

Yet Stanley, a dedicated publicity-seeker, could never keep out of controversy. First he was forced to write to *The Times* to defend himself against a campaign of vilification in the French press, which alleged that while in Paris he was provocative and insulting to Brazza.[22] Then he became embroiled with the Baker family in a dispute over the military performance in the Sudan of Lupton Bey and Baker Pasha (Sir Samuel's brother), whose army had been annihilated by the Mahdi.[23] Leopold had to warn him to be quiet, as his outspokenness on these matters *pari passu* with a lecture tour on the Congo might lead to an accusation that the Belgian King was meddling in the Sudan.[24]

Stanley's relations with Brussels now began to enter a period of uneasiness that was to persist for the next three years. He took it hard when his personal recommendation of Julian Arnold (Sir Edwin of the *Daily Telegraph*'s son) as Strauch's secretary was ignored.[25] In retaliation Stanley took his time about replying to Strauch's offer of a new contract from the AIC, offering an immediate £500 a year as a retainer while in Europe and specifying the future maximum time to be spent in Africa as two and a half years. In addition, the royalties from his proposed Congo book would be his, provided he published nothing without prior approval from Brussels.[26] This *douceur* seemed less impressive when Leopold a few days later sent a sheaf of sentences to be omitted from Stanley's first draft of the book and suggested that the entire project would be better shelved until after international recognition of the Association, now a distinct possibility in the light of moves to organise a general Africa conference in Berlin.[27]

While Stanley stalled on the renewal of his contract with the AIC, he kept up a correspondence with Leopold's secretariat about the proposed Congo railway, advised on British half-pay officers who might be suitable for service there, and kept in touch with his successor de Winton.[28] A welcome relief from the toil of working on his speeches to be launched at British industrialists was the interview he conducted in Sackville Street to select another of the success stories of the Congo, Herbert Ward. Ward described the encounter as follows:

> The room in which I was received impressed me as characteristic of the man. There were here no ornaments or bric-à-brac, nor were the walls hung with guns and trophies of the explorer. Everything spoke of earnest, tireless work; floor and tables bore traces of it, littered as they were with manuscripts, maps and scattered papers and pamphlets, while amid the confusion everywhere around I detected the famous Congo cap, which has figured in so many illustrations, thrown carelessly on a sideboard.[29]

Stanley began by expressing doubts about how the new recruit would stand up to the climate. Ward explained that he had been in Borneo, which particularly interested Stanley because of Leopold's obsession that the British treaties with the Sultan of Borneo formed a precedent for the AIC. His objections melted away: 'Well, after all, the Congo is a sanatorium compared to Borneo.'[30]

On 18 September Stanley delivered the pilot version of his commercial speech to the London Chamber of Commerce. He spoke of the record of the AIC under its various manifestations, how it had unlocked the Congo to free trade, how a Confederation of tribal states would be good for business. The lecture was enthusiastically received.[31] But ever at his elbow lurked the spectre of Brussels. For the Manchester speech, perceived as crucial, he had to submit his draft to Leopold, who returned it with deletions: there was to be no mention of the Anglo–Portuguese treaty and nothing critical said about Germany, for it was on Bismarck that Leopold now chiefly depended.[32]

Stanley was beginning to find the pace of work punishing. As he explained to Mackinnon when accepting an invitation to his castle at Balinakill, he had engagements in Brighton from 11 to 13 October, had three speeches to deliver in Manchester from 21 to 23 October, then had speaking engagements in Edinburgh. In addition, he had to hold himself in readiness in case he was needed at the Berlin Conference in November which had hardened into a fixture. Despite being a fast writer, he was beginning to feel under unconscionable pressure.[33] But the success of the three Manchester speeches, to the Chamber of Commerce, the Manchester Athenaeum and the Manchester Geographical Society, set the adrenalin flowing properly again.[34] Addressing the Chamber of

Commerce in Manchester Town Hall on 21 October, Stanley was on his very best demagogic form. He asked his audience to imagine a market for cotton vaster even than India, one where millions of Congolese might be wearing a cotton garment. Such was his advocacy that the Chamber of Commerce at once began to lobby the Foreign Office to back Leopold and the Association[35] The *Manchester Guardian*, which had been agonising over the implications for foreign relations with France and Portugal, was won over, though with reservations.[36] Stanley told his friend James Hutton, president of the Chamber of Commerce, that 'he had been rather afraid Manchester had drifted into old fogeyism and senility. Her loud manifestations and eager expressions of gratification at the prospect of the new market prove the reverse.'[37]

From Manchester Stanley proceeded to a short working holiday with Mackinnon at Balinakill.[38] Mackinnon himself had visited Leopold in Brussels the month before to co-ordinate tactics.[39] Then it was time to proceed to Berlin, if he was wanted there. But it was precisely this that was uncertain during October and early November. Leopold's deviousness and dog-in-the-manger attitude led to a diplomatic tangle which took weeks to sort out. The problem was that the AIC, having no standing in international law, could not be invited to the Berlin Conference. Stanley was an employee of the AIC, but the Americans, with justifiable pride, wanted such a distinguished 'fellow-American' on their delegation.

The American Minister at Berlin and the man designated as their representative at the Conference was John A. Kasson.[40] On 20 October he wrote to Stanley as follows: 'Can you hold yourself at liberty to be present at Berlin a week before the meeting of the Conference on West African affairs and during its deliberations . . . this action will be in harmony with the interests which you represent [a reference to Stanley's divided loyalties as between the Association and the USA].'[41] As each delegate would also be allowed an associate, Kasson thought of Sanford and sent for him. A further US official, W. P. Tisdel, was also accredited as 'US representative to the State of the Congo'.[42]

Now ever since the idea of the Berlin Conference had been mooted, Leopold had been wooing Kasson, but he did not want Kasson to put either Stanley or Mackinnon fully in the picture on US–Belgian relations. Kasson's invitation to Stanley cut across his scheming, and Leopold issued a hasty note of regret that Stanley could not be released to the US delegation. Perplexed, Kasson conferred with Sanford in London about this unexpected development. Sanford suggested turning the tables on Leopold by a theatrical *coup de main* while he was in Brussels with the King. He had Kasson cable him requesting Stanley's presence yet again; this gave Sanford the opportunity to break off his talks with the King and endorse the request.[43] Leopold dithered and finally agreed, provided Stanley signed the new contract, which he had not yet done: Leopold thus revealed one of the motives for his dog-in-the-manger attitude. In a memorandum in early November he revealed other reasons. Stanley would muddy the waters at Berlin since it would be open to representatives of other powers to point out that one of the US delegates was scarcely a dispassionate debater of the future of the Association in the Congo; he was indiscreet and might reveal secrets; he did not get on with Kasson and was secretly strongly disliked by Sanford.[44]

Meanwhile Stanley added another twist to the story by requesting leave of absence until the following spring to attend such conferences as would help his book – a clear indication that he personally wanted to go to Berlin. He offered to return to the Congo in 1885 provided that his AIC salary was raised to £1000 p.a. Sanford felt that the way to cut the Gordian knot was to ask Bismarck to invite Stanley, but at this all Kasson's diplomatic hackles rose: it was not for Bismarck to say who should or should not be in the US delegation and anyway Stanley had been invited as an expert explorer, not an official member of the delegation.[45]

When Stanley pressed to know whether he was to go to Berlin, Leopold's officials stalled, on the fatuous ground that it was not yet clear whether such co-opted 'experts' would be welcome in Berlin. Stanley decided to cross over to Belgium to speak to Leopold in person.[46] Meanwhile Leopold contested Kasson's position with the argument that since Stanley worked for the AIC, and the AIC had not been invited to the Berlin Conference, the invitation *had* to emanate from Bismarck. The subtext of all this was that the Belgians wanted Stanley at Berlin as *their* observer, *not* as a member of the US delegation, and considered it important that Kasson should acknowledge their prior rights over the great explorer.[47] Leopold got his way and the request was forwarded to Bismarck.

Bismarck for his part saw good propaganda advantage to be gained from Stanley's presence in Berlin. He was a popular and almost legendary figure who would arouse enthusiasm in Germany for overseas ventures now that the Chancellor had decided to go for colonies and claim the fatherland's right to a place in the sun. He immediately replied with his permission. Leopold had no option then but to allow Stanley to proceed to Berlin, cautioning him, however, to be prudent and be guided by Sanford.[48]

Kasson meanwhile had withdrawn his invitation to Stanley on grounds of AIC opposition. It took further cables and messages to sort out the mess. Not until 11 November was it crystal clear that Stanley would, after all, form part of the US delegation. As a *quid pro quo* Sanford and his wife talked him round to the idea of renewing his contract on the terms required by Leopold.[49]

Before leaving for Berlin Stanley had to sort out his domestic arrangements. Dualla was falling out of favour, and Baruti, the boy from the Soko tribe he had brought back with him to be a second Kalulu, was proving far more intractable than Kalulu had ever been. One night when Stanley was absent, Baruti asked the explorer's housekeeper to give him a certain choice dish from the larder. When she refused, he became violent, seized her baby and rushed upstairs. At the landing he held the baby over the banisters and threatened to drop it unless his demand was granted.[50]

This was the troubled context in which an American woman of Stanley's acquaintance introduced him to a seventeen-year-old apprentice of German descent at Sackville Street, one William Hoffmann, destined thereafter to be a constant and troublesome feature in Stanley's life. Hoffmann later gave an account of his introduction to Stanley. He was working on the Congo book in his study and a bright fire was blazing. 'Well, my man,' said Stanley, 'can you speak German?' 'Yes.' 'Will you accompany me to Germany, as I am going to attend the Berlin Conference?'[51] Thus did Hoffmann become Stanley's manservant. But the master–servant relationship got off to a bad start. At Charing Cross, when they boarded the Berlin express, Stanley felt hungry and sent Hoffmann off to buy some sandwiches. By the time he came back with them, the train had gone. Left penniless, Hoffmann had to get the stationmaster to wire ahead to the coast to say that he would be on the next train. When he caught up with his master, Hoffmann was treated to the special tongue-lashing Stanley reserved for feckless or incompetent servants of whatever rank.[52]

Stanley and Hoffmann reached Frankfurt at 5 a.m. on 15 November and Berlin later that day. He put up at the Hotel Royal and started familiarising himself with protocol for the US delegation.[53] Immediately there arose a clash of personalities between Stanley and Tisdel, who disagreed violently with his estimate of the economic potential of the Congo and claimed to know as much as Stanley about African affairs.

When Sanford took Stanley's side, Tisdel stormed off and quit Berlin without taking part in a single session of the Conference.[54]

There was much to research and digest before the first sessions of the Conference got under way. Stanley was not privy to all Leopold's secret thoughts and devious manoeuvring but he knew that the key to ultimate success was Bismarck, who formally recognised the AIC on 8 November, thus at one level throwing down the gauntlet to the British championing of Portugal. At Berlin, Bismarck and Jules Ferry made common cause in resentment and suspicion of the 1882 occupation of Egypt by Britain. Bismarck and Ferry shared the conviction that without colonies they would decline to the level of a fourth- or fifth-rate power like Spain.[55] Additionally in the French case *l'honneur* and Brazza's prestige were at stake.[56]

But cutting across these political considerations were the economic ones. At this level free-trading England and Germany were ranged against protectionist France and Portugal, thus introducing contradictions into the pre-existing political alliances. Free trade benefited the great powers of the day, as it always does. The inertia of power was bound to secure an automatic advantage for the imperial giant (Britain) or its great industrial rival (Germany). Indeed Lord Salisbury later justified his imperialism as a pre-emptive strike against the endemic French tendency towards tariff walls.[57] Protectionism is the reflex action of the ascending, declining, threatened or second-rate power; significantly in the twentieth century when the USA became *the* great power in the 1930s, Britain switched to protectionism.[58]

After being introduced as a technical delegate for the USA, Stanley at once plunged into the Conference maelstrom. He argued for a broad commercial delta 380 miles wide from the mouth of the Loge River to 20° S, latitude, within which freedom of trade would be guaranteed, and argued that the same freedom should be established to within 1° from the sea coast, from latitude 5°N. up to and inclusive of the River Zambezi.[59] As against the Portuguese desire for a much narrower outlet, Stanley suggested that the northern limit of the proposed free-trade area be placed at Fernan Vaz. In fact this proposal originated with the British delegation, but it was thought to have a better chance of success if Stanley, not the Foreign Office, introduced it.[60] Stanley impressed his listeners with a lucid explanation of the two senses of the term 'Congo basin', geographical and commercial, the point being that a narrow geographical definition might well deprive the trade of the Upper Congo of its natural outlet.[61] Kasson was especially impressed by the performance of his fellow delegate: 'He [Stanley] went to a chart suspended in a room, and immediately engrossed the interest of every delegate, by a vivid description of the features of the Congo basin; and finally of the country necessary to go with it under the same regime to secure the utmost freedom of communication with the two oceans.'[62] But Stanley's definition was resisted by France and Portugal, and the limit was eventually set to the south of Fernan Vaz, at Sette Camma.

Not all participants shared Kasson's enthusiasm for Stanley's approach. The explorer's clear mind could not deal with the fudging and compromise so necessary to diplomacy. Because he lectured and hectored the delegates on the need for crystal clarity in the Congo and hence for formal agreements, official representatives felt themselves browbeaten into writing home for explicit instructions, so that the net effect of Stanley's interventions was to delay proceedings. Also, his air of omniscience irritated those with no particular axe to grind on the east-coast trade area, so that they tended to make difficulties just to put him in his place.[63]

Stanley's overwhelming aplomb came from the knowledge that he had both Kasson's overt support and the secret backing of Bismarck. The fact that the Conference accepted the principle of a free trade area and to some extent went along with Stanley's definition of it was hailed by the explorer as a great triumph, and he entered his first major social engagement, dinner with Bismarck, in a mood of exultation. There was just one other guest that night (24 November 1884) – a Hamburg merchant named Woerrmann, member of the Reichstag and delegate to the Conference, a man mainly interested in West African commerce. Bismarck introduced Stanley to him as a glittering example of what a solitary hero could do to open up unexplored territory.[64] Stanley's glowing mood that evening is evinced in his journal entry:

This evening I had the honour of dining with Prince Bismarck and family. The Prince is a great man, a kind father, and excellently simple in his family. The Princess adores him, says little and that always in a deferent [sic] manner. The Prince listens in a benevolently paternal way, pats his big dog or plays with his ears, with his pipe held negligently downward, which seems to me, when with an encouraging smile he leans towards his wife – a sign of the usual habits of husband and wife. I gathered by their attitudes and behaviour a better idea of their domestic life than I should by ever so much description. The Prince asked many questions about Africa and proved to me that in a large way he understood the condition of that continent very well.[65]

Stanley later exaggerated his role at the Berlin Conference. In fact a large number of African issues were discussed on which Stanley had no knowledge or could contribute little – the Niger question for instance. It gradually became clear that Britain was prepared to recognise the AIC in return for opposition to the internationalisation of the Niger basin.[66] And when Stanley did re-enter the fray, on 30 November, he seriously embarrassed Leopold by giving away too much about his ulterior motives in the Congo. He effectively revealed the plan for a railway by arguing that concessions for developing the infrastructure should be given to the actual occupiers in Africa, thus alerting rivals to what was in Leopold's mind.[67] When the gaffe was pointed out to him later, Stanley rewrote the incident. His version in *Congo* simply states blandly: 'I made a speech about the religious and missionary enterprise in the Congo basin.'[68]

So marginal was Stanley to the main proceedings that Kasson raised no objection when Stanley departed on the evening of 30 November to keep a long-standing engagement in Edinburgh. He paid a flying visit to the Foreign Office in London to report the growing *entente* between Bismarck and the British delegation, following which the Foreign Office instructed Kirk to use his influence with Barghash to recruit another 400 Zanzibaris for Congo service.[69] Then Stanley sped on to Edinburgh for his speech at the inauguration of the Scottish Geographical Society. He was in Edinburgh on the 3rd and 4th, then Glasgow on 5–6 December.

This proved one of Stanley's least happy ventures. Stanley regurgitated his Manchester arguments, presenting the Congo as a cornucopia of commercial opportunity. His speech was full of commodities, prices and statistics.[70] In the audience was the Scottish explorer Joseph Thomson, who was known from his published work to be critical of Stanley.[71] He could not see the great trading future that Stanley outlined and at the banquet afterwards Thomson took the more famous man to task: 'I have to express the melancholy feeling I have for the last few days entertained as I listened to Mr Stanley, on seeing how the iron heel of commerce has entirely knocked romance out of African travel. There were days when there was romance in African travel, but the soul-less [sic] march of commerce has been gradually trampling out that, and we must apparently consider that the days of African romance are pretty well gone. It is pitiful that such should be the case . . . We have come to look upon the palm-tree, not in regard to its artistic effect, but upon the quantity of oil that it is to produce. If this sort of thing is to go on, I should prefer to go to the North Pole.'[72]

When Stanley bridled at this portrait of him as a mere money-grubber, Thomson pressed home the attack in the Scottish press. He accused Stanley of being thin-skinned and lacking a sense of humour: 'It has been said that Scotsmen require a surgical operation to impart a joke to them. Are we to claim Mr Stanley as a countryman from the apparent development in him of this interesting peculiarity?'[73] Privately he was much more caustic. In a letter to Bates at the RGS, Thomson developed the theme of his dislike: 'There is one thing certain, however, that they [the Scots] are not inclined to dance to Stanley's piping. Even in Glasgow the merchants are shaking their heads over this windbag that he has been trying to inflate and in Edinburgh the people have been quite delighted with the little bit of fun I had out of him. He has not made a single friend and has succeeded in repelling everyone by his insufferable egotism.'[74]

Stanley was soured by his Scottish experience, even though he fulfilled his commitment by going on from Edinburgh to speak to the Dundee branch of the Scottish Geographical Society.[75] But the scepticism and even hostility he encountered, so tellingly in contrast to his treatment in Manchester in October, scarred him. When he recalled the events in early 1885 he was especially bitter about the way the *Scottish Geographical Magazine* had highlighted Thomson's remarks and those of other hostile commentators:

In old times we are told the Caesars in their triumphal chariots were accompanied by a skeleton that they might not forget in the midst of their triumph how vain after all were all these temporary elevations. My Scotch friends doubtless with the view to conveying a moral to me put forth my address, and my speech, and then show me my skeleton made more hideous by falsehoods. The moral is plain, the philosophy is good, but the taste and the spirit of it all is censurable.[76]

On 9 December a chastened Stanley was back in London, where he dined with Mackinnon and an assortment of Foreign Office mandarins and other notables.[77] Then he proceeded to Brussels, fortified by the news that the Royal Treasurer Gazelot had just informed him that his salary would be the £1000 p.a. he had asked for. In this roundabout way he learned that he was still in favour with Leopold, who indeed received him well and told him he was pleased with his performance at Berlin.

The time in Brussels was spent plotting how to leak to the Foreign Office Minister Julian Pauncefoote the French design to take from Belgium all the coastal territory from Sette Camma to the Loango.[78] Stanley reported his impressions to Sanford: 'I saw the King. He is pale, probably from confinement indoors, otherwise charming and polite as usual and in no way dispirited, so far as I can judge.'[79]

While Stanley returned to the fine and dry weather of Berlin in December 1884, Leopold had at last decided how to prise England away from Portugal. Fearful that if he made the concession on the Congo basin demanded of him, he would simply be asked to make yet further concessions, he threatened to pull out of Africa altogether, leaving chaos behind. Since he had already signed the *droit de préférence* with France, this would leave the Congo behind French Customs barriers, and this would have been the end result of the sinuous Foreign Office policy.[80] As Stanley wrote to Hutton on 10 December: 'I am off tonight for Berlin. We are going to the wall sure, if England will not act with Germany.'[81]

Leopold's bluff worked. On 17 December Britain recognised the Association and, following a full meeting of the plenipotentiaries, Italy, Austria–Hungary, Russia and Spain followed suit.[82] But still France and Portugal remained aloof. The French were pressing hard for the annexation of the Kwilu-Niari lands, on the grounds that the treaties signed by Stanley's agents were with vassals of Makoko and therefore invalid.[83] Leopold was in principle prepared to cede these territories but only in return for an indemnity of five million francs. When the conference adjourned for the Christmas holidays, Stanley was therefore sent back to London for a further session of arm-twisting at the Foreign Office. In particular Strauch wanted immediate permission from the British to enlist 500 Zanzibaris and 350 Chinese coolies for Congo construction work, as well as a couple of hundred sepoys for 'policing' duties. This was urgent, since the contracts of service of many of those at the Congo posts were near to expiry and their departure before replacements arrived would entail the abandonment of all the hard-won stations at Vivi, Isangila, Manyanga, etc.[84]

During the Christmas holiday break from 23 December to 5 January, Stanley was back in London lobbying Lord Granville, stressing the absolute necessity not to allow French protectionism to ruin commercial opportunities on the Congo.[85] He received an invitation to speak at banquets in German cities and Leopold, pleased with his tireless work with Granville, granted him leave to attend, provided he made no reference, even indirect to Brazza, for alienation of the French at such a crucial time could cost the King the Congo.[86] Here again Stanley paid the penalty for his crepuscular status, always the man in the middle. While Brazza was a French national hero, Stanley was doomed to fall between the three stools of Belgium, Britain and the USA, each with a claim on him but none prepared to embrace him as a true son. His irritation found expression in a letter to Sanford, witheringly ironical about the necessity to mouth 'effectless . . . pointless . . . platitudes'.[87]

On 5 January the Berlin Conference resumed proceedings and at once passed a resolution prohibiting the slave trade in the Congo basin; an attempt to prohibit the sale of liquor also was defeated.[88] On the 7th Stanley was banqueting in Cologne, and on the 8th and 9th he lectured to enthusiastic audiences in Frankfurt and Wiesbaden.[89] He was about to return to Berlin when Sanford advised him that the Conference was suspended for a week. Stanley stayed put on the Rhine: 'I do not see the necessity of yawning over dullness there, as I can do it with so much more freedom here.'[90]

He was back in Berlin on the 19th for the banquet given by Bismarck for plenipotentiaries and delegates to the Conference. It was at this time that he met the future Kaiser Wilhelm in Potsdam. There was a general feeling by now that the final lap of the Conference had been reached, but the last days of January saw Stanley firmly in harness. On 28 January Sanford persuaded him, much against his will, to write a long letter to Bismarck criticising Portuguese policy in general and on Kabinda in particular.[91] He made a speech to the Conference on the wealth and resources of the Congo which later attracted much criticism. In this he claimed that the population of the area was forty-three millions, and cited Wissmann, Schweinfurth and even Tippu Tip as evidence.[92] In fact the best estimate of the Congo's population in 1885 puts it at between twelve and thirteen millions, but Stanley in mitigation could cite Brazza in his defence, for Brazza made a rough estimate of fifty millions.[93] He was at one with Brazza too in his exaggeration of the wealth of the Congo. Stanley estimated the potential value of trade to be £70,000,000. Of course for this to be achieved a railway was needed all the way to Stanley Falls; Stanley dealt briskly with Sir Edward Malet's suggestion that a line from Vivi to Leopoldville alone would be enough. When the Netherlands delegate made the mistake of mentioning Cameron's name in connection with the suggestion that canals could be used, Stanley snapped back that this was only possible between Lakes Mantumba and Leopold, if the delegate knew where that was.[94]

At last in early February, Bismarck and the British 'squared' France.

Leopold agreed to cede the Kwilu-Niari territories for an indemnity and permission for the Association to run a six million francs lottery in France. The French concluded a treaty with the organisation on the very day that news of Gordon's death in Khartoum came in.[95] It remained now only for the Great Powers to bludgeon Portugal into acceptance in return for a face-saving strip of territory to the north of the Congo mouth; without English support, now that Britain had thrown in with Bismarck, there was little else the Portuguese could do.

On 15 February Portugal signed the convention and on the 21st the French neutrality resolution was adopted. There remained the formalities, such as the recognition of the Association by Sweden and Belgium itself.[96] Then on 26 February came the formal plenary session of the Conference with Bismarck in the chair. The Berlin Act of this date declared the Congo and its tributaries to be a free trade zone from the Atlantic to the Indian Ocean and the whole area was designated as neutral. All the powers were pledged to aid missionaries and put down the slave trade. The only worrying feature for Leopold was that an International Commission was set up to oversee Congo navigation and raise loans for its expenses, thus conjuring visions of a possible rival to the AIC. All in all it seemed a fairly sweeping triumph for Leopold and his henchmen. The one minor cloud was that although Sanford signed the treaty, it was never ratified by the USA. Already the Department of State was distancing itself. Senator Morgan wrote to Sanford at the conclusion of the Conference: 'I very much regret that Mr Freyling-hausen [the Secretary of State] has been so reticent about the Congo. Not that I could feel neglected in the matter but because you and Mr Stanley deserved something better than to be carefully hid away from sight as if you had purloined Congo and were trying to deliver the country over to us or somebody else in a sort of illegitimate way.'[97]

Stanley spent the dog days of the Conference putting the finishing touches to his *Congo* book. He had to forward each chapter to Brussels for approval; Leopold got out his blue pencil and deleted all incriminating evidence. His primary aim was to cover his tracks but he also insisted that Stanley tone down what he had to say about the state of the expedition when he arrived back in Africa in December 1882 and that he omit the offending officers' names. 'Your book coming out after the close of the Conference must be written in a peaceful spirit towards everybody. You must not allow a single sentence, nay a single word to be written that would hurt the legitimate pride of any power.'[98]

What general conclusion can we come to on Stanley's performance at

Berlin in 1884–5? He had shown his usual mixture of fidelity to Leopold and indiscretion. Opinions of him were as varied as ever. One of the diplomats, Sir Rennell Rodd, noticed that Stanley always spoke with real affection about blacks but that there was something about him that belied his words.[99] Leopold's quondam trusted adviser Emile Banning said that Stanley was hopelessly ignorant of the subtleties of diplomacy, that he exaggerated the wealth of the Congo and that his optimism, common to all men of action, was strangely at odds with his reiterated pessimism on the many obstacles to a Congo railway. But Banning did at least acknowledge Stanley as a peerless explorer: 'With incomparable fatuity M. Brazza considered himself as a rival to Stanley and the French pretended to take the comparison seriously.'[100]

Stanley felt magnanimous enough after the conclusion of the hard slog of negotiations to reopen contact with Harry Johnston, now that the Portuguese gaffe had been safely subsumed in history. Humorously rehearsing the many barbarous epithets – 'pirate', 'murderer', 'forger' – he had attracted during his career, he again extended the hand of friendship to his young protégé: 'Let us both promise to begin – I to stop pirating, murdering and forging at once and for ever; you never to make a promise unless you mean it and when it is once made to pride yourself on keeping it for ever.'[101]

Yet if Stanley could relax, his royal patron could not. Once the Berlin Conference had welcomed the new state into existence, Leopold's next step was to get Belgium to confer on him the crown of the Congo. The snag here was that Article 62 of the Belgian Constitution forbade a Belgian king to accept the throne of another state without the two-thirds majority assent of both chambers of the Assembly. This was why Borchgrave warned Stanley not to refer in his book to Leopold as the sovereign of the Free State, since his status had not yet been clarified; instead the book should be dedicated to 'all friends of Africa'.[102]

Leopold faced the humiliating possibility of being denied by his own Parliament what had been granted to him by the Great Powers. To convince the Assembly that there would be no conflict of interest, the King gave assurances that he would be absolute ruler in the Congo and that Belgium itself would be committed to nothing, neither money, administration nor military force. The Belgian nation was then faced with the choice of humiliating its King in the eyes of Europe or letting him have his way. The outcome was predictable. Only one deputy voted against the bill, but all who voted for made it clear that the Congo was purely Leopold's affair and would never return to the notice of

Belgium.[103] A modern writer has aptly summed up the resulting situation:

> One feels obliged to re-emphasise just what an incredible arrangement this was. The Congo had not been taken as a colony by Belgium, nor was Leopold to rule it as King of the Belgians. A brand-new state had been created essentially by fiat out of a vast African territory, unbeknown to the overwhelming majority of the people who lived there. And a private individual, whom an even greater number of those people had never heard of, had been given that state to own personally and had been made its king. 'The sovereignty of the Congo is invested in the person of the Sovereign,' a Belgian lawyer of the time wrote. 'His will can be resisted by no juridical obstacle whatsoever.' Leopold II could say with more justification than Louis XIV did: '*L'Etat c'est moi.*' Leopold himself, somewhat later, put it even more bluntly: 'My rights over the Congo are to be shared with none; they are the fruit of my own struggle and expenditure . . . the King was the founder of the state; he was its organiser, its owner, its absolute sovereign.' Perhaps an American newspaperman at that time summed up this peculiar situation most succinctly: 'He possesses the Congo just as Rockefeller possesses Standard Oil.'[104]

7

THE conclusion of the Berlin Conference and the beginning of the 'scramble for Africa' in earnest provides an opportunity for an overview of Stanley as 'man of Africa'. Though his last great African journey was still to come, the essential pieces in the jigsaw puzzle were already in place by 1885. Certain questions virtually pose themselves. What was the impact of Stanley on African society (and the Dark Continent on him)? How does he relate to the theme of imperialism in general and Leopold's Congo in particular? Given that he covered such vast areas (modern Zaire, Tanzania and Uganda), what traces did he leave behind him in African folklore? What sort of a reputation did he have and were there any legends of Stanley?

It does not take exceptional insight to perceive that Stanley was only truly himself when in Africa, that he assumed a heroic size there and shrank back to normal human dimensions when in Europe. After 1871, whenever Stanley was away from Africa there was a distinct impression of a man working at half-throttle, someone killing time and going through the motions. This throws into paradoxical relief Herbert Ward's judgement that the influence of Africa on Stanley was almost entirely baneful. Ward felt that experience in the Dark Continent reinforced Stanley's belief in the efficacy of brute force and naked power, gave him an excessively pessimistic view of mankind, and also influenced his prose style, since the habitually flowery speech of Africa fed back its colour into Stanley's own idiom, producing a tendency towards archaic language and euphuism.[1]

But Ward missed one vital point in his assessment. Africa was Stanley's salvation, and not just because it enabled him to rise high and far from a Welsh workhouse to a knighthood, world-wide fame and great wealth. It had a therapeutic effect also. Stanley's struggle with the Dark Continent was an objective correlative of his struggle with the dark forces within himself. It is even possible to speculate that, like Conrad after him, he might have drawn a kind of sustenance from the Congo itself.[2] And it is certain that Stanley introduced the Congo into European imagination as the quintessential symbol of the 'heart of darkness'.[3]

There is another point that Ward failed to bring out, Stanley's pessimistic view of human beings and their capabilities was partly mitigated by his generally high opinion of the black man. Naturally this sympathy operated within the general context of the common Victorian notion of the 'effortless superiority' of the white man – it would be anachronistic to expect otherwise, and of the men of the nineteenth century arguably only Thaddeus Stevens in the USA attained to a genuine empathy with blacks. Stanley's real feeling for the indigenous African *was* paternalistic, as was Livingstone's, but there is in his writings none of the contempt and dislike that disfigure the work of Sir Richard Burton or Sir Samuel Baker. Even Joseph Thomson, who liked to pride himself on his peaceful progress through the continent, as against Stanley's conquest with Sniders and Remingtons, eventually came to embrace a form of racial prejudice more like Burton's sentiments than anything to be found in Stanley.[4]

Stanley frequently singled out one or other of the *mangwana* for special praise: Uledi, Baraka, Wade Hefeni and many others are the subject of encomiums throughout his writings; particularly during his five years building the Congo Free State (1879–84) he often contrasted the superior intelligence of his African aides with the white flotsam and jetsam of Europe that was sent out to him.[5] Few things irritated Stanley more than references to 'niggers' or suggestions that the African was a benighted savage, incapable of normal human emotions. He described blacks as capable of great love and affection, with a full sense of gratitude and other noble traits. He found them in general clever, honest, industrious, docile, enterprising, brave and moral: 'in short equal to any other race or colour on the face of the globe.'[6] As he wrote in his journal in October 1883, commenting on the Bangala chieftain's love for the grandson whom Stanley was holding for ransom: 'I have seen hundreds of instances which absolutely contradict that absurd statement of Monteiro that the Africans know neither love, affection nor gratitude. Monteiro, I know, has been endorsed by Captain R. F. Burton – but Burton would endorse anything that was uncomplimentary to the African. I know not which to wonder at most – the impudence of Monteiro or the credulity of his stupid readers.'[7] It has to be remembered, too, that Burton-like views were entertained by many of Stanley's white collaborators and contemporaries on the Congo: the missionary Bentley described the Bolobo as innately cruel, drunk and immoral, while Liebrechts considered that the intelligence of the African was used mainly for evil purposes.[8]

But Stanley was not just impressed by the innate goodness of the black man; this could after all be subsumed in paternalism with the added rider 'until corrupted, just like children'. He declared himself fully convinced of the African's intellectual equality with the white man. Among the Irebu in June 1883 he listened to a brilliant piece of narration from an African storyteller: 'The story as a story was capitally related; as a comedy it was surpassingly well done and proved that in this faraway part of Africa there must have been many a Shakespeare and Milton, who have mutely and ingloriously died unwept, unhonoured and unsung by the ignorant civilised world.'[9] And as for ability in business: 'In the management of a bargain I should back the Congoese native against Jew or Christian, Parsee or Banyan, in all the round world. Unthinking men may perhaps say cleverness at barter, and shrewdness in trade, consort not with their unsophisticated condition and degraded customs. Unsophisticated is the very last term I should ever apply to an African child or man in connection with the knowledge of how to trade . . . I have seen a child of eight do more tricks of trade in an hour than the cleverest European trader on the Congo could do in a month.'[10] Stanley was a Victorian paternalist only in that he was convinced of the superiority of European *culture*.

Any assessment of Stanley as 'man of Africa' must deal with his impact on indigenous societies and the reputation he left behind. Yet this is peculiarly difficult to gauge and quantify. Generalising, we may say that his effect was greater the longer he stayed in a given locality (as in the Congo in 1879–84) or when he came into contact with the more solid tribal organisations like that of Mutesa. But properly to measure the force of his advent on aboriginal societies, we need to set him in a context defined by general African views about the white man and his qualities and powers.

The most common basic view entertained in nineteenth-century Africa about whites when they were encountered, before familiarity bred cynicism and envious contempt, was that they came from the land of the dead, were spirits and could therefore work magic spells. On one linguistic analysis 'Mpoto' – 'the land of the white man' – really means 'the land of the dead'.[11] So, for example, the missionary Grenfell working on the Juapa in 1885 was called 'Bedimo' ('ghost').[12] Charles Bateman who worked for Leopold on the Kasai reported that the Bashilele people called him 'Chienvu' – the reincarnation of a former chief of that name.[13] Associated with this was the idea that white men had powers over death since they came from the land of the dead itself. Harry Johnston and Lt. Orban were once asked by a chief to send back a man from his village who had just died.[14] Another gloss on the almost universal belief that white faces were the mark of a spirit was the idea that to work for such spirits in itself meant death.[15] This engendered a general fear but also the sanguine attitude that the white man could control the weather at will; Bateman, arriving at a strange village in the middle of a thunderstorm, once claimed to have started it so as to impress the villagers with his power.[16]

Tying in whites with the spirits of dead ancestors produced some interesting results. The horrors of the slave trade could be palliated by the notion that slaves went to America, died, then as spirits worked at producing sums of wealth unknown in the land of the living. When the distinction between Europe and America began to impinge, a different variant appeared. This was that when rich Africans died they went to Europe and became white. The cloth with which they were buried was their merchandise when they came back to trade, so the differential wealth of European and African traders could be explained in magical terms.[17]

Another belief about whites was closely associated with the usual mode of their arrival – aboard steamers. It was widely believed that the pale-faced strangers lived beneath the sea, where they wove cloth in great quantities. It has been suggested that this belief arose because Africans would see an approaching ship mast first, then hull and only finally the entire ship.[18] The first steamers the Bangala saw made them think that their owners were water kings, Lohengrins of the Equator, and that the ships were drawn by huge fish or hippos; the engine room was envisaged as a vast casserole where food was prepared. But the steamers – 'Kumba' as Mata Buiki called them – were not the only source of wonderment to the Bangala. Since they often saw the white men go down to the bottom of the ship to get pearls, *mitakos* and other merchandise, they believed that the men of the Mpoto (the West) descended into the bowels of the steamer to open up a door and thence fetch their treasures up from the bottom of the river.[19] A variant on this farther downriver was that it was water-sprites, distinct from the white man, who wove the cloth they possessed.[20] This was why when Stanley arrived, the Bangala at first hesitated to trade with him; they feared that if they accepted his gifts, the Likundu or evil spirit would restrict their wealth in future to those exact gifts.

The steamer motif also fed into the notion of whites as spirits since the steamer gave them the power to go away and come back again at great speed. In 1883 the first name the Bangala gave to Stanley was Midjiji (Ghost). This was all part of the general African disbelief in physical laws in favour of magic.[21] But it was clear that the coming of the powerful strangers was received with gloom. One of the most powerful African myths was that of a golden age before the coming of the white man. In this era all animals lived together peacefully. But the golden age was shattered by man's sinfulness: animals turned and rent one another and the final apocalypse was denoted by the coming of the Ibanza or white wizards.[22] Yet, as with most myths of the apocalypse (Norse *Ragnarok* for example), the gloom was lightened by hopes of a new age, when the elements or wild animals would destroy the interlopers and herald the dawn of a new Eden.[23] The hope was sparked by the high mortality of Europeans in Africa which eventually prompted a more sophisticated response from the Congo peoples: that Europe must be a very unsavoury place indeed, since its inhabitants preferred death by disease in Central Africa.[24]

The white man, then, at the very least was perceived as a being with enormous knowledge and talents deriving from magic or superior fetish.[25] In an ironical but poetically justified inversion of European cultural chauvinism, Africans actually expressed surprise that the strangers had human feelings![26] To some extent the worst fears about whites in this regard were laid to rest when the first white women and children appeared on the Congo – a convincing proof of normality.[27]

All the great African explorers left behind them traces in the local folklore of their coming and a reputation that could vary from saintliness to aggression and brutality, as in the case of Livingstone and Sir Samuel Baker respectively.[28] Speke too had made a very favourable impression on the tribes with whom he came in contact; this was confirmed by Livingstone, and Frank Pocock in 1876 reported that Speke was 'all the rage' in Uganda and Karagwe. Some have gone so far as to assert that he was the most popular of all European explorers in Central Africa.[29] Stanley's name, as might be expected, excited mixed reactions. Where he was compelled by the momentum and logistics of his expeditions to press forward at great speed, clearing the way with Sniders or Winchesters, his reputation tended to be that of a fearsome demon. When he was able to build up the trust of the locals slowly and over a long period, a very different picture emerged in the local folklore.

An awareness of place and time is all-important in assessing Stanley's niche in African folk memories. On the Livingstone expedition Stanley made little impact on Nyamweziland. Like Burton and Speke before him (significantly Speke's great reputation was in Uganda rather than Tanzania), he was not really distinguishable from an Arab. The first white man to make an impression in the Tanganyika lands was Philippe Broyon; only on the second Stanley expedition did his name begin to be whispered.[30]

On the 1874–7 expedition Stanley came into contact with major African rulers like Mutesa and Mirambo, who were clearly impressed by him. In general, the higher the level of social organisation, the better the records of Stanley's visits – hence his name lived on in Uganda and Unyoro, especially as he tarried there longer than elsewhere on the *Through the Dark Continent* journey. Lesser chieftains tended to be intimidated by the size of his columns; these both bred envy and created serious pressure on precarious food supplies.[31] Naturally, all the Stanley variables were interrelated: the sense of urgency which did not permit a leisurely, peaceful progress was a function of the size of his parties, and this in turn was a function of the lavish sums with which he had been equipped by Bennett. And the endurance of his name in Buganda was itself part of a process whereby the solid structure of Mutesa's social system owed something to the presence at his court of knowledgeable, sophisticated aliens, whether Arab or European.[32] The only caveat that should be entered against the persistence of Stanley's reputation in Uganda was, as he pointed out in the early 1880s, that the story of his time with Mutesa in 1875 was attenuated by the rapid turnover of court personnel: 'almost all the notables of the country mentioned in *Through the Dark Continent* have perished and those who were at that time mere pages at the court occupy their positions.'[33]

But it was during his arduous five years founding Leopold's Congo state that Stanley's reputation among Africans acquired a stability and fixity. His fame was mixed, with some oral traditions emphasising his dark side, others his positive aspects. Simplifying, we can whittle down the different, heterogeneous strands to three: Stanley was a hard and ruthless man, he was just, he was wealthy.[34] Interestingly and characteristically, Stanley was as indifferent to his reputation among Africans as he was to the criticisms of him at home by white liberals. When Herbert Ward asked him what impression the arrival of his flotilla had made in

1879 on the tribes of the Lower Congo, Stanley replied insouciantly: 'In this world we can't stop to think about the impressions we create – no time for that sort of thing.'[35]

The hardness and ruthlessness are well attested. Stanley's *wangwana* said to Livingstone's servants at Ujiji: 'Your master is a good man – a very good man; he does not beat you, for he has a kind heart; but ours – oh! he is sharp – hot as fire.'[36] Many an African who had tasted the lash from 'the little master' could tell the same story. In the 1920s there were still Africans alive who had known Stanley and could provide vivid testimony to his hardness.[37] Despite the lack of overt hostilities, the 1883 expedition by Stanley's flotilla to Stanley Falls, and his demonstration of the power of the Krupps gun, left him with a local reputation as an aggressor, second only to Tippu Tip in ferocity.[38] Later, on the Emin Pasha expedition, oral tradition credited him with having cut a swathe of destruction through the Ituri rain-forest.[39] Col. George Williamson, a US Civil War veteran in the service of Leopold's Congo in the late 1880s, reported that Stanley's name 'produced a shudder among the simple folk when mentioned; they remember his broken promises, his copious profanity, his hot temper, his heavy blows, his severe and rigorous measures by which they were mulcted of their lands.'[40] The missionaries too testified to the fear of Stanley and his henchmen that pervaded the Congo basin.[41]

But this aspect of Stanley should be seen in perspective. Congo missionaries were riven with factionalism. One clique strongly supported Stanley and all his works and depended for their success on his support.[42] Naturally the 'out' groups exaggerated his notoriety among the tribes for their own purposes. Much of the fear engendered by whites on the Congo arose *after* Stanley had left the area and the full brutality of Leopold's minions was unleashed. The problem here was that the term Bula Matari was widely used to denote both Stanley himself and the Association he represented, so that any atrocities committed by the Belgians tended to be laid at the door of Bula Matari. And there is no serious question that Stanley could be compared with genuine men of blood like the German Karl Peters who finally fulfilled Stanley's fantasy of violent revenge against the 'insolent' Gogo by machine-gunning them in droves.[43] Known to Africans as Mkonowa-Damu – 'the man with the blood-stained hands' – Peters was eventually recalled as Imperial High Commissioner (Kilimanjaro district), asis brutality revolted even the not normally squeamish German authorities in Berlin.[44]

But against the 'forceful' aspect of Stanley can be set his reputation for justice. Three witnesses will suffice, all of them admirers, but critical ones, of the explorer. The missionary A. M. Mackay reported: 'Whenever I find myself in Stanley's track, I find his treatment of the natives had invariably been such as to win from them the highest respect for the face of a white man.'[45] Ward found that his name 'acted as a talisman throughout the Congo country. By millions of these savages his name is uttered with respect almost akin to fear.'[46] And this was Harry Johnston's verdict: 'No disparaging word has ever in my hearing fallen from the lips of an African. He was generous, kindly, sympathetic and just, only severe to wrongdoers; absolutely uncursed with that odious British pride and snobbishness which seals up the black men's sympathies and confidences.'[47]

The two strands of harshness and fairness represented Stanley's Janus face, and he sometimes traded on this ambiguity to achieve his goals. He was helped in this by the fact that he had appeared on the Congo in two very different guises: in 1877 as the Ibanza, sailing in canoes, dealing out death from a hundred bullets and crushing all who stood in his path; and in 1880–83 as Bula Matari, the dispenser of trade goods, the Solonic law-giver, the Solomonic arbitrator.[48] It was a mammoth task to persuade the tribes that the two men were one and the same. For the African a man's very identity was guaranteed by his enduring characteristics: his pacific or bellicose nature, whether he travelled in a canoe or in 'the house that walks on water', and so on. How could Bula Matari and Tandelay be one and the same? The Ibanza of 1877 had traded in brass rods while Bula Matari traded in bales of cloth. The only judicious conclusion was that Tandelay, the first to appear on the river, had been sent by Bula Matari; this meant that Tandelay was merely Bula Matari's vizier or First Minister.[49] Stanley turned this incredulity to his own advantage when settling the Irebu civil war in 1883. Reluctantly 'conceding the truth', he warned the Irebu that although he, Bula Matari, was a man of peace, if they did not compose their differences, he would summon his war-chief Tandelay from the lower river to return with his host of deadly 'lightning sticks'.[50]

Which of the two faces of Stanley – that of Tandelay or of Bula Matari – dominated in African consciousness is hard to determine but one good 'control' in elucidating how the Africans actually felt about him was in the degree of fidelity and loyalty they were prepared to give him. Wissmann thought that the ultimate test of an African explorer, given the hardships produced by the necessary evil of porterage, was whether his porters were prepared, in the main, to stick by him.[51] No explorer could expect a nil or even low rate of desertion but, when all allowances have been made, Stanley scores remarkably highly in this area. The key to this was that he actually liked Africans. He had no time for those, like Thys and Bateman, who maintained that the African was feckless and shiftless, with no thought for the morrow, treacherous (always ready to make alliances with the white man to defeat rivals), and gluttonous.[52] To a greater extent than any African traveller after Livingstone (except perhaps Weeks) he genuinely enjoyed the company of his 'dark companions'.[53]

The third aspect of Stanley's reputation among Africans – that of a man of wealth – is perhaps the most securely anchored in the evidence of oral tradition and, arguably, the most important. The combination of the mysterious and impressive steamers and the plethora of trade goods they disgorged was irresistible.[54] Stanley related the mixture of awe and cupidity with which the Irebu greeted *En Avant*. They thought its paddle-wheels must be turned by some twenty men concealed at the bottom of the ship. More sophisticated observers guessed that the secret must be the 'big pot' (the boiler) because the engineer was forever stoking up the fire. But what was he cooking there?' 'Perhaps,' concluded the Irebu, 'if we had also big pots in our canoes, and we had some of the white man's medicine, we need not toil any more with tired arms at our paddles, and suffer from aches and pains in our shoulders.'[55]

Wealth was crucial in establishing the reputation of the white man in general and Stanley in particular. In Usukuma in 1889 Stanley, driving vast herds of cattle through East Africa with the Emin Pasha column, acquired the prestige of being a harbinger of meat and plenty. The local folklore said that for this reason, if he ever returned, men would flock to him.[56] Among the Bangala Stanley had a reputation as a man who introduced the *mitako* or brass rod as a unit of currency, thus contriving a dual system, for before the Bangala used the *manyango* (copper).[57] Riches were considered all but definitional of the white man. For this very reason the Congo missionaries initially had a thin time of it, for they were white men without wealth. Only when their medical expertise became widely known did they win favour.[58]

Africans could never understand the secret of European wealth, for they operated on a kind of proto-Marxist labour theory of value, in terms of which, with limited human labour to add to natural resources, the store of wealth available to a community could grow only slowly. With barter too they were limited to a circulation of existing goods. Totally alien was the Western notion of the creation of 'wealth' by credit, of buying stocks 'on margin' or creating an intrinsically non-existent effective demand by devices like credit cards. Exploitation in the classical economic sense they would learn from the whites and then only when they were its victims. Hardly surprisingly, then, when Stanley tried to explain to the Irebu how a complex Western trading system worked they were mystified and exclaimed: 'We know how to trade but our wealth does not increase.'[59] Convinced that the total wealth of an area could not be augmented by trade, they concluded that Stanley's wealth was a purely personal attribute of the man himself which could be explained only in magical terms. It was a short step from this to the belief that Europeans could distribute gifts in unlimited quantities without growing poorer.[60]

The stories and legends about Stanley that survive in African oral tradition almost invariably fasten on one or more of this trio of attributes: hardness, justice, wealth.[61] But the full blast of the legend of Bula Matari was felt in those societies where Stanley had irrupted like a thunderbolt (Soko, Bangala, Irebu, etc). Where he was a distant figure, his local fame was a faraway echo of this. A good example was at Manteke which was founded in 1879 by Henry Richards of the LIM but which Stanley himself did not visit until 1883. Here he was simply known in oral tradition as 'the second white man'.[62] Yet along the Congo proper his fame was such that oral histories dated events around his coming in 1877 much as we might use 1066 or 1789 as historical markers. Glave mentions that if a thief was haled before a village council for stealing a chicken, he would give an account of his personal history by invoking the universally known formula: '*Arlekaki Tendele mboka bis kaza kala*' – 'When Stanley passed our village a long time ago.'[63]

This brings us to a consideration of the most famous name by which Stanley was known in Africa – Bula Matari (properly Matadi) – 'the breaker of rocks'.[64] Both Stanley and his wife were immensely proud of this sobriquet which seemed to connote the Nietzschean morality of strenuousness by which the great explorer lived; the fame of the name was such that a tributary of the Upper Congo was named for it – Maia Boula Matari.[65] The appellation sped through Central Africa by bush telegraph, to the point where in Ujiji by 1882 there was already a legend that this was where 'Father David' had met the 'Stone Breaker'.[66] But in fact the Congolese did not really intend it to refer to the sledgehammer incident at Vivi and still less to the dynamiting of Ngomi mountain. Instead it was meant to denote a ruthless individual whose head was so hard that he could break rocks with it.[67] When other evidence suggests that the Bangala – Stanley's 'Ashanti of the Upper Congo' – were thoroughly cowed and genuinely frightened by him[68], the balance of the Sirius-like ambiguity of Stanley's reputation seems to tip decisively towards the dark side. On the other hand there is this testimony from the independent Congo's first Prime Minister Patrice Lumumba – scarcely a man one would have imagined with much sympathy for Leopold's right-hand man: 'Stanley gave us peace, human dignity, improved our standard of living, developed our intelligence, made our spirit evolve.'[69]

The question of the *impact* of Stanley on African society is a different one, more elastic and imponderable and subdividing into direct and indirect effects. But something of the same rule of thumb holds good: his impact was the greatest where he stayed longest. Arguably though, the relationship with advanced African societies is the inverse from the reputational situation, for Stanley and those who came after him were able to transform weaker social systems miraculously and almost overnight, whereas the stronger, more cohesive societies resisted the incursions of the West much longer.[70] Uganda still held its own in the late 1880s while Kabba Rega of the Bunyoro fought a gallant guerrilla warfare against the colonising power right through the 1890s.

While Stanley was still a technical explorer, his impact was as limited as that of any other occasional visitor to the great African courts; as has been well said, 'These men, and even Livingstone, were customarily regarded in a light similar to that in which the court of Imperial China examined envoys from the West.'[71] But when he returned to the Congo in 1879 as the standard-bearer of Western civilisation and the harbinger of its motor-force, capitalism, the dislocating effect on traditional society was immediately apparent. Unwittingly, Stanley was delivering Central Africa to the rapacious maw of the most blatant system of exploitation the world had seen since the Ancient World. The rate of change was astonishing. According to Thys, the Bangala were transformed out of all recognition between 1877 and 1887.[72] Even those who had no inkling of the later horrors to be unleashed on the Congo in the form of 'red rubber' and the official terrorism of Leopold's corporate 'Free State' noticed the rapidity of change. First the economic system of the Congo was transmogrified; then the older customs and modalities were broken down to produce a social system functional to Leopold's desire for plunder.

The first effect was the simplest. By bringing in large amounts of brass, Stanley and his European aides caused a devaluation of the brass rod currency even as they introduced it to tribes where it had been unknown before.[73] In the 1880s the *mitako* became shorter and prices rose. The value of the brass rod was declining in proportion to its length, causing general price inflation; at the same time prices were fluctuating in real terms because of changing supply and demand in response to the arrival of European traders. After the Berlin Conference the Great Powers, hand in hand with private trading concerns, made a concerted effort to strangle native competitors. On the Congo the impetus to drive the Bobangi out of business by any means necessary reached the point where bloodshed was inevitable, and duly followed in the late 1880s and early 1890s.[74]

Stanley himself played a part in this process. In 1883 he gave medals and payment in kind to the chiefs of Kinkanza to make them local managers and suppliers of labour, especially porters. The payment was a pig and a goat to those in the existing tribal hierarchy. But when some of the chiefs protested that the medals were 'bad medicine' and refused to co-operate, Stanley simply went behind their backs and supplanted them with more pliant individuals who were prepared to play the Association's game. This tied tribal hierarchies to a cash nexus rather than old customs and traditions and eventually had the effect of replacing matrilineal succession by succession through the deceased chief's younger brother or sister's son.[75] Stanley was impatient with any local customs or folkways that interfered with his purposes. One of the traditions on the Lower Congo was the maintenance of political clientelage through the import and distribution of alcohol. When a chief demanded rum in return for his services, Stanley was able to seek general European legitimation for his destruction of the ancient ways by portraying the chief as a bibulous, boozy scoundrel.[76]

The Congolese were well aware of the threat to their traditional way of life posed by the presence of white men trading as far up as Stanley Pool and then breaking into their monopolies on the Upper Congo. They threatened to disrupt the so-called 'Great Congo Commerce' – the flow of trade from the coast to Stanley Pool and beyond, whereby ivory was exchanged for goods imported by the European traders at the Atlantic estuary to the Congo.[77] The Berlin Treaty of 1885 removed the last barrier to the process. The Free State declared itself the owner of all land not actually in use by the 'natives' and reserved for itself the definition of 'use'. While formal slavery was abolished, corvée and the requisitioning of labour was introduced. Local traders were crushed, the tribal chiefs bought off by making them 'managers'. Local cults were suppressed in favour of Christianity, and in return decades of sleeping sickness were ushered in. The Africans meanwhile were denied assimilation into the capitalist, bureaucratic and industrial institutions at any level except the most menial. But their very social structure made unity against the Europeans difficult, and the division of labour ruled indigenous modernisation on the Japanese model out of court. The only solution, as the great African chief Mirambo saw clearly, was to unite all of East and Central Africa under a handful of paramount chiefs, perhaps himself, Mutesa and Kabba Rega, to form a formidable and impenetrable military block. But until such a day came, Mirambo could see no alternative to an alliance of convenience with Tippu Tip and the hated Arabs.[78]

Such were the momentous consequences of Stanley's epic 1877 voyage down the Congo. Yet his indirect impact was even more startling. He was the first explorer to force a switch of trade from the historic long-distance trade routes, largely because by his very success in venturing into the unknown in 1876 and conquering all obstacles he opened the door to Tippu Tip and his slavers.[79] This, if anything, was the indictment that Hyndmans and others should have brought in 1878 instead of nitpicking over the technicalities of Bumbire. Until Stanley opened up the Congo and the Aruwimi, the tribes lived in security from Tippu Tip and his Arabs. By the mid-1880s Tippu was using his 'Manyema hordes' to crush the Soko and other peoples in the Stanley Falls area. The London press were later to pick up this point and contrast the responsible patient twenty-year stint Kirk had put in with Barghash with Stanley's glory-hunting, publicity-seeking forced marches, all guns blazing. Stanley, it was alleged, should have stayed in one area as Kirk and Livingstone did, 'but Stanley had other work to do'.[80]

When Stanley proceeded to the 'rescue' of Emin in Equatoria, the more perceptive analysts pointed out that the effect of that expedition would be to open Equatoria too to the slavers.[81] But it seems unnecessarily harsh to blame Stanley for consequences that he could not have foreseen. Once again we are in the quagmire of Popper's 'unintended effects'. Even Livingstone himself fell foul of this particular trap. His blockade-breaking in 1858 when he used a show of force to browbeat chief Tengani into opening up the Shire River also had the effect of letting the slavers in.[82] But Stanley's indirect impact was far more significant than this, for by removing the barrier to Tippu Tip and the Nyangwe Arabs Stanley triggered a minor version of the disastrous *mfecane* of southern Africa in the early nineteenth century. Once on the Congo, Tippu Tip's Arabs penetrated every tributary and byway and were soon in collision with the mighty Luba empire of Katanga.[83]

Stanley's impact becomes even more significant if we regard the long-distance trade that he so disastrously affected as an 'African mode of production' analogous to the Asiatic mode that Marx explicitly recognised. It has been trenchantly argued that long-distance trade was itself a mode of production, possibly *the* dominant mode of production in pre-colonial Africa.[84] Here we return in effect to the debate on wealth between Stanley and the Irebu and its implications. According to the Western view, a mode of production by definition must produce a surplus value. Long-distance trade, on the other hand, is a mere transfer of wealth from one society to another.[85] Here we confront a clear conflict between traditional and Western notions of what constitutes wealth. A proper assessment of Stanley's indirect impact must await a more comprehensive resolution of this technical issue.

The question of Stanley's relationship to imperialism is easier to resolve, for the golden age of his explorations antedated both imperialism proper and the 'scramble for Africa'.[86] Stanley *was* an imperialist in the 1890s but his active career was then over and his place had been taken in Africa by active exponents of empire like Lugard, Rhodes and Milner. Stanley is best seen as a precursor of imperialism, a man who laid foundations that were later used by others for different purposes.[87] He could scarcely be considered an imperialist in any of the classical senses, since no European nation recognised its 'manifest destiny' in Africa until after the Berlin Conference, and the 'scramble' was arguably triggered by Leopold's own dreams of personal empire. As Lord Salisbury recorded: 'When I left the Foreign Office in 1880, nobody thought about Africa. When I returned to it in 1885, the nations of Europe were almost quarrelling with each other as to the various portions of Africa which they could obtain.'[88]

Economic imperialism – the notion of colonies as a necessary outlet for the export of surplus capital, so as to prevent a domestic crisis of under-consumption – lay almost twenty years in the future.[89] Besides, Leopold's motive was not the health of Belgian capitalism but his own aggrandisement. His unlocking of the Congo was part of a massive scheme of personal booty: 'The Congolese system was too viciously wasteful, too recklessly short-term in its conception, to deserve even the term of exploitation. It was no more than a prolonged raid for plunder.'[90] As a final irony, Leopold came to Africa by accident after disappointment in the Philippines and elsewhere. The idiosyncratic nature of the monarch's enterprise in the Congo partly accounted for its unhappy history.

The classical model of economic imperialism required stability as a precondition for foreign investment. But Leopold was merely interested in turning himself into a combination of absolute monarch and Rockefeller. So far from being an agent of imperialism, Stanley was merely used as 'a decoy by a subtler mind than his, and became the unconscious instrument of the most colossal invasion of human rights the world has ever witnessed.'[91]

But if Stanley was the mere agent of a royal plunderer, the relationship was an uneasy one. He was Hercules to Leopold's Eurystheus and the fraught relationship of official master and employee showed that Stanley was an unruly and unreliable subordinate. He wanted to go slowly in the Congo and build on solid foundations; Leopold wanted him to rush ahead and plant the flag of the Association everywhere along the Congo, be the foothold never so precarious. Leopold dreamed of sucking out from Central Africa vast wealth that would enable him to be the most powerful man on earth, with the charisma of kings and the dollars of Carnegie. Stanley looked forward to the day when the Union Jack would flutter over the domains that he had discovered. Both men needed each other. In the early days only Stanley could have secured the foothold for Leopold's undisclosed Promethean ambitions in Africa. Yet only Leopold could send Stanley back to the continent that had made him. He had come to the end of the line with Bennett and knew that he was too controversial a figure in England to be employed by the RGS on any of its expeditions. Stanley was the sorcerer's apprentice. The position he and Leopold found themselves in may be likened to the mutual exploitation of the German Nazis and the giant German corporations (Krupps, I. G. Farben), each trying to mould the other to its own purposes. When Stanley most truly became an agent of imperialism, by contrast, was when he turned away from Leopold and embraced Mackinnon and the British East Africa Company.[92]

But as a precursor of imperialism, Stanley did demonstrate in a spectacular way that Western technology was a vital necessary condition for the conquest and subjugation of Africa. Few people ever gave more convincing proof of the saying current at the time among the *wangwana*: '*Bunduki sultani ya bara bara*' – 'The gun is the Sultan of Africa.'[93] The period of Stanley's active life in Africa (1870–90) saw the most spectacular revolution in firearms technology in history.

The switch from muzzle-loading rifles to breech-loaders – a key element in the Prussian victory over Austria in 1866 – also dramatically widened the technological gap between European and non-western peoples. It accounted for the British victory over the Ashanti in 1873 after two campaign defeats on level technology and the final defeat of the aboriginal peoples and the closing of the frontier in both North and South America.[94] The key rifles of this type were the French *chassepot* (famous from the Franco-Prussian War), the Sniders used by Stanley in 1874–7 and the American Martini-Henry and Peabody-Martinis. All these used metallic cartridge cases and steel barrels instead of iron as in the older weapons and could be quickly reloaded from a prone position.[95]

But the breech-loader was scarcely perfected when the first repeating or magazine rifle was introduced. The first, the Winchester, was used by the Turks in the war against Russia in 1877–8. In all these small-bore magazine rifles the use of smokeless powder became the norm. The discarded breech-loaders then entered Africa in large numbers, with the Europeans able to maintain their technological gap. Stanley found Emin's troops in 1889 armed with breech-loaders. This development alarmed Europe's pro-consuls. Kirk's successor at Zanzibar, Euan-Smith, told Lord Rosebery in 1888 that if a large-scale arms trade in breech-loaders developed in East Africa, pacification of the indigenous inhabitants would be impossible.[96] The scale of the problem can be appreciated when it is realised that in 1885–1902 a million firearms and four million pounds of gunpowder, plus millions of caps and rounds of ammunition, entered the German and British spheres of influence in East Africa.[97]

After the pilot Winchester came the Mauser (1884), the Mannlicher (1885), the Lee-Metford (1888) and the French Leber. Meanwhile there was significant development in another sphere: the machine gun, which made its début with the Gatling in the American Civil War.[98] Stanley took a Krupps variant of this to the Congo in 1883. But the real breakthrough came in 1884 with the first machine gun to be operated by propellent gases instead of a handcrank. The gun, patented by Hiram S. Maxim in 1884 and adopted by the British army in 1889, contained only one barrel. Since smokeless cartridges were consistent in their energy output, the loading could be done by gas pressure or by recoil instead of with a crank. The Maxim, unlike the Gatling and its derivatives, was light enough for infantry to carry, it could be set up inconspicuously, and it spat out bullets at a rate of eleven per second; its sole drawback was that it could really be used only as a defensive weapon.[99] Stanley was always at the very forefront of weapons technology, for he took a Maxim gun with him to Africa in 1887 – a full two years before it came into use with the British army. There can be no serious question but that Stanley's reputation on the Congo derived in part from the awesome weapons he was able to deploy.[100]

There is a final area where the justifiability of imperialism, the impact of Stanley and the morality of Western penetration of Africa all merge. Stanley always tried to legitimate his involvement in Leopold's shadowy schemes on the grounds that by his nation-building in the Congo he was walking in Livingstone's footsteps and liberating Africa from slavery. But did the indigenous African see it like that? The fact was that it was the Europeans' wealth and military power that impressed the African most, not their religion and culture. By and large Africans genuinely respected Arabs, even when they feared and envied them. The slave trade, such an anathema in Western eyes, was merely an extension of the domestic slavery sanctioned by tribal custom. Islam too was attractive: unlike Christianity, it was untouched by racial bias and it accepted the African perception of the role of women. Islam and African tribalism were at one in accepting a plurality of wives and a general chattel status for females; the Muslim religion itself required no more than the mouthing of a few rote-learned words. Best of all, Islam put prestigious firearms in its converts' hands and the Muslim paradise, with its four luscious virgins assigned to each male member of the faithful, was infinitely more appealing than the anaemic and ethereal Christian heaven.

Moreover, on any analysis the Arabs did more for the African than Leopold and his henchmen did. The Arabs taught the more advanced tribes administration. With scribes working in Arabic, they were able to offer enlightened local rulers the elements of a modern bureaucracy. They spread Swahili as a common language through East and Central Africa. They were responsible for a revolution in African diet, having introduced mango, orange and avocado trees, beans, onions, garlic and tomatoes to the continent. Indeed some British colonial administrators later regretted that the Arabs had not established an empire over the entire area, thus providing the incoming European overlords with a sophisticated class with which to collaborate.[101]

These issues formed the subject matter of a number of debates Tippu Tip conducted in the 1880s with Europeans, notably Vangele and Becker. Tippu spoke with contempt of the great zeal Europeans had to abolish at once everything that it had taken the Arabs and Africans centuries to build up. He challenged Becker to explain to him the difference between African slavery and Russian serfdom. In his view, his own slaves had a better deal than the proletariat of Europe's cities. At least, slaves as they were, they had full bellies, while the European employee, if he was lucky enough to find employment and be tied to a master, had the 'freedom' to languish from lack of proper payment and the 'privilege' of watching his children die of starvation. Tippu made the further point that Christian arguments about the dignity of freedom were so much humbug in a continent where a slave could be happy while the 'free' tribesman was at the behest of some murderous chieftain. There was far less racial prejudice between Arab and black than between the white man and the black man; he himself would not treat a black slave the way he had seen Stanley treating his own whites. You Christians believe in the morality of work, he taunted, yet the black man left to himself is lazy and prefers to steal his bread rather than earn it. How then did Christians square 'freedom' with the 'morality of work'? His final point was that European aspirations for the eventual independence of Africa were, if not false and hypocritical, a recipe for disaster: 'Independence for the African is nothing else but licence, theft, brigandage, debauchery, madness and misery. Just see what will happen in the future.'[102]

These views could perhaps be dismissed as the self-serving statements of a merciless slaver, if the later record of Leopold's Congo did not far eclipse in ferocity anything Tippu had been able to compass. Yet even as they stood, they received support from some more thoughtful observers in Europe. In 1888 the journalist E. Belfort Bax wrote in the London *Star*:

> Would that the English democracy at least could be made to take sufficient interest in this African question to see the infamous trans-actions of philanthropists and explorers through all their cant of anti-slavery and the like. Would that one could bring down to them the fact that the Arab slave trade at its worst is but an idyllic dream compared to the state of things which Mr Chamberlain recommends as a panacea for the slave trade – to wit, the forcing of civilisation, i.e. modern capitalism in its worst form, upon an unwilling and primitive population accustomed to simple conditions of life. Everyone that has gone into the business in the least knows well enough that the whole business of Stanley, Emin & Co is being machined by a ring of capitalists greedy for cheap labour, cheap ivory and markets in which to shunt cheap home-made goods. The Arab slave trade, besides being a convenient handle to disguise the nature of the undertakings in question, is as far as it goes often really an obstacle to their immediate success. Hence the exaggerated and highly coloured pictures we are daily receiving of the horrors of the slave trade.[103]

There was a moral dimension here similar to the one Marx famously explored when examining the coming of capitalism in India. While at one level one hailed the destruction of benighted superstitions like that of Hanuman the monkey (or in this case the African slave trade), one deplored the ruthless and inhuman way in which traditional societies were eviscerated in order to integrate them with an international capitalist system. It was typical of Stanley the ruthless technocrat that such moral dilemmas never arose in his mental universe, or if they did they were at once discarded as mere armchair abstractions, a waste of time for the man who would master the 'woodenheaded world'.

8

F ROM Berlin Leopold's nagging about the *Congo* book followed Stanley to Brussels and back to Sackville Street. At the beginning of March Stanley had an interview with the King about the book. Leopold was still concerned that if recalcitrant officers were named, future would-be recruits would be deterred from African service. Stanley found the monarch's behaviour boorish and added a waspish aside in a letter to Sanford that the implicit portrait of the King in his book would do nothing to enhance his reputation.[1] As it turned out, Stanley scored a minor satisfaction, since Leopold's final corrections arrived too late to be included in the book. Moreover, the order to emphasise in the preface that he was still in the King's service seemed to Stanley to sort ill with the general prescription for maximum discretion.[2]

The final proofs and corrections were in his editor Marston's hands on 23 April 1885 after some particularly troublesome work on the Congo maps.[3] These last-minute corrections were done at Newstead Abbey in Nottingham, where he was visiting the Webbs whom he had not seen for seven years.[4] He had other claims on his time too: Dualla had left him to get married after six years' service and he was on the look-out for a young Somali aged between sixteen and twenty with a knowledge of English. But the interlude was a pleasant one, as he told Mackinnon: 'It is an unequalled treat for me to breathe a little country air after my close confinement in London and Berlin . . . oh dear! England is lovely, and it is a crime in L. Low & Co. my publishers to keep me indoors proofreading – it is only a wee bit more cool than on Congo today, and everything looks so lovely.'[5] His antennae ever sensitive to any change in ambience, Stanley soon sensed the only tiny cloud on the horizon: 'Mrs Webb, though she is not quite so cordial as in old times to me for some reason, is a model lady fit to sit in the presence of queens.'[6]

From Newstead Stanley proceeded to Liverpool to embark on a

transatlantic visit for a trip to the USA about which he was remarkably cagey to Mackinnon, saying no more than that it was business not pleasure. What had happened was that his American publisher Harper had warned him that a Philadelphia rival was putting out a pirated edition of the *Congo* book, since the rights of foreign authors were not protected in the USA. It turned out that Stanley had not after all been through the necessary formalities to be considered a US citizen; mistakenly he assumed that service in the Civil War and the oath of allegiance he took then were enough. It was therefore necessary to present himself to the proper authorities in the USA for a formal naturalisation process. The trip was a typical Stanley lightning in-and-out affair. He left Liverpool on 23 April, obtained his citizenship papers on 15 May and on 25 May was back in London.[7]

Finding no word awaiting him there from Brussels on his future employment in Africa, Stanley now started to fret. He had arranged all his baggage and even bought two donkeys on the assumption of an imminent return to Africa. Well, when was this return to take place? He had expressed some anxiety on this score even before he left for the USA as he told Sanford: 'May I ask at what time the Association requires me to go to the Congo? I had a curious letter from Count Borchgrave the other day who said he noted I had not mentioned a word about my engagement while Col. Strauch at Berlin asked me not to mention the fact on account of the hostility by French and Portuguese. What does it all mean?'[8]

What it all meant was that, unknown to Stanley, France and Portugal had agreed to recognise the Association at Berlin only when given personal guarantees from Leopold that Stanley would never be sent back to the Congo. Since Brazza was still in Central Africa, this was France's way of getting its revenge on the man who had outwitted and humiliated their national hero. It is also the clearest and most remarkable testimony to Stanley's importance in the struggle for mastery in Africa. Leopold naturally did not tell Stanley that he had bargained away the explorer's future to secure his own ends and raised no objection to the gloss Stanley put on the leave of absence granted to him – that is to say, that when it ended on 1 June 1885 he would immediately return to the Congo. The only answer the explorer received to his enquiry was a curt two-liner from Borchgrave that his services would not be needed for quite some time.[9]

Stanley wrote back sternly to point out all he was doing for the Congo Free State in England. He mentioned the 'intolerable expense' (some

£500) of getting all his tropical kit together, ready to leave for Africa at a moment's notice.[10] This time the reply was a resounding silence. On 24 June Stanley wrote again, this time to Leopold to complain of Borchgrave's stalling. He was not favoured with a direct reply, but four days later Borchgrave wrote another short note to the effect that it was impossible to say exactly when the explorer would be sent back to Africa.[11] Strauch was tempted to tell Stanley flat out that he could never return to Africa under Association auspices because of opposition from France and Portugal. But Leopold's reflex action was secretiveness, so he opted for keeping Stanley on ice. He explained to Strauch that it was not a good idea to reveal to Stanley the pledge he had given the French and Portuguese; he needed him as a second string to his bow in case Brussels *had* to send him back, for example, if de Winton fell ill or key men like Janssen and Valcke succumbed to fever or the climate. Strauch disagreed and favoured sending Stanley out anyway. Leopold clinched the debate by pointing out that Stanley could only go out to the Congo if he was put in the picture about the royal pledge to France and Portugal, and if he knew that, he would (justifiably) feel so hurt and resentful that his future utility and loyalty would be in question.[12]

Meanwhile in the privacy of his journal Stanley fumed at the treatment meted out to him. 'How long am I to remain a victim to suspense? Are my expenses in vain? Does the King wish to send me to the Congo or does he not? Is it true, as I have heard, that the French stipulated before signing the treaty with the Association, that I was not to return to the Congo?'[13] He felt very bitter that Sanford had persuaded him to renew his contract, that he had then cut short all his engagements in England and even crossed to the USA incognito, while all the time Leopold was playing false with him. It was clear that the King's attitude was: 'We are grateful for past services of Mr Stanley but we think we can carry out the administration and all further work on the Congo without further aid from him.'[14] Stanley professed not to care whether he went back to Africa or not; what mattered was certainty and predictability. If he knew for certain he was not wanted he could make money out of lecturing; he accordingly decided to take Borchgrave's letter as a prolonged extension of leave.

He therefore kept a high profile in the relevant English circles. If ever he felt unwilling to fulfil a social engagement, he hinted darkly that Leopold had given him secret orders not to attend.[15] Sometimes the cry of wolf concealed a real wolf. Such was the case when Baroness Burdett-Coutts pressed him to attend a meeting at which the British government's 'betrayal' of Gordon in the Sudan would be discussed. Stanley was always willing to wade into any discussion on Gordon but on this occasion he received explicit orders from Brussels that as an employee of the Congo state he had to steer well clear of this particular controversy.[16] Stanley therefore picked and chose what parties to attend and which contacts to make, using Leopold as the perfect excuse. He accepted honours from the Baptist Missionary Society for his support in the Congo. He addressed the Anti-Slavery Society.[17] He received ovations at the RGS anniversary dinner on 8 June, and attended the reading of de Winton's paper on the Congo the day before.[18] He corresponded with Cardinal Manning about a Gordon memorial; the Catholic Church had condemned the policy of non-intervention in the Sudan, as it meant leaving the peoples there to savagery.[19]

But overall Stanley was a deeply unhappy man. Not only, it seemed, had Leopold double-crossed him, but the King was also dragging his feet over the project dearest to Stanley's heart: a Congo railway.[20] Stanley's feverish interest in this amounted at times to obsession. He drew up a detailed scheme for a 52-mile track between Vivi and Isangila on the right bank to get round the most fearsome cataracts, and another 95-mile track to link Manyanga and Stanley Pool on the left bank.[21] At their meeting in Brussels in March 1885 Leopold gave Stanley permission to take soundings in England and, if possible, to form a syndicate to finance the 150 miles of track. In concert with Hutton and Mackinnon he soon managed to raise £400,000; a detailed synopsis was despatched to Brussels and won the King's qualified approval.[22]

But Leopold, as ever, was playing a double game. He wrestled with the problem of how to sign an agreement with British capitalists to get the much-needed railway while maintaining political control. The problem was that the proposed railway company would have to be given land concessions to lay track and total rights along the railroad. Leopold solved the dilemma by stalling Stanley's syndicate with a provisional agreement while he cast about for ways of raising the money himself.[23]

Even for a past master of tergiversation and prevarication, Leopold excelled himself in 1885. First he delayed answering Hutton for two months. Then he told the syndicators that the matter could go no further until a report from a Belgian survey team was received.[24] But Stanley kept up the pressure, maintaining a high profile in the English press for the idea of a narrow-gauge Congo railway while trying to pin Leopold down to details.[25] Leopold then uncoiled a fresh serpent of problems. He wriggled ingeniously with the idea that any dispute between the state

Stanley in the uniform of the Congo Free State, wearing his self-devised 'Stanley cap'

Mission canoe descending the Upper Congo

'Home is the hunter.' Stanley after his last great African exploration

The Commandant's house at Vivi Station which even had its own wine cellar (one of Stanley's lecture slides)

Novice explorers celebrate on a dead hippo (one of Stanley's lecture slides)

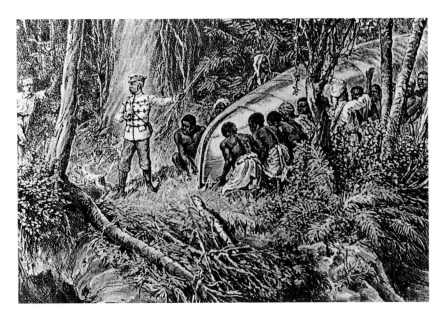

Stanley directing a boat to be carried to the river (one of Stanley's lecture slides)

King Leopold II in the uniform of a
Lieutenant-General with the Grand
Cordon of the Order of Leopold

Stanley giving final instructions to
Barttelot on his departure from
Yambuya, 28 June 1887 (from a sketch
by Herbert Ward)

Interview of Barttelot and Jameson
with Tippu-Tip at Stanley Falls
(from a sketch by Herbert Ward)

The meeting of Emin Pasha and
Stanley at Kavalli's on 29 April 1888

The Emin Pasha Relief Committee, with William Mackinnon standing centre and Sir Francis de Winton seated on his right

Four of 'Stanley's men' – pioneers in the Congo. From left to right: E. J. Glave, Alfred Parminter, Herbert Ward and Roger Casement

Dorothy, Lady Stanley

Sir Henry Morton Stanley KCB

The American lecture tour. The special car at Monterey, California, March 1891

The grave in Pirbright churchyard

'How are the mighty fallen.' The huge metal statue of Stanley, founder of the Belgian Congo, now lies face down in a parking lot in Kinshasa

and the railway company be settled according to the law of the Free State; since the Congo constitution had not yet been drawn up, this amounted to offering the syndicate a pig in a poke. Then he added a further layer of obfuscation by insisting that the company buy the rails for the track in Belgium; this elicited the perfectly reasonable answer that this was a matter for the contractors.[26] Only in 1886 did he finally throw off the mask and reject the British syndicate's proposals on the (spurious) ground that a railway monopoly was contrary to the Berlin Act and that an agreement with the railway company would compromise the sovereignty of the new Congo state.[27] The real reason for his opposition was that by now there were *Belgian* capitalists interested in the railway project. The Belgian syndicate was led by thirty-seven-year-old Captain Albert Thys who, by a dynamism rivalling Stanley's, managed to raise one million francs to form the Compagnie du Congo pour le Commerce et l'Industrie (CCI). By the time Stanley had departed on the Emin Pasha expedition, in May 1887, Thys had set out for the Congo to implement Stanley's brainchild. After a year's energetic work there he replaced Strauch as Administrator-General of the Association.[28]

Leopold's strategy was high-risk. He needed capital to sustain the infant Congo state but was unwilling to relinquish his own iron grip on the territory. Since the Berlin Act forbade import duties and Leopold (as a further sop to the humanitarians) had banned the sale of alcohol in his African domain, bankruptcy loomed by 1886. The original idea of a 20-million franc lottery in France, agreed at Berlin, went into abeyance with Ferry's fall from power. Turning down the British railway syndicate and stalling for time until a Belgian company was in place was an act of fanaticism or courage, depending on one's point of view.[29] Once again 1887 proved Leopold's lucky year, for a bond issue was arranged in the nick of time. The King persuaded the Belgian government to authorise an issue of 150 million francs' worth of premium bonds, eighty million of which were to be offered on the French *bourse*. A guarantee for prospective shareholders was provided by the *moral* support of a consortium, including the Banque Nationale (the Belgian state issuing bank).

It can be seen that Stanley was a small cog in the mighty wheel of Leopold's machinations. Nevertheless, in Stanley's inner world the refusal to send him back to the Congo and the underhand way the King had scuttled all his hard work on the railway was tantamount to betrayal. However measured his later statements, he never really forgave the monarch for his treatment in 1885-6. That was bad enough. But the

twelve months from July 1885 on also brought Stanley bitter disappointment and unhappiness in his private life, making this period in his life
in many ways the nadir of his career.

It is not clear why, after so many years in the emotional wilderness,
Stanley should have decided on his return from the Congo in 1884 that
he needed a wife. Perhaps he felt that his social position in Anglo-Saxon
society could only be secure if he possessed the outward trappings of
respectability. Perhaps the guilt at the repressed homosexual side of his
personality was becoming too great to bear. Or perhaps the desperate
need for affection (existing side by side with a morbid fear of any woman
who might provide it) began to overwhelm him. Whatever the reason,
certain it is that on his return to Europe Stanley was actively looking
around for a partner, as he informed Leopold during the 'debriefing'
sessions of September 1884.

His first fumbling overtures nearly brought disaster. Much of the
evidence has been suppressed or destroyed but, reading between the
lines, it is clear that he was the victim of a blackmail attempt from a
woman, almost certainly involving a paternity suit. At the end of December
1884 he wrote to inform his friend Alexander Bruce that he had cancelled
all his engagements and would appear no more before the British public;
he intended to make a permanent abode in Belgium 'where . . . I shall
at last be able to live without the fear of an absurd and ridiculous scandal
instigated by a demented woman . . . I cannot permit myself to be
dragged to a police court at the instigation of every woman that has a
mania . . . I have examined the whole affair thoroughly, and I find that
although two minutes would be sufficient to prove the whole thing a
fraud, yet as it cost me from 1872 to 1878 to disprove the effect of Sir
H. Rawlinson's impudent letter to *The Times*, a dozen years might elapse
before I should be able to recover the lost ground in the esteem of those
who at present profess esteem.' Worst of all was the thought of the field
day his enemies would have: 'Cameron and Markham will be in their
glory.'[30]

The affair was somehow hushed up, or the woman did not go through
with her threat. It is easy to see how Stanley could have been prey for a
blackmailer, for in the company of women he was impossibly gauche
and reserved. He explained the problem himself in a letter in August
1884: 'I have lived with men, not women, and it is the man's intense
ruggedness, plainness, directness, that I have contracted by sheer force

of circumstance . . . I wish to say, my dear friend, that I am absolutely uncomfortable when speaking to a woman, unless she is such a rare one that she will let me hear some common sense. The fact is, I can't talk to women. In their presence I am just as much of a hypocrite as any other man, and it galls me that I must act and be affected, and parody myself . . . It is such a false position that I do not care to put myself into it.'[31]

One woman who qualified as a 'rare one' was the German writer and painter Marie von Bunsen, to whom Stanley was introduced shortly after his dinner with Bismarck. Scion of a diplomatic family, she spoke perfect English so was able to make a shrewder assessment of him than would otherwise have been possible. At first sight she found Stanley disappointing: he was short, broad, circular with a tanned face, keen dark eyes (the whites were rather yellow), grizzled hair, short moustache and strongly marked features. 'His manners at first seemed more than simple; he hardly looked at me and sat down uncouthly. I talked for all I was worth and tried every kind of topic; he hardly responded.'[32]

Two days later at the American Thanksgiving festivities Stanley was virtually dragged up to her by Sanford. He mumbled in his aloof, indifferent, stiff way that he was to have the pleasure of taking her in to dinner. This time she was able to pierce the carapace of reserve to some extent. She found that he had no small talk or witty conversation and spoke as if giving a public lecture. He told her of the affectionate nature of Africans, of how the beauties of nature made up for loneliness in the Dark Continent, of his ordeal because of the apathy of his white companions, and that the Bible and Shakespeare were his constant companions. He was especially bitter about his treatment in 1872 and 1878 and said that when nobody believed he had found Livingstone tears rolled down his cheeks. After the dinner Sanford congratulated Marie on her marvellous success in getting Stanley to come out of his shell. Several people later told her that Stanley had been interested in her as a possible wife, though her overall opinion was not sufficiently favourable. She never recanted the judgement passed after the first meeting: 'He impressed me as being of the tough Conquistadore type with the outward habit of a disgruntled farmer and the phraseology and vocabulary of an American journalist.'[33]

Marie von Bunsen was clearly too formidable a woman for someone with Stanley's problems, so predictably the encounter led nowhere. Back in England Stanley took to conducting a postal flirtation with an Austrian woman who had written to him through his publishers but would not reveal her name. But with both sides boxing clever and neither giving anything away this brush with 'The Unknown Madame or Mademoiselle' also came to nothing.[34] Stanley became despondent at the thought that though he could tame Africa and subdue the most ferocious chieftains, he could make no progress with women. It even caused him anguish to dwell on others' marital felicity. In July 1885 he wrote to Sanford: 'Don't for pure charity conjure up beatific visions of domestic bliss. I have always maintained your right divine to be proud and happy, but it is unkind to twit a doomed bachelor like myself.'[35]

But in June 1885 Stanley's fortunes suddenly took an unexpected turn. Gertrude Tennant, widow of a wealthy landowner and sometime Tory MP for St Albans, ran one of the fashionable London salons, where political, artistic and literary celebrities mingled. Aged sixty-six (she died at ninety-nine in 1918), she was one of Victorian London's *grandes dames*, and Edwin Arnold of the *Daily Telegraph* was a frequent visitor at her soirées. At her daughter's suggestion, she asked Arnold to bring Stanley with him to dinner on 24 June.[36] Stanley accepted the invitation but, as it turned out, Arnold himself could not attend, so his place was filled by no less a person than Gladstone. At dinner Gertrude Tennants's daughter Dorothy (always known as 'Dolly') sat between Africa's greatest explorer and the 'Grand Old Man'.[37]

Dorothy Tennant was the only woman of any importance in Stanley's actual life (as opposed to the fantasies he wove around Virginia Ambella, Katie Gough-Roberts and Alice Pike). Edwin Arnold described her as 'tall and statuesque, handsome in face and figure. She moved like some goddess of old story.'[38] Aged thirty-four and single at the time of the dinner engagement, she was in her own way as much an oddball as Stanley himself. She kept a detailed diary, addressed to her father who had died a dozen years before. The normal form of ending her daily entry was to sign off 'Goodnight, dearest' or 'Goodnight my darling'. It would doubtless be facile to talk of an 'Electra complex', especially since Dorothy was abnormally close to her own mother, even to the point of sleeping in the same room, but there was undoubtedly something more than a little eccentric about Dolly. It is surely significant that one of her contacts in the art world, Sir John Millais, used her as the model for a painting called *No!* which shows a girl on the point of sending off a letter rejecting a proposal of marriage.[39]

For as well as being a society hostess Dolly was an amateur painter of some repute; her work was hung in the Royal Academy in the late 1880s. She specialised in painting Grecian nymphs and London urchins, the latter a subject doubtless suggested to her through her activities on the outer fringes of Beatrice Webb's Fabian circle. Her canvases seldom exceeded a foot in height but she mounted them in gilt frames so deeply recessed that it was said that the beholder had an immediate sense of distance. Her London gamins were taken straight from the street; she would offer them a good dinner and a cash 'tip' to pose for her. The urchins' naïvety charmed her. Once when the door to her house was opened by a flunkey, one of the lads asked Dolly: 'Why does your brother dress in that rummy way?' The same boy, having eaten dinner, told her in full innocence: 'My eye, but yer mother can cook!'[40]

Such was the woman who distracted Stanley's attention from Gladstone, with whom, in any case, he never got on. The evening was a great success. 'What a charming lady Miss Dorothy is!' Stanley wrote to Arnold. She for her part reacted in what can only be described as an overripe way. Her diary that evening 'told her father': 'So much for succeeding. I am astonished at succeeding. Oh God help me. Do help me. What am I to do?'[41] She wrote to tell Stanley he should feel free to call at Richmond Terrace any time he wished.

The Tennant establishment in Richmond Terrace was situated in a cul-de-sac, prolonging the line of Downing Street towards the Victoria Embankment. It was eminently peaceful: only the clip-clop of hooves, the jingle of bells on the bridles of cab horses or the sound of a steamer siren on the Thames occasionally punctuated the tranquillity. Stanley was nothing loth to return, but Dolly began by overplaying her hand. She slipped from the formality of 'Dear Mr Stanley' to 'My dear Bula Matari' before the reserved Stanley was ready for such familiarity. She had to return to 'Dear Mr Stanley' before he was tempted to return. Partially to make amends, she wrote to propose an oil-painting of his head: 'I would let you be very comfortable, you shall smoke . . . and feel just as though you were in your own tent.'[42]

Stanley accepted, but before the sittings could begin he had to keep a prior engagement with Mackinnon in Balinakill. He did not enjoy the interlude, apart from the one-night stopover in Glasgow with the Bruces. He suffered from facial pain, a recrudescence of the toothache in Brussels in November 1882, and found the damp, cold climate on Mackinnon's estate completely unsuited to him.[43] He was glad to return to London and the company of the Tennants. With some reservations Stanley approached the double doors of Richmond Terrace by a short flight of stone steps with a fanlight above. In the hall was a gaslight, then the vestibule opened out into lofty rooms with vast mantelpieces and velvet, tasselled curtains, which were drawn across the fireplaces in summer. She took him through the library, to the left of the entrance hall, through the dining-room and to her 'birdcage', a small room which she used as a studio. Here Stanley sat while she painted, and a friendship developed.[44]

Dolly left a full physical description of Stanley, and her close scrutiny and painterly eye make it worth having as a detailed record of the explorer at the age of forty-three. She found him both older and younger than his years in looks with an erect carriage, deep chest and thick short arms. He had small hands with short, round, broad-tipped, round-cushioned fingers, and short, thick legs. He had a short, well-proportioned nose, lips that were at once sensitive and determined, and a very big head, with a well-shaped forehead and thick throat. Whenever he entered a room full of people he held his head slightly tilted backwards, in a self-conscious posture.

> His chin is very square and would be a beautiful chin but for a slight thickening come to form an under chin, not of superfluous fat, but rather the muscular throat of a man prematurely aged . . . his face is somewhat marked, I should say by exposure to sun, by fever, by responsibility, by anxiety. His smile is what the French call 'caressant', his eyes look tender and sorrowful, he laughs softly, and just a little self-consciously, as he throws his head on one side . . . He uses his hands very much when talking, not violently, for he is calm deliberation in person, but he slowly emphasises or illustrates what he is saying with his hand. When excited, he raises his arm and brings down a fist with spasmodic strength.

Like all observers of Stanley, Dolly was most impressed by his eyes:

> The eyes are mysterious, his look most expressive and most searching. His look has something intense and penetrating. The upper lid, or rather brow beneath the eyebrow, tilts over the eye, giving a sort of earnest grandeur to his expression. The white of his eye is troubled and murky, slightly bloodshot, and yet the eye shines out clear, with the observancy of some keen-sighted bird who is watching you, listening to you rather with the eye than with the ear.[45]

The intimacy deepened that afternoon to the point where Stanley told her about Alice Pike. He had just finished telling her the story when her mother came in, spoke about the oddity of Gordon's never marrying and concluded: 'I am sure he must have been jilted by some girl in the past of whom no one has heard yet.' Stanley's and Dolly's eyes met as if to say, 'What a coincidence!'[46] Stanley's conclusion, expressed to Alexander Bruce, was 'Barkis is willing, but she may not be.' Dolly, though, was deeply touched: 'I wish Alice had died because then, though separate he could have thought of her with love, and he would not have mistrusted mankind. I felt so sorry for him, not because of this only, but there is a loneliness and disappointment about his life which he will not allow.'[47]

By the time of the second sitting two days later, Stanley was confiding to her his bitterness about Leopold and the myopic Belgian xenophobia. He boasted that he had written his *Congo* book in stretches of eighteen hours' writing at a time. After a long session from 11 a.m. to 2.30 p.m. Stanley came very close to hinting what was in his mind: 'I feel in the depths of my heart that I have been denied what I should have enjoyed with rapture – see, I have no house, no one of my own to care for me.'[48]

The sittings went on until mid-August when the Tennants departed London for the season. Stanley occupied himself with moving into his new chambers at 160 New Bond Street which he had rented unfurnished, then spent £900 doing them up to his own taste.[49] Then, at the beginning of September, he departed for a holiday in Switzerland. At Ostend, before proceeding, he cabled ahead to request an interview with Leopold, but this was refused.[50] He was at Zurich, Lausanne, Berne, Fribourg and Geneva in a densely packed two-week trip which he claimed did wonders for him: 'I feel quite set up. Muscles dense and hard, appetite excellent, carriage firm and stout.'[51] Then he heard from Leopold, who claimed to have been waiting for news from England, when all members of Stanley's syndicate in England had been waiting for him.[52] From Geneva Stanley took the express to Paris and thence to Brussels where he had an audience with the King, and meetings with Van Neuss, Thys and Van Etvelde, Administrator for Foreign Affairs of the Congo State. By coincidence, just before he left Geneva he received a letter from Sanford, advising him to abandon his celibate state and think about marriage. Stanley replied with typical secretiveness: 'Where are the pretty girls you wrote me about? I have not seen one to talk to.'[53] But after his talks in Brussels his mood seems to have darkened for he wrote again to Sanford in more sombre vein. 'I cannot be punished more than I have already. With the womankind Fate has decreed that I shall have little to do in this world, perhaps because I am reserved for exquisite pleasure in the next.'[54]

Fortunately the correspondence with Dolly enables us to chart the reasons for the change of mood. Dolly wrote to him from Staffordshire to tell him she was going to visit Newcastle. Stanley replied from Switzerland with lengthy screeds and later, from Belgium, with ironic amusement at an incognito visit he had made to the Congo Exhibition in Antwerp: 'I have no correspondent living that I should take the trouble to write to so lengthily but yourself.'[55] But meanwhile in Newcastle Dolly had met Burt, MP for Morpeth, the only ex-miner in the House of Commons, who took her down a mine and explained the pitiful conditions in which his brethren worked. Dolly wrote to Stanley: 'I felt glad to know what I felt intuitively somehow, that the future of England depends upon the working man.'[56]

Stanley was displeased with Dolly's enthusiasm for the proletariat. He always had a strong antipathy to socialism, hardly surprisingly in the case of one who had come so far from the workhouse, since such individuals invariably feel that 'levelling down' diminishes their own status and achievements. Stanley's understanding of socialism was in any case elementary: he equated it with the technically classless primitive societies of Africa before the rise of a State in which the task of government becomes the responsibility of full-time officials – in this respect at least he would have agreed with Engels on the meaning of class.[57] He wrote back to Dolly with a homily about the superiority of Nature to human society – a clear hint that he thought social inequality a manifestation as natural as gravity. And he 'punished' her by an inconsequential flirtation with Jeanne Orianne, daughter of the commander of the Belgian Gendarmerie Nationale.[58]

But Dorothy Tennant was a spirited woman. She struck back by some acerbic remarks on Leopold that went beyond anything Stanley would have permitted himself. And she defiantly reiterated her commitment to the cause of the common man: 'The coming elections somewhat excite me. Politics are dangerously fascinating, even putting aside all the higher considerations. If I were a man I would throw myself into the arena, fight for the people and deserve the title of "Procurator of the Poor". As it is, I look on eagerly and hopefully.'[59]

The incipient storm between them blew itself out. While Dolly and her mother relaxed at Hunstanton in Norfolk, Stanley on his return from Brussels headed north again. After short stops at Manchester and Glasgow, he joined Mackinnon in Tarbert to help him with electioneering – for the electorate had now broadened considerably following the 1884 Franchise Act.[60] Then it was on to Balinakill for relaxation and excursions on the loch in Mackinnon's steamer. On his return to London his letter of thanks for the holiday was exuberant. He claimed his lungs and entire body had been renewed and strengthened, that he was taking to his letter-writing chores like a duckling to a pond and was quite prepared for eighteen hours a day of desk work. 'Nothing in all my past life equals it [viz. the holiday]. It has been one long enjoyable and joyous holiday, cold winds, wet weather, wet decks and wet feet notwithstanding.'[61]

The fact that he got back to London and immediately collapsed with a bilious attack and raging headache tells a slightly different story, as does his world-weary missive to Sanford: 'I have no plans. I am simply trifling my time in unproductive work, dining out being among them.'[62] November 1885 was not a good month for Stanley. He should have been basking in the generally favourable reception of his *Congo* book. Though the story lacked the brazen drama of his previous books on Africa, Leopold's pruning and blue-pencilling had at least prevented Stanley's worst excesses in the way of personal attacks on rivals and critics. Even Kirk received the book well: 'You cannot read Stanley's book without imagining what the position of these natives should have been left to such masters as were at Vivi.'[63]

There were, however, two vociferous critics of the book. Peschuel–Loe-sche resented the unflattering (but accurate) picture Stanley had painted of his Congo work and published a polemical anti-Stanley pamphlet in Germany. Leopold advised Stanley that he would have it answered by his German friends, that Stanley was on no account to enter the fray and that he was to avoid public discussion 'with a man so inferior to yourself as Peschuel–Loesche'.[64] But Stanley had already entered the public arena to joust with his second critic – the American Tisdel who had stormed out of the US delegation to the Berlin Conference the year before. Tisdel had made an extended trip to the Congo in 1885 and now launched a splenetic attack on Stanley as a fantasist, a man who was using his reputation as an explorer to mislead and bamboozle the gullible over the alleged mineral wealth and natural resources of the Upper Congo.[65] When this broadside produced no response, Tisdel twisted the knife in the wound. He cited a long list of authorities including de Winton, Parminter, Verney Cameron and Chavannes (Brazza's secretary) who disagreed with Stanley's estimates and added, as if privy to great secrets: 'If His Majesty the King of the Belgians will relieve me from the bond of secrecy imposed by him at my last audience, I shall not hesitate to give some interesting facts communicated to me by His Majesty.'[66]

This was too much for Stanley. Leopold or no Leopold, he was not going to stand idly by and see himself defamed. His problem was that he could not positively assert that the Upper Congo was a land flowing with milk and honey. So he resorted to nitpicking and personal abuse of Tisdel. Of Tisdel's report he said: 'It fills about twelve and a half pages of the consular reports, yet I have discovered that there are over fifty errors which are either the result of ignorance or caused by an unworthy motive of some kind.'[67]

It was a relief for Stanley to renew his visits to Richmond Terrace, once Dolly and her mother had completed their peregrinations. On 23 November Stanley went to tea and held court among a bevy of admiring young men. Dolly noted: 'We all sat round Stanley. I like to hear his deep decisive voice, his commanding enunciation.'[68] As for Stanley, the real object of his visits was as far away as ever from being achieved. He had revealed his true motives earlier in the year to Bruce:

Do you think I am making any progress in this *affaire du coeur*? I cannot see it. I am easily rebuffed and very sensitive. If she proposed to me it might be very different but I have to propose to her, do you know I rather think I will not have the courage. And then, there is a mother in this case, and I am rather afraid of her. I think it would be a boon to shy people like myself, if there were no such people as mothers. I find them sadly in the way. Having brought eligible people up – they insist on interfering at the wrong time. My bachelorhood is solely due to these mothers.[69]

The letter was a classic of self-deception and transference of guilt. The only mother to whom his bachelorhood was due was his own.

But Stanley was in earnest about advancing his suit, however timid it might be. He took the advice of Baroness Van Dornop and slept with a piece of wedding cake under his pillow 'with all the firm belief of childhood in the goodness of Santa Claus'.[70] The charm seemed to work, for in December 1885 there were definite signs of progress in the relationship. Fascinated by the name 'Bula Matari', Dolly had made for him a tiny silver token for his watch chain with a monogram bearing the legend of a Greek capital delta crosed with a T.[71] Another invisible Rubicon seemed to be crossed when Dolly consented to come with her mother to tea at Stanley's rooms at 160 New Bond Street, although the explorer was so terrified at the thought of being alone with the 'Queen of Ragamuffins' (as he affectionately termed Dolly) and her mother that he pressed Mackinnon into service as a kind of male chaperone and minder.[72]

Yet he would have been less pleased if he could have glimpsed the contents of Dolly's diary. On 7 January 1886 she attended Millais's wedding and noted: 'I wonder whether I shall ever marry. I do not see anyone I would wish to marry.' She claimed to need a wise, hardworking and tall (!) man; some of her male friends had two of the three attributes but none all three (it is clear which Stanley did not possess!). She drew up a short list of possibles, on which were Arnold, Stanley and a M. Coquelin, 'whom I now see and hear from rarely, it is true'. But despite finding no one eligible, she confessed to a 'fierce longing to be understood and cared for'.[73]

For all that, the deepening friendship with Stanley continued. On 9 January the explorer paid another visit to Richmond Terrace, and again Dolly put him under the microscope of her minute observation. Once more she noted the cold, silent, disdainful public persona – a veneer that concealed a tenderness he dared not show, marked by a strong feeling for children, slaves and the oppressed or dispossessed. She noted that he habitually spoke slowly, tensely and emphatically; the timbre of his voice was agreeable, he had a slight American accent, and he had a mannerism whereby he strongly accentuated the last syllable of words. 'He comes into a room with his head thrown backwards and a rather curious step. He says "good day" to you with great solemnity and ceremony, bowing whenever you offer him a chair.'[74]

Obliged to reciprocate the Tennants' hospitality, Stanley increasingly sought the avuncular support of Mackinnon to coach him in the small change of etiquette in polite society. A gift of cheese from the Scotsman produced a typical response: 'it will do to put on the table and show my lady friends what a friend I have in the north.' Gradually Mackinnon himself became a regular feature at the Tennants' dinner parties whenever he was in London. The first such invitation showed Stanley in nervous, half-facetious mood, fretting about whether Mackinnon and Dolly would get on: 'Miss Dorothy does not know much about big ships though she has undertaken a picture where there is a sailor standing near a shroud bidding goodbye to his native land.'[75] Stanley meanwhile honed his social graces to perfection by inviting other guests to his rooms in New Bond Street. A frequent visitor was Mrs French Sheldon, an admirer seven years his junior, qualified as a physician and married to a wealthy American businessman. A letter to her in January shows Stanley trying to be a man of the salon: 'Mrs Dickens and the Misses

Roche are invited to tea on Sunday afternoon at 4.30 p.m. Won't you and "Shell" [Mr Sheldon] come and bring Mr Wellcome also, that we may not be outnumbered by the young of the fair sex.'[76]

In private with Dolly, Stanley continued to fume about his treatment by Leopold – the 'weak stomached' monarch, as he described him to Mackinnon.[77] His frustration and anger reached a peak in January 1886 following a prolonged but abortive meeting with the King (together with Hutton and Mackinnon) in which he attempted to disentangle the layers of obfuscation Leopold was throwing around the Congo railway project. During these discussions Leopold deliberately made no mention of Stanley's personal position.[78] On 16 January Stanley wrote a personal letter to Leopold that expressed real anger about his own treatment, the delays to the railway proposal, and most of all about the fact that he was barred from Africa. He mentioned the expense he had already been put to, Leopold's implicit acceptance that he would be returning to the Congo by pressing him to renew his contract, and the rumours of a gathering Anglophone xenophobia in the work of the Association. This alarmed British capitalists and prevented their investing in the railway syndicate. Stanley ended by reminding the King of the promise he had made as far back as 1878 – that if the Congo venture prospered, Stanley would be named Director-General of the State, and asked for a clear and unambiguous reply about his future.[79]

Leopold hated it if anyone pointed the finger at him and accused him, even implicitly, of duplicity. Stanley's letter was perfectly justified, but Leopold reacted to it as if Stanley had made reference to the King's debaucheries or the virgins he liked to deflower in the Palace. The tone of injured innocence in the reply has an emetic quality: 'The King has been surprised by your reply and grieved to see you doubt his sentiments towards you.' Stanley ought not to listen to calumnies about the Congo nor credit the easy canard that he had enemies at the Belgian court. As proof of this, Leopold offered to prolong his contract into the 1890s; he reiterated that he did intend to use him again in the Congo but could not fix a date as yet.[80]

This assuaged but did not satisfy Stanley. The King, he felt, should make a clean breast of it and admit that he could not employ Stanley in a Belgian colony because of domestic public opinion. Not that Stanley would accept even that judgement: how could he harm the nation he had built himself? 'It is as much my child as it is the King's.' Anyone who observed the failure of the German Loango expedition in 1873–5, and the perennial Dutch opposition to any foreign penetration in the area, could not but come to the judicious conclusion that by Stanley, and by Stanley alone, was the Free State created, certainly not by the Belgian mediocrities Leopold had sent out to help him.[81]

So in private Stanley fumed. The letter from Leopold confirmed all his worst fears about the 'Belgianising' of the Congo. This posed serious problems for him. He could not serve under a Belgian, for was he not Bula Matari? At the age of forty-five, he was aware that time was running out. Did Leopold seriously think that £1000 a year could compensate for the awesome ordeal of his five years in the Congo? If he was to be condemned to indolence and atrophy by not being able to return to Africa, no amount of money could compensate for the loss.[82] But publicly Stanley returned tokens of fealty and confidence in the King.[83]

There was scant sympathy for Stanley's plight in Brussels. Among Leopold's courtiers there was a widespread but usually unspoken view that the 'American' was already too big for his famous African boots. When Stanley wrote to thank Leopold for the extension of his contract until 1895, and the award of the Grand Order of Leopold, he still expressed an expectation of returning to Africa.[84] Count Devaux was sufficiently taken aback by Stanley's 'impertinence' to send the following to Mackinnon, noteworthy for its arch insinuation of Leopold's sexual excesses in the closing remarks:

> Stanley wrote a very polite letter this time to thank the King for his Order. I am sorry to hear that he is unwell and I am convinced that his dyeing his hair has something to do with it. I have seen so many brains and stomachs affected by the dyeing of the hair. He does not seem to me to have a right and fair appreciation of his situation. In the first place there is certainly some difficulty for the King to say *now* and *at once* what he will do with him. It may be that he is more necessary here than in Africa for some time on account of the railway affair. On the other hand the Congo is being transformed into a new shape . . . It is not very easy in such a state of things to decide what precisely Stanley's [role] may be in the course of time. One thing is certain – the *exploring* period is over or very nearly so. Stanley is no more to be a pioneer. He must now get into the garments of a state's man *[sic]*. I don't see why he frets in that way and why he does not confide in the King who after all has not treated him so badly. There is certainly no *man* in Belgium who has been treated the like of it.[85]

Devaux's letter mixes nonsense and shrewdness in a perplexing manner.

It was true that Stanley was ill: since the beginning of January he had been ill almost constantly with gastritis and indigestion. He himself blamed the malady on incesssant letter-writing and desk work, which meant no exercise and hence poor health. That was certainly a more plausible scenario than Devaux's absurdities about hair-dyes. But the real reason was hinted at later in the Count's letter. Not only was Stanley the victim of Leopold's deviousness and duplicity; there was also in Stanley's mind the fear that his day was over, that even if he was sent back to Africa it would be in some tiresome administrative capacity, that the days of exploring new segments of the 'Dark Continent' were already in the past.

In February Stanley's ill-health gave cause for concern. He spent one wretched evening at dinner at the Tennants' with Gladstone (now Prime Minister) and Mackinnon, but scarcely touched his food; he later told Dolly that the mere sight of it nauseated him. When the two Tennant ladies went to visit him next day, they found he had been ill all night; the *grande dame* had to play Florence Nightingale.[86] After two weeks without significant improvement, Stanley's doctors recommended a trip to Mediterranean sunshine.[87]

At the beginning of March Stanley set out for Nice but on the road to Folkestone, he had a dangerous relapse of stomach inflammation. A local doctor got him strong enough to return to London, where Sir William Jenner, the eminent physician, tended him.[88] It was decided that sea air would do the patient good, so Stanley departed for the Granville Hotel in Ramsgate to convalesce prior to continuing his European trip. After three days in Ramsgate his London doctor was convinced that a complete cure had been effected and departed for London; all pain in Stanley's stomach had disappeared. The explorer put himself on a strict, salubrious regime. He had a fine suite of rooms overlooking the Channel and there he slept soundly for seven to eight hours every night. He was on a milk diet and told Dolly that since the beginning of March he had lost 27 pounds: 'Congo weight without the Congo fibre!'[89] He walked for three to four hours a day, 'laying in a good stock of ozone'. Indeed the only after-effect of his sound sleep was a slight stiffness in his joints from all the walking.'I stick to my milk diet, as I am still timid of taking anything that might possibly renew the agony suffered at Folkestone.'[90]

But there was no escaping the exigencies of Leopold, even when he was ill or convalescent. After leaving him unconsulted for months, the King suddenly reactivated his faithful agent in England at the very time stomach cramps were bringing him to a standstill on the Folkestone road. For the monarch's interest had been awakened by Gladstone's speech at the culmination of the Commons debate on the Sudan, in which the GOM made it clear he wanted no British confrontation with the *mahdiya*. Leopold saw a chance to get by the back door into the mansion whose front door Bismarck had slammed in his face at the Berlin Conference. Covering his tracks as ever, he asked Stanley to write to Brussels, as it were spontaneously, proposing that the Congo State lease the Sudan at an annual subsidy of £200,000. Leopold would pledge himself to put down the Mahdi's followers and remit to Egypt the annual revenue of £600,000 which used to be paid to Cairo before Mohammed Ahmed cut the umbilical cord. Stanley was to play up the 'saving savages for Christianity' angle and word the letter in such a way that Leopold could present it to the British as an unsolicited suggestion coming from an African expert.[91]

The resultant Stanley letter, written in Ramsgate, was a minor masterpiece of dissimulation. He began by claiming that the Sudan had fascinated him ever since he met Linant de Bellefonds in 1875, and that if Verney Cameron had solved the Lualaba/Congo riddle, he himself would have gone north to join hands with Gordon. There followed an unusual (from Stanley) encomium for Gordon's 'rightdoing' in the Sudan and a typical lecture from Stanley the geographer, in which he pointed out that Equatoria province was as near to the Congo as to the Nile and that Cairo itself was nearer to Europe than to Gordon's former gubernatorial domain. He argued that the obstacles that beset Gessi and Baker did not exist on the Congo, and that with the Sudan in the grip of the Mahdists, Christianity's only hope was the annexation of Equatoria by Leopold. He underlined the fact (all-important to Leopold) that under Gordon the Sudan returned a revenue to the Khedive, of which £70,000 was clear profit. Stanley then 'besought' Leopold to use his formidable military capacity and suggested that if Britain baulked at outright annexation, a deal could be cooked up whereby Leopold did the job and presented the bill to Egypt.[92]

Here was an embarrassing poser for Stanley's fellow-diner at the Tennants', William Ewart Gladstone. He handed the letter to the Foreign Secretary, with a note scrawled in the margin: 'What answer does Lord Rosebery advise?' Rosebery was a good match for Leopold, as his answering minute shows. 'That we do not contemplate any further operations in the Sudan ourselves and that it was mainly the method in which that surplus of £70,000 was extracted that led to the Sudan rebellion.'[93]

Once he had recovered his health at Ramsgate, Stanley returned to London, packed his effects and was on the 8 a.m. train out of London on 23 March. He arrived in Nice at 5 p.m. the next day. Ironically, 24 March 1886 saw the last of his mother Elizabeth Parry. Stanley had kept in touch spasmodically over the years, and saw her last in August 1884 at the Langham Hotel in London just before he crossed to Belgium to confer with Leopold. The same Dr Pierce who had delivered Stanley in 1841 attended her at death and buried her in Bodlewydden churchyard. When he heard of her death, Stanley at once sent a cheque to clear Dr Pierce's account and defray all funeral expenses.[94] So passed the woman who more than any other person was responsible for Stanley's twilight sexual identity.

At the Hôtel des Anglais in Nice Stanley discovered Flaubert's *Salammbô* for the first time. His old friend Edward King, who wrote the preface to a new English translation, dedicated the edition to him, in the hope that he would find this dark African tale of interest. King knew his target. Stanley was enraptured; he found the book better than all other historical novels he had devoured, among them *Ivanhoe*, *Ben-Hur* and *The Last Days of Pompeii*.[95] He was in good spirits generally. He joined a family of Scots from Dumbarton for prayers and psalm-singing, protesting that his piety was sincere, and was entranced by the Mediterranean, which he pronounced a panacea for all who were ill: 'I who knew it so well and had gaily toyed with the sunshine and sea of these shores when younger – how could I have forgotten it?'[96]

Continuing on his tour, Stanley reached the Hotel d'Italie in Florence on 3 April and spent the weekend there exploring and 'walking his feet off'.[97] Stanley was bowled over by Florence; not even Ruskin, he said, could do justice to its beauties – but he was taken aback by the contrasting squalor and filth of its inhabitants and the prevalence of fleas. His letter to Mackinnon on 6 April is full of violent mood swings, one moment enthusiastic about some architectural masterpiece, the next curmudgeonly and pessimistic: 'I wonder whether you have carried with you this thought. That whenever God has been most gracious to man or most bountiful of his creatings, there we find man most regardless of them.' He speaks of his hope that Italian sunshine will mean the end of the dark days of his illness, then touches on the subject that almost certainly triggered them in the first place. He says he could have been spared *all this suffering* (italics mine) if Leopold had been only as generous to him as he was to the *wangwana* and simply given him indefinite leave, so that he could have enjoyed himself.[98]

On 7 April he left Florence for Rome, where he stayed at the Hotel Costanzi. He enjoyed the sightseeing immensely – for all his globetrotting this was his first visit to the Eternal City. He drove along the Old Appian Way to the catacombs of St Sebastian, distinctly put out by the pious Latin mumblings of the monks in his party.[99] Crossing the Tiber put him in mind of a favourite author, Macaulay. The sheer weight of antiquity overwhelmed him: 'One comes across such grotesque scenes at Jerusalem, in Egypt, in Uganda and in Rome, but our true feelings in the presence of graves, tombs and memorials of the dead may not be spoken.'[100] But Rome also showed the dark side of Stanley. He entangled himself in a somewhat absurd verbal campaign of vilification of Gladstone. The trigger was a letter from Dolly in which she declared she was turning against the idea of Home Rule and distancing herself from the GOM.[101] This plugged into an inferno of pent-up hatred for Gladstone that had been festering in Stanley's mind. In successive letters to Dolly and Mackinnon he inveighed against the 'treason' involved in espousing Home Rule: 'after the public utterance of the vile treason, Mr Gladstone can never be regarded by me more than as a traitor to his own country.'[102]

After a final banquet given him in Rome by Prince Teano, who introduced him to a princess 'who I think excels the famous Greek Helen in beauty', Stanley departed for Naples on 12 April and stayed there for ten days, visiting Pompeii, Herculaneum and Ischia.[103] He spent the best part of his letters to Dolly in further attacks on Gladstone; he was not even prepared to concede him the eloquence his political enemies credited him with.[104] But Dolly gave as good as she got; to some extent the correspondence was a return of their clash the previous year over the working class and indeed at the end of her long, impassioned defence of Gladstone's integrity she conflated the two themes. Stanley had jeered at the 'levelling down' involved in the extension of the franchise by the 1884 Act. Not so, she replied, it was simply giving the counties what the boroughs already enjoyed. She also condemned Stanley's 'elitism' (though the term did not exist then): 'I can speak from experience of the capability of the Welsh miner and the Northumberland miner to vote intelligently – I should say that these men were more thoughtful and earnest than thousands in the towns who before were privileged to vote.'[105]

Stanley replied with a long apologia for his position, laced with heavy irony: 'I have received your admirable defence of Mr Gladstone with wondering eyes and bated breath. What power there is in faith. While any was left in me I also was brave and strong in the cause of the good and true.'[106]

Stanley had soured the effect of limpid Mediterranean sunlight by his gratuitous verbal assault on Gladstone. Suddenly, as if it were nemesis for his hubris, the tour itself went sour on him. When he arrived in Milan from Naples, he found that his protective cover was blown and the incognito was no more. Instead of being able to wander alone in ancient ruins, he found himself lionised by Milanese society, so that he could not even manage to see the sights properly. He was given a reception by the town council and the geographical society and showered with medals and diplomas: 'My neck became quite limp with bowing so much – and my back has a faint lumbagoid feeling still.' He was bitter that the Italians would not leave him alone; like many who dream of fame when young, he found that the reality turned to ashes in his mouth. And because he was Bula Matari, who had braved the rigours of Africa, it was thought that no physical feat was beyond him. He railed at the necessity of having to climb up 400 steps to the top of the *duomo*, which left him with 'fever of the muscles . . . yet what could I do? Strangers fancy that because I crossed Africa I could easily go up the Duomo . . . my dear Mackinnon, pray take a friend's advice. Don't cross Africa if you can possibly live without doing it – for if you come back safe, your friends will ask you to become a member of Alpine clubs, and Lawn Tennis clubs and other muscle-fever clubs.'[107]

Stanley decamped from Milan as soon as politeness permitted and went up to a hotel at Menaggio on Lake Como. But here too he had no peace; there was always someone at his elbow, nudging him with 'That is Bellagio,' 'This is Menaggio.' His bland description to Mackinnon masks the real anger he expressed to Dolly: 'The Milanese and Comoese were getting too exuberantly hospitable altogether for a convalescent, and so I had to depart from Italy by express.'[108]

From Lake Como he took the express through St Gothard to Paris, where he sought protective cover in his beloved Hôtel Meurice. His mood was grim, for he now felt that his vacation had been ruined: 'All Europe is crowded. The hotels, the lakes, the trains, each public conveyance and caravanserai – and the people talk of depression of trade. Why, Paris is full. The Grand Hôtel and the Hôtel du Louvre turn people away, and they say the times are dull and out of joint. Why, I never saw the times so gay or so prosperous. People find money to throw away, despite its reported universal scarcity.'[109]

The curmudgeonly mood continued when he returned to London in the first week of May. He was reunited with Dolly at a Thames-side lunch aboard Mackinnon's ship *Manora*, but a week later at Richmond Terrace, at lunch with James Bryce and others, Stanley was the only one present who opposed Home rule. Dolly's attempt to convert him to the cause failed, as her cryptic diary entry hints: 'People are very passionate on the subject, frantically for or against.'[110]

There was bad news waiting for him, quite apart from Leopold's continued footdragging on the Congo railway scheme. At Stanley Falls station Captain Deane, who had replaced Wester, had allowed himself to become embroiled in open confrontation with Tippu Tip. Deane refused to give up a woman who had fled from the Manyema to the station for his protection. When the Arabs made threats, Deane opened up on them with the Krupps gun. This was arrant stupidity. Heavily outnumbered, Deane and the garrison could put up only token resistance when Tippu Tip ordered the post sacked in retaliation; Deane was lucky to escape with his life.[111]

Stanley spent a dull and frustrating June in London before he and Mackinnon decided to take another trip across the Channel to see if they could ginger up the railway proceedings. They paused on the way back to take the waters at Hombourg-les-bains. Their luck was in on 15 July, for an hour after their crossing on a smooth sea to Dover, a ferocious gale blew up and raged along the Channel.[112] From London the two men proceeded to Scotland. They embarked at Greenock on one of Mackinnon's steamers for a house party at Balinakill for fifty guests, including Dolly and her mother.[113] The party was followed by a cruise around the Scottish Isles. The Tennants enjoyed Scotland so much that they stayed on, visiting friends, when Stanley left for London.

It was the proximity to Dorothy Tennant on the cruise that finally decided Stanley to nerve himself up and ask for her hand. In mid-August he took the plunge. 'I wrote a letter to Miss T,' his journal records cryptically.[114] But he dithered for two days before he signed and dated it and sent it off to Scotland. The letter, which reads at times like a Jane Austen parody, reveals Stanley at his most gauche and vulnerable.

You have dropped phrases in my hearing which have induced me to think that possibly I did not love in vain; if I have misconstrued them the punishment is mine . . . knowing how woefully ignorant I am of women's ways, I restrained myself, lest by giving expression to the ardour that possessed me, I should unknowingly give offence to one I had learned to esteem, admire and love with all my heart and soul ... Thus I went to you and came away, visit after visit, always perplexed and doubting, never certain of anything, but that you were the noblest and brightest of your sex and that I loved you ... You are in need of nothing. I cannot advantage you in anything, therein I am poor, helpless, trembling. I am only rich in love of you, filled with admiration for your royal beauty ... I have sat and brooded for hours over the possibilities and impossibilities, which confidence alternating with diffidence pictured ... For all the world I would not wound your feelings, nor offend any delicate susceptibilities. Nevertheless, bear without offence this declaration of mine, and tell me honestly, and candidly, to put an end to this exasperating doubt of mine ... When I leave you I become miserable and unfit for company, and memory of you obscures all things else.[115]

The letter was not well planned. Stanley said nothing about his future African plans and made the tactical error of agreeing to be bound without demur to whatever decision Dolly made. The answer was rejection. The letter turning down his proposal does not survive (almost certainly because Dolly later destroyed it) and she appears to have given no specific reasons. Stanley suspected that it was his origins and early life that told against him, but almost certainly this is rationalisation. It is most likely that a number of different considerations weighed with Dolly. In the first place she was not 'in love' with Stanley, as her diary entries show clearly, and she was perhaps a little young for a hard-headed marriage of convenience. She realised that she and Stanley were poles apart on a number of important issues of fundamental principle (Gladstone, the workers, etc.), and that marriage to such a strong-willed man would mean submerging the independent part of her personality. Also, she wanted a 'proper' marriage and did not relish being an explorer's 'grass widow'. In their many conversations Stanley had repeatedly expressed the hope of returning to Africa. She might have been prepared to consider him if he had been willing to promise never to return to Africa, but he would not. A judicious conclusion would seem to be that neither party felt old enough to settle down on the other's terms.

The rejection from Dolly coincided with the final collapse of hopes for the railway syndicate. Leopold was able to throw off the mask as soon as he had a consortium of Belgian capitalists in place.[116] Not even a flying visit to Brussels and a personal plea to Leopold from Stanley could alter his resolution, and on 13 September the news that the contract would be awarded to a Belgian consortium was made official.[117] Leopold's action was a particular blow, for Stanley had told Dolly melodramatically that he would go abroad if his suit was turned down. Ignoring the fact that he could have been put on the spot if Leopold had called him for African service *and* Dolly had accepted him, he poured out his bitterness about both tormentors to Mackinnon:

> I have been living ever since my book left my hands last year in a fool's paradise. That woman entrapped me with her gush, and her fulsome adulations, her knick-knacks inscribed with a 'Remember Me', her sweet-scented notes written with a certain literary touch which seemed to me a cunning compliment to myself – as I detected a certain kind of effort, her pointed attentions to me . . . on leaving her presence I was buoyed up with some letter or despatch from Brussels which kept me on the stretch of expectation always. 'We do not know exactly when we shall need you, but we shall let you know – my dear Mr Stanley – in ample time to prepare.' So I lived, constantly hoping, hoping here and hoping there – and after all both have come to nothing. I look back with regret that nearly sixteen months of my life have been lost through these artful people.[118]

Bitterly disappointed and taking the collapse of the railway project as the last straw in his disillusionment with Leopold, Stanley sought oblivion in work. He signed a contract with the impresario Major Pond for an American lecture tour that would net him £40,000; this would be followed by a tour of Australia that would bring in a similar amount.[119] But first, remembering the débâcle of his lectures in the USA in late 1872, he would try out his material on English audiences. Beginning at Harrogate on 29 September, Stanley swept through the country for a month, enthralling audiences with the most exciting yarns he could produce on the Dark Continent. When the tour ended in London on 15 November, he crossed to Queenstown to take the steamship *Baltic* to the USA. Departing on 17 November he was in New York for his first speaking engagements on the 27th and 29th, at the Lotus Club and Chickering Hall.[120]

At the back of his mind Stanley still nursed the hope that a summons would come to recall him to his work in Africa. Before he left on the *Baltic*, he had been told by Mackinnon that there was a project afoot to send an expedition to bring Emin Pasha, governor of Equatoria, out of Africa and the grip of the Mahdists. This was grist to Stanley's mill, for he had always wanted to lead an expedition into the northern, eastern or north-eastern corners of the Congo, to discover new resources and fix the national boundary.[121] He told Mackinnon that if the project took shape he was ready to put himself at its head 'at a moment's notice . . . without hope of fee or reward', regardless of the financial losses he might have to take from cancellation of his American tour.[122]

December saw Stanley in Massachusetts and Connecticut. His old friend Mark Twain went to Boston to introduce him on the lecture rostrum and entertained him 'rather elaborately' at Hartford, where Stanley also lectured on the 8th. Twain suggested to Stanley that he write an autobiography while he was on tour. With his stenographic abilities, he could write it in just 105 days, while riding the cars and the book should net him $50,000.[123] But on 11 December at St Johnsburg, Vermont, Stanley received the telegram he yearned for. Mackinnon's cable told him the Emin Pasha expedition was on, and the committee had offered him the leadership.[124] Stanley telegraphed his acceptance immediately, booked passage, and was back in England on Christmas Eve, ready for the greatest challenge of his life.

9

EQUATORIA province was a ghost from the past for Stanley. It was in 1875, while at Mutesa's court, that his sphere of influence and that of Gordon had intersected. And now in December 1886, Gordon's successor as governor of the province, Emin Pasha, was to draw him back to the area and, for the first time since 1877, take him into unexplored regions of Africa.

Equatoria was an Egyptian province in the extreme south of the Sudan, where the Nile emerges from Lake Albert. It was Khedive Ismail of *Aida* fame who first tried to establish effective control over the area. Sir Samuel Baker was appointed its governor from 1870 to 1873, followed by the even more illustrious figure of Gordon, who was governor from 1873 to 1876. Both men set themselves in vain to extirpate slave trading in the area. Primitive technology and transport, the ineffectiveness of local armies and the vast distances involved made this a hopeless task. After the rapid incumbencies of two American and one Egyptian governors, the man known to history as Emin Pasha was appointed to the office in 1878.

Emin Pasha was no more the governor's real name than Henry M. Stanley was his would-be rescuer's. He was born Eduard Carl Oscar Theodor Schnitzler in Silesia in 1840. After qualifying as a doctor, Schnitzler left Prussia to seek a new life in an alien culture. He entered Turkish service as a medical officer and travelled widely through the Ottoman Empire. Thereafter he always referred to himself as Emin Bey. In some ways he was a Prussian epigone of Burton. Like him he had an unquenchable love of the exotic and was an outstanding linguist. He spoke French, English, German, Italian, modern Greek, Turkish, Albanian and (most importantly) Arabic and several African languages. He was also a man of unquenchable scientific curiosity, a highly talented botanist and zoologist.[1]

In 1875 he came to Khartoum as a physician. The following year Gordon invited him to become chief medical officer in Equatoria. His great success with the Africans – for he was completely devoid of feelings of European superiority – led Gordon to recommend him as governor. But Emin Pasha was unlucky. His tenure of office was immensely complicated by the great Mahdist uprising which began in 1882. The Mahdi's victory over the forces of Hicks Pasha in 1883 ended effective Egyptian rule in the Sudan. It was followed by the disaster of Gordon's relief expedition to Khartoum, culminating in Gordon's death there in January 1885.

Cut off in Equatoria, Emin decided to retreat to the extreme south of the province, where he reckoned himself safe from the ravages of the *mahdiya*. In July 1885 he arrived at Wadelai station, where he made his headquarters. Wadelai was on the west bank of the Nile, about 35 miles north of Lake Albert, and was chosen to enable Emin to maintain contact with Zanzibar. The first cause of the Emin Pasha expedition can be located in the letters Emin proceeded to pour out to his east-coast contacts and especially Alexander Mackay, the leading Church Missionary Society agent in Buganda. Mackay persuaded Emin to stay put in Equatoria, on the grounds that there was a good chance his beleaguered enclave would be annexed by the British.[2] This heartened Emin, who saw the British Empire as civilisation's best hope. He had no confidence in his fellow-countrymen, and still less in Leopold's Belgians; the Congo State was anathema to him, and in 1883 he had tried to extend Egyptian dominion into the Mangbetu country, expressly to pre-empt the encroachment of the Association.[3]

Mackay forwarded Emin's letters to British officials in Zanzibar, who passed them on to London. They were full of pleas for help from the British.[4] Still feeling guilty about their failure to rescue Gordon in 1884–5, sections of the British élite, with press and popular backing, began to toy with the idea of an expedition to snatch Emin from the jaws of the Mahdists, thus gaining at least token satisfaction for their murder of a great British hero. The idea of Emin as a 'second Gordon' began to be promoted by *The Times* and other organs.[5] Extension of British influence inland made sense to men like Mackay and Frederick Holmwood (Acting British Consul-General at Zanzibar); they had long argued for abandoning the traditional policy of supremacy on the coast in favour of concentration on the upper Nile and the Lake Victoria region.[6]

Yet the decision-makers at the highest reaches in British politics were not at all keen on the idea. Gladstone in 1886 reiterated his resistance to any idea of reviving a British military presence in the Sudan, even under camouflaged Anglo–Belgian auspices.[7] When the Home Rule crisis brought about the fall of the GOM, the Tory Prime Minister who took over, Lord Salisbury, proved equally hostile. If Emin had to be rescued, he reasoned, and Emin was a German, why then it was Berlin's business and nobody's else's.[8] Moreover, if a private expedition under Stanley's direction was financed by British capitalists, Salisbury wanted it clearly understood that there was no question of the British government's bailing out Stanley if he got into trouble; he would be as much on his own as the Christians in Buganda had been after Bishop Hannington's assassination in 1885.[9]

But Salisbury was led to modify his originally vociferous opposition by four main considerations. In the first place, Mackinnon argued that here was a golden opportunity for British businessmen to avenge themselves on Leopold's perfidy over the railway syndicate. Not only was there a possibility of huge profits if the cache of ivory Emin reportedly had at Wadelai could be transported to the coast; in the long term, important commercial concessions could be wrestled from the tribes for British trading companies in East Africa.[10] Secondly, after the massacre of Christians at the Kabaka's court, Buganda seemed a 'busted flush'; British interest in East Africa needed a new focus and Equatoria could well be it. Thirdly, Sir Evelyn Baring (British Consul-General in Cairo) pointed out that the relief of Emin was important for Egyptian interests and self-respect; whereas the Egyptian government lacked the resources to bring Emin out itself, it would be willing to provide £10,000 towards an Emin Pasha relief expedition to be headed by Stanley.[11] But it was the fourth argument that really weighed with Salisbury. African colonialism after 1884 represented the outer projection of European conflicts and incontestably the new interest the Germans were showing in East Africa was worrying. Mackinnon and Sir James Fergusson at the Foreign Office plugged away at the motif that the Emin relief project could turn the flank of Bismarck's offensive in Africa. Reluctantly Salisbury acquiesced in the idea of an expedition, provided it was not under the auspices of Her Majesty's Government.[12] The combination of Mackinnon's money and the Egyptian subvention enabled Salisbury to get himself off the hook on which he was impaled by public opinion, without lifting an official finger.

While Stanley was in America, Mackinnon set up an Emin Pasha relief expedition committee and began feasibility studies. Stanley had promised him that the cost of the expedition would not exceed £20,000 and Mackinnon was confident that he, Hutton and his other financial contacts could raise the money. In return for this outlay they could hope to establish their commercial position in East Africa by opening a direct trade route to Victoria Nyanza and the Sudan. It was not far-fetched to expect that these territories could be governed under charter in the same way as the Royal Niger Company operated; on the way to relieve Emin, Stanley was to negotiate treaties and concessions with the chiefs between Mombasa and Wadelai.[13]

But was Stanley the right man to head the expedition? Some thought the Scottish explorer Joseph Thomson had good claims and Thomson himself pressed hard to be considered as an alternative to Stanley.[14] It was in vain. Mackinnon's was the dominant role on the EPRE committee, and he was determined that to Stanley would go the palm. Thomson was bitterly disappointed by the decision and spitefully pointed out that he was being passed over in favour of an American citizen. For a while he sulked and raged, then reflected and offered himself as Stanley's second-in-command. Stanley claimed to have supported him for this but, whatever the case, Thomson was turned down.[15] It is interesting in the light of Thomson's assiduous propaganda portraying himself as the man of peace as against Stanley's man of war, that the CMS missionary Mackay thought that Stanley was far the better choice. He wrote to Emin as follows: 'Whether Stanley or Thomson will be in charge of the caravan I cannot of course say. Most probably the former . . . Thomson has, I fear, more inclination for mere exploration than for relieving those in trouble.'[16]

So by the time Stanley docked in SS *Allen* at Southampton on Christmas Eve 1886, preparations for the Emin Pasha relief expedition were already well advanced. Stanley was given full discretion over the expedition's personnel, organisation and equipment.[17] The only remaining major question was which route the expedition would take. Ever the precisian, Stanley had already sketched out a number of possible itineraries, with the costs attaching to each.[18] Some of these routes were unlikely, such as the one through Abyssinia or the direct route through hostile Buganda. More promising was the idea of sailing up the Zambezi and the Shire Rivers to Lake Nyasa, thence to Lake Tanganyika, a south-north crossing, and then on to Lake Albert and Wadelai; the problem here was the probability of large-scale desertions. Thomson's 1883–4 route through Masailand, from Mombasa to the north-east end of Lake Victoria, thence through Bunyoro to Wadelai, was on paper the best of all, but Stanley felt he would not be able to get through without severe and sustained fighting.[19] An itinerary from Bagamoyo to Wadelai via the south side of Lake Victoria was vulnerable to the charge of trying to annex German territory.

On 29 December, at a meeting of the EPRE committee in Stanley's rooms at New Bond Street (attended by Mackinnon, de Winton, the explorer Grant, A. J. Kinnaird and the Hon. Guy Dawnay), Stanley expressed his reservations about all these routes on the ground that the desertion rate would be unacceptably high. Instead he proposed sailing from Zanzibar to the Congo mouth, steaming upriver to Stanley Falls and then cutting across to Lake Albert. This would trim the manpower and *matériel* requirements back to 600 porters and fifteen whaleboats, whereas for his second choice (Bagamoyo to Wadelai via Lake Victoria) he would need 800 carriers, fifty transport donkeys, twelve riding animals and a steel boat. But the committee plumped for Stanley's second choice, for two main reasons: the Sultan of Zanzibar was known to be hostile to the Congo Free State and would veto the recruitment of porters for use on a Congo route; and the expedition would become snarled up in Free State affairs and thus unable to promote British interests.[20]

It now remained for Stanley to cross to Brussels to get Leopold to release him from his contract; if the King played dog in the manger, there would be no Emin relief expedition, at least not with Stanley at its head. Stanley had already foreseen difficulties here and had attempted to make straight the ways with a formal request to be allowed to lead the expedition. He recapitulated the unhappy history of his employment with Leopold since the passing of the 'deadline' for further African service in June 1885, especially since the disappointment over the railway he would have expected to hear something but 'nothing but a cold disappointing silence'.[21]

Leopold was in two minds about Stanley's application. Though he knew all about Stanley's antecedent unhappiness, and had even half expected a request from Stanley to be released from his contract, he was still toying with the idea of putting the explorer in command of a punitive expedition to regain Stanley Falls and march on the Arab capital of Nyangwe. Strauch felt that the Free State did not yet have the resources for a successful war on the Arabs. But Leopold's overall sentiment on Stanley's arrival back from the New World was to turn down his request for the Emin Pasha command in return for a firm commitment to send him with a major military expediton against the Congo Arabs.[22]

Belgian public opinion, in so far as it was at all engaged by Leopold's African exploits, naturally assumed that, since Stanley was in the King's service, it must have been the monarch who summoned him back from the USA for work on the Congo.[23] Perhaps the plan that Stanley had put to the King in September 1884 – of extending the Congo State's boundaries to Equatoria and paying the costs by the rubber and ivory the expedition could uplift – was about to be revived under the pretext of 'rescuing' Emin.[24] The analysts were not far wrong. Strauch had vetoed the original plan on the grounds of difficulty and expense but, with money from Mackinnon and the Egyptian government seemingly sloshing around in London, perhaps this time Leopold could pull off a coup by sending a *Belgian* expedition under Stanley to relieve Emin in return for a subsidy of, say, £60,000.[25]

Immediately after the EPRE committee meeting on 29 December, Stanley took the evening train to Calais and arrived in Brussels at 6.30 a.m. on the 30th. Three hours later he was in conclave with Leopold. Stanley summed up the tension at the beginning of the meeting as follows: 'It was a harrowing meeting . . . since the close of the Berlin Conference in February 1885 – the King has been keeping me on tenterhooks . . . in a few minutes I let him perceive how much he had wounded me by this curious conduct of his.' Leopold was emollient. He told Stanley he always wanted to send him back to Africa and hinted, without being explicit, that it was French opposition that had prevented him. 'Well, Mr Stanley, I confess it has been hard upon you but it could not be helped. Circumstances were such that I could not employ you as I had intended. *Haut politique*, you know, to which we must all bend.'[26]

After these soothing preliminaries, the King came straight to the point. He could release Stanley from his contract *only* if the Emin expedition proceeded up the Congo. The nimble-minded Leopold had already worked out that it was quite possible to achieve his Equatoria ambitions without contributing a penny himself – always the scenario he liked best. If Mackinnon and the other paymasters accepted these terms, he was willing to postpone the 'important mission' he intended to entrust to Stanley. Leopold's confirming letter to the EPRE committee was uncompromising: extra expense notwithstanding, the committee would either have to send Stanley out via the Congo or find another leader.[27] Mackinnon and his associates had no realistic option but to accept the itinerary imposed on them. Stanley received his formal instructions a few days later: 'The Congo State has nothing to gain by the expedition for the relief of Emin Pasha passing through its territory. The King has suggested this road merely so as to lend your services to the expedition, which it would be impossible for him to do were the expedition to proceed by the eastern coast.'[28]

Back in London at the New Year, Stanley tested the waters in Foreign Office circles with regard to Leopold's demands. On 5 January he saw Sir Percy Anderson and argued Leopold's case as follows: they would be using riverborne transport to within 500 miles of their goal, the itinerary was quicker and would allay German fears; most of all, the Kabaka, hearing of the expedition's approach, would be constrained from harming English and French missionaries. Anderson promised to consult Lord Iddesleigh (the Foreign Secretary) and let Stanley have an answer on the 8th. All roads led back to Iddesleigh. When Stanley approached Admiral Sir Francis Sullivan about using a Royal Navy ship to get the expedition to the Congo, the Admiralty simply replied that it was awaiting its cue from the Foreign Office.[29]

Meanwhile Stanley and the EPRE committee had to sift through the hundreds of applications to join the expedition; more than eighty were received on New Year's Day alone.[30] By the end of the first week of 1887, some of the officers had been selected. After very strong representations on behalf of Major Edmund Barttelot and Lt. William Stairs, Stanley agreed to take them provided Lord Wolseley raised no objection and gave them a good reference.[31] A. J. Mountney Jephson was on the point of being rejected by the committee when he produced his 'ace in the hole' – a donation by his patroness the Comtesse de Noailles of £1000 towards the expedition. Even so, de Winton, a powerful voice on the committee, thought Jephson was too much of a 'masher' to stand up to the rigours of Central Africa. Stanley's dissenting opinion is interesting, underlining once again his mania about neatness and personal appearance, as well as being self-contradictory: 'I differ with him for I don't think how a man dresses matters a bit. It depends on the nature of the man within them [sic]. I am positive that the skulker and the malingerer affects the mean dress mostly while the dandy white or dandy black have always stood up to the mark.'[32]

Other additions to the expeditionary personnel including J. Rose Troup, Captain Nelson and James Jameson, another man who was taken on only after subscribing £1000 to the expedition. Among those turned down were Sir Claude de Crespigny and the Marquis of Queensberry.[33] The Foreign Office meanwhile requested Holmwood in Zanzibar to recruit immediately up to 500 *wangwana*.[34] Arrangements were made with Baring in Cairo for the free issue of 400 Remington rifles and ammunition, plus 200 loads of ammunition to be taken to Emin.[35]

Mackinnon's steamship line had to provide all the ocean shipping for the run from Zanzibar to the Congo and for the transport of ammunition to Zanzibar, after P & O declined to carry such an explosive cargo.[36] The Zanzibar mailship was diverted to carry supplies, and the Eastern Telegraph Company offered to transmit all the expedition's cables at half-rate. Stanley himself sent orders ahead to Zanzibar to collect large quantities of cloth handkerchiefs, beads, wire, brass, iron and copper for trade in Africa. In the end the expedition set out with 27,262 yards of cloth, 3600 pounds of beads and forty porter-loads of choice provisions from Fortnum and Mason's.[37]

The most impressive aspect of the expedition was the amount and quality of firearms it took with it. Altogether there were 510 Remington rifles with 100,000 rounds, fifty Winchester repeaters with 50,000 cartridges, 2 tons of gunpowder, 350,000 percussion caps, 30,000 Gatling cartridges and 35,000 special Remington cartridges.[38] In addition the very latest addition to the arsenal of conquest was donated: a Maxim machine gun, which could fire 600 rounds a minute as against a maximum of 200 by any other machine gun. Stanley and Stairs went to inspect the gun in the grounds of Hiram Maxim's residence at Thurlow Lodge, Norwood. After trying out the firing mechanism, Stanley declared himself delighted. He put Stairs in charge of the gun and said that it 'would be of valuable service in helping civilisation to overcome barbarism'.[39]

Other offers were not so welcome. The African Lakes Company offered the expedition full facilities if it would adopt the Zambezi–Tanganyika route, but it turned out their 'facilities' were virtually nil: 'This is sheer impudence,' thundered Stanley, 'or are they fishing for advertisement.'[40] Nor were the personnel coming forward very much to Stanley's liking. One who perplexed him was William Bonny, a former army sergeant, who was one of the very first to volunteer for the expedition.[41] After three weeks of agonising Stanley made his decision. On 7 January he wrote in his journal: 'Have finally agreed to accept William Bonny as Doctor's Assistant. It is much against my will, but I have been unable to resist his pertinacity . . . there is a peculiar stodginess about the man that prevents me from anticipating any valuable service from him.'[42]

By the end of the first week in January, Sir Julian Pauncefoote at the Foreign Office was able to tell him that the Remingtons and ammunition had already left Suez for Zanzibar. But just when all appeared to be proceeding smoothly, Leopold put another spoke in the wheel. He announced that he could not put all his Congo steamers at the disposal of the expedition, as he would need some for the normal business of the Congo State. The EPRE committee declared this new condition unacceptable and sent a special courier to Leopold with a letter to ask exactly what he *was* prepared to give.[43] This was a blow to Stanley. The committee was already hostile to the Congo itinerary and now here was Leopold with his nitpicking Fabian tactics ruining the one solid merit the Congo route had; it was essential for Stanley to have *all* his flotilla for the journey up to Stanley Falls. He made it clear that he would not commit himself to taking the Congo route until Leopold put all his steamers at his disposal and he no longer had to worry about water transport.[44]

Leopold sent the EPRE committee assurances of his support, but couched in terms that were still not entirely unambiguous.[45] It was only after Stanley's second interview with him, on 15 January, that this aspect of things was cleared up to the explorer's satisfaction and he wrenched from the King a statement of full backing for the expedition.[46] Now it was time to square the Foreign Office. Unfortunately the promised interview with the Foreign Secretary never took place, for the day before it was due to happen Lord Iddesleigh dropped dead from a heart attack. However, it was known that Iddesleigh had favoured the Congo route, since it spared him from angry representations from the French and Germans.[47]

On 13 January Stanley went with Baroness Burdett-Coutts to receive the freedom of the City of London.[48] Then he travelled Dover–Ostend *en route* to Brussels to beard the (literally) bearded lion in its Brussels den; he was accompanied as far as Dover by Barttelot, who was going on ahead to Egypt.[49] On the 15th he had a two-hour audience with Leopold, when they spoke mainly of Tippu Tip. The King seemed to harbour a murderous spite against the Arab leader for the sacking of Stanley Falls station and wanted to pursue him to the death. Stanley pointed out that in the present state of Free State resources, that was a pipe dream. Much better would be to use Tippu Tip for the monarch's own ends. Stanley suggested biding time – revenge is a dish best eaten cold – but meanwhile offering Tippu (who would be referred to in correspondence as 'Number One') the governorship of Stanley Falls under the Belgian flag. Leopold acquiesced grudgingly. For once he had revealed the dark side of his personality, as Stanley noted: 'Though His Majesty is about as perfect a gentleman as I have ever seen, yet even he, considerate and just as his nature is – is not without vindictiveness.'[50] It was typical of Stanley's love of playing one side off against the other that he allowed no hint of the proposed arrangement with Tippu Tip to reach British ears, so that the Foreign Office remained apprehensive that Leopold intended to use the Emin expedition to recapture Stanley Falls from the Arabs.[51]

Stanley left Brussels at 5.30 p.m. on 15 January and was back in London early next morning. But if he thought to compensate for the nights sleeping 'on the cars' he was disappointed. At 2 a.m. on the morning of the 17th he was aroused from his sleep by an insistent hammering on the door of his apartments in 160 New Bond Street. At the door was a policeman to tell him that Rose Troup was in gaol for assaulting a brother constable. Since Troup was to be tried before a magistrate at 10 a,m, on the 17th and knew that a man of Stanley's reputation would tip the scales in his favour, he requested his presence. Piqued by this intrusion on his repose, Stanley sent Hoffmann with a note to de Winton, asking him to assume the onus.[52]

On the 18th Stanley travelled with de Winton to Sandringham to see the Prince of Wales. They had tea, a visit to a model dairy, dinner, then Stanley with the aid of maps gave a fifteen-minute talk on the itinerary to the dozen or so guests, before retiring for billiards and cigars.[53] In the morning the Prince said goodbye very amiably and made him a present of a silver cigar case. That evening in London there was a farewell banquet at Burlington House, and afterwards the Webbs of Newstead appeared to wish him a personal Godspeed.[54]

On 20 January the rest of Stanley's officers left England in the *Navarino*: Nelson, Jephson and Stairs in charge of the Maxim gun (Barttelot was already in Egypt).[55] Also due to depart was the troublesome black boy Baruti, whom Stanley intended to return to his Soko kinsmen. In charge of Baruti Stanley had placed Bonny, so that it was a shock when James Grant the explorer returned from Fenchurch Station with the black boy in tow and the news that Bonny had left him at the station for hours, hungry and cold, after depositing him on the platform and saying he would be back in a few moments. Next day Bonny appeared and Stanley taxed him with his misdemeanour. At first Bonny tried bluster and said the date on de Winton's instructions had been wrong. 'This won't wash,' replied Stanley laconically. 'Where did you go?' Bonny's next version was that, as he had never seen the Crown Jewels and could well die in Africa, he had gone to the Tower of London on a sudden impulse. Realising that this was a cock and bull story, Stanley's instinct was to sack Bonny then and there but his hand was stayed by the reflection that as yet the expedition had no doctor. He therefore contented himself with a severe warning to Bonny that one further such 'mistake' would lead to his being sued as a runaway. There was an Australian steamer at Plymouth which was scheduled to be at Suez before the *Navarino*. Stanley ordered Bonny to catch it forthwith.[56]

On the evening of the 21st, after dining with Mackinnon, Stanley drove to Charing Cross Station for departure on the high adventure of rescuing Emin. He was seen off by large cheering crowds, who pestered him to know when he would return. 'As soon as I can,' was the laconic reply. The trio of de Winton, Mackinnon and Hutton accompanied him as far as Cannon Street, then he was left alone with Hoffmann, Baruti and his own reflections.[57] Stanley reached Brindisi at 4 a.m. on 24 January, to find a telegram from James Gordon Bennett asking him to carry his yacht club flag across Africa! 'I cannot refuse him, though it is a ridiculous whim.' At Brindisi he embarked on the P & O steamer *Tanjore* for Alexandria.[58]

He was at Alexandria at 6 a.m. on 27 January. There surgeon T.H. Parke volunteered his services as expeditionary medical officer. To test his resolve Stanley gave him a somewhat abrasive answer: 'If you care to, follow me to Cairo, and I will talk further with you. I have not the time to argue with you here.'[59] At 10 a.m. he took the train for Cairo, where he was met at the station by Evelyn Baring, effectively Viceroy in Egypt. On the way to his house Baring told him that the German explorers Schweinfurth and Junkers had influenced the Prime Minister, Nubar Pasha, against the Congo route on the ground that it would take too long. Nubar and the Khedive were also worried that the expedition now seemed to be a purely exploratory venture, in no way concerned with Egyptian prestige, and they therefore failed to see why they should foot the bill.[60]

Stanley in lordly fashion replied that de Winton, Grant and other experienced people had endorsed the Congo route and that he preferred their opinion to the Germans'. A meeting that evening with Schweinfurth did nothing to palliate Stanley's distaste; he contrasted himself, the disinterested rescuer of Emin, with Schweinfurth, an axe-grinder of German imperialism. He repeated that he wanted to avoid fighting – his reputation as warmonger was bad enough already – but that an east-coast approach would certainly mean conflict, with the people of Ankole, Karagwe and Bunyoro at least.[61]

Next morning Stanley breakfasted with Nubar Pasha and Mason Bey, the circumnavigator of Lake Albert in 1877. Nubar agreed to write to Emin to order him to pull out of Equatoria, since the Egyptians could no longer afford to sustain him there. But it became clear that the rumours were true and the Egyptians were threatening to withdraw their offer of £10,000.[62] Stanley fared better with the second German, Junker, whom he was able to talk round to the Congo route.[63] The two conversed for many hours; in his report of the meeting Stanley gives a valuable clue as to what may have made the rapport possible: 'He seems a quiet little man, about 5' 5" high [!] with a Russo-German cast of features . . . he impressed me as a frank and honest man and I am sure his book will be interesting.'[64]

But both Schweinfurth and Junker thought that the presence of the Maxim and the Remingtons meant that Stanley intended to cut a path of destruction to Emin, which demonstrated to Stanley's satisfaction that they possessed no judgement outside their own narrow field: 'We carry African currency to buy food, arms to defend our charges and wits to use as occasion might need.' This led him into a disquisition on the use of force. He noted that press reports had Emin fighting his way out to Uganda to general praise: 'it is strange that the press is willing to applaud Emin for using force to come out while it is very ready to condemn me if I use force to reach him.' He reserved the right to use force and claimed that, as the territory of the Congo State extended as far as Lake Albert, it was nobody's business but Leopold's if he did. He ended his apologia by using the arguments of Bentham, whom he habitually derided. It was necessary on this expedition to weigh up the greatest good of the greatest number, not just Emin's men against hostiles but present losses against future gains: 'I fancy the posterity of the present wild Aruwimi tribes will have reason to rejoice that the unreasoning portion of their ancestors retired before our rifles.'[65]

Next day Stanley dined with General Stephenson, Commander-in-Chief of British forces in Egypt. Present also were Junker, Schweinfurth, Valentine Baker and others. Junker provided a character sketch of Emin and warned that he would be most unlikely to withdraw from Equatoria even if ordered. Junker's portrait made it clear that Emin was no hero, merely a prudent and conscientious scholar and administrator.[66] Coffee with Mason Bey next day tended to confirm this negative picture of Emin. Baker expressed doubts about the Remington ammunition sent to Zanzibar and suggested that the Egyptians would not be above palming him off with already condemned cartridges.[67]

On the first day of February Baring took Stanley to see the Khedive: 'a short, stout man like his father Ismail, good-looking, and I should say amiable.'[68] Although Stanley later claimed to have 'won round' the

Khedive and Nubar to the Congo route, the truth was that Lord Salisbury had ordered Baring to override the Egyptians and give the Emin expedition his full support. It was behind-the-scenes pressure by Baring that effected the conversion Stanley attributed to his own eloquence.[69] It was agreed that, whereas the Khedive basically wanted Emin to return, he left it open to the Pasha to sever his Egyptian connections if he wished to stay on in Africa.[70]

After the audience with the Khedive, Baring took Stanley on to General Grenfell's to test the quality of the ammunition. Grenfell professed himself astonished at Baker's allegations and said he would carry out exhaustive examinations immediately. As a result of the tests, Stanley wired Mackinnon for 50,000 rounds of fresh ammunition.[71]

Next day he breakfasted with the Khedive: 'at table he showed a pleasant side of character. His laugh is hearty and good-natured. He protests his patriotism.' The Khedive gave him a letter for Emin which promoted him to Brigadier-General but also allowed him to decide his own fate, with the proviso that if he stayed on in Africa it was on his own head.[72]

Stanley's work in Egypt was now finished and at 11.45 a.m. on 3 February he left Cairo for Suez. Huge crowds saw him off; the sixty-one Sudanese troops recruited for the expedition by Baring came marching to the railway station with flags flying and music playing. At Zagazig he was joined by Parke, whom he had finally decided to take on as the expedition physician. Jameson joined them at Ismailia. All paths were now converging on the *Navarino*. Bonny and Baruti were expected on the *Garonne* at Suez and at Aden Barttelot would join them.[73] The party would then be complete, except for Rose Troup and a few others who were proceeding directly from Liverpool to the Congo.[74]

This time all went to plan. Bonny and Baruti arrived at Suez on 4 February. The combined party (Stairs, Jephson, Jameson, Nelson, Parke, Bonny, Baruti, Hoffmann, the Syrian Assad Ferran and sixty-one Sudanese) sailed in the *Navarino* for Aden to pick up Barttelot. Stairs whiled away the boredom of the cruise down the Egyptian littoral by drilling the Sudanese. Hoffmann meanwhile was heard to enquire if it was really the Red Sea down which they were steaming. 'Yes,' replied Stanley. 'Well, sir, it looks more like a black sea than a red one,' was his ingenuous answer.[75]

They arrived at Aden in the small hours of 12 February and changed ships, as the *Navarino* was going on to Bombay. Barttelot came on board the new steamer SS *Oriental* with twelve Somalis whom he had engaged.

Also, Stanley was held to his absurd promise to Gordon Bennett when the agent of the British India line brought him the flags left behind by the *Herald* proprietor.[76]

They steamed down to Zanzibar, stopping *en route* at Lamu and Mombasa. At Lamu they saw, at the entrance to the harbour, a pile of human skeletons, said to be the result of a battle between the Somalis and Gallas (respectively the clients of the British and Germans) which the Somalis won. They also received word of the German Oscar Lenz who had just crossed Africa. Lenz had originally been sent out to rescue Emin and had proceeded up the Congo as far as Stanley Falls. Finding himself unable to obtain men there, he had made his way back via Lake Tanganyika and Zanzibar. It always irritated Stanley when anyone else achieved a trans-Africa journey, so not surprisingly his journal reference is suitably waspish: 'Having failed in his purposes he will doubtless visit the Congo with his blame – at least it has been the habit of all failures of late.'[77]

At Mombasa, reached on 21 February, Stanley noted that the best place for the Mackinnon concession he was trying to wring from the Sultan would be on the right-hand side of the northern entrance to the harbour.[78] But the *Oriental* made but a short stop here and pressed on to anchor in Zanzibar roads at midday on the 22nd. The expedition transferred to berths on the *Madura*, which was to take them round the Cape and to the Congo. Stanley himself lodged with Consul-General Holmwood.

There could be no mistaking the changes that had come over Zanzibar since his last visit eight years earlier. Cables had been laid to Aden, Mozambique and Cape Town. There was a broad carriageway in the centre of the town, full of horses and carriages, and many new buildings, including a palace and a clock tower. Hoffman was entranced: 'Along the wide, well-made streets of the city, lit by oil-lamps, went stately horses and carriages. I could see steam-rollers, lamp-posts, shop-fronts, all as modern and ordinary-looking as possible. Save for the hordes of black men clustering down on the quayside, and the rich, tropical vegetation, we might have been arriving at an English port.'[79]

But it was the warships at anchor in the bay that denoted the more profound change, a change in the entire political complexion of the area. Bismarck's late bid for colonies was already producing sensational results. In 1884 Peters led a small party into the East African interior and concluded twelve treaties in six weeks in which the chiefs alienated land 'for all time'. After the Treaty of Berlin, the Kaiser (on 27 February

1885) issued a charter extending his 'protection' to all the Peters territory. Peters then formed a German East African Company and transferred to it the treaty rights of 1884. Barghash protested vehemently to the Kaiser; in answer five German warships anchored in Zanzibar roads in August 1885. Kirk meanwhile had been ordered by London to encourage Barghash to accept a German protectorate; in view of the French threat to Egypt and the success of the Mahdi in the Sudan, Gladstone wanted no quarrel with Bismarck. In 1886 a joint Franco–British–German commission investigated the Sultan's claims to territories in East Africa; following German pressure the three commissioners recommended that the Sultan should be allowed to possess merely the ports on the mainland and a ten-mile coastal strip opposite Zanzibar.[80]

Almost the first person Stanley met in Zanzibar was Tippu Tip, whom he had last seen in December 1876. Tippu had aged a lot in ten years: his hair was iron-grey and his beard white but at 6 foot 2 inches he still had a commanding presence and, with Barghash's castration by the Germans, was *the* power in Africa between Lake Tanganyika and the Upper Congo. Tippu had been in Zanzibar since November 1886 discussing the implications of the Berlin Act with the Sultan. Barghash had confided in him the possibility of having to withdraw to Manyema from Zanzibar if German pressure became too great.[81]

The news of the sack of Stanley Falls station after the imprudent action of Captain Deane had appalled Tippu and his first thought was that he ought to travel to Belgium to discuss differences with Leopold. On arrival in Zanzibar, finding Barghash a spent force, he was compelled to assume the mantle of Arab leadership himself and began negotiations with Holmwood. He warned him that the Arabs of the interior would resist to the death any attempt by Europeans to wrest their possessions from them by force. On the other hand, he welcomed British help in composing his differences with the Belgians, even suggesting that the Association appoint a competent officer to deal with Arab relations.[82]

Tippu Tip's position was immensely complicated. In general he liked Europeans and had had satisfactory meetings and conversations with Cameron, Vangele and Becker. But he could not abide Stanley at any price. Stanley he saw as a congenital liar, a man without a shred of honour or integrity, one who went back on his word, did not keep his bargains and was a worse slave driver to his men than any official slaver. His only use for Africans, said Tippu, was as human sacrifices; when he was not using them as cannon fodder, he was hurling them into the darkness of Tartarean forests from which they could not extricate themselves.[83] Beyond this, Tippu had a personal grudge against Stanley. In 1876, when Stanley launched into the unknown north of Vinya-Niara, Tippu had prophesied that the white man would never be seen again. His triumphant emergence at the Congo mouth had led to loss of face and credibility for the Arab leader.[84] It was partly Stanley's role as Leopold's agent in the Congo and partly Deane's headstrong aggression that made Tippu Tip so angry with the Belgians, and there was no question but that he was strong enough to maintain himself against all comers in Central Africa.[85]

Such was the situation when the two men met on 22 February. Superficially all was politeness. Stanley began by offering Tippu the governorship of Stanley Falls under Belgian auspices, as agreed with Leopold on 15 January, under the mistaken impression that the Arab leader was short of money.[86] Tippu asked, reasonably enough: 'How can you give me what's already mine? What do you want in that country anyway?' Patiently Stanley explained the terms of the 1885 Berlin Treaty. Tippu snorted with contempt. What right had Europe to take his country and give it to Leopold? Stanley shrugged: as for that, Tippu should ask the Sultan or the Consul-General; he himself had nothing to say on the matter.[87]

Tippu then calmed down and asked why Leopold wanted him. Stanley argued that Tippu and Leopold had a common interest in keeping out other white interlopers. The only conditions the Belgian King exacted were flying the flag of the Congo State, allowing a Belgian resident, and prohibiting the slave trade between Stanley Pool and Stanley Falls. In return, Tippu would receive a salary of £30 a month as governor of the Falls. Most importantly, Stanley wanted to hire 600 porters from him at $30 a head, with a $1000 bonus payable on successful completion of the hiring; this made $19,000 in all apart from the monthly salary from Leopold – surely a better deal than an uncertain war against the Belgians. Tippu hesitated about accepting. He went away and consulted with Barghash. Was not the salary insulting and derisory? Barghash advised that it would be wise to accept even if the Belgians were paying a third of the amount, for as governor at Stanley Falls, Tippu Tip could still command the destinies of Central Africa.[88]

Tippu returned for further talks with Stanley. The sticking point seemed to be that Tippu did not want Leopold to extend as far as Stanley Falls but Leopold was insistent on it. Disappointed that the proffered money did not seem to be having the desired effect, Stanley warned that if Leopold could not extend as far as Stanley Falls, his Congo State would collapse. If that happened, France would step in to fill the vacuum and would have no compunction about sending a major army of conquest up the Congo.[89] This point, made with forceful asseveration, chimed in with Barghash's advice. With great reluctance Tippu agreed to Stanley's terms. He had other motives, revealed later. The principal one was concern for his commercial future. German pressure was already leading to Zanzibar's downfall and a steep decline in Arab profits from the Congo trade. By this concession to the Europeans, Tippu hoped to open a new pipeline for his trade into Equatoria. On 24 February he signed a contract with Stanley. Barghash witnessed the signing and gave presents to the two signatories: a gold watch and 2000 rupees to Tippu and a diamond-embossed ring to Stanley.[90]

When this contract became public knowledge in Europe, Stanley was vilified by liberal opinion for doing deals with a known slaver.[91] But in his own terms he had pulled off a great coup. Forced to proceed by the Congo route by Leopold, Stanley knew that he faced well-nigh insuperable labour problems unless he had Tippu Tip's co-operation in securing porters.[92] Without this co-operation, he would have to give the Arabs at Stanley Falls a wide berth, since it was far too dangerous for European interests to run the risk that the expedition's vast arsenal of arms and ammunition might fall into Tippu's hands.[93] In a word, despite Stanley's bluster to the EPRE committee, it was Tippu and Tippu alone who made the Congo route a viable proposition.

But the agreement with Tippu Tip was not the only fruit of Stanley's brief sojourn in Zanzibar. There was also the question of the Mackinnon concession. On 23 February Stanley had a private audience with the Sultan on this subject. As he drove to the palace, many of his old followers among the *wangwana* lined the route and called out: 'Yes, it is he!'[94] Stanley was bored, as ever, with protocol at Barghash's now increasingly fairy-tale court, so he came to the point very quickly, presented his credentials from Mackinnon and the letter in which Mackinnon asked for a commercial concession as a counterpoise to the Germans. Stanley played the German card very skilfully; he warned the Sultan that when he returned in three years' time he fully expected to find Zanzibar part of German territory. He advanced an argument peculiarly calculated to appeal to the weak and vacillating Barghash: even if he did not trust Mackinnon, why not simply play off the British against the Germans? His eloquence found its mark. Holmwood had been plugging the selfsame line even before Stanley's arrival, so it was not difficult to persuade Barghash to come to an 'in principle' agreement.[95]

After a farewell dinner at the consulate on the 24th, the *Madura* weighed anchor next morning, groaning with human bodies. Tippu Tip was to accompany the expedition to Stanley Falls to be installed as governor and took a hundred of his men on the voyage. In addition, 623 *wangwana*, two Syrians and twelve Somalis drew four months' pay in advance and were then marched straight to the ship to prevent bounty-jumping.[96] Together with nine Europeans and sixty Sudanese, all in all some 800 passengers thronged the gangways of the steamer on its passage south. It was perhaps hardly surprising that just two hours after clearing Zanzibar harbour, a ferocious battle broke out between the Sudanese and the *wangwana*. Stanley's officers had to wade in among the combatants with clubs to restore order.[97]

When the vendetta between the two groups was temporarily settled by physical separation, with the Zanzibaris in the fore quarters and the Sudanese in the aft, Stanley had the leisure to reflect on the calibre of officer he was taking with him to Central Africa. Rose Troup, who had worked for Stanley in the Congo, was travelling out directly. James Jameson, who had virtually bought his ticket with the £1000 subscription, was the most delicate-looking of the party. Obsessed with natural history he seemed of no great force of character, amiable and quiet: 'still the same nice fellow we saw, there is not a grain of change in him – he is sociable and good.'[98] The twenty-one-year-old Lt. Stairs of the Royal Engineers Stanley found much more impressive mentally. He was painstaking and industrious, and was already making real efforts to communicate with his men by learning Swahili. Nervous, excitable, warm-tempered, Stairs 'is a splendid fellow, painstaking, ready, thoughtful and industrious – is an invaluable addition to the staff.'[99]

The thirty-eight-year-old Captain R. H. Nelson of Methuen's Horse, a veteran of the Zulu war, likewise elicited little comment from Stanley, except to say that he was modest, unpretentious, good-natured and undistinguished. Surgeon Parke, too, was damned with faint praise. A charming gentle-mannered Irishman, he sometimes gave Stanley the impression that English was not his native language and that he was not over-bright – a verdict he was later to reverse.[100]

But from the very earliest days the two officers who most engaged Stanley's attention were Mountney Jephson and Barttelot, the second-in-command. Stanley began to note his antipathy towards Barttelot as early as 26 February, when he noticed his deputy's tendency to exceed his authority and usurp functions reserved for the expedition's leader. There was nothing wrong with his physical courage: a major in the 7th

Fusiliers, he was a veteran of the Second Afghan War and Wolseley's Sudan campaign and, at twenty-seven, was tough, wiry and a born fighter. But outside his knowledge of army life in Africa and the tropics, he was an ignoramus, a pure military automaton who did not read or think. The combination of fussiness and autocracy in Barttelot overcame the obvious advantage (in Stanley's eyes) of his short stature – he was just 5 foot 4 inches tall. 'Barttelot is a little too eager and will have to be restrained. He is a little unsound in discipline, and there is a lurking aggressiveness in him which may lead to open rupture – unless a thorough African rupture makes him more amenable. There is plenty of work in him, but you can well understand how lovely this quality would be if it were according to orders. The most valuable man to me would be him who also had Barttelot's spirit and go in him and could come and ask if such and such work had not better be done. It at once suggests thoughtfulness and willingness, besides proper respect.'[101]

Jephson, who was different from all the others in having no previous experience of tropical travelling or soldiering, quickly won Stanley's esteem. He was plucky and very strong and distinguished himself during the brawl between the Sudanese and Zanzibaris. He was a great reader, had a fine memory and possessed the art of small talk. As he was socially well connected, it was not surprising to find him and Barttelot, with a host of mutual friends, boon companions in the *Madura*. But where Stanley took an almost instant dislike to Barttelot, conversely he took an immediate shine to the twenty-seven-year old Jephson, who had the added advantage of not being too tall (5 foot 7 inches in his shoes, as Stanley, always obsessed with other men's height, records): 'There is a great deal in Jephson the thin-voiced whose manner is so affectedly deprecatory. His manner is actually fierce when aroused, his face becomes dangerously set and fixed . . . [he is] gallant and plucky. But he is a man of whims and humours, thin-skinned – awfully so – prone to nourish resentment – and remember small grievances. I believe he has a keen scent for the latter, would in fact scent a grievance where you would least expect one. This comes from too much feminine society, because manliness would despise pettiness – which is a fault with prettiness and over self-admiration. Jephson will be either made or marred if he is with this expedition long.'[102]

But if Stanley disliked Barttelot and was fond of Jephson, the man who intrigued him most in the whole party was William Bonny, the forty-year old former sergeant of the Army Medical Department. Enigmatic and well-travelled (everything from soldiering in South Africa to coffee planting in Brazil), Bonny had already fallen foul of Stanley over the Baruti business. Stanley oscillated between not knowing what to make of him and fearing that he would be his most mistaken appointment. Certainly he had stood the heat so far better than any of the whites. So at this stage Stanley contented himself with an anodyne assessment: 'Bonny is the soldier. He is not initiative [sic]. He seems to have been under a martinet's drill . . . is Tommy Atkins par excellence, stolid and steady, with not an idea in his head, beyond so many months will give him so many months' pay.'[103]

The passage from Zanzibar to the Cape also gave Stanley the opportunity to ponder the many 'contradictions' in the enterprise on which he was launched. Very different interests were at play on this expedition, all of them apparently irreconcilable. First there was the British position. Mackinnon, baulked of a railway on the Congo, had now decisively switched his attention to East Africa and wanted to ape Leopold by making his British East Africa Company a second Association – that is to say, he wanted treaties with East African chiefs and trade stations on the Congo model.[104] To this end he was prepared to use Emin as his agent if the Pasha agreed to come out of Equatoria. Salisbury, for his part, thought Mackinnon's ideas chimerical but saw the need to counter German influence in East Africa.[105] The Egyptians, having lost the Sudan to the Mahdists and unable to persuade the British to reconquer it for them, wanted to retain a foothold in Equatoria or, at the very least, retrieve some prestige by getting Emin and the Egyptian garrisons back to Cairo.[106]

Secondly, there was Leopold. The King wanted to extend the boundaries of his Congo State to the Nile and to this end was prepared to create Emin governor of a new Belgian enclave on the Upper Congo/Nile watershed. The monarch wanted a harbour on one of the great lakes and a secure military bastion against possible invasion by the Mahdists.[107] He claimed to see no conflict between his ends and those of Mackinnon and the British, but this was almost certainly an example of the King's bogus naïvety. There *was* a conflict between Mackinnon's aims and Leopold's, and between the ends of both these men and the Egyptians, and not just in the sense that a Congo itinerary for the relief expedition seemed to tip the balance in favour of Congo interests over East African ones.[108] Which side was Stanley on? Almost certainly the answer is, his own. He did not confide the scope of Mackinnon's ambitions to Leopold, nor Leopold's offer to Emin to Mackinnon, though enough must have slipped out to make the King realise wearily that of the rival bids for Emin's services that of the British magnate would probably beat his.[109] Stanley was playing both ends against the middle, manoeuvring for personal advantage. Ever the opportunist, Stanley's main aim was the enhancement of his own reputation and glory, though if he had to choose between the interests of the two men, he was psychologically likely to opt for Mackinnon, for Leopold had hurt and humiliated him in 1885–6 and the Scotsman had not. The itinerary he proposed to take, outward up the Congo and homeward through East Africa, seemed an acceptable compromise between the exigencies of Leopold and Mackinnon but was in fact most clearly calculated to help Stanley. It is a tribute to his often-derided political skills that he had won over general opinion to this mixed route by the time he left London.[110]

The international prospect was already impossibly cloudy. Even France became involved; it entertained a deep suspicion of the real motives of the Emin Pasha expedition and suspected Anglo–Belgian collusion to carve up the uncharted and unclaimed areas of Central Africa. The suspicion was reinforced in 1888 when, with no news from Stanley, there was talk of a fresh British relief expedition; the French suspected that Stanley's 'disappearance' was part of a previously con- certed plot to allow the British to send large-scale military forces to the area.[111]

Yet even apart from all these considerations, there were two obvious jokers in the expeditionary pack, as Stanley shrewdly saw. One was the huge cache of ivory Emin was supposed to have at Wadelai. It was the prospect of laying hands on this that made susbscriptions to the EPRE committee so plentiful.[112] Yet Stanley the master administrator quickly did some sums on the *Madura* that exposed the hollowness of such hopes. Junker had estimated Emin's ivory store at 75 tons, worth £60,000 at 8-shillings a ton. This seemed a fortune well worth possessing. But a realistic logistical assessment soon showed the treasure to be located in cloud-cuckoo-land. If each of Tippu Tip's porters realistically carried a load of 38 pounds apiece, only £6600 worth would be brought to the Falls. Once deductions of £3800 had been made for transport, pay and bonuses, only £2800 would remain, on which freight and other charges would be payable. Unless the ivory fetched an unexpectedly high price in Europe, even a couple of round trips would not realise more than £6000. Therefore the high profits envisaged by armchair speculators in Europe would not materialise.[113]

Even more of an imponderable factor was Emin himself. The relief expedition was always bedevilled by a fundamental ambiguity and uncertainty about what exactly 'relief' meant. Did it mean that Stanley was to escort Emin and his Egyptian troops back to Cairo, or did it imply merely the delivery of supplies and ammunition? The problem, as Stanley saw it, was that if Emin accepted none of the three propositions put to him, from the Khedive, Leopold or Mackinnon, what was his position then? 'If he refuses all three, then he and his force must undertake an independent role, and live on the country as they best can and Emin will be a kind of white Mirambo living on violence and cattle lifting. What a prospect for Gordon's lieutenant!'[114]

Stanley would not have been reassured if he could have read Emin's correspondence while the expedition laboriously threaded its way towards him. All Emin's letters to Kirk, Felkin, Mackay and others seemed to contain the recurrent phrase 'Help us quickly or we perish.'[115] But this did *not* mean, as Stanley so consistently presumed it did, that Emin wished to leave Africa. What he wanted was to stay in Africa because he personally loved the continent, preferably under the British protectorate that Kirk and Mackay had long urged on him as his best chance in the future. Emin was high in his praise for Stanley when he heard he was on his way. 'I have always felt the greatest admiration for Mr Stanley as an explorer; his intrepidity, his pluck and his kindly regard for his followers have always commended my hearty sympathies.'[116] But he made it clear that he had no intention of following Stanley out of Africa; his reading of the relief expedition was that Stanley would deliver the stores and ammunition and then depart: 'If, however, the people in Great Britain think that as soon as Stanley or Thomson comes I shall return with them, they greatly err. I have passed twelve years of my life here, and would it be right of me to desert my post as soon as the opportunity for escape presented itself? I shall remain with my people until I see perfectly clearly that their future and the future of our country is safe.'[117] From December 1886 until April 1888 both the men with assumed names lived in a twilight world of mutual misunderstanding that was eventually to have explosive effects.[118]

· 10 ·

THE *Madura* slowly made its way south, past Mayotte Island of the Comoro group. Stanley made sure all his officers had specific tasks to occupy their time. Parke had overall responsibility for the Sudanese, Bonny was in charge of the donkeys and goats, while Stairs, Nelson, Jephson, Jameson and Rose Troup were in charge of 117 *wangwana* each. Barttelot's task was to deliver rations in gross to each officer daily, for distribution to his group. Every day a muster was held to allow the officers to familiarise themselves with the men. And from 26 Feburary to 4 March Parke vaccinated everyone on board against smallpox.[1]

Annoyed that all the officers seemed to be keeping journals, Stanley by and large held himself aloof from them. He spent most of his time with Tippu Tip and Jephson. Already rumours were running around the ship of Tippu's animus towards Stanley, how Stanley on leaving him in 1876 had promised to make him a rich man but instead sent him his photograph![2] Stanley broached the subject of Tippu's discontents, only to find the Arab raging about the conduct of Captain Deane. This was an old bone of contention. Tippu had brought three Krupps shells to Zanzibar and ostentatiously produced them to Stanley as proof of the type of bombardment his men had sustained from Stanley Falls station. Stanley tried to pour oil on troubled waters; was Tippu really going to generalise about white men from the consequences of a single hothead's exaggerated sense of 'honour' over a woman; was this not another instance of the phenomenon Tippu himself must often have seen, the 'young buck' on the rampage? He pointed out to Tippu that once he was governor of Stanley Falls, there would be no need to see the white men he so disliked.[3]

Stanley had given Tippu Tip and his ninety-six followers free passage all the way from Zanzibar to Stanley Falls on the calculation that it would

161

not then be open to the Arabs to try to persuade the *wangwana* to desert. His attitude to Tippu was generally cynical and even at this stage of the expedition he was planning to double-cross him if that became necessary. 'If there is no ivory, I shall be indebted to Tippu Tip for the sum of £3600 . . . at the same time I shall not risk the expedition for the sake of ivory.'[4]

But it was Jephson with whom Stanley spent most of his spare time. Jephson found Stanley remarkably quick at grasping ideas and astonishingly lucid in his capacity to express them: 'he has such a wonderful gift of word painting . . . such a keen sense of the ridiculous.'[5] Again, as with Livingstone, Burton, Bruce and many others, we observe Stanley's natural rapport with fellow-Celts, as opposed to the born and bred Englishman. The Jephsons of Mallow were, like the Burtons, an Anglo–Irish family.[6] But Jephson soon learned that there was a dark side to Stanley and a diary entry on 28 February indicates the general drift:

I had a great argument with Stanley. He seemed to think that the only thing worth doing was to succeed, no matter how, in anything you undertook and that success was everything, whilst I contended that failure was sometimes a nobler thing than success – circumstances made it so . . . Stanley seems to have no sort of patience with anything which does not succeed. Of course such a feeling is splendid, how could great things be done without a great deal of that feeling, still if one has *only* that feeling it leads to a great deal of injustice and intolerance towards other people who have not been so lucky in succeeding as he has done.[7]

The *Madura* reached Cape Town on 8 March after a cruel buffeting in high seas around Durban and Port Elizabeth.[8] They took on ammunition, coal, stores and livestock, bearing in mind that on the ten-day run to the mouth of the Congo they would consume 120 sheep and goats. Stanley went ashore for a short walk but so many people stopped and stared at him that after buying a few books he was glad to retreat to the security of the ship. His distaste for Cape Town was underlined when a deputation of humanitarians from the Chamber of Commerce came aboard to seek assurances that he was not planning to massacre the indigenous peoples he encountered. Stanley replied tartly that he had no intention of robbing Africans or seizing their food and goods; the

Remingtons were there as a 'failsafe' weapon, just in case he had to force passage through to Wadelai.[9]

The sensation of Cape Town was Tippu Tip, whom Stanley had allowed to go ashore in company with Hoffmann provided the party took no photographs – already Stanley was wary of possible future rival memoirs.[10] It was not just his height but the retinue of his wives (thirty-five of the ninety-six followers were Tippu's women) that excited the curiosity of Cape journalists.[11] Tippu Tip himself was enormously impressed by his first real view of white civilisation; until now, he admitted, he had thought all white men fools.[12] In the light of Tippu's remarks about the chaos into which Africa would descend if blacks were ever given their independence, there is considerable dramatic irony in his admiration for the artefacts of South Africa.

Jameson, the lover of flowers and wildlife, brought back to the ship from his shore excursion a number of dogs, conjuring memories of the five Stanley had taken with him in 1874–7. Stanley chose a male fox terrier and Jephson a white mongrel. 'I have named mine "Randy",' Stanley wrote, 'after Randolph Churchill because of his stirring speech at Bradford in 1886, with the sentiments of which I heartily agreed. Jephson called his "Bill Sikes", for his low breeding and sullen looks.'[13] But it was soon Jephson's turn to reveal his dark side. After just four days he grew tired of his pet for being smelly and low-bred and for being ribbed about him by his messmates. He tied two iron bars to the dog and dropped him from a port-hole. Stanley was always sentimental (though not necessarily compassionate) about animals, and the incident upset him: 'Meek and voiceless creatures like Bill Sikes are often the subject of contumely in this world, then people get an idea in their heads, that their existence is intolerable and exercise a pressure against them, until they are crowded out.'[14]

The *Madura* weighed anchor at 5.30 p.m. on 10 March and began to creep up the western coast of South Africa; again there was stormy weather immediately after leaving the Cape but, mercifully, this soon abated.[15] On the 14th there occurred the first death among the *wang-wana*, from dysentery. As on the trip down to the Cape, Stanley spent much time closeted with Tippu Tip, and hammered out with him an agreement that once at Leopoldville, Tippu would go on ahead, collect the promised porters, and rejoin Stanley at Yambuya village, at the confluence of the Congo and Aruwimi. The only jarring note at present was the strong antipathy Stanley felt for Tippu's favourite son-in-law, Salim bin Masoud.[16]

On 18 March 1887 the expedition arrived at Banana to find that the telegraph cable had recently broken, so that neither Stanley's cables nor Leopold's instructions had arrived and nothing was ready for them.[17] After disembarking its vast quantities of humans and *matériel*, the *Madura* continued on its ocean-going way. For the 108-mile voyage to Matadi (on the opposite bank from Vivi) Stanley chartered from the Dutch and English trading companies the river-steamers *Albuquerque* and *K. A. Niemann* and the paddle-boat *Serpa Pinto*. The agents of the English house depressed his officers with tales of the Congo authorities' incompetence and food shortages ahead.[18] This irritated Stanley, already 'decidedly grouchy' after the initial bad news. Fred Puleston, who met him at Banana, found Stanley extremely reserved and brusque, pessimistic, obsessed with the coming trial but full of forebodings. He snapped at Puleston and his two English companions: 'I am surprised that you gentlemen do not invite my men ashore and ask them to point out their last resting places.'[19]

At Boma Stanley's mood darkened further. Liebrechts had succeeded de Winton as governor of the Congo State, but downriver Valcke and Parminter held undisputed sway. After their antecedent turbulent relationship, it was not surprising that Valcke was cordial but awkward with Stanley and seemed to delight in giving him the bad news of famine and steamer shortages at Leopoldville. 'Valcke I feel sure has vented some malice in so glibly giving me such an extinguisher. For a junior to find himself in power, and able to thwart his once formidable senior, would be more than human not to let his gentle malice be exercised ... Valcke's malice peeped out (and I am sure he must have felt good) when he said, "And I have to remind you, Mr Stanley, that the boats were only to assist you if they could be given without prejudice to the service of the State." '[20]

Stanley proceeded upriver to Matadi, fuming inwardly at the obstacles in his path. If only half of what Valcke had told him was true, it was quite obvious that Leopold was hampering the expedition rather than helping it. He oscillated between blaming Leopold for duplicity and censuring the EPRE committee for not having opted for the Congo route in the first place. But at all events, 'our prospects are of the blackest.'[21]

At Matadi the scattered segments of the expedition reunited. A Portuguese gunboat brought in Barttelot and the Sudanese and Jephson and his quota of the *wangwana*. Nelson and Jameson marched their contingents overland, while Valcke and Parminter brought the rest of the Zanzibaris up to Matadi in Association boats. Then Valcke translated the orders he had received from Strauch. The only commitment seemed to be to provide the steamer *Stanley* and a lighter. Stanley raged inwardly when he thought of the time the EPRE committee had spent trying to ensure that Leopold could not pull the stunt he now seemed to have pulled. He particularly bridled at the statement that the committee 'solicited the aid of the King'; but for Leopold's obstinate intervention, the expedition would have set out from Bagamoyo on the east coast route! 'I observe that Valcke is not so much to blame as Strauch, though I still fancy that "putting a spoke in our wheel" has given him a great delight.'[22]

At Matadi too Puleston met Barttelot for the first time. He noticed that he and Stanley did not get on; they were too much alike, both impatient and domineering. Given Stanley's foul humour, Puleston had a strong intuition that something would go badly wrong on the expedition.[23] It did not take a person of exceptional insight to intuit that. Every item of bad news Stanley received seemed to whip him into a frenzy. When the missionary Comber offered to lend him the steamer *Peace*, then at Stanley Pool, but with certain restrictions, Stanley noted angrily in his journal: 'I am becoming suspicious of both State and missionaries. There is a false ring about their promises.'[24]

It was doubtless the deep anger and frustration Stanley felt that turned the overland march to Leopoldville into a nightmare experience for all. It was the rainy season when they set out on 25 March to follow the south bank route overland to Stanley Pool, and many of the party were new to the perils of heat, swamps and crocodiles. The caravan route, which wound round the thirty-two cataracts between Matadi and Stanley Pool, was a mere footpath, 40 inches wide, winding through grass several feet high. In the early stages of the march there was no particular shortage of food, though the descent of 800 armed men on small villages taxed their resources as well as causing some alarm. Stanley had issued a 25-day iron ration, but his men supplemented this by bartering blue beads, brass wire and cloth handkerchiefs for a wide variety of foodstuffs: pigs, fowl, goats, fresh and smoked fish, hippo meat, eggs, potatoes, nuts, shrimps, even rats and locusts. There was also abundant sugar-cane, tobacco and palm-wine, while pineapples were in European terms literally ten a penny.[25]

But the Sudanese found the going tougher than they had expected. They also regarded portering as beneath their military dignity and were mutinous and insolent. Barttelot, in charge of them, complained that Major Chernside, who recruited them in Egypt, must have deliberately picked out the greatest scoundrels he could find.[26] Barttelot answered their recalcitrance with brutality. He struck and punched them and threw the ringleaders into the river, so that their clothes drifted off downstream and their ammunition was spoiled. Stanley reprimanded his second-in-command: 'The Sudanese are rather trying to get along with, being of stubborn temper and sulky. Still, it is early times to maul people and I had to admonish Barttelot and to explain to him that we must not expect too much from the people at the outset.'[27]

Every morning camp was struck early and pitched again in the early afternoon. The column was already beginning to straggle and often different contingents made separate camps for the night. There was rising mortality. Within a week of arrivng at Banana nine of the *wangwana* had died, most of them from Nelson's company – a fact which Stanley attributed to their having been located near the boilers on the *Madura*.[28] Stanley himself was very ill, being attacked by both diarrhoea and bilious fever. Two officers established themselves in his estimation at this time, surgeon Parke by his assiduous attentions and Jephson by jumping into a stream to guide the bearers of the hammock containing the prostrate expedition chief.[29]

On 28 March the column ran into a caravan headed by Herbert Ward, whom Stanley had recruited for Congo service in 1884. After three years in the Congo State Ward was preparing to leave for Europe when he heard of the Emin Pasha expediton from the missionary Charles Ingham. Knowing of the shortage of porters, he collected 300 men and intersected Stanley's party, offering to place the porters at Stanley's service provided he himself was taken on. His account of the meeting provides a graphic account of the Emin Relief expedition on the march:

> I had broken camp early one morning, and was marching rapidly along ahead of my caravan, when in the distance coming over the brow of a hill I saw a tall Sudanese soldier bearing Gordon Bennett's yacht flag. Behind him, astride of a fine henna-stained mule, whose silver-plated strappings shone in the morning sun, was Henry M. Stanley, attired in his famous African costume. Following immediately in the rear were his personal servants, Somalis with their curious braided waist-coats and white robes. Then came Zanzibaris with their blankets, water-bottles, ammunition belts and guns. Stalwart Sudanese soldiers with dark-hooded coats, their rifles on their backs, and innumerable straps and leather belts around their bodies; and Zanzibari porters bearing iron-bound boxes of ammunition, to which were fastened axes

and shovels as well as their little bundles of clothing, which were rolled up in coarse sandy-coloured blankets . . . At one point a steel whale-boat was being carried in sections, suspended from poles which were each borne by four men; donkeys heavily laden with sacks of rice were next met with, and a little further on the women of Tippoo-Tib's harem, their faces partly concealed and their bodies draped in gaudily-covered cloths; then at intervals along the line of march an English officer with whom, of course, I exchanged friendly salutations; then several large-horned African goats, driven by saucy little Zanzibari boys. A short distance further on, an abrupt turn of the narrow footpath brought into view the dignified form of the renowned Tippoo-Tib, as he strolled along majestically in his flowing Arab robes of dazzling whiteness, and carrying over left shoulder a richly-decorated sabre, which was an emblem of his office conferred on him by H. H. the Sultan of Zanzibar.[30]

Yet this impressive parade masked an ever-escalating brutality. On 3 April there was another fight between the Sudanese and the *wangwana*. The Zanzibaris were having to lug 65 pounds of ammunition, four days' rations of rice and their own kit, while the haughty Sudanese carried their rifles only. While the *wangwana* stuck to their task stoically, the Sudanese were always complaining. To avoid further conflicts Stanley had to order Barttelot to keep his Sudanese a day's march ahead of the Zanzibaris. He was already regretting having brought the Sudanese along. They were meant to be an earnest of Egypt's intentions towards Emin and his garrison, but nobody had warned Stanley how pig-headed and contumacious they were.[31]

Problems with the Sudanese continued. At Banza Mateka mission station, run by Mr and Mrs Richards (two of the few Congo missionaries for whom Stanley had any time), and again at Lukungu station, four days' rations of potatoes, bananas, Indian corn and palm nuts had been assembled for the expedition, but the Sudanese simply gorged their supplies, then threatened to desert if they were not given more food.[32]

Stanley often pondered what his position would be if the Sudanese actually did desert *en masse*, but meanwhile he had discipline problems on all sides, not just involving the unruly men of the Sudan. The *wangwana* came to him with complaints that Nelson was striking them crippling blows on the legs and shins; Stanley had to reprimand Nelson.[33] But Stanley employed different standards according to whether it was he or his officers who did the chastising. Barttelot recorded with relish:

'Stanley as rearguard got on A1. He flogged loafers and they all kicked amazingly.'[34] Parke, usually uncritical of Stanley, confirmed that he speeded up the daily rate of march by flogging loiterers.[35] Jameson, who had originally regarded beating porters as not fit work for white men, changed his tune after a while and recorded this verdict on Stanley's flagellation exploits in the rearguard: 'How he did lay his stick about the lazy ones, and the Somali whacked away too! It was a sight for sore eyes to see the lame, sick, halt and the blind running with their loads as if they were feathers; and I was delighted to see some of my men catch it hot, after I had been told by Mr Stanley himself not to strike them.'[36]

But predictably the worst offenders against Stanley's disciplinary code were always the Sudanese, and it was on this issue that Stanley first came into serious conflict with Barttelot. On 5 April one of the Sudanese soldiers came to Stanley to show him a black eye – the effect of a punch from the Major. Stanley sent for Barttelot and rebuked him. The Major did not deny the punch but said he was taking his cue from Stanley. 'I have seen you do it.'

Stanley glared at him for a moment, until he was satisfied that the response was spontaneous and not a calculated piece of insolence. Then he gave Barttelot a lecture on the difference between his 'exemplary' violence and the Major's gratuitous brutality. He pointed out that his own punishments were always public, proclaimed and explained: 'I sometimes affect a great rage, or I taunt them with irony but I don't pitch into them like a pugilist. Besides, I speak their dialect perfectly. I give them notice that I am coming and if they don't scamper I call out to their headmen to start them. There is method in what I do, and no scars are left.'[37]

Barttelot listened to the homily in silence, but there was something about his 'body language' Stanley did not care for. He decided to seek an early pretext to take the Major down a peg or two. Meanwhile Stanley took out his anger on another target. This time it was Bonny, who had been out of favour ever since the Baruti/Tower of London incident.[38] On the pretext that Bonny's marching was sloppy and mechanical, Stanley humiliated him in front of his charges by calling out: 'Hello, Bonny, wake up, my son. You will mistake the mouth of a hippopotamus for a doorway if you go on nodding in that way.'[39]

On 8 April the Sudanese again threatened mutiny. Stanley warned them that if they deserted, he would give the order in the country around that these were Bula Matari's enemies and should be shot on sight. When the Syrian Assas Farran claimed to be exempt from the daily chores imposed on the Sudanese, Stanley dubbed him ringleader of the troubles and threatened to spit him with a bayonet. In an attempt to pour oil on troubled waters, Barttelot apologised to Stanley for the problems the Sudanese were causing, but Stanley rounded on him and said all was the fault of the Major's poor leadership. If he had to shoot the Sudanese for desertion, he, Stanley, would see to it that Barttelot's name was blackened with Lord Wolseley.[40] When Barttelot blazed defiance at this threat, Stanley picked out the laziest of the Sudanese and ordered the Major to take them on ahead to Leopoldville by forced marches, threatening dire sanctions if they lost a single load. The order was a clear, calculated act of vindictiveness, as judicious onlookers admitted.[41]

The nightmare continued. By mid-April the expedition was sustaining losses on every day's march: from illness, desertion, and pilfering of rifles, ammunition and stores. Fever was cutting a swathe through the remaining Sudanese, and Hoffmann was delirious with it. The Sudanese were both skeletal in appearance and beyond the control of their officers; only the fear of Stanley drove them on. When a third box of Remington ammunition was lost in Parke's company, Stanley had to reprimand Parke, one of his favourites.[42] Salim bin Masoud gave further evidence of fractiousness by an altercation with Jephson (he had already clashed with Stairs) in the course of which Jephson threatened to throw the Arab into the river. Tippu Tip intervened to silence his refractory subordinate but then complained to Stanley of Jephson's behaviour. When Stanley called Jephson in for a talking-to, he in turn did not respond well to his leader's admonitions.[43]

On top of all this came a letter from Liebrechts at Leopoldville, which showed how deeply the EPRE committee had been gulled by Leopold. There was also a grudging missive from Bentley about the loan of the *Peace*, whose tone Stanley bitterly resented after all he had done for his mission.[44] The stress of all this found Stanley at his most irrational and punitive. First he humiliated Jameson in front of his men, in the process making him the victim of the most barefaced duplicity. Stanley had ordered Jameson, over his protests, to flog on the sick. When one of the chiefs fell ill on the march, Jameson urged him on, whereat Stanley rushed up with surgeon Parke and proceeded to play the part of the concerned, compassionate leader as against Jameson's brute.[45] It was a frequent Stanley ploy on this expedition to give secret orders to his officers to act in a draconian way, then to intervene himself in compassionate guise as the angel to their devil; if necessary, Stanley would take the *mangwana*'s side against his own officers, even when they had merely faithfully carried out his orders. This was pathology itself: Stanley was determined there would be no Frank Pococks, with a special relationship with the men of Zanzibar, on this expedition.

18 April was a black day even on this dark-limned trek. Three separate incidents revealed Stanley at the very limits of rationality. When yet another box of ammunition went missing. Stanley arbitrarily identified one of the porters as the culprit and gave him a hundred lashes. Even while he was being beaten, the man protested that *his* ammunition box was in camp, which later was proved to be the case. Jephson remarked cryptically: 'It was rather an extreme measure but he knows best what to do, I suppose.'[46] Stanley then proceeded to chain and padlock all the chiefs or porters together, and lectured the trussed *wangwana* on how such ammunition losses in 1877 would have meant their death by firing squad. Seeing Jameson looking on disapprovingly, Stanley warned him that if any more such losses occurred, Jameson would be dismissed. Jameson went to Stanley's tent afterwards and protested bitterly about this censure.[47]

Next Stanley summoned Jephson to his presence and warned him that he would not allow the expedition to be jeopardised through the shortcomings of its officers. He was disgusted with his officers' racialism and their talk of 'niggers' and so on. But if he made Jephson the official recipient of the proof of his toughness, it was Baruti who (literally) received the sharp end that day. When Hoffmann came in to tell his employer that Baruti could not be found to carry the master's lunch basket, Stanley ordered the boy found and flogged. Baruti, who had already in London demonstrated his martial spirit, and was now a strapping lad of fifteen, tried to resist the flogging, whereat Stanley took out his hunting knife and threatened to rip him up if he did not submit to his punishment. Stanley then laid on with the whip himself.[48]

On 20 April the main column caught up with Barttelot's tardy Sudanese. Disgusted at their slow progress, Stanley ordered them to halt and to forgo the privilege of marching a day ahead of the porters. On the other hand, he warned Barttelot that he would be held personally responsible for any fisticuffs between the Sudanese and the *wangwana*. At this Barttelot fell into a towering rage. Two men with volcanic tempers were glowering at each other but, as ever, Stanley could see just one point of view: 'The Major's temper is not improving, and if he's thwarted in the least, he gets extremely saucy. One of these days I shall have to put a bridle on his fluent tongue, for an outburst of bad temper is sure to provoke, in the end, something similar in others if too oft indulged.'[49]

Barttelot tried to strike back at the leader by initiating a whispering campaign. When Stanley accused his officers of opening the Fortnum and Mason's box, Barttelot noised it about that this was to mask the fact that Stanley was surreptitiously helping himself to the luxury goods.[50]

At last, on 21 April, the month-long ordeal was over and the expedition trooped despondently into Leopoldville. For the last six days of the march Stanley had enjoyed the company of a man later to become both famous and infamous: Roger Casement. Casement, then aged twenty-three, was in Congo service as superintendent of the boiler irons for the steamer *Florida*. 'He is a good specimen of the capable Englishman,' noted Stanley.[51] But the expedition itself already presented a tatterdemalion picture: the losses from death, desertion, pilfering and wastage had been severe. The strong liquor imbibed at Lukunga station came close to killing some of the white men. Hoffmann had had three attacks of fever in a month, but with no chance to convalesce – since his master halted for the illness of no man save himself – he had kept himself going with doses of quinine so strong that he was temporarily struck deaf.[52]

Nevertheless, Stanley was determined to enter Leopoldville in heroic style. He mounted his Europeans on the fine Muscat donkeys they had brought from Zanzibar and had Tippu Tip march at his side, resplendent in a white fez and yellow *djoho*. He belittled his heavy losses by saying that if he had taken the eastern route to Wadelai, he would already have lost over a hundred men through death, sickness or desertion.[53]

But what he found in Leopoldville appalled him. The extent of Leopold's perfidy became clear. His much-trumpeted 'help' was revealed as a sham. There were no steamers to take the expedition on upriver. No preparations had been made, even though Leopold had insisted on the Congo route.[54] Even worse, famine was raging throughout the Stanley Pool area. There was adequate food for only about one-third of the expeditionary force. Food shortages were partly a result of the Association's already growing reputation for brutality which had driven many of the indigenous food producers into the bush.[55] But they were also due to the fecklessness of the missionaries who had not planted a single crop of bananas, rice or maize since Stanley had been in Leopoldville three years earlier, despite the fertility of the soil; they existed on hippo meat and their motto seemed to be 'Let be everything – struggle no longer.'[56]

There was a pressing need for the expedition to get out of the Stanley Pool orbit and into the Upper Congo where they could reasonably hope for more abundant food supplies. This meant requisitioning the available shipping in Leopoldville and environs. Accordingly, Stanley's first call was on Bentley of the Baptist Missionary Society to get final agreement to hiring the *Peace*. When Bentley raised difficulties on grounds of deficient parts for the steamer, Stanley became angry. Suspecting that the missionaries had deliberately sabotaged the craft so as not to have to lend it, he raged at Bentley: 'If any disaster befell the expedition through the delay, it would be laid to the account of the Baptist Missionary Society.'[57]

The Baptist Missionaries had always supported Stanley. If they were reluctant to charter their steamer, how much more resistant would the Livingstone Inland Mission be, for this society had always opposed Stanley and held itself aloof from all his endeavours. Since the end of 1884 the LIM had had its own steamer *Henry Reed* at Stanley Pool, a rival to the *Peace* of the BMS.[58] It was this ship that Stanley was now determined to get his hands on. But Dr Sims and Mr Billington proved tough adversaries. When Barttelot and Jephson visited them to negotiate for the loan of the *Henry Reed*, Billington claimed that the ship needed to be painted and that in any case he needed it to go downstream, as he was to be married shortly. Sims tried to negotiate a quid pro quo whereby he would be allowed to accompany the expedition to Stanley Falls to set up a mission there. When this was refused, both men flatly turned down the request. Billington added insult to injury by claiming that he had consulted the Bible and found therein an injunction not to assist the Emin expedition.[59]

Stanley's anger came bursting out of every fissure at this response. He rehearsed the many favours he had done the LIM. In 1881 he had saved their missionaries Clarke and Lanceley from starvation. Again, in 1883 Sims, after trying vainly to negotiate on his own account with the Stanley Pool chiefs, approached Stanley for an LIM site, which was granted. In 1884 he extended the grounds belonging to that mission and even gave permission for a branch mission at Equator station.[60] Now he asked a favour from *them*, this was how it was requited! All his bitterness came pouring out: 'Mr Billington was only hungering after the carnal pleasures of marriage with a person whom he never saw before . . . what cantankerous, ungrateful people these missionaries are!'[61]

On the evening of 22 April Stanley, together with Jephson and Barttelot, dined with governor Liebrechts. Patiently Stanley explained his position to Liebrechts and put him in the picture on the new Brussels policy towards Tippu Tip. He made the point forcefully to Liebrechts that if his expedition was forced to stay at the Pool for lack of river transport, he could not guarantee their good behaviour. He also hinted darkly that if necessary he would seize the steamers by force and defy the Congo State to oppose his 800 Remington-wielding men.[62] Liebrechts was in a peculiarly difficult position. He knew that Leopold was in fact double-crossing Stanley, since the King, foreseeing that Stanley might try to commandeer *Henry Reed*, had ordered Valcke to take the ship on an exploration of the Ubangi, to pre-empt its use by the Emin expedition.[63] As so often, Stanley's hard-driving methods meant that he was on the spot before the order could be implemented. But Liebrechts also knew that Stanley was well capable of carrying out his threat. Also, it was clear that total starvation would soon overtake Leopoldville if this huge force was allowed to remain.[64]

Stanley left Liebrechts's table confident that he had sold his message well: 'I think Liebrechts is on our side but we shall see.'[65] Next morning he sent him an official letter, formally requesting the requisitioning of the *Peace, Henry Reed* and *Florida*, so as to remove the threat of famine and disorder from Leopoldville; he was willing to pay double the normal hiring rate (i.e. £100 per month).[66] Liebrechts responded swiftly to this and signed the necessary order. Billington responded to this by removing the valves and pistons of the *Henry Reed* but, unluckily for him, one of the locals found them and informed Stanley.

The seizure of the missionary steamers was a typical example of Stanley's ruthlessness and iron resolve. Later Liebrechts tried to pretend that the decision was forced on him by Stanley, but Rose Troup, who witnessed all the negotiations, quite correctly pointed out that it was not possible for the governor to shirk responsibility for his own signature.[67] Nevertheless the boldness of his action shook the protocol-minded European residents of Leopoldville. So alarmed were the missionaries that Bentley asked the British consul at Loanda to register the *Peace* so that thenceforth they could invoke British protection against requisitioning.[68] Stanley smirked in triumph and wrote in heavy irony: 'Billington can now proceed to marry his bride with the consciousness that in his absence the mission is making money.'[69] He sealed his triumph with an acidulous letter to *The Times* inveighing against 'ingrates' among the missionaries.[70] Billington, though, was predictably heart-broken: 'If it is possible to love an inanimate object, I love the *Henry Reed*. And now to think she should be committed to the hands of such ruthless "ne'er do wells" and become the habitation of whoremongers and harlots.'[71]

Stanley additionally secured the *Florida* – a vessel belonging to the Sanford Exploring Expedition, which Sanford against Stanley's advice had set up in December 1886 in disillusionment with Leopold; this seizure too was controversial, and when Stanley later damaged the *Florida*, Sanford sued his erstwhile comrades in the EPRE committee.[72] The proximate cause of Stanley's getting his hands on *Florida* was that it was in the charge of his old friend Swinburne at Kinshassa. Its acquisition meant he had a viable flotilla at last. He invited Casement to a champagne breakfast to celebrate the launching of the *Florida*. The explorer sat on an old camp chair outside a hut, his bronzed features lit up by the bright, piercing eyes. They ate cold roast fowl, brown ship's biscuit and milkless tea. Then Stanley opened the champagne and puffed contentedly on his cigar.[73] A little later at Kinshassa the two men met up again, and Casement rather boldly asked Stanley if it was possible for a white man to travel unarmed through Africa, as Caillie had done in North Africa in the 1820s. Stanley was, as ever, scathing about such hypotheticals and counter-factuals: 'You might perform the journey from Matadi to the Pool on stilts, Mr Casement, and I have no doubt you could accomplish the remainder of the distance on your head if you liked to devote enough time to it, but what good you would derive from it, or anyone else, when you emerged at Zanzibar, I don't really know.'[74]

Tippu Tip meanwhile was finding profitable employment in quizzing Ngalyema about the ivory trade of the Central Congo. Ngalyema greeted his 'brother' Bula Matari effusively, but his long list of complaints about the increasing savagery of the white men at the Pool bored Stanley; he was glad to hand the chieftain over to Tippu.[75]

On 25 April Stanley struck camp and marched overland to Kinshassa, after holding a muster that revealed a loss of fifty-seven men, thirty-eight Remingtons and 50 per cent of their implements (axes, spades, shovels, etc.) during the twenty-eight-day march on the Lower Congo. Stanley rationalised this by claiming that most of the losses accrued from bounty-jumping, and that the desertion rate would have been many times greater on the eastern route.[76]

While Barttelot and Parke with 153 men took the one officially authorised steamer, the *Stanley*, upriver, at Kinshassa the leader supervised the overhaul of the *Florida*. Stanley was still in sour mood, angry that his chief ship's engineer was ill with fever: 'It is hard lines for me when I have paid him wages from London to Leopoldville and a first class passage, drawing four months' pay for nothing and the first day he is wanted, he falls ill.'[77] But Casement, noticing that the dog Randy's tail was docked, asked what had befallen him and received a bizarre tale. Tired of the spartan fare on the slog to Leopoldville, Stanley one night cut off the dog's tail and made soup out of it for him and Nelson. They then served up the cooked tail for Randy to eat, and the fox terrier demolished his own tail in short order![78]

At last, on 1 May, the flotilla was ready to start upriver. With three commandeered ships under his aegis, Stanley allowed himself to feel slight confidence. The feeling was reinforced by a conviction that nature and the elements were on his side. Although it was the rainy season, there was fine weather every morning and the rain, as if on cue, began to fall only at around 2 p.m. The river was neither too high nor too low, tornadoes occurred solely in the evenings when they were safely moored. Even the riverine pests, mosquitoes, gadflies, tsetses, crocodiles and hippos, did not seem so vicious as on previous occasions. The only minor hitch was that they had to return to Leopoldville for repairs to the *Peace*'s boilers and rudder, which continued to give them trouble.[79]

On 5 May they caught up with Parke and Barttelot at Mswata; they had arrived four days earlier to lay in a store of provisions. There was more trouble with the *Peace* and from 7 to 10 May additionally they had to carry out extensive repairs on the *Stanley*. But when the flotilla got under way, it made an impressive sight. First came the *Henry Reed*, carrying fifty men and a hundred loads and towing two barges containing another fifty men. Next in line was the *Stanley*, carrying 160 men, 400 loads and six donkeys, and towing the *Florida*, which contained 160 men, a hundred loads, and six donkeys. Bringing up the rear was the *Peace*, with fifty men, a hundred loads, towing two barges with thirty-five men. All in all there were 590 men, 700 loads and twelve donkeys.[80] Yet even this armada did not exhaust the complement of expeditionary *matériel* and manpower. Stanley had to leave two depots of stores and men behind. The first, to his intense chagrin, was left in charge of Rose Troup.[81] The second, under Ward and Bonny, was at Bolobo station.

After fattening up on the abundant food at Bolobo station, where he left the least healthy of his men, Stanley took the flotilla on to Equator staion, where he met up with another of his old favourites, E. J. Glave, and Alphonse Vangele.[82] But just before they arrived at Equator an incident had occurred which seemed to cast doubt on the entire future of the Emin project.

By the common consent of all who participated in the expedition, a pall of gloom hung over the flotilla as it slowly beat up the Congo. The *wangwana* could not always be prevented from raiding villages, looting and pillaging.[83] But to prevent this meant flogging and beating, for which many of the officers had no heart. To make matters worse, no word of encouragement or praise ever emanated from Stanley's lips. He had a talent for always finding something to criticise, for ignoring ninety-nine good things to fasten on the one bad one. Barttelot testified: 'the harder we worked, the glummer Stanley looked. After a long march, no smile from him or word of any sort, except to say, "You have lost a box" or some sneer of that sort.'[84] Stanley also consistently sided with the Africans against their officers, while reserving the right to mete out condign punishment to any *wangwana* who displeased *him*. He was domineering and autocratic and always took his meals alone in his own tent at night.[85] He had none of the qualities of true leadership, of inspiring men to an *esprit de corps*. No one would ever have called *him* with affection, as Shackleton's men called their leader, 'the boss'.

Stanley's version of this state of affairs was that since most quarrels started from trivial causes – because people in close confinement got on each other's nerves – the best policy for himself was to eliminate the possible triggers. As for failure to praise, Stanley made a virtue of this and claimed that with professionals praise was unnecessary.[86] But these protestations masked the fact that Stanley shunned intimacy, never had any close friends, and found it next to impossible to relate to another human being as an equal. The instinct to dominate was too strong. Significantly, of all his officers he got on best with Parke, a physician of some ingenuity in whom there was a hard core of professionalism for Stanley to respect. On the other hand, Parke was temperamentally a respecter of authority, any authority. Stanley was the leader, and for Parke that was good enough. His account of his time with Stanley is Panglossian in tone and slides over some of the more unsavoury incidents on the expedition with an enviable myopic facility.

Stanley's jottings on his officers' qualities, as the flotilla continued on the Upper Congo voyage, are most revealing of his state of mind. He saw clearly that none of them had a particle of affection for him, but they had by and large given him prompt and implicit obedience, which was what he wanted most. 'I can get love any time I ask for it, but in this daily struggle against all forms of death, it is the confidence that whatever strength there may be in my force, it is mine to wield, direct and guide, when and how it is needed, and on the instant.'[87]

Nelson he found too querulous and 'would gladly add violence to a talk'. His one reservation about Parke was that he was too much under

Nelson's influence. At this stage he had a warm feeling for Stairs, though he noted his acerbity and ability to wound with a telling word. Bonny was largely a write-off in Stanley's mind; it had been a grievous mistake to let himself be imposed on by the man's pleadings. Barttelot was suffering from the culture shock of Africa and the conviction that there was a war brewing between England and Russia, which he would miss through this adventure with the 'niggers'. As for Jephson, Stanley's attitude at this stage was amused contempt: 'Were I to open even a chink for jaw I think we should soon become a bemuddled debating society. Jephson, I know, is chock full of effervescent gabble which if I were to uncork would be my death.'[88]

These comments help to illuminate the acrimonious clashes that came to a head as the flotilla neared Equator. At Mswata on 5 May one of the best *wangwana* headmen came to complain that Barttelot had taken to prodding 'malingerers' with a spiked stick and showed the wounds he himself had sustained. Stanley immediately sent for Barttelot and remonstrated with him. Stung by the criticism, Barttelot poured out a flood of bitterness about the tasks he was expected to perform on the expedition. Stanley tried to sidestep the altercation by remarking that there were better ways of punishing a man than poking at him with a spiked stick, which could kill or disable. When Barttelot wanted to argue the point, Stanley fixed him with one of the steely glares that had faced down Ngalyema, Mata Buiki and a dozen others. 'Let us drop the subject right here,' Stanley said icily. 'I have said my say.'[89]

A week later Stanley confided to Stairs that he was thinking of leaving behind a Rear Column when he got to the Aruwimi River. At Leopoldville Stanley had told Liebrechts that he had not yet decided between three routes to Wadelai: via the Oubangi-Welle; via Stanley Falls and the Mboura; or up the Aruwimi.[90] But in fact all along he had favoured the Aruwimi approach; he simply wanted to play his cards close to his chest and keep the Congo State guessing. The question was, who should command the Rear Column? Stanley wanted Stairs but he also intended to leave Barttelot behind as a punishment for his unsatisfactory behaviour. Stairs, reasonably enough, pointed out that he, an army lieutenant, could not command a major, whatever Stanley's wishes. Very well, asked Stanley, who will stay with Barttelot? You? Stairs answered firmly that he would rather be sent home. Jephson, then? No, said Stairs, there would be a furious row within twenty-four hours. Who then? Stairs recommended leaving Jameson as Barttelot's second-in-command, assisted by Bonny; Ward and Rose Troup would bring their contingents up to base camp later, when the *Stanley* was sent downstream to fetch them.[91]

This seemed good advice to Stanley. Next day he told Barttelot of his decision. The Major, naturally, was much cast down and read the move, correctly, as punishment. Stanley tried to sugar the pill by saying that the halt at base camp would not last long – only until Tippu Tip supplied the promised porters.[92] But Barttelot was secretly very angry. It was clear to him that he and Jameson were *personae non gratae*: 'it is my belief, if he thought he could get rid of us, he would; he sticks at nothing.'[93]

Yet on 20 May, when the most serious breakdown in communication yet between Stanley and his officers took place, Barttelot found himself in the unusual role of peacemaker. The problem arose from gross indiscipline on the 15th when both Sudanese and Zanzibaris ran amok and looted a village about 12 miles north of Bolobo.[94] Jephson and Stairs, hitherto among Stanley's favourites, began to confiscate all the goods they could identify as looted. When the *wangwana* resisted this 'expropriation', Jephson lost his temper at their impudence and hurled some of their food and bedding overboard. Since this happened on the *Stanley*, the leader summoned Jephson and Stairs to give an account of themselves. A bizarre altercation then took place at voice-tops, since Stanley was standing on the deck of the *Peace*, calling out to his two officers on shore.

Stanley began by asking Stairs for his version. Stairs in some exasperation pointed out that he and Jephson were forever having to beat back the Zanzibaris from looting villages; this particular incident was only one of several. Stanley then repeated the *wangwana*'s charges of routine and gratuitous violence. At this Stairs lost patience: 'Oh well, if you like to believe them in preference to what I say, you are welcome to do so. You will only be acting according to your custom.'[95] Stanley then called to Parke to witness the sequel. He called Jephson forward. Jephson approached the bank with pallid face and blazing eyes.

Stanley bawled out impatiently to Jephson to give his side of the story. Jephson yelled back at him. 'You are not to shout at me in that way, sir!' At this Stanley exploded and he railed at Jephson. 'You goddam son of a sea-cook! You damned ass, you're tired of me, of the expedition, and of my men. Go into the bush, get, I've done with you. And you too, Lieutenant Stairs, you and I will part today; you're tired of me, sir, I can see. Get away into the bush!' Next Stanley boomed out to the *wangwana* that if either Stairs or Jephson gave another order, they were to be tied to trees. Seeing the look of contempt on Jephson's face, Stanley then completely lost control. 'If you want to fight, goddam you, I'll give you a bellyful. If I were only where you are, I'd go for you. It's lucky for you I am where I am, you goddam impudent puppy.'[96]

This torrent of rage can be seen as mixture of stress, anxiety, fear of failure, unconscious resentment of Jephson's 'silver spoon' and paranoid delusion, though Stanley, typically, rationalised it as a case of his officers 'trying it on'.[97] But he was clearly shaken by his own over-reaction, for when Barttelot came to see him around noon to ask if the decision about Jephson and Stairs was irrevocable, Stanley hesitated and said: 'As regards myself it is.'[98] Barttelot thought he detected a measure of bluster in the words and pressed on with his self-appointed task as mediator. Stanley asked him to sit down, then launched into self-justification. First of all, he wished to say that nobody was indispensable, except Parke, and if anyone wished to join the dismissed duo, he was free to do so. All he was trying to do was to train a new generation of explorers to take over from him, since he himself was getting old. He took the opportunity to criticise his officers sharply; they did not know the country or the language, knew nothing of man management and relied on violence alone; but for the presence of Bula Matari the expedition would already have disintegrated.

Calmly and uncharacteristically, Barttelot rolled with the punches. When Stanley insisted that the confrontation with Stairs and Jephson had been a 'set-up', Barttelot denied that there were any cabals and assured him that Jephson and Stairs both deeply regretted what had happened. In that case, snapped Stanley, they should come and apologise. Barttelot departed, and a little later Jephson and Stairs came to apologise. Stanley 'magnanimously' reinstated them and summoned the headmen of the *wangwana* to tell them that the 'little masters' were once again in command and that their policy on looting must be heeded. Writing up the incident that night in his journal, Stanley recorded surprise at Barttelot's admirably statesmanlike behaviour; he was the very last person Stanley would have imagined as a mediator. He sensed, too, that he himself by contrast had appeared to disadvantage.[99]

His suspicions were certainly shared by his officers, all of whom were disgusted that Stairs and Jephson had been obliged to apologise for a fiasco that was entirely of Stanley's making.[100] Jameson recorded his verdict in stupefied incredulity.

'I had no idea until today what an extremely dangerous man Stanley was. Could there be anything more inciting to mutiny than what he had told the Zanzibaris? He forgets one thing, however: that if they dared to lift a hand to one of us, there would be a terrible lot of them shot, which would rather weaken his expedition. It is a curious fact, when one thinks over it, that the very men who complained to Mr Stanley ought, by his own orders, issued when we left the Pool, to have been severely flogged.'[101] Barttelot concurred with this estimate. 'The missionaries, two of them, who heard the disturbance, and the captain and engineer of the *Peace*, never heard such language or witnessed such a disgraceful scene before. I believe this is Stanley's method of carrying on in Central Africa, but I had judged him pretty well before, and was not surprised so much at his conduct.'[102]

At Equator station Stanley found more to excite his contempt, not just the missionaries from the LIM but Vangele's taste for administration over exploration. When Stanley proposed to him an exploration of the Welle, Vangele reacted coolly. Stanley recorded scornfully in his journal: 'that is the way with most men. They crave for chances of distinction. The opportunity comes and they turn their heads away. It is too perilous a job! Well, nothing great was ever achieved without braving danger, or incurring trouble and pains.'[103]

By 30 May the expedition was at Bangala station, 547 miles above Leopoldville, 892 miles from the Atlantic, with just 488 more miles to the planned base camp at Aruwimi rapids. After the initial problems with the *Peace*, including an occasion when Stanley gashed her forward section by running her on to a reef, the steamers had settled down to a slow chug, which involved huge woodcutting details at night for fuel, In the end the engineer on the *Peace* got her into effective running order by capping the upper safety valve so as to stop steam escaping.[104] But Stanley was worried that he was now badly behind schedule. He had expected the entire expedition to be completed by December 1887, within the budget of £20,000 even though many in Britain had warned that he was being absurdly sanguine in such an estimate.[105] He claimed in Cairo that he could get to Wadelai via the Congo in 157 days from Zanzibar, yet already a hundred of those days had passed. Even if he got to the Aruwimi rapids in sixteen days, he would still be 360 miles from Lake Albert – leaving him an average of 12 miles' marching a day to reach his target on time, which he frankly conceded was impossible.[106]

It was time for some sober, realistic calculations and Bangala, with its ample food supplies, was a good place for reflections and lucubrations. Van Kerkhoven, the station chief, was away but Baert, his deputy, entertained them liberally. Stanley marvelled at the transformation of Bangala in ten years. Cannibalism, the ordeal by poison and the sacrifice of slaves to a dead chief were all things of the past, and Stanley could comfort himself with the thought that he had been Providence's chosen agent to bring light into such darkness.[107] It was in eupeptic spirits that he sat down with Tippu Tip and Barttelot to plan the next stage of the expedition.

The gist of Stanley's talk with Tippu Tip concerned the number of porters needed to bring the cache of ivory out of Equatoria and the exact logistics of this – dotting the 'i's and crossing the 't's of their Zanzibar agreement.[108] Barttelot received orders to accompany Tippu to Stanley Falls to supervise hs formal induction as governor and to bring back the first of the porters. Stanley himself would set up base camp at Yambuya, 96 miles up the Aruwimi past its confluence with the Congo, where the Aruwimi cataracts began.

Stanley's voyage to Yambuya was accomplished without incident and he arrived at the village on 15 June. At the Aruwimi confluence Baruti was reunited with his kinsfolk among the Soko. On board the *Peace* he called out to one of the tribesmen milling around in canoes that he was the youth's brother. The young man was sceptical until Baruti told him that he had a bite mark on his arm under the tattoo where he had been mauled by a crocodile when a little boy. The two brothers then embraced heartily. Stanley commented: 'Some say the African has no love, no gratitude, no affection, but there is a sight that speaks for itself.'[109]

On 16 June, at river journey's end, Stanley took his flotilla across to the south bank of the Aruwimi and asked permission to billet in the village of Yambuya. The tribesmen were reluctant and a palaver began. But when he seemed to be getting nowhere after a couple of hours. Stanley lost patience and ordered a forced occupation of the village. The landing of the armed *wangwana* was accompanied by a cacophony from the steamship whistles, designed to inspire fear. When the defenders broke and fled, Stanley, now mindful of public opinion in England, rewrote the incident so as to make it appear that the locals were overawed by the steamer whistles *alone*.[110]

Stanley next converted the abandoned village into a heavily fortified camp, surrounded by a ditch and a double wooden palisade. He fretted about the fact that he was eight days behind schedule, 'all owing to the wretched little steamer the *Peace*' and its allegedly incompetent crew and engineer. Naturally he did not mention that he had been in error by underestimating the length of time the expedition would take or that he himself had caused a major delay near Bolobo by running the steamer on to a reef. But he did recognise that failure to conciliate the local

Tungu peoples put their future food supply at risk and he dreaded to think what kind of a fist Barttelot would make of conciliating fractious tribesmen. It seemed the last straw when his protégé Baruti decamped with two Winchesters.[111]

Nelson and Jephson were kept busy collecting wood to fuel the *Stanley* and *Florida* for the return trip, to pick up Rose Troup, Ward, Bonny and their contingents. Parke lost caste in the leader's eyes by telling a story which revealed that he was incapable of remembering the simplest orders – an ominous sign. But most of all, as the days slipped by and there was no word from Barttelot, Stanley began to fear that he might have been the victim of treachery by Tippu Tip at Stanley Falls. Or else, the Major's hot temper – epitomised by an infamous pistol-whipping of a mutinous Somali during the Gordon relief expedition – had erupted and caused an armed clash with the Arabs and Manyema at the Falls.[112]

But if there had been any treachery, it was on Stanley's side. Yet again Tippu Tip had allowed himself to be duped. His disenchantment began immediately on arrival at Stanley Falls. There was a serious clash with the local tribesmen. Tippu called on Barttelot to help him put a defiant village to the torch. Barttelot replied that he had strict orders from Stanley not to become involved in quarrels between blacks and Arabs.[113] This angered Tippu, but his rage grew when he asked for the supplies of gunpowder Stanley had promised him for the arming of his men. Barttelot said he had none; all the powder had been left with Rose Troup at Kinshassa. This was a clear breach of the agreement with Stanley. He put it to Barttelot that since there was no powder at the Falls, and his men were already hard put to defend themselves against hostiles, how could they possibly come up and join Barttelot and the Rear Column at Yambuya? That was a practical point; the morality of 'no powder, therefore no porters' spoke for itself.[114]

There was yet another aspect to Stanley's failure to keep his side of the bargain. There was already considerable resistance among the Manyema to the idea of helping Stanley and the Emin expedition. Tippu's deal with Stanley was as fiercely criticised by his own people as a 'sell-out' to the Europeans as it had been in Europe on the grounds of its being a Faustian compact with a slaver. Said bin Habib, the local magnate, refused to recall his raiding parties at Tippu's request when the Arab tried faithfully to implement the terms of his governorship.[115] Tippu could perhaps have made his writ run if he had brought the gunpowder but failure to do so seriously dented his credibility with the Manyema. In despair at his humiliation Tippu later threatened to return to Leopoldville for his powder, bill Stanley and return with the ordnance, or else return to Zanzibar in disgust if the material was not handed over.[116] Tippu was particularly incensed at Stanley's duplicity, for he had noticed all the way along the route to Stanley Pool how cheap gunpowder was; he could have bought any amount on his own account.[117] But on the Upper Congo it was scarce and if he tried to obtain some immediately from Stanley at Yambuya, he knew that the explorer would try to drive a sky-high bargain for its sale.[118]

If the failure to give Tippu his gunpowder was the hinge on which the entire fate of the Rear Column turned – and Stanley must have known that without it Tippu would not meet his side of the deal and send porters – whatever possessed Stanley to act in such a self-destructive way? Here we enter the world of what Leopold liked to refer to so glibly as *haute politique*. Stanley knew very well that if he gave Tippu Tip the gunpowder, he himself would fall from grace in the Belgian monarch's eyes, as it would postpone the day of reckoning between the Belgians and the Congo Arabs. On the other hand, if he failed to deliver the powder and thus fell foul of Tippu Tip, the Rear Column would be doomed to impotence. The fiasco that later attended the Rear Column was, then, a direct result of Stanley's duplicity, of his attempt to have his cake and eat it. Stanley knew this very well, but later tried to cover his tracks so that the finger of indictment could not point back to him.[119]

Barttelot made his way back to Yambuya in some consternation, angry that Stanley's explicit orders had wrongfooted him with Tippu.[120] He was even angrier when he learned from his brother officers that Stanley had been worrying about his safety; he took that as a slur on his military abilities.[121] But Stanley trumped his ace by working himself into a fine lather over the fact that Tippu would not perform on a promise; in Stanley's world it was perfectly permissible for him to demand 600 porters *now* while Tippu waited for ever for his powder.[122] Stanley's frustration was increased by the realisation that his fears about the food supply were beginning to be borne out; for six days before Barttelot's arrival, Stanley and his officers had had nothing to eat except rice, beans and manioc.

A pall of gloom hung over the base camp. Iskander, one of the two Syrians, died of exhaustion following repeated attacks of malarial fever. While the *Peace* and the *Henry Reed* were prepared for departure, Stanley sat down with Barttelot to brief him on his duties while the Advance Column was away. He stressed that the camp would have to be well defended at all times, for there was a potential threat from the Arabs as well as the Tungu. He cautioned the Major against undue pugnacity, but the interview on 25 June (lasting from 2 to 4 p.m.) did not impress Stanley with his intellectual qualities.[123]

But there was more to be said for Barttelot's position than Stanley allowed. Again and again the Major pressed him about Tippu Tip's reliability. Stanley obliquely hinted that that was why he had not supplied him with gunpowder, keeping his own arrangements with Leopold right out of the conversation. He reverted to his original itinerary, as agreed in London. A quick dash to Lake Albert would lead to a meeting with Emin about the end of July or a little later. The refugees and the ivory would return to the Congo estuary, while Stanley and the *wangwana* pressed on through East Africa to Zanzibar.[124] Stanley himself would return to base camp to pick up the united Rear Column before completing the trans-African journey.

Yet Barttelot remained unclear about his orders. Was he to wait at Yambuya for the reinforcements from Ward and Rose Troup and the 500–600 porters promised by Tippu Tip, or should he attempt to follow Stanley? Stanley knew well enough that without aid from Tippu, the Rear Column could not advance. He also realised that his own actions had made such aid unlikely, to say the least. But he struck a histrionic posture and declared that if the Arab would not 'co-operate', they could manage without him.[125] This was a rationalisation of the fact that Stanley had already decided to press on to Lake Albert without waiting for Tippu. He expected to arrive back at Yambuya in November, then take the Rear Column back to Lake Albert with him – all predicated on the idea that the journey to the lake would take no more than two months.[126]

Stanley's journal makes it quite clear that he expected Barttelot to await his return some time in November 1887.[127] In normal circumstances, his grotesque underestimate of the difficulties that lay ahead would have been plain to see and he would have been convicted *nem.con.* of the very amateurish incompetence he so excoriated in others. But Stanley was nothing if not lucky, and now luck played into his hands in such a way that he was able later, after a fashion, to cover the traces of his own spectacular blunder. For Barttelot now pleaded and cajoled to be allowed to follow in the leader's footsteps if certain conditions obtained. Stanley relented and agreed to blaze a trail for Barttelot to follow.[128] But he was only *definitely* to follow if Tippu Tip provided the full complement of porters – a contingency Stanley knew to be next to impossible.

To underline his instructions, Stanley laid out four hypothetical cases. Barttelot had full authority to advance when the steamers returned with

Troup, Ward and the rest of the Rear Column *and* when all 600 porters arrived from Tippu Tip. If the Arab supplied part of this force, Barttelot was to use his discretion about advancing. Nothing was said about the scenario where Tippu provided *no* porters – which Stanley must have known was the most likely outcome. It was clear that marching in relays would involve Barttelot's having to throw away too many loads, so the logic of the 'no porter' situation was that Barttelot would have to remain in Yambuya. This was anyway Stanley's original wish, for he authorised Barttelot to remain in base camp, *whatever the circumstances*, if he thought it best. This was the unequivocal implication of his parting words to Barttelot: 'Goodbye, Major, I shall find you here in November when I return.'[129]

By toying with the idea that he might after all follow his leader, Barttelot unwittingly opened a Pandora's box of ambiguity and uncertainty. This enabled Stanley when writing his public account of the expedition in *In Darkest Africa* to cover up his own poor judgement and leadership by asserting that he always imagined Barttelot would follow him and was flabbergasted when he did not. Stanley was never more 'economical with the truth' than when rewriting the history of his final conferences at base camp in June 1887.

· 11 ·

ON 28 June 1887 Stanley and the vanguard left Yambuya for the unknown. They were plunging into the uncharted 'Dark Continent' just as fully as in December 1876 when Stanley left Tippu Tip at Vinya-Niara. 389 men with 360 rifles descended into the gloom of the Ituri forests. Behind them lay the Rear Column proper at base camp with 130 men under Barttelot and Jameson, plus another 131 under Ward at Bolobo.[1] Bonny was left behind as 'doctor' to the Rear Column. With Stanley went Stairs, Nelson, Parke and Jephson. Stanley had revised his optimistic forecasts of being able to march 12 miles a day, and had now set a realistic target of the end of December as the date when he would be at the shores of Lake Albert.[2]

Stanley was not to know that he was embarking on his most taxing and hellish expedition yet. His 1887 plunge into the Ituri rain forest was the most dreadful ordeal any European explorer of nineteenth-century Africa ever faced. Less than half of the expedition's manpower would survive, and for much of the time the survival of the rest of them was touch and go. The problem was that the Ituri had never been crossed by Europeans, yet Stanley's scant intelligence led him to believe that after a few weeks' march the forest would give way to parkland, enabling him to make the sort of daily progress he had clocked up in 1874–7.

But in fact the Ituri was a green hell of 50,000 square miles. Rivers like the Ituri (the Upper Aruwimi) flowed from the plateau of the Nile/Congo watershed through a dense forest of tangled vegetation, matted lianas and oozing, clotted undergrowth that exhaled noxious miasmata and squelched underfoot. Lofty forest giants reached a great height and formed an overarching canopy through which shafts of sunlight seldom penetrated. Marching in such conditions was a hot, sticky, steamy affair, like being permanently in a Turkish bath.[3] They had to use machetes to hack their way through the impacted, interpenetrated undergrowth; even the donkeys shivered with fever.

On the first day they experienced temperatures of 86°F in the forest. More worryingly, there were immediate signs of hostility. The first village they came to was deserted and the ground was bristling with skewers, the points turned upwards to cut and gouge the feet of the intruders. Stanley divided his force into two columns, then sent the first forward on a kind of minesweeping operation, while the other column covered them with the Remingtons. While the work of plucking up the skewers was in progress, the men were assailed by a cloud of tiny arrows.[4]

On the second day out, Stairs became very ill. Some spears were thrown into the camp perimeter at night, showing that the hostile tribesmen must have penetrated well within the picket lines. Next day the agonisingly slow advance continued. Every time one of the *wangwana* climbed a horse or mule to see if skewers lay ahead in their path, arrows whined and whistled past his ear. At 3 a.m. on the morning of 1 July the entire encampment was aroused by the howling of a madman, shrieking that the strangers were not welcome and would be enslaved.[5]

Progress was so slow that on the 2nd Stanley decided to make for the river bank and follow it past the rapids. Stanley's contempt for Parke's naïvety continued; the surgeon assured them that forest bees had no sting but had scarcely uttered the opinion before he was badly stung himself.[6] On 4 July they struck the Aruwimi River, only to be ambushed a second time by the Bahungi people, this time hidden in overhanging trees. A second fight took place; when the enemy fled, the expedition found a goat tethered in an abandoned canoe – this provided a welcome meat ration for the leader and his officers.[7]

So far the hostility had been explicable on the grounds that Stanley and his men had been mistaken for Arab slavers; the cane skewer was the main line of indigenous defence against them. When Stanley launched a *Lady Alice*-style portable steel boat (carried in sections) on the river, this inference was strengthened. There was almost immediately a river fight between the expedition boat party, containing twenty men, and a flotilla of eleven canoes. Under steady Remington fire, the locals abandoned their canoes and fled. After a day's halt in a camp by the riverside, amid swarms of multi-coloured butterflies, Stanley divided his men into a land and a boat party. Stanley travelled by boat, while Jephson commanded the land contingent.[8]

The river here was about 800 yards wide. There were crocodiles in abundance in the water, but no hippopotami, which Stanley attributed to the lack of edible grass. The march routine was four hours' progress between 6.30 and 10.30 a.m., two hours' rest, then marching again until 3.30 p.m. Already many of the men were suffering colds from a rain storm. Dejection and demoralisation were beginning to creep in: 'So many impediments are met – impervious swamps, stiff thorny under-growth and a bewildering mass of creepers and lianas, creeks, sloughs etc. so that our progress is but one mile an hour.'[9] Every yard had to be fought for by the billhooks of forty pioneers in temperatures that were still as high as 96°F at 4 p.m. On the other hand, the boat could complete a day's land journey in two hours.

On 10 July they came to Banalya, a cluster of seven villages near the rapids. Again Stanley ordered a few days' rest, for even those who had departed Yambuya strong and healthy now looked jaded. In Banalya, as elsewhere in the Ituri, the villagers fled to the opposite bank with their goats and valuables. The expedition then occupied the huts and ate the abandoned manioc. The rest enabled Stairs to recover his health after fourteen days of being carried in a litter. Stanley noted the poverty of bird life here as compared with the Congo.[10] But the awesome forest itself revived the feelings he had first experienced north of Nyangwe in 1876:

What attracts my wonder in these terrible forests is the venerable ancientness of Time, and how with deathly stillness, it can speak to my heart of my own utter nothingness, and unimportance of no more worth, note, or use than that to add my body – a little heap of corruption among the dead leaves, the withered and withering branches. The atmosphere appears to me weighted with an eloquent dumb history which I read, and hear, and see and inhale until the secretest cell and smallest vein on my body feels its influence, and out of which it has driven for the time all remembrance of self, all knowledge of identity, perception of visible things or matter, all extraneous consciousness to give place to the overwhelming fact.[11]

On 13 July they pressed on to another settlement at a bend in the river. Again Stanley had to call a halt because of the pelting tropical downpour and the exhaustion of his men. No meat was to be had at any price. On all his expeditions so far Stanley had been able to count on eating meat at least twice a week, but in the Ituri there seemed nothing available but roots, manioc and vegetables. Though many tracks of elephant, buffalo and wild boar criss-crossed their track, they never sighted any game.[12] Quite apart from the difficulty of traversing the Ituri rain forest, Stanley had overestimated the resources likely to be available to him under its sunless canopy. The population of the forest was about 3.75 per square kilometre at this time.[13] This very sparse population lived at subsistence level, so there was no surplus to trade with European travellers.

By mid-July, the river party had grown in size to five canoes and the steel boats, carrying seventy-four men and 120 loads. As Stanley's supply of canoes increased, so did his sick list to fill them. Inevitably he ascribed this tendency to malingering. But given the fury of the elements, this was an unnecessary hypothesis. Between 16 and 17 July it rained seventeen hours non-stop. Morale was plummeting all the time: the men had no meat, their clothes were sopping wet and most were unable to sleep through the incessant downpour. Most demoralised of all was the handful of Somalis, to the point where they lacked the spirit even to light a fire.[14]

They continued to creep slowly along the river. Some days the land party could manage no more than 400 yards' progress from dawn to dusk! Stanley cursed himself for not having brought the fifteen whale-boats, which would have enabled him to cover 20 miles a day.[15] All along the river their approach was signalled by the sonorous booming of drums fashioned from hollow logs: 'the absence of all other sounds lends peculiar power to their voices and the boom of their drums.' They took their first casualties on 20 July when two of the *wangwana* went missing with two rifles, almost certainly killed while straggling.[16]

Stanley's officers were all performing well, with the exception of Parke, who lost his way in the forest when he was officer of the day in charge of pioneers. Stanley was especially pleased with Jephson, who had made an almost incredible (Stanley's word) transition from the London man-about-town to seasoned African explorer in a mere six months. His direction of pioneers was exceptionally able. This detachment of forty sickle- and machete-wielding veterans had the toughest job in the expedition. Every morning it left camp half an hour ahead of the column to clear the way through the jungle.[17]

Further slight lightening of the gloom came when they started to move beyond the orbit of the Aruwimi slavers. Here the only non-indigenous peoples were Manyema brigands who burnt villages barbarously and fought fire with fire by planting the local pathways with poisoned skewers. There was a slight thawing in the unremitting hostility that had attended the expedition so far. The local people were the Bali and the Bira.[18] They would call out to Stanley's party: 'Go up river, oh son of the sea.

We suffer also for we have no food.' Just occasionally, though, Stanley was able to barter for some chickens and eggs.[19]

The roofs of the huts the expedition stayed in were infested with rats, mice and beetles, but there was a worse threat to frayed nerves in this part of the rain forest: a plague of bees and wasps. On 25 July they experienced the worst these insects could do. From the clouds of wasps above one of the Aruwimi cataracts, Stanley dubbed it Wasp Rapids. That morning they set out from their camp near an elephants' watering hole to negotiate the cataracts. While the boats were in the most dangerous part of a narrow boiling channel, one of the men steadied himself by grasping at a branch overhead, and accidentally disturbed a wasps' nest. The angry insects at once sallied out to punish the intruders. The sequel was terrible. The churning, seething river was as wild as the sea and required all their attention, but meanwhile the wasps were at them, inflicting horrible bites. The *wangwana* had no choice but to endure stoically the most frightful wounds. With their eyes glued to the water, they were forced to allow the insects to settle and sink their jaws into skin. Stanley and Jephson, fully clothed, fared better than their dark companions. At last, some 200 yards beyond the rapids, the wasps left them as suddenly as they had come. In the 'post-mortem', Hoffmann was held to be to blame for having made a sudden movement in the canoe that forced the Zanzibari to cling on to the branch overhead; he was the object of much bitter laughter. The remaining *wangwana* had the ingenuity to find another route past the wasps, but the Sudanese and Somalis, blithely reckoning that lightning would not strike twice, suffered a second ferocious attack on their passage through the rapids.[20]

The sufferings sustained from these aerial tormentors necessitated another halt. Stanley's coxswain was in a high fever from wasp stings, and squadrons of forest bees continued to zoom and dive around them. The sole consolation was that the bees' and wasps' mastery of the lower skies seemed to have scared off the mosquitoes, for there were few of these on the river.[21]

A visit from the chief of the Bira seemed to open up the possibility of large-scale trading with the locals, but their extortionate demands led the *wangwana* to begin selling axes, billhooks, machetes and even cartridges for food. Stanley took a prisoner to enforce better bartering terms and, as a second string to his bow, sent 170 men under Nelson, Jephson and Parke across the river to try to find an alternative source of supply. Some supplies were brought back but not before an incident when one of the Zanzibaris fell into an elephant pit. His cries brought the locals running, he shot one of them, and the man fell across the pit, making a kind of human awning.[22]

By the beginning of August, Stanley had fourteen canoes and the steel boat at his disposal, enough to convey three-quarters of all their baggage. He ordered the canoes lashed together in twos and, after stowing ten days' provisions on board, he set off upriver. But the Somalis and Sudanese at once revealed themselves to be useless canoeists. The Somalis were attacked by hornets, abandoned their canoe and lay down depressedly on the river bank until Stanley's bodyguard got them to their feet by lashing them with switches. The Sudanese fared even worse. They managed to capsize two canoes, containing twelve rifles and ten loads of beads and ammunition. Fortunately, Stanley's divers dredged up six of the rifles and all the ammunition.[23]

Hard on the heels of this misfortune came the first death through heart failure, the loss of a further straggler and the demise of an exhausted donkey. The stench of death was all around them; the mounds of decaying corpses in one deserted village kept them at arm's length, lying on the forest floor instead of in the huts. Next it was the turn of Stairs's men to capsize canoes. Two boatloads of guns and trade goods went to the bottom. Jephson's divers recovered thirteen cases of ammunition and five rifles, but even so the losses were serious: seven Remingtons, two boxes of Maxim ammunition, five cases of cowries, four of beads and one of copper wire. Since leaving Yambuya, they had now lost fifteen rifles. Stanley's usual punishment for those who lost canoes was to put them in the overland party.[24]

On 4 August they reached the obstacle of Panga Falls, but though these were 20 feet high, they had got to the bottom of them by the afternoon. Stairs, who had been put in charge of the pioneers for his misfortune with the canoes, retrieved his reputation by valiant man-hauling of canoes overland round the cataracts. But on the way to Nejambi rapids another canoe capsized, with a loss of eleven rifles and nine bales (though all but two of the rifles were later recovered).[25]

By 9 August food shortages were again becoming acute. Stanley sent out three detachments in different directions to forage. They brought back barely enough food for one day, and a Zanzibari was wounded in the throat by an arrow into the bargain. Another of the *mangwana* died of dysentery and several more were at death's door. An attack from a hippo could be shrugged off, but by now the rapids were so difficult that the land party was starting to get into camp before the river party. On the 12th another Zanzibari died of gunshot wounds – probably suicide.

Stanley himself was going down with fever and awoke every morning with aching limbs. There was now a desperate need of food.[26]

With hungry bellies and a daily lengthening sick list, the last thing the expedition needed was a clash with hostile tribesmen. Yet at Avissiba rapids on 13 August they had to stand and fight their grimmest battle so far. The *wangwana* blazed away madly at the hostiles, who replied with showers of arrows, one of which wounded Stairs just below the heart.[27] Some of the *wangwana* made a flank attack and captured a flock of seven goats, but their shooting had not been accurate enough to dent the attackers' confidence. A pep-talk from Stanley that night did the trick. When the Avissiba peoples renewed their onslaught next day, 300 rounds of accurate firing rapidly thinned their ranks: 'a few straight shots had effected in a few minutes what the indiscriminate and wasteful firing of the day before had not.'[28]

Heaps of enemy slaughtered did not compensate in Stanley's mind for the seven wounded in his own party in the two fights and the close call of Stairs, who had to have the poison from the arrow wound sucked out by Parke. And still there was no solution to the gnawing food shortages. On 14 August, tired of the *wangwana*'s ineffectual and unpunctual foraging, Stanley sent out Parke, Jephson and Nelson on a major reconnaissance for provisions. While he continued along the first-class track on the river bank (even though Stairs was seriously wounded, Stanley would not stop), he sent this foraging column inland with the orders to bring back food at all costs. All the time his sick list grew; two more *wangwana* died of dysentery. Even the man of iron was beginning to despair: 'I am not running despair [sic], but if I give rein to my fancy, I see a very dark outlook indeed . . . If 389 picked men, such as we were when we left Yambuya, are unable to march to Lake Albert, how can Major Barttelot with 250 men make his way through this endless forest?'[29] He estimated that he was still no more than a third of the way to the lake shore.

On 18 August, with no word from Jephson's party yet, Stanley sent out scouts to investigate. The news they brought back filled him with apprehension. Instead of looping round and swinging back south towards the river, Jephson had lost his bearings and was heading diagonally away from them in a north-easterly direction; each day that passed increased the gap between the two forces. Railing at the stupidity of his officers, he summoned his most reliable headman Saad Tato and sent him out with another party to intercept the Jephson caravan and guide it back to the river.[30]

A sick and dispirited Stanley waited anxiously while the death toll around him mounted. Two of his men died of tetanus from the arrow wounds and another of dysentery. On 18 August there was another pelting tropical storm; 'had we not enough afflictions without this pelting rain?'[31] By the 20th he was beginning to fear the worst; he was sure that Jephson's judgement was not good enough to deal with any serious problems that might have befallen his column. But after six days he was more resigned than angry: 'I am not as savage with Jephson now. I think his sufferings must be as great as mine are. Had he returned on the second or third day there would have been a scene.'[32]

At last, at 5 p.m. on the 21st Saad Tato led back the bedraggled Jephson column, which itself had sustained three fatalities (two from arrow wounds, one from dysentery). The entire episode had been a monumental error on Jephson's part, and Saad Tato's rescuing party itself had been in danger and had skirmished with hostile bands. Stanley's relief was so great that his reception of Jephson was mild. The young man recorded in his diary: 'I expected to be met by reproaches and angry words but Stanley was very quiet and nice about my having led the expedition astray.'[33]

Stanley at once helped Parke to tend the wounded. The most serious cases were those who had taken arrows in the throat or windpipe. Even when the poison was sucked clear instantly, death from lockjaw could follow. With his manpower being eroded, and not yet half-way to his goal, Stanley was apprehensive but no longer depressed, as he had been when both Jephson's and Saad Tato's parties were away and in danger. Attending the sick 'must have exorcised a malign influence over me . . . the last few days had begun to fill me with a doubt of the expedition.'[34]

The united party marched to the foot of Mabengu rapids and camped there. A general muster showed 373 still alive, but fifty-seven of these were sick. Morale was low, the men were exhausted and the struggle for food was too protracted. Indiscipline was increasing. When they found food at the Nepoko rapids on the 26th, the men would not be warned not to overindulge and gorged and stuffed themselves. When this was followed by the wild firing off of guns in camp, Stanley issued a warning that future offenders against the code of conduct would be severely punished. But the very next day the land and river parties failed to link up. Stanley's mood was savage: 'A native who would surrender was shot this afternoon. He had a dozen freshly poisoned arrows and a bundle of "corked" slugs in canoe.'[35]

And still all around them loomed the dark, forbidding Ituri. Hoffmann recorded his awestruck impressions.

The mighty African forest, with its gigantic trees through which scarcely a ray of light could penetrate, with its tangled, thorny undergrowth, seemed to do everything in its power to impede our progress. We had to cut our path every inch of the way with bill-hooks, knives and axes, through the close network of creepers, through the fleshy tendrils of lianas, through the thick plantations of sugar-cane. Crossing deep swamps, we had to keep a war eye open for motionless objects on the edge of the water; objects which looked like logs of wood but were more probably lurking crocodiles, and pick our way carefully among the razor-edged oyster shells that were strewn across the bank.[36]

On the last day of August Stanley was supervising the cutting of a track past the rapids so that they could portage their boats when a scout came running into camp breathlessly to announce that Emin Pasha was approaching. 'Emin' turned out to be a Manyema Arab in a canoe with nine slaves. The Manyema spent a night with them and explained that ahead lay an Arab settlement at the village of Ugarrowa's, headed by Abed bin Salim. Next morning they were gone before daybreak, leaving behind them the body of a murdered seven-year-old boy and with five Zanzibari deserters.[37]

The coming of the Manyema and their precipitate departure made two things clear to Stanley. One was that the burned and deserted villages the expedition had encountered had not been examples of spontaneous abandonment. It was clear that the locals would regard his party as slavers, so that hopes of food were vain. He would have to act like the Manyema themselves to avoid starvation. Hence the pattern of occupied villages, appropriated canoes, food seized at gunpoint, women and children held as hostages in a cycle of ruthlessness that appalled Jephson and opened his eyes to his leader's true nature.[38]

The second implication of the proximity of the Manyema was that there was now an incentive for their kin the *wangwana* to desert. Immediately after the coming of the Manyema party Stanley noted a growing propensity to desertion by men taking away arms and ammunition. Six men, three rifles, three boxes of ammunition and a tin of biscuits went missing the day after the Manyema decamped. Next day was even worse: five men unaccounted for, a box of cloths and a box each of Remington and Winchester ammunition vanished. So far he had avoided draconian punishments when the deserters were brought back, but he realised that once he left the river and carriers were at a premium, this problem would become acute. Unless the dribble of manpower ceased, he would be forced to employ capital punishment to preserve his own credibility. He summoned the *wangwana* headmen, who were against severity but could suggest no concrete way to arrest the tide of desertion.[39] 'It is getting patent daily that severe measures will have to be adopted to stop this desertion and theft of ammunition – we have now lost five boxes of ammunition by theft and are short of 48 rifles – almost a rifle per day.'[40]

When four more deserters were reported on 4 September, Stanley was reduced to removing the rifle springs of men he considered unreliable, in the hope that would-be absconders would think twice about decamping with useless rifles. He also tried to staunch the haemorrhage of ammunition by appointing a special overseer of cartridges and powder.[41] Insult was added to injury when a man was caught red-handed trying to desert with one of the Fortnum and Mason's boxes. Stanley wanted to hang him but the most the headmen would agree to was that, like other deserters, he should be put in chains. Jephson showed himself more of a hardliner on this occasion even than his boss: 'If I were Stanley I should hang the man whether the chiefs wished it or not, he will never stop desertion until he does.'[42]

But still the desperate food shortage continued. Stanley's men found a woman with two children hiding in the bush, who was able to impart the name of her tribe but also confirmed that there was no food to be had in the forest. By 12 September no one had eaten for three days. The men were walking skeletons: 'Achmet the Somali is reported to be dying. It is a wonder that he has lived so long, being a dreadful object of bones, covered with a skin.'[43] When they camped by Hippo Rapids – so called for the large numbers of hippopotami there – Stanley tried in vain to bag one for the pot. In desperation, Stanley got off a shot at a bull elephant but succeeded only in wounding him.[44]

And still the skirmishing continued. The arrows being fired at them were getting longer – now around 20 inches in length. The *wangwana* shot dead two warriors who glided by in a canoe, but other similar craft floated past, causing fears for the fate of any stragglers. Another Zanzibari pioneer was bitten by a snake as he cleared a way through the bush. On 14 September two further desertions were recorded – thirty men had now gone missing since the muster roll of 23 August when Jephson's column returned.[45]

At last, on 16 September, gunshots signalled that contact had been made with the Manyema of Ugarrowa's. Later that day Stanley came into the adobe settlement (containing 300 people and eighty guns) and greeted Ugarrowa, who as a boy had accompanied Speke and Grant on their expedition of 1860–63. Stanley made camp on the left bank facing Ugarrowa's and pondered his next move.[46] The first disappointment was to learn that the food supply was exiguous here too. But he at least secured enough for a few days. Until his departure on the 19th, he was in negotiations with Ugarrowa for the care of fifty-six sick and dying men he intended to leave behind at the settlement. He also wrote a letter to Barttelot, which he hired Ugarrowa's people to deliver to Yambuya; however, the couriers were turned back at Wasp Rapids by the hostility of the tribesmen.[47]

Ugarrowa showed Stanley his cache of ivory and gave him his first sight of the Mbuti pygmy people.[48] He also co-operated in a scheme to cut down the desertion rate. First Ugarrowa warned the *wangwana* that he would not harbour any refugees from the column once it moved on. Then he was an amused spectator while Stanley and the Zanzibari headmen enacted a charade. Stanley condemned one of the chained deserters to death as an example to the others. The headmen then begged and besought him to commute the sentence. With much theatricality Stanley 'allowed himself to be persuaded' and the man was set free. The friends of the condemned were so overcome with emotion that they set up a cry of fidelity to Stanley, promising to follow him unswervingly to Lake Albert: 'Death to him who leaves Bula Matari!' arose the chant.[49]

Sadly it was a case of 'the devil a monk'. The very next day after the departure from Ugarrowa's three deserters were brought in. Ugarrowa, furious that his words had not been heeded, flogged the men and sent them back to Stanley in chains. This time Stanley felt he had no choice but to go through with the execution; if desertions continued at the September rate, there would be nobody left by the end of the year. Stanley called his men together for a general assembly and addressed them. He argued that the deserters had to die for the general good and the safety of all. Lots would be drawn, and whichever of the three drew the fatal number would be hanged by the other two. So it was done. The unfortunate victim, Mabruki by name, was selected; the other two, still chained, hauled him up.[50] All hands witnessed the execution. But the hanging proved a messy business. The first tree-bough over which they strung the rope snapped under Mabruki's weight. He had to be strung up a second time and died within two minutes. The sight of the hanged man was so sickening that Stanley decided to exercise mercy with the other two and commuted their sentences, to relief and satisfaction from the *wangwana*.[51]

After just five days into the wilderness after Ugarrowa's, having left fifty-six sick behind there, Stanley found himself with another fifty ailing men on his hands. Hunger was again a problem and there was a desperate need of fresh meat. They were in elephant country now and Stanley comforted himself with the idea of bringing down a tusker to provide the entire party with steaks. They could hear hundreds of the great beasts trumpeting in the forest, but could seldom get near them, as the noise of the human caravan frightened them off.[52] Stanley managed to get off a shot at one but merely wounded it. A few days later Stairs wounded another, was charged by it and almost gored. In partial compensation a few days later he found a gazelle trapped in a game pit.[53] Also, a captive woman was brought in who swore that slightly inland there was a great abundance of plantain.

As hunger oppressed them, so too did the dank gloom of the mighty forest. Stanley described it as a wall of trees, extending the distance from Inverness to Plymouth, lashed together with an impenetrable undergrowth of creepers, some 12 inches in diameter. Temperatures ranged from 80° to 92° F. Rotting vegetation and the trunks of fallen forest giants were 'buried in masses of creepers of the most vivid green, netted by hundreds of lianas, and ten fathoms' length of calamus. Then every mile or so the dark, sluggish, winding creeks . . . covered over with lilies, with a sickly perfume strangely mixed with a nauseous effluvium of pitch-black mud.'[54]

Hardly surprisingly, the river party, even after struggling with boiling rapids, frequently got far ahead of the land contingent. For this reason, and because navigation by canoe was becoming increasingly difficult, Stanley proposed abandoning the river. They were having too many narrow escapes. On 4 October the boat was nearly wrecked and a canoe was swept twice beneath the waves.[55] But Uledi (of *Through the Dark Continent* fame), volunteered to be a pathfinder canoeist. However, one decision Stanley did take at this time. With a half-starved force and a mounting desertion rate – the hanging of Mabruki had had only momentary exemplary effect – Stanley lacked the capability to carry the sick in litters. He therefore resolved to leave behind Nelson, who was ill with ulcerous feet and legs, together with fifty-two other sick men and eighty-one loads, while the main column pressed on to the nearest Arab settlement.[56]

The decision to abandon Nelson was the most signal example so far of Stanley's utter ruthlessness and it caused consternation in the minds of the other officers.[57] But it solved nothing. Three days after leaving Nelson and his party behind, Stanley held a muster, which recorded 213 souls present (as opposed to 224 on the 6th). Eleven men had deserted in three days, all of them crazed with hunger. There were numerous traces of game now: wart-hogs, buffalo, antelope, elephants, but though Stairs, Jephson and Stanley all tried their hand at tracking these animals they had no luck. Stanley managed to wound an elephant but it got away.[58]

Desperately hungry, and intermittently attacked by wasps and showers of torrential rain, Stanley confessed he had never encountered hardship like this on any of his previous expeditions. The marvel was that Randy the terrier was still going strong. But the leader's journal is eloquent of the most frightful anxiety they all felt as death by starvation began to loom as a distinct possibility.

10 October. A few only of foragers across river have returned. They bring nothing having found nothing . . . I ate my last bean, last grain of Indian corn and of rice, and very last portion of everything solid foreign to this soil and this morning the horrid emptiness of the stomach gave me real anxiety and had to be filled with something lest the muscles exercise upon itself . . . I tried a handful of potato leaves, bruised fine, with a beautiful fruit large as a prize pear . . . and a cake made by a captive woman of the woodbean flour.

11 October. Our weakness is most pitiable – but there is courage in our people yet.

13 October. Nine have died since yesterday.

The expedition was now so debilitated that when men deserted with guns and ammunition, Stanley was too dispirited to send posses after them. Even the 'beautiful fruit' turned out to be an illusion, for Hoffmann who ate it ravenously was then violently sick. In agonies of hunger the officers tortured themselves with the devising of *haute cuisine* menus. None of them had ever before realised the importance of food; as Stanley remarked: 'prayer precedes meat but praise comes after.'[59]

By 15 October it was clear to all that death was not far away. Stanley left a party on the river in the boat and himself struck north into the forest. After a terrible day's march, he killed and ate his sick donkey. That night he overheard the *wangwana* talking; they were all convinced they would die and that hope of striking an Arab station was illusory. Randy was now getting weaker and weaker. Stanley dared not feed him scraps, for the Zanzibaris would have murdered him if they thought he was getting anything they could eat. When Stanley let the terrier wander free in the forest, he frequently returned with signs of combat with some denizen of the gloom. The only bright spot was the stoicism and endurance of his officers, though this was variable. The only man who never criticised the leader with a look or gesture was Parke. Jephson was tough but mutable, while as for Stairs: 'I do not quite believe him to be friendly. Sometimes I catch something in his looks which forbids me let myself go in overpraise.'[60]

On the 17th their hopes were buoyed up by questioning of a forest dweller who revealed that there was an Arab post just one day's journey away. Next morning, after a chilling trek in thick, cold mist, they heard singing and shouting in the distance. As the mist cleared they found themselves in a clearing on the outskirts of the town of Ipoto, surrounded by people jabbering away excitedly in Arabic and Swahili. They were saved. After thirteen days without any food grown by man, 192 men had survived.[61]

It turned out that Ipoto was under the command of a runaway Zanzibari slave called Kilonga-Longa, a rival of Ugarrowa. The Manyema here had far outstripped Tippu Tip in devastation of the environment. The coming of the Arabs on the Upper Congo and Aruwimi had produced ecological disaster. It was their depredations that had brought the expedition to the brink of disaster from starvation. Tippu Tip, Ugarrowa, Kilonga-Longa – it all formed a pattern: 'Half a dozen resolute men, aided by their hundreds of bandits, have divided about three-fourths of the great Upper Congo forest for the sole purpose of murder, and becoming heirs to a few hundred tusks of ivory.'[62]

At first Stanley and his men were well received and treated hospitably. The *wangwana* gorged themselves to the point where their stomachs reacted negatively to the overeating. But when it became clear that the expedition had nothing to offer in return for its demands, the Manyema attitude hardened. They refused to part with food except for trade goods and threatened to shoot any of Stanley's men found pillaging their plantations.[63] In response the *wangwana* began to sell their clothes, then their ammunition changed hands within three days. Stanley realised with alarm that the Manyema were trying to disarm the expedition by buying up its rifles and cartridges. Stanley began by bluster, demanding that the Manyema return the rifles. When they ignored the request, he turned his anger on his men. He held a muster and sentenced to twenty-five lashes anyone who could not produce his gun and ammunition. One man was flogged on the spot. Yet immediately afterwards word was brought that yet another man had sold his rifle for food. This time Stanley hanged the culprit, one Jumah, as an example to the others. This show of 'strength' finally impressed the Manyema and they agreed to return five of the rifles.[64]

Relations with the Manyema continued tense. One of the *wangwana* was speared to death while raiding a cornfield, and Stanley gave another a public flogging of 200 lashes for stealing. Stanley's sadistic side emerges in his bland comments on the affair: 'the scars will last on his body till death, and for the time being he is utterly disabled.'[65] Fortunately for Stanley his negotiations with the grasping Manyema were materially assisted when Uledi and the river party came in, for Uledi was a master diplomat. While Stanley was confined to bed for a day with a slight fever, Uledi traded enough goods to enable a forward march to be made.[66]

Stanley's mood at Ipoto was deep black. Jephson recorded: 'We see very little of Stanley, he stays in his hut all day and we remain near ours. This evening he came up whilst we were at dinner and remarked that we seemed to be doing very well in the way of food, we told him that except the coffee, everything we were eating we had bought with our own clothes – he turned the subject violently.'[67] The leader's anxiety now centred on the abandoned Nelson. By 26 October he had an agreement with the Manyema that they would assist Jephson to go back and find Nelson. The party would consist of forty *wangwana* and thirty Manyema. To seal the pact Stanley made brotherhood with Ismaili, the most important of the headmen (Kilonga-Longa was absent), and signed an agreement with him, witnessed by Parke.[68]

Next Stanley told his officers what his plans were. While Jephson accompanied the relief party back to find Nelson, he would press on. Parke would remain at Ipoto to tend Nelson and the other sick when they came in. Jephson asked and got permission to follow the leader once he had rescued Nelson. Stanley agreed, provided Parke remained in Ipoto with Nelson and the sick. For greater protection he would leave the Maxim gun behind. He himself would return for them in three months. Parke did not relish the prospect of a further period of short commons among the treacherous Manyema, but accepted without demur. Privately he was bitter that Stanley was leaving him and the sick as, in effect, hostages, at the whim of Kilonga-Longa – hostages moreover who stood more chance of being relieved by Barttelot and the Rear Column than by Stanley himself.[69]

Jephson was even more disgusted at the dispositions Stanley suggested, and the disgust showed. On the 26th Stanley doled out Nelson's food for six days – a good-sized plateful of coarse hard flour and one small chicken.[70] Jephson describes the sequel: 'When this was brought in, he remarked that it was an ample allowance for that time. I said nothing but I think my face must have expressed the disgust I felt at the scandalous smallness and meanness of the allowance, for a few minutes after the food was taken away to my hut, he sent another small chicken for me to take on – it was very fortunate for me and for Nelson as well that I had sold my clothes for food, we should have been on short commons indeed had we depended entirely on Stanley.'[71]

On 28 October Stanley himself marched on from Ipoto through heavy rain, accompanied by Manyema guides. Their insolence towards the *wangwana* irked Stanley and he seethed inwardly, but he had to curb his tongue, since Jephson, Parke and Nelson were all in the power of the Manyema.[72] Everything about Ipoto had angered Stanley. When would the European powers combine to bridle Arab arrogance and clear the slavers out of Central Africa? The first essential step was a treaty to ban the sale of gunpowder. 'It is simply incredible that because ivory is required for ornaments or billiard balls, the rich heart of Africa should be laid waste at this late year of the nineteenth century, signalised as it has been by so much advance, that populations, tribes and nations should be utterly destroyed. Whom after all does this bloody seizure of ivory enrich? Only a few dozens of half-castes, Arabs and Negros, who, if due justice were dealt to them, should be made to sweat out the remainder of their piratical lives in the severest penal servitude.'[73]

Stanley and his men stumbled and fell over prominent tree roots. To get to the village of Bukiri they had to cross a log 'bridge', 20 feet high, between the edge of the forest and the village. But gradually the going improved. The forest was more open, so that they could cover one and a half miles an hour as opposed to half a mile an hour in the depths of the Ituri. For the first time billhooks were not constantly needed. They enjoyed brilliant sunshine every day and a thunderstorm at night.[74] After crossing the confluence of the Ituri and the Epuru, they entered a well-populated area, the domain of the Balese tribe.[75] Once past the dreadful orbit of the Manyema, food was plentiful again. They could get bananas, corn, goats, chickens, flour and beans: 'for the first time since leaving the Congo we were assured of being able to fill the ravenous stomachs of all our followers.'[76]

The one blot on the horizon was the insolence of Khamis, chief of the Manyema guides. Tension grew between the Manyema and the *wangwana*, especially after Khamis slapped Saad Tato in the face. Stanley asked his headmen not to retaliate for the moment but to bide their time. The time came on 10 November, as their pace quickened to two miles an hour over firmer ground which absorbed the rain. To the sounds of crashing timber all around them as forest giants breathed their last, Stanley warned Khamis that since they were now out of Ismaili's territory, henceforth the *wangwana* had his blessing to retaliate for any slight.[77]

On 10 November Stanley called a halt while Khamis and a mixed party of Manyema and *wangwana* scouted ahead for food. Stanley was so plagued by fleas that he pitched his tent in the middle of a village street to try to be rid of them. Four days later Khamis came back, laden with flocks of goats; he had sent on his own men to loot and pillage, since Stanley had forbidden the Zanzibaris to do so. After a day's gorging, Khamis and his men left without fulfilling their contract to escort the expedition to Lake Albert. They left behind a store of ivory, which Stanley sent after them, to remove any pretext for Khamis to 'badmouth' the white man with Ismaili.[78]

Scarcely had Khamis left than Jephson came into camp. Cunningly foreseeing that it would take Barttelot nine months to cover the ground Stanley had marched in three, Jephson had made it a point of understanding that he be allowed to escape the anathema of beggary into which Stanley had cast Parke and Nelson.[79] His mood when leaving Ipoto on 26 October was grim: 'I know Stanley will make no allowance for these difficulties even if he allows there are any, he always slangs one indiscriminately so one must just make up one's mind to grin and bear it.'[80] Three days later he found Nelson, who told him he had been unable to sleep at night because of anxiety ever since the others left him. This was hardly surprising. Only five of the fifty-two men who had been left with him were alive and two of those were dying; of the others seventeen were dead and the rest had deserted.[81]

After burying thirteen boxes of ammunition, Jephson and Nelson arrived back at Ipoto on 3 November. Nelson soon found that his plight had improved only marginally. Stanley had made no arrangements with the Manyema chiefs to feed his officers. Stairs, in charge of the Maxim gun, had had to sell his clothes. Parke was particularly incensed that

Stanley had not even bothered to say goodbye to him. As Jephson remarked bitterly: 'It is really quite wonderful how little Stanley seems to care about the welfare of his officers, he seems to take no interest whatever in what they do or how they manage to get on. I think it is a mistake his having European officers under him, he should merely have Zanzibari chiefs and see to all the work himself.'[82]

Not surprisingly, then, when Jephson and his forty-eight men caught up with the main column, the letters he brought from Parke and Nelson were full of bitterness and recrimination towards their leader. Nelson upbraided Stanley for having made no arrangements for their food at Ipoto: 'What are we do to do? Die of hunger? Surely we deserve a little better treatment than this . . . what would people at home say?'[83] Stanley waved the point aside. He snapped only when Parke's letter told him that Ismaili was already trying to evade the terms of his sworn contract. 'If ever a man had cause to pity himself, I have!' he exclaimed.[84]

Next day he sent out Stairs to reconnoitre the route. One of the *wangwana* named Simba was wounded in a fracas with the locals, then blew his own brains out, to the disgust of his comrades who said he was too poor to have the presumption to commit suicide.[85] Uledi came in with more news about Ismaili's bad behaviour, and a muster on 23 November produced just 175 men – 285 had left Ugarrowa's.[86] Stanley felt some remorse about his treatment of the people of Ibwiri. They had treated the expedition well, but the *wangwana* had requited their kindness with looting and pillaging.[87]

On the 24th the expedition marched on from Ibwiri. Food was still plentiful and the forest became less dense. By the 30th they were trekking through mixed country, part forest, part parkland.[88] Stanley delighted in the new sensations: a new specimen of arrow, 2 foot 6 inches long with a spear-shaped three-inch point; the most plentiful tobacco crops he had yet seen in Africa; and his first sighting of black cattle with a white face.[89] On 3 December they reached the main Ituri River and finally on 4 December they emerged well and truly from the forest gloom. The five-month Hobbesian war of all against all was over. Stanley describes the moment. 'We emerged upon the plains, and the deadly gloomy forest was behind us. After one hundred and sixty days' continuous gloom, we saw the light of the broad day shining all around us and making all things beautiful. We thought we had never seen grass so green or country so lovely. The men literally yelled and leaped with joy, and raced over the ground with their burdens. Ah, this was the old spirit of former expeditions successfully completed all of a sudden revived.'[90]

They proceeded across the rolling plain, largely untroubled by the heavy rain. Stanley looked forward now to seeing Lake Albert which had intrigued him ever since he read Philip Gosse's book during the 1882–3 home leave from the Congo. In particular he wanted to see the 'large donkey' which Harry Johnston later identified as the okapi.[91] But just when they thought they had left all cares behind them, they ran into the stiffest indigenous military resistance so far. At first the people Stanley calls the 'Abunguma' watched them sullenly as they crossed the eastern Ituri by a suspension bridge, which would admit just one man at a time. Then came skirmishing and a half-hearted night attack on the camp. Finally, when the expedition got to the foot of Mount Mazamboni, the Abunguma, 'the most populous tribe since the Bangala', decided that matters had gone far enough.[92]

On 9 December the expedition was camped on a strong position on a hilltop, fortified by a thorn boma. Stanley decided not to move until the locals made friends with them or, alternatively, until they were taught the power of European technology. When all peace negotiations broke down, Stanley ordered a punitive sortie. He divided his force into three. Jephson and thirty riflemen were told off to the left, Uledi detached to the right, while Stairs led the centre. Stairs and his men confronted the enemy across a broad stream. The crackle of gunfire echoed across the undulating grasslands. At first the tribesmen faced the onslaught bravely, and loosed showers of arrows at their tormentors, confident in the watery barrier between the two forces. Seeing this, Stairs ordered the charge and led his men across the stream in a rousing onslaught. They gained the far bank and opened up a withering fire on the now faltering tribesmen. They pursued them into banana plantations and villages which they put to the torch. Uledi meanwhile had discovered a path leading along a mountain spur and after ascending 500 feet came on to and above the right flank of the enemy. Catching them in a natural killing ground, they opened up with the Winchesters and did awesome execution. Finally Jephson's party emerged from the left ravine, effectively catching the hostiles between three fires. It was a classically successful textbook military exercise.[93]

Chief Mazamboni next announced he would make a final decision for peace or war after seeing the quality of Stanley's trade goods. Two yards of scarlet cloth and a dozen brass rods, however, proved less than efficacious, so battle was resumed. Between 9 and 13 December four more pitched battles took place, with the enemy trying to cut off the rearguard and taking severe punishment from the Winchesters in the process. On the 12th Stanley himself killed a man who was yelling on a hillside with a shot fired from fully 600 yards away.[94]

On 13 December Mazamboni's men followed them at a respectful distance, out of rifle range, as the column threaded its way down to the lake shore. Excitement was running high with the Europeans. Stanley described the situation. 'At 1 p.m. we resumed our march. Fifteen minutes later I cried out, "Prepare yourselves for a sight of the Nyanza." The men murmured and doubted and said, "Why does the master continually talk to us in this way? Nyanza indeed! Is not this a plain and can we not see mountains at least four days' march ahead of us?" At 1.30 p.m. the Albert Nyanza was below them. Now it was my turn to jeer and scoff at the doubters, but as I was about to ask them what they saw, so many came to kiss my hands and beg my pardon, that I could not say a word.'[95]

But the euphoria of gazing down from the plateau on to the great lake soon turned to puzzlement and disillusionment. Where was Emin with his levies? Questioning of the peoples by the lakeside revealed that they had not seen a white man since Mason Bey's circumnavigation ten years earlier.[96] This awakened Stanley's worst fear: that Emin might meanwhile have made his own way to Zanzibar, thus destroying the point of the expedition. He did some quick calculations. It would take four days to get to Wadelai by water, but he had no canoes, so the point was academic. By land it would take twenty-five days, and because of his aggressive policy towards the Lake Albert peoples he would probably have to fight all the way. With only forty-seven cases of cartridges left, a running fight all the way to Wadelai would leave them with just twenty-five cases to hand over to Emin – a plain absurdity for a 'relief' expedition.[97]

So it was that, paradoxically, the Emin Pasha relief expedition was in need of relief itself. On 14 December Stanley informed his officers that for the time being the search for Emin would have to be abandoned. He proposed returning to Ibwiri, building a fortified camp, then sending out detachments to gather up all the far-flung pockets of manpower along the trail, Parke and Nelson at Ipoto, the men at Ugarrowa's, and so on, even to the Rear Column itself. Once the entire expedition was reunited at Ibwiri, they could make a second, more determined attempt to find Emin.[98]

This announcement caused his officers intense disappointment. Stairs and Jephson argued that this meant turning back on the very brink of success. Jephson pleaded to be allowed to cross the lake to Wadelai, but

Stanley rejected this as too risky.[99] As reinforcement for his decision he pointed to the continuing hostility of the lakeside peoples; by day they were sullen and suspicious and by night they went in for sneak attacks on the camp. How could the expedition guarantee its food supply in these conditions?

The decision to retreat contained some rationality, but only on premises which themselves logically precluded the original decision to split the expedition and leave behind the Rear Column. In his fanatical desire to reach Lake Albert at any cost – and fanatical is the only word to describe such a blithe failure to think through the consequences of his actions – Stanley swept aside inconvenient facts and obvious considerations which returned at the lakeside to strike him with force. It may be, as has been suggested, that Stanley was embarrassed to meet Emin with his expedition in its current ragged state, but this hardly explains the disappointment at not meeting the Pasha at the lake.[100] More likely, having redoubled his efforts as he lost sight of his goal, simply to brave out the horrors of the Ituri, Stanley found himself driven on by the 'automatic pilot' of constant action and did not stop to correlate means and ends until he reached the notional 'end' of his journey.

Retreat to Ibwiri meant further clashes with Mazamboni's truculent people. Some part of the motive for Mazamboni's aggression comes through in the verbal exchanges recorded on 15 December. 'A man and his wife came within a bow shot from the shore . . . "Which way did you come from? Ituri? Ah, that proves you to be wicked people. Who ever heard of good people coming from that direction? If you were not wicked people you would have brought a big boat like the other white man and shot hippopotamus like the other man." '[101] This was the Bula Matari/ Tandelay syndrome in reverse. Mason, who had arrived in a steamer, was a good man, a man of wealth. Stanley, who had arrived on foot and with no wealth, was bad.

The retreat turned out to be every bit as perilous as Stairs and Jephson had feared when arguing against it to Stanley. They were detained at first by a severe rainstorm, but when they got under way they were at once plagued by a shower of arrows from small marauding parties. Mazamboni's men no longer offered combat in pitched battles, but adopted a kind of guerrilla, hit-and-run warfare. In response Stanley tried to burn off the attackers by long forced marches. In addition to the usual day's travel, he insisted on a further five hours' trekking from 5 to 10 p.m. At the end of this the exhausted *wangwana* would simply flop on the grass and sleep where they lay, the cold nights of the grasslands notwithstanding. Mazamboni's men constantly nudged and prodded the rear, moving in at the first opportunity to spear the sick and straggling. Even hunting was difficult. There was an abundance of game, especially kudu and hartebeeste, which was easy to kill, but there was the ever-present danger of ambush to the hunters.[102]

Stanley was not the kind of man to take *la petite guerre* lying down. His patience snapped when he saw a sick straggler being speared about 500 yards behind the column. He decided to ambush the ambushers. Saad Tato and four of the best sharpshooters were positioned behind a rock for an ambuscade. They poured lead into their pursuers and momentarily shook their resolve.[103]

Next day things seemed to be looking up with the lucky find of a vast store of grain and beans, enough to provide every man with five days' provisions. But just as the officers were congratulating themselves on this piece of serendipity, Stanley through his binoculars spotted a fresh ambush in tall grass. He swerved the line of the column away, and his sharpshooters again foiled an enemy attempt to fall on the rear. Tired of this war of attrition, and unable to afford the steady drip-drip in loss of men and ammunition, Stanley decided on a policy of search and destroy. He sent out a mobile column of eighty of his best men to plunder every village around, strip it of its livestock, then burn it to the ground. Mazamboni's men took to watching the expedition from afar and giving it a wide berth.[104]

By 23 December they were at the main ford of the eastern Ituri. Now on the borders of the Balese country, Stanley was startled to find that the locals had destroyed all bridges and taken away all canoes. To cross the river, he had his men construct a crude suspension bridge as far as an island in mid-river. A violent hailstorm assailed them while they were crossing, but the bridgehead on the island gave them a toehold. There they constructed rafts of banana stalks to get them to the other side.[105]

Through his interpreters, Stanley warned the locals that he would be returning and if the bridges were still down there would be a reckoning. This 'Christmas message' was pure Stanley. 'Those unacquainted with these people might think we should be grateful for crossing and march off without molesting them. I have the best will in the world to do so, and if but a child came and expressed regret, I would forgive all but if I go and leave them unpunished, my people will certainly suffer, and I shall bear the loss.'[106]

By noon of 26 December they were all on the far side of the Ituri

River. Little else disturbed the tenor of their march for the next two weeks, and on 6 January they came to the familiar approaches of Ibwiri.

· 12 ·

THEY found Ibwiri abandoned but with plenty of food in store. This, together with a stash of fine wooden boards, gave Stanley the incentive to build a stockaded camp. By 18 January 1888 the stockade, henceforth known as Fort Bodo, was complete. The main problem about the fort was its infestation by rats, fleas, mosquitoes and, above all, red ants. These were a constant menace in the Ituri forest, as Stanley noted: 'to the living the red ants are a nuisance. Twenty times a day while on a march we have to cross their columns and then only do the Zanzibaris break into the double quick to avoid them – but woe betide the unlucky man who stumbles and falls over their lines.'[1] But the ants were not only a danger to moving columns. They seemed particularly attracted to Ipoto, as Parke recalled on 19 January: 'A column of ants, of about four inches in width, and densely marshalled, has now been continuously passing through my tent for nearly twenty-four hours. So the length appears to be unlimited.'[2] But troublesome as the red ants were, they were not so deadly as the black variety. Marching in military squares 12 – 15 inches wide and 100 feet long, black ants were more likely to eat anything in their path than live and let live.[3]

Once the stockade was completed, Stanley despatched Stairs to Ipoto to rescue Nelson and Parke. Whatever the provocation, he was not to open fire on the Manyema unless they had actually spilt the blood of expedition personnel. Stairs returned on 8 February with the tattered remnants of the Ipoto contingent, the steel boat and the Maxim gun. There were just sixteen survivors. Eleven men had died of starvation and the Manyema had tried to starve out the others to get their guns.[4] Parke and Nelson shocked Stanley by their appearance, Nelson particularly so: (he) 'walks like an old man of ninety. Yet he eats well and would naturally eat much more if food was properly cooked and of European quality.'[5]

Picking up from camp gossip that the British officers felt very angry at his cavalier attitude to their sufferings, Stanley insisted that Parke and Nelson write an official account of their time at Ipoto. This was a typical Stanley tactic. He always liked his officers to write down their version of any controversial incident, defying them in effect to criticise him. If they criticised him, he would find means to victimise them. If they did not, but complained later, Stanley would use the 'official account' to which they had signed their names to rebut any criticism of himself. Stanley also suspected Stairs of manoeuvring behind the scenes to influence the *wangwana* headmen. When he proposed returning to look for Barttelot and the Rear Column, the Zanzibari chiefs opposed the idea and exhorted him to try to find Emin once more.[6] Stanley was in a ticklish spot. He had urged his men forward on gruelling forced marches with the promise of meeting the Pasha at Lake Albert; but when they got there, the locals said they knew nothing of any white man. There was an issue of credibility here that Stanley was trying to duck; he could not face the embarrassment of a second fruitless search for Emin.

He therefore opted for a middle-of-the-road strategy. He sent out Stairs again, this time to bring up the men who had been left behind at Ugarrowa's and Barttelot's Rear Column, on the assumption that Barttelot 'must' by now have got as far as Ugarrowa's. Stairs departed on 16 February. Two days later Stanley complained of a large glandular swelling on his left arm, and next day he was attacked by a violent pain in his stomach and the familiar symptoms of African fever.[7] The pains spread to the abdomen, liver and gall bladder. Parke, who was in constant attendance, examined him and found inflammation of the left axillary gland. He made a general diagnosis of impacted gallstone and aggravated African fever – the very same illness that had brought Stanley to the brink of death on three previous occasions (one of them in New Bond Street). Stanley was in a critical condition from 19 February to 16 March.[8]

Stanley had only a confused recollection of that time. He could not praise his physician enough – 'Dr Parke has been most assiduous in attention and gentle as a woman in his ministrations' – but in his conscious intervals he was violent, unpredictable and raged at his officers mercilessly. In one of his fits of anger he hit Hoffmann over the head with a stick. Hovering near death, in his lucid moments while sipping soup or having poultices applied, he lashed out physically and verbally at all in sight. He told Jephson he was guilty of 'overweening pride – pride of birth and pride of self' and suggested that instead of his soft life he should have spent three years before the mast by the time he was eighteen. He also spoke of himself in a way that drew stupefied incredulity from Jephson: 'He made himself out to be a St John for gentleness, a Solomon for wisdom, a Job for patience and a model of truth. Whereas I do not suppose a more impatient, a more ungentle and more untruthful man than Stanley could exist. He is most violent in his words and actions, the slightest little thing is sufficient to work him into a frenzy of rage, his sense of what is honourable is of the haziest description and he is certainly a most untruthful character – "o wid some power the giftie gie us".'⁹

By 13 March Stanley was able to walk for the first time in three weeks. Parke lanced the tumour in his arm, out of which a great mass of pus discharged. On 16 March he took his first extended walk without being supported and thereafter convalesced rapidly. By the 25th of the month he was well enough to travel. Stanley decided to return to the lake to try once more to make contact with Emin, without waiting for Stairs to return. The cultivation in the fields around Ford Bodo had produced prodigious results, so that there was no longer any worry over food supplies.¹⁰

On 2 April Stanley, Jephson, Parke and 126 men with the steel boat set out for the return march to Lake Albert; Nelson and another forty-nine invalids were left behind at Fort Bodo. The expedition was unopposed at the Ituri except for a handful of warriors who shot a few arrows at them, which fell short, then retired. On 11 April they emerged from the forest into the grassland. The switch from darkness or twilight to brilliant sunshine was hailed with shouts of joy, by none more so than Parke, who had endured 289 days in the fuliginous gloom of the rain forest. The euphoria of the experience led Parke into one of his rare moments of indiscretion: 'Dr Parke and Mr Jephson not taking the advice of the Zanzibaris respecting the light-coloured tobacco leaves, smoked them and became qualmish and uncomfortable therefrom.'¹¹

Next day, when they occupied a Besse village, the locals tried to counterattack but were quickly dispersed by a skirmishing line of sharp-shooters. East of Besse they lost their way and had to steer straight across the grassland to the Undussuma peak, scene of their struggle with Mazamboni's on 10–11 December the previous year. Stanley put out peace feelers to Mazamboni and this time his overtures were recipro-cated. Mazamboni's men explained that the hostilities were another case of mistaken identity. The area in which they lived was a favourite target for Kabba Rega's raiders from Bunyoro; Stanley's men had been mistaken for them. The explanation led to a general reconciliation. First Mazamboni's courtiers apologised for the events of last December. Then Stanley made blood brothers with Mazamboni himself.[12]

Mazamboni then introduced Stanley to the other tribal leaders of the area: Gavira and Kavalli. Between them the three chiefs controlled a large area extending from the lake shore to the neighbouring plateau and the grasslands to the west. As he learned more, Stanley made interesting ethnological discoveries relating to the power politics of the region. It seemed that two entirely different tribes coexisted on the grassland. A Hamitic race of hunters and warriors had begun to encroach on the preserves of the agricultural matrilinear peoples some time in the eighth or ninth century AD and had achieved total conquest by the beginning of the seventeenth century. These taller, slimmer Hamitic peoples (called by Stanley the Bakuma), characterised by longer heads, narrow noses and thin lips, lorded it over the original Babira (of Bantu stock). But masters and servants were forced into a closer symbiosis by the ever-present threat from Kabba Rega and his warriors.[13]

All three chiefs had news of Emin. Mazamboni told him that someone answering the Pasha's description – 'Malleju' ('the bearded one') – had been on the lake since Stanley's visit. At Kavalli's the young chief actually handed over a packet that Emin had left behind. The letter was wrapped in an oilcloth and a fragment of *The Times* for April 1886.[14] What had happened was that Emin, under threat from both Kabba Rega and the Mahdists, at first received garbled reports in Wadelai of a white man raiding the area on the western shores of Lake Albert. He had assumed that this could not be Stanley(!). When the reports became too insistent to be ignored, Emin and a detachment of his soldiers sailed south from Wadelai to Mswa on the south-western corner of the lake at the end of January. But interrogation of the lakeside peoples threw up the same unsatisfactory answers that Stanley had received a month before. Just in case it was Stanley that was looking for him, Emin left a letter with Kavalli. He did not have the resources for a full-scale search for Stanley and, between Kabba Rega and the Mahdists, had problems enough in his own province.[15] The letter he left behind asked Stanley to send a messenger to the north-west shore of the lake, where he would be picked up by one of Emin's steamers. The letter came as a very great relief to Stanley's officers, tired as they were of chasing shadows, though Stanley himself remarked sourly that it was a very cool message indeed from a man supposed to be in the last extremity.[16]

Stanley at once ordered Jephson and Parke to launch the steel boat

Advance on Lake Albert and go in search of Emin. From Mswa Jephson sent a note to Wadelai to tell Emin that this was indeed the Stanley expedition. Emin at once ordered his steamers south.[17] On 27 April Jephson and Emin met at Mswa. Emin was effusive in his thanks to the British for their efforts; Jephson for his part was deeply impressed by the intelligence and sincerity of the Pasha; he contrasted his humanity and popularity with the ruthlessness and aura of fear that surrounded Stanley.[18] It only remained now for Jephson to escort Emin back for a meeting with Stanley that would, on paper, emulate the sensation of the 1871 Ujiji meeting with Livingstone.

Stanley meanwhile left Kavalli's camp at Bundi, 5000 feet above sea-level, overlooking the southern end of Lake Albert, for the descent to the lake itself. Katonza and Komubi, the chiefs who had harassed the expedition at the lake shore on 13–16 December, hearing that the trio of most powerful chieftains had made obeisance to Stanley, followed suit and made their submission; again their excuse for previous hostilities was that they thought Stanley's men were Kabba Rega's.[19]

They descended to the lake which, like Lakes Tanganyika and Victoria, was alive with crocodiles.[20] Stanley amused himself by placing pieces of meat on the roof of a conical hut, just an arm's length away, and noting the boldness of the kites, who would swoop down, grab the meat and fly away before anyone could touch them. He was beginning to warm to Lake Albert's peculiar charms: 'I have often smiled at the rhapsody of Sir Samuel [Baker] on his discovery of the Albert Nyanza, perhaps oftener after Mason's mysteriously brusque way of circumscribing its "illimitability", but I can feel with him now some sympathy despite its known length and breadth.'[21] But Stanley still felt angry that Emin had not taken proper steps to meet them in December, which could have saved them five days' fighting and four months' loss of time. His mood was fluctuating and temper uncertain, and Jephson recorded a typical incident just before he left for Mswa: 'Stanley got in a great rage with the men today and as they were not working as well as they might he fired at two of them, he just grazed the heel of one of the men and took a piece off about the size of a sixpence, a quarter of an inch more would have shattered the bone of the foot and made him lame for life; Stanley really is not responsible for what he does when he gets into these fits of passion.'[22]

On 29 April Jephson, Emin and his friend and confidant Captain Casati loaded the steamer *Khedive* with provisions and livestock and took the *Advance* in tow. That evening on the lake shore Stanley saw through his field glasses a large steamer approaching. At 8 p.m. the trio rowed ashore. The *wangwana* were so excited that they fired off their guns in welcome.[23] A bespectacled figure walked up to Stanley's tent and said in excellent English: 'I owe you a thousand thanks, Mr Stanley. I really do not know how to express my thanks to you.' Stanley replied: 'Ah, you are Emin Pasha. Do not mention thanks, but come in and sit down. It is so dark out here we cannot see each other.'[24]

In his journal Stanley provided a fuller account of the historic meeting:

At the door of the tent we stood and a wax candle threw light on the scene. I expected to see a tall thin military-looking figure in faded Egyptian uniform, but instead of it I saw a small spare figure in a well-kept fez and a clean suit of snowy cotton drilling, well ironed and of perfect fit. A dark lively beard bordered a face of a Magyar cast though a pair of spectacles lent it somewhat the appearance of an Italian, or Spanish appearance. There was not a trace in it of ill-health, or anxiety – it rather indicated good condition of body and peace of mind.[25]

Emin did not look his age (forty-eight) but nearer thirty to thirty-five. Casati, though younger, looked gaunt, care-worn, anxious and aged. He too wore a suit of clean Egyptian cotton and a fez.

Five bottles of champagne had been given to Stanley at Stanley Pool to toast the occasion of his meeting with Emin. Unlike at the famous meeting with Livingstone, this time Stanley did not forget them, possibly because two had already been opened to celebrate the first sighting of Lake Albert. The remaining three bottles were now uncorked and the five Europeans sat talking and drinking far into the night.[26]

With the first great European Africanist Stanley had 'found' there was instant rapport. With Emin there was an equally immediate failure to communicate. As soon as Jephson handed him Stanley's letter at Mswa, Emin recorded in his diary that he had no intention of leaving his province.[27] Yet during the first day's conversation he made no mention of this. Stanley began by revealing that the Khedive's orders were that if the Pasha stayed in Equatoria, he did so at his own risk. Stanley then tried to sway him in favour of returning by asking him what would happen when he grew old or died. Emin said his problem was that he could not leave unless he had carriers for the women and children of the Egyptian garrison. They can walk, riposted Stanley brusquely. Emin then raised difficulties about food supplies. By mutual agreement the subject was deferred. Stanley noted with some irritation: 'I am unable to gather from long conversation with Emin Pasha his future intentions. When a return is proposed to him, he taps his knee, shakes his head and smiles in a kind of "we shall see" manner. I do not think he can make up his mind easily to leave this country, where he has lived like a king.'[28]

In retrospect it is hard not to be fanciful and contrast the noonday meeting with Livingstone at Ujiji (on the eastern shore of a lake) with this encounter in darkness and candle-light (on the western shore of a different lake). Even the words 'we cannot see each other' were to prove prophetic.[29] Almost all the variables that made the Livingstone/Stanley meeting result so happily were different in this case. True, Emin was just 5 foot 7 inches tall, so did not present a threat at this level – Stanley, ever-obsessive about the height of men he met, noted down the stature of Emin and Casati on two different occasions.[30] But Livingstone had been a devout Christian, whereas Emin had embraced the Islamic faith. Emin was a brilliant linguist, botanist and zoologist – an academic, in a word – while Stanley never truly mastered any language other than English and had the plain man's impatience with sciences that did not have an immediate pragmatic value. The perfect choice of explorer to 'rescue' Emin, if he had only been twenty years younger, was the linguist and orientalist Sir Richard Burton.

There was a sense in which Emin and Stanley were at once too alike and too unlike. They were alike in that both were rootless individuals who had reinvented themselves. Eduard Schnitzer had become Emin Pasha; John Rowlands had become Henry Stanley. Both had denied their origins and found fame and solace in Africa – African exploration always contained this element of a desire to return in effect to childhood and so transmogrify the experiences of actual childhood. But there the similarities ended. It was no accident that Stanley's 'socialisation' should have been in the America of the expanding frontier and 'manifest destiny'. He represented the aggressive, thrusting, technologically superior West, contemptuous of 'inferior' cultures and desirous of making them over, via Christianity, capitalism or overt imperialism, to the comforting embraces of 'civilisation'. Emin, by contrast, had explicitly chosen to be a man of the East, a man ready to submit to Fate, kismet, *baraka*, the will of Allah. For Emin everything was written; for Stanley nothing was. Stanley was all energy, incessant activity and the will to dominate. Emin's nature showed itself in indecision, changes of mind, procrastination, a tendency to let matters drift or problems solve themselves, to attain his ends indirectly or by intrigue rather than by bluster or brute force.[31]

Emin was far superior morally – in his concern for others and his genuine love of Africa (whereas Stanley loved Africa for what it gave him). But Stanley's Promethean will made things happen in situations where Emin could only wring his hands.

On 30 April the two contingents marched to Nsabe to make permanent camp further along the lake. Stanley thought the *wangwana* cut a much more impressive figure than Emin's Sudanese. While Emin sent out for more food and bearers – there was no game nearby – Stanley handed over the Remington ammunition and suggested that the joint forces dig in behind an entrenchment, in case Kabba Rega, with his 1500 riflemen, decided to try conclusions. The *Khedive* steamed off to bring up reinforcements, while Saad Tato and the best of the hunters scattered far and wide in search of prey.[32] Then the two leaders settled in for a further round of talks.

The talks proved very difficult. At first Stanley brought the maximum pressure to bear to get the Pasha to return to England, or at least Egypt. Emin finally came clean and admitted that he did not want to leave, especially having regard to the people in his care. He adduced the new argument that if he ordered the Egyptians and Sudanese to pull out, they might mutiny. Stanley in reply tried psychological warfare, speaking of the need for the Pasha to make a will for, depending on whether the Mahdists or Kabba Rega killed him first, he would need to leave his accumulated back-pay to someone.[33] But Emin was tenacious. All he wanted was the ammunition and supplies to maintain himself where he was. His soldiers did not want to leave Equatoria and he did not want to leave *them*. Besides, they could have withdrawn to the east coast at any time since the Mahdiya started.[34]

In the back of both men's minds were unstated considerations and motives. After the trauma of 1872, Stanley did not want to return to England a second time without his 'quarry', perhaps to be accused once more of being a fraud and impostor. Emin, on his side, was shocked and appalled at the small scale and general condition of a 'relief' expedition which seemed to be in need of relief itself.[35] Stalemate ensued.

On 3 May Stanley tried again. Reluctantly he unveiled the two possible commissions for Emin if he stayed in Africa, from Leopold and Mackinnon. Since, he argued, Egypt lacked the military resources ever again to be able to control Equatoria, the choice for any rational man in Emin's situation had to narrow to these two. Leopold's offer, made orally to Stanley, was for Emin to remain governor of Equatoria under the aegis of the Congo State.[36] Emin turned the offer down flat. He argued that the idea was implausible for a number of reasons. He himself could not change flags without the Khedive's permission as he was in the service of Egypt. Moreover, distance and logistics meant that the Congo could not help Equatoria against the Mahdists or Kabba Rega; they had their own dispute with the Congo Arabs to settle and could not even defend Stanley Falls![37]

What about the British, Emin asked? Did they not have an interest in Equatoria? The snag here, Stanley confided, was that Equatoria was 500 miles too far inland. Unless Britain undertook the conquest of Uganda, an east-coast corridor to Equatoria was too perilous; no government would be prepared to make expensive outlays on such an indefensible province.[38] This was the point at which he introduced the Mackinnon scheme. He proposed that Emin and the élite of his troops should accompany the expedition to the Kavirondo area of Lake Victoria, there to be established as the nucleus of Mackinnon's British East Africa Company. Without bringing pressure to bear on Emin, he advised him that this was a far better offer than Leopold's.[39] If Emin accepted, once he was established in Kavirondo, Stanley would lead the relief expedition through Masailand to the coast and then get formal approval for the actions he had taken as Mackinnon's plenipotentiary.[40]

This proposal allowed Emin the leeway to stall that he had been seeking throughout the talks. He said that a decision was possible only after he had consulted his Sudanese, for he could not be seen to be, nor did he wish to incur the charge that he was, running out on them.[41] Emin's real motive was to find a plausible pretext to stay on. Stanley tried to cut the Gordian knot by sounding Casati on his opinion, for Casati's view was known to have great weight with Emin. However, this tactic foundered on the obvious rock that Casati understood no English and his French was even worse than Stanley's.[42] Besides, he had his own reasons for disliking Stanley. He was at Kabba Rega's court, just starting to make progress in negotiations with that potentate, when news of the Emin expedition arrived in Bunyoro. Kabba Rega read this development as an attempt by the combined European and Egyptian forces to conquer Buganda and Bunyoro. Casati was lucky to escape the kingdom with his life.[43]

It was left that Emin would tour Equatoria seeking the opinions of his soldiers on a return to Egypt, while Stanley went back to find his Rear Guard. Should the Sudanese prove reluctant, as was most likely Emin would try to win them over to Mackinnon's Kavirondo scheme. At this stage Stanley was very keen that Emin should opt for this solution, and spoke in grandiloquent terms of the Imperial British East Africa Company. This had a capital of £400,000 already subscribed, there were plans for a railway from the east coast to Lake Victoria, and the IBEA would soon become a second East India Company.[44]

How plausible was the Mackinnon solution? According to Stanley, some Egyptian officers came to his tent on 4 May to tell him that they wanted to go back home, never mind Lake Victoria, but 'the Pasha does not want to return – he is happy with his travels about the country and bird studies and such things but we . . . wish to return.'[45] This seems to be a case either of Stanley deceiving himself or misunderstanding what he was told. Emin, who knew his men's minds intimately, realised that they did not want to move *anywhere*. He had tried to persuade them before to trek off south towards safety or home but they had refused; it seemed, then, that even the Lake Victoria idea was a pipedream.[46] Besides, Sudanese morale was poor. They had expected an army of deliverance and found instead a motley gallimaufry of scarecrows. To counteract the poor image his 'relief' expedition had presented, Emin wanted Stanley to come with him on the provincial tour. But Stanley was now obsessed with the fate of the Rear Guard, so offered to send Jephson instead.

Emin stayed with Stanley almost a month, and their political discussions petered out after the first week. Much of the rest of the time Emin spent telling Stanley bizarre stories about Gordon's period as governor and his notorious eccentricities. He revealed that the hero of the British people was an opium addict and attributed to this habit his sexual abstinence, for opium was said to make men impotent, as was the root of the Lymphaca lotus, with which Gordon also dosed himself. Stanley always liked it if someone played the iconoclast with Gordon's reputation but Emin unwittingly deepened Stanley's dislike for his Islamic deviancy, when he said, as though between normal heterosexual males: 'I cannot conceive how mortal man could restrain himself from sexual intercourse.'[47]

Stanley's distaste and resentment for Emin deepened over their time together. He was most annoyed to find that the Pasha was not in desperate straits, so that there had been no real need for the Advance Column to put itself under such pressure to reach him. In this way Stanley transferred the guilt for his own hard driving, which had caused so many fatalities, on to Emin himself. Also, it was quite clear that assembling Emin's people for the putative march to Lake Victoria was going to take a very long time.[48] To salve his angry feelings, Stanley allowed himself to be patronising in his journal about Emin's scientific flair and curiosity: 'The Pasha is so exceedingly industrious that all kinds of work seem agreeable to him. It is pleasant to observe at his quarters aneroids laid out in shade but truly exposed to air, thermometers, dry and wet bulbs properly arranged . . . His journals are a marvel of neatness and fine writing as though he aimed at obtaining a prize for order, neatness and accuracy. Such a man as this would be invaluable for such expeditions as I have led since 1874.'[49]

In other respects the sojourn at Nsabe was a pleasant one. Saad Tato and his young assistant Mabruki performed wonders on the big game trail. They bagged two buffalo on their first day out, but not before one of them had gored Mabruki.[50] Next day Saad Tato shot four roan antelopes, amply replenishing the meat supply. When food supplies again started to run low, towards the end of the second week of May, the *wangwana* started to loot and pillage. The local Balegga refused to take their incursions lying down, and in one raid two of them were killed and another two badly wounded. Two days later another of the *wangwana* was found dead and his Winchester missing. Stanley remained uncertain how to react to these events: 'I am never quite satisfied as to the manner of these accidents, whether the natives or the Zanzibaris are the agressors. The latter relate with exceeding plausibility their version of the matter, but they are such adepts in the art of lying that I am frequently bewildered.'[51]

On 14 May the *Khedive* returned with supplies. Emin gave gifts of cloth to Stanley and his officers. His apparent affluence served to rub salt in Stanley's wounds, since he had left his own reserve supply of clothing at Yambuya with the Rear Column. But one worrying sign was observed when the *Khedive* arrived. Instead of possessing natural authority, Emin seemed to be reduced to pleading and wheedling with his men to get them to do his bidding. If there was one thing Stanley despised in a leader, it was a man who coaxed and cajoled his followers instead of browbeating and overawing them. But Emin's methods seemed to work. He sent the *Khedive* back to Wadelai and it returned on 22 May with its sister ship the *Nyasa* and a reinforcement of eighty Sudanese soldiers.[52]

The stay at Nsabe also provided Stanley with the unwonted luxury of reflection on the grandeur of nature in Africa. On 6 May a ferocious storm blew across the lake, churning up the whole face of the Albert into foam, spray and white rollers. A week later they were hit by a tornado.[53] Nights in Africa always particularly intrigued Stanley and the

Emin expedition prompted him to a vintage Stanley purple passage:

> By nine o'clock the men, overcome by fatigue, would be asleep; silence ensued, broken only by sputtering fire-logs, flights of night-jars, hoarse notes from great bats, croakings of frogs, cricket-cheeps, falling of trees or branches, a shriek from some prowling chimpanzee, a howl from a peevish monkey, and the continual gasping cry of the lemur. But during many nights, we would sit shivering under ceaseless torrents of rain, watching the forky flames of the lightning, and listening to the stunning and repeated roars of the thunder-cannonade.[54]

An aspect of nature not so welcome was the discovery of two small brown snakes of a coppery tint in his tent on the morning of 20 May. Perhaps by an association of ideas he made Emin a parting present of two mongooses. Stanley was irritated by Emin's less than gracious acceptance, for he complained that in general the animals were a nuisance; they knocked over instruments and spilled ink. They also had a mania for eggs, to which they reacted like dogs to aniseed.[55]

On 23 May the *wangwana* entertained Emin and his men to a farewell dance. Stanley and the Pasha made their final plans for a rendezvous later that year. In eight months' time Stanley's entire force would muster at Fort Bodo, ready for a march to Lake Albert, where Emin would have assembled all his people for the journey to Lake Victoria. All ideas of taking Emin's cache of ivory back via the Congo were laid aside.[56] Stanley made his farewells to Emin, then briefed Jephson, who was to accompany the Pasha, privately. He was to use all his powers of persuasion to convince the garrison to return to Egypt, insinuating that they would not be paid unless they reported to Cairo.[57]

To show his good faith, Emin made Stanley a parting present of 130 Madi carriers from Equatoria. Superficially, the two men parted on good terms.[58] Stanley's force departed for Fort Bodo on the morning of 24 May. But a short way along the road the Madis deserted *en bloc* and fired a shower of arrows at Stanley's men as a Parthian shot. Parke dropped one of them in his tracks with a well-aimed rifle shot, but this simply precipitated the flight of the deserters.[59]

The day had begun badly, but a little later a great silvery-topped mountain peak was pointed out to Stanley. This was the Ruwenzori, the fabled 'Mountains of the Moon', a staple of African legend since the days of Ptolemy. All ancient accounts of the source of the Nile spoke of its headwaters being located around a lake system and a range of snow-capped mountains. Until 1888 no such mountains had been found in the lake areas, though the discovery of Kilimanjaro by the Germans alerted the more perceptive geographers that the old stories might contain a grain of truth.[60] Stanley later claimed that he had succeeded in getting the first recorded sight of the Mountains of the Moon by a European.[61] But in fact Jephson and Parke had seen it first, on 20 April while on their way to Lake Albert with the boat. Parke records in throwaway manner the true first sighting of the Ruwenzori: 'On the march we distinctly saw *snow* on the top of a huge mountain situated to the south-west of our position. As this was a curious and unexpected sight, we halted the caravan to have a good view. Some of the Zanzibaris tried to persuade us that the white covering which decorated this mountain was *salt*; but Jephson and myself were satisfied that it was snow.'[62] But it was ever Stanley's practice to belittle the achievements of other explorers or to downgrade the feats of his fellow travellers. He did not bat an eyelid when Emin wrote to him: 'Allow me to be the first to congratulate you on your most splendid discovery . . . It is wonderful to think how wherever you go, you distance your predecessors by your discoveries.'[63]

Even later that day Stanley was amazed to see Kavalli with 400 warriors hurrying towards them on the road. It transpired that Emin had told the local tribes he was proceeding against Kabba Rega in Bunyoro but, because of the loss of manpower to Stanley, he had to call on their levies to assist him. Stanley was concerned that Emin seemed to be playing straight with nobody: 'His conduct to Kavalli reminds me somewhat of a suspicion that though he is fair in words, he appears to dislike doing what he promises . . . Emin strikes me as being rather heedless or weak in carrying out intentions and promises.'[64]

On 26 May Stanley learned that the chiefs Musiri and Kadongo intended to attack his column between Gavira's and Mazamboni's. This was very bad news, for he had just 111 rifles and ten rounds each to reach Fort Bodo, 125 miles away. To make every shot count, he decided he would have to 'take out' the two hostile chiefs successively: 'it was held by Thomas Carlyle that it was the highest wisdom to know and believe that the greatest thing which necessity ordered to be done was the wisest, the best and the only thing wanted there.'[65] Fortunately at this moment a further eighty-two Madis, sent by Emin to replace the deserters, caught up with him at the foot of the plateau. He decided to rope them together, then untie them when he had placed three or four

hostile tribes between himself and Emin.[66] Next he carried out a
precision raid on Kadongo's village which succeeded perfectly. On the
road to Gavira's after the raid they ran into Mazamboni's brother. Stanley
impressed on him that the expedition expected Mazamboni's aid in
chastising Musiri. Fortune was with Stanley that day. On arrival at Gavira
he found the eponymous chief ready to join in the attack; then, an hour
after sunset, Mazamboni himself came in with 1000 warriors. With this
powerful force, Stanley swooped on Musiri's village. He found another
empty village. Forewarned of the attack, Musiri's men had decamped
and taken their herds. But there was a full granary to reward the
assailants, and Stanley was jubilant that he had brushed yet another
enemy from his flank without any waste or ammunition.[67]

The victory war dance that followed contained the finest music and
the most impressive balletics Stanley had seen so far, and was crowned
by a message of submission from Musiri.[68] After taking detailed notes
on the ethnology of the area, Stanley pressed on to Bodo at a great pace.
After their mauling in April, the Besse people left them well alone. On
4 June they were at the Ituri and the expedition members, some 224
strong (with 101 Madis and 111 wangwana), began to drive across the
river the livestock Mazamboni had given them. Suddenly a large crocodile
appeared and started to make for the swimming cattle, its saurian head
held above the water as if intending to swallow a cow or donkey. Stanley
fired at the marauder and appeared to score a direct hit, for the crocodile
at once sank beneath the waters and troubled them no more.[69]

On 8 June they entered Fort Bodo to find Stairs awaiting them. He
had experienced another nightmare journey back through the rain forest
to fetch the sick and ailing from Ugarrowa's. Only fourteen of the fifty-six
left behind remained after the trek to Fort Bodo. This meant that of the
389 souls Stanley had led away from Yambuya a year before, just 169
remained.[70] Stanley was alarmed at the physical condition of the men
at Bodo. Ahead of them loomed a 1000-mile return march, which only
the fittest could hope to survive. He spent a week handpicking 107
volunteers, each carrying twenty-five days' supply of Indian corn. To cut
down on baggage and loss through sickness, he intended to march to
the Rear Column himself, with no white companions.[71] But first he had
to make sure Fort Bodo was well defended against any conceivable
combination of Manyema and tribesmen. He fortified it strongly and put
Stairs in command. This elevation gave Stairs the boldness to suggest
that perhaps the non-appearance of the Rear Column at Ugarrowa's was
because the Belgians had detained the *Stanley* downriver. Stanley scouted

the suggestion. If anyone was to blame, the prime candidates were Barttelot and Tippu Tip.[72] He recorded his intuition that the entire Emin Pasha relief expedition was ill-starred: 'Evil hangs over this forest as a pall over the dead; it is like a region accursed for crimes; whoever enters within its circle becomes subject to divine wrath.'[73]

The more Stanley brooded over the course of the expedition – and brood he did all the way from Nsabe to Fort Bodo – the less satisfactory everything seemed to him. There could be no denying that splitting the expedition and leaving a Rear Column had been an egregious error. That was bad enough, but the *mésalliance* with Emin seemed even worse the more he pondered it. In the course of their numerous conversations Emin had been unable to hide his disappointment that the 'relief' expedition provided neither a secure route to the coast, nor ammunition and other goods in sufficient quantities to enable him to maintain himself in his province, nor even a guarantee from Egypt or Britain of Equatoria's continuing existence. From Emin's point of view, the arrival of the so-called relief expedition was simply a further drain on his resources, and in its laughably inadequate size and resources it affected adversely his credibility in Equatoria – especially as Stanley refused to show himself in person and unfurl the legendary banner of Bula Matari.

From Stanley's point of view, Emin's lack of grip on his province was deeply worrying. He seemed shot through with weakness and false pride.[74] He also seemed to be labouring under the illusion that the relief expedition had been sent out because of his reputation as a scientist, not because he was perceived as the man who had inherited Gordon's mantle and was heroically holding out against the Mahdi's dervishes. How else explain his curious remark to Casati regarding the specimens he had sent to the British Museum: 'Who would have thought that a bird and a butterfly would have proved so useful to my people?'[75] This sort of thing excited Stanley's particular derision. He had the man of action's contempt for visionaries, dreamers and practitioners of theoretical or non-applied sciences and repeated the familiar charges that the scientific mentality cared more for abstractions than feelings and for 'Man' than flesh and blood human beings.[76] The seeds of the later apocalyptical breakdown in relations between the two men were already there in May 1888.

On 16 June, taking 208 of the 283 men at Fort Bodo, Stanley set out for Yambuya, by now desperately anxious about the fate of the Rear

Column. Stairs and Nelson were left behind to await Emin and Jephson, prior to the general rendezvous on Lake Albert. With Stanley were Hoffmann, 113 *wangwana* and 95 Madi porters. Parke was to accompany them as far as Ipoto to bring back the loads left there.[77] Stanley took such a large body with him to Yambuya on the best-case scenario that the non-appearance of the Rear Column was solely due to Tippu Tip's not having kept his word about the carriers. Even so, he hoped that Barttelot had *some* at least of the promised men, otherwise the full impedimenta of the expedition could not be brought to Lake Albert.[78]

But deep down Stanley was apprehensive that some far worse disaster than Tippu Tip's non-feasance had overtaken the Rear Column: mass desertions, the foundering of steamers, maybe even an attack on Yambuya by Tippu and the Manyema. But he told Parke that whatever he found, he would go no farther west than Yambuya. If Rose Troup, Ward and Bonny had failed to arrive with their loads, that was the end of the matter; in no circumstances would he go down to Stanley Pool after them.[79]

The march back to Ipoto was as gruelling as Stanley had feared, though accomplished in a much shorter time than the outward journey. 'The cries of the leaders indicate the nature of the obstacles to be met through the forest. We hear "red ants afoot!; a stump! spikes! a pitfall to right! a burrow to left! thorns! Those ants! lo, a tripping creeper, ware nettles! A log below! a hole! slippery beneath! Look out for mud! Those ants! red ants on march! Ware ants! a log! spikes below!" '[80]

At Ipoto, reached on 22 June, the healthy, well-fed appearance of Stanley and his men frightened Kilonga-Longa and his Manyema into an apology for their previous behaviour. Nineteen out of thirty of the purloined Remingtons were brought to Stanley, though only fifty of the 3000 cartridges were returned. Stanley had no time to chastise the Manyema so, accepting their apologies, and leaving Parke behind, he plunged into the forest again on 25 June. They ferried across the Ituri in canoes, entered the previous October's wilderness and reached Nelson's starvation camp. Only the hope of meeting Barttelot drove them on through the green hell. But Stanley was pleased with progress. A distance it took them thirteen days to cover in October 1887 when starving they could now cover in four days with full bellies.[81]

At Nelson's camp they dug up the buried stores and ammunition, which were still in good condition. On 29 June they left the river route to take a shorter, inland route, steering south-westerly by compass through the trackless woods.[82] On 2 July they struck the Lenda River and crossed by a tree bridge. But on the other side the pattern of starvation, desertion and sneak attacks by poisoned arrows reasserted itself. The first to drop in their tracks through hunger were the Madi carriers, who had jettisoned their corn supplies to lighten their loads. Other Madis, unused to the forest, were severely wounded in the foot by spikes and had to be carried. Whenever the expedition came upon a plantain plantation they would rush upon it and devour it like locusts.[83]

On 7 July they were tormented by a tropical downpour. As Stanley made camp in the pelting rain 'in the bosom of the untraversed woods' he decided that his decision to strike inland had been a mistake. When next day he found some women who offered to guide him to Ugarrowa's, he jumped at the chance. But after three days' hewing and hacking at the unyielding jungle, they found themselves back at the camp they had occupied three days earlier, exactly where they had encountered their 'guides'. Seeing that they had expended so much energy merely to walk in a circle, the *wangwana* declared the women traitors and called for their execution. Stanley resisted the call, took further bearings and two days later steered them by compass to their old camp on the Ituri opposite Ugarrowa's.[84]

Ugarrowa's itself they found deserted; the chief had returned to Stanley Pool to sell his huge stock of ivory. They were now in desperate straits from hunger. Not only was the village where they had hoped to replenish their supplies an abandoned husk, but when they pressed on to Aruwimi Falls they found that Ugarrowa's men had eaten all the food in the area on their westward trek. By great good fortune the expedition located a single plantain plantation, which gave them the wherewithal for a few more days' marching. Setting out on 16 July, in seven hours they got to the rapids above Navabi Falls and found their old camp at Avamburi landing place. It was full of the skulls of refugees from Ugarrowa's marauders. Since several of the Madi had also joined the ranks of the dead, Stanley halted here for two days and buried the dead in a mass grave.[85]

After a seven-hour march they came on 20 July to camp above Bafaido cataract. Here another Matadi, whose foot was skewered, lay down and took a stoical farewell of his comrades. Finding a store of canoes, Stanley embarked the expedition and started to negotiate the cataract. They made just 2 miles' progress next day, which they spent battling the rapids – which claimed another two men in its boiling waters.[86] A further two *wangwana*, who went absent without leave to look for plantains, were cut down by the local tribesmen.

By 25 July they were at the Bavikai rapids at the mouth of the Nepoko River. Stanley was growing weak from lack of meat, having subsisted for so long on a diet of bananas and plantains. Hearing from the spies he habitually kept among the *mangwana* that the Zanzibaris had been having considerable luck catching and eating goats and chickens, he issued an order that any meat caught must be brought to him. In this way he soon tasted his first fowl for weeks and quickly felt restored in vigour.[87]

But always the horrors of the terrain oppressed him. On 26 July he recorded his impressions in his journal:

> I was never so sensible to the evils of forest marching as on this day
> – my own condition of body being so reduced owing to the mean and
> miserable diet of vegetables on which I was forced to subsist made me
> more than usually sympathetic. At this time there were about 30 naked
> Madis in the last stages of life, their former ebon black was changed
> to an ashy grey hue ... Almost every individual among them is the
> victim of some hideous disease, tumours, scorched backs, foetid
> ulcers, are common, others are afflicted with chronic dysentery, and a
> wretched debility caused by insufficient food ... the ground was rank
> with vegetable corruption, the atmosphere heated, stifling dank, and
> pregnant with the seeds of decay of myriads of insects, leaves, plants,
> twigs and branches.[88]

On 27 July they portaged their canoes over Avugadu rapids and pressed on to Mabengu. Armies of bats swarmed around them at night. By the end of the month they reached Avisibba, scene of the battle with the cannibals with poisoned arrows a year before. They found the remains of their deserters from that time, who had been killed and eaten. A forlorn little girl they happened on spoke of a major engagement between the Avisibba people and Ugarrowa's men, who had passed that way a few days before.[89]

After camping at an island above Nejambi rapids, Stanley ordered the canoes passed through the cataracts on the left-hand channel. Some of the *mangwana* tried getting through on the right-hand branch and were swept away and drowned. The next obstacle was Panga Falls, which also had to be portaged. They struggled to complete the task in pouring rain but by 5 August had a flotilla of nineteen canoes below the falls. They now entered the area where they had encountered the stiffest armed resistance on the outward march. Sure enough, dozens of skirmishes ensued, and the *mangwana* took casualties from poisoned arrows. By now fresh traces of Ugarrowa's men were everywhere in the form of gutted villages and devastated fields. Stanley decided to overtake Ugarrowa by rapid passage on the river. He split his force, gave thirty-five to his chief guide Rashid to take overland, then pressed on with his flotilla of canoes to overtake Ugarrowa at Wasp Rapids.[90]

On 10 August Stanley's men caught up with Ugarrowa's force. It consisted of fifty-seven loaded canoes, and among their number were the couriers Stairs had sent from Ugarrowa's to get news of the Rear Column. Driven back by local resistance at Avisibba with the loss of four of their number, the couriers had sought refuge in the bosom of the Manyema marauders.[91] Ugarrowa himself received Stanley with great kindness and sympathy, and provided him with canoes enough to take his entire party downriver. Stanley waited until Rashid and the land party arrived, then embarked his entire force on 12 August.

Persistent drumming followed them to the Mariri rapids, but the hostiles kept their distance. Floating past their outward land camps, they came to Bunganeta Island. Stanley now recognised all the landmarks and, sixty days out from Fort Bodo and just 90 miles from Yambuya, congratulated himself on his rate of progress. His original estimated time of arrival at Yambuya had been 3 September[92], so he was two weeks ahead of schedule. But still there was neither sign nor word of the Rear Column.

Suddenly, on 17 August, Stanley rounded a bend in the Aruwimi River near the village of Banalya and saw a European-style encampment. Through his field glasses he made out white clothes and a red flag. He ordered his canoeists to paddle with all their might for the shore. As he got closer, Stanley saw that the camp was stockaded. At the gate Bonny suddenly appeared. There followed a dramatic dialogue.

'Well, Bonny, how are you? Where is the Major? Sick, I suppose?'
'The Major is dead, sir.'
'Dead! Good God! How dead? Fever?'
'No, sir, he was shot.'
'By whom?'
'By the Manyema–Tippu Tib's people.'
'Good heavens! Well, where is Jameson?'
'At Stanley Falls.'
'What is he doing there in the name of goodness?'
'He went to obtain more carriers.'
'Well then, where is Mr Ward, or Mr Troup?'

'Mr Ward is at Bangala.'

'Bangala! Bangala! what can he be doing there?'

'Yes, sir, he is at Bangala, and Mr Troup has been invalided home some months ago.'[93]

This bare recital did not do justice to the gruesome facts. Within hours Stanley learned that the Rear Column had been overcome by disaster so complete that he, the superstitious Welshman, was inclined to attribute its collapse to the forces of darkness and the malign work of the Evil One.

· 13 ·

WHEN Stanley marched from Yambuya into the unknown horrors of the Ituri forest on 28 June 1887, he left behind him the latent elements of potential tragedy. The *origo mali* was Leopold. Since the King had not provided a flotilla of boats so that the expedition could proceed together, Stanley was forced to leave behind at Leopoldville the bulk of his ammunition. This meant that once at Yambuya Stanley could not fulfil his side of the bargain with Tippu Tip and give him the gunpowder he required. Since Tippu in turn refused to implement his side of the contract unilaterally, there were not enough porters for the entire expedition to proceed, even though it had already dropped astern two separate detachments, under Rose Troup at Kinshassa, and Ward at Bolobo. Everything would still have worked out well if Stanley had returned as promised in November 1887, or even if he had returned six months later. But his lamentable underestimation of the difficulties he would face in getting to Emin, and the ambiguity and imprecision of the orders he left with Barttelot, combined to produce a disaster which gave new meaning to the cliché about 'The Dark Continent'. Jephson once said of the Emin Pasha expedition: 'the whole story is a very dark one, as dark as any of the many dark stories connected with African travel.' Within this darkness, the experience of the Rear Column counts as the ninth circle of hell.

Yet perhaps Stanley's worst mistake of all was the appointment of Barttelot to command the Rear Column. In retrospect, as Stanley later saw, Barttelot was wholly unsuited by temperament to exercise a difficult command in conditions of maximum stress.[1] Hot-tempered and autocratic, Barttelot could get on with none of the other officers except Jameson. He also continued to smart at the humiliation, as he saw it, of being left behind at Yambuya by Stanley as a punishment.[2] Additionally, he hated and was hated by the *wangwana*. The word 'nigger' was never far from Barttelot's lips and he had actually been reprimanded on this score by Stanley himself. 'He was completely at sea when dealing with the black' was Ward's verdict.[3] Rose Troup put it more strongly: 'It did not take me long to discover that he had an intense hatred for anything in the shape of a black man, for he made no disguise of the fact. His hatred was so marked that I was seized with great misgivings concerning his future dealings with them, more particularly when he would have to handle Tippu Tib's men.'[4]

Six weeks after Stanley's departure, on 14 August, the *Stanley* brought both Ward's and Troup's contingents up to Yambuya, but not before the rear of the Rear Guard had itself come close to disaster. With men packed on her like sardines, the *Stanley* hit a reef while coming upriver. The fore compartments filled with water and had the bulkheads not been watertight, the ship and its complement would have gone to the bottom in seconds. They were a long way from the shore, with a fast current running, but there was no panic, largely because the men did not realise the danger they were in. Troup got the men off in canoes and spent a nervous night aboard himself. Next day the canoes had to take off 150 loads before the *Stanley* got off the sandbank; then three days were spent fitting a new plate.[5]

Once the detachments were united at Yambuya, Barttelot had to face the fact that he had under his command the dregs of the expedition: the malingerers, skrimshankers, troublemakers and the genuinely sick; Stanley had taken the manpower's gold and left the dross. Out of 271 men at Yambuya, perhaps 165 were in a condition for porterage. In camp were 660 loads, 493 of which had been brought up by Troup. There were four times as many loads as men, so real progress was only possible when Tippu Tip sent his bearers. By the time the *Stanley* arrived, there was no sign of them.[6]

Stanley had told Barttelot he would return in November. The Major's wisest course, then, was to sit tight and wait for the leader to return. But his force was beset by illness and food shortages – the only readily available source of nutrition was manioc, which grew in abundance around the camp. There was a danger that inactivity and inanition would finish off the Rear Guard before Stanley returned. Stanley *had* permitted Barttelot to follow in his footsteps if Tippu Tip supplied *all* 600 of the promised porters. If he merely supplied *some*, he had left it open to Barttelot to make a very slow advance using relays of porters. Barttelot's real problem was to decide how long he should wait for Tippu to supply the promised men.

These, then, were the adverse conditions confronting the Rear Column. They were condemned to enforced idleness and food shortages, they were beset by sickness and a hostile environment, uncertain both of Stanley's return and Tippu's intentions. In addition, they were commanded by a racialist martinet, who was at daggers drawn with most of his officers, and who was a harsh and unyielding disciplinarian. The mixture was inherently combustible.

A further decline in their fortunes became apparent the day after the arrival of the *Stanley* when the presence of a force of Manyema in close vicinity to the stockaded camp became known. These Manyema were raiders and slavers, operating independently of Tippu Tip. They were a threat to the Rear Column, not so much directly as because they diverted the precious supplies of fish, palm oil and other foodstuffs from the local villages to their own camp and threatened the locals with death if they traded with the expedition instead. Barttelot interviewed the headman of these Manyema, who told him that Tippu Tip had already sent the promised 500 porters to Yambuya, but that opposition from hostile tribesmen had first detained, then finally dispersed, them when their gunpowder ran out.[7]

Barttelot at once decided to send Jameson and Ward to consult with Tippu Tip at Stanley Falls. After a five-day journey they arrived, were treated with conspicuous friendliness by Tippu, and sent on their way with a promise that he would let them have more men, though possibly not as many as in the original party. He sent back his nephew Selim bin Mohammed to take over as chief of the Manyema encampment, so that relations between the two camps could be conducted through official channels.

The two men returned, confident that the porters would soon be with them. Ward collapsed with an attack of dysentery that kept him *hors de combat* for six weeks, to Barttelot's disgust. He noted in his diary: 'Ward a little better, he ain't much of a chap.'[8] Barttelot hated Ward for his intellectual superiority and his genuine feeling for, and ability to get on with, the Africans *he* so detested.

But as the weeks went by, and no carriers arrived from Stanley Falls, Barttelot began to fret over the presence of the nearby Manyema. Not only were they a threat to his food supplies and a standing reproach to him – since they massacred the locals with impunity and when these appealed to him for protection, Barttelot found himself frustrated and impotent, bound by Stanley's 'non-intervention' instructions – but their free and easy lifestyle tempted the *wangwana* to desertion. In response Barttelot's discipline became more and more draconian.

A never-ending cycle of brutality began. Two Zanzibari deserters, Bartholomew and Msa, were given 150 and 100 lashes respectively. What this meant can be gauged from Glave's description of a Congo flogging:

The *chicotte* of raw hippo hide, especially a new one, trimmed like a corkscrew, with edges like knife-blades, and as hard as wood, is a terrible weapon, and a few blows bring blood; not more than 25 blows should be given unless the offence is very serious. Though we persuade ourselves that the African's skin is very tough, it needs an extraordinary constitution to withstand the terrible punishment of 100 blows; generally the victim is in a state of insensibility after 25 or 30 blows. At the first blow he yells abominably; then quiets down, and is a mere groaning, quivering body till the operation is over, when the culprit stumbles away, often with gashes which will endure a lifetime ... I conscientiously believe that a man who receives 100 blows is often nearly killed, and has his spirit broken for life.[9]

Having survived this ordeal, the two men deserted again, were recaptured, and sentenced to further punishment. Msa received 150 lashes, and Bartholomew was given the 'lenient' punishment of 75 strokes, since he was still tender from the previous flogging. Next it was the turn of the Sudanese to taste Barttelot's wrath. The theft of a goat led to the arrest of the Sudanese soldier Burgari Mohammed. He received 150 strokes then, since he had tried to implicate another man, was fined nine months' pay and sentenced to another flogging as soon as he had recovered from the first one. Until then he had to walk up and down in the sun every day in chains. Burgari escaped, was recaptured, and tried for desertion. The death penalty was proposed. Jameson and Troup argued against this, but Ward and Bonny were for it, so the luckless Sudanese was executed by firing squad.[10]

An even more notorious instance of brutality concerned the *mangwana* interpreter John Henry, who made the mistake of stealing Barttelot's revolver. Barttelot at once sentenced him to be shot, but the *mangwana* threatened to desert in a body if the execution was carried out. After a furious altercation in which Barttelot fumed, blustered and threatened the Zanzibaris with excommunication from their native island, he 'commuted' the sentence to 300 lashes. John Henry died from the effects of the savage flogging two days later.[11]

Troup, Ward and Jameson were by and large civilised and compassionate men, but Barttelot had a rival for brutality in Bonny. Shortly after Stanley returned to Banlaya, Stanley inspected the victim of one of Bonny's 150-lashes sentences, for theft. One of the sick was emitting a noisome foetor and Stanley asked to see the man's 'ulcer'. He lifted his loin cloth for an answer and 'the sight was enough to sicken a hyena, even. Never in my life have I seen anything so awful. The seating parts or buttocks were two deep hollows in which maggots swarmed and a saucer might easily have been put into either hollow.'[12]

At the beginning of October, with Ward still ill and Bonny down with fever, Barttelot decided on another visit to Stanley Falls. He took Troup with him to try to beard Tippu Tip in his lair. Tippu told them that local manpower was now exhausted on his own slaving and ivory expeditions; the porters would have to come from Kasongo, in the heartland of Tippu's 'empire', a month's journey upriver towards Nyangwe.[13] At the beginning of November the two white men returned to Yambuya with empty hands, save for a herd of goats and flock of chickens. To keep up the pressure, Barttelot ordered the recently recovered Ward up to Stanley Falls to complain about the behaviour of the local Manyema. He found that Tippu had already departed for Kasongo, ostensibly to find the porters.[14]

By December the Yambuya camp of the Rear Column was a shambles. The white men took it in turns to succumb to rheumatism, fever and biliousness. Thirty-one *wangwana* had already died of malnutrition and scurvy and the effects of eating raw or improperly cooked manioc. The manioc tuber contains a form of cyanide, and only careful preparation and cooking can eliminate the poison. The tired and listless *wangwana* had no time for such niceties. The result was giddiness, fainting, stomach cramps and nausea in the short term; in the long run the results were degeneration of nervous tissue, paralysis of the optic nerve and blindness.[15] Salim bin Rashid, one of Stanley's veterans, confirmed that it was the unremitting diet of manioc that helped to explain why Stanley found only sixty out of 271 alive when he returned to Yambuya in August 1888. 'There is another thing I wished to say and that is, we have been wondering why we who belong to the continent should die and the white men who are strangers to it should live. When we were on the Congo and other journeys, it was the white men who died and not we. Now, it is we who die, a hundred blacks to one white. No, master, the cause of death is in the food. The white men had meat of goat and fowl and fish and lived, and we who had nothing but manioc died.'[16]

Christmas passed and New Year 1888 dawned, and still no news from Stanley. Barttelot was now beside himself with anxiety and frustration. He discussed the possibility of advancing without *any* of Tippu Tip's porters, but Rose Troup, the expedition's transport specialist, advised him that with their existing manpower it would take twelve days to advance 4 miles. For want of anything better to do, Barttelot decided on a fourth excursion to Stanley Falls. This time he took Jameson and the Syrian interpreter Assad Farran with him. In mid-February 1888 they reached Stanley Falls to find that Tippu Tip was still absent in Kasongo. Barttelot decided to send Jameson downriver to find him, this time with an additional request for 400 fighting men.[17]

Back at Yambuya in March 1888 Barttelot revealed the thinking behind the request for fighting men. He now intended to take a flying column in search of Stanley, accompanied by Tippu Tip's warriors, while the rest of the Rear Column retired under Rose Troup to Stanley Falls station.[18] The snag was that this was directly contrary to Stanley's orders. So Barttelot decided to send Ward down to the Atlantic coast to cable the relief committee for further instructions. This was a peculiarly eccentric decision, both because whatever the committee replied it would not materially affect the basic problems he confronted at Yambuya and because, if his own plans worked out, he would anyway not be there to receive the answer telegraphed to Ward. The official Barttelot explanation was that the committee might have news of Stanley from the Zanzibar coast and might want to withdraw the entire expedition.[19] The real reason for Barttelot's action was pathological.

By spring of 1888 there were clear signs that the stress of inactivity and uncertainty at Yambuya was beginning to unhinge Barttelot. Without Ward and Jameson to guide him, he lurched into pointless, angry confrontations with Selim Mohammed and the Manyema. Troup's sickness began to exasperate him: 'Troup, sick as per usual' was a typical diary entry. In April a rip-roaring row between Troup and Barttelot led to Troup's retiring to his tent for six weeks in an Achilles-like sulk. Bonny described the confrontation: 'There was a big row between Barttelot and Troup, each accusing the other of certain things. Barttelot charged Troup with being a drunkard and having been in police courts, etc., Troup charging Barttelot with having been kicked out of the Egyptian army, etc. ... Barttelot ordered Troup to leave the camp. Troup said, "You are not head of this expedition." '[20]

Another example of Barttelot's unbalanced mental state was his decision to send all Stanley's effects downriver as part of the process of
freeing the would-be 'flying column' from unnecessary baggage. Not
only did Barttelot send down to Bangala Stanley's spare sets of compasses
and maps and the provisions which had been hauled up from the Atlantic
at such cost: he even sent down Stanley's spare clothes and his favourite
pair of trousers![21]

But worst of all examples of Barttelot's paranoia was his increasing
preoccupation with poison. He became obsessed with the fact that all
five of Stanley's white comrades on his first two expeditions had perished
and began to concoct a theory that Stanley had deliberately made away
with them. One day Barttelot was discussing the drowning of Frank
Pocock with Bonny. ' "The Major asked me . . . if I did not think you
to be a poisoner like Palmer of Rugeley and I asked why. 'It is odd, you
know,' he said, 'that not one of his white companions ever returned
home from his expedition, and I suspect that he did away with them to
hide the truth.' " '[22] The reflection led by an association of ideas to the
notion of getting rid of his chief tormentor among the Manyema.
Barttelot told Bonny one day: 'I want to poison that nigger Selim bin
Mohammed.' Bonny was so alarmed at this that he took all dangerous
drugs out of his medicine chest and hid them.[23]

This is the context in which Barttelot's extraordinary order to Ward
should be seen. The nearest place from which a cable could be sent to
the Emin Pasha relief committee was 1500 miles away: the Portuguese
posts of Sao Thome or St Paul de Loanda. The journey there was
arduous and, on the first stretch to Bangala, perilous since the route lay
through unsubdued areas. It is not stretching a point to imagine that
Barttelot may genuinely have hoped Ward would not survive. There
seems to have been a peculiar animus by Barttelot towards Ward. Bonny
claimed that Jameson inflamed the Major against Ward by hinting to
him that Ward had embezzled brass rods for his personal profit, but the
true evil genius of this whispering campaign is likely to have been Bonny
himself.[24]

But whatever the genesis of Barttelot's paranoia and hatred, there
could be no mistaking its reality. Four days after setting out, Ward was
overtaken at the Lomami River settlement by an extraordinary letter
from Barttelot, which read as follows: 'WARD – I am sending this to warn
you to be very careful in the manner you behave below – I mean as
regards pecuniary matters. I shall require at your hands a receipted bill
for everything you spend, and should you be unable to purchase the

champagne and the watch, you will not draw that £20. The slightest attempt at any nonsense I shall be down upon you for. I have given you a position of trust, so see that you do not abuse it. You will send me a receipt of this letter. EDMUND M. BARTTELOT, Major.' Ward replied, 'Consider letter gross insult and will demand explanation and satisfaction on my return.'[25]

Despite the insult, Ward behaved heroically. The journey downriver was far the worst in his three and a half years' Congo service: there were heavy thunderstorms every day, he had to canoe on rivers engorged with rain and trek through grass 18–20 feet high. When he got to St Paul de Loanda and cabled the EPRE committee, the answer came back, predictably: obey Stanley's orders.[26]

Ward then hastened to return. He was at Stanley Pool on 11 June, caught the steamer *En Avant* for the upriver journey and on 3 July met Rose Troup coming downriver, on his way home after being manoeuvred by Barttelot into requesting sick leave. The captain of Troup's ship handed Ward another amazing missive from Barttelot: 'SIR – On arrival at Bangala you will report yourself to the chief of the station, and take over the stores from him belonging to the Expedition. You will remain at Bangala till you receive orders from the Committee concerning yourself and the loads . . . On no account will you leave Bangala while you remain in the service of the Expedition, till you receive orders from home . . . Should you bring a telegram of recall for me, you will make arrangements with the chief of Bangala to forward it to the Falls, where a messenger awaits it. You will not, however, send any other message after me, nor will you on any account leave Bangala station unless you receive orders to that effect from the Committee – EDMUND M. BARTTELOT'[27] That was effectively the end of the Emin Pasha expedition for Herbert Ward.[28]

Barttelot's friend Jameson meanwhile had a superficially more placid journey, to see Tippu Tip in Kasongo, but the consequences were even more sensational than Ward's abortive journey. Jameson got a very warm welcome from Tippu, for he was one of the few Europeans the Arab really liked, by contrast with Barttelot, whom he detested cordially, even more so than he did Stanley.[29] In fact Tippu even confided in Jameson that, as far as he was concerned, his contract to supply carriers was with Stanley, not Barttelot, therefore the Major had nothing to do with the matter. Another of Tippu's grievances, extensively aired during the time at Kasongo, was that the Belgians had sent no representatives or 'residents' to visit him at Stanley Falls with his insignia of office; other wealthy Arabs, such as Said bin Habib, openly scoffed at this 'gubernatorial office' that provided Tippu with no visible signs of authority and at the Belgians who did not even deign to send a steamer to visit their 'governor'.[30]

At last, on 5 May 1888, Tippu started back to Stanley Falls with his good friend Jameson, to see if he could at last get the Rear Column under way. But at Riba-Riba, an Arab settlement half-way to Stanley Falls, an event occurred that would ever afterwards besmirch the memory of the Emin Pasha expedition. The date was 11 May. Tippu and Jameson had been discussing cannibalism, and Jameson ventured to suggest that the whole idea was an invention, a 'traveller's tale' or tall story. Tippu looked solemn and reiterated that the practice was a daily reality. The sequel is described by Jameson:

He then said something to an Arab called Ali seated next to him, who turned round to me and said, 'Give me a bit of cloth and see.' I sent my boy for six handkerchiefs, thinking it was all a joke, and that they were not in earnest, but presently a man appeared, leading a young girl of about ten years old by the hand, and then I witnessed the most horribly sickening sight I am ever likely to see in my life. He plunged a knife quickly into her breast twice, and she fell on her face, turning over on her side. Three men then ran forward, and began to cut up the body of the girl; finally her head was cut off, and not a particle remained, each man taking his piece away down to the river to wash it. The most extraordinary thing was that the girl never uttered a sound, nor struggled until she fell. Until the last moment, I could not believe that they were in earnest. I have heard many stories of this kind since I have been in this country, but never could believe them, and I would never have been such a beast as to witness this, but that I could not bring myself to believe that it was anything save a ruse to get money out of me, until the last moment.

The girl was a slave captured from a village close to this town, and the cannibals were Wacusu slaves, and natives of this place, called Mculusi. When I went home I tried to make some small sketches of the scene while still fresh in my memory, not that it is ever likely to fade from it. No one here seemed to be in the least astonished at it.[31]

Meanwhile at Yambuya, Barttelot's anxiety and paranoia was increasing daily. He became convinced that the Manyema under Selim bin Mohammed were planning an attack on Yambuya. His diary for early April is peppered with anxious remarks: 'Salem means mischief.' 'Things look black.' 'Perhaps my days are numbered.'[32] He decided on yet another visit to Stanley Falls, this time to enlist the help of Tippu's deputy Bwana Nzige in the 'coming conflict' with Selim. Nzige assured him he would recall Selim, if that would put his mind at rest. Twenty-four hours later Barttelot set out on the return journey. On arrival he found there had been no Arab attack nor any serious pretence of one. When Selim came to tell him that he had been recalled, even this clear evidence of Arab good faith did not satisfy Barttelot. Like all in the grip of paranoid delusion, he simply used evidence contrary to his illusory thesis as inverted supports for the initial paranoia. Hence: 'Salem Mohammed came to see me, and told me he was going away down river . . . this may be a blind. I have sent men out to watch him.'[33]

It is worth stressing the absurdity of Barttelot's fears. If either Tippu or Selim had wished to destroy the Rear Guard encampment at Yambuya, they could have done so easily. Tippu Tip later reacted with anger to the suggestion that he had deliberately sabotaged the Rear Column. He pointed out that if he had so wished, he could have wiped out the entire expedition, Stanley included; it was not his policy to hinder someone he disliked, he simply killed them.[34]

On 8 May another dimension was added to the complex relationships between the Arabs at Stanley Falls and the Europeans at Yambuya. The Belgians finally put in an appearance in the shape of the steamer *AIA*, conveying Lt. Van Kerkhoven and the engineer Werner, together with the escort Ward had left at Bangala. It was almost as though the Congo State had exercised telepathy and picked up Tippu Tip's bitter complaints to Jameson.[35] After three days at Yambuya, *AIA* steamed off to Stanley Falls. A few days later Barttelot too decided to make yet another visit to the Falls, to await Jameson's return. On 22 May Tippu Tip and Jameson arrived to find the Major and Van Kerkhoven ready to talk serious business.

Tippu Tip at once informed Barttelot that he could let him have 400 men, not the 800 originally promised, provided they were not asked to carry loads heavier than 40 pounds per man. This was a shock to Barttelot, but next day all was explained. The Belgians were attempting to divert the spread of Tippu's sphere of influence towards Bangala by putting him in the picture about the Mobangi-Welle River, allegedly rich in ivory. Tippu played both sides against the middle. He told Barttelot that Belgian pressure meant he would have to detach half of the 800 porters for use in this expansion towards the north. But he told Van Kerkhoven that he saw right through the Belgian's game. He would not be distracted from his own plans to pacify the Congo as far down as Bangala. The discussions between the Belgian and the Arab became strained, then heated, until by 7 June word was all over the Falls that there had been the most frightful row between Tippu and Van Kerkhoven. Tippu declared that as inheritor of the Sultan's mantle he intended effective occupation of the Upper Congo territories. Van Kerkhoven replied that he would shoot any man of Tippu's who ventured near Bangala.[36]

Faced with these cross-cutting rhythms, Barttelot made one of his few sensible decisions and accepted that the 400 porters represented all that he could hope to get from Tippu Tip. He and Jameson cut across country with Muni Somai, the Manyema headman who was to lead the porters into the Ituri for them. They had contracted him for £1000 and guaranteed the sum personally, in the case the EPRE committee raised a cavil. Tippu Tip and Van Kerkhoven made a stately progress to Yambuya (which the Arab had not yet visited) on the *AIA*. On the way they met the *Stanley*, bringing the Belgian 'resident' for Stanley Falls, M. Haneuse. The *Stanley* then followed them up the Aruwimi to Yambuya. The Belgian purpose in sending Haneuse was not to boost Tippu's status at the Falls and to support him against recalcitrant Arab rivals; it was simply to spy on him, against the day Leopold was ready for his decisive military move.[37]

Once at Yambuya Barttelot and Jameson put in a week's strenuous labour to make all ready for the advance into the Ituri. But Barttelot's problems with Tippu Tip were not over yet. On 7 June, when the expedition was all but ready to depart, Tippu examined the loads for the Manyema and found them a few pounds overweight (the heaviest was 45 pounds). He refused to allow the bearers to proceed unless the loads were repacked at the agreed weight of 40 pounds. This apparent nitpicking was the Arab's revenge for Barttelot's failure to complete his side of Stanley's agreement. He did indeed hand over the promised gunpowder, but the ammunition caps were found to be 80 per cent faulty. Not only could they not be delivered to Tippu; Jameson and Barttelot actually had to buy 40,000 new ones from the Arab![38]

At this eleventh-hour intervention from Tippu, all Barttelot's pent-up wrath burst forth. Vangele witnessed the sequel. He described Barttelot as raging at Tippu Tip like the successive waves of the sea battering at a storm-tossed ship. Barttelot's behaviour was brutal and arrogant. Tippu Tip blinked his eyes nervously but behaved correctly.[39] Apparently, though, he had ordered his men to shoot the Major if he laid hands on him. All Barttelot's rage was in vain. Tippu insisted that the loads be dismantled and repacked, even though this meant in many cases that airtight tins of powder and cartridges had to be opened and soldered up again.[40] But finally all was completed to general satisfaction. On Monday 11 June, Barttelot, Bonny and Jameson marched out of Yambuya in Stanley's tracks, almost a year after his departure. With them went twenty-two Sudanese, 115 *wangwana*, 430 Manyema and 150 camp followers (women and slaves).[41]

One final action Barttelot took before leaving. Jameson had complained to him that Assad Farran, the Syrian interpreter, was a venal man of no fixed loyalties. Barttelot dismissed him on the grounds that he was utterly useless and a valetudinarian. He made Assad sign a statement in which he swore not to divulge any information about the expedition. but Barttelot and Jameson had unknowingly made a very powerful enemy, a man who in the future was to contribute materially to sustaining Stanley's version of the Rear Guard disaster against that of its chief and second-in-command.

One of the pressures contributing to Barttelot's eventual mental breakdown was the apprehension that Stanley and the entire Advance Column had perished. When a whole year passed without anything being heard of Stanley by the outside world, European opinion began to share Barttelot's fears. Many newspapers confidently reported that Stanley was dead.[42] The fear was that he had been lured to his death by the Arabs; his previous experience would not have made him proof against such perfidy, since it was all with African kings, not slavers.[43] This canard led to a fully-fledged debate between the leading Africanists on Stanley's likely fate. The Egyptian government felt convinced that he was dead.[44] Joseph Thomson, the man passed over for leadership of the expedition, declared: 'I unhesitatingly express my conviction that he and his entire party have been annihilated to the west of the Albert Nyanza,' (doubtless the wish was father to the thought).[45] Circumstantial evidence of Stanley's death seemed provided by reports that the Mahdists had taken white men prisoner, and that some Snider rifles had been captured, until someone pointed out that Stanley had taken no Sniders on this expedition, only Remingtons and Winchesters.[46] Joseph Thomson proceeded to trump his own ace by saying that Stanley could not have been taken prisoner by the Mahdists, since he had already been massacred in the Ituri forest.[47]

These fears were not shared by the more thoughtful British analysts. Harry Johnston thought that the explanation was that opposition from forest tribes had turned Stanley northward into the Upper Welle.[48] Cameron too was convinced Stanley was still alive, as were de Winton, Mackinnon and the other members of the EPRE committee.[49] In France official pessimism was tempered by Brazza's view that Stanley had gone to the White Nile and was making treaties there.[50] But the greatest consensus in favour of Stanley's survival was found among Austrian and German geographers and explorers, all of whom, except for Peters, thought he was safe. Wissmann was all along confident that Stanley was not dead, on the grounds that if he was, some news of this would already have surfaced in Africa.[51] The man in the best position to know the likely truth, Rose Troup, now returning convalescent from the Congo, hinted that he could say a lot, had he not been gagged by the terms of the engagement of the EPRE officers, which forbade them to utter on the subject until six months after Stanley had published his own account. He did, however, allow himself to comment that he was too much of a believer in Stanley's pluck, willpower and, above all, luck, to think that he had perished. But he added ominously – a hint of the controversies to come – 'Though I am not afraid for Stanley, I am for his fellow white men. Somehow or other, Stanley has got a singular knack of always coming back alone.'[52]

But the uncertainty that was entertained by everybody in Europe, including Leopold and Queen Victoria,[53] soon led to a conviction that a second Emin Pasha relief expedition should be sent out. The Germans scented a golden opportunity to extend their sphere of interest westward to Lake Albert, and a German expedition was prepared under Peters and Wissmann.[54] The Belgian explorer Jacques Becker also laid plans for a journey to the Congo to learn what had happened to Stanley; Leopold meanwhile concluded that his best hope of furthering his Congo interests lay in throwing in his lot with the German expedition.[55] All this activity caused a flurry in London. Sir Samuel Baker warned of the blow to British prestige if the Germans finally succeeded in relieving Emin, and talk arose of a second British Emin relief expedition under Joseph Thomson, routed through Masailand.[56]

But already in the columns of the British press a backlash against the whole idea of the Emin Pasha relief expedition and ventures like it was beginning to be discernible. The pointlessness of relieving someone who had constantly asserted that he did not wish to be relieved, and the baneful indirect consequences of opening up further segments of Africa to the slave traders, were frequently stressed.[57] De Winton and the EPRE committee were increasingly forced on to the defensive. De Winton wrote many letters to *The Times* to defend the Congo itinerary and to divert attention towards the threat from the Peters/Wissmann expedition: 'what use is the German expedition? Is another nation to reap the harvest sown with British blood and British treasure?'[58]

The tone of the criticisms was increasingly severe. The *Cork Examiner* saw the Emin expedition as simply an excuse for gigantic plunder.[59] In 1889 anxiety about the eventual fate of the expedition and criticism of it continued, especially when Stanley's first despatches began to be received.[60] Stanley's admission that he had hanged men caused as much furore as the Bumbire incident a dozen years before, and again the query arose, under what authority or sanction of international law Stanley had ordered these executions.[61] Others criticised the tone of his despatches: ' "He has sustained heavy losses of men" – as though he and not the poor fellows themselves deserved pity on account of their deaths.'[62] A devastatingly cynical article appeared in the London press in April 1889:

It is impossible not to admire Mr Stanley's pluck and endurance. But I venture to question the use of marches like his into the interior of Africa. The plea was that Emin Pasha wished to be relieved. He does not want to be. He is only desirous to be left alone. What benefit, then, is it to the cause of civilisation that a white man should hire a vast number of carriers and undertake an expedition, in which half of them die of fatigue, and some are hanged for wishing to desert, in order to force his way through tribes by burning their villages and shooting them? The net result seems to be that it has been discovered that one lake is not so deep as it was a hundred years ago, that another lake lies to the south of the first, that there is a very dense forest, mainly inhabited by dwarfs, on the road to these lakes, and that somewhere in the vicinity of this forest there is a high mountain (hitherto unknown), the top of which is covered with snow. All this is, no doubt, interesting. But is it worth impressing carriers who die of fatigue or are hanged, shooting dwarfs, and destroying villages? I should like to hear a carrier or a dwarf on the subject.[63]

Yet all this was mild beside the controversy over Barttelot's brutality which broke out when Assad Farran, the Syrian interpreter dismissed by the Major as 'quite useless', arrived in Hull on 18 September 1888. His detailed allegations against Barttelot created a sensation. He also told the story of Jameson's sketching the cannibal feast.[64] Immediately the Barttelot family, the EPRE committee and other interested parties sprang into action to deny the allegations and state that they were actuated merely by spite and hatred because Barttelot had dismissed Farran.[65] In Paris Brazza proposed to deal with the issue by racial prejudice. No one should take Farran's word for anything, he declared, as he was a Syrian: 'They are, as a rule, an arrogant, offensive lot, with very little breeding and even less probity.' As for Jameson's having taken part in a cannibal feast, that was a bagatelle; these were common on the Congo and in any case how was he supposed to stop it?[66]

Pressure was brought on Assad Farran by Burdett-Coutts of the EPRE to retract his remarks. It was pointed out to him that in his contract was an article stating that he would forfeit six months' pay if he criticised any of the expedition's leaders. Since Farran arrived without a shirt on his back, it did not take much persuading to get him to withdraw his charges. The letter of retraction read as follows: 'I, Assad Farran, late interpreter with the Emin Pasha relief expedition, declare that the alleged severities towards his men of which Major Barttelot has been accused were an exercise of discipline which was rendered absolutely necessary, in the interests of the expedition, by the circumstances in which Major Barttelot was placed at the camp at Yambuya, and by the mutinous conduct of his men.'[67]

This 'confession' at once caused uproar in the press. The *Liverpool Echo* wanted to know whether money had changed hands to exact this retraction, and whether Farran had been sufficiently independent to speak the truth. It also pointed up the absurdity of the EPRE committee's actions. If Farran was a pathological liar, as the Barttelot family alleged, what was the point or value in Burdett-Coutts's getting him to retract and sign a fresh statement, one so obviously drafted by the said Burdett-Coutts?[68] The *Star* pointed out that all the way from Hull to London Farran had talked most freely about Barttelot's barbarities; only under threats from the EPRE committee did his story change. It expressed its impatience with the rhodomontade about 'absolutely necessary discipline'. The only serious question was whether Barttelot had in fact behaved in the barbarous way Farran charged.[69] But the greatest absurdity in the committee's actions was pointed out by a correspondent in *Pall Mall*. Having quoted the letter of retraction, the writer went on: 'The Committee of the Emin Pasha Relief Expedition have not, it is clear, much sense of humour . . . For a native interpreter, who was dismissed by Major Barttelot as an "utterly useless" and "very inferior" fellow,

Assad Farran has a very pretty English style, and a really gratifying sense of English "discipline".[70]

As yet, however, the Emin expedition was merely controversial, not notorious. The row over Barttelot's severities and Jameson's actions, the question marks over Stanley's judgement or the motives of the expedition's authors raised in 1888–9 were but the advance ripples of a *tsunami* of excoriation that would overwhelm Stanley and his collaborators in 1890.

When Barttelot marched out of Yambuya on 11 June, he was not so acutely aware as Jameson that he was in for big problems with the Manyema.The particular individuals Tippu Tip had got together were insufficiently socialised in Arab ways, so that neither Tippu himself nor the headman actually on the march, Muni Somai, had much control over them. They were utterly unsuitable for the role Barttelot had cast them in. They found the work uncongenial, refused to move on for days on end, and generally took the line that they would proceed only on their own terms. There was considerable friction between the Manyema and the *wangwana*. The *wangwana* despised them for carrying lesser loads, but feared their numbers and their cannibalism. Soon the march was wracked with familiar problems: there were fights between the two factions of carriers, the trackers lost their way, there were threats against the lives of the Europeans, and a smallpox epidemic broke out. On the fourth day of the march fourteen of the *wangwana* deserted with twelve of the most precious loads.

By this time Barttelot was, by common consent, no longer truly responsible for his actions.[71] He decided to return to Stanley Falls (yet again!) to acquire chains with which to fetter the runaways and deserters. After a 300-mile trip in eight days Barttelot reappeared at the Falls to Tippu's stupefaction. He obtained the chains and in addition requested and received sixty-eight replacement porters.[72] By 15 July he was back with his main column at Banalya, where Bonny (acting commander) had brought it to camp. Jameson was still five days in the rear with the tardy Manyema.

Barttelot now entered a period of steep mental decline. When his boy servant Soudi tried to desert, the Major kicked him and beat him so badly that the boy died of his injuries. He took to going about the camp with a pointed stick, jabbing and poking the men with it. Bonny relates that he actually beat a man to death with it. He took to facing out the recalcitrant Manyema by staring at them and showing his big front teeth in a hideous rictus; on one occasion a Manyema woman annoyed him, so he bit her in the shoulder.[73] On 17 July Manyema began to celebrate the Festival of the Moon and began firing their guns off wildly. One of the shots narrowly missed Barttelot and the Major chose to take the incident as an assassination attempt. He caught the offender and punished him severely.

At about 10 p.m. on 18 July an insistent drumming began, accompanied by the noise of singing. Barttelot sent his boy to stop the noise. It ceased. But early on the morning of the 19th a Manyema woman started beating a drum and singing. This time the Major sent some Sudanese out to quell the disturbance. Hearing firing commence, Barttelot got out of bed and snatched up his revolver, telling all within earshot that he would shoot the first man he found firing. Barttelot pushed his way through the crowds of Manyema to where the offending woman was beating the drum and singing. He ordered her to stop. Just then a shot rang out from a loophole in a house opposite, occupied by Sanga, the husband of the woman. The bullet passed through Barttelot's heart; death was instantaneous.[74]

From the screaming that ensued, Bonny feared a general massacre was imminent. But when the noise ceased, he ventured out, saw what had happened, examined the corpse and buried it in the forest, after sewing the body in a blanket. Then he sent a note to Jameson to tell him what had occurred.[75] Jameson hurried up to Banalya, made a note of the goods still unlooted – for Sudanese, *wangwana* and Manyema alike had gone on the rampage in the confusion after the murder – then hurried to Stanley Falls to request help in the apprehension of Sanga.

Uncertain what to do next, once at the Falls Jameson consulted his friend Tippu. To his amazement, Tippu jumped out of his chair and said dramatically: 'Give me £20,000 and I and my people will go with you, find Mr Stanley, and relieve Emin Bey.'[76] This was a demand so steep as to amount almost to extortion, but as Jameson saw it he had little option. Without the Manyema the expedition could not go forward, but only Tippu Tip in person could overawe them and get them to do their duty. Jameson agreed to the sum in principle, but decided to descend to Bangala to see whether the committee's telegram to Ward contained any guidance or leeway that might enable him to agree to the sum requested without footing the bill himself.[77]

First, however, he had to attend the trial of Sanga. Caught hiding in the forest, Sanga was conveyed to Stanley Falls for trial. The hearing took place on 7 August before a tribunal consisting of Tippu Tip, M. Haneuse, M. Baert and two other minor Belgian functionaries. After Jameson's evidence, there was little defence Sanga could mount. Tippu had advised Sanga that his only chance was to plead that there had been a general Manyema conspiracy to assassinate Barttelot, and that he had been assigned to carry out the deed.[78] Sanga, however, chose to stick to the truth: that he had shot the Major because he seemed to be menacing his wife. The court found him guilty by unanimous verdict and he was taken out and executed by firing squad.

Jameson now prepared to depart for Bangala. But the Belgians, who had heard of Tippu Tip's plans to accompany the expedition to Equatoria, began to think of their own insecure position if he departed, and protested that as governor of the Falls he had a duty not to leave his post; his contract with Stanley was to supply the expedition with porters, not go on it himself. They insisted that if Jameson found no positive instructions at Bangala, he would have to descend to Banana to cable Brussels for Tippu's furlough.[79]

Tippu Tip was ever afterwards convinced that the Belgians had poisoned Jameson to ensure that such permission could never be forthcoming. There is certainly something mysterious about Jameson's last days. He left Stanley Falls in good health on 9 August and on the 17th he died in Ward's arms at Bangala, officially from haematuric fever.[80] The other possibility is that Jameson, learning at the Falls that Assad Farran's tale about the cannibal feast was all over the Congo and would soon be the talk of Europe, simply lost the will to live. But his sudden death added yet another strange twist to he already macabre story of the Rear Column.

Stanley certainly perceived it in this light. Later he was to reflect on the occult 'synchronicity' of the date 17 August 1888 – for on that day he arrived at Banalya to discover the chaotic world of the Rear Column, Jameson died at Bangala, while far away in Equatoria Emin and Jephson were taken prisoner by the Mahdists. As he recorded with the superstitious awe of the true Celt: 'This is all very uncanny if you think of it. There is a supernatural *diablerie* operating which surpasses the conception and attainment of a mortal man.'[81]

· 14 ·

STANLEY'S immediate reaction to the guilt he felt when Bonny recounted the sombre tale of the Rear Column was to claim that Barttelot was always supposed to follow him as soon as possible and he could not make out why this had not happened. Why, he asked, had Barttelot only started in June 1888 on a journey he should have begun in August 1887? The seven visits to Stanley Falls by Barttelot and his comrades accounted for 1200 miles of travelling which could have been spent on forward marching.[1] To Jameson (now dead) he wrote: 'I cannot make out why the Major, you, Troup and Ward have been so demented . . . all of you seem to have acted like madmen.'[2] To Mackinnon he told the same story, preparing the ground for the music he would have to face when he returned home: 'My opinion is that the entire lot – except Bonny – have shown themselves utterly incompetent and lack brains altogether. They had positive instructions from me what to do. The first report from deserters settled them. From that time to my meeting with them they have acted like madmen.'[3]

He then began to grill Bonny for information that would redound to the discredit of Barttelot. Naturally, this was not difficult to find. In the light of Barttelot's conduct, he asked, why did not Jameson or Bonny, or somebody, relieve the Major of command? Bonny replied, reasonably enough, that anyone trying to take over could have been arrested and shot as a mutineer. He attributed his own survival to the favour Barttelot showed him for keeping his mouth shut. Jameson, additionally, had his own reasons for not opposing Barttelot. Barttelot knew all about the cannibal incident – indeed, so did everyone on the Congo – and had it to hold over Jameson. Finally, even if they had relieved Barttelot of command, they would have had his blood on their hands, since the *wangwana*, no longer in fear of the firing squad, would have murdered the man they hated so at the first opportunity.[4]

What about the *wangwana*, Stanley persisted. Why were they not given at least occasional supplies of meat to arrest their death toll? Surely Barttelot could have bartered rods and beads to get a meat supply? Ah, said Bonny, the Major expressly refused to do this, so as to punish the Zanzibaris for pilfering axes and other tools and selling them. What was in the Major's mind, asked Stanley. Bonny replied that he was obsessed with 'kudos', chafed at being Stanley's Number Two and so tried to find out as much as he could to Stanley's detriment. His abiding hope was that if he waited long enough, news would come through that Stanley had perished in the forest; he would then take command of the expedition, find Emin, and become one of the youngest colonels in the British army.[5]

Bonny's analysis chimed in perfectly with Stanley's own reading of Barttelot. He had reprimanded the Major on the way upriver for his insatiable hunger for kudos and had quoted him the couplet:

Not once or twice in our fair island story
Has the path of duty and honour been the road to glory.

It was a long-standing Stanley motif that, influenced by Bentham (who found the word 'duty' 'disagreeable and repulsive'), the English cared more for kudos than duty. All his officers on the expedition dreamed of winning a Victoria Cross or Albert Medal, but were not prepared for a diet of rice and beans which might actually be the means of achieving those honours. Barttelot, in Stanley's analysis, had foolishly set himself on a collision course with Tippu Tip, when *realpolitik* meant that without Tippu there would not just be no expedition, but not even any Yambuya encampment. If Tippu could be faulted, it was in having promised more than he could deliver – when he was cool and dispassionate, as opposed to when he was making propaganda, Stanley could see that the provision of 600 carriers was a tall order. With these thoughts in mind, Stanley proceeded to a justification of his own conduct *vis-à-vis* the Rear Column.

I parted from the Major in the confident belief that he was inflexibly resolved to march eastward soon after the arrival of the expected steamers. His face was aglow with resolution, his grip was firm as he clasped my hand and wished me his farewell. He was such a simple, honest, active soldier that none of us in the Advance had any doubt of him. He was a man who hated meanness, dawdling, shirking, malingering . . . of a small figure, wiry and tough – with a square resolute face on which courage was writ large – he was the very ideal of a jockey of Mars, a good type of those who rode so gamely with Cardigan, through the flames of Muscovy's cannon . . . He was a gentleman and always bore something subtle about him that marked him as one. Proud and decided, fastidious and severe but upright and sternly just. It's a perfect riddle to me why such a man as this yielded to the fascination of Tippu Tip and broke his promise.[6]

It is interesting that at this stage in the expedition Stanley was disposed to absolve Tippu Tip from all blame. Indeed the letter he wrote on the 17th, inviting the Arab to join him, was cordiality itself. 'Emin Pasha has ivory in abundance, cattle by thousands, sheep, goats, fowls and food of every kind. We found him to be a very good and kind man . . . If you go with me it is well. If you do not go with me it is well also . . . whatever you have to say to me, my ears will be open with a good heart, as it has always been towards you.'[7] Stanley thought he knew the right bait with which to attract Tippu, but the Arab, having had a possible £20,000 snatched from his grasp by Jameson's death, had no intention of following Stanley gratis.[8]

Three days after his arrival at Banalya, Stanley moved from Banalya to a camp at Bunganyeta Island in the River Aruwimi, about 14 miles upstream. Stanley's aim was to separate the *wangwana* from the Manyema, who were now riddled with smallpox.[9] Here Stanley brooded on another matter. Rashid had found a letter lying in water which turned out to be a confidential letter from Stairs to Barttelot, sent from Fort Bodo in June. The dispatch had been entrusted to Wadi Mambruki, who drowned. When the *wangwana* fished his cartridge pouch on to the shore, they found the message inside. In the letter Stairs bitterly criticised Stanley for his insouciance towards his sick officers. He accused him of needless brutality, raiding villages in reprisal for a few harmless flights of arrows, and forever reserving the best provisions for himself. Its comments were notably hard-hitting:

Stanley has got the name all about these parts of being the meanest man ever given life. It's pretty well true . . . Stanley treated us all from first to last in a perfectly damnable manner as regards food; he has at times had all sorts of things given him, not one of which we ever got unless one of us went and shamed him out of the thing. Emin gave him a devil of a lot of whisky and tobacco for us which we have not seen, and so on, till every one of us have quite given up any idea of ever getting anything from him . . . Stanley will chisel like the mischief and want all the provisions for himself at Yambuya; he gives in at once, though, if he is stuck up to on this point.[10]

Bonny was soon able to attest the truth of these observations. On Bunganyeta Island he fell ill and asked Stanley if he could have some goat or chicken. Stanley said he had no meat but on the very next day he killed a goat and pointedly offered Bonny none.[11] But Stanley always based his selfishness on the small print of the officers' contract which spoke of a 'fair share' of European provisions. This did not mean an *equal* share with the leader; in every army the general drew more allowances than the brigadier, and so on. Stanley failed to realise that in his punctiliousness he was actually conceding the substance of Stairs's indictment.

The short march to Bunganyeta had revealed to Stanley the low morale and wretched equipment of his men.[12] For a week he tried to build them up into a credible fighting force for the long trek through the forest gloom to Fort Bodo. Then on 29 August the expedition set out. Stanley had 462 men and 254 guns. 283 of the men were carriers. He divided them into a land party and a river party. There were just enough men to carry all the loads.[13]

They got through Mariri rapids and were at south Mupe on 4 September when Tippu Tip's emissary Selim bin Mohammed caught up with them to say that Tippu would not be coming with them, and that he was in no way responsible for the disaster that had overcome the Rear Column. Finding that his honeyed words had had no effect on Tippu, Stanley lost his temper. He raged at Selim that whereas Tippu could not hurt him, he could hurt Tippu, so that he might like to reconsider the question of following him. Then the *mangwana* headmen came to Stanley to say that Selim had been trying to inveigle the Manyema back to Stanley Falls. Selim promised to return with Tippu's further answer within forty days. Stanley said this was humbug: the Arabs had no intention of keeping their word and had caught up with him simply to lure the Manyema away. Selim asked if he could take away the Manyema who wished to leave. Stanley adroitly turned the tables on him: since he was supposed to be returning in forty days, he could pick them up then.[14]

Stanley's analysis – correct as it turned out – was that although the Arabs were cold-blooded killers, they would only murder white men or other Arabs if motives of revenge were afoot. This meant that he had seen the last of Tippu and his men. The sight of Selim bin Mohammed triggered memories in Bonny of Barttelot's obsession with him. He told Stanley that Barttelot had prepared petrol at Yambuya, ready to pour over all the stores and ammunition ready for ignition if it came to a last stand, so that 'those accursed Arabs' would gain nothing by their treachery.[15]

Next day Stanley discovered that the Madis were going down with smallpox after contact with the Manyema at Banalya. The *wangwana* had been inoculated on the *Madura* but were not proof against general debility. The first desertions began, followed by the first deaths from hostile action: two of the Zanzibaris went on a raid on a Batundu village and were slain. A few days later a party of nine scavengers (five Manyema, three *wangwana* and a Sudanese) were ambushed and speared to death[16].

On 8 September they were at 'Elephant Playground' and on the 11th at Wasp Rapids. Here Stanley waited for the land party to come in, before making a new division of forces. 192 expedition members would proceed by canoe while 262 went overland. But heavy losses continued to be taken. On the 13th a canoe capsized and two boxes of powder and beans went to the bottom. One of Emin's Madis sustained a bad wound from a spear launched at his back by a crouching tribesman. Primitive surgery revealed that none of his vital organs were harmed, so Bonny simply stitched him up again.[17]

The toll from smallpox and hostile action continued. On 18 September one of Stanley's best men, Jabu, was shot dead by an arrow from a hidden tribesman. On the 20th another Madi was speared in the woods and a Manyema woman received an arrow in the groin from which she later died. A Zanzibari dropped dead in his tracks from weakness, bringing the death toll for that one day to three. On the 21st another two *wangwana* were killed. During September additionally three men had been drowned in the Ituri and one committed suicide by drowning to avoid the ravages of smallpox. His most daring foragers, including one Stanley refers to as 'a veritable Jack Cade', usually returned from their raids with horrible wounds from poisoned arrows.[18]

Initially Stanley was puzzled at the continuous hostility on the Ngula River in September and the showers of poisoned arrows that daily assailed the river column.[19] He made the best of it by telling himself that at least he did not have to administer the death penalty for desertion

– the locals were doing that for him. Questioning of prisoners revealed that the new boldness and aggression of the people on this stretch of the journey – who had given him no trouble on the first journey – were due to their successes against Ugarrowa's party earlier in the year.[20]

Stanley did not crack on the pace in the early stages, so as to give his men a chance to collect food against the great barren wilderness ahead, but even so they found victuals hard to come by. The craving for meat led on 16 September to a swimming race between an entire company of his men and a bush antelope. but when they caught it and speared it, it proved far too small to make any difference to hundreds of meat-hungry mouths.[21]

And still the fatalities went on. A 100-strong foraging party returned on 22 September, laden with bananas, but there were many stragglers left in the forest. 'Till long past midnight, guns were fired as signals and great ivory horns sounded loud blasts which travelled through the glades with continued rolling echoes.'[22] When a muster was held, four more men were discovered dying in agony from arrows coated with poison. During the first forty-nine days of this march Stanley lost forty-four men killed – an average of almost one a day.

They portaged their way slowly past Panga Falls and Nejambi rapids to Avisibba and Engwedde – the stretch of river with its numerous islets that gave them so much trouble the first time. A local woman gave birth squatting on the river bank; the *mangwana* recommended that the child be killed there and then.[23] By the 30th they were at the upper rapids of Avugadu. Stanley noted in his journal: 'If I were twenty-five years younger I might live to see this primeval forest widely open and this track of mine a broad highway.'[24] Still the missiles continued. Two of the arrow-wounded recovered well, but a Manyema woman who had taken seven pointed shafts in the back died, to the grief of the husband. Stanley noted the incident down as further evidence against those who claimed Africans had no feelings.[25]

Stanley's mood during this first month in the wilderness, as they were subjected to the swathes of smallpox (sometimes fifteen fresh cases in a single day) and the attrition of enemy arrows, was black and sombre. When a second *mangwana* committed suicide by hurling himself into the rapids, Stanley simply remarked coldly: 'He was one of the most worthless men in the expedition. . . . I have fourteen or fifteen men of no earthly use to us, themselves or anybody else . . . Most of these people suffer from indigestion which has induced debility. Good food or a daily allowance of meat would soon cure them, but alas we have none of these things.'[26] His harshness is also shown by an explicit linking of himself to the exploitation of Africa. He quoted Sir James Mackintosh and said the words could equally well apply to Central Africa: 'Not an acre of land has been brought into cultivation in the wilds of Siberia, or on the shores of the Mississippi which has not widened the market for British industry.'[27]

And still he fumed away about the intercepted letter from Stairs. It particularly riled him that Stairs had said his officers had to hide their illnesses from him, for to be ill was a crime. He chewed over the phrases 'the meanest man', 'a cheat', 'a bad lot'.[28] To assuage his anger he took to inviting Bonny to his tent for long sessions of gossip and debate. Under pressure from Stanley, Bonny admitted that his January 1887 story about leaving Baruti to visit the Tower of London was a phoney. He was in fact trying to avoid his third wife, who he discovered had married him bigamously, and who was trying to waylay him at the station. When Bonny decamped, the woman stood guard over Baruti until the 'white-haired gentleman' rescued him, when she gave up. What had happened to the other two wives, Stanley queried. Both dead, Bonny told him.

'A third wife!' said Stanley. 'There must be something fascinating about you for the women. I have not been able to get one wife yet and you have had three. Well, well, there is no accounting for women's tastes, is there?' Bonny then further admitted that when Stanley had openly chided him for his listlessness on the journey between Matadi and Stanley Pool he had actually been under the influence of opium. Further probing elicited the intelligence that Bonny was a genuine opium addict; he had picked up the habit in India and now smoked it every day. Stanley confided in his journal that he had misjudged Bonny: 'A man who has succeeded in securing three wives to himself must be a man of character.'[29]

Moving up to the confluence of the Ngaya with the Ituri, at Little Rapids, in early October they were assailed by a tornado. Further attacks from poisoned arrows persuaded Stanley to cross to the south bank of the Ituri, but in another fight with the forest peoples a man was wounded with a poisoned shaft.[30] On 10 October they had a bizarre encounter. A dense cloud of moths, extending from the water's face to the forest canopy, 80 feet high, blanketed the entire expedition, flying at a rate of 3 knots. The cloud was 'so dense that before it overtook us we thought that it was a fog, or, as scarcely possible, a thick fall of lavender-coloured snow.'[31]

They proceeded through Hippo Broads to Amiri rapids, where a Zanzibari headman was so badly stung by wasps that he despaired of life. Stanley dosed him with carbonate of ammonium while Bonny injected him with a hypodermic. The man made a good recovery, but ominously there were now signs that the *wangwana*'s immunity against smallpox was beginning to fail.[32]

By the second week of October Stanley was tiring of Bonny's company, even though the ex-sergeant provided him with someone to moan to about Hoffmann's shortcomings: 'Stanley said that every man on the expedition had a better character than his servant William who was a fearful thief and liar.'[33] But Bonny himself soon came under the verbal lash. Stanley told him that after nearly two years' service with the expedition, there was no evidence that his services had any value, and that an automaton would have done just as well.[34] Faced with this onslaught, Bonny did what he always did when Stanley was in this mood: he diverted him on to the subject of Barttelot's crazed behaviour, especially his action in sending Stanley's precious effects downriver. But he recorded ruefully in his diary: 'Of course I must believe that the man [Stanley] treats me with the greatest contempt . . . he is just the man for the work he has undertaken but he should be alone or without white men.'[35]

Stanley's negative attitude to Bonny did not improve when he discovered that the sergeant had appropriated Barttelot's notorious pointed stick and was using it to chastise the men in his detachment. After he had severely wounded one of the *wangwana* with it, the man broke it across his knee and swore that but for Allah he would have retaliated directly on Bonny. Stanley haled Bonny before him and reprimanded him for unnecessary brutality; this one incident gave him a very clear light on what daily life at Yambuya must have been like.[36]

Disciplinary problems were mounting too. Stanley had taken two milch goats with him for their milk, but one night three of the *wangwana* overpowered the goatherd and slaughtered the animals for their meat. Stanley punished them with twenty-four strokes of the switch each, followed by fettering in the chaingang. He felt positively murderous that this act of indiscipline had deprived him of milk for the rest of the trek.[37]

After Amiri rapids there were more losses through enemy action. Out of twelve foragers sent ahead of the main body, three returned wounded and two were posted missing, believed dead.[38] They now began a march through a land empty of food, sustained by the thought that they had ten days' rations in hand. On 23 October they came to Ugarrowa's which, as on the inward 1888 journey, was deserted: 'A crop of rice seemed to be growing in the big courtyard but the grains had all been picked by the birds.'[39]

On 25 October they moved to a camp opposite the mouth of the Lenda River. The Ituri was in full flood, so that even crossing a creek entailed a soaking. A terrible storm battered at them. They were 160 miles from the grassland, and so far had existed mainly on roast plantain. Stanley looked forward to the pleasures of being free of insect bites, especially from the ubiquitous red ants.[40] The only consolation was relative immunity from snakes. After 24,000 miles of travelling, only two men had been bitten by serpents, neither fatally. But whenever they cleared the ground in the forest, they realised the danger they had fortunately escaped. Whipsnakes, puff-adders and horned snakes were killed in numbers. The Ituri itself swarmed with water snakes and in the forest were tiny snakes akin to the Indian *krait*, no longer than earthworms but supremely venomous and greatly feared by the locals. Around Fort Bodo, additionally, there were pythons and fanged ground snakes.[41]

On the 27th Stanley took the fateful decision to take a more northerly route to Lake Albert, avoiding Ford Bodo altogether.[42] This was despite the fact that provisions were already runing low and ahead of them stretched the uninhabited track of forest which contained Nelson's 'starvation camp' and where they had all suffered so fearfully before. In the ensuing days they captured a number of pygmies (whom Stanley weighed and measured for his Victorian 'scientific' public), who told them that the Manyema had stripped the region of food.[43] The clearing at Andaki on 2 November confirmed the bad news. They cut their way with billhooks through overgrown plantations choked with weeds. They were lucky to find an elephant track running parallel to the Thuru River, along which they made good progress – lucky, because at this point the river itself was impassable because of the rapids whose roaring they heard all around them in the forest gloom.[44]

By 4 November Stanley was growing anxious. Food supplies were running very low, there were thirty men on the sick list with ulcers, tumours, smallpox and fever, the desertion rate was growing, and stragglers were being left behind on the trail. When Stanley detailed two Sudanese to carry Osmani, a member of Emin Pasha's bodyguard, as he was feverish, he was found next morning quite dead, in circumstances that suggested to Stanley that the Sudanese had simply strangled him to be rid of the burden.[45] Bonny was worse than useless. When he was not flogging the men, he had other non-expeditionary matters on his mind.

He had found himself a Manyema concubine, whom he wanted to take with him even on foraging forays; Stanley's dislike of both Bonny and sexuality dictated a firm refusal.[46]

Starvation now threatened. 'I am getting more and more anxious. This is the fifth day since we had food supplies, which means for many two days' hunger.' Despite the *wangwana*'s fatalistic *'Inshallah'*, Stanley knew the end was not far away. He ordered a halt while a large party of foragers was sent out.[47] To keep up his men's spirits, on the 8th he distributed a cupful of flour to each man, and surveyed the sorry state of his expedition:

> Not long ago most of these men, now crippled with wide-spreading ulcers, tortured with pain and emaciated from hunger, were fine robust fellows, but disease and hunger have made terrible ravages among them. Some few of them have been skewered in the feet, by the deadly native skewers in the plantations, other in their heedless scramble over the logs in the clearings have abraded their shins, others have had their feet gashed by oyster shells in the creeks they forded, and these wounds through dirt have become ravenous ulcers. Constant showers, morning dews, wading through mud have also had ill-effects. The fatigue of burdens and the heat – it was 94°F. yesterday, have compelled them to fling themselves down anywhere for rest and the sudden chill of the damp ground has caused many a fever, which rendered them incapable of looking after their rations.[48]

When the foragers did not return to 'starvation camp' after a week, Stanley came as close to cracking as he had ever been in all his African travels. Taking Hoffmann and a party of men with him, he set out in a desperate search for the missing foragers.[49] He also took a loaded revolver and a full dose of poison, determined to commit suicide if he could not find them.[50] But the day after leaving 'starvation camp' Stanley's party ran into their comrades, bringing back up to five days' supplies of plantain. Stanley had learned a bitter lesson. From now on there would be no attempts at short cuts, they would cleave to the route they knew. He ordered a return to the river, prior to striking for Fort Bodo.[51]

When they reached Kilonga-Longa's ferry, they found the hostile tribes had destroyed all the canoes and the river was in full flood. They began to follow the Ihuru River northwards along an elephant track: 'this forest is a little more open than that we have lately passed through.' But momentary joy in the beautiful effect caused in the forest by the rays of the afternoon sun was cut short by the intelligence that the chief of the Manyema had jettisoned four loads (67 pounds) of the precious European provisions. There was nothing he could do about it now, but Stanley swore vengeance for later. The Manyema had brought nothing but trouble. Among other diseases caught by contact with them was mumps, now in evidence as the small pox epidemic waned.[52]

Porters continued to die but the loads remained the same. Every one of his porters was now ill from an endless list of maladies: ulcers, body pains, headaches, rheumatism, fever, gastritis, and many other ailments. Some respite was afforded in mid-month by the finding of a huge plantation of bananas but, still under intermittent arrow fire from the hostile forest-dwellers, Stanley on 17 November ordered Bonny ahead to try to find a ferry over the Ihuru.[53]

On the 20th came fresh armed conflict, between Stanley's rearguard and a tribal regiment. The hostiles fled under a lashing of lead from the Remingtons, leaving behind one dead and two wounded. Next day the pangs of hunger began to grip them once more. Stanley confessed that he was feeling half-crazed from the effects of not having tasted meat for a month: 'I cannot help thinking that vegetarians would soon abandon a vegetable diet were they subjected to our experiences in this forest. The strength of us whites soon declines if we are without meat for some days.'[54]

Bonny returned without success in his hunt for a ford across the river. Stanley's personal relations with him remained cross-grained and sour. He was still irked by his diary-keeping (a rival record) and warned him that if he was to be shot by accident (!) the survival of his diary might depend on its freedom from personal anecdote. When Bonny asked why they always displayed Gordon Bennett's yacht club flag, Stanley told him that it was his understanding in 1886 that Mackinnon had arranged for Bennett to foot the expenses of the expedition. It was on that understanding that he had accepted its leadership and carried Bennett's flag across Africa, only to learn later that the *Herald* proprietor had not contributed a penny to the expedition.[55]

22 November saw the expedition again seriously short of food. A heavy shower of rain contributed to the general demoralisation, and there were further desertions. A soup made from two gallons of water and two tins of Liebig meat extract provided but temporary relief for aching stomachs. Some of the men were by now truly maddened by hunger pangs. A Madi managed to crawl to Stanley's tent, attracted by the light of a candle.

Hearing him groan, Stanley rushed out and found a naked body writhing around in the mud, seemingly incapable of purposive movement. When the man saw the candle flame, his pupils dilated and he attempted to grasp the light with his hands. He was lifted up and taken to the campfire where he eventually recovered.[56]

With the men on their last legs, they were scarcely able to repel another attack, which left one tribesman dead and two wounded. Fortunately the foraging party returned at noon on the 24th with forty-six loads of plantain and a goat which was used to make a thirty-gallon stew. As so often, Stanley's men made themselves sick with overindulgence. It was a recurring pattern on these expeditions for the porters to throw away their reserve provisions after a 'blow-out', then to find themselves starving three days later.[57]

At last, on 1 December, Bonny found a place where a pontoon bridge could be thrown across the Dui River. Bonny and Rashid performed heroically in constructing the bridge, and the expedition crossed over. Still attacks continued. At the beginning of December a Manyema and Bonny's African servant succumbed to poisoned arrows.[58] And now starvation as severe as that just after Ugarrowa's once again overtook them. The news that Bonny had at last located the Ihuru River was not enough to lift the general gloom that hung over the camp. They were once again in a 'starvation camp', once again awaiting the return of a desperate foraging mission. All their provisions were exhausted, largely because his men had trusted the word of a local woman who told them there was a village with food nearby.[59]

By 14 December the foragers had been absent six days and hopes of survival were again fading. A young boy died and the condition of the other followers was most disheartening. Two more Madis expired and the last surviving Somali was on the point of terminal collapse. Stanley broke open the officers' box, took out the scanty contents and mixed them with water in a tin bath to make a thin gruel. But the words with which Stanley described his compassion betrayed a remarkable imperviousness to the suffering around him: 'These constant sights acted on my nerves until I began to feel not only moral sympathy, but physical as well, as though there was *a contagious weakness*' (italics mine).[60]

Stanley agonised about whether to wait for the overdue foragers and so risk starvation or strike into the jungle after them. In the end Bonny volunteered to stay behind with ten men and ten days' provisions while Stanley and the others went in search of the foraging party. A council was called which adopted the plan. After slaughtering the only remaining goat to make soup as sustenance for the trek to come, Stanley led out sixty-five souls on the search for their lost comrades. Bonny was left with twelve men, twelve women and forty-five sick with instructions to maintain strong defences. In all minds was the unstated conviction that the leader was engaged in a forlorn quest. At 1 p.m. on the 14th Stanley led out his bedraggled column. He considered himself doomed as surely as when he had determined on suicide the month before. The situation he left behind him was piteous, for 'the sick and feeble were condemned inasmuch as it was impossible to do the slightest service for them in the difficulty we were in. They could not follow us to obtain food, nor could they share the meagre diet necessary for the garrison of the camp and the preservation of goods.'[61]

Stanley's contingent spent the night of the 15th in the open forest. Next morning they arose stiffly from an unsettled sleep amid the dew. Soon after resuming the march Stanley heard voices in the distance and called for silence. Within minutes his men were embracing the returning foragers. Again they had escaped death by a whisker. After gorging themselves on bananas and plantains, the united force arrived back in 'starvation camp' at 2.30 p.m. on the 16th.[62]

With stomachs replenished, they struck out towards the Ihuru River, then followed its course to Fort Bodo, which they reached on 20 December. It had been a very near-run thing. The fatalities were horrific. Between Banalya and Fort Bodo, Stanley had lost 105 persons out of the 462 that left with him at the end of August.[63] He himself was down to 127 pounds in weight, having lost 50 pounds since arriving in Africa. Parke described the arrival of the bedraggled survivors as follows: 'Mr Stanley looked cadaverous and ragged to an extreme degree – and I never felt so forcibly as now how much this man was sacrificing in the carrying out of a terribly heavy duty which he had imposed upon himself. He might very well have been living in luxury within the pale of the most advanced civilisation, housed in some of its most sumptuous mansions, and clothed with its choicest raiment, and here he was, I had never before so fully believed in Stanley's unflinching earnestness of purpose and unswerving sense of duty.'[64]

Fort Bodo did not exactly provide the relief from care Stanley had been looking for. Although Stairs had local matters well in hand, Jephson had not arrived and there was no news from him. Word of the death of Randy in June did not improve the leader's temper. He set about putting his subordinates in their place. Stairs he punished for his 'treachery' by giving him all the dirty work to do. On Christmas Day he sent him out on a foraging expedition and, when he returned from this, sent him out again to seize enough canoes for the Ituri crossing.[65] Hoffmann was already in disgrace after being caught redhanded in theft in the Ituri. After his first act of stealing, Stanley simply reprimanded him and purged his anger by flogging six of his men who had not fallen in quickly enough.[66] After the second, Hoffmann had to sign a confession, in Bonny's presence, that he was guilty of theft and lying.[67]

Stanley's most turbulent relationship was with Bonny. He enjoyed the sergeant's 'rough diamond' qualities and his quickness in debate and sometimes engaged him in discussions about the Bible, Wolseley or Gordon.[68] He was particularly amused at a discussion between the two medical men Parke and Bonny about the appropriateness of the phrase 'landing in the water' – a subject which arose when Bonny was giving his eyewitness account of the sinking of the *Princess Alice* in the Thames in September 1878.[69] But most of the time Stanley was markedly antagonistic to Bonny. On his return to 'starvation camp' with the foragers on 16 December, Stanley gratuitously told Bonny he regretted giving him fifteen cups of rice on 9 October.[70] He continued to be irritated by the sergeant's keeping a journal and reminded him of the 'six-month' clause in his contract, adding with asperity that he would do better to keep his mind on the day-to-day work of the expedition. Bonny retaliated next day by asking permission to travel to the Welle River and thence to the Congo and home. Stanley dismissed the suggestion as ludicrous. He took it as proof that Bonny was no better than the other failures in the Rear Column. He accused Bonny of being both useless in general and cruel in particular. He had often heard Bonny's ferocious floggings and accused him of 'the deliberate and ferocious murder – it deserves that name' of a Sudanese soldier who had stolen a piece of meat.[71]

Bonny's request led Stanley to call all his officers together and make a general speech about the pitfalls of the search for kudos – the flaw that had destroyed Barttelot.[72] The unconscious motive for his speech was his intense dislike for the idea that anyone but himself should explore new regions. Then, after resting at Fort Bodo over Christmas, he established a camp at Kandehore on the far side of the Ituri River, and began to transfer the loads from Fort Bodo in stages, still occasionally under attack from showers of arrows. Repeated marches got the loads to the edge of the grasslands – there were not enough men to move the stuff all in one go. There he left Stairs and Parke with the sick and the loads and pressed on to Mazamboni's country. At Mazamboni's he received a letter from Jephson to say that he was at Kavalli's. Jephson's letter also explained the zigzag pattern of his fortunes since parting from Stanley in May 1888. It soon became clear why he had not been at Fort Bodo.[73]

Emin's garrisons had imagined that Stanley was bringing large-scale assistance but the shock Emin and Casati felt when they saw the bedraggled 'relief' expedition sent ripples back into Equatoria province.[74] Rumours about their future fuelled the uncertainty felt by the Sudanese and Egyptian soldiers. When word came through that they might have to withdraw altogether, Emin's garrisons burst into revolt. When Emin and Jephson arrived back in Equatoria to drum up support for the Kavirondo scheme, they were arrested. The rebel council then formally deposed Emin, and for some time his life and that of Jephson hung in the balance.[75] Unable to agree on their next move, the rebel leaders were rapidly approaching stalemate when the Mahdists took a hand. The ripple effect of Stanley's expedition had by now reached Khartoum, where the Khalifa too imagined it to be a major military enterprise, presaging an attempt to reconquer the Sudan.[76] Abdullah's hordes swept into Equatoria.

In panic at this new development the rebel officers released Emin and Jephson, who retreated to the south of the province. While pitched battles were fought between the Sudanese garrisons and the Mahdists, Emin and Jephson tried to get ready the people who wished to leave the province, as agreed with Stanley. By the end of 1888 Equatoria presented a confused state: the north of the province was in Mahdist hands, the middle sector was held by the rebels who had deposed Emin, while the ex-governor himself maintained a toehold in the extreme south.

All this would have been enough to convince any rational man that Jephson had excuse enough for not adhering to Stanley's schedule. But instead of accepting that all actions have unintended consequences, that no one can predict the future, that at least the imbroglio in Equatoria was not on a par with the chaos of the Rear Column's year in Yambuya, Stanley raged at the failure of the world to conform with his minutely laid plans. There is a volume of egocentricity, and a smidgin of madness too, in the way Stanley reacted to Jephson's tale as simply a perverse and malicious refusal by Equatoria province to do his bidding. All Stanley could see was Jephson's 'indecision': 'If I had hesitated at Banalya, very likely I should still be waiting for Jameson and Ward, with my own men dying by dozens. Are the Pasha, Casati and yourself to share the same fate? If you are still victims of indecision, then a long goodnight to you all.' With heavy irony he asked Jephson to wait at Kavalli's 'if you consider yourself still a member of the expedition subject to my orders.' After an immensely long screed, Stanley thought it better to add a postscript. But instead of toning down any of what he had said before, he added a series of gratuitous and patronising remarks about members of the Rear Column: 'Jameson paid a thousand pounds to accompany us. Well, you see, he disobeyed orders and we left him to ponder the things he had done. Ward, you know, was very eager to accompany us, but he disobeyed orders and was left at Bangala, a victim to his craving for novel adventures. Barttelot, poor fellow, was mad for Kudos, but he has lost his life and all – a victim to perverseness. Now don't you be perverse, but obey, and set my order to you as a frontlet between the eyes, and all, with God's gracious help, will end well.'[77]

Jephson's mild remarks in his diary on the receipt of this missive considerably understate the case against Stanley: 'His letter to me is in many ways greatly wanting in common sense and I think the way he speaks about the officers of the Rear Guard is not very pleasant.'[78] The only thing that can be pleaded in mitigation of Stanley's brutal letter – and even then it can only be partial mitigation – is that he was still reeling from the horrors of his third and worst journey through the black and green inferno of the Ituri (he was the only white man, apart from Hoffmann, to make the journey thrice). As he told Mackinnon: 'this has been the nearest approach to absolute starvation in all my African experience.'[79]

The horrors of the Ituri made him determined that at all cost he would strike for home by the eastward route. But the presence of large numbers of Kabba Rega's men on his flank in that case meant he *had* to have the extra protection of some at least of Emin's Sudanese. This reinforced his original conviction that, having returned once without his quarry (Livingstone) and had been reviled as a consequence, he would not go back empty-handed a second time. Emin, who was a much shrewder judge of human beings than Stanley imagined, already knew what was in Stanley's mind. He felt bitter that Stanley's coming had not only brought him no aid or comfort but had actually precipitated both the revolt in Equatoria and the Mahdist offensive there. Angrily he reflected on the pressures Stanley was bringing to bear to effect a complete withdrawal from his beloved province: 'For him everything depends on whether he is able to take me along, for only then, when people could actually see me, would his expedition be regarded as totally successful. To Stanley's chagrin, when he went on the expedition to find Livingstone, he experienced what it meant to leave behind in Africa the main object of his expedition. This time he would rather perish than leave without me! Therefore Stanley urged Jephson, during his own absence, to try everything to persuade me to leave. So, here again, we have only egoism under the guise of philanthropy.'[80]

Stanley for his part was determined both to force Emin to go with him and to avoid any further encounters with the Ituri. At Mazamboni's he was able to allow himself the luxury of recollecting in tranquillity the African forest that he would never see again and its peculiar moods and noises: 'No stillness even at midnight. Never-ending clicking of crickets and the chorus of frogs. Also a distinct audible movement of insects, creeping, crawling, hopping or biting some crisp material. Doleful and oft-repeated cries of the lemur, calculated to disturb the nerves of the timid. A tribe of monkeys may be migrating or a solitary chimp assuring himself by striking at trees. Sometimes a dead tree falls with a startling crackle or booming fall. The decayed branches of trees often fall down. This can often make the forest echo with a crash like a musket shot.'[81]

Such memories were to become increasingly distant. In January 1889 Stanley set his face away from the primeval-mysterious blackness of the African forest and towards the dappled sunlight of Africa's vast plains and grasslands.

· __15__ ·

J
ANUARY 1889 was a fallow month for Stanley. While he waited for a reply from Jephson, he established base camp at Kavalli's in rolling country that reminded Bonny of the Transvaal, where he had served earlier.[1] The sick list of 124 remained in Ituri ferry camp under Stairs's command – clearly this was further punishment for Stairs's 'impudent' letter to Barttelot.[2] When Kabba Rega's allies the Balegga massed to attack the white man's camp, 1500 of Gavira's men with sixty rifles met them on a mountain overlooking the lake and, after sharp resistance, put them to flight.[3]

With the Balegga on his flank as an irritating gadfly, Stanley ordered Nelson to deputise for Stairs and test the Maxim gun. Like all machine guns this proved unreliable and did not work satisfactorily. One obvious defect was that the canvas-belt contracted when wet, making it difficult to introduce cartridges. Another was that the tin which contained the water for keeping the barrel cool was detachable and could be lost. If this one item was lost through theft or accident, the entire gun was useless. The Maxim's one great advantage was that it was very light and could be carried by just four men even during a forced march. The Remingtons too were a superior weapon; unlike their 'rival' the Martini-Henry rifle, they did not have a tendency to jam.[4]

On 28 January Stanley celebrated his birthday and allowed himself some self-congratulation: 'I am forty-eight years old today. If I were asked whether the privations of the last two years had affected permanently my physical vigour and elasticity – I should feel bound to say that at present I am not conscious of it.'[5] His mood alternated between buoyancy and anger. On the one hand he was aware that prising Emin Pasha out of Central Africa was not going to be easy and he raged at the Pasha's 'ingratitude'. On the other, he was quietly confident that he would eventually manage to winkle Emin out of his stronghold. Since the news of the revolt in Equatoria his intentions had changed. It was no longer feasible to imagine that Emin, with his diminished resources, could establish himself at Kavirondo. This meant that he had to take the Pasha to Zanzibar, by force if need be. Gone was the jaunty insouciance in the Ituri forest, when Stanley had declared he did not care whether Emin returned or stayed, as instanced by this jotting by Bonny: 'Stanley said yesterday that Pasha thinks that some of the Expedition members would like to stay with him. Well, let them as far as I am concerned. I should not care if the lot remained with him.'[6]

But what Stanley said in the depth of the Ituri, when he was uncertain whether he would survive, was one thing. His view of the matter when he reached the grasslands and learned of the revolt in Equatoria was quite another. Jephson was not the only one who felt the full force of Stanley's wrath in January 1889. Emin also received a letter, dated 17 January, asking for a reply within twenty days as to his intentions: did he, or Casati, or others intend to proceed to the coast, for Stanley's expedition could not be expected to remain inactive at Kavalli's indefinitely.[7]

This letter, and the insulting one to Jephson, caught up with the pair on 26 January at Tunguru, where they had fled from Wadelai in December.[8] Emin replied next day, accepting the fresh ammunition and gunpowder Stanley had brought him from Yambuya, but renouncing further aid, since Stanley's ultimatum precluded the gathering of all those Sudanese and Egyptians who might want to take advantage of the offer of an escort to Zanzibar. He bade Stanley adieu and wished him a safe homeward journey. It was quite clear he had no real intention of accompanying the expedition. Jephson then said goodbye to Emin and prepared to return to his leader's side at Kavalli's. The idea that this was farewell rather than *au revoir* hung in the air between him and Emin, though Casati promised he would bring the Pasha down to talk to Stanley within a few days.[9]

On 6 February Jephson arrived at Kavalli's and gave Stanley a full report of his nine months with Emin. According to Jephson, the Pasha's soldiers were eager to leave Equatoria: 'no one keeps Emin Pasha back but Emin Pasha himself.' Jephson also added a piece of information which Stanley stored up for future use: he told him that most of Emin's Egyptian officers were 'animals who have been sent from Khartoum for nefarious practices'. Stanley was scathing about Jephson's good opinion of Emin personally and pondered the 'riddle' the Pasha was presenting. Why did he want to try to hang on by the skin of his teeth in Equatoria, when his officers had made it clear by their revolt that they did not want him?[10]

Stanley now decided that he would force Emin to accompany him. He dashed off an angry, threatening letter, but Jephson persuaded him not to send it and compose instead something more diplomatic. Stanley then sat down and indited a despatch 'after a style which probably Chesterfield himself would have admitted was the proper thing, which my friend Jephson pronounced was "charming" "nice" and "exquisitely sweet".'[11] The gist of this epistolary 'masterpiece' was a request that Emin extricate himself from Tunguru and come down to Mswa for a further conference.[12] Meanwhile Jephson ingratiated himself with Stanley by a story purporting to show that the real obstacle to Emin's falling in with Stanley's plans was his *éminence grise* and evil genius Casati. Jephson's report, as filtered through Stanley, ran as follows:

I find Casati more impossible than ever. I asked him whether he would go with us tomorrow, and he replied he would rather wait. I then asked, 'How many loads have you?'

'Oh,' he answered, 'you know I have very few things. All my things were taken by Kabba Rega; perhaps I may want eighty carriers.'

Vita the apothecary wants forty carriers, and Marco the Greek trader wants sixty, so at this rate our Zanzibaris will be killed between here and Kavalli's. The Pasha remonstrated with Casati for taking all his grinding-stones, earthern jars, bedsteads for his boys and women, etc., upon which he said: 'Mr Stanley has offered to take all our loads.'[13]

So pleased was Stanley with this tale that he invited Jephson to take his meals with him, an honour that had never before been extended either to Jephson or to any of the other officers.[14] He confided his fears that Mahdists would take advantage of Emin's softness to infiltrate themselves into his party and thence into the expedition's camp. Already he was preparing a master strategy to force Emin to come with him, and this notion of betrayal and treachery by a fifth column was central to it.

At bottom Stanley wanted to bear away Emin to the coast as a trophy, both to avoid a repeat of the 1872 experience when he had returned without Livingstone and to salvage something from an expedition whose failure and notoriety so far would surely breed a multitude of questions in England. Emin would not consent to go unless his conscience was clear about 'his people'. But a horde of ragged Egyptian civilians and assorted hangers-on would be a drain on the expedition's resources and would create no very favourable impression on arrival in Zanzibar. Stanley had to find the equilibrium point: just enough followers for Emin to feel justified in leaving, but not so many that they acted as a drag on the chain to the expedition.

To a large extent Emin played into his hands. Having decided not to leave his province, he should have remained deaf to the siren songs from Kavalli's. But on 13 February he wrote to inform Stanley that he had arrived at Nsabe. The reason for his journey was to accompany Selim Bey and some of his other Sudanese officers, who wanted Stanley's assistance against the Mahdists, and needed Emin as an interpreter.[15] Stanley at once sent Jephson down to the lake to escort Emin's party back to Kavalli's. On 17 February a large party trooped into Stanley's camp. With Emin were Casati, Marco, Vita Hassan, Hawashi Effendi and Osman Latif, plus the first detachment of genuine refugees, those who were prepared to accompany Stanley to the coast. Additionally, Selim Aga and a deputation of officers came to discuss joint operations against the Khalifa.

At the first interview, where Emin acted as interpreter, Stanley made it plain that the officers could expect no help from him in Equatoria. He told them their choice was simple: either remain and survive on their own devices, or accompany him to the coast. Selim and the officers then asked for sixty days' grace in which to prepare their families and effects for the march to the coast. Stanley answered simply that all who wished to go with him should assemble at Kavalli's. Again Stanley was playing a double game. He needed a minimum of sixty soldiers to stiffen his force against possible attacks from Kabba Rega, so was prepared to temporise to acquire them; but he never had any intention of escorting out the entire loyal Equatoria garrison. Emin was anyway doubtful that Selim and the others actually would follow Stanley out of Central Africa.[16]

Selim departed with an assurance that the expedition would wait at Kavalli's until all those who wished to avail themselves of the safe-conduct to Zanzibar and Egypt had assembled there. The *wangwana* were now given the unwelcome task of transporting the baggage belonging to Emin's party from the lake shore to base camp at Kavalli's. Meanwhile the other contingents trickled in: Nelson and his column, and Stairs with the Ituri camp convalescents, another twelve of whom had died.[17]

To sustain the increasing numbers of people arriving to occupy the 190 huts at Kavalli's – by 18 February there were over 500 and this quickly rose to over 1000 – Stanley sent out raiding parties to requisition cattle and supplies. He was ruthless in his collecting, raiding and burning surrounding villages if they resisted. For these distasteful forays he tended to use Stairs – his punishment for the Barttelot letter continued.[18]

But the real bone of contention at Kavalli's was the baggage of the refugees which the *wangwana* were supposed to haul up from the lake shore to the plateau. Friction soon arose between the men of Zanzibar and the arrogant Egyptians and Sudanese, who treated the *wangwana* as their personal servants. Even more seriously, Emin's followers had completely ignored Stanley's injunction to keep their baggage to an absolute minimum. 'That was a rash promise of mine to convey all their property,' Stanley remarked ruefully.[19] Emin had demanded 380 loads for himself, Casati, Vita Hassan and Marco the Greek, but in the event this total was exceeded. Casati brought eighty loads, Marco sixty and Vita Hassan forty, but Hawashi Effendi, the Egyptian officer who had commanded at Dufile before the Equatoria rebellion, arrived with ninety-four. Not only did most of this comprise bric-à-brac and rubbish, but there were items that could not be condensed into loads: 10 gallon jars for making *raki*, wooden bedsteads, 20-gallon copper cooking pots and grinding stones weighing 80 pounds each.[20]

Two reports from Stanley illustrate the problem. 'There is an old Saratoga trunk, which was borne by two men. I tried to lift one end of it, and from its weight I should say it contains stones or treasure. What a story that old trunk could tell since it left Cairo! How many poor natives has it killed? How much anguish has it caused? The Zanzibaris smile grimly at the preposterously large size of the boxes they have to carry. They declare there are thousands of such cumbrous articles yet, and that they will be kept here for ten years.'[21]

Again, on 22 February: 'Marco the Greek merchant reached camp today with Bonny's escort. He is a fine, manly looking fellow. He has also an eye to comfort I see. In his train are domestics carrying parrots, pigeons, bedsteads for himself and harem, heavy Persian carpets, oxhide mats … and, oh horror, he has also brought three hundredweight of stone to grind corn with, as though the natives here could not lend us any number of stones. He has also brought ten-gallon pots to make beer in, and for use as water vessels. If all the refugees are similarly encumbered, we shall, I fear, be employed for months carrying this litter.'[22]

To help solve the problem of baggage transport Stanley started to exert leverage on the local tribes. His raids for cattle became more extensive. On one day alone Stairs brought in 125 head and their protesting owners.[23] Stanley purloined more cattle than he needed to feed the swelling throng at Kavalli's in order to achieve a corvée. The tribesmen were told they could have their cattle back if they helped in transporting the loads from the lake shore up the escarpment.

But Stanley was playing a subtle game as he got the impedimenta of Emin and his followers hauled up the plateau. For a start, it was unnecessary for all the effects to be taken to Kavalli's ready for sorting for the march to the coast. The sorting process could, and should, have been done at the lake shore. Moreover, Stanley could have requisitioned vast amounts of local labour by blackmail. But he did neither of these things. He recruited just enough local labour to ensure that the *mangwana* were not overwhelmed by their burdens, but not so much that their onerous task was relieved and their complaints stifled. He intended to screw up Zanzibari anger to such a pitch against the Egyptian and Sudanese ingrates that when he finally played his trump card, the *mangwana* would be willing and zealous collaborators. The machiavellian ploy worked. Discontent and demoralisation among the porters grew. The headmen remonstrated with Stanley, but he feigned impotence: 'I am aware of what is going on. But what can we do? These people are our guests. We are bound to help them as much as possible. We indeed came here for that purpose.'[24]

By 10 March the Zanzibaris were at the point of open mutiny. Nelson's contingent was sent for yet another back-breaking trip to Lake Albert to bring back sacks of grinding stones and heavy pots. The men's patience snapped and they mutinied. Some of the mutineers called out, with reference to the Egyptians and Sudanese: 'Shoot them all and let us go to Mazamboni's!' The *mangwana* expected that Stanley would take their side, as he had done in many similar situations, even against white men. But Stanley ordered the disloyal men to fall into line. He then disarmed them of their rifles, gave the eight ringleaders sixty lashes each and a further five to twelve lashes to thirty of their boldest accomplices. He then roped them all together back to back against the flagpost and left them there all day until they had apologised.[25] Hassan Bakani was given ten strokes of a cane for going absent without leave, and was so aggrieved that he threatened to shoot himself, as another of the *mangwana* had done a few days previously. He rushed into his hut to find his gun, and it took the strength of five men to restrain him.[26] Tensions were mounting noticeably in camp, but all was grist to Stanley's mill.

One interested observer of Stanley's methods was Casati, who 'read'

Stanley earlier and more shrewdly than his friend Emin. He left an account of 10 May which is much what the rabbit would leave if it could record its encounter with the snake:

> The punishment was inflicted in a bold, frank, confident manner; and to one of the guilty men, who in a frightened faint voice answered the call, he said in a grave voice, while blows rained down: 'My name is Stanley Bula Matari and not only Ibrahim like yours.' Stanley is a man remarkable for strength of character, resolution, promptness of thought and iron will, Jealous of his own authority, he does not tolerate exterior influences nor ask advice. Difficulties do not deter him, disasters do not dismay him. With an extraordinary readiness of mind he improvises means, and draws himself out of a difficulty; absolute and severe in the execution of his duty, he is not always prudent, or free from hasty and erroneous judgements. Irresolution and hesitation irritate him, disturbing his accustomed gravity; his countenance being usually serious. Reserved, laconic and not very sociable, he does not awaken sympathy; but on closer acquaintance he is found very agreeable, from the frankness of his manner, his brilliant conversation, and his gentlemanly courtesy.[27]

On 28 February Emin, who had gone with Selim back to Equatoria, returned with his loads and his six-year-old daughter Ferida, fruit of a union with an Abyssinian woman lately dead. Stanley always had a soft spot for children and was much taken with the pretty little six-year-old with large beautiful black eyes and the 'colour of a Portuguese'.[28] But for Emin himself, though his overt relations were cordial at this stage, he entertained nothing but contempt. Stanley regarded him as a materialist, suffused with 'scientism', far more interested in the skulls of the dead than the fortunes of the living: 'He certainly has but little sympathy for anyone but himself and I fancy his best friendship does not extend beyond verbal expression . . . Emin has not taken any interest in a single Zanzibar or Sudanese in this expedition . . . as regards any particle of what is divine that may be found in them, Emin simply yawns – though always politely.'[29]

He even saw fit to compare Emin to Bonny – only a person of Stanley's purblind prejudices could have produced such a grotesque equation. Stanley was rapidly losing patience with Bonny's routine brutality to his servants which, despite the sergeant's protestations of innocence, he had been able to verify with his own eyes. Of Bonny he said: 'Barring one man I knew when a boy, the most cantankerous fellow I have ever met. Black man equally with the white falls under his displeasure.' Then came the ludicrous comparison with the gentle Emin: 'It is in this curious way of showing how aggrieved he is, that the Pasha, for reasons even more puerile than those of Bonny, closely resembles him. One grievance is linked to another, until the chain of grievances becomes portentously long and one day I become suddenly aware of the fact that I am an unspeakable tyrant, and altogether too wicked to breathe the same air with them.'[30]

Stanley's murderous hatred of Emin, because the Pasha had dared to oppose his will to his own, and because he refused the 'privilege' of being forced out of the province Stanley was supposed to be coming to 'relieve', and was not suitably 'grateful', found expression in obsessive point-scoring against the supposed imbecility of all the whites who surrounded him. Parke, the man who had saved his life, Stanley described as an intellectual simpleton away from his medical textbooks; he scoffed at the ignorance of a man who thought that Arthur Young, the eighteenth-century traveller, had been up the Congo![31] But always it was Emin who was the chief focus of his derision. Stanley contrasted himself with the Pasha by saying that Emin wished to know only the Africans' external measurements and dimensions while he wanted to probe the secrets of their souls; for this reason Emin was absurdly trustful where he, Stanley, was sceptical and cynical. As time went on, his interest in the taxonomy of birds and fossils drew from Stanley a neurotic irritation:

I never see him handle these subjects which consume his time and occupy him so absorbingly without being reminded of a model house-wife. The way he holds them up to view is finicky – with the little finger of his hand uplifted. He is painfully clean and dainty in his habits. His handwriting is so minute as to require a magnifying glass to read. His journals are scrupulously free from blots, as they may well be from the manner he holds his pen, and the deliberate care with which he dips it into the ink. His delicate and slender fingers are naturally fitted for delicate and dainty tasks, for handling the fittings of a watch, fine needlework, or to put the finishing touches to a miniature. He is so short-sighted that though he writes so minutely, he cannot see the face of a man twelve paces off, and I think his nature is such that he finds more interest in an ant than in an elephant, in the colours of a butterfly than in the moods betrayed by a man's face.

271

A true naturalist would find as much interest in the greater as in the lesser.[32]

As the stream of refugees trickled in, the March pattern of daily life at Kavalli's followed February's but in enhanced form. In one day Stairs and Jephson requisitioned 310 head of cattle.[33] The expedition made periodic forays into the territory of the Baragga, to cow these allies of Kabba Rega and uplift cattle, as also against the Milindra people, old enemies of Emin and Casati.[34] They discovered chimpanzees in the Baregga hills, so all the white men (including Emin) went picnicking there to collect zoological specimens. Emin Pasha had already assembled an impressive collection of local fauna and flora, including the original chimpanzee skull that first triggered the excursion.[35] But it was this very collection that so irked Stanley. Emin spent all his time with it and none with his people. This explained why he had not a particle of control over them and, by extension, why Equatoria province was in such a mess when Stanley arrived. But all of Emin's actions played into Stanley's hands. He told the *wangwana* he sympathised with their plight and agreed with them about Egyptian arrogance: 'It is riling also to see the Egyptian officers congregating in special groups each day, smoking their cigarettes and making their reflections on our slavishness.'[36]

15 March brought the denouement at Kavalli's a stage nearer. Stairs arrived from the lake with Shukri Aga, another of Emin's senior officers and second only to Selim Bey in importance. Shukri conferred with Stanley and Emin on the flexibility of Stanley's original twenty-day deadline as vouchsafed to Selim Bey. Difficult negotiations ensued all that day, at the end of which Stanley set a definite date of 10 April for the departure of the expedition on the homeward trek. Stanley wanted Shukri to sign a written document, but instead Shukri gave him his hand as a sign that his promise would be kept religiously, without a written pledge.[37]

Stanley's mood continued grim. At a general inspection on the 20th some of the men's rifles were found to be in an execrable state. Stanley ordered them cleaned and primed on pain of severe flogging; he could not risk misfiring Winchesters and Remingtons if it came to a shoot-out with Kabba Rega's 1500 riflemen who, Stanley discovered to his horror, were armed with Sniders, Henry-Martinis and Jocelyn and Stars – firearms individually not that much inferior to his own and wielded by a force that would outnumber his effectives by some three to one.[38] Bonny too was becoming a running sore. 'Bonny has been engaged in another miserable squabble with the Zanzibaris about a female servant. He is so aggressive and positive in his disputes that he requires to be silenced sharply in order that the other side may be heard. I believe he is deteriorating rapidly.'[39]

On 26 March Emin received a letter from Selim Bey to say that there had been a further mutiny at Wadelai. This meant that it was no longer possible for those loyal to Emin to maintain themselves in the province, so that they would now certainly be accompanying the expedition. The only snag was that, owing to uncertainties in the war-torn province, more time was needed. The 'twenty-day' deadline, and even the extension granted to Shukri Aga until 10 April, was no longer feasible. Stanley reacted to this news much as he had reacted to Jephson's story of the earlier revolt in Equatoria: it was simply an excuse or a pretext for delay or incompetence and did not merit further consideration.[40]

Yet this time Stanley's impatience was a machiavellian pose. He had never had the slightest intention of waiting for Selim Bey and his levies, delay or no delay, and had deliberately set a deadline which Selim could not meet. Genuine relief for the stricken province of Equatoria was the last thing on Stanley's mind. He needed Emin as his trophy and a sprinkling of his troops to make the expedition viable against Kabba Rega's raiders. Anything more than that was an encumbrance and an irrelevance. Now Selim had played into his hands and given him the excuse to do what he intended to do anyway. With the deadline fixed and irrevocable, the remaining part of Stanley's strategy could be implemented: an internal *coup d'état* that would leave Emin shorn of all power and influence even over his own troops.

Emin was an *ingénu* fallen among rogues. Throughout February and March his journal is full of entries bespeaking respect for Stanley's dynamism and leadership qualities.[41] When he received Selim's letter, with its intelligence that all the garrison would now follow Stanley and Emin out of Equatoria, he went to Stanley's tent with the good news, beaming with joy. 'What did I tell you?' he said. 'You see, I was right! I was sure they would all come.'[42] He was shocked to find that Stanley did not view the news in the same light at all. Stanley was adamant that whatever Selim said, the expedition would move out on the morning of 10 April. He explained that he had a duty to the EPRE committee, which was spending £400 a month just to keep the expedition ticking over in Africa, and to his officers who were keen to return to their normal careers. All this could not be set aside for the convenience of Selim and his men. Stanley thus revealed to anyone more perceptive than Emin one prong of his double-toothed strategy. The other he then hinted at by saying that in any case he suspected the good faith of the men Selim was bringing back; their most likely motive was to overpower the expedition and seize rifles.[43]

At this Emin started to hedge and asked for an extension of the deadline. Otherwise, he averred, he simply would not know what to tell his own officers. Stanley proposed calling a full council of his officers to discuss the matter. When Stairs, Nelson, Parke and Jephson were assembled, Stanley addressed them in a nudging speech, which hinted very strongly at the answer he wanted them to give Emin. He rehearsed the incompetence of the Pasha's men, spoke of their traitorousness and unreliability, and hinted at Emin's own gullibility and incompetence. Emin had had nine months to organise an exodus, yet when the expedition returned from the horrors of the Ituri, it found Emin and Jephson the prisoners of Mahdist sympathisers. He pointed out the Pasha had originally accepted that twenty days constituted 'reasonable time' for Selim to return, yet in thirty days he had managed to get no farther than Tunguru with one-sixteenth of his men. Shukri Aga was also well behind schedule at Mswa. The original twenty days had been extended to forty-four, yet still the Egyptians pleaded for more time. Then Stanley played the ace he was to use continuously for the next fortnight: the fear of conspiracy. There were already conspirators in the camp, awaiting their opportunities to seize the expedition's goods and rifles in the Mahdi's name. If they waited for Selim, all they would do would be to strengthen the hand of this faction. Was there, then, a case for extending the deadline beyond 10 April?[44]

One by one the officers said there was not. Emin then asked if he could reasonably be acquitted of the charge of having abandoned his people if he marched out on 10 April without waiting for Selim. All but Nelson overruled this objection. Nelson alone seemed keen to sustain the argument that a hasty departure would mean a failure in duty towards the Equatoria garrisons, but Stanley silenced him with an angry look.[45]

Stanley's hectoring performance at the 'conference' was a *tour de force* of insulting behaviour and specious logic. Emin had had to sit through a rant, in which he and his people were excoriated as being either traitors or imbeciles. Stanley's illogicality almost defied belief. His listeners were expected to accept both that the men Selim and Shukri were gathering were Mahdists to a man, actuated by a desire to destroy the encampment at Kavalli's, *and* that it was still worth waiting for them until 10 April! It was almost a textbook demonstration of the leader's insincerity and bad faith. Parke had often been derided by Stanley as an ignoramus, but he was not so stupid that he could not put two and two together and see that there was something badly wrong with his leader's logic.[46]

When his officers dispersed, Stanley asked Emin to wait behind for a few more private words. To sugar the unpalatable pill, he revived the idea of Emin's becoming Leopold's governor on the lower Congo, but this time contingent on his returning to Zanzibar first. As an alternative, there was the prospect of being governor of Mombasa under Mackinnon's IBEA company, at a salary of £700–800 a year.[47] It remained unclear whether the Egyptian and Sudanese troops could also be employed by Mackinnon, but in any case they were primarily an Egyptian government responsibility; Emin, by contrast, had been given *carte blanche* by Cairo – he could either return there or make his way to any new appointment.[48] Significantly, Stanley did not raise the question of the original Kavirondo offer and Emin, after the Equatoria revolt more suppliant than independent entity, was too embarrassed to mention it.[49]

But Emin was now disgusted and disillusioned with Stanley. Not only had he been subjected to a barrage of direct insult and wounding innuendo but, for the first time, he began to get the measure of Stanley's breathtaking duplicity. He asked for time to consider and swept from the tent. Typically, Stanley carried self-deception and mendacity into his own private journal. All he could see, or claimed to see, was Emin's ingratitude. 'We believed when we volunteered for this work that we should be met with open arms. We were received with indifference, we were led to doubt whether any people wished to depart . . . instead of meeting with a number of people only too anxious to leave Africa, it was questionable whether there would be any, except a few Egyptian clerks.'[50]

By the end of March the *wangwana* had completed the transfer of effects from the lake. Nelson came up from the lake with 132 men – the mutinous company that Stanley had cowed on the tenth. In six weeks they had conveyed 1355 loads to Kavalli's. The number of refugees at the camp stood at nearly 600. Jephson came in with fifty-six locally recruited carriers. The cattle raids continued, but the supply was beginning to dwindle. By now the scavenging parties were returning with fifty or sixty cows per foray, as against an average of several hundred a month before.[51] On 1 April Stanley despatched Stairs (inevitably!) to Mazamboni's to form an advance depot for the onward trek.

On 31 March Emin returned with Casati to express serious reservations about proceeding with Stanley. A long debate ensued, ranging over political and ethical theory, dealing with law, duty, honour and morality. Ever the practical man, Stanley despised this sort of disputation. He thought that Emin and Casati were dishonest and were simply casting around for a philosophical peg on which to hang a decision they had already taken on quite other grounds. Emin was adamant that his men would do all in all as he would. Stanley begged leave to differ and thought that only about half would be swayed by the Pasha. The Egyptians and Sudanese had no intention of yielding to Emin's authority in any true sense but would play along with him for their own purposes. Once again, Stanley's journals are full of contempt and barely-contained rage towards the Pasha. 'Should any accidental violence be the consequence of our delay – the whole must be attributed to Emin Pasha, inasmuch as he is the sole cause of our having been delayed so long here . . . the least apparent submission of his people to the Pasha makes him run over with love towards them, though to any of us here it is a base farce.'[52]

By now Stanley was beginning to identify Casati as the principal obstacle to his plans: 'The Pasha pays great respect to Casati's opinion, who is only a reflection of the Pasha himself.'[53] Stanley began to get Casati more firmly in his sights when Emin again came to say that Casati had advised him to stay with his people. 'What people, please?' asked Stanley sardonically. Did the Pasha mean the people who had already revolted and gone over to the Mahdists or did he refer to those who intended future treachery? Emin shrugged and suggested that Stanley should talk to Casati via an interpreter. As expected, this interview revealed an adamantine resolve on Casati's part to stay put and an unshakeable conviction that the pledge Emin had given his officers at Mswa overrode anything Stanley had elicited from him by browbeating. Stanley objected that Emin's troops did not seem to see it that way. Casati said that a commander should never abandon his post. Agreed, retorted Stanley, as long as his troops don't rebel. And what about the countervailing duty to the Khedive? None of this budged the Italian one inch.[54] For a while Casati usurped Emin's role in Stanley's journals as 'Public Enemy Number One'.

What I have gleaned hitherto of Casati's character is that in some points he resembles the Pasha. He is more African than Emin even, for Emin has some regard for his dignity, while Casati appears to have none. He hobknobs with the Egyptian clerks and officers daily, takes coffee and smokes with them while in his dress he is as slovenly as a European could well be. I have only seen him at a distance, he has not ventured to exchange the ordinary courtesies of the day with any of us. His household consists of nine blacks and were it not for his colour, there would be no difference between master and servant – such is the equality preserved in his house. At first I was much affected by it – as it was so anomalous – but we have got used to it by this. His choice of a hut also among the Egyptian rabble, the whispers of the Pasha about his eccentricities, the fondness he shows for a black female child – have all contributed, unconsciously, to cause him to lose caste among us. I may be misjudging him, but he certainly is an odd character.[55]

Stanley's particular animus was aroused by the fact that every time Emin went to confer with Casati, he came away depressed and wanting to stay on. What was Casati's motive, he wondered? 'Can it be that life in Italy was harder than we have any conception of? That the fleshpots of Wadelai appear to him preferable? . . . I am quite content in my own mind with the surmise that life in Italy, after the freedom, licence and gratuitous bounties of Equatoria, has no charms for Captain Casati, but it is the case of Emin that always puzzles me.'[56]

This was a reference to a conversation when Emin told him he would prefer to be, like Livingstone, an unfettered rover of the great African spaces. He would be quite happy never again to be subject to the stifling conventions of Europe, if he could just get regular newspaper reports from Europe. 'No,' said Emin, 'I don't wish to return to Europe, I remember its restrictions, its tiresome etiquette, and the pettiness of its bye-laws. I could not breathe in an over-ruled atmosphere after the freedom of Africa. Oh yes, I know what the return to Cairo means. I should have plenty of sugared phrases for a short time and then be relegated to the corner of a coffee house, and soon forgotten. None of that, thank you, for me.'[57]

On the evening of 3 April Emin came to Stanley's tent for another chat. They talked for an hour, between 5.30 and 6.30. Emin told him that all but four of his servants had declined to go on with him, and one of those was accompanying Emin merely in hopes of recapturing a stepdaughter whom Casati had taken into his household and treated like a pet. Stanley was interested in anything that concerned the man now considered Emin's evil genius and asked for further details. Emin explained that the soldier in question was not the girl's natural father, so Casati denied his rights in the case. Emin deplored Casati's obstinacy and feared that the brooding stepfather meant him no good. All this was yet another consequence of the 'morbid attachment of Casati to his servants male and female'.[58]

But Emin soon proved to be tarnished with the selfsame fault, if fault it was. About an hour after Emin had left him, Stanley happened to be passing the Pasha's tent. Inside he heard a furious row going on; his own name was mentioned several times. Shortly afterwards Mohammed Effendi, whom Stanley had identified as the disputant with Emin, came striding up to him with a crowd of followers to demand 'justice'. Patiently Stanley began to unravel the dispute. It turned out that Mohammed's wife had fled to Emin's protection and was now Ferida's nurse. Mohammed wanted her back. Stanley promised a decision when he had heard all sides to the story. First he summoned the wife, who said she had left her husband because of his brutality. Then he sent for Emin, who stressed how important the woman was to his daughter's well-being. Stanley asked to be given binding powers in the case and Emin acquiesced. Stanley promised a decision next morning.[59]

This judgement of Solomon took the form of a written contract to regularise marital behaviour. The woman was to return to her husband, provided he apologised to Emin. She was to continue to attend Ferida by day, then return to her husband by night. Mohammed himself was pledged not to beat her or call on her services during the day. Even so, Emin had to command her several times to return to her husband before she reluctantly consented to do so. Stanley advised Mohammed to tie her up until she came to heel. At the end of the interview, the woman finally took down her veil and Stanley saw that she was very beautiful. 'I little expected to have such an interesting and beautiful female figure in any book of travels of mine.'[60]

Stanley had long been casting about for a pretext to deprive Emin of any independent power and reduce him to a cipher. The opportunity came at last when the boy Sali, Stanley's spy, reported that there had been an attempted theft of rifles, and that only two out of fifty-one of Emin's men intended to accompany him. Stanley now resurrected the spectre of Mahdist conspiracy. His frequent hint that the men Selim and Shukri Aga wished to bring into camp were fifth columnists was now extended to the proposition that the enemy was already within, and that the attempted theft of rifles portended a general mutiny in the camp, in advance of the arrival of the other 'Mahdists'. To understand Stanley's actions on 5 April 1889, we have to understand that the obsession about 'conspiracy' denotes, not paranoia, but hardheaded calculation.

That morning Stanley stormed into Emin's tent and accused his people of being on the brink of mutiny. There was a vile and murderous plot afoot, said Stanley, which only the efficiency of his secret agents had forestalled. As a result, Emin and all the Egyptians and Sudanese would be immediately evacuated to a camp 3 miles away, and then allowed to accompany the expedition only when they had taken a formal oath of allegiance. Emin was too stunned to ask the obvious questions: how many rifles had been stolen, come to that, had *any* been stolen, did not the whole structure of 'conspiracy' rest on the say-so of Sali? Instead he feebly asked to be allowed to consult Casati. Stanley insisted he had to have an answer right there and then. The *wangwana* would that very day go round the camp to announce an immediate departure. All who resided or dragged their heels would be expelled from the camp. Alternatively, the Pasha might like to set out that very day with an advance guard, leaving Stanley to deal with the 'mutineers'.[61]

'The Pasha during all this time was shaking his head in that exasperatingly melancholy manner – which has always seemed to me to betray the pitiable weakness of character which has wrecked the fine forces of men he commanded.'[62] Emin said he could not consider the first possibility, of being expelled from camp. As for the second, he was not ready to move out at a moment's notice, his schedule was predicated on the agreed departure date on the 10th. Very well, Stanley persisted, what do you suggest? Emin repeated that he could not be ready before the 10th. At this Stanley lost his temper and said he was tired of the Pasha's excuses. He had been packing for fifteen days and was still not ready, did not like Stanley's proposals but could suggest nothing himself. Stanley stamped his foot on the ground and said in a convulsed voice: 'I leave you to God, and the blood which will now flow must fall upon your own head!' After several more angry exchanges – which Emin described as being like scenes in a madhouse – Stanley stormed out of the tent in a rage, exclaiming: 'I am resolved, Pasha, I am resolved.'[63]

At this Emin took fright and came running out of the tent after Stanley to ask what he could do to make matters right. Brusquely Stanley informed him that the time for pacific solutions was past. He ordered him to sound the trumpet for general muster. When, after ten minutes, there was no sign of the Egyptians and Sudanese, Stanley sounded the alarm signal and ordered Jephson to take No. 1 Company with sticks and beat out every single one of Emin's men on to the square. Now at last the reason for Stanley's apparent harshness towards the *wangwana* as they protested about lugging the heavy loads from the lake became clear. He had tuned them to a fine pitch of indignation, so that they were now more than willing to fall on their tormentors from Equatoria. The men of Zanzibar laid about them with gusto. The release involved in such an unexpected revenge led to many sore heads and aching limbs on the other side.[64] The *wangwana* blocked all exits from the camp, pulled down tents around the ears of the laggardly, and laid bare heaps of merchandise and cases of ammunition. Stanley went into his tent and re-emerged almost at once, rifle in hand and cartridge pouch on his belt. Emin too disappeared into his tent and came out with long field boots on, as if he was ready to march.[65] 'For the first time in years the Egyptians and Sudanese had to form a decent line. Not until they had formed it with military precision was a word said to them.'[66]

When Emin's men were standing apprehensively to attention, Stanley pitched into them with a flood of rhetoric. Looking straight at Osman Latif, whom he suspected of being the leader of the Egyptian opposition, Stanley said he had heard the men of Equatoria were anxious to prove their mettle. Well, if they wanted a fight they could have one right now. Stanley worked himself up into a lather and shrieked at them. 'If you have the courage, point your gun at my breast. I am alone and unarmed.' Blind fury made him unaware of the palpable absurdity of the statement. Not only did he have a Winchester rifle in his hand, but behind him was a solid wall of *wangwana*, their guns pointing at the Egyptians and Sudanese, their trigger fingers itching to avenge the many slights they had taken on the chin throughout February and March. When Osman Latif denied that there was any conspiracy, Stanley lashed out again. In that case, what is the meaning of your arrogant behaviour, the theft of rifles, the plots, and the threats not to accompany Emin? He wound up in minatory vein. 'My orders alone are to be obeyed here, and whoever resists I will kill him with this gun, and trample him under my feet. Whoever intends to start and follow me, let him pass to this side.'[67]

Stanley then ordered all who intended to accompany Emin to step to one side. All did so, out of fear of being shot dead on the spot. Next Emin's servants were sent for. All likewise stepped aside, with the exception of Selour, whom Emin identified as the chief conspirator. Stanley pretended that he wished Selour taken out and shot immediately. What about a trial, protested Emin. We can have a trial if you will consent to point out the other conspirators, Stanley replied. Emin was reduced to defusing Stanley's rage by pointing out other 'conspirators' who were placed under arrest. Histrionically making an effort to calm himself, Stanley told the other men on the square that any further sign of rebellion or revolt would be dealt with by the firing squad.[68]

The dramatic events of 5 April represented a kind of *coup d'état*, in which Stanley, using an entirely fabricated conspiracy theory, gelded Emin Pasha and thoroughly browbeat and subdued his men. To achieve this, he used the pent-up anger of the *wangwana*, who by obeying the leader's orders so willingly (for their own ends) simply gave a massive demonstration of Stanley's naked power. He had effectively manipulated all actors in the drama. His officers, after initial puzzlement, backed his actions once the 'details' of the 'conspiracy' were divulged. Emin himself was left both shaken by the revelation of the true nature of the man he had to deal with and shaking with rage at his own humiliation. 'Today for the first time in my life I have been covered with insults,' he told Casati. 'Stanley has passed every limit of courtesy, but I have promised not to speak, so can say no more.'[69] In the privacy of his journal he raged at the treatment meted out to him. Still accepting the reality of the conspiracy, he noted with bitter irony, redolent of the usual contempt of the academic for the Grub Street scribbler, that Stanley could have made his point 'with fewer scenic effects and journalistic rhetoric . . . Stanley is created to converse with Zanzibaris, he should never include Europeans on his expeditions.'[70] But he decided to tread carefully. After the day's traumatic events Jephson had a private word with him. He warned him not to make the mistake of thinking that the day's insult was the utmost Stanley could do if provoked; the Pasha had not yet plumbed the depths of the man nor realised the extremes of which he was capable.[71]

Yet what Jephson saw as high drama and Emin as tragedy, Stanley, secure in his overwhelming victory, was inclined in retrospect to view as farce. He had decisively broken the will of Emin and Casati and the 'effete' Egyptians, whose long slothfulness in Equatoria had made them incapable of fight or opposing their wishes to his. The tone of Stanley's reflections that night establishes beyond question that the entire 'conspiracy' was a charade and that his rage was pure histrionics – but significantly the kind of thespian performance only available to one who could tap in at will to a reservoir of anger stored up since childhood.

The farce is over and has succeeded admirably, for I think the Pasha's followers are pretty thoroughly impressed. Even the Pasha himself wakened up and the acted vigour has been like champagne to him. Once I came near breaking down and spoiling all by laughing. Osman Latif Effendi's wrinkled old mother – who must be somewhere between seventy-five and eighty years old – came up to me in the midst of my tragic display and jabbered Arabic most volubly to me, as though I were a born Arab, upon which with an impatient wave of the hand I said to her in English, 'Get out of this, this is not the place for old women.' She lifted up her hands in horror, gave a little shriek and cried 'A Allah' in such terms of terror that I came near betraying the fact *that my sternness was only affected* [italics mine]. Everyone else guffawed loudly at the poor old thing as she beat a hasty retreat from the terrible scene.[72]

Next day a kind of appalled tranquillity lay over the camp. Emin Pasha was incommunicado on the grounds of ill-health (he was broken and depressed), while Casati was no longer speaking to him because Stanley had found in favour of the soldier in the matter of the little girl Casati claimed as ward. But there were clear signs that the Egyptians, doubtless in fear of their lives, were at last making serious preparations to march.[73]

In an attempt to defuse tensions, now that he had got his way, when Mazamboni's men came to entertain them with a farewell dance on the 8th, Stanley arranged a fight between the Sudanese champion and Zanzibari challengers. The idea seemed decidedly risky to Bonny: 'I think Stanley committed a grave blunder in thus furnishing such a breach of discipline which might have ended in a general rising of Arabs against Zanzibaris. I was never more surprised in my life when the fight was ordered by Stanley.'[74]

But once again Stanley proved a shrewd judge of men. He used the occasion to display his 'evenhandedness', thus convincing the Sudanese that he was not an automatic ally of the *wangwana*. Omar, a giant of a Sudanese sergeant, took on three Zanzibaris in a duel with clubs and laid them all out. The enraged *wangwana* then rushed him, which gave Stanley and his officers an opportunity to intervene and separate the combatants. The Zanzibaris responsible for ordering the assault were placed in the guardhouse. Selour was sentenced to two dozen lashes for using a shovel during the fracas. On the other hand, Omar was sentenced to carry a box of ammunition on his head until the wounds of the men he had knocked out healed. The same sentence was visited on three more of his countrymen. Amazingly, this 'solomonic' judgement, ending an affray Stanley had himself ordered, was received with general approbation.[75]

No obstacle now remained to the expedition's departure for the east coast. On 10 April, as agreed, it threaded its way out of Kavalli's. The caravan was 1510 strong, including 230 *wangwana*, 130 Manyema, 350 plateau tribesmen, 200 of Kavalli's people plus 600 of Emin's followers, including 268 women and 105 children, and requiring 397 carriers for their effects. Nelson, commanding the Rear Guard, had orders to fire the encampment as he left it. The resulting inferno could be seen for miles.[76]

What Stanley described as a 'splendid blaze' was not viewed in that light by Selim Bey when he finally staggered in to Kavalli's to find a gutted husk. Despite many letters pleading for an extension because of the revolt at Wadelai, Stanley ignored all Selim's correspondence and left him to his own devices. When Selim moved down to Kavalli's, his force of ninety men and 300 women and children was repeatedly attacked by the plateau tribes in revenge for Stanley's humiliating cattle raids and the forced labour Stanley had requisitioned for carrying his loads.[77] If any of these porters deserted, Stanley simply carried out further raids to make up the numbers.[78] The upshot was that Selim was marooned at Kavalli's until 1891 when Emin returned, now in German service. Selim refused to speak to him for his 1889 'treachery' and told the Pasha's companion Stuhlmann that, unlike the perfidious Emin, he remained an Egyptian subject, bound to the government in Cairo, not an adventurer who sold his birthright for a mess of pottage.[79]

Wherever Stanley went, it seemed, he left a trail of destruction, not just in the form of smoking villages and dead tribesmen but in the ravages he made in personal relationships and the feelings between man and man.

· 16 ·

J UST three days after the hurried departure of the expedition, Stanley
fell seriously ill with gastritis. The column came to a halt at
Mazamboni's. What neither the pleas of Selim Bey nor the exhor-
tations of Emin could bring about Stanley's illness now achieved.
Parke injected his patient with morphine but could not hover over him
in attendance as he had done the year before. Soon after the inception
of Stanley's malady, Parke, Jephson and Bonny all went down with fever,
making the last two-thirds of April another limbo period.[1]

Relations between the humiliated Emin and Casati and the British
remained tense. Particular resentment was felt that the duo did not
bother to visit their fellow white men when sick. Parke noted acidulously
on 26 April: 'Captain Casati is very retired; he has never come over to
this camp, even to enquire for Mr Stanley or any of us.'[2] Emin, however,
sent further messages asking Stanley to wait until Selim came up. This
merely served to rile the valetudinarian Stanley, who conducted further
versions of a conspiracy theory, this time one in which Selim was in
league with a fifth column already on the march, which had instructions
to slow down its rate of progress. It seemed to have escaped him
that the only thing slowing down the expedition was his own illness.
Nevertheless, from his sickbed Stanley gave orders, over Emin's protests,
that the Pasha's followers should have the mainsprings removed from
their rifles.[3]

Further bad feeling was caused when Emin refused to abide by the
decision of a court martial that the ringleaders in the 'plot' should be
executed by firing squad. He tried to pass the buck to Stanley by asking
for *wangwana* sharpshooters to do the deed. Not wishing to widen the
rift between the two sections of the expedition, Stanley refused the
request and told Emin to get his own men to do it. Emin said he had no
men who could shoot well enough to dispatch the victims humanely and

used this as an excuse to commute the sentences to flogging. Even Jephson started to lose patience with the Pasha at this point. He felt he had been made a fool of, and made to serve on a six-hour court martial for no purpose.[4]

It was probably this background that made Stanley determined that the next delinquent, whosoever it proved to be, would face the supreme penalty. When Stairs – who continued to get the dirty work – returned with the deserter Rehan, who was guilty in addition of theft of rifles and incitement to desert, Stanley was insistent that he had to die. In his published account of the expedition, Stanley claimed he advised a non-capital punishment, but this is inconsistent both with other eyewitness reports and with the general context; only Stanley was likely to have pressed for a death sentence, certainly not Emin, and the only one of his officers likely to have argued for hanging (Bonny) had no influence.[5]

Stanley, still on a milk and water diet and unable to stand, dragged himself to the court martial, held in open session, at which Rehan was sentenced to death by a tribunal composed of Stairs, Nelson, Jephson and Parke; the leader cunningly took no direct part himself. Stanley offered to spare him if any of his *mangwana* colleagues spoke up for him but, after 5 April, everyone was edgy and suspected Stanley of wishing to identify 'conspirators'. More than anything, it was the atmosphere of witch-hunt in the camp that doomed Rehan. Stanley turned this tragedy too to his own benefit by insisting that all Emin Pasha's men attend the execution, so that they could witness his 'impartiality'.[6]

The actual execution contained echoes of the first hanging in the Ituri forest, in September 1887. The rope used for the lynching – for such in effect it was – had become so rotten with exposure to wet and damp that it broke when Rehan had been hoisted about a foot from the ground. Four plies were then spliced together for the second attempt. While all this went on, Rehan displayed not a scintilla of hope but looked on, apathetic and indifferent. The renovated noose was then attached and the victim was drawn up to a height of some 14 feet from the ground, in which position the body was left suspended for the night.[7]

Emin continued more enigmatic than ever. There are even signs that he had decided to play the Stanley game of obfuscation back at him. He complained of lack of carriers, then when Stairs went to investigate the problem, Emin told him that his people did not deserve any help, but that if Stairs was short of the odd porter, he would send him a slave or two![8] Emin's behaviour gradually alienated his erstwhile allies among Stanley's officers. Even Jephson found the Pasha offhand, rude and ungrateful. Ruefully he recorded his reappraisal. 'The Pasha is in his way as dangerous a man as Stanley and tried to put one in very nasty positions; only he does it in a meaner and more ungenerous way than Stanley does, and that is saying a good deal. For the past three days I have not gone to see the Pasha. I can no longer trust myself to remain quiet under his rudeness.'[9]

The wheel came full circle when the man Stanley had once likened Emin to emerged as a virulent critic. 'Bonny, after falling foul of every white in the expedition with abuse, gave me his opinion of the Pasha which is the reverse of flattering. They have fallen out about the birds they collect and Bonny is dissatisfied with his share. It seems that he shoots the birds and the Pasha's people prepare them, and in consideration of shooting them he obtains half the collection. He is so angry that he calls the Pasha a vile swindler!'[10]

Emin's raw state after the mauling from Stanley on 5 April is attested to from a variety of sources. Casati was no longer speaking to him. Next Emin compounded this misfortune by turning on Vita Hassan the apothecary and accusing him of having instigated Mohammed Effendi to make the scene at Kavalli's which ended with Stanley's judgement of Solomon and the return of his wife on a nocturnal basis.[11] Nor was Emin's state of mind improved when Stanley came to him with circumstantial evidence that one of his officers (Ibrahim Effendi Eltram) was a traitor – the most obviously bad apple in a thoroughly rotten barrel, as Stanley put it. His correspondence was said to prove that Selim Bey too was a traitor, who wished to detain the caravan only to deliver it to the Mahdists.[12] Stanley then rubbed salt in the wound by adding as a Parthian shot that he would have acted against the 'mutineers' long before 5 April, but for fear of humiliating the Pasha! Stanley's version was that the events of 5 April were forced on him as soon as he realised that Emin was virtually alone in his desire to leave.[13] This was gall of a high order. Not only had Emin *not* desired to leave, but the humiliation on the 5th had been consummate. One can only speculate on Stanley's actions had he not been constrained by 'consideration' for the Pasha's feelings!

Of course this was yet another example of Stanley's spectacular ability to lie even to himself. We can form some idea of how far Stanley's polished publications were from the raw actuality. In *In Darkest Africa* there is no entry corresponding to Stanley's entry under 6 May in the 'Personal Journal' of the Emin Pasha expedition – the journal that Stanley considered publishing later. This journal entry deals with the arrival of Shukri Aga and tells how he returned from a raid with twenty-eight prisoners in tow. The 'Personal Journal' entry is as follows: 'I am getting pretty sick of these Egyptians. I would rather they themselves should perish than that they should harm these people who have been so loyal and good to us.' Thus does Stanley portray himself as the true humanitarian, sickened by the brutality he sees around him. But the original undoctored journal puts a very different slant on this event. Here Stanley says that the 'bush people' deserve no mercy but they could well be left alone but for the excessive demands and rapacity of the Egyptians and their families. His main objection to such raids is not their inhumanity but the *trouble* they lead to – a pragmatic rather than humanitarian consideration. The original unvarnished diary entry read as follows: 'I really think they had better die rather than we should unnecessarily inflict misery or common injustice *even to beings so low in the human scale as bush people* [italics mine].'[14]

At last, on 8 May, Stanley felt well enough to press on from Mazamboni's, though for the first few days of the journey he was carried in a hammock made of hide.[15] Again he refused to heed the Pasha's entreaties that he should wait for Selim Bey. And he refused to extend to Jephson the care he had lavished on himself. From 10 to 27 May Jephson lay ill with a fever that oscillated between 102 and 105°F. But where Stanley had been in the cool of a tent at Mazamboni's, Jephson was jolted and jarred in an unwieldy hammock borne by clumsy porters.[16]

Once on his feet, Stanley strode purposefully at the head of the column, a pipe in his mouth, a stick in his hand, guiding the destinies of 1500 people with his adamantine will. Ahead of him was thrown out a party of *wangwana* scouts with local guides. Behind Stanley and his men came Jephson and his company, then Emin and his people, escorted by another company. The families of the Egyptian officials, their servants, carriers and dependants, plus the Manyema recruited at Yambuya, were in the rear. Last of all came the rearguard, alternating between Nelson's and Stairs's company. The march began at sunrise and continued until 11 a.m. without halts. By that time the head of the column would have reached the night's resting place, but usually the rearguard did not get in until 4 p.m.[17]

The pace was the usual blistering one set by Stanley in his African journeys and within days stragglers and sick were being left behind, many of them cursing the day they had first heard of the Emin Pasha relief expedition. Pleas for stopovers were met with the argument that since even three or four days' rest would do little to alleviate the misery of the worst cases of illness, it was press on or abandon the march altogether. Part of the reason for Stanley's haste was to make sure that Selim Bey and his party could not catch up. If they did, Stanley had a contingency plan ready. He would disarm them as traitors and, if they objected, attack them as foes.[18]

For all that, the first few days of the march were the easiest. Since Mazamboni was escorting them to the limits of his territory with 300 warriors, the expedition was allowed free range in the luxurious banana and plantain plantations. In return Mazamboni received forty head of cattle and sixteen tusks of ivory, averaging 52 pounds each.[19] Then they began a slow ascent to a spur above the Balegga valley. On their left rose the slopes of mountains, a range 70 miles along, among which the snowy peak of Ruwenzori was clearly visible. To their right, in a westerly direction, the forest, black as night, kept company with them. They were seldom out of sight of the advancing capes and receding bays of the dark wooded mass. Once on the spur they saw how narrowly they had avoided being swallowed up by the forest. They continued the climb to the uplands at 5000 feet.[20]

Seeing that the Egyptians marched at half his rate and abused the officers he sent back to hurry them on, Stanley predicted heavy casualties once they ran into enemy forces. The first brushes came sooner than he expected. As soon as Mazamboni's warriors turned back at the frontier, on 10 May, Kabba Rega's élite *warasura* warriors saw their chance. While bathing in the river, Emin's men were attacked. Fire was returned and three of the enemy killed, though not before they had shot Casati's servant Okili dead through the head.[21]

Now deep in enemy country, Stanley sent out two heavily armed parties of 120 men each to forage, one under Stairs, the other under Nelson and Bonny. The main column slogged on through a cloud of mist, the product of a violent rainstorm on the night of the 11th.[22] Already on the march there were clear signs of man's inhumanity to man. The rearguard executed a man for 'spying' without even referring the matter to Stanley. Bonny told of a baby abandoned in tears on the road by one of Emin Pasha's women. Stanley asked what Bonny had done about it. 'Why, I left it there. What else could I have done with it?' Stanley gave him a withering look. Even by his own lights Bonny was stupid, for Stanley was sentimental about children and would have given the sergeant money for the child. The sentimentality comes out clearly in a eulogy Stanley delivered on the boy Tukabi who absconded twice from his father to join the expedition, as he wanted to see the land where guns and gunpowder were made. 'Such a boy as this must be a wonderful fellow. I ought to mention that he appears to be a singularly bright little fellow with very intelligent eyes.'[23]

The expedition was now heading south into the valley of the Semliki, the river that linked Lakes Albert and Edward. All of this was land that no white man had seen before.[24] 'From the temperate and enjoyable climate of the regions west of Lake Albert we descended into the hot-house atmosphere of the Semliki valley – a nearly 3000 feet lower level. Night and day were equally oppressively warm and close and one or two of us suffered greatly in consequence.'[25] Stairs, Jephson and Bonny were the main victims, but Stanley himself suffered from a high temperature and a two-day fever.

As they wound their way down into the valley, Nelson came to meet them with news that Kabba Rega's forces were massing on the far side of the Semliki to dispute passage and had taken all the canoes. The situation required all Stanley's skill. Through his binoculars he spotted an unguarded canoe on the other side of the river. Under covering fire Saad Tato and Uledi swam across and retrieved it. Saad Tato received an arrow wound and had to be patched up by Parke, but at least the pair had succeeded in bringing back the precious canoe. While the *warasura* fired showers of arrows at them, Bonny and the five best shots in the expedition paddled across and established themselves in a beachhead. The canoe was sent back and further detachments of half a dozen men were ferried across in relays. The beachhead became a genuine bridgehead and some fifty crack shots were pouring lead into Kabba Rega's warriors. Stanley found two more canoes and stepped up the ferrying. On the afternoon of the 18th an arrow attack by the *warasura* on the canoe ferries led to a general engagement with Nelson's one-hundred strong company, in which Kabba Rega's men were completely routed. By the afternoon of 19 May, 1168 souls, 610 loads of baggage, 235 cattle and three canoe-loads of sheep and goats were safely across the Semliki.[26]

But on the other side it took the expedition five days (three of marching, two of rest) to get just 16 miles inland from the Semliki. One day they marched for six hours through quagmires of mud in the thick, gloomy forest of Awamba, which Stanley found in many ways worse than the Ituri because of its excessive humidity.[27] One village was so badly infested with gnats that he regretted occupying it almost at once. His irritability found a focus in Bonny. 'I had to reprimand Bonny, gently, in consideration of his pluck at the Semliki ferry, for choosing the best house in the village for himself when it should have been reserved for the Pasha. He replied that as Jephson had taken all the milk he thought it was to be every man for himself. Jephson being so pitifully weak after his long bout of illness, I had to tell him not to presume so much.'[28]

But it was the Egyptians who most excited Stanley's scorn during the gruelling march on the other side of the Semliki. They would start the day well, then collapse after about an hour. Utterly unaccustomed to a rainy zone and the effect of precipitation on the roads, the Egyptians floundered through the quagmires in an agony of misery and demoralisation, only making progress at all because the rearguard whipped and prodded them on. One Egyptian, sapped by 12 miles of mud, sat down on the road and refused to go any further, saying he would prefer to die. Women abandoned their children in woods off the trail where they could not be seen or heard. Stanley was the terminus for a never-ending stream of complaints, from the rearguard at their thankless task in chasing up the laggardly Egyptians, and from the Egyptians, via Emin, who complained of cruel usage by Stanley's officers.[29] Stanley noted bitterly. 'I wonder what the well-fed sentimentalists of England would say were they in my place on such a day as this! It is cruel work altogether, cruel for the rearguard who wish to get to camp, and rest out of the rain and mud and the fatigue of waiting and urging on men who break out into insolent abuse of them in return for their well-meant efforts ... the number of women with infants and small children straggling in the mud, wet to the skin, and hungry, give a heartrending aspect to the expedition.'[30]

Matters came to a head when another Egyptian called Hamdan tried the 'sit-down strike' method on Nelson in the rear. Nelson simply left him there, with the result that that night rumour flew the Egyptian camp that Nelson had shot Hamdan. Stanley decided to have it out with Emin. Not surprisingly, he found the Pasha still smarting under the impact of 5 April. Emin said he had witnessed with his own eyes the cruelty of Stanley's officers towards his own people. Stung by this aspersion, Stanley asked cuttingly why Emin did not take fifty men and act as the rearguard, and see how he liked going without food for twelve hours only to be cursed for his pains. Emin snapped back at him: 'I wish to God I had not consented to come with this expedition.' 'I quite believe you,' replied Stanley with heavy irony, 'though for what sane reason only God and yourself know.'[31] Emin glowered at him and accused him of taking the expedition on much too fast, without sufficient halts. Stanley stalked off but got his revenge that night in a choice journal entry in which he rehearsed all Emin Pasha's sins. Babies had been thrown into the woods, women left behind and Egyptians abandoned on the road, but Emin took no interest whatever. Immune to the splendours of Ruwenzori, uninterested in the natural phenomena of hot springs, salt lakes or even the pygmies, Emin's gaze lit only on birds, beetles and butterflies. Stanley fed the line to Hoffmann, who faithfully reproduced it in his book. 'His gallant rescuer might be dying, his men might all desert him, but bring him a rare bird, an unknown beetle, a strange flower, and he would immediately become wrapped in a sort of divine ecstasy from which it was impossible to rouse him.'[32]

Stanley's response to the sufferings in his rear was typical. He made the sentimental gesture of having all the children brought to the space around his tent at night, for greater security, then regretted the gesture when their crying kept him awake all night.[33] Then he looked around for a focus for the anger he felt towards the Pasha; by an association of ideas natural to him his choice fell on Bonny, who had allowed large numbers of the cattle to stray while they were in his charge. Bonny evidently replied to the reprimand with a form of 'dumb insolence', for Stanley recorded: 'His bearing often puzzles me. It is not what could with justice be called insolent or defiant, but it suggests that everybody is in the wrong but himself – and that if he liked he could prove unutterable things to everyone's discomfiture.'[34]

Some respite from hardship was offered at Ugarama, where the people were delighted to hear that Stanley's herds of cattle had been seized from the allies of Kabba Rega. Here food was plentiful, since terraces were cultivated up to a height of 8000 feet. There was a great abundance of fruit, millet, yams, corn and sweet potatoes. Then it was an easy passage until the end of the month through Batama and Bukoko. But one untoward event soured the more favourable turn of events. Two separate parties went out skirmishing, the *wangwana* for game and the Manyema for ivory. Mistaking each other for enemies, they became involved in a fratricidal shoot-out that left a man killed and eleven wounded. Suppressing his anger, Stanley consented to accept an apology from Kilonga-Longa's men.[35] But his mood did not improve when there was yet another erroneous armed clash on 30 May, this time between Shukri Aga and the locals who had mistaken his men for *warasura*. Altogether fatalities amounted to four killed and eight wounded in the expeditionary personnel.[36]

By the first week in June, the supply of livestock was down to 104 cattle and thirty sheep and goats; neither the forest nor the rank grass of the Ruwenzori suited the beasts. They were now splashing through cold streams, at their nearest point yet to the snow-capped Ruwenzori – which the pygmies regarded as the seat of their gods.[37] Stanley decided to send out a party to attempt an ascent of the lofty peak. His first choice to lead the climbing party was Jephson, but Jephson no sooner recovered from one fever than he went down with another. Nelson was the fittest officer to hand – he had even gained ten pounds in weight since leaving Mazamboni's – but since he now did the job of two officers, Stanley could not spare him. Reluctantly, he decided to send Stairs, who was still in disgrace and normally the expedition's white dogsbody.[38]

Emin and Stairs set out to conquer Ruwenzori. Emin's weak lungs forced him back after just 1000 feet of steep climbing, but Stairs managed to get to nearly 11,000 feet before lack of oxygen forced him back.[39] The main column meanwhile descended the precipitous walls of the Rami-Lulu gorge, traversed the narrow level, then ascended the wall-like slope on the other side. They entered a forest, whose variety exceeded the Ituri but which, like the Ituri, contained numerous hostile peoples. A Madi chief was speared on the first day, and skirmishing continued until Stanley pitched camp in a dry forest glade and opened negotiations with the local Bakonjo people.[40] He discovered that the local Konjo and Nande tribes had retreated into the forest to escape the superior Hamitic peoples. But when the Bakonjo learned that Stanley's expedition were sworn enemies of the Bunyoro, they welcomed them with open arms and sought their help against their ancient foes.[41] Soon the Konjo were fast friends and provided an escort through Mtsora and Muhamba, the edge of the lowlands.

Before beginning the ascent of the next range of mountains, Stanley tried to guard against the possibility of massacre in the rear by forming Emin Pasha's men into a company of fifty-four riflemen. Predictably the attempt foundered on Egyptian sullen un-cooperativeness. Casati asked for his servant to be excused and Stanley rashly consented. Then all the other Egyptians joined in refusing to release their servants. Angrily Stanley ordered the arrest of Vita Hassan, Marco the Greek and Basili, the chief clerk. Emin, who stood to lose his bodyguard of six armed retainers, went to Stanley to complain.[42]

Stanley received his overtures coldly and said that if everyone took the same selfish attitude, there would soon be no defence left. Just then Shukri Aga came in to say that the Egyptians were regarding Emin's request as a test case and would not co-operate if Stanley made special concessions to the Pasha. 'I see your example has been speedily followed,' said Stanley sardonically. 'If you were unwilling to control this rabble, why did you bring them with you?' Emin shrugged and said he could not stop them. Stanley asked him if he wanted to see his people massacred. Emin replied: 'I don't care for that and I cannot help whatever may happen. I must have my own people. I dare say they are very sorry they came along, and I am very sorry I ever came too.' Stanley accused him of being an ingrate. Emin stormed off in a rage. His parting words were: 'Do as you please and you may leave me behind any time you like.' 'No,' Stanley shouted after him, 'it is as *you* please.'[43] Both men were in a towering rage. Emin turned on his heels and repeated; 'I think you had better leave me here, I wish you had never come to help me.' Stanley bawled back at him: 'You are a most thankless and ungrateful man.'[44] Once again Stanley had won a propaganda victory over the Pasha, for all his officers, especially those who toiled in the rearguard, approved Stanley's actions and felt that Emin's refusal to co-operate was unreasonable.[45] He also won his point and formed the recalcitrant Egyptians into a rifle squad.

On 15 June the expedition left the plain and began the ascent into the mountains. The landscape reminded Stanley of the lower Alps as viewed from Berne. Next day they descended a long hill to the River Ruvehari in the plain of eastern Usongara. Stanley remarked on the poor condition of their cattle and Nelson told him this was due to Bonny's incompetence. Stanley summoned Bonny to his tent and got Nelson to repeat the charge. When he heard the accusation, Bonny rounded on Nelson and called him a 'damn liar' and a 'professional vilifier'. 'He had charged Stairs to him of being afraid of his men, Jephson of being the cad of the expedition, Dr Parke of being ignorant of his duties and of being unprofessional, that he had said the most horrible things of the Pasha, though he was glad to dine with him, and had not even spared me.'[46]

At this obvious instance of pure malevolence, Stanley told Bonny to shut up. Even if everything he said was true, it was irrelevant to the charge and did not excuse his neglect of the cattle. He ordered Bonny to apologise to Nelson. Instead of doing so, Bonny lashed out and landed a blow. Within seconds the two men were writhing around on the floor of the tent, punching and gouging. Stanley fired a shot with his revolver to bring them to their senses, then ordered them to their feet. They obeyed sheepishly. Again Stanley ordered Bonny to apologise and again he refused. Stanley ordered him to be confined in his tent under close arrest. When Bonny had been marched off, Stanley apologised to Nelson for the sergeant's behaviour.[47]

Even more than previously, Bonny was proving a thorn in Stanley's flesh. He could not understand why the man had such an exalted opinion of himself. He was plucky, was a good bridge builder, he kept his records methodically, and to his credit he had his behaviour in 'starvation camp' in late 1888 and the courageous way he crossed the Semliki into a possible ambush. But on the debit side he was hopeless at managing blacks, had an ungovernable temper, was churlish, vindictive, sly and vain. Stanley decided to keep him in isolation for a few days as a 'cooling-off' period.

The march east was already threatening to turn into a full-blown nightmare. Not a day passed without some personnel problem; the external threats almost came as a relief. He learned that the Egyptians had captured ten local women for the satisfaction of their lusts and ordered them released. 'Who was responsible for this behaviour I did not think it was polite to enquire too closely, as I do not wish my journal-keeping friends here to know things of this kind which would not reflect on the expedition as a whole.' One small consolation was that just after he had taken a photograph of Ruwenzori, Emin came to apologise for the behaviour of his men. The two shook hands and Stanley said that as far as he was concerned all disputes between them were now closed. But when Emin asked to be released to go his own way, Stanley refused.[48]

As the expedition approached Rusesse, a herd of twenty-five cattle was taken into its possession. Then they trekked on to Katwe, where Stanley discovered the salt lake of Katwe and the saline flats around.[49] Here they ran into a large party of musketeers and spearsmen belonging to Ruvara, a vassal of Kabba Rega's. These warriors were routed after a short, sharp fight, following which a flotilla of canoes belonging to Ruvara's foes approached to offer friendship if Stanley would burn Katwe village. He was happy to oblige. In return chief Kakuri, Ruvara's rival and enemy, appeared next day with food, which enabled the expedition to rest while Stanley explored Lake Katwe. Circumnavigating the lake in a canoe on 18 June, Stanley saw a large black panther slaking its thirst at the lakeside, but was unable to approach close enough to get off a shot.[50]

On 20 June they pressed on from Katwe, skirting the salt lake, then proceeded over a plain flat as a billiard table to Muhoyka, a village equidistant from the lake and the mountain: 'a dry and hot land, the ground was baked hard, the grass was scorched – the sun, but for the everlasting thick haze, would have been intolerable.'[51] On the other hand, marching on the plains involved no thorns, stones, roots or red ants. When they reached the River Rukoki the vanguard received a volley from Kabba Rega's musketeers who lay hidden in ambuscade in a thick brake of reedy cane. Stanley ordered a charge which soon drove the *warasura* pell-mell from the rushes. Then he sent Nelson's company, one hundred strong, out with his local allies to track the enemy and overhaul then. After a 12-mile pursuit without finding them, Nelson broke off and returned to the column.[52]

On 25 June they crossed the Nsongi River and began plodding into the uplands. There was desultory firing at them from *warasura* on hilltops, but the real threat to the expedition came from a quite different source. Ague and fever caused by drinking adulterated rainwater decimated the expedition. 200 persons reported sick. Stanley himself was prostrate for four days, with a temperature as high as 104°F. Emin, Parke, Jephson and Hoffmann also succumbed.[53] As if sensing that the expedition's pulse had faltered, on 28 June the *warasura* launched their fiercest attack yet on the rearguard. They took heavy casualties from the repeating rifles and sheered away suddenly. This proved to be the last serious encounter with Kabba Rega's raiders.[54]

With fever still running through its ranks, the expedition descended to the level terrace at the foot of the eastern walls of the basin of Lake Edward. By now they had travelled along the northern, north-western and eastern coast of Lake Edward. They were received with friendship and hospitality by the local chief, and Stanley used the halt to discuss the future path to Zanzibar. Situated as they now were on the borders of Ankole, they had three choices: they could strike across Buganda; go the long way round via Ruanda and Lake Tanganyika; or traverse Ankole south-west to the southern tip of Lake Victoria, then follow Stanley's 1874-5 route to Bagamoyo. Since Buganda was known to be in turmoil and Ruanda was an unknown quantity, it was thought best to opt for the Lake Victoria route.[55]

On 4 July they left Lake Edward. The level plain assumed a rolling character, dotted with trees. Soon they were among hills, trekking on an upward gradient. Stanley approached Ankole, ruled by Ntare, with some apprehension. But the king proved just as fearful of the expedition. He was suitably impressed by the power of the Maxim gun, the expedition's numbers were not such that his territory would be laid waste, provided he got rid of it quickly, and besides Stanley had checked his own enemies, the *warasura*. As a result, a kind of non-aggression pact was agreed and Stanley received permission to cross Ankole. He later claimed, mendaciously, to have been ceded all soverign rights in Ankole by Ntare.[56]

After warning his men to be on their best behaviour, since they were now among friends, Stanley commenced the climb up to the pass of Kinyamagara. Then the expedition descended into a long winding valley running parallel with the eastern shore of Lake Edward. On 10 July they reached Katara in a land teeming with lions and leopards. At night a hyena dragged off one of the goats.[57] At Katara an event pregnant with significance for the future took place. A delegation of Christian rebels approached him to solicit his help in deposing Kabaka Karema and replacing him with Mwanga. But Stanley was dubious. He knew very well that Mwanga was the author of the murder of Bishop Hannington in 1885 and he doubted the sincerity of his conversion to Christianity. So Stanley stalled, promising an answer when he had traversed Ankole.[58]

With Emin, Casati, Stairs and Jephson all prostrate with fever, Stanley was irked to find that his old nemesis Bonny, one of the few with the constitution to fight off the diseases of Africa, was up to his old tricks. Stanley haled him in for another ferocious dressing-down over the loss of twenty-four cattle, caused when Bonny abandoned his post. But Bonny was as insolent as ever. 'He shrugs his shoulders, departs to bed and acts as though it were no concern of his that the cattle perish or are lost. Yet there is no man on this expedition, white or black, who will make more clamour, or grumble more fiercely, if his rations are in the least stinted.'[59] This raises the obvious question: why did Stanley put up with him? Almost certainly the answer is that he already foresaw the furore that would break out in England over the expedition and wanted Bonny's evidence against Barttelot as a reserve weapon,

Bonny's particular imbecility was simply one species of a widespread genus in the expedition. It passed Stanley's understanding how his men could go in for petty pilfering after they had been treated so well by the people of Ankole, themselves not far from the bread line. Here were over 1000 people, living free, with no *hongo*, tax or blackmail being levied. The innate goodness of the African was daily apparent. One day a feverish Bonny fell into a ditch. A passing African spearman could have killed him with impunity, but instead went and fetched a half-gallon gourd of fresh milk, gave it to Bonny to drink, then helped him from the ditch and on his way. Apart from Stairs, who had a genuine rapport with Africans, his officers seemed unable to reciprocate these friendly feelings, but complained if Stanley reined in their brutality and whispered that he preferred blacks to whites. Well, enough was enough, Stanley concluded.

The next case of looting would be visited with exemplary punishment.[60]

The expedition wound through hill country and through a pass in the Ruampara mountains into the narrow, winding Niamianja valley – a land stiff with cattle. All the leading expedition members were constantly up and down with fever; Stanley suffered another three-day bout from 17 to 20 July. 'The ascent to the eastern plateau was marked by an increase of cold and many an evil consequence, fevers, colds, catarrhs, dysenteries and paralyses. Several times we ascended to over 1000 feet above the sea, to be punished with agues, which prostrated black and white by scores. In the early mornings at this altitude hoar-frost was common – blackberries were common in north-western Ankole, 5200 feet above sea level.'[61]

At Niamianja village the rearguard was menaced by tribesmen, but Uchunku, the prince-royal of Ankole, coming fortuitously on the scene for a blood-brotherhood ceremony with Stanley, chased them off. But the favourable conditions experienced during the crossing of Ankole seduced Emin's men into a bad mistake. Some Nubians deserted and four Egyptian officers, tired of the rigours of the march, asked permission to stay behind. Clearly foreseeing the consequences, Stanley agreed. No sooner was the rearguard safely gone, than the locals set on them and stripped them naked.[62]

This was not the only such incident on the march through Ankole. Some children who were left behind by Emin's people were immediately seized and enslaved by the locals.[63] Jephson, once in Stanley's words a 'confirmed Eminist', was becoming more and more disillusioned over the Pasha's indifference to the fate of his people. 'Gordon spoke truly when he said a man should return to Europe every three years, otherwise his sense of morality (in the broad sense of the word) would gradually adapt itself to that of the country in which he lived. The Pasha is a striking example of the truth of Gordon's remark. Someone defines morality as a tissue to the growth of which a hot climate is not conducive. I think it was Lord Beaconsfield.'[64] Jephson was becoming sickened by all the barbarism he saw on the march that seemed to leave Emin unscathed. Not only were laden porters cuffed, pummelled and lashed by their Egyptian and Sudanese overlords, but their treatment of women was supremely callous. 'Poor women, young girls from twelve or thirteen, with ulcered limbs, heated with fever, and footsore, would be seen miles away from the column, loaded down with sheer rubbish, that neither had value nor use for anyone.'[65]

After the blood-brotherhood ceremony with Uchunku, Stanley gave the prince a demonstration of the power of the Maxim gun. Its rapid firing sent Uchunku into boyish ecstasies and he had to clap his hand over his mouth to suppress his delight.[66] But Stanley's officers were already impatient to be away from Ankole. The huts in which they received hospitality were alive with rats, bugs and fleas, so that they turned out in the morning like boiled lobsters – an invariable concomitant of sleeping in huts rather than tents. The rats had a playful habit of dropping from the ceiling on to sleeping men, sometimes right on top of their noses.[67]

But, as they prepared to cross the Alexandra Nile, just 125 yards wide, in the valley of Mavona, prior to entry into Karagwe, Stanley had more serious matters to ponder. A second deputation from the Uganda Christians arrived to solicit aid in their civil war.[68] Stanley later rewrote the incident so that it appeared he had been lobbied only by the Christians of Ankole. In fact it was the Christians of Uganda and Mwanga himself who asked for aid. Stanley's decisive refusal to become involved provoked yet another angry scene between himself and Emin, who urged him to take the expedition to their aid. Stanley again lost his temper and raged at Emin. 'We are much too weak. You do not know Uganda, if you think that with our force we could go to Buganda.' Emin then volunteered to go with just his own people, but Stanley vetoed that suggestion too.[69] Only afterwards, when he learned that he had fluffed a chance of extending British influence into Buganda, thus leaving the way open for the Germans, did Stanley doctor his account of this incident.

Almost as soon as the expedition had set foot on the soil of Karagwe, a leopard carried off one of the Manyema women.[70] In Stanley's mind the bad omen was soon occluded by the familiarity of the surroundings. Here were the Magata hot springs he had visited in 1876, and here too he was welcomed by chiefs and headmen who had known him then.[71] It was also one of the few areas of Africa where rhinos throve in abundance – again echoing the experience in 1876. Stanley saw three of the beasts feeding on a hill and fired at them, only to see them gallop off unharmed. The Nubian hunters had better luck and downed four of the pachyderms. They brought a baby rhino into camp as a mascot, but it proved so aggressive that it had to be despatched forthwith.[72]

They began climbing again, along the grassy ridges of the Ruanda borders, making for Kafurro. In Karagwe they were received with the same kindness as in Ankole, but Stanley's boasts about his friendship with the king drew a contemptuous diary entry from Jephson: 'All this talk of kings and emperors and princes of the royal blood, with their residences, courts and palaces sounds all very well in books of travel, but it is nothing but bosh and it conveys a very false idea to the people for whose instruction the book is published.'[73]

Mutual contempt was very much in the air on the trek through Karagwe. Casati became so ill that he had to be carried in a hammock by six bearers. Emin purged his bad feelings towards his old friend by confiding in Stanley during the evening halts what he termed Casati's 'weirdness'. Casati would never ask the women of his household to do any work for him, since they were widows and he did not want to incur the charge of exploiting husbandless women. Casati also regularly gave his property away to his black followers and burdened himself with the care of a little black girl who was no relation.[74]

But Emin's disenchantment with Casati was merely at an abstract level. It was otherwise with Stanley's feelings for Hoffmann and Bonny which reached breaking point as the expedition threaded its way up and down the Karagwe hills. It was now clear to all that Hoffmann was a kleptomaniac who spent all his time trying to maximise the theft of as many items as possible from the widest possible range of people. A board of inquiry was convened to consider his conduct. He was found guilty and dismissed from the expedition, but allowed to draw rations as far as the coast. Stanley itched to do the same with Bonny who 'gives me as much trouble in his way as a dozen Hoffmanns'.[75] But Bonny was too valuable to Stanley to ditch in this way.

On they plodded, over dreary wastes of sere grass on mountain and valley, prey to flailing sleet and bitter cold. On 10 August they descended 800 feet to the narrow basin at the head of Urigi Lake and next day left the confines of Karagwe. There was now heavy mortality and loss through desertion; a muster revealed only 800 left out of the 1500 who had quit Kavalli's.[76] One of the *mangwana* decamped into the wilds even with thirty months' pay owing to him. In the rearguard Stairs and his men found Emin's people so exhausted that they had to build grass fires and revive them in the warmth before they were fit to continue.[77]

All this took place in Karagwe where, by the generosity of the rulers, the expedition enjoyed free living. Once they crossed into Kavari, problems of dearth and morale were accentuated, and this led directly to one of the most ugly incidents in the entire eastward crossing of Africa. At the village of Mutara on 12 August, a Sudanese soldier shot one of the locals dead and wounded two others during a looting raid. The tribal elders formed a deputation and came to Stanley to complain. He ordered all the Sudanese mustered and asked them to point out the culprit. At first there was a conspiracy of silence, but then he threatened to impound their accumulated pay at Zanzibar to make good the villagers' losses. At this the Sudanese informed on the culprit, one Fathel Mullah. Stanley handed him over to the tribesmen to do what they wished with him, justifying his action as follows: 'If we get a reputation for being predatory and violent after the manner of Fathel Mullah, the chances of the expedition's reaching the coast will be scant.'[78]

Stanley described the incident in his book, but had the effrontery to add: 'He was marched away and we never knew what became of him.'[79] In fact the man was put to death with hideous tortures, as Stanley knew. The full reality of this unsavoury incident is conveyed in two descriptions, respectively by Parke and Jephson. Parke described the sequel to Stanley's unsolomonic judgement.

> They greedily rushed upon him and seized him – as only savages can do – with eyes blazing with demoniacal delight, and a horrible grin of vindictive satisfaction displaying their white ivory-like teeth, which gnashed with the rage they were about to quench in his blood. It was a horribly thrilling sight to see him dragged off by his captors. He had a most scoundrelly-looking face, and they hauled him off, in spite of his abject entreaties, to spear him to death, as is their custom, for it is 'blood for blood' with these people. He certainly was an atrocious ruffian, and thoroughly deserved his horrible doom; still it was a dreadful scene as he was brought off to receive the treatment that awaited him at the hands of the executioners.[80]

And here is Jephson's sombre assessment:

> The guides tell us that the natives will all collect tonight from the villages round and have a feast and drink quantities of *pombe*. They will have the prisoner bound in their midst and the women will all insult and beat him and when the men have drunk sufficient *pombe* to madden them, they will rush on him in a body and hew him to pieces. That is their custom. A horrible fate certainly, I cannot conceive a much worse fate, but it is a fate he has brought on himself and one which he richly deserves.[81]

Only Casati grasped that there was a pathological element in Stanley's behaviour. How could the man who claimed to have inherited Livingstone's mantle sanction the savagery of *lex talionis*? If he wanted to appease the tribal elders and mete out exemplary punishment, he should himself have had Fathel executed by firing squad. To explain such mindless cruelty, the word 'sadism' hovers in the air. It was as if Stanley's hatred for Emin and his people finally found a focus in a single sacrificial victim. Emin was urged to intervene to plead for clemency, but was too broken by his many scarring conflicts with Stanley to have the stomach for the task.[82]

The despondent expedition trekked east from Lake Urigi to the base of the Unya-Matundu plateau, then up to Kimwani where they were well received by chief Kajumba. On 15 August they came in sight of Lake Victoria. A quick survey of its south-western fringes confirmed that the lake was even larger than Speke and Stanley's original estimates.[83] They began a march across flat land from which the lake had receded twenty-five years before. This was lion country and at night many of the beasts roared at a respectful distance from their camp fires. Stanley patted himself on the back at the thought that 'Providence' had cleared a path for him through territories that had been ravaged by civil war in 1887-8.[84]

In this land of Uzuija the general health of the expedition began to pick up and fevers became less common. But losses of cattle were frequent, through Bonny's incompetence. Stanley recorded his disgust: 'A master at shirking duty, a framer of plausible excuses whenever addressed upon any palpable dereliction of duty. He is simply unteach-able, and yet he always bears himself as though he were undeniably right, whatever fault he may be convicted of.'[85]

At Amranda above Lake Victoria they turned east for the English mission station at Usambiro. On 28 August they were met by Alexander Mackay, the Scottish missionary, himself an accomplished amateur explorer.[86] Stanley took to Mackay straight away and called him a 'second Livingstone'. Mackay was a man of small stature (inevitably Stanley noted the detail!), with long brown hair and a rich auburn beard, dressed in white linen and a Tyrolese felt hat. It was doubtless the likeness to Livingstone that made Stanley go overboard for him, since it was a long time since he had allowed himself to praise a man so. 'God knows, he has passed through hard times in Uganda – when his bishop was murdered, his pupils tortured to death, and the Uganda hero turned his eye of death on him. And yet I see why the little man did not flinch, and his blue eyes unblinkingly regarded the monster. Brave little Mackay! Spirits of his kind, whatever the size of their bodies may be, cannot be daunted or cast down.'[87]

At Usambiro mission station the expedition remained from 28 August to 17 September for rest and recuperation. It was very necessary. Parke was down with ophthalmia that stayed with him until the coast and prevented him from completing his diary.[88] All were exhausted and famished. But Stanley, at Mackay's behest, had to deal harshly with some of the expeditionary personnel who started selling slaves to the locals. He mustered the entire party and warned that anyone found guilty of this offence would be kept in chains as far as the coast, then turned over to the consul for imprisonment.[89]

There was plenty of food at Usambiro, and Stanley often contrasted the groaning board of dinner at night with the fare in 'starvation camp' in the Ituri. He began to catch up with the news, some of which had unfavourable implications for his expedition. Anglo-German rivalry in East Africa was now at fever pitch, and Peters had been sent out from Berlin with a fully equipped force to rescue Emin. The EPRE committee in London had also sent out a second British expedition to the east coast to find Emin, on the assumption that Stanley was lost. Stanley was incensed at this, as it seemed a slur on his own abilities: 'I certainly must blame those responsible for sending Jackson to relieve me at Wadelai, before they heard that I needed relief.'[90]

His anger at these two developments helps to explain how firmly he set his face against any collaborationist endeavours, even when vehemently urged by Mackay. Mackay wanted the Jackson and Stanley expeditions to unite, then intervene in Uganda, replacing Kalema (backed by the Moslems and Arab slave traders) with Mwanga and the Christians and incidentally blocking German expansion. Thus would religion and trade go hand in hand: 'If you have Buganda you have the lake, and there you will find the only market for ivory.'[91] But Stanley reiterated his implacable opposition to the idea of intervening in Buganda, and he warned that the Jackson expedition, unless armed to the teeth, would be at risk not just from Kalema but also from the Mahdists and Kabba Rega.[92]

Stanley was now more than ever determined to take Emin to the coast, so that it could be clearly seen that it was he, not Jackson or Peters, who had rescued Emin. He feared that Emin had pro-German sympathies and would defect to Peters if the expedition made contact with the Germans. If Stanley collaborated with Jackson, he also feared that his lustre would be dimmed and his glory halved.[93] Nor would Stanley consent to halt at Usambiro against the day that clearer light could be shed on the increasing complexities of East Africa. When Mackay asked him to remain until rumours of a war between German forces and Arab slavers could be verified, Stanley refused adamantly.[94]

But Emin saw a chance now to force Stanley to show himself in his true colours. He sought him out and resurrected the Kavirondo project, now, with the coming of the Jackson expedition, eminently feasible. Blandly Emin asked when he and his people could expect to be escorted to the north-eastern corner of Lake Victoria. It took Stanley a moment to recover self-possession, then he answered that the proposal had been made originally only on the premise that Emin would withdraw sufficient men from Equatoria to make the project viable.

'Then am I to understand you refuse to keep your promise?' Emin asked.

'I beg your pardon, Pasha, but you force me to say that I made no promise to take you alone there.'

'It does not matter, Mr Stanley. I knew you would never keep your promise and besides my life is always at my own disposal and I can end it when I like.'

'May I ask what you mean by that, Pasha?'

Emin made no verbal reply, but Stanley claimed that his intention was clear from the look on his face. He asked Emin what terrible secret he possessed that made him take that tone. The Pasha made no reply but stalked from the tent.[95]

The first two weeks of September were spent catching up on press reportage of the Emin relief expedition. For the first time Stanley realised how unfavourable was the publicity at home. He began to jockey for position in the post-mortem stakes that were certain to come. He devoted much of his correspondence to blistering attacks on Emin, portraying him as both an ingrate and a comic-cuts shortsighted naturalist who had not been worth the trouble of saving. Emin replied in kind in his correspondence.[96] Learning that the Jackson expedition was on the north-eastern shore of Lake Victoria, Stanley laid plans for his own caravan to leave Usambiro before Jackson could meet him or hand him any new orders. He left behind a cold dry letter.[97] This drew from Peters the comment: 'Not a greeting to his countrymen, not a word of counsel or of suggestion to Jackson and his colleagues!'[98]

After a sumptuous dinner, complete with rare wines, given in their honour by Mackay on 14 September, the officers mustered the expedition and found just 559 souls ready for departure to the coast – little more than a third remained of the crowd who had left Kavalli's in April.[99] On the 18th they trekked out of the mission station in a south-easterly direction; Mackay accompanied them for a mile on the road. Despite

Stanley's pleadings, he declined to accompany them to the coast, prefer-ring, like Livingstone, to remain with his work in Africa.[100]

The week after leaving Usambiro turned out to be the most perilous in the entire homeward journey. In February 1875 Stanley had crossed Usukuma without major hazard and with simply routine payments of *doti*. But now he ran into stiff opposition. Perhaps this was partly due to the fact that his earlier crossing of Sukumuland had been at the height of the rainy season, whereas now he marched in the boiling sun. Perhaps too the spread of trade goods and firearms had made the Sukuma peoples at once more avaricious and belligerent. The plethora of missionaries between Bagamoyo and Lake Victoria had inflated the going price for *bongo* from ten cloths to the equivalent of £270 for three days' transit. Whatever the reason, it was here that the expedition encountered the toughest military challenge in the entire three years. 'That first week's journey southwards from Msalala and Lake Victoria was in some ways the most terrible part of the expedition,' Hoffmann recalled.[101] At first Stanley was inclined to shrug off the showers of arrows desultorily loosed in their direction as simple high spirits. But he changed his tune after a narrow escape at the village of Ikoma. Mackay had told them that the English ivory trader Stokes had a store of European provisions there. Expecting the inhabitants to be friendly, Stanley neglected to take the usual precautions and stumbled into an ambush. Desperate hand-to-hand fighting ensued, in which Stanley had his rifle almost torn from his hands until two of the *wangwana* came to his aid. So far from obtaining provisions, the expedition had to fight its way out of the village, leaving ten dead, to avoid being overwhelmed.[102]

A three-day running fight ensued: 'the entire population appeared to have turned out to obstruct, annoy and assault the column at any favourable point or opportunity.'[103] In one skirmish seven of the Sukuma people were killed; in another, Stanley's men captured 130 head of cattle and goats. And all the time overhead the sun shone with extraordinary fervour. The faces of the defenders were baked and their lips cracked with the heat. The grass along the route was so short that the roots themselves were eaten by their hungry animals. A thunderstorm on the afternoon of the 23rd came as a welcome relief.[104]

The climax of the testing fight in Sukumuland came on the afternoon of the 24th. Three separate enemy detachments approached, intending to attack on right, left and centre. The caravan was now short of food and water and Stanley's patience was at snapping point. He ordered his men to form a square, with women, children and non-combatants inside the laager. Then he brought up the Maxim gun. Waiting until the enemy had advanced to within 300 yards, he gave the order to open up. The Maxim raked along the enemy ranks, dropping warriors by the dozen. After this devastating exhibition, the Sukuma peoples kept their distance. They tracked the column from afar, yelling war-cries and firing off flintlock muskets into the air.[105]

Tired and hungry, in need of water and rest, after seven nerve-wracking days the expedition entered the territory of the friendly Sinyanga and dropped the enemy astern. Stanley's relief was palpable. 'This September will be memorable with us for the many crosses we have had to bear. Its earlier days stand out as in a dream. They were so pleasant and our anticipations were delightful. Alas, five days' fighting, sufferings from thirst, the heat of the sun which focused all its power directly on us, the vile water, all combined with this days's particular fatigues and rank offensive smells to try our temper greatly.'[106]

For the first few days of October Stanley was sick. After a halt to accommodate the leader, the expedition pressed on through Usongo and Singwizi. Their track led through scrub plains and thorny jungles, and the pace finally saw off Osman Latif's old mother, who had been carried in a hammock all the way from Lake Albert. Predators abounded, and Stanley gave this account of a typical night: 'Lions, jackals and the brays of our donkeys made this night hideous and few of us had any sleep despite fatigue.'[107]

On 18 October two French missionaries from Bukumbi, Fathers Schynse and Girault, overtook the column and sought permission to accompany it to the coast. Next day the Manyema fell in with a caravan belonging to Tippu Tip and started west on their homeward journey.[108] By this time the rate of progress of the expedition had slowed down and its composition was different from the force that left Lake Albert. First came Stanley and two companies of *wangwana*. A third Zanzibari company formed the rearguard. In the middle were the Wanyamwezi porters Stanley had recently recruited and the racial pot-pourri that made up the tired and huddled masses from Wadelai – such of them as still survived. The Sudanese had now been given the task of herding the cattle, down to eighty head.[109]

They were heading directly south-east through a country teeming with lions, all the more plentiful now since a Masai invasion had scared off the indigenous Ikungu hunters. There were many giraffes which the lions preyed on, and Stanley's hunters 'bagged' one of the beasts for a communal supper. Also to be seen were packs of wild dogs, ferocious enough to bring down a solitary lion unprotected by his pride. As if this was not enough, four tribes of bandits were known to infest the region. And above all there was the unremitting heat. 'The sandy paths through the jungle on account of the great heat are almost unbearable to the carriers of the caravan. The thorns have also been a nuisance and our people are not at all happy looking. Though they are not stinted in meal and meat, they mostly all look seedy and thin.'[110]

Schynse noted that there was bad blood in the expedition between the Europeans and particular animus against the 'pile of corrupt and useless Egyptians'. But he himself took comfort from the fact that the chief of the Kabarata who had insulted him last year was very subdued in the presence of such a large caravan and assured Stanley that he was the white man's best friend. Schynse also learned the reason for the Sudanese keenness to drove the donkeys, goats and cows through the heat, despite their (the Sudanese) reputation for idleness. Meat supply apart, all domestic animals cost four times as much at the coast as in Usukuma.[111]

On 26 October the expedition reached the territory of Stanley's old enemies, the Wagogo. At once thefts and skirmishes became commonplace. The Sudanese lost their goats in one raid. When Stanley tried to buy the predators off with ivory, they demanded wood. His men cried out for him to give them lead, but he settled for twenty-six *doti* of cloth.[112] The trek through Ugogo's red soil was as tedious as on the three previous occasions Stanley had traversed their territory. The Gogo peoples alternated outrageous *hongo* demands with the barefaced theft of guns. Stanley recorded ruefully: 'Ugogo has been a bitter land to travellers for generations. In the whole of Africa there are few people so insolent. However, it is not likely I shall ever see Ugogo again, but I should esteem it an agreeable task to bring this people to a sense of their long wrong-doings.'[113]

The expedition wound its way down from the plateau for the eight-day crossing of the vast and arid Ugogo plain. As they picked their way across rocky terrain, they were assailed by taunting Wagogo, by wind, dust and thirst. Even when they pitched their tents under baobab trees they were assaulted by clouds of red dust. In Nyangwira, the most populous part of Ugogo, Stanley again bowed the head and paid a substantial *hongo* to the one-eyed ruler Mukenge. There were some tense moments while Stanley bartered in a grove of palm trees near the chieftain's kraal. Stanley did not want to have to swivel the Maxim gun into action for a few *doti*, while Mukenge hesitated to attack such a large caravan.[114]

It is a bitter irony that Stanley, so often under attack in England for

over-reaction to tribal 'impudence', should on this occasion have been
singled out by Peters for a different and opposite kind of criticism. The
bloodthirsty Peters, who later solved the Gogo 'problem' by slaughtering
them in hundreds, accused Stanley of egregious weakness, especially
given that he had a Maxim gun with him. When Mukenge redoubled
his demand for *hongo*, Peters argued, Stanley should have used the
opportunity to take the strut out of him. Instead Stanley meekly sent him
four times the usual *doti*. This was a bad mistake, Peters thought, since
it inculcated the idea that whites would always pay tribute; if a large
expedition containing nine white men bowed the knee, what hope was
there for other travellers?[115]

Schynse too was intrigued as to why Stanley, who according to Emin
was a man of force and blood, should have swallowed Gogo 'insolence'.
One afternoon as Stanley sat under a tree smoking his pipe while his
tent was being erected, Schynse raised the matter with him. Stanley said
they were near journey's end and he had too many women and sick in
the column to make it worthwhile engaging the Wagogo; had any of the
tribes further inland tried his patience in this way, it would have been a
different story, however. 'If this was the beginning of the expedition, I'd
give them a *hongo* in lead,' he confided. 'After fifty-three skirmishes, I'm
philosophical. I'd like to come back here and sort them out. I don't mind
paying normal *hongo* but the Wagogo are thieves. They still try to stop
us getting water, in spite of the *hongo*, the chief reckons he's not
responsible for anything.'[116]

But even Stanley in pacific mood had his sticking point. When the
Gogo people tried to deny the caravan the use of their wells, Stanley set
men with loaded guns to impress the point that he must have an
unimpeded water supply. The Wagogo backed off, asking only that the
waterholes where they took their own herds should be inviolate.[117]

After Nyangwira Stanley struck off from the main caravan route to try
to avoid excessive demands for tribute. Their route was still determined
by waterholes, and food was short unless they wished to pay the Wagogo's
extortionate prices. The soil was a sandy gravel and Stanley marvelled
that the cattle remained in a good condition, even though he could not
make out what they found to eat. At night they camped on hills and
eminences and at day descended into the acacia-dotted plain – so flat
that in the rainy season it was completely waterlogged.[118]

On 8 November they came to the border of Ugogo and Masailand.
Stanley turned sharply south-east, with a chain of hills flanking him to
the north, then crossed the chain when it turned south. Ahead of them

was only the final plateau. But as they passed through this no man's land – where the population was part Masai, part Gogo and part Wanyamwezi – they sustained the fiercest enemy attack since the last week in September. Masai raiders came charging in on the camp in search of cattle. Surprisingly, this time it was the *wangwana* who panicked and the Sudanese who held firm. A steady fire which dropped two warriors in their tracks broke up the assault within minutes.[119]

Next day they passed the Masai encampment. Yesterday's would-be plunderers watched them go sullenly. They crossed the Kambi plain, breasted another chain of hills and descended into another plain where they made out the distant flags of Mpwapwa.[120] Mpwapwa was now the extreme eastern outpost of German power. There to meet them was Lt. Schmidt of the Imperial German Army, who commanded a garrison of four whites and one hundred Zulu mercenaries. Schmidt broke out champagne for them. For the first time since Kavalli's Emin unbent and looked happy. Stanley caught up with international press comment and sent off a shoal of letters.[121]

After pausing for a couple of days to allow Schmidt to attend his second-in-command who was ill with dysentery, the expedition set out again. Since this part of East Africa was now recognised as German territory, the rest of the journey was supposed to be in the nature of a triumphal tour, in which Schmidt would show off his guests. The first few days of the march, up and down hills, were taxing but once they entered Usagara proper they found it a paradise after Ugogo. The presence of German troops had produced a new deference towards whites, so that the expedition no longer went in fear of enemies, but enjoyed the placid spectacle of teeming herds of buffalo, gazelle and antelope.[122]

On they went, through places familiar to Stanley from 1874 and his very first African journey in search of Livingstone eighteen years earlier: Makata, Simbambwenni, Mrogoro. 'The change in the aspect of the country since we touched the slopes dropping down to the Mukondokwa valley is marvellous. Instead of the dry and arid outlook on either hand and thorny jungles we have come among slopes and plains bedecked with lilies, which effuse a delightful fragrance.'[123]

Stanley was already nervous that the presence of Schmidt and the Germans might lure Emin away and even questioned the Pasha about his future intentions on 17 November.[124] But there was one welcome slice of serendipity for Stanley from the German presence. On 22 November Schmidt began to distribute to the whites the European provisions that Wissmann, German commander-in-chief in East Africa, had forwarded. Tired of waiting his turn, Bonny pushed to the front to demand his share in his customary bully-boy style. To Stanley's delight, Schmidt gave him the most ferocious tongue-lashing. How dared Bonny claim as of right something which was given by the Germans as a gift and over which he, Schmidt, had absolute prerogative?[125] What Stanley, for his own prudential reasons, dared not do the Germans now did for him.

On 29 November, just a few miles from the coast, at Mswa, Stanley ran into a younger version of himself in the form of Thomas Stevens, reporter for the *New York World*. When Stevens, whose previous exploits included trying to cycle across Africa and riding a mustang across Russia, arrived in Zanzibar, Wissmann told him he would not be allowed to interview Stanley on the march, as this privilege was reserved for German correspondents. With Stanley-like persistence, Stevens crossed from Zanzibar to Bagamoyo, only to be taken prisoner by Wissman's assistant Baron Gravenreuth, who released him after he had given his word of honour he would not try to find Stanley. The officer in charge of Stevens, admiring his pluck, released him from his parole, with the result that Stevens raced ahead to Mswa and scooped both the German correspondents and his rival Vizetelly, who had been sent out to 'find' Stanley by Gordon Bennett and the *New York Herald*.[126]

Stevens described the scene at Mswa: 'Big tents and little tents, groups of little grass huts which the African porter or soldier constructs for himself at every camp, were scattered over a large space, on a gentle slope, between the thorny environs of a hidden village and a dry ravine. Egyptian flags, crescent and stars on a red ground, floated lazily from tent-poles.'[127] He secured the first interview with Stanley, but Vizetelly was able to scoop him later by offering Stanley £2000 for the first *published* interview.[128] Stanley never allowed sentiment to interfere with business. He took Gordon Bennett's money while having an infinite personal preference for Stevens.[129]

In 2 December Stanley gave a celebratory dinner for his officers and Emin and Casati. Next day the Pasha seemed to have mellowed sufficiently to make a chat feasible. Now that he was at the coast, Emin seemed to have lost his irritability and eremitic propensities. He told Stanley that he had half decided to accompany Casati to Naples where they could build a villa. Appropriately enough, to signal journey's end, their conversation was interrupted by the booming of the cannon at Zanzibar which could be heard across the channel and inland. Next day

Wissmann himself appeared on the other side of the Kingani with horses for the ride to Bagamoyo. Leaving the expedition to catch them up later, Stanley, Emin and Wissmann rode to Bagamoyo, where they arrived at 11.30 a.m. on 4 December.[130] After nearly three years in which he had aged thrice that amount, Stanley once again gazed on the limpid waters of the Indian Ocean.

17

IN Bagamoyo Wissmann had prepared a sumptuous banquet for the homecomers. He had his own reasons for being delighted at the arrival of Stanley with Emin, since it cut the ground from under his compatriot and rival Peters who, having got a head start on him, was nonetheless denied the glittering prize of having 'rescued' Emin.[1] The banquet was laid out in an upper room and the guests included Emin and Casati, Stanley and his officers, the German and British consuls, representatives of the two East Africa companies, and the captains of the German naval squadron that hovered in Zanzibar waters to remind the Sultan of the time of day.

Stanley went to the banquet at 7.30 that evening (4 December) and virtually collided with Emin on the stairs. He noted that Emin was flushed with wine, but attributed this to the fact that the Kaiser had sent him a telegram of congratulation and awarded him the Order of the Crown. Upstairs, to the strains of a mediocre orchestra, there were many champagne toasts and the cables of congratulation to the expedition were read out. Unnoticed, Emin slipped from the room. The next thing Stanley observed was his 'eyes and ears' Sali running into the room, calling out that the Pasha was dead. It turned out that Emin had gone into the next room and stepped out of a window 15 feet above the ground. His fall was not, as Sali first reported it, fatal but it could well have been but for a steep lean-to roof below the window which broke his fall. Schmidt had then been summoned. He found Emin unconscious, badly bruised and bleeding from the ears. After failing to rouse the Pasha by dowsing him with cold water, Schmidt sent for a stretcher party. By the time Sali arrived at the upper room with the news, Emin was ensconced in the German hospital with severe concussion and a suspected fracture of the skull.[2]

The official version of this unfortunate accident was that Emin, notoriously shortsighted, had mistaken a low window for a door. But Stanley was convinced that Emin's fall was a suicide attempt. 'It is true that he had partaken freely of champagne that day but just a minute before the accident – as we call it – he had delivered a perfectly sensible – even brilliant speech ... the balcony wall was quite three feet high, and as it was freshly built, it bore the marks of his heels. If he did not purposely climb on that wall, it is an absolute mystery to me how the mortar had the impress of his heel.'[3] What, then, could the motive be?

Stanley had long suspected that Emin's habitual vacillation, his desire to remain in the province that had repudiated him, his foot-dragging on the return journey, especially at Mackay's mission station, his reluctance to return to Egypt even to collect his £6000 back pay – all this pointed to a hidden motive. This motive he claimed to have uncovered on arrival in Bagamoyo in December 1889. There waiting for Emin was a letter from the wife he had abandoned in Silesia in 1875, taking all her money and valuables and leaving her destitute. Her attempts to pursue him through the courts had failed because Emin had hidden himself away in Equatoria, safe from European judicial processes. But Stanley's 'rescue' had dragged him back unwillingly into the orbit of civilisation to face the censure of the world. By all accounts, the letter from Emin's wife did not make pleasant reading.[4]

The truth of all this is probably impossible to retrieve, but Emin's accident – if accident it was – removed him at a stroke from British influence and delivered him to his fellow-countrymen, to whose cause he was anyway inclining. Stanley at first demanded that Emin be transferred to Zanzibar on a British warship, but the Germans insisted their patient was too ill to be moved. Typically, Stanley then washed his hands of Emin. He paid a perfunctory visit to him in hospital and was satisfied from the fact that the Pasha shook his head that he did not have a fractured skull. Then he departed for Zanzibar, where after a 2½-hour crossing he landed at 11.30 a.m. on 6 December.[5] Parke and Jephson stayed behind a bit longer to tend to Emin; before departing for Zanzibar Jephson solemnly renewed his old friendship with the Pasha and urged him to return with them to Egypt. Emin said he would never forget that Jephson had been his comrade in captivity in Equatoria in 1888 but sentiment alone could not induce him to go to Egypt.[6]

In Zanzibar Stanley found a further shoal of telegrams awaiting him, from Leopold, Gordon Bennett, Queen Victoria, Kaiser Wilhelm and many others. The Kaiser managed to reinforce his claim to East Africa even as he congratulated the hero: 'that your way home led you through territories placed under my flag, gives me great satisfaction.' Queen Victoria had all along followed the epic journey with great interest.[7] Now she indicated her pleasure in the clearest possible terms: 'STANLEY, Zanzibar. My thoughts are often with you and your brave followers, whose dangers and hardships are now at an end. Once more I heartily congratulate all, including the survivors of the gallant Zanzibaris who displayed such devotion and fortitude during your marvellous Expedition. Trust Emin progresses favourably. VRI.'[8]

In Zanzibar Stanley was the guest of the new consul Euan-Smith, who behaved towards Stanley impeccably while being in other respects just as cross-grained an individual as his predecessor Kirk.[9] Stanley spent until 29 December writing an official report of the expedition that Euan-Smith would forward to London. He did, however, make the unStanley-like mistake of visiting Parke in hospital – Parke was now down with blackwater fever. The result was a Christmas spent in bed with fever himself.[10]

From time to time he made efforts to prise Emin out of his bolthole in Bagamoyo. Both the Pasha and Casati declined passage on the official Egyptian ship which arrived at Bagamoyo to pick up the Sudanese and Egyptian survivors of the African crossing. When Stanley sent Sali across the straits to find out how Emin was getting on, he saw further evidence that the Germans were playing the same trick he himself had used to secure Emin – a form of compassionate arrest. When Sali handed Stanley's letter to a German officer, the officer ordered Sali out of Bagamoyo and threatened him with hanging if he was found there again.[11] Stanley sent Stairs and Jephson over to verify the tale and dissuade Emin from accepting service with the Germans. Neither man was able to speak to the Pasha save in the presence of four German officers.[12] Emin was further incensed against Stanley by the reports reaching him of Stanley's unflattering character portrait and he repaid the 'compliment' in kind.[13] Stanley fumed at the unfortunate conse-quences of Emin's fall. Apart from the 'trophy' motivation, Stanley wanted Emin out of East Africa for another reason. He was still hoping that Mackinnon would invite him to lead an expedition from the IBEA base at Mombasa to set up on Lake Victoria the kind of stations he had established for Leopold on the Congo. If Emin joined German service, there was a good chance that the combination would forestall him.

Euan-Smith watched his guest with a kind of awed fascination. He noted the uneasy relations between Stanley and his officers and the antipathy for Emin.[14] To end the slave trade Stanley argued for an arms embargo to Africa by all European powers and a railway from Mombasa to Lake Victoria. But the consul evidently found the company of his guest bracing and stimulating: 'Stanley has now been a guest in my house for nearly a month and we have talked "Africa" until the most unpronounceable names are now familiar in every mouth as household words. His hair is as white as snow. When first I saw him he looked dreadfully *usé* and done up but the rest and good living have worked a wonderful change for the better in his appearance.'[15]

Two events of significance took place before Stanley departed for Mombasa on 29 December. The first was of the nature of the 'dog that barked in the night'. The future great man of Africa Frederick Lugard made a point of avoiding him. 'Between ourselves I did not care greatly about meeting Stanley. Letters of his that I had seen [not published] had made me feel disinclined to fall down and worship him, so I went up country again.'[16] This was a straw in the wind, indicating that Stanley's reputation was about to go into a nosedive in English élite circles.

The second represented one of Stanley's more serious miscalculations. He decided to institute a suit against Tippu Tip, alleging breach of contract for his failure to provide Barttelot with porters at Yambuya.[17] He lodged an indictment in consular court asking to have Tippu Tip's assets in Zanzibar (some £10,000) frozen pending the outcome of the suit. The court decided that the suit could not proceed without the Sultan's consent, as Tippu Tip was his subject. On 23 December the Sultan gave his consent and the suit proceeded. A hearing was fixed for 26 December. But since Tippu was absent and his son Sef bin Mohammed refused to appear in his place, consular judge Cracknall decided that Tippu should be given six months' grace, from the date of reception of a subpoena, to appear and answer the charges. Stanley could not wait either, so he left a written deposition countersigned by Bonny, dated 27 December.[18] The court placed under injunction the £10,000 paid by Becker to Tippu's agents for the sale of ivory. Informed opinion in Zanzibar held that Stanley's litigiousness would merely alienate the Arab to the German side.[19]

Hearing of this development, Leopold craftily saw a possibility for Belgian expansion at the expense of the Germans. He wrote to Tippu to ask him to visit Brussels for talks; in return Leopold would see that the damages suit was waived.[20] He had consulted legal and African experts about the affair, who assured him that the contract with Stanley was so vaguely worded that it could not possibly constitute grounds for a lawsuit.[21] Tippu received Leopold's letter before the subpoena from

Zanzibar and was predictably angry. His hatred towards Stanley was now at white heat. In 1891 he grudgingly came to Zanzibar to defend himself against the charges. At Bagamoyo he met Stairs and Moloney *en route* to Katanga. Tippu denounced Stanley as the most notorious liar on the continent and warned that if he returned to the Congo or East Africa again, he would be at high risk of assassination.[22]

On arrival in Zanzibar Tippu Tip hired a lawyer who easily rebutted Stanley's charges and entered a countersuit for reimbursement of all goods provided to the Emin expedition by Tippu. Over Stanley's enraged protests, it was decided to seek accommodation. Both sides withdrew their suits, and so the ill-advised litigation ended. Mackinnon was so disillusioned with Stanley over his precipitate suit (entered into without consultation with the EPRE committee) that he refrained from offering him further employment.[23]

On 29 December Euan-Smith accompanied Stanley on a warship across to Mombasa, where he was to take passage to Egypt. 'It has been very pleasant having Stanley with us for the last three weeks. We have done our best to fatten him up. I think he has really enjoyed himself, though he is looking forward immensely to the reception which awaits him in Europe. He is wonderfully well and hearty and I can see that he is quite prepared to come out to Africa again should fitting work be found for him.'[24]

On New Year's Day 1890 Stanley with his four officers and Bonny, plus the ubiquitous Sali, boarded the steamer *Katoria* for Suez.[25] Stanley was still suffering from a cold he had picked up in Zanzibar and the infected lungs plagued him for three weeks. The very idea of writing a book on the Emin expedition filled him with dread in Zanzibar as he completed its 'synopsis' in the form of the official report to Euan-Smith. He told himself he would take the first steps once at sea, but on the *Katoria* he was given a 7 × 5½ foot stateroom, into which he had to squeeze his seven boxes. Serious work would have been impossible even if he was not liable to disturbance every few minutes from the waiters.[26]

Eight days later the ship was at Aden and on 13 January they were at Suez. Here Bonny was expected to take his leave of the others, but he insisted on being put up in Cairo at the expedition's expense despite a fierce rebuke from Stanley. In Zanzibar Bonny had distinguished himself at the Grand Hotel by conduct that was far from exemplary. 'There is a good deal of drinking going on, and rows alternate with fevers,' Stanley recorded laconically over Christmas 1889. But Bonny went on to higher things. A fist-fight with a Dr Charlesworth landed him behind bars, from which he was released only on the understanding that he was forthwith permanently expelled from Zanzibar. It was a tremendous relief for Stanley when Bonny finally quit Cairo on 25 January. 'A specious rogue' was Stanley's final summing-up, but he realised that he was also a rogue whose testimony he might well need in the future.[27]

As the *Katoria* came to anchor at Suez, Stanley stood on the quarter-deck, dressed in grey tweed. His figure was very much slighter than it had been when he was last here three years earlier. His close-cut hair was now almost completely white and threw into relief the bronzed face, hard-set lips and cold grey eyes. He spent the night of 13 January at the British India Agency, then at 7 a.m. next morning boarded a special train that whisked them all to Cairo. They arrived on one of the wettest days ever known in the Egyptian capital. Water was 2 feet deep in some streets.[28] At the station to meet them were Sir Evelyn and Lady Baring, Sir Francis and Lady Grenfell and a host of ambassadors and Egyptian dignitaries. Stanley was then conveyed in a private carriage to the Khedive's residence, where they discussed Emin at length. Then it was on to Shepheard's Hotel where, because of the flooding, planks had to be laid from Stanley's carriage to the fourth step of the hotel entrance which led straight on to the verandah. In the evening there was a banquet attended by the ailing Nubar Pasha. Stanley replied to the toast with a motif he was to develop further in his book *In Darkest Africa*, alleging that his success was due to 'the finger of that Great Power – call it chance, fate, Providence or what you will.'[29]

After a period of socialising, rest, and posing for group photographs with his officers, on 25 January Stanley started work on the book that would eventually become *In Darkest Africa*. But finding the atmosphere at Shepheard's Hotel uncongenial, on 1 February he moved to the Hotel Villa Victoria to begin concentrated work.[30]

From the very earliest days Stanley's friend and editor Edward Marston had seen that the controversy surrounding the Emin Pasha expedition would make Stanley's account of it a potential bestseller. He had to beat off severe competition to retain the British rights.[31] The competition for the American rights to the book was also very severe. In the end it narrowed down to a two-horse race, between Harper Bros and Scribner Bros. After sealed bids had been invited, the palm went to Scribners, who paid a £40,000 advance.[32] Given that huge sums of money hung on the outcome of his labours, Stanley asked Marston to come to Cairo so that he could be on hand for daily consultations.

Marston found Stanley ensconced at the Hotel Villa Victoria, situated in the most beautiful part of Cairo, near the Ezbekiyeh Gardens. Surrounded on all sides by fine, newly built mansions, the Villa Victoria comprised three separate buildings, forming three sides of a quadrangle, in the centre of which was a garden of huge palms and orange trees, criss-crossed by walks. One of the orange trees, laden with ripe fruit, looked straight into Stanley's workroom. In the very centre of the garden was a fountain surrounded by tropical and oriental plants; Marston thought it a veritable lotus-land. Stanley was in the part of the hotel farthest from the street, in a fine suite of rooms on the ground floor, very handsomely furnished in the oriental style. There was a large lofty reception room and an equally large and gracious dining-room. Here Stanley girded his loins for the writing of his *magnum opus*.[33]

Stanley approached the task with trepidation. 'I knew not how to begin. Like Elihu, my memory was full of matter, and I desired to write that I might be refreshed; but there was no vent. My right hand had lost its cunning and the art of composition was lost by long disuse.'[34] He found it hard to hit his old stride again. Sometimes he could write nine folios an hour, at others he could scarcely manage a hundred words. But gradually the old skill returned and he started to cruise at his old speed. He had copious notes and diaries to write from, and from 8 a.m. to 11 p.m. every day he toiled away, hardly ever going out, even for a stroll in the gardens. He wrote at a tremendous pace, never stopping to amend or blot, and throwing the wet sheets away from him as soon as they were finished. As he frequently forgot to number his sheets, it was laborious to piece the day's work together again. He had an eccentric habit of lying on the floor while writing, resting on his left elbow while scribbling with his right hand. Stanley was able to take the strain of this all day long, where most people would soon have become exhausted through muscle tension.[35]

But the barriers to Stanley's completion of the herculean task were not just physical and mechanical. Psychologically, he faced the daunting task of exculpating himself from responsibility in the many dark incidents that had besmirched the image of the expedition. The Rear Column disaster aside, there was the appalling casualty list to explain. 708 *wangwana* set out with Stanley from Zanzibar in February 1887. Only 210 returned in December 1889.[36] Of 555 of Emin's followers who had joined him at Kavalli's, only 290 reached the coast. Of the sixty Sudanese whom Stanley had taken to the Congo only twelve survived and one only of the thirteen Somalis lived to tell the tale.[37] Ulcers, fevers, fatigue, debility, abandonment, straggling and skirmishes had done for the rest.

Arguably Jackson had achieved more with less cost, less pomp and less bloodshed.[38] The greatest irony was that not a pound of Equatoria's rich hoard of ivory ever reached the coast. Emin told Father Schynse with great bitterness that the lust for ivory had always been the main motive of Stanley and Mackinnon.[39] This might well have been true of Mackinnon, but if so he was sorely disappointed. Most of it was dumped into the Nile during the civil disturbances in Equatoria and the rest passed into the hands of the Mahdists.[40] Against this were some substantial achievements in exploration and geography: the Ituri, the Semliki, Ruwenzori, etc., but scarcely enough to atone for the fearful loss of life.

Stanley naturally skated lightly over the dark side of the expedition, except when to deal with it was unavoidable, as with the Rear Column, in which case he threw the blame for the fiasco on to anyone and everyone but himself. He presented the expedition as an achievement in the heroic mould. By the middle of February he was in full flight with the writing. 'I am sailing now right ahead with scudding sails set, and fair weather. Two months' more steady work will see me through. If I had this book on my back in England, I should be unfit to go into society.'[41]

For two months Stanley rarely ventured out of his room even for a stroll in the garden. He refused to go for a drive with Parke and on the one occasion he consented to an excursion to the Nile, with Marston, he was so restless and preoccupied that after half an hour Marston was glad to let him flee back to his sanctuary. At lunch and dinner he would be agreeably chatty for an hour then disappear to his cloister. The only drink he touched was Apollinaris water laced with a tablespoonful of brandy. His abstemiousness led him to neglect his rare lunch and dinner guests, as he never thought to offer them anything to drink. Nothing irritated him more than a tap at the door when he was working. He sometimes glared tigerishly even at Marston, who was of necessity a frequent and privileged intruder. He terrified Sali by roaring in agony if ever the black boy brought him a telegram, so that in the end Sali simply poked the offending cable into the room on the end of a bamboo pole and bolted. Stanley excused his curmudgeonly behaviour like this: 'When my work is accomplished, then I will talk with you, laugh with you and play with you or ride with you to your heart's content, but let me alone now for heaven's sake.'[42]

The one intrusion on his time Stanley permitted was to Miss E. M. Merrick, who had been commissioned by Sir John Elliott and the RGS to paint his portrait. Even so, he was an impatient sitter, alternating between taciturnity and garrulousness. And he fussed over the details.

When the sittings were over, he would place a large looking-glass next to the portrait to compare his likeness. Next time Miss Merrick would be handed notes on which would be written instructions: 'Nose not straight enough', 'Forehead too low', 'Hair too grey', etc. He was inordinately vain about his eyes. 'Take care of my eyes,' he told her, 'for Stanley's eyes are known all over the world.' On one occasion he consented to give an interview to a Belgian journalist while he was sitting but soon regretted it. He became exasperated with the questions about his private life and boomed at the questioner: 'If people would only try and discover what Stanley has done and not who Stanley is, they would be saving themselves much time and trouble.'[43]

As he hit his stride and the writing progressed more fluently, Stanley became impatient of any and every interruption, however necessary. He wrote tetchily to Mackinnon: 'There are a lot of idlers in Cairo who pester one to death, sit with one for half an hour for nothing. I have not a word to say to them except monosyllables – and it is quite amusing to watch one resolved to bore me to the utmost limits and I resolved to be patient.'[44] But for many of the interruptions from Marston Stanley had only himself to blame. All the photographs he had taken in Africa turned out to be either under- or over-exposed. He had not written the first few chapters (before Marston arrived) in copying ink. And he clashed with Marston's artist Joseph Bell, who insisted on naturalistic accuracy in the illustrations. On one occasion Bell and Stanley were discussing an illustration of a porter crossing a river with a donkey.

'Did the porter carry a rifle?' asked Bell.

'Of course,' replied Stanley.

'And in what hand did he carry the rifle,' Bell pressed him, 'seeing that one hand is already engaged in guiding and helping the donkey and the other in swimming for dear life?' Stanley scowled at him. He had no sense of humour where his own glory and reputation were involved.[45]

At last, after fifty days, the task was completed. The 900-page book, compiled from 903 foolscap sheets of manuscript, had been written at the rate of 8000 words a day. Since in the same time Stanley had also written 400 letters and fired off one hundred telegrams, it is hardly surprising that the writing of the book was hailed by many journalists as a more astounding feat than the expedition itself.[46]

Most of the writing time not spent on the book during February–March 1890 was devoted to analyses of the officers who had accompanied him through the valley of the shadow of death. Although Stanley liked Parke best at a personal level – because he had not breathed a word of criticism of his leader – the man he considered the best officer was Stairs, and he now regretted that he had not placed him in command of the Rear Column, Barttelot's seniority notwithstanding. Stairs was remarkably quick at getting the hang of things; he could improvise and think on his feet. Most of all, he was the one white whom the Africans truly respected: 'He was a man to them with a big "M", with his superior wits ever on the alert, sharp, active, ready, with every sense at instant command.'[47]

Nelson, too, made great strides and at the end was physically the toughest of them all. As yet, however, Stanley was ambivalent about Jephson. His generosity and sociability were offset by hotheadedness. Jephson operated on a short fuse; hence his nickname among the Africans 'Bubu-rika' ('the cheetah') – denoting his tendency to spring at them if they did not obey instantly. 'He has a deal to learn yet before he is capable of commanding men.' But Stanley admitted his besetting fault as a commander when he confessed to Mackinnon: 'I never permitted myself in Africa to indulge in laudation of any act however well done.'[48]

But even beyond these jottings, Stanley did manage to deal with an avalanche of letters and telegrams in Cairo, sometimes by having Marston answer for him.[49] In other cases he had no choice but to take pen in hand himself. There was the suit against Tippu Tip to deal with, the question of payment and compensation for the survivors of the expedition, wranglings with Sanford over the lease of the *Florida* and considerable routine correspondence with the EPRE committee.[50] Stanley was glad when the burden of writing was lifted and he was able to take ship for the French Riviera at the end of March.

At Cannes he was Mackinnon's guest on board his yacht.[51] Then he took the train to Belgium there for a week in April he was treated by Leopold and the Belgians almost as though he were a visiting head of state.[52] All of this he had dreaded and he endured it with an inner loathing. 'I am angry with myself that, conscious of my physical and mental unfitness for such a life, I do not utter a decided "no" and depart to leave myself in some quite retreat.'[53] Yet even in Belgium the vista was not unclouded for, with *In Darkest Africa* yet unpublished, Stanley was propelled into the headlines as a stalking horse in the growing Anglo-German rivalry over East Africa.

In allying himself with Mackinnon, Stanley became involved in a head-on clash between German ambitions for an African colony running east-west across the continent and the idea of the map painted red from the Cape

to Cairo which was the dream of Mackinnon, Harry Johnston and Cecil
Rhodes. Although Stanley was not an ideological imperialist as they
were, he did believe in annexing valuable territories, and it was his proud
boast at the end of the Emin expedition that he had made treaties with
six different rulers through whose lands he passed on the march from
Lake Albert, ceding suzerainty to Britain.[54]

But the Germans challenged the validity of the 'treaties', pointing out
(rightly) that non-aggression pacts and blood-brotherhood ceremonies
were not the same things as treaties yielding sovereignty. Stanley was
asked to justify his claim to have signed treaties. He produced two
different arguments. One was that he had had to make the treaties
informally, since Emin and Casati were with him. The other was that
his call for the annexation of the territories was made independently of
his agreement with the chiefs.[55]

The issue came to a head after the Peters expedition into the interior
of East Africa, in the course of which he signed a formal treaty with
Mwanga, pretender to the Ugandan throne – the man who had unsuc-
cessfully solicited Stanley's assistance. The English and German press
whipped up the Stanley-Peters rivalry into a re-run of the Stanley-Brazza
affair a decade earlier. It was alleged in England that Peters' pretensions
in Uganda were bogus in the light of the Stanley treaties. Stanley
meanwhile claimed that everything between the Aruwimi and the eastern
shores of Lakes Victoria and Tanganyika was British by right of effective
occupation, viz., his marches during the Emin expedition.[56]

The position of the protagonists, Peters and Stanley, was immensely
complicated by the lukewarm support each man received from his
respective government. Stanley lamented that he could not compete with
Peters if he had support from Berlin while Mackinnon had none from
London.[57] But in fact opinion in Berlin was very far from monolithic.
Bismarck's line was that Germany already had enough African possessions and in any case he did not want friction with Britain just
because Stanley and Peters wished to re-run the Stanley-Brazza game.[58]
London's view was that Stanley's 'treaties' would have to be watertight
in international law before the Empire took on Germany over the issue.
Both the sorcerers' apprentices tugged at the leash. Peters claimed it
was an open secret that the German Emin Pasha expedition was a
colonialising enterprise.[59] Stanley aggravated the situation by making
inflammatory speeches about the disputed territory in the lake country.[60]

Both Lord Salisbury in England and Bismarck in Germany wanted to
play down their rivalries in East Africa. Hatzfeldt, the German ambassa-

dor in London, assured Salisbury that Uganda and Wadelai and all places to the east and north of Lake Victoria were outside the sphere of German colonial ambition.[61] But behind the scenes in both countries powerful forces manoeuvred to bring about a head-on collision. On both sides the Royal Family was inclined to take the hawkish view. The young Kaiser Wilhelm was sympathetic to Peters, and when he dismissed Bismarck later in 1890 he was inclined to give 'the German Stanley' his head. Opponents of Salisbury's 'softly-softly' approach warned Queen Victoria that to allow Germany to dominate the Lake Tanganyika region might lead to a dip in the Tory government's popularity so disastrous that the dreaded Gladstone would be returned to power. Salisbury found himself having to write private memoranda to the Queen, explaining his opposition to Stanley's ideas.[62]

When Stanley arrived back in England at the end of 1890, the pace of controversy hotted up. In speech after speech he warned that the Salisbury government was letting slip a great opportunity in East Africa. The combative Salisbury, after taking discreet soundings from Leopold, decided to hit back. In a speech at the Merchant Taylors' Banquet on 22 May 1890 he poked fun at the 'African lion' then at the very height of his popularity.

Mr Stanley has warned you that the British government is doing terrible things – that it has surrendered vast forests and tremendous mountains and great kingdoms which he has offered the British public to occupy; and he gives you mysterious hints in order that you may interfere in time or – if you do not interfere – that you may be satisfied to submit to his threat that the Company with which he is connected will abandon Africa to its fate.[63]

But in fact all the time Stanley was speaking with forked tongue. To his large audiences he spoke of the chances being squandered after he had laid the foundation with his treaties. Yet to the Foreign Office he conceded that he had no written treaties that would stand up in international law.[64] When the Germans challenged Stanley to make good his boasts, the Foreign Office intervened to say that Stanley was irrelevant; he was a private explorer, not a British official, so that nothing he did could bind the British government.[65]

This official smokescreen masked considerable irritation in Whitehall that Stanley had embarrassed the government and brought it into collision with Germany on the strength of a will o' the wisp. Sir Percy Anderson of the Foreign Office produced the underestimate of the year when he minuted with regard to the conflicting claims: 'If there is a liar about (and there must be one), I should be surprised to learn that it is Stanley, though of course it may be.'[66] The likelihood that Stanley was the liar became certainty when Stanley produced the map of his journeys in *In Darkest Africa*. It became clear that the larger British pretensions could not be sustained even on the basis of first possession. Mackinnon suffered yet another disappointment in his famous protégé.[67]

There was considerable irony here. At Bagamoyo Stanley had told the reporter Stevens that hardly anyone except himself kept promises. 'Mr Stanley said also, that he believes that in every profession and every walk of life, simple, straightforward truth always triumphs over falsehood and deceit.'[68] He went on to say that the secret of Bismarck's success was that he never lied, and that his truth-telling was received with incredulity by other diplomats. Apart from the grotesque humbug of Stanley's presenting himself as a mythical George Washington, one can only smirk at the retrospective insight that it was Bismarck himself who a few months later was the victim of Stanley's penchant for 'expedient exaggerations'.

The Anglo-German dispute of 1890 over East Africa was settled in the end, not by rhetoric or propaganda from Stanley or anyone else, but, predictably, by *haute politique*. This time Britain won the battle for spheres of influence in East Africa. Faced with a possible war with France and Russia, Berlin needed British support. In return for the cession of Heligoland to Germany, the Kaiser consented to a British sphere of influence from Uganda to the Congo boundaries and a British protectorate in Zanzibar. The entire area between Mozambique and the British sphere of influence became German East Africa – virtually identical to the Tanganyika of the post-World War One mandated territory, except that German East Africa included Ruanda-Urundi.

One final consequence of the Anglo-German conflict in 1890 and Stanley's role in it was that Emin Pasha threw in his lot with his compatriots. Since Stanley had beaten Peters to the punch by getting to Emin first, the only way the Germans could retrieve their laurels was by suborning Emin in turn away from the British. The paths to this objective were made straight by Stanley's sustained jeers and jibes at Emin, which not only further enraged the Pasha against Stanley and all his works but destroyed Emin's credibility with Mackinnon and the IBEA Company.[69]

Yet there is evidence that Emin was reluctant to become a German agent. On 13 March 1890, now fully recovered from his injuries, he had a long conversation with Euan-Smith. He began by rehearsing the history of his dealings with Stanley. He confirmed that he had turned down the idea of service with Leopold, since he remained convinced that the Congo State would either collapse or fall into the hands of the French. He attacked Stanley for failing to honour the Kavirondo promise, not allowing him to join the Jackson expedition, and for failing to help Mwanga in Uganda. He lamented the fact that Stanley's calumnies had ended his chances of working for Mackinnon's IBEA Company and he was considering writing a book to present his side of the case.[70]

In fact it was not Stanley's opposition that damned Emin. Both Euan-Smith and Kirk had independently come to the conclusion that Emin as a British agent would be more liability than asset. Even as they spoke, Euan-Smith had within his gift the post of Administrator-in-Chief of the IBEA Company, and Mackinnon himself was in favour of the appointment, as an irritated journal entry from Stanley shows clearly.[71] But Euan-Smith thought Emin utterly unsuitable for the post, and in this opinion he was backed by Kirk, finally in full agreement with Stanley about something. Kirk wrote: 'I am glad we are rid of Emin – he has been a grossly exaggerated man and would have been to us a fearful encumbrance – I have little doubt he will become more German than the Germans themselves – for after all he is I believe or was a German Jew and one with not a particularly bright record until he got on under Gordon. Of course he is a remarkable man and a scientific man but no administrator.'[72]

The sequel was predictable. Unless he was to return to Europe – which he always refused adamantly to do – Emin now had no choice but to accept the service which Wissmann offered him at £1000 a year.[73] Wissmann coaxed Emin into a substantial propaganda assault against Stanley and the British. First, Emin wrote to the Sultan to complain about the personal discourtesy meted out to him by the British.[74] Next he wrote a letter dissociating himself from Stanley's suit against Tippu Tip.[75] Since the German intention was obviously to swing the injured Tippu over to their cause, Stanley was forced to advise Euan-Smith that the only way to trump Germany's ace was by abandoning the lawsuit and freeing Tippu's assets so that he would not be permanently alienated.[76] He neglected to point out that the entire mess involving both Tippu and Emin had arisen in the first place because of his own injudicious treatment of them.

When it was learned in London that Emin had entered the service of Britain's rivals after so much blood and treasure had been spent by the British in getting him out of Equatoria, there was a predictable outcry.

At this stage the version that Emin was a mere ingrate was almost universally accepted, for Stanley was riding high in popular esteem.[77] Even Stanley saw that Emin's service with Germany turned his expedition into a thing of farce, though he could never admit this publicly.[78] But in the short term the 'betrayal' played into his hands by stoking the fires of anti-German feeling in England. Only when the full Emin expedition scandal broke in the columns of British newspapers at the end of 1890 did the more thoughtful analysts attempt a reappraisal.

Emin got his wish to become, like Livingstone, a wanderer over Africa. If his fall at Bagamoyo on the evening of 4 December 1889 was, as Stanley suspected, a form of death-wish, Emin's unconscious desires soon found fulfilment. In October 1892 he was deep in the Ituri forest when he became the first victim of the imminent war between Leopold's Congo and the Arab slavers. On the orders of the Arab chief Kibonge he was murdered while under a safe-conduct. But the cynics maintained that after 1889 Emin was always a mere shadow of his former self, that he had been 'killed' in all but physical form by Stanley's brutal treatment of him.[79] Stanley's fall from grace was like Lucifer's. He had begun his career by revering the one true man of Africa in his era, and ended it by destroying another such *rara avis* – surely the appropriate term, given Emin's predilections. Stanley's life was now in steep decline in more senses than one.

· 18 ·

STANLEY arrived at Dover from Belgium on 26 April 1890 to
be greeted by the Mayor and Corporation as 'Henry Mortlake
Stanley'. The pressmen who were there to accompany him
on the train journey to London found him looking very bored. With
snow-white hair and a 'Chinaman complexion' like unburnt clay, he
puffed away phlegmatically at his cigar.[1] Once in London he had a string
of social engagements to fulfil, the most important of which were with
the Royal Family.

As early as February de Winton had written to him about the immense
interest in his affairs by Queen Victoria and her family.[2] Leopold too
was primed to let the Queen know the very second Stanley had completed his private talks in Brussels.[3] Consequently, Stanley's first social
engagement was at Sandringham where, in company with Mackinnon,
de Winton and Parke, he gave an after-dinner lecture on Africa to the
future George V.[4] On 3 May he attended a reception at St James's Hall
in the presence of the Prince of Wales and other royalty. Finally, on the
6th he was received at Windsor Castle in private audience by the Queen
herself. She found him more prepossessing than in 1872 but still
remarkably cagey about his future plans.[5] But Victoria was swept along
by the current Stanley-mania. Not only did she commission a portrait
of Stanley's head from the painter Angeli, but she toyed with awarding
him a knighthood then and there. De Winton advised her that it would
be better to wait until after the publication of *In Darkest Africa*, as the
book was likely to be controversial. So she contented herself with sending
him a jewelled portrait of herself.[6]

The diary of engagements gave Stanley scarcely a moment of leisure.
A reception by the EPRE committee was followed by a banquet and
speech at the Royal Geographical Society. Then came dinners and
banquets from a variety of sources: the Corporation of London (who

gave him the freedom of the City); the Turners' Company, the Chamber of Commerce, the Merchant Taylors, the Fishmongers' Company, the Savage Club, the Society of Expatriate Americans.[7] In the speeches he gave to these assemblies, Stanley largely followed the line he had given to Vizetelly of the *New York Herald* at Msua, stressing the discoveries on the Aruwimi and in the Ituri, the attempted ascent of Ruwenzori, the charting of Lake Albert and Lake Edward. The providential theme was again well to the fore: 'A veritable divinity seems to have hedged us while we journeyed . . . a higher plan than mine . . . the vulgar will call it luck, unbelievers will call it chance but deep down in each heart remains a feeling, that of a verity there are more things in heaven and earth than are dreamed of in common philosophy . . . their [his companions] diet has been all the time what the legal serfs of Sing Sing would have declared infamous and abominable and yet they live.'[8]

In the speech to the Royal Geographical Society he concentrated on the gains of the expedition, anticipating the criticism to come. Apart from the new discoveries, he had unlocked huge quantities of rubber and gum to trade, had opened up the farthest recesses of the Dark Continent to Christianity and had established that in the Aruwimi there were 10,000 million more trees than mankind knew about before.[9] Not all his listeners were that impressed by this hectoring way with statistics. One journalist reported acidly: 'Except that it will furnish some new Catullus with a fresh comparison for his demand of kisses from some new Lesbia, we see nothing particularly interesting in the 10,000 millions.'[10]

May, June and July 1890 saw Stanley's reputation at its apogee. For now the few voices raised in opposition were crying in a wilderness. John Burns, later to be the first working-class Cabinet Minister in Britain, waxed incandescent at the proposal to give Stanley the freedom of the newly constituted London County Council, and John Bright made a vigorous defence against Stanley's contemptuous attack on the Quakers' work in Africa.[11] But almost everyone else joined in the uncritical adulation for a great expedition successfully accomplished. The sensation continued with the publication of *In Darkest Africa* on 28 June. This was a bestseller that outstripped by far the considerable success of his earlier books. 150,000 copies were sold, and impresarios in North America and Australia at once began clamouring for the explorer's presence in the lecture halls.[12] Stanley spent June in a triumphal progress through Scotland. He collected the freedoms of Edinburgh, Glasgow, Dundee, Aberdeen and Manchester, and attended degree ceremonies at Edinburgh and Oxford where he was awarded the honorary LLD and

DCL respectively. The conferring of similar doctorates at Durham and Cambridge was held over until the autumn to accommodate his bulging engagement calendar.[13]

Among those who had watched with trepidation Stanley's perilous three-year odyssey in Central Africa and followed the many newspaper accounts of his death was Dorothy Tennant, the woman who had rejected his marriage proposal in 1886.[14] On Stanley's return she ventured a wish to see him. She began the letter formally but ended with 'Bula Matari, do not be too proud to come.'[15] He did not answer this, but on 3 May at a crowded party she tried again. She grasped his hand and whispered, 'Come to me.' But he rebuffed her coldly: 'It is hard to say it – I must decline the pleasure of approaching you . . . you will do wisely and well to leave me alone.'[16] On 6 May she made a further overture, explaining that she just wished to say goodbye and to tell him that his letter of proposal in 1886 had always been sacred to her.

> What I wrote to you in '86 was only true in this sense. Suppose a wild, uncultivated tract of land and suppose that one day this land is ploughed up and sown with corn. If the field could speak it might say: 'I have never borne corn, I do not bear corn, I shall never bear corn.' And yet all the while the wheat lies hidden in its bosom. When you were gone, when you were out of reach, I slowly realised what you had become to me, and then great anguish filled me. I then made myself a vow that I would train myself to strive to become wiser and stronger, better, gentler and then, when you came back I would see you and tell you all quite simply, and say 'Truly I have never cared for anyone but you. I did not know it when you wrote to me, for till you wrote the possibility of your caring for me had never even occurred to me. But at that time I was not worthy of your love. Now I believe I am, let me help you and take care of you, and be everything in the world to you.' But there was vanity in this, for it presupposed your still caring for me.[17]

Stanley replied from Windsor, where he was the guest of Queen Victoria. He explained that he had been humiliated in 1886 as if he had been a base-born churl in the presence of a queen. 'I worshipped you as a goddess and the goddess spurned me . . . please take this as an explanation, and not as recrimination . . . had such possibilities approached me in 1886, I would have been delirious with joy, nothing in all the wide world would have been so blissful.'[18]

On 7 May the two met at an evening party. Dolly told him she would be his wife if he still loved her.[19] But now it was Stanley that was playing hard to get. He replied curtly next day: 'let us be good friends.'[20] This cold douche thrown in her face made her redouble her efforts. She wrote again, explaining that she realised what he meant to her only after he had departed on the Emin expedition. She had taken a vow to make herself morally and spiritually worthy of him, which was why she now accepted an equal pain in rejection to that he had suffered in 1886. 'Oh Bula Matari, listen to me. If I made you suffer I have expiated the wrong done. Remember the difference between us. You were a man, you knew more of life, you had loved before. I was a girl unacquainted with love . . . Yours was only a flower, a rose you say which I crushed. But my love is a flame which will never die, it began so small a spark you could not see it light, now it burns like the altar flame never to be extinguished [her underlining].'[21]

Having received the obeisance he required, Stanley allowed himself to admit to his emotional need for a wife. On 13 May he made a formal proposal of marriage. The note containing this reached her at Richmond Terrace at 4.30 that afternoon. She wrote back at once.

My own beloved Bula-Matari,
It is all true – and not a dream and I am really to be yours. If you did but know how I love you, how intensely I love you. I am afraid of my joy, after so much unhappiness it seems too much light.[22]

Next day she called on him at 34 De Vere Mansions and after a short talk, they agreed to make their engagement public. Two days later Stanley came to see her mother and brought along a diamond engagement ring for Dolly. The news travelled swiftly among the London socialites. Baroness Burdett-Coutts at once invited the explorer's fiancée to the Turners' banquet. The following Wednesday Dolly and her mother attended a party at the Foreign Office, then withdrew from society to prepare for the wedding. Press reporting of the event tended to be on the waspish side. Many, then and later, asserted that Dorothy Tennant was too good for Stanley.[23] Others drew attention to Dolly's opportunism. Apparently a picture she was exhibiting shortly before the engagement had been priced at £200. The secretary of the gallery received an offer of £170 and wrote to Dolly to advise her to take it. He was surprised to receive a curt note by return, ordering him to accept not a penny less than £200. Then he read in the press of the engagement to Stanley and everything fell into place.[24]

Great fun was also had with Stanley's admission to the Savage Club that in Africa he had been as chaste as Galahad.[25] One columnist remarked: 'An interesting fact, doubtless, and very comforting, maybe, to the wife of his bosom: but of what public concern? Who cares much whether he preserved his virtue intact or ran riot in the jungle?'[26] Private comment too tended to be critical. Beatrice Webb, an acquaintance of Dolly's, found the public engagement vulgar.[27] Frank Harris, told that the charming Dorothy Tennant was to marry the 'lion of the season', remarked that a truer description was that she was about to marry the king of beasts, for Stanley always seemed to him a force without a conscience.[28]

More tact and sensitivity was shown by Frederick Myers, the English poet and founder-member of the Society for Psychical Research, who had married Dolly's sister Eveleen in 1880.[29] He wrote at once with his congratulations and an assessment of his sister-in-law. He found her spoiled, impetuous and not always wise. Against this she offered, as few other women did, cheerful, loving, helpful and intelligent companionship. Welcoming Stanley as his brother-in-law he went on: 'You will understand that it is not your fame that makes me feel this. Nothing would be more disagreeable to me, as an intimate member of the Richmond Terrace group, than to have a new and overwhelming fame and importance suddenly plunged down beside me in the family, unless that man were one whom I could myself honour and care for his personal and private qualities.'[30]

What assessment can we make of this whirlwind courtship and engagement? Is is very clear in retrospect that in 1886 Stanley had unconsciously willed the rejection that Dorothy Tennant had meted out to him, just as he had done earlier with Virginia Ambella, Katie Gough-Roberts and Alice Pike. This is the hidden subtext of the letters where he had seemed to go out of his way to pick fights with her over Gladstone and the working man. This was part of the syndrome of simultaneous attraction and repulsion that characterised all Stanley's dealings with women. He had not counted, however, on the boomerang effect of Dolly's conversion while he was on the road to Wadelai. The torrent of poignant regret and damned emotion she released on him swept away his defences for the moment. But the unconscious was to strike back before the wedding, as we shall see.

Dolly in her own way was as much a pyschoanalytical study as her would-be husband. There is something bizarre and disconcerting about the way she refers to herself in 1886 (when she was thirty-four) as a 'girl'; arrested development seems a mild term in the circumstances. And there is surely much unconscious significance in the symbolism of the field of corn. 'I have never borne corn, I do not bear corn, I *never shall* bear corn [her underlining].' This seems to denote either an admission of barrenness or a morbid fear of childbirth and points forward to the scarcely surprising eventuality that her marriage with Stanley was childless. The unconscious impetus of her feelings towards Stanley seems to be the need to find a surrogate father, after years of corresponding with the dead original.

I sometimes realise how little I really know of life, and passions and tragedies and all the turmoil. Thank God you will take care of me and shield me and keep me from harm. I dread the world, the real world. Of course, the world of London parties is only like play-acting. What I shirk from is dealing with the rough outside world, being deceived by people. I see by reading and observing how people drift into being bad and miserable. I hate the world. Oh keep me close to you, put your arms around me. Don't think I can stand alone. People here called me 'self-sufficing', they say I am independent, I did not invite confidences. But it was not really so, only I felt there was more dignity in standing aloof so long as I could not, would not, lean for ever on anyone I met. But you are beside me now, my rock, my prop, my bulwark against the great breakers of life.[31]

Dolly's implicit conditions for the marriage contained the unspoken assumption that it meant the end of his career as African explorer. Harry Johnston, his old friend and admirer, was urging this consummation on both partners in the run-up period to the marriage. On 6 June he wrote to Stanley as follows: 'Go no more to Africa. You have now secured – surely – enough glory for your lifetime and for history. Sit down therefore and enjoy yourself for the rest of your natural life. I called you once in a magazine article "The Napoleon Bonaparte of exploration". Well, you have now won your Austerlitz. Stop short and do not risk a Moscow or a Waterloo.'[32]

In similar vein he addressed Dolly a little later. 'I am so glad you are going to marry him, and I think you will be happy in so doing *if* [three times underlined] you don't go to Africa. *Don't go to Africa* [three times underlined]. Your mission is to reconcile Stanley to England, where he must reside as "Agent General" for Africa. Stanley must go into Parliament and you must help him, nurse him, encourage him, entertain for him, and generally be that real helpmeet to him that only a good wife can be. So will his career meet with its true fruition.'[33]

Dolly replied the same day. 'The future lies before me a dark unexplored continent. I have never questioned Mr Stanley about it – but – I confess to you – I have my hidden away fears. I *dread* Africa. I have read far too much about it not to dread Africa. But if he *must return* – I go with him. If duty urges him to return I shall not *dare* dissuade him. Your words therefore greatly console me. You make me hope that possibly he may not consider it his bounden duty to return to Africa.'[34]

As the day scheduled for the wedding drew closer, the unconscious 'failsafe' mechanism which would ensure an escape from actual intimacy, rather than the fantasy of the 'ideal woman', was triggered. Stanley felt violently ill and there was doubt whether the ceremony could proceed as planned. The official diagnosis was gastritis, but why the explorer should have been attacked at this precise time, rather than in Cairo when he was under enormous pressure to finish his book, was not explained. Certainly his letter to Mackinnon at the beginning of July hardly indicates *coup de foudre*. 'Were *she* the ugliest little mortal in existence, I think I would marry her, provided I could get some excuse for breaking away from this weary, frivolous world of writers of letters upon nothing.'[35]

Until the very morning of 12 July, a question mark hung over the wedding. Then on the morning itself Stanley struggled out of bed and, supported by Parke, tottered into the carriage that would take him to Westminster Abbey. Despite the drenching rain, huge crowds had gathered outside the Abbey to witness the event; the police had great difficulty controlling them. Inside, every one of the Abbey seats was taken. 5000 people had been refused admission tickets, but even so many a leading light of London society was reduced to standing in the aisles. Among those present were Gladstone, the Lord Chancellor, the Speaker of the House of Commons, dozens of dukes and duchesses and, as groomsmen, Parke, Stairs, Jephson, Nelson and even Bonny. There were representatives of the military and exploring worlds. The ceremony was conducted by two Deans and a Bishop and the Master of Trinity, Cambridge, gave the marriage address. Best man was Leopold's representative, the Comte d'Arche.[36]

The first sensation of the day was when Stanley hobbled up to the altar on a walking stick, still too ill to be present in anything but body.

There he sat in an armchair and awaited his bride. Then Dolly swept into the Abbey on the arm of Sir John Millais. She wore a dress of white silk and satin and from her neck dripped a panoply of jewels: a diamond necklace from Mackinnon, a diamond locket from Queen Victoria, a bracelet from Leopold, and a sapphire and diamond bracelet from Stanley.[37]

Stanley suffered agonies until the service was over. Then he was helped to his carriage outside and the newly-weds drove the short distance to Richmond Terrace, still through immense crowds. 'The police struggled in vain to keep back the fighting, shouting, maddened people,' Dolly wrote in her diary. 'I felt so faint and dreaded seeing some horror, some terrible accident. I closed my eyes and only opened them when I felt the carriage go rather quicker. A reinforcement of mounted police had come to the rescue.'[38]

After an inspection of the wedding presents[39] the couple departed with Parke to Waterloo Station, there to entrain for Hampshire. Louisa, Lady Ashburton, had lent them Melchett Court in the New Forest for the honeymoon, though Stanley continued so ill that he could scarcely write, much less consummate his marriage.[40] Gradually, over a month he began to recover and take walks in the countryside. 'We might be in the great Congo forests for all that we see once we enter the woods.'[41]

The real honeymoon did not take place until August, when the Stanleys departed for Maloja in Switzerland, via London and Paris. And it is at the Hotel Kursaal in Maloja that we get our first important clues to the reality of the Stanley marriage. The evidence is in two parts. In the first place, Stanley absolutely insisted that he would not go to Switzerland on honeymoon unless Jephson came too as a 'minder'.[42] By now he had fastened on Jephson as yet another in the long series of young male companions he always needed at his side. Not since Albert Christopherson in the Congo had he found a man who fitted the bill so well. Jephson, who was bemused by the request to accompany the honeymooners, but was flattered by Stanley's interest, inadvertently tapped into some of Stanley's deeper feelings when he prodded his leader for assurance of his esteem and affection. Stanley wrote back: 'You remember the crossing of the Lufu . . . well had I been in condition to indulge in a sentiment which was near to the tip of my tongue I think I should have revealed pretty clearly my kindly feelings towards you. You remember your leading the caravan one day . . . I came near adding "Come to my arms, Jephson."'[43]

The second part of the evidence is in the form of the cancelled passages in Stanley's private journals. Dorothy Stanley suffered from the disease that seemed to beset the wives of African explorers – for we observe the same syndrome with Isabel Burton, Lady Lugard and the wife of Sir Harry Johnston: a desire to expunge the true record so as to present to the world an idealised version of the husband-hero. The journal recording the events of Stanley's private life contains several passages scored out in ink by Dolly. On one page, however, relating to the honeymoon trip to Switzerland, the ending of one entry is legible: 'I do not regard it wifely, to procure these pleasures, at the cost of making me feel like a monkey in a cage.'[44]

Taken together, the two pieces of honeymoon evidence seem to point to a conclusion that is wholly unsurprising in terms of the sexual profile of Stanley adumbrated below (see pp.394-96). Stanley's schizoid personality, which prevented him from integrating love for a woman with carnality, extended into a bisexual limbo where he was incapable of active participation in either heterosexual or homosexual intercourse. He combined a desperate need for love with a desperate fear of intimacy. Attracted to female beauty and grace, yet horrified by the sexuality of women, Stanley was at the same time incapable of out-and-out homosexuality. The coexisting heterosexual and homosexual impulses both remained at a latent repressed level. When he was finally called upon to satisfy a wife, Stanley in effect broke down and confessed that he considered sex for the beasts. The unconscious motive for getting himself rejected by four different women was made manifest. The presence of Jephson in the selfsame hotel where this tragic marital breakdown was being played out suggests that Stanley used the homosexual elements in his own personality as a kind of rudder to maintain his psychic equilibrium.

But to the outer world Stanley maintained the fiction that his was a blissful marriage. 'Dolly is better than fine gold. She is infinitely better than any conception I had of her. She knows something of everything, and when she does not allow her politeness to restrain her, she is wise in her remarks.'[45] And at the mundane level Stanley enjoyed his time in Switzerland. By chance Sir Richard and Lady Isabel Burton were staying at the same hotel; the two explorers had many stimulating discussions about Africa and their contemporaries, though Dolly found Burton's cynicism and forthrightness hard to adjust to.[46] Stanley also wrote an introduction to Jephson's book on Emin Pasha and the rebellion in Equatoria. Jephson was thrilled at the master's praise and at the prospect that his preface would secure it an American sale.[47] It seems clear that the influence of Jephson and Burton tugged one way and Dolly another, for Stanley told Mackinnon: 'I have no immediate purpose of going to Africa as I am bound by my lecture tour but there might come a time when having fulfilled all my engagements I might think European life too dreary to be endured.'[48]

From Maloja they went south to Lake Como, then on to Milan and Monza where they were met by Casati and his long-time patron Captain Camperio who entertained the Stanleys regally at his delightful country house La Santa near Monza. Casati had mellowed in his attitude to Stanley and was now inclined to agree with him about the shortcomings of his old friend Emin Pasha.[49] After Monza the Stanleys travelled to Geneva, then on for a sentimental stay at the Hôtel Meurice in Paris. The European jaunt ended with a four-day working sojourn with Leopold in Ostend.[50]

On 8 October the Stanleys arrived back in England. Jephson related that Parke met them at the station but could hardly get a word out of Stanley as 'he was in such ecstasies at again meeting his mother-in-law'.[51] Given Stanley's normal contemptuous impatience with elderly females, this was a surprising development, but strong bonds had evidently been forged between him and Gertrude Tennant. When Stanley told his would-be mother-in-law of his engagement to her daughter, she advised him that she would not give her consent unless she was taken completely into the family. A tearful scene ended with Stanley giving her *carte blanche* in his household. This gesture completely won the old lady over. She told Mrs French Sheldon that she loved Stanley as a son and was confident that her daughter would be in safe hands: 'it is a great privilege for any woman to be linked with a character and a career like Mr Stanley's.'[52]

The bonds with Gertrude Tennant were tightened when it was announced that she would accompany her daughter and son-in-law on the coming lecture tour of the USA. An interesting spectacle of dependency ensued. Dolly had her mother at her side and in compensation Stanley took Jephson with him. After degree ceremonies at Cambridge and Durham and visits to Cardiff and Swansea to receive the freedoms of those cities, the Stanleys travelled to Liverpool to take ship for the USA on the White Star liner *Teutonic*.[53]

On 6 November, in bright sunshine, the SS *Teutonic* entered the Verrazano narrows at the entrance to New York. Pressmen were taken out to the steamer on a lighter and thronged about Stanley with notebooks and questions. Dolly tried to shield him from their enquiries and draw him away to look at the scenery, sweetly frowning on all who questioned him. But the ploy was stymied almost at once when a thick blanket of fog descended on the *Teutonic* and she had to feel her way like a blind man up the bay to the White Star Pier.[54]

Major Pond had arranged lectures in 110 cities, to recoup the expenses of the aborted 1886 tour. Most of the speaking engagements were in cities on the east coast, and Pond confidently expected an enthusiastic turn-out, especially as controversy over the Emin expedition was reaching its height. In its early stages the tour lived up to expectations. Once again Stanley was lucky. Historians of the West often single out 1890 as the year of the closing of the frontier. Americans now had to look elsewhere for an outlet for their blood-and-thunder impulses which they had hitherto indulged with the tales of Davy Crockett, Wild Bill Hickock and Kit Carson. The 'Dark Continent' provided the perfect focus.[55]

Having been out of the USA (except for lightning visits in 1874, 1885 and 1886) for eighteen years, Stanley was unprepared for the vast changes that had overtaken the country in that time and at first suffered from a form of culture shock. He found the noise and pollution of New York almost intolerable. The streets were criss-crossed with tramlines, telegraph posts with myriad wires cut across the skyline, the city streets were forever being dug up to enable some fresh cable to be laid, and a forest of billboards assailed his eye. Worst of all was the elevated railway. 'The man who invented the hideous "Elevated" deserves to be expelled from civilisation . . . the view from our hotel window shows me the street ploughed up, square blocks of granite lying as far as the eye can see, besides planking, boarding, piles of earth and stacks of bricks. I counted one hundred and seventy-four lines of wire in the air, rows of mast-like telegraph poles, untrimmed and unpainted, in the centre of the American metropolis! What taste!'[56]

The Stanley party toured the eastern seaboard and proceeded into Canada in a special Pullman car named 'Henry M. Stanley'. Stanley chafed at the pace of the lecture circuit. Pond would allow him no rest between engagements and kept the press on his tail, 'sometimes on the car and *of both sexes* [his underlining].'[57] By Christmas Day 1890 they were in Omaha, which he had known so well in 1867. Then it had been a frontier town of 11-15,000 inhabitants but now it contained 140,000 people and sprawled over ten times the area. As in all the cities Stanley had visited, Omaha manifested in its architecture the new craze for conspicuous consumption which often resulted in houses far superior to anything seen in English cities.

But if Stanley was impressed by the wealth of America, he was much less so by its people. 'With all their inventiveness and gifts for improving dead matter, the living man – the American man himself – black or white does not strike me as having improved at all morally or mentally. He is richer, prouder, more independent in bearing, but he still retains the same rudeness of manner.' He contrasted the modernity of American hotels with their staff. 'The servants are simply the most untrained, undisciplined, loutish and ill-bred of their kind in the world. The newspapers are still the same sensational crime-loving journals I knew long ago, ugly, dirty-looking, preposterously coarse in language, slangy and licentious ... I suppose there are six times more churches in America now than in 1867 but I have been looking anxiously for some moral results of all the preaching and praying – and so far my search has been in vain.' Worst of all aspects of the USA was the noise: 'The noisiest streets in the world. They are really murderous in their intensity – such hissing, grinding and rolling of trams every minute throughout the day or night is most wearing on the nerves.'[58]

They returned to New York for a series of lectures in January. Stanley renewed acquaintance with General Sherman at the Press Club banquet and was saddened a few weeks later in Chicago to hear of his sudden death.[59] By the beginning of February Stanley was seriously regretting having taken on such a strenuous tour. He quarrelled bitterly with his agents about the crushing workload and when Pond refused to relent, decided to hit back in his own way. He was asked to name his own time for a reception at the Chicago Press Club and, though he had three free days in the week, he fixed on Sunday, thus outraging the local religious communities. When Pond put his foot down and insisted on a weekday, Stanley then peevishly limited himself to a mere 1½-hour appearance at the reception.[60]

March 1891 saw him in the far West. All the proposed lectures in Texas were cancelled, not because of the Rear Column controversy but because it had been revealed that Stanley deserted the South for the Unionists during the Civil War. In the western states his speaking engagements were far-flung: Omaha, Sioux City, Denver, Colorado Springs, Salt Lake City, San Francisco, Los Angeles, Oakland, Stockton, Sacramento, San Jose, Fresno and Los Angeles again. The Californian newspapers infuriated Stanley by quoting his height as, variously, 5 foot 3 inches and 5 foot 4 inches: 'the truth is I am five feet, five and a half inches in my socks,' he huffed indignantly.[61] But the high spot of the tour for Stanley was when he was able to show Dolly around the scenes of his youth in New Orleans, Chattanooga and Nashville.[62] Thence they returned to New York where Major Pond gave them a farewell dinner at the Lotus Club on 11 April. Four days later they sailed to Liverpool.[63]

The lecture tour had netted Stanley some £12,000 but he found it, particularly in its later stages, a veritable *via dolorosa*: 'enduring the breaks on my privacy because they are a necessity; each time invoking more patience, and beseeching Time to hurry on its lagging movement that I might once more taste of absolute freedom. Meanwhile, what pleasure I obtain is principally in reading, unless I come to a little town, and can slip, unobserved, out of doors for a walk. I often laugh at the ridiculous aspect of my feelings, as I am compelled to become shifty and cunning, to evade the eager citizens' advances. I feel like Cain, hurrying away with his uneasy conscience after despatching Abel, or a felonious cashier departing with his plunder!'[64]

Immediately on return to England, Stanley sought sanctuary at the South Wales retreat he had acquired – Cadoxton Lodge. By now he had decided that, although the marriage could never be a union of blood and passion, the Tennant connection gave him the serenity and tranquillity he needed; even his mother-in-law Gertrude had stood up wonderfully well to the rigours of American travel. He expressed his satisfaction with Dolly thus: 'I loved her but yet I dreaded after all, for I knew her so little. I feared she was gushing and shallow, and a mere society product. But had she been moulded to fit my nature, she could not have been more perfect than she is. She is always May – sunshine with a promise of rain. She is extremely sunny in disposition, yet sensitive, easily affected by joy or sorrow. She is brimming over with gladness, is gay, sportive, irrepressibly merry, but so quick are her sympathies, that if she sees or hears anything suggestive of pain or sorrow, she seems to yearn to soothe, control and heal. This excessive womanliness is a new thing to me in her, for I had only regarded her brilliant externals.'[65]

Dolly, for her part, though she lacked a passionate lover, at least had someone on whom to lavish the devotion she had hitherto expended on a phantom. Like Isabel Burton, she dedicated herself to building up the legend of her husband, denying, striking down and effacing anything and anyone that contradicted the mythical picture. She also had to suppress her own previous opinions and view of the world so as to fit in with Stanley's. An incident in the first year of her marriage shows how far she had travelled from the *ingénue* who fretted about the plight of miners and proletarians. The parents of Stanley's 1874-7 companions the Pococks had by 1890 been reduced to terrible straits. At seventy-four

Henry Pocock was too infirm to continue his work as a fisherman and his wife, a year older, was going blind. Remembering Stanley's eulogy about 'his brother' Frank, Henry Pocock wrote to Stanley to ask for financial assistance. The letter found him convalescing at Melchett Court after the wedding. On 5 August 1890 Dolly fired off a monumentally insensitive reply: 'Mr Stanley is sorry he cannot assist you – he has so many and great demands on him that he is quite unable to respond to the innumerable appeals made to him for money. Night and day he is assailed, just as though he had a great fortune.'[66]

Incensed at the plight of the elderly Pococks, Henry Smetham took up the cudgels on their behalf in a vigorous campaign in the *Chatham and Rochester News*. He pointed out that the couple lived in Upnor with a widowed daughter who earned her bread by hard toil and campaigned for a fund that would provide the old folk with 12-15 shillings a week as long as they lived. He added that the amount in question was no more than the cost of firing off a single gun on ceremonial occasions: 'That one should be done and the other neglected is a disgrace to mankind – and what we are pleased to call civilisation – and runs near to blasphemy to that God we hypocritically pretend to serve.'[67]

Smetham's campaign for a Pocock fund threatened to mushroom into a scandal, breaking on the public as it did simultaneously with the most unsavoury revelations about the Emin expedition. Stanley acted quickly, but his letter is a masterpiece of humbug and obfuscation in his familiar style.

> Dear Sir,
> In Detroit I had the pleasure of meeting a relative of the Pococks, who brought most vividly to my mind the sad end of Francis. I urged my wife to remind me of the matter on reaching London. This she has done, and in consequence I send you £50 towards your needs. The *Daily Telegraph* and *New York Herald*, in whose service your son died, should treble the sum, and do something to atone to you for the great loss you sustained.[68]

This was typical of the Stanley method. Do not admit that you are doing something under duress, but claim that it was your idea all along. If a tragedy occurs, the victim is in the service of a newspaper or a committee. If a triumph is achieved, this is because Stanley is the leader. Small wonder that there was little room for Dolly's erstwhile sympathy for the underdog if she wished to live in harmony with her beloved Bula Matari.

The Pococks, however, were fortunate. Stanley's gesture started the ball rolling, so that in the end enough was raised to carry the old couple comfortably through the few years remaining to them.

Stanley could afford to be generous, for on top of the income generated by the American tour, he secured another useful £2000 nest-egg on his return by making a similar tour around Great Britain and Ireland. Hull, York, Bradford, Sheffield, Cambridge, Liverpool, Cheltenham, Gloucester, Bristol, Swansea, Caernavon, and Canterbury were just some of the venues in a breathless two-month whistlestop.[69] At last he was free to take a holiday and at the end of July 1891 he travelled with his entourage to his favourite place of relaxation: Switzerland.

This time they were at the Grand Hôtel des Alpes in Murren. Stanley did not really care for the altitude of the resort (4900 feet) which was too cold for him. But he enjoyed himself with Gertrude Tennant while Dolly lay in bed with a chill: the two used the latest invention, the telephone, to talk to each other from neighbouring hotels and the now doting mother-in-law told him: 'Bula Matari, you are an angel.'[70] Yet he was an angel destined to fall from grace. One Saturday morning they set off for a picnic at a spot about an hour's drive from the hotel. Stanley was showing Dolly's sister's little boy how Africans threw spears. As he swung round with the projectile, he lost his balance, fell heavily and snapped the fibula near the ankle. He was in great pain and had to wait a long time for a stretcher. He was then taken to hospital where he was flat on his back for three weeks before being allowed up on a pair of crutches, with his broken leg in plaster of Paris. For the rest of his stay in Switzerland he was pushed around in a wheelchair.[71]

It is possible that Stanley's accident might have been triggered by some unconscious self-destructive impulse, for it is curious that a man who had never injured a limb during four different expeditions in Africa totalling a dozen years, in which he had hacked through jungles, waded across swamps and scaled precipitous mountains, should have come to grief in a Swiss glen. Perhaps the trigger can be sought in a depressing encounter with the press just before the fall. Special correspondent Aubrey Stanhope of the *New York Herald* received orders from Gordon Bennett to go to Switzerland to investigate rumours that the great explorer's marriage was on the rocks. Perhaps someone during the American tour with sensitive antennae had intuited that the marriage was not all it might be, or Stanley himself had let drop some half-clue. At any rate Stanhope did not approach his assignment with much relish;

he described it as 'quite the most disagreeable' he had ever been called upon to carry out.[72]

The plucky Stanhope went up the mountain on mule-back to Stanley's eyrie at Murren. When he explained his mission, Stanley exploded with rage. But he was in a difficult position. He could hardly send packing a representative of the newspaper that had made his own fame and fortune. Besides, if he did, Bennett might well decide to stoke up again the embers of the dying Rear Column controversy. Stanhope tried to let him off the hook. 'Suppose,' he suggested, 'you go and ask the women what they say about it. They instinctively know what is best to do in such matters.'[73]

Controlling his anger, Stanley went to consult with his wife and her sister Mrs Myers. They indignantly repudiated the rumour. Stanhope asked for a written statement. Stanley produced the following: 'I have no hesitation in saying that each day of our married life has been one of pure content and unalloyed happiness.' Still Stanhope was not satisfied. Respectfully he pointed out that the affidavit was not countersigned by his wife. Almost at breaking point, Stanley went in to see Dolly and came back with her statement which read as follows: 'I am very much astonished and disgusted with reports in a New York newspaper that my married life is unhappy and that I am separated from my dear husband. It is indeed high time that a stop should be put to such a shameful fabrication. Is there no protection from these newspaper insults?'[74]

Back in England, the Stanleys spent two months at Wimpole Rectory at Royston near Cambridge – placed at the explorer's disposal for the late summer by Lord Hardwicke. As Stanley recovered from the broken leg, he was attacked suddenly by gravel and African fever. His physician Sir Henry Thompson put him on an ascetic diet of vegetables, fruit and poultry; nothing sweet, no red meat and no wine was permitted. Thompson's diagnosis was that because Stanley's stomach got used to the primitive fare of Africa, it could not adjust to the rich food of Europe.[75]

Next it was time for another gruelling lecture tour, this time in Australasia. Dolly had originally decided not to accompany her husband after the unpleasant American experience, but two considerations urged her on. First, Stanley was still hobbling on crutches and would need careful nursing. Secondly, not to go would be to fuel the rumours of separation and infidelity in the Stanley marriage that continued to circulate. Gritting her teeth, Dolly prepared for the journey to the southern hemisphere. After a quick visit to Leopold at Ostend, they boarded the SS *Arcadia* in the Mediterranean. But not before Stanley was involved in a potentially fatal accident. The train taking them to Brindisi was derailed in Italy; the engine, van and four freight trucks in the front of the train were wrecked (without loss of life) and Stanley's compartment was next to the van. Had this been overturned, it might have gone hard with him as he was still lame and on crutches.[76]

The sea voyage to Australia was long, confining and monotonous. It turned out to have been a bad mistake to pick up the liner in the Mediterranean. The ship was packed to the gunwales, with 345 first-class passengers alone, and all the best staterooms and most comfortable seats in the dining-room had been taken by those who embarked at London. There was just a single one-day stopover, at Colombo. The experience did nothing to whet Dolly's appetite for exotic lecture tours. She complained bitterly about the heat, the weather and the slow pace of shipboard travel.[77]

Stanley began his lectures as soon as they arrived in Australia and delivered one daily except on Sundays. There was plenty of sightseeing to be fitted in also; Dolly was raised momentarily from her gloom by the sight of Sydney Harbour Bridge and by a meeting with the former policeman, now magistrate, who had captured Ned Kelly. But she was deeply unhappy. She lamented that since her marriage she had been in her own home for just three weeks: 'a woman is never at home but at home.'[78]

Stanley followed his usual pattern of rotating three lectures on his most exciting African journeys (omitting his five years with Leopold). He was ten days in Melbourne, three in Ballarat, two in Geelong, then in Brisbane and Sydney (where he encountered the only real press criticism).[79] At the end of the year the Stanleys crossed to New Zealand where they were royally entertained by Sir George Grey, a passionate Stanley admirer.[80] They returned via Tasmania and wound up the Australian tour in Melbourne and Adelaide.[81]

It was an exhausted party that arrived back in England in April 1892. But by now the triumphant African lion of two years ago was in danger of sinking to the level of a pariah dog. Stanley's reputation had sunk to an all-time low following the prolonged controversy over the Emin Pasha expedition and its dark epitome in the form of the Rear Column. Stanley, always a superstitious man, felt almost as though he were confronting the gibbering shades of Barttelot and Jameson and that they clamoured for blood.

· 19 ·

THE Emin Pasha expedition had been controversial ever since its inception but criticism of its various aspects reached the zenith in late 1890 as Stanley began his US tour. Stanley was censured for many different things: the self-regarding and self-justifying account he gave of the expedition in his book; his employment of Tippu Tip as governor of Stanley Falls; the huge loss of life on the expedition; the fact that he had camouflaged an essentially profiteering and freebooting enterprise in a cloak of humanitarianism and religiosity; the unfavourable impact of the expedition on Africa; and, most of all, the scandal of the Rear Column.

To some critics the very 'methodology' of the Emin expedition was wrongheaded. Jackson argued forcefully that Thomson, not Stanley, should have been chosen to lead it. Stanley had grossly exaggerated the perils of Masailand and had used his own peculiar employment contract with Leopold as a lever to force the expedition to proceed by the Congo route. From this one decision came the 'double-cross' by the Belgian state, the horrors of the Ituri and the fiasco of the Rear Column.[1] Peters, the most vociferous critic of Stanley, argued that the original mistake was compounded with numerous other contingent errors made by the leader during the course of the enterprise: the decision to employ Tippu Tip, the failure to assist Mwanga, the mendacious identification of Ruwenzori with the 'Mountains of the Moon' and most of all the use of force to compel Emin to go to Zanzibar. Peters described the Stanley expedition as being 'like working an equation with totally unnecessary circuitous ways and formulas . . . neither the ostensible nor the real object has been obtained . . . even the Mahdi himself could not have been more injurious to the civilising of the Upper Nile than Stanley has been in reality . . . if Stanley had stuck fast in the swamps of the Aruwimi, Emin Pasha would at this day, according to all human calculation, be still in Wadelai in a perfectly secure position . . . therefore it must be stated that Stanley's enterprise has been absolutely hurtful in its effects for the general interests of humanity, and for the special interests of England.'[2]

When Stanley published his own account of the expedition in *In Darkest Africa*, the huge commercial success of the book soon gave way to doubts and misgivings engendered by the very tone of the whirlwind fifty-day production. Particular exception was taken to Stanley's insistence that he was the agent of Providence and God's elect, that his survival was evidence of some divine favour.[3] Stanley added to this motif on his American tour when he declared: 'I am back from the gloom of a country much of which is unknown to the glory of One that is the Light of the World.'[4] When Stanley taunted England with no longer possessing any Drakes or Raleighs the London *Star* retorted: 'He seems to be unaware that since those glorious days of piracy moral ideas have advanced somewhat . . . without stigmatising the Sunday-school sentiments about Providence which Mr Stanley sent home from time to time for the "unco guid" as necessarily humbug, it is plain, in the light of his general character, that even under the most favourable construction they are only thinly veiled egoism, and that of a very bullying and offensive kind.'[5] Another reviewer queried how the constant references to God's providence were to be squared with the 'supernatural diablerie' Stanley claimed to see at work in the destruction of the Rear Column. The fact was that Stanley left a rearguard full of invalids in the power of an Arab he considered unreliable, in the charge of an inept hot-tempered officer, in the middle of hostile, malaria-ridden country. Surely the thesis of the Evil One was supererogatory?[6] Yet others queried the concomitance of the alleged Christian feeling alongside a ruthless commercial insistence that no other members of the expedition could publish their accounts until six months after Stanley's 'official' version had appeared.[7]

Stanley's references to God and Christianity were considered particularly unacceptable in the light of the ruthless *realpolitik* attitude he had displayed during the expedition. Criticism focused on three areas: Stanley's seeming indifference to the slave trade and Tippu Tip's role in it; the fact that the one real concrete result of the expedition was to enlarge the area open to slavers; and the commercial motives behind the expedition.

According to one estimate, three-quarters of the 680 porters used by Stanley on his expedition were slaves.[8] This caused an outcry in the

Aborigines' Protection Society in 1890, and Stanley's friend Henry Wellcome had to battle against many angry interruptions at a special meeting of the Society to point out that it was impossible for any African explorer to determine with certainty who were and were not slaves; even Livingstone on occasion had been forced to employ slaves.[9] As for Tippu Tip, this was largely a red herring peddled by men who basked in gross ignorance. The Belgian Vangele had already testified on his return to Brussels that Tippu acted impeccably throughout towards the expedition, despite being under considerable provocation from Barttelot.[10] If any blame attached to the hiring of a known slaver as governor of Stanley Falls, such censure must be laid at Leopold's door, not Stanley's. Stanley also ingeniously conflated Christianity with the decision to use Tippu by quoting the biblical passage that there is more joy in heaven over the one sinner who repents.[11]

The critics were on firmer ground in asserting that Stanley's expedition had blazed a trail for slavers to follow. Until Stanley opened up the Aruwimi and Ituri, the tribes there had held their own against the slavers. His penetration of their forest fastnesses sealed their doom.[12] The same was likely to be true of Equatoria; the only question to be resolved was whether the Arabs and the Manyema or the Mahdists would be master there. Before Stanley's coming Emin ran a successful state in Equatoria. Stanley's advent destroyed all that.[13] What made this so unacceptable was his *realpolitik* approach, which seemed to deliver to the West the worst of all possible worlds. In his despatches Stanley took Captain Deane to task for his conflict with the Arabs at Stanley Falls: 'the error of judgement which induced Captain Deane to defy the Arabs for the sake of a lying woman who had fled from her master to avoid punishment.' The *Saturday Review* took Stanley sternly to task for this. 'We are not rabid against slavery, but we very seriously trust that no Englishman will ever fail to commit similar "errors of judgement".'[14]

The third indictment, that the Emin Pasha expedition had been a 'humanitarian' blind to mask commercial freebooting, was the toughest to rebut. It seems clear that there were two main economic motivations to the expedition, one of short-term profit, the other of longer-term economic imperialism. The short-term objective, seizing the estimated £112,000 worth of ivory that Emin had in Equatoria, was a disastrous failure, but this result did not prevent critics asking whether the British public had not originally been gulled into enthusiastic support for a 'rescue' attempt that was more concerned with retrieving elephants' tusks than a short-sighted Prussian naturalist.[15] The long-term objective was to establish a British commercial empire on the headwaters of the Nile. This was why the offer to set up Emin and his followers at Kavirondo on Lake Victoria had originally been made by Mackinnon. His IBEA Company was to be a means of arresting Germany's progress eastward and Leopold's westward.[16] Of course, the two economic motives overlapped, for Mackinnon hoped to finance the nucleus of his commercial empire out of Emin's ivory.[17]

One of the reasons for the ultimate downfall of the Emin expedition, in terms of its real as opposed to ostensible goals, was that it was a geopolitical mess. Officially designed to tweak the noses of the Mahdists in the Sudan by whisking away Emin from their grasp, the expedition's real purpose was to establish British power unofficially in the Lake Victoria region. The expedition thus faced in three main directions: westward towards the Congo, where it complicated the relations between the Congo State and the Arabs; northward towards the Sudan, the Khalifa and the Mahdists; eastward towards the German sphere of influence. The expedition was consequently embroiled in matters of high politics which could be resolved only by war or nation-state diplomacy. The problem to the west was resolved by the Congo-Arab war of 1893; that to the north by the Omdurman campaign in 1898; that to the east by the Anglo-German accord of 1890. In more senses than one, then, the Emin expedition was a 'mission impossible'. The kind of economic imperialism Mackinnon had in mind needed a much clearer field to operate in than was available to Stanley in 1887-9.

There is another point to be made in fairness to Stanley and against his critics. 'Stanley has triumphed, but Central Africa is darker than ever,'[18] was a frequent motif of his enemies. But the same critics were not at all pleased when Jephson argued that the corollary to such criticism was to leave Africa to its own devices; he argued that Emin's regime in Equatoria had paid scant attention to the interests of the indigenous blacks and that, in drawing up a balance sheet on the expedition, it was the fate of the aboriginal peoples that should form the centrepiece.[19] This drew a broadside from the 'Thunderer', though the logic of its leader-writer seemed to have been derived from Lewis Carroll: 'The soil, too, itself has rights, as well as savages who live upon it. If it cannot obtain from its aboriginal occupants the measure of development to which it is entitled by its intrinsic capabilities, it will invite strangers to supply its wants.'[20]

All in all, the controversy over the general consequences of the Emin expedition resulted in a draw or stalemate. Even if it was accepted that the entire idea had been misconceived and foolhardy right from the beginning, this was not something that particularly brought Stanley into the dock. As the leader of the expedition, he was the agent of others, and it was the Mackinnons, Huttons, de Wintons and Burdett-Couttses, to say nothing of Leopold and his ilk, who merited the greater censure. Stanley could have maintained his (scarcely unblemished hitherto) reputation intact, had it not been for the ferocious controversy over the Rear Column that gathered steam towards the end of 1890.

In October and November that year, finally released from the legal shackles that had bound them hitherto, the two most virulent anti-Stanley factions published their accounts. First came the posthumous memoirs of Barttelot, as edited by his family; then followed Rose Troup's account of his time with the Rear Column. The substance of the charge in these books had already been anticipated by Casati. The Italian alleged that it was precisely greed for ivory that had led Stanley to the seemingly inexplicable decision to divide the expedition and leave behind a Rear Column; only thus could he hope to recruit enough porters to fetch out of Equatoria the fabled hoards of ivory: 'Instead of sending an exploring detachment to the lake [Albert] under an expert and daring officer, and remaining himself behind to direct the more important work, thus securing the triumph of the undertaking, his inordinate desire for doing everything himself, and his ardent wish not to let a crumb of glory fall into the lap of others, impelled Stanley (forgetful of the charge which had been entrusted to him and not to others) to give summary orders, placing between himself and the principal column an enormous distance, an impenetrable forest, silence and doubt, for long consecutive months.'[21]

The Barttelot book charged Stanley with 'malignity, ingratitude, desertion and misrepresentation' and drew from the press the clamour that Stanley ought to cancel his US tour to answer the charges.[22] The *Birmingham Post* described the published Barttelot diaries as leaving the 'impression of the perfectly frank, full and unreserved utterances of an English gentleman'.[23] The battleground had now moved beyond the simple point first advanced in 1889 by the Barttelot family, that Stanley had left the Major imprecise instructions.[24] The charge had become a threefold one: Stanley had misled Barttelot and all his other officers, who thought they were engaged on a humanitarian mission when their real objective was to enrich the Mackinnon IBEA Company; he had made a disastrous error by plunging into the Ituri forest without taking his entire force; he was responsible for what had happened to Barttelot, since he took all the best men with him, leaving Barttelot with the sick and cripples and the ticklish problem of getting Tippu Tip to provide porters.[25]

Stanley could have met these allegations with a discreet silence or a dignified rejoinder. But this was not his way. At first he tried the tactic of pretending that the Barttelot family's charges were infantile and beneath contempt. If he himself was at fault for appointing Barttelot to command of the Rear Column, 'I would then say that if Major Barttelot had not been born, he surely had never existed, therefore the fault lay with his parents; or, if the British government had not seen fit to elevate this young man to the rank of major, I would not have supposed him to be capable of commanding a few hundred men.'[26]

Since this sophistry failed to blunt the daily criticisms of his leadership, Stanley moved on to phase two of his campaign. He gave an interview to the London correspondent of the *New York Herald* shortly before his departure for the USA. Looking out over his gold-rimmed spectacles and puffing at a cigar throughout the interview, Stanley claimed to have the hidden story of the Rear Column. He had not revealed it before out of regard for the Barttelot family, but since they had repaid his compassion with vindictiveness, he now wanted to set the record straight. The gist of the matter was that Barttelot had been killed rather than murdered, and he had incontrovertible proof of this in reports from Ward and Bonny. Why, then, did you not divulge this material in *In Darkest Africa*, asked the reporter. I did not want to blacken Barttelot's name, replied Stanley, but in view of the Barttelot family's attitude he now saw that his reticence was misplaced.

The reporter asked him what he meant by saying that Barttelot was killed rather than murdered. Stanley said that if the man who shot Barttelot had been tried before an English jury he would have been found 'not guilty'. When the *Herald* man pressed him further, Stanley with many a wink and nod asked him to consider what were the grounds in English law for a verdict of 'justifiable homicide'. Without saying so in so many words, Stanley left the clear impression that Sanga had shot Barttelot because the Major had taken his wife into concubinage.[27]

The cunning of this ploy was that it plugged into rumours that had long been current about the sexual behaviour of white men on the Congo. Some even hinted that the inactivity of the Rear Column for eleven months was due to sexual bewitchment by the houris whom Tippu Tip had sent to Yambuya to beguile the whites.[28] But Stanley's critics sensed they had their man in a trap. Since he claimed to have doctored the true evidence about Barttelot when he published *In Darkest Africa*, it followed that he must have it; he should therefore produce it to substantiate his flimsy story.[29] You can suppress evidence and not make charges, or you can produce your evidence and make charges, the critics pointed out gleefully in anticipation of a decisive victory over Stanley; what you *cannot* do is make charges *and* suppress your evidence.[30] It was generally considered that Stanley had gone too far this time and fallen into a trap of his own making.[31]

The row between Stanley and the Barttelot family was the news sensation of autumn 1890. Even Queen Victoria followed it with a horrified fascination though she was later to find the Rear Column story 'too horrible to write about'.[32] The French in particular rubbed their hands in pleasure at this internal crisis in 'perfidious Albion' and called for a lawsuit or tribunal to determine the true facts about the Rear Column.[33] *Le Figaro* crowed triumphantly: 'Now that an Englishman and not a Frenchman like de Brazza; not a German like Peters and Emin Pasha; not a Russian like Dr Junker; nor an Italian like the Catholic missionaries, but an out and out genuine son of Albion makes accusations against Stanley, the British public condescends to listen.'[34] Foreign criticism simply enraged the British press further against Stanley, who was accused of besmirching Britain and the Empire in the eyes of foreigners.[35]

All Stanley's enemies rushed in for the kill they sensed was imminent. The *New York World* suggested that Stanley's real motive for abandoning the Rear Column was diplomatic. Stanley was sent to Equatoria to spike Germany's guns. Because he was in a race with the Germans he had to press on at full speed and leave the Rear Column to its fate; additionally, Emin was pulled out of Equatoria to prevent the province from passing under German protection.[36] The French explorer du Chaillu was canvassed for his opinion; it was known that he was angry with Stanley for not having, in *In Darkest Africa* given him credit for the first discovery of the pygmies. Du Chaillu expressed his opinion forcibly that the motive for Sanga's killing of Barttelot was absurd: 'those blacks do not shoot for their women. On the contrary, they will give them to you with open hands. No black would think of killing a white man for such a trifling offence in Africa.'[37]

The indictment against Stanley seemed overwhelming when Rose Troup brought out his account of the Rear Column within weeks of the life of Barttelot; Troup's would have been the first set of memoirs in the field had not Stanley secured an injunction in line with the six-month clause.[38] But Troup took ample revenge in his book. He bitterly attacked Stanley for leaving Barttelot in charge at Yambuya, for the confusion of his orders. In newspaper interviews he accused Stanley of being muddled in his facts about the Rear Column and relying entirely on hearsay. As for the slaying of Barttelot, Stanley's story about a sexual motive was utter nonsense. The shot was fired at point-blank range and was a spontaneous reaction to the fact that Barttelot raised a club to Sanga's wife. The general consensus on the Troup revelations was that they hammered another nail into the coffin of Stanley's reputation.[39]

Stanley's first reaction was weak. He accused Troup of cowardice in not deposing Barttelot and taking over command, even though he could have been shot for mutiny had he attempted to do so. His appeal to Ward also fell on stony ground. Although Ward when interviewed showed a desire to keep out of the entire controversy, he revealed his hand by speaking of Barttelot's death as 'murder' (rather than 'justifiable homicide' as in the Stanley version) and spoke of the expedition's taking Emin prisoner rather than rescuing him.[40] But in the euphoria of having rebutted the sexual innuendo against Barttelot, Stanley's opponents overlooked the fact that Troup's book was highly critical of Barttelot. This was a dormant volcano waiting to erupt.

Only those who knew not Stanley thought that this would be the end of the affair. The explorer Grant had a shrewder appreciation than most of the likely outcome. 'I have never blamed Stanley, who will come out of it, I have no doubt, with flying colours. He is not the man to put himself in the wrong, and when "scratched" will show desperate fight and quite right too . . . the correspondence of the Barttelot family shows them all to be burnt by the same iron – they look upon natives as only fit to be kicked and shot – they would never take a native's word – oh no – Mr Stanley has no right to believe in them!'[41]

With exquisite timing Stanley coaxed all his enemies to reveal themselves by appearing to have no answer to the fresh spate of criticisms. Then he unleashed his Caliban. It will be remembered that none of Bonny's eyewitness accounts had yet seen the light of day. Suddenly, at the end of the first week of November, all Britain reeled under the impact of the new disclosures about Barttelot, made by a man who had actually been present during the darkest days of the Rear Column. Bonny told the world that, far from being a perfect English gentleman, Barttelot was as close to a raving lunatic as anyone outside an asylum could come. He had gone around camp with an evil leer on his face, poking people with a pointed stick. He had kicked the boy Soudi to death and shot a soldier for stealing goat meat. He had beaten one man's brains out and crept up behind a Manyema chief and stabbed him in the back. Finally – which led to his death – he had kicked Sanga's wife in the stomach. In addition, he had accused Stanley of being a poisoner, tasted a bit of potassium cyanide on his tongue to see if it could be detected in coffee, and announced that Stanley had actually murdered the Pocock brothers during the 1874-7 expedition.[42]

Even while the public sat stunned under the impact of this dark tale, the Stanley counterattack began. Numerous anti-Barttelot witnesses came forward to attest to the circumstantial truth of Bonny's account. Captain Stanhope, who had seen Barttelot in action at Yambuya, endorsed the Stanley-Bonny account.[43] A correspondent from Cairo reported that Barttelot's army colleagues who had served with him in Egypt were unanimous that he must have been justly slain.[44] Ward, too, fell into the Stanley trap. Riled that Stanley had accused him also of cowardice in not relieving Barttelot of his command, he started another hare by accusing Governor-General Jannsens of the Congo Free State of incompetence in not sending his idle steamers up the Aruwimi to relieve the Rear Column.[45] This simply had the effect of drawing Jannsens too into the Stanley camp; he declared roundly that all Congo forces fully supported the Bonny/Stanley story.[46] Stanley's brother-in-law Frederick Myers wrote in triumph to the EPRE committee that a comparison of the Barttelot and Bonny diaries showed the Major as 'a mean and jealous spirit throughout . . . one cannot accept Barttelot as a specimen of the generous though headstrong British officer. He was plainly a spiteful and self-seeking person.'[47]

But the evil genius of Bonny had not yet finished weaving its spell. He pointed out artfully that Barttelot's vile temper at Yambuya had an organic connection with Jameson's monumental error in sketching the cannibal feast, since this story ran up and down the Congo and Barttelot feared that he would be held responsible for his friend's indiscretion and lose his commission.[48] By this time it was two years since the Jameson story had first surfaced, and most of the public had forgotten it, if they had ever known it in the first place. Foreseeing that if the Jameson story again hit the headlines, it would drag the Major down with it, the Barttelot family made the bad mistake of launching an attack on Assad Farran, the Syrian who had first broken the story, calling him a liar who hated the Major 'with true Eastern intensity'.[49] The general bemused reaction was: who is Assad Farran? *The Times* soon indulged that curiosity by printing in full Assad Farran's 1888 affidavit on Jameson and Barttelot.[50]

Here was startling ammunition for the pro-Stanley camp, since Farran's account of Barttelot's brutality and Jameson's monstrous act of inhumanity predated by a full two years the public controversy over the Rear Column. Immediately there were signs of a swing back in public opinion in favour of Stanley.[51] In vain did the anti-Stanley faction exclaim that the charges against Jameson were incredible, or recruit Rider Haggard to say that he knew both Stanley and Jameson and would prefer to take the word of the latter.[52] Bigger guns sounded on the Stanley side, confirming the Jameson story in detail. Schweinfurth confirmed Assad Farran's story from his private sources, while the *Indépendance Belge* endorsed it from the archives of the Free State and referred readers back to an 1888 issue setting the case out in detail.[53] The French pounced on another glorious chance to rub the noses of the British in the mire. 'These stories certainly interfere with the Biblical varnish with which pious England likes to cover her most selfish enterprises. They make it difficult to continue the campaign of vilification which the British press wages against the proceedings of our countrymen. Ah! if one of them had been guilty of any one of these acts which seem to have constituted the daily life of Mr Stanley, what cries, what fits of anger, what indignant expostulations would have broken out among our virtuous neighbours! ... Let us compare our countrymen with the English. We have fewer angelic pretensions; but on which side is the spirit of humanity?'[54]

Faced with this powerful backlash, the supporters of Barttelot and Jameson tried to shift the ground of the debate on to the reliability of the sources for the cannibal feast story. One target was the Assad Farran affidavit. 'Before whom was the affidavit sworn? It is a novelty to have that sort of legal business transacted in the heart of Africa. Nor were we aware that the natives of those parts were sufficiently civilised to not only know the meaning of affidavits, but to be capable of drawing them up in their own handwriting.'[55] But this sort of legal nitpicking was effectively disposed of by an Australian correspondent with first-hand knowledge of the Congo. He pointed out that a judicial enquiry would exclude much vital material because of the rules of evidence: 'if all history was to be credited only on such evidence as a judge receives at *nisi prius*, history would be nearly a blank page.'[56]

In any event, the case for the defence of Jameson was soon blown sky-high by a singular error on the part of the Jameson family. Hoping to clear her late husband's name, the young Mrs Jameson published a private letter in which Jameson admitted to being the (albeit unwitting) cause of the girl's death and cannibalism.[57] Some of Stanley's attackers made a 180-degree turn. *The Globe*, previously one of Stanley's sternest critics, tore holes in Jameson's defence that he thought the locals simply wanted to get *doti* from him when they offered a sacrificial victim in return for cloth. 'If that was his belief, it appears extremely singular, to say the least of it, that he should have at once agreed to be victimised.' Nor could it be believed that he gave cloth to all who asked, so he must have done it to satisfy a morbid curiosity. Also, why did he not intervene when the girl was produced?[58]

Further grist was added to the Stanley mill when it was pointed out that the EPRE committee had actually had the private letter to Mrs Jameson in its hands when it forced Assad Farran to make his retraction; in other words it forced him to retract what it already knew to be true.[59] Not surprisingly Myers again pounced. In further letters to Mackinnon he pointed out that it was now universally accepted as a plain fact that Jameson was guilty as charged of the cannibalistic incident. 'It is plain that the diaries were written under the moral influence of Barttelot and coloured by Barttelot's hatred of Stanley.' He scoffed at Andrew Jameson's statement in *The Times* that his brother had behaved like a gentleman and that there was not a vestige of proof to the contrary. Myers commented: 'one wonders still further in what school of gentility Mr Andrew Jameson's notions have been formed.'[60]

The Jameson family were reluctant to accept the overwhelming verdict that their most distinguished scion had penetrated the heart of darkness. Mrs Ethel Jameson pestered the EPRE committee for all relevant documentation, including Assad Farran's denial under duress that her husband had sketched the cannibal feast.[61] Then she and Andrew, her husband's brother, set out for Zanzibar to try to get a different version from Tippu Tip. Euan-Smith, firmly in the Stanley camp, jaundicedly reported her arrival in February 1891. 'She is rich, pretty, about 24, and does not seem to object to the notoriety cast on her – she probably will soon write a new book.'[62] Andrew Jameson travelled inland as far as Mpwapwa but with scant results for his cause. Not until Tippu himself arrived in Zanzibar did Mrs Jameson get satisfaction. As loyal to Jameson in death as he had been in life, Tippu roundly denounced Stanley as a liar and said that the cannibal story was an absurd fabrication.[63] Alas, on this occasion it was Stanley who was right and Tippu wrong.

Stanley's counterattack had seen off the Barttelot and Jameson families decisively but his obfuscatory tactics did not entirely escape notice. The *New York Herald* commented that in the maelstrom of scandal surrounding Barttelot and Jameson, some of the original charges concerning the management of the Rear Column seemed to be slipping from sight.[64] A London commentator put it more trenchantly: 'Mr Stanley came in like a lion last spring. It can hardly be said that he goes out like a lamb, for there is nothing that is very lamb-like in his composition. We must seek some other comparison. Shall we say he goes out like a cuttle-fish, which covers its retreat with a cloud of darkness?'[65]

The truth was that, Samson-like, Stanley was able to pull down the entire temple of the Emin Pasha expedition with him but could not arrest his own crash. Not even his closest friends could exculpate him from negligence or errors in his handling of the Rear Column. The very strongest case for the defence had to contain some criticism. This comes through clearly in the judicious assessment made by Harry Johnston. First he placed Stanley in context as a true Africanist, in contrast to the present Congo officialdom. Next he ventured the conjecture that Barttelot in the latter stages at Yambuya had been insane – a common sequel to fever in the Congo. Then he pointed out that nobody had ever been able to pin on Stanley the charges of terrible brutality that had stuck to Barttelot and he reminded his readers of what those terrible floggings involved. 'It means the man's whole back, shoulders and thighs would be a pulpy mass of churned-up flesh, that the nervous system would receive such a shock that the flogged man would probably die of the effects, if he did not succumb quicker to the injuries sustained by his kidneys and other internal organs, which the flogging over the small of the back would most certainly affect.'[66]

But he blamed Stanley for the imprecision of his orders to the Rear Column. Insofar as they ordered an advance, they were impracticable given the human jetsam he left behind. 'We can scarcely understand how it is he expected the wretched rearguard, under much greater difficulties, to make the same journey seven times over which he had barely succeeded in effecting on the first occasion ... History will ... say that at worst Mr Stanley made a few regrettable mistakes, and did not bestow sufficient care on the condition in which he left the Rear Guard ... but that he accomplished magnificently one of the most splendid feats performed in this or any century – the rescue of Emin Pasha and three journeys through the trackless forests of the Congo. History will say of Stanley that he was the Napoleon Bonaparte of African exploration, with all Napoleon's greatness and some of his failings.'[67]

This was essentially the judgement the Emin Pasha committee came to when it drew up its final report. Lavish praise was poured on Stanley, but his handling of the Rear Column was criticised. Predictably, Stanley found this intolerable. He could never bear *any* criticism, no matter how intermingled and overgrown by praise. He told Mackinnon he found the final report a disgrace and an insult to him and all the survivors. He had been accused in the press of maligning the dead who could not answer back; now the committee had inverted this and by raising *nil nisi bonum* to a new power, had left him angry and speechless. 'As the pamphlet now stands, it is a condemnation of us who lived, and a defence of those who are dead. The dead do not require any defence, they require sympathy, forgiveness and peace, and the living require only justice.'[68] To make his displeasure palpable he signed himself 'Yours faithfully' instead of the 'Yours ever' he had used with Mackinnon for a decade; relations continued frosty for a couple of months.[69]

Yet however much he blustered, Stanley could hardly fail to see that the controversy over the Emin expedition had irretrievably tarnished his reputation. His chances of honours in Britain or further commands in Africa had been significantly reduced. As one of his critics remarked in 1891: 'It is improbable that, in any case, he will have the chance of leading another English expedition; but if he ever induces another English gentleman to serve under him, that Englishman's relatives will have a good case for putting him under restraint as a lunatic.'[70]

Worst of all crosses for Stanley to bear was that his religious and devotional sentiments were no longer taken seriously. Early reviewers of his book contrasted his harsh and punitive actions with the religious saturation of the sentiments in which he described his pagan worship of power. Insofar as there was a religious sensibility present, it was that of a Celtic heathen: 'that his belief in the supernatural is strong almost to superstition is evident to anyone who knows him or is familiar with his writings.'[71] Troup's darts were particularly aimed at this aspect of Stanley. He confessed himself surprised at the abundance of providential religiosity in *In Darkest Africa*, as he had seen no signs of either overt Christianity (in the form of prayers) or its implicit variety (in the shape of devoutness or compassion).[72] Indeed he had seen precious little vestige of elementary humanity. Troup once exasperatedly exclaimed that Stanley had no more philanthropy in him than 'my boot'.[73]

Stanley had only himself to blame for the frequent charges of humbug he incurred. He actually had the effrontery to say that he foresaw ultimate good from the Rear Column controversy, since the quest for truth proved European moral superiority.(!)[74] His Nietzschean high-mindedness also left people cold. The *Star* described Stanley's 'Gospel of Enterprise' as being cant of the same order as Carnegie's 'Gospel of Wealth'; 'it is impossible to believe that the thinking portion of the working classes have the smallest inclination to make a hero of this man.'[75] But it would be a mistake to set his religious sentiments down to humbug. Stanley's God was always the wrathful chastising Yahweh of the Old Testament, not the Jesus Christ of the New. The conflation Yahweh/Wotan – most appropriate for a Nietzschean – emerges clearly in the kind of missionary he admired. Always it was the men of action, the Livingstones and the Mackays, he preferred, not the preachers or contemplatives.

After the bruising experience of the Rear Column controversy, it was only to be expected that Stanley's later career would be mired in shallows. Since it was the *New York Herald* that launched Stanley on his career as African explorer, it is appropriate for that organ to have the last word on the tattered shreds of reputation left to Stanley in 1891. 'Whatever else these terrible charges and countercharges may have done or left undone, they have killed African exploration as a profession.'[76] If Stanley was to have any future in Africa, it would have to be sought in the career of another Nietzschean 'superman', someone else who regarded himself as inhabiting a special sphere of morality, beyond good and evil. In the Europe of the 1890s that meant one man: Leopold of Belgium.

· 20 ·

THE return of Stanley from the Emin Pasha expedition brought to a head his latent conflict with Leopold. Both were men who understood only power, dominance and manipulation; both therefore were exercised to discover a way to exploit the other. Leopold still laboured under the illusion that it was he, not Mackinnon, who loomed largest in Stanley's future African plans.[1] Stanley fostered the illusion and presented the results of the Emin expedition as a great boon for Leopold's Congo: he had secured peace with the Arabs by appointing Tippu Tip as governor of Stanley Falls; he had demonstrated that a great revenue could be drawn from the Ituri forest; and he had extended the territory of the Free State to Lake Albert.[2] Leopold meanwhile was full of praise for Stanley's Promethean achievements; he told Mackinnon that there was scarcely a single one of Africa's mysteries that Stanley had not solved.[3]

But in their intimate letters and journals the two men told a different story. From the Shepheard's Hotel in Cairo in January 1890 Stanley wrote to tell Mackinnon what he really thought of the King. Explaining that in no circumstances would he ever work for him again, he went on: 'I have strong objections to his ingratitude to me in 1885 and 1886. I do not feel like forgiving him for imprisoning me in my room for two years awaiting orders.'[4] Stanley's anger was increased by the reflection that at forty-nine he was past his peak as an African explorer; in the limbo of 1885, when he was still forty-four, it would have been a different story. 'It may be that he has at last made up his mind to that great mission he has so often referred to verbally and in writing. I think, however, that though he remembers "Time is pressing" when he needs me, he forgets how time has flown with me . . . I feel like an old man today.'[5]

Leopold's position was different. He still saw a use for Stanley's abilities, provided he could not interfere with his own nefarious schemes

357

in the Congo State; perhaps a position as viceroy in the as yet un-conquered territories of Katanga, Aruwimi or Manyema might be the answer?[6] But Stanley knew Leopold too well by now to consent to be shunted into a backwater; to the monarch's consternation he flatly turned down all such 'minor' African appointments.[7] Next Leopold thought of making Stanley the Belgian plenipotentiary to the 1889-90 anti-slavery conference. Again Stanley rebuffed him, saying he had no interest in a commission that was a mere talking shop and a waste of time. His health was a further barrier, and he would need rest and recuperation before returning to Europe from Egypt.[8]

Leopold, whose spies kept him well informed on all matters, knew very well that Stanley's health was robust – vigorous enough to allow him to work sixteen hours a day on his book. He chose to comment ironically on Stanley's valetudinarian status in Cairo.[9] This irritated Stanley and he noted with asperity in his journal that Leopold was one of those people who never accepted illness as an excuse. When de Vaux, Borchgrave's predecessor, was suffering from kidney disease, Leopold seemed amazed that he could not work like a Trojan. In 1882 and again in 1884 Leopold had been impatient when Stanley was prostrated from the after-effects of African fever. Now, after three years on the Emin expedition, Stanley was again expected to need no rest. 'I fear this promise of a big undertaking is but a bait to draw me home the quicker.'[10] Here was a case of the biter bit. No one had less sympathy for ill-ness (in *others*) than Stanley himself; it was but poetic justice that he should suffer under the lash of another autocrat with Erewhonian lean-ings.

Stanley's instincts on the international conference for the suppression of the slave trade were sound, for this was yet another of Leopold's stalking horses to mask his base economic designs. It will be remembered that in 1887 Leopold had persuaded the Belgian government to authorise a premium bond issue. When the bonds came on the market in February 1888 Leopold had to purchase large numbers of them himself to hold share prices steady. But by the time the second instalment of the premium bond issue was ready to be floated, their quoted opening price was less than the market price of the first batch. Even though the Belgian government offered to purchase them, only a third of the second issue was taken up. By late 1888 it was clear that Leopold could not raise enough on the stock market to pay for the day-to-day administration of the Congo, especially since the only permitted tax (export duties) pro-duced negligible amounts.[11] Meanwhile other financial possibilities were non-starters. Ferry's offer of a 20-million franc lottery in 1885 was not honoured by the incoming Freycinet administration in France and it was not until 1888 that the French Bourse authorised a loan lottery.[12] The Rothschilds turned down Leopold's application for a loan, which led the King to weep crocodile tears over the financial community's lack of confidence in him.[13]

From Leopold's point of view there were some interesting straws in the Congo wind if he could only keep the Free State solvent for a while longer. The Belgian railway group led by Captain Albert Thys (in whose favour Leopold had double-crossed the Hutton/Stanley/Mackinnon consortium in 1886) had by entrepreneurial dynamism raised a million francs and formed a Compagnie du Congo pour le commerce et l'industrie (CCCI). After a year Strauch was sacked as administrator-general of the EIC and Thys appointed in his place.[14] Following this, Leopold gulled Belgian minister Bernaert into making a 10-million franc loan to the railway syndicate. This, plus help from foreign capital, led to the formation in July 1889 of the Compagnie du Chemin de Fer du Congo (with 71 per cent of the capital from Belgian sources). Additionally three new companies were formed: for trading, cattle-raising, and the purchase of ivory and rubber (Société Belge du Haut Congo).

To parlay his bets until the potential wealth of the Congo could be released, Leopold advanced a troika of ideas. There was political action to get a direct loan from the Belgian treasury. There was (most important of all for the future) the creation of a new economic system for the production of wealth by the Congo state apparatus itself; alienating 'vacant lands' to the State enabled Leopold to construct a state monopoly. And there was an attempt to revise the clauses of the 1885 Berlin treaty that prohibited the levying of import duties.

As before, Leopold tried his old trick of pretending to be concerned with humanitarian ideals, so as to mask his sordid cupidity. His aim was to set up protectionist barriers in the Congo under the guise of stamping out the slave trade. But Leopold had gulled his audiences once too often. To the King's annoyance the Dutch immediately saw through to his base motives.[15] More seriously, so did Emile Banning, one of the architects of the Berlin treaty and erstwhile admirer and supporter of the King; a decisive rift between the two men followed soon after.[16] This was a serious check to the monarch at the very time that he was beginning to win the propaganda battle for Belgian public opinion and suck the parliament into his Congo quicksands. He needed a powerful opinion-former and who better than Stanley, in early 1890 still the unsullied 'hero' of Emin's rescue, not the tarnished angel he was to appear a year later.

Stanley was quite prepared to play Leopold's games as long as they did not conflict with his own interests. He produced a paean to Leopold that satisfied the King but committed him (Stanley) to nothing. 'What does the greatness of a monarch consist in? If it is the extent of his territory, then the Emperor of Russia is the greatest of all. If it is the splendour and power of military organisation, then William II takes first place. But if royal greatness consists in the wisdom and goodness of a sovereign leading his people with the solicitude of a shepherd watching over his flock, then the greatest sovereign is your own.'[17]

Such was the background when Stanley made his week-long visit to Leopold between 19 and 26 April 1890. The King treated his most famous agent as visiting royalty and used the visit to 'sell' the Congo, pointing out that Stanley on the Emin expedition had discovered ground-nuts, tobacco, cattle, copper, iron and gold: 'in the recent scramble we have drawn the winning ticket'.[18] After a day of banquets and junketings the two men got down to serious talking on 20 April. Leopold sat with his back to the window on one side of a marble-topped table. Stanley sat facing him. Time seemed to have stood still since the last audience more than three years earlier, except that Leopold's brown beard was now white from ear to ear and his own hair, then iron-grey, was now 'as white as Snowdon in winter'.[19]

Leopold posed detailed questions about the country between the Aruwimi and Lake Albert. Stanley painted a glowing picture of the rubber to be extracted there and proposed an elephant reserve in the Ituri, where herds would still remain when every single pachyderm had been exterminated elsewhere; it must be stressed that his interest was in the continuance of the ivory trade, not nature conservancy. He also argued that the ferocious tribes of the area could be brought round to white rule by the kind of patient and fair treatment he had shown to the Bangala and the Soko on the Congo.

In the afternoon the subject switched to Emin, and Stanley poured out his now familiar litany of criticism of the ill-fated Pasha. When he mentioned with contempt Emin's excessive liking for women, it is legitimate to assume that the famed libertine and roué Leopold suppressed a smile. When the talks resumed the next day it was Emin's troops, especially the 6000 left behind at Kavalli's under Selim Bey, that most engaged Leopold and he discussed the feasibility of sending Belgian officers to incorporate this legion of the lost into the Congo armies.[20]

In the afternoon Stanley raised the project dearest to his heart: the suppression of Arab slavery and the destruction of Tippu Tip's power between Stanley Falls and Lake Tanganyika. He stressed to Leopold that this was much more important than the proposed Welle exploration and would need no more than 2500 troops to accomplish. Besides, if the slavers were not halted in their tracks they themselves would ascend the Welle and make common cause with the rebels in Equatoria. If this combined force in turn linked arms with the Mahdists, all Africa would be carved in two and all Leopold's plans turned to dust. How long would the total project take, Leopold asked? About a year, Stanley replied, and he felt compelled to add that the lands south of Stanley Falls to Tanganyika were much more valuable commercially than the Nile littoral the King seemed to hanker after.[21]

The morning of the fourth day was spent discussing boundary disputes with the French. At one point Leopold rang a bell and van Kerkhoven, one of Stanley's Congo veterans, came in, to be briefed on Stanley's plans for the occupation of the Welle. In the afternoon Stanley went to the anti-slavery conference in Brussels to give an address on the methods used by the Arab slavers. He told the delegates that the key to suppression of the slave trade was an arms embargo; neither Arab slavery nor Mirambo's empire would have been possible without guns and gunpowder.[22]

It was not until the fifth day of their talks that Leopold finally unveiled his proposed future plans for Stanley. Others could expel the Arabs and deal with the French but 'there is only one man capable of making my secret mission a success and that is *Stanley*, the *great explorer* and *founder* of the *Congo State*.' Leopold spoke the words artfully with a smile, his arms riding up and down histrionically as he put strong emphasis on certain words. He then revealed that he wanted Stanley to command a military expedition to defeat the Khalifa and take Khartoum.[23]

Stanley's first reaction was that such an idea was a chimera. But would you undertake it if you had sufficient resources, Leopold persisted? Of course, Stanley replied. Leopold went on to assert that he had the money to achieve the project, and make Stanley a rich man into the bargain. Stanley tested out the proposition by telling the King that he would need 12,000 European troops. At this Leopold's face fell and he asked how many black troops could do the job instead. Stanley looked grave and assured the monarch that this would be a task for 50,000 crack troops, all from élite squads.

Can't you do with less, asked a disappointed Leopold. Stanley replied that the absolute minimum would be 5000 whites and 10,000 blacks. A disconsolate Leopold shook his head and said white troops were out of the question but he could rise to 20,000 blacks from the warlike tribes of the Congo. At this Stanley grimaced and pointed out that such men would have to be collected from their tribes, then welded into a fighting force. They would then be fighting the best army in Africa on hostile soil, outnumbered four to one. To achieve success against those odds, four years' hard training would be required, by which time Stanley would be too old to command.

While Leopold was still absorbing this disappointment, Stanley moved in for the knock-out blow. Patiently he explained the logistics of the Congo. Apart from the distances to be covered, there was food, transport and subsistence; even 1000 men would need fifty whaleboats to carry them, to say nothing of the army of porters and back-up staff. Besides, his own experience of white officers on the Congo made Stanley doubtful they would stay a four-year course. For all these reasons the capture of Khartoum from the Congo was an impossibility with Leopold's current resources. If he had 5000 seasoned Egyptian troops, the case might be very different. Then he would seize and fortify Fashoda before pressing on to Abba Island and thence to Omdurman and triumph. Even so, he would be talking about a campaign lasting six years and costing one million pounds sterling.

Leopold was downcast and the disappointment showed in his words. 'I was under the impression that a man like you would have been more eager for such an adventure as the taking of Khartoum than it seems you are. You might have had £100,000 for yourself if you had consented to the enterprise.' Stanley retorted that he was always eager for fame, glory and adventure but he could not do the impossible; it would be unworthy of him to minimise the obstacles to such a project just so as to flatter the King.[24]

Stanley was thoroughly enjoying the chance to revenge himself on his erstwhile reluctant taskmaster and the opportunity was enhanced during the sixth day of his visit. They got down to the business of discussing the boundary between Mackinnon's sphere of influence and the Congo. Mackinnon had proposed the Semliki River but Leopold complained that this gave the British an unfair advantage and twitted Stanley about showing favouritism to Mackinnon. Stanley tried to divert Leopold's attention by asserting that his long-term advantage was best secured in the Ituri forest. But has not all this been devastated by the Arabs, objected

Leopold? At present yes, Stanley replied, but the potential once the Arabs have been expelled is enormous.[25]

As Leopold was beginning to suspect, Stanley was indeed manoeuvring to place all the cards in Mackinnon's hands, just as he had promised Mackinnon he would.[26] Even though he saw no necessary territorial conflict between Leopold's claims and those of the IBEA Company, he was determined to give Mackinnon the benefit of every doubt and to ensure that Selim Bey's men passed into the service of the British, not the Free State.[27] So, even as he paid lip-service to the King in the royal palace, he was avenging himself for the slight that had rankled since 1886. Had Leopold known his man through and through, he would have realised how dangerous it was to make an enemy of Stanley.

The upshot of this six-day conference was the signature of a treaty between Leopold and Mackinnon (dated 24 May 1890, with Stanley signing on behalf of the Congo Free State). This laid out spheres of influence, with the Congo territory extending as far as the Nile at Lado (the Lado enclave) on the left bank, with the IBEA on the right bank commanding territory down to Lake Tanganyika. Leopold also tried to manipulate Anglo-German rivalry to his own advantage by suggesting that German East Africa would be more secure if the Free State's boundaries extended as far as Bahr-el-Ghazal.[28] But both the Mackinnon treaty and the German machinations foundered on the reef of the Anglo-German agreement of June 1890, defining respective interests in East Africa, which gave Britain the western watershed of the Nile. Leopold's response to this was to send the explorer Becker to Tippu Tip with proposals for a secret treaty whereby Tippu would receive 200,000 francs in return for his ivory and the establishment of three ports in the Bahr-el-Ghazal and one on the Nile itself. Tippu flatly refused.[29]

1890-91 saw further developments in Leopold's African designs in which Stanley was a (sometimes unwilling) agent. In July 1890 Leopold published his will, showing the personal 'sacrifices' the King had made for *'la gloire belge'*. The Belgian Parliament then voted the King a 25-million franc loan over ten years, interest-free. At the end of ten years Belgium was entitled to repayment in full or annexation of the Congo State. In the same month the Brussels Anti-Slavery Conference ended with a tacit agreement to allow Leopold to undertake the conquest of the Congo Arabs. At the same time, he used Great Power apathy towards the internal slave trade to persuade the international community to let him levy import duties so that he could fight the slavers. Queen

Victoria was bombarded with letters to this effect.[30] Stanley was pressed into service too, though unfortunately for the King, his order to Stanley to write to *The Times* on the issue coincided with the full flowering of the Rear Column controversy.[31] Stanley stalled again. First he asked for documentary evidence on the budgetary shortfall to be made up by import taxes. Leopold claimed that he did not have the necessary documentation in the archives.[32] Next, as a quid pro quo Stanley asked for the official Free State report on Jameson's cannibal feast. Leopold failed to send it on, anxious not to be embroiled in the controversy, so Stanley neglected to write the letter to *The Times*.[33]

However, Leopold's campaign for import duties was ultimately crowned with success. An agreement was reached in February 1891 that Leopold could levy a 10 per cent *ad valorem* import duty across the board. But the King's duplicity fooled fewer people as the years went on. When Stanley was again reluctantly persuaded to speak in favour of suppression of the slave trade during his American tour of 1890-91, his critics hit back with the Monroe doctrine and charges of humbug. Aside from the fact that the USA was pledged to avoid entanglements outside the hemisphere, anti-slavery rhetoric from the Europeans was cant – they wanted American resources to help prop up their own economic interests in Africa. Nobody could be less interested in the reality of slavery than Leopold.[34]

But Leopold was determined to extract the last pound of flesh from Stanley's American visit. He asked him to lobby the US Senate on the import duty question and a US-Congo accord. Despite waiving an extradition treaty, the King had not been able to overcome Senate objections. So he suggested a modification of the 1884 US declaration in the form of additional clauses or amendments. He asked Stanley to try to get a special session of the US Senate to ratify all treaties relating to the Congo, using a press campaign ostensibly aimed at other objectives. How, he asked, could anyone in the USA – the home of protectionism – object to a picayune secondary tax of 6 per cent on alcohol? 'What can be done? I know Americans do not like to be bothered with affairs outside their magnificent continent, but they have commercial and other treaties with various powers European and African ... could you not explain this through the American press without giving it the appearance of being suggested by foreigners, for the United States do not like the counsels of the foreigners.'[35] Stanley carried out the commission perfunctorily with a few interviews with Secretary of State Blaine and other luminaries on Capitol Hill.

Leopold by now easily had enough money to support the existing Congo State. But it was his overweening ambition to expand into Katanga and on to the Nile that first led him to the monstrous evil of the extraction of a super-surplus value. The first step was an order in 1891 prohibiting the indigenous inhabitants of the Congo from hunting elephants for ivory or tapping wild rubber. Instead a state monopoly in these commodities was created. It was Banning, now a ferocious critic of Leopold, who pointed out that such a monopoly was not only against the interest of the native population but was expressly forbidden by the Berlin treaty; the Congo was supposed to be policed by the EIC so that the powers could practise free trade there, so Leopold had no right to be buying and selling through a state monopoly.[36]

After attacks from the powers and within Belgium, Leopold was forced in 1892 to modify his position to the point where the Free State divided the 'vacant lands' into three zones, including one where, theoretically, there would be free trade. In fact in the 'free trade zone' a form of bogus competition went on between Leopold's front companies.[37] This head-on collision between the principles of monopoly and free trade fed into the growing clash between Belgians and Arabs. Leopold had to cut out the private trader and ensure that the Arabs sold only to state agents. Seeing the danger looming, Tippu Tip showed Leopold's letter of instruction to the British consul at Zanzibar. In retaliation, and on the principle of sauce for the goose and gander, the British and Germans continued to offer arms and ammunition in exchange for ivory, despite the Brussels protocol signed in 1890.[38] But by 1893 three and a half million francs' worth of ivory was sold in Antwerp, plus one million francs' worth of rubber (this was to double within two years).

In 1891 Leopold tightened his grip on Katanga. An expedition under Stairs was sent to add the territory to the Congo State. Meanwhile Leopold despatched another expedition under Dhanis to occupy Portuguese territory to the south. An explosive confrontation ensued, in the course of which Leopold worked out a madcap scheme for sending a gunboat up the Tagus to hold Lisbon to ransom. The mission was entrusted to Liebrechts, who refused to implement it on grounds of its inherent insanity.[39] Nevertheless a diplomatic settlement in 1891 left Leopold in possession of much of Dhanis's conquests.

Yet since Katanga's copper would take years to exploit, Leopold again schemed to push his frontiers to the Nile, proving that his proposal to Stanley for a conquest of the Sudan was no isolated flash in the pan. Partly he dreamed of becoming the heir to the Pharaohs. But mostly he coveted the vast elephant herds in the southern Sudan and saw Khartoum as the gateway to the Nile, which would give the Congo State an outlet to the Mediterranean, so that it was approachable from both the Atlantic and Mediterranean.[40]

Leopold began by sending van Kerkhoven in command of an expedition up the Welle to Wadelai. Van Kerkhoven himself was killed during the bloody progress to the Nile but his second-in-command Lt. Milz made contact with the survivors of Emin's forces and in October 1890 arrived on the bank of the Nile; his successors, however, were driven off three years later by a revolt among Emin's officers. The next Nile development was in 1892 when Salisbury pressed Leopold to renounce the agreement with Mackinnon. Leopold referred Salisbury disingenuously to a Foreign Office communication of May 1890 appearing to show that the British government had no objection to the accord. Further examination showed that it was *commercial* rights not sovereignty that was being referred to.[41]

But at this point Leopold received unexpected help when France decided to occupy Fashoda. Britain was now prepared to use Leopold as his forces were *in situ*. In return for the recognition of the Anglo-German agreement, Leopold was offered the lease of Bahr-al-Ghazal and the left bank of the Nile as far north as Fashoda. Leopold then tried to dicker, so as to get Belgian possession guaranteed as long as Belgium was a monarchy. As a concession the left bank up to Fashoda was leased during Leopold's lifetime and Bahr-al-Ghazal on normal notice.[42] This led to angry reactions from France and Germany. The French objected to the Congolese barrier across her line of advance. The Germans protested at the article which allowed Britain a strip of the Congo territory for the passage of the mythical Cape-Cairo railway. Britain was eventually forced to abandon this corridor.[43] Finally, the 1892 Liberal government refused to allow Rosebery to support Leopold against France, so in August Leopold signed a new treaty with France, allowing him just the Lado enclave.

Where was Stanley in all this politicking? Once again Leopold looked in vain for any support. In 1892 Stanley, a zealous partisan of Lord Rosebery, was engaged in a long-running feud with Sir William Harcourt over the future of Uganda. Stanley campaigned on Rosebery's side in the press and told the British nation that the East African market for African goods could amount to twelve million consumers.[44] The debate between Rosebery and Harcourt supporters became acrimonious. Horace Waller, Stanley's old adversary from 1872, accused the IBEA

Company of supporting the slave trade.[45] Harcourt himself had been one of Stanley's bitterest critics during the Rear Column controversy.[46] When Mackinnon met Harcourt and Bryce at the Stanley's home in Richmond Terrace, the sparks predictably flew. The general opinion of Harcourt in Stanley's circle can be gauged from a remark by Mounteney Jephson: 'Harcourt is a politician who goes whichever way the wind blows, even when there isn't any.'[47] Harcourt responded by hitting below the belt. 'I think it a salutary lesson that the Stanley-Emin relief expedition has opened the eyes of the British public a good deal to the importance of these philanthropic-missionary-civilising pretenders. As long as you keep to simple missionaries attending to their own work or discoverers like Livingstone going unattended amongst the savages they are safe enough. But when you come to militant bishops that want annual expeditions, plundering and robbing and killing right and left, it is quite a different thing.'[48]

In the end, although Gladstone had assured Leopold that Britain would definitely be evacuating Uganda, Rosebery's influence was such that Sir Gerald Portal was sent out to establish a protectorate. Gladstone made the mistake of canvassing Stanley's opinion on this expedition and received for his pains a self-righteous screed about how the government would have done better to listen to him in the first place. As Dorothy Stanley remarked: 'I told Mr Gladstone he might keep the letter, he cannot have liked it much.'[49] And it was typical of Stanley in this mood that he would be cold and aloof with potential allies like Lugard, who came to see him about Uganda, but who was regarded by Stanley as too much of a rival for African prestige.[50]

1893 saw a partial *rapprochement* between Stanley and Leopold, both because the King was able to turn Stanley's feelings of jealousy towards rival Africanists to his own account and because Leopold was pursuing policies close to Stanley's heart. This was the year Leopold finally unleashed his forces under Dhanis against the Congo Arabs and Stanley gave the King his enthusiastic support.[51] When the Belgians emerged victorious, Stanley took all the credit on himself. 'Few in this country know that I am the prime cause of this advance of the Belgians against the Arab slave-raiders. Indeed, people little realise how I have practically destroyed this terrible slave-trade, by cutting it down at its very roots. I have also been as fatal to Tippu-Tib, Rashid, his nephew, who captured Stanley Falls from Captain Deane, Tippu-Tib's son, Muini Mubala, and lastly Said-bin-Abed . . . as if I had led the avengers myself, which I was very much solicited to do.'[52]

The other aspect of the *entente* between Leopold and Stanley concerned Cecil Rhodes. Ever since the publication of Arnot's *Garanganze* in 1889, Rhodes had been interested in Katanga's copper. His champion Harry Johnston, who shared his dream of a map of Africa coloured red from the Cape to Cairo, was a fervent champion of the proposed Cape-Cairo railway and in 1890 published maps showing the boundary of the Congo Free State falling short of Katanga. It was this action that led Leopold first to protest to Salisbury and then to send Stairs in 1891 to stage an annexing *coup d'état* in Katanga.[53]

In 1893 when Leopold moved against the Congo Arabs, opinion in Britain at first inclined to the view that the King was an invader and aggressor; the British continued to supply the Arabs with guns and ammunition from the east coast. Leopold had the idea that Stanley might be able to energise Cecil Rhodes on the Belgian side in return for a railway concession in Katanga.[54] Stanley replied at once. 'With regard to Mr Cecil Rhodes, I beg to say that my personal acquaintance with him extends only to a three hours' conversation with him while at dinner one day last November, during which he gave me reason to believe that he had long ago conceived a highly flattering impression of me. Since 1890 I had looked forward to this meeting, as both of us had mutual friends, who were good enough to carry to me Mr Rhodes's great admiration for my road-making in the Congo and to convey to him my commendations of Mr Rhodes's abilities as a a financier, statesman and imperialist.' He warned Leopold that Rhodes was hostile to the Congo Free State both because of the 1891 Katanga seizure and because of the ideological anti-Leopold fuel supplied by H. H. Johnston.[55]

Leopold replied by return to propose a scheme whereby Rhodes would pressurise the British government to recognise the 1890 Mackinnon treaty, in return for which the King would guarantee him facilities for his trans-Africa telegraph line, possibly including an annual subsidy to maintain the telegraph in Uganda and a defensive treaty against the Mahdists.[56] Stanley duly passed on the offer to Rhodes, but Rhodes's suspicion and dislike of Leopold was too great to be overcome.[57] However, Stanley showed his independence from the King by backing Rhodes to the hilt in his war against Lobengula and the Matabele at the end of the year.[58]

Relations between Stanley and Leopold continued superficially cordial until 1895. If anything, it was Leopold who acted deferentially. His agents tried to place an ailing Bonny in the Congo service on Stanley's recommendation, and the King solicited the explorer's opinion even on such matters as the construction of the new harbour at Heist, near Ostend.[59] But in 1895 a major crisis erupted when the Belgian Captain Lothaire arrested the British trader Charles Stokes in the Congo on charges of gun-running. After a hearing before himself and a brother officer, Lothaire led Stokes out to an immediate execution. The affair caused a sensation in England and lowered public esteem for Leopold's controversial Congo State even more.[60]

Stanley had met Stokes in Cairo in 1890 and was very fond of him.[61] Alarmed by the outcry in England, Leopold had Liebrechts (now Secretary of the Interior for the Congo State) send Stanley the relevant documents, in hopes that he would make another of his interventions in the columns of *The Times*.[62] But when Stanley read the transcripts of the 'trial' he was appalled. There had been no proper court martial; Lothaire had acted as judge, jury and executioner. Nor could he see what the pretext for a death sentence was; not even Stanley could be persuaded to see that the illegal sale of a few percussion muskets merited the supreme penalty. White men should never swear away each other's lives in Africa, even if Lothaire's actions were not expressly prohibited by the 1894 Anglo-Congolese treaty.[63] In sum, Lothaire's actions were utterly indefensible and a serious blow for all well-wishers of the Congo State. If the documents he examined ever became public, he warned, the scandal in England would be tremendous.[64]

But although Stanley could not defend Leopold's actions over the Stokes affair, he was psychologically incapable of accepting the flood of atrocity stories that now began to flood out of the Congo, exposing a vista of carnage, murder, rape and mayhem not perceived in Europe since the Thirty Years War.[65] He used the bogus argument that the silence of 'six hundred' missionaries in the Congo meant that conditions there could not be as black as they were painted: 'are all the rest of these missionaries paid by the State to keep silence?'[66] The argument was singularly spurious. There were not 600 missionaries in the Congo and those that there were maintained a discreet silence about atrocities out of fear of the wrath of Leopold.

In 1896 when further horror stories reached Europe, Stanley continued to brush them aside in public.[67] A particularly grave series of allegations was published in September 1896 by Captain Salisbury and Mr Parminter, both of whom had resigned in disgust from service with the Congo State.[68] Stanley did his best to rebut them, but as ever he was a bull in a china shop and the newspapers refused to print his 'refutation' as originally written on the grounds that it contained libellous material.[69] Still in a state of willing disbelief Stanley explained to Leopold his theory that the ancient foe, the Dutch House, was responsible for the black propaganda that was utterly destroying the credibility of the Free State in Britain. But his private letter to Leopold betrayed his conviction that there was substance to the stories. 'I would suggest to Your Majesty that something should be done to prevent the continuous supply of Congo sensations because 1905 is not far off, and people, fed as they are with stories of atrocities, will be apt to believe that some of them must be true and that the State ought to be suppressed in consequence . . . if England can be persuaded that the Congo government is a disgrace to civilisation, there will undoubtedly be a third Power which will move for the downfall of the State.'[70] Leopold was sufficiently taken aback by this that he promised to suppress all irregularities in the Congo – needless to say the promise was not kept.[71] Although Stanley continued to support Leopold in public – as for instance in the introduction to Guy Burrows's book on the Congo – privately he characterised Leopold's rapacity as 'an erring and ignorant policy'.[72]

The extent to which the two men were far apart emerged from a meeting in Brussels in April 1897. Stanley suggested as a means of dampening down the chorus of international disapproval of the Free State a High Tribunal to deal with all matters affecting foreign subjects in the Congo. Leopold bridled at the suggestion. This would place power in the hands of men who had no commitment to the Congo State. It would be too expensive and the Tribunal might actually demand that the construction workers be properly fed (this from Leopold's own lips)! Besides, how about other nations accepting such interference? Would it be accepted in Cuba, in the Philippines, in Russia? Suppose France sent judges to British Africa or Ireland; imagine the uproar? No, the root cause of the British press campaign was, and always had been, simple hatred of the Congo State; after all Britain was the very last nation to afford recognition in 1885.[73]

One brushed aside Stanley's careful suggestions at one's peril. Stanley brooded on the latest snub. It seemed all the more unacceptable as, in 1896, after the Italian invasion of Abyssinia collapsed at Adowa, Stanley had backed Leopold's scheme for moving into the Italian sphere of influence in Eritrea and Ethiopia, against the advice of friends like Lord Cromer (formerly Sir Evelyn Baring) who saw straight through the King's machinations.[74] The consequence was that although Stanley continued to follow avidly the advance of the Congo railway (completed in 1898), he had little more to do with Leopold.[75] The last contact

between the two was when Stanley approached the King for a contribution towards the planned Livingstone monument. The man who had
made a personal fortune of £2 million in six years through unspeakably
brutal exploitation and rapacity sent – just £20.[76] If ever there was an
evil genius in Stanley's life, capable of darkening an already black inner
psyche, it was surely Leopold II, King of the Belgians.

· 21 ·

O N return from Australia Mrs Stanley determined to distract her husband from further thoughts of Africa by encouraging him in a political career. First she had to clear up the uncertainty about his nationality, which had prevented his being knighted in 1890. Correspondence with Lord Salisbury produced the information that the 1870 Naturalisation Act required a potential British subject to have had five years' residence in the United Kingdom. By the skin of his teeth Stanley established his eligibility; between 1872 and 1892 he had spent five years and twenty weeks domiciled in Great Britain. On 20 May 1892 he took the oath and was readmitted to his native nationality.

With the aid of Alexander Bruce, Dolly then persuaded him to become Liberal-Unionist candidate for North Lambeth in the 1892 election.[1] Ten days before the poll the Stanley bandwagon rolled into action. But Stanley was a disastrous candidate. He consented to speak at working-men's clubs but regarded asking any man for his vote as degrading. Totally lacking the common touch, he was ill at ease and irritable during the campaign. To make matters worse, he fought on a highly reactionary platform on imperialism, social discipline and vehement opposition to Home Rule, which in a constituency like North Lambeth was bound to seem aggressive and confrontational.[2]

His first attempt to woo the voters was a disaster. He was unused to the rough and tumble of political meetings and became disturbed and uncoordinated under a hail of heckling and booing. Sensing that he was losing his temper, the crowd stepped up the booing and taunting until nothing else could be heard. He stopped talking, folded his arms and glared fiercely at his tormentors.[3] Dorothy Stanley, perceiving that the entire campaign stood on the brink of disaster, burst into tears and twice tried to rise to her feet only to sink back into her chair. Her evident distress had an effect on the audience, which started to calm down. But before Stanley could resume his speech, she got to her feet and cried out: 'When all of you and I are dead and forgotten, the name of Stanley will live, be revered and loved.' This outburst was greeted with peals of laughter and cries of 'Shame'. Eventually the police had to eject four hecklers before Stanley could limp through to the end of his speech.[4]

On 27 June he addressed the electors from a cart. Again his reactionary sentiments were in evidence. First came a blistering attack on Gladstone and Home Rule and a corresponding encomium for Joseph Chamberlain. Referring to the movement for an eight-hour day, he said that if he had worked only eight hours a day, he would never have got ahead of the Germans in Africa and added 200,000 square miles of land to British territory. He was just getting down from the cart when he remembered an old political trick. 'I had forgotten my duty. Gentlemen, let me introduce my dearly beloved wife, late Miss Dorothy Tennant. She is a descendant of the greatest liberal the country ever knew – Oliver Cromwell.'[5] In this way he linked his wife, formerly a fervent Gladstone supporter, with the anti-Irish movement, for Cromwell was the most hated figure in Irish historical demonology.

Stanley's opposition to Home Rule won him friends in press circles previously his most severe critics.[6] But it did not impress the electorate. The climax of the campaign came on 29 June when his winding-up meeting in Hawkeston Hall, Lambeth was howled down by the opposition. The platform was stormed, the speakers forced to flee. When Stanley and his wife got into their brougham, the enraged crowd tore off the door of the carriage. The predictable election defeat followed. Much against his will, Stanley allowed Dolly to persuade him to remain as the Liberal-Unionist candidate for the constituency.[7] He accepted a banquet from the Chamberlain faction and pledged himself to their service in the next election. This effectively precluded any African engagements, which was what Dolly had been aiming at all along.[8]

The Stanleys assuaged the bitterness of defeat with a cruise on Mackinnon's yacht through the Scottish lochs to the Clyde.[9] Then Stanley entered a limbo period for some three years, lecturing in England, Scotland and Ireland on African issues and contemporary social questions. His stance on domestic matters was always that of a deep-dyed reactionary. In the 1893 coal strike he launched a bitter attack on the miners: 'if I had any money to spare at the present time, it would not be given to men who were determined to be sulky and who, to spite the coal-owners, preferred to starve.'[10] He wrote on Africa and boosted the sales of his friends' travel books by writing introductions for them.[11]

He developed a fondness for East Anglia and Cambridgeshire. In 1894 a succession of malarial attacks led him to spend more and more time at seaside resorts, first on the Isle of Wight, later at Monte Carlo.[12]

The years 1893-94 also saw the demise of many of his closest friends. First was Sir William Mackinnon who, Stanley alleged, died prematurely of a broken heart after shabby and ungrateful treatment from the British government.[13] Then came the deaths of surgeon Parke, the missionary Charles Ingham and his wife – with both of whom Stanley was particularly friendly, General Beauregard, his old commander at Shiloh, and, most grievous loss of all, Livingstone's son-in-law Alexander Bruce.[14] Few clues remain as to Stanley's private life in this period, after Dolly's excisions. We learn that he helped his brother-in-law F. W. Myers organise a parapsychological conference (he referred to Myers as 'a rare mind') and that Dolly had a superstition which prevented her ever from travelling on a Sunday. It is also clear from her addiction to the drug secephonal that she suffered from chronic insomnia.[15]

1893 was a bad year for Stanley, quite apart from the deaths of so many of his friends. A painting trip to Tuscany, with an itinerary from Turin to Rome via Siena and Florence, ended traumatically just when Stanley thought he had secured a new friendship. John Addington Symonds, the celebrated author and Italianist, met Stanley in Rome and enchanted him with his brilliant conversation. Stanley made a dinner date at the Café Roma next day, but two hours later a message came that Symonds had been taken violently ill; he died two days later. Stanley was in bed for a week with shock. The experience turned him against Rome. He complained of the strain on his nerves of the racket from the stone pavements and the effect of the dreaded Roman fever on his health.[16]

He returned home to find another headache awaiting him. When Stanley cut short his American lecture tour in 1886 to head the Emin Pasha expedition, Major Pond, the impresario, had accepted the convenient fiction that Leopold had summoned Stanley back to Europe. The truth of course was that he had returned of his own volition. Now it transpired that another party was involved – a London-based American called Greenleaf Webb Appleton, who now sued for non-payment of fees due after introducing Stanley to Pond. Appleton alleged that only Leopold's contractual lien on Stanley's services justified the cancellation of the 1886 lectures and that it was Mackinnon and the EPRE committee, not Leopold, who had summoned Stanley from the USA; therefore he was bringing an action for breach of contract.[17] Stanley was forced into the humiliating position of having to ask Leopold to lie for him to get himself off the legal hook – this partly explains the change of attitude towards Leopold in evidence after 1893. The case was eventually settled out of court on the judge's ruling that the plaintiff was entitled to commission only on the original 1886 fees, not the enhanced ones for the 1890-91 lecture tour.[18]

1895 was a significant year in Stanley's life. In June Parliament was dissolved and electioneering commenced. On 15 July 1895 Stanley at last secured the prize Dolly was hoping for when he was elected MP for North Lambeth with a majority of 405. But his first weeks in Parliament led to further disillusionment. He complained about the accommodation and the facilities offered to Members and was contemptuous of the intellectual and personal qualities of most of his colleagues. Of all the luminaries of whom he left pen portraits in his diary (Redmond, Dollon, Harcourt, Balfour, Haldane, Austen Chamberlain, Curzon, Dilke), it was Sir Charles Dilke who impressed him most.[19] He even noticed with irritation that the doorkeeper addressed him with the words 'Mr Stanley, I presume.' The mock banter and verbosity of the House irked him and he recorded a particularly damning verdict on 20 August: 'The criminal waste of precious time, devotion to antique customs, the silent endurance of evils, which, by a word, could be swept away, have afforded me much matter of wonder.'[20]

But Stanley was providing a very one-sided picture. The truth was that Parliament did not suit him nor he Parliament. A natural man of action, he believed in solving issues by administrative order or the gun, not by talk and debate. His arguments on all topics outside Africa lacked subtlety and finesse and he was soon marginalised as an obscure backbencher of reactionary stripe, his close-cropped white hair and red face making him a quasi-military archetype of the Colonel Blimp figure. He was a poor public speaker on an election platform, since he lacked the ability to improvise and could only orate in the style of his public lectures. In the House this disability was magnified and he was by common consent an indifferent parliamentarian. His first intervention, on the Sudan, was undistinguished, and when he tried to make an even-handed speech on the Stokes affair, his rhetoric was so boring and prolix that the Speaker cut him off.[21]

After just a month of this Stanley took himself off on a three-month tour of the USA. Starting at New York, he swept through Canada, the West and the South (where he paid his final visit to New Orleans).

Outwardly he pretended that the trip had been a success: 'I have but lately returned from a lengthy American tour which I much enjoyed. It has added considerably to my stock of knowledge and made me quite ten pounds heavier.'[22] But in the privacy of his journals he railed against the 'general mediocrity' prevalent in America and the indifference of people to him. He found it hard to adjust to the fact that he was already a virtually forgotten figure.[23]

The significant thing about Stanley's tour to the USA was that Dolly did not accompany him; nor did he accompany her on her 1895 holiday in Switzerland. Again, interestingly, 1895 saw a brief resurgence in Dolly's diary-keeping which she had abandoned on marriage to Stanley.[24] Taken together, all this suggests that the Stanley marriage went through some sort of crisis in 1895. The resolution was interesting, for it took the form of the adoption of a sixteen-month-old child called Denzil, the son of an ex-governess whose husband had died, leaving her penniless. So as to permit the woman to resume her career as a governess, the Stanleys agreed to become the adoptive parents of Denzil. The decision was taken, Stanley explained cryptically, because 'we have concluded we are not to be blessed with children'.[25] The reality was almost certainly that there was no physical basis to the marriage, that it was a union that existed purely on a companionable quasi brother-and-sister level.

After returning from the USA Stanley resumed his increasingly unpalatable duties in the House. His contributions during his five years as a Member became fewer and of decreasing significance. He spoke on the Armenian massacres and on the plans for a reconquest of the Sudan, even clashing with Dilke on the issue on one occasion.[26] He had a few words to say on the railways being built from the Zambezi to Lake Nyasa and through Uganda. But it was perhaps significant of his own parliamentary bankruptcy that his last intervention in the House, in 1900, was on the subject of trustees for liquidated companies and the assignment of debts.[27] Stanley lifted a corner on his essential passivity in a letter to Henry Johnston, with whom he had first discussed the idea of entering Parliament on the Congo in 1883: 'I have not so many illusions as I had in 1883, but if ever there comes a time for honest and straight speaking, I will do my level best, to protect against wrongdoing, meanness and cowardice. I have a fund of warm indignation always in reserve against Dilkism, Laborism and Little Englandism, but I am too old and self-contained to let it out on every occasion, besides we have plenty of good speakers who will be able to deal effectively with the more opinionated opponents, and I would rather listen, than engage in unnecessary discussion.'[28]

However, at the beginning of 1896 Stanley was briefly in demand for his opinion on the Anglo-American crisis over the Venezuela-British Guiana dispute. As a man who had had both nationalities and a career straddling the two great English-speaking nations, Stanley's attitude was, suitably, 'a plague on both your houses'.[29] Otherwise, his journalistic output tended to be limited to questions affecting the future of Africa and the role of the British Empire.[30] He was as much on Joseph Chamberlain's side on the issue of imperialism as he had been over Irish Home Rule; Chamberlain had reciprocated the admiration by appearing as a supporting speaker in North Lambeth during the 1895 campaign. In fact it was arguably the encouragement from Chamberlain that kept him going during the onerous five years in the House. One night he came home from the Commons and announced to Dolly: 'Well, I could live for Balfour, but I could die for Chamberlain. He says what he means to do – and why – and then he does it.'[31]

Meanwhile at Richmond Terrace Dolly endeavoured to turn their home into the kind of salon over which her mother had once presided. Luminaries from the worlds of exploration, politics, the arts and sciences rubbed shoulders with the ageing explorer. Apart from his great friend Mark Twain, Stanley had contacts with Trollope, Ruskin, Sir George Trevelyan, G. A. Henty, Holman Hunt, Sir Frederick Leighton and Auguste Rodin. Among explorers he corresponded with Nansen, Sven Hedin, Gerhard Rohlfs and even Carl Peters and George Schweinfurth.[32] Another visitor was the inveterate diner-out Henry James, who had a line to the Stanleys through their mutual friendship with Garnett Wolseley. James indeed bracketed Stanley with Marco Polo as the two discoverers in history who had had the most wondrous adventures.[33] James was also involved in another Stanley contact. Dolly's mother, then Gertrude Collier, was the daughter of a naval attaché at the British Embassy in Paris. During vacations at Trouville she became a friend of Flaubert's and in 1877 Flaubert introduced her to Alphonse Daudet. When the Daudets came to London in 1895, they knew no one except Henry James and the Tennants, mother and daughter.[34] Through this dual contact they were introduced to Stanley, whose enthusiasm for French literature was marked. Daudet described the set-up at Richmond Terrace. There Stanley held court, surrounded by fanatical admirers and old comrades from his expeditions. Outside this circle Stanley was shunned as a man of ferocity and anger.[35]

Two other views of the Stanley 'court' are available to us. Marie von Bunsen, the woman Stanley had allegedly been attracted to in Berlin in 1884, saw him during an 'at home' in London. 'He was standing in the background, flattened against the wall, embittered, like a whipped dog.' She intended to go across to talk but she was intercepted on the way over and when she looked for him again, he was gone.[36] A more complimentary picture comes from Mark Twain. 'Stanley is magnificently housed in London, in a grand mansion in the midst of the official world right off Downing Street and Whitehall. He had an extraordinary assemblage of brains and fame there to meet me – thirty or forty (both sexes) at dinner, and more than a hundred came in after dinner. Kept it up till after midnight. There were cabinet ministers, ambassadors, admirals, generals, canons, Oxford professors, novelists, playwrights, poets and a number of people equipped with rank and brains.'[37]

But lack of action and frequent illness in 1896 made Stanley increasingly restless. He had a particularly severe attack of malaria during a trip to Spain in June 1896. Fever and gastritis produced alarming symptoms of agonising pain, acute breathlessness and shivering so violent that the bed he lay on would shake and the glass on the table vibrate and ring.[38] A visit to Budapest and Vienna in April 1897 failed to cure his malaise – a mixture of physical illness and boredom[39] – so Dolly looked around for other challenges that would not involve a return to the Congo whose spell she so dreaded. An invitation to be present at the opening of the Bulawayo railway in South Africa in the autumn of 1897 seemed to present a risk-free opportunity to give Stanley the illusion that he was once more a man of action. Dolly worked hard to set up a journey that she could somehow control from afar.

Once again Dolly did not accompany her husband, though this time, with Denzil in her charge, she had an excuse. Instead she rehired Hoffmann, who had rehabilitated himself from disgrace by hard-working service in the Congo in the early 1890s. Hoffmann and Stanley left Southampton on 9 October 1897 in the SS *Norman*, in company with the Duke of Roxburghe and five other MPs. The voyage turned out to be one of the most disagreeable Stanley had ever made. The ship was packed to the gunwales and the din and cacophony on board from morning until night was almost deafening. The noise continued so disturbing at night that Hoffmann was often obliged to knock on the doors of adjoining cabins to request that Stanley be allowed a little sleep.[40] Stanley also missed Denzil and his feeling for children came through strongly in the very real grief he felt when a nine-month old girl died of meningitis and was buried at sea.[41]

As they neared the Cape, Stanley claimed to be able to smell again the continent he had last seen seven years before.[42] Once at Cape Town they boarded a 'State Pullman' – an ordinary corridor train of six coaches with three persons in a carriage instead of the normal four. This was by far the slowest train journey Stanley had ever made in his life; the 1360 miles to Bulawayo took three days to complete at a top speed of 19 m.p.h. They chugged along through Wellington, Kimberley, Vryburg and Mafeking to Matabeleland but still managed to miss the opening ceremony at Bulawayo, since a train ahead of them ran off the rails and delayed the Pullman for a decisive four hours.[43]

Arriving just in time for the evening's festivities, they found their hotel, the Palace, only half finished. Stanley was lucky enough to get a finished room but Hoffmann was reduced to sleeping in an uncompleted partitioned area. To Stanley's fury Hoffmann disobeyed an explicit instruction about never letting his master's boots out of his sight. Next morning they witnessed a confused mêlée in the hotel corridor with men struggling to sort out 500 pairs of boots which had all been taken away and cleaned indiscriminately.[44]

All in all, especially as Cecil Rhodes was incommunicado, sulking in his tent after the humiliating failure of the Jameson raid the year before, Stanley found Bulawayo a disappointment. It was a boom town with miners and prospectors arriving daily to look for gold, but the Wild West atmosphere Stanley would have relished thirty years earlier (and did) now left him cold. He set off for Johannesburg and was annoyed when the train was delayed at the Transvaal border while Kruger's officials spent from midnight to dawn combing through the passengers and their luggage. At Vereeniging he consented to an interview with a journalist from the English-speaking *Standard and Diggers' News* who wrote up the meeting as 'How I Found Stanley'.

> Was the mild silver-haired gentleman . . . really the much advertised Mr H. M. Stanley, MP, DCL, LLD, PhD . . . who . . . has through grit and a great deal of attitudinising and *mise-en-scène* made himself famous . . . who discovered Livingstone (when he was not lost), who found Emin when that Equatorial dignity did not want to be found . . . and who has so picturesquely if unconvincingly fulfilled the star turn in the Bulawayo advertising troupe? . . . This is Mr Stanley's first appearance in the Transvaal, and he has been retained by journals

paid to deprecate and abuse this country. We will not say that Mr Stanley has a 'Darkest Transvaal' in preparation, but we cannot quite rid ourselves of the suspicion that the Republic will be held up to the world – well, not in the kindliest manner.[45]

The reporter was not wrong. In Johannesburg Stanley listened to the grievances of the Uitlanders and, though he rather despised them, began to be won over to the idea that only armed force could secure the British future in South Africa.[46] On 23 November he moved on to Pretoria and there, at 5.30 a.m. next day, he had a private interview with Transvaal President Paul Kruger. Kruger was sitting on his stoep drinking coffee and had set aside half an hour for the audience with the famous explorer before departing on an election campaign. Stanley was impressed by his rugged, rock-like massiveness but less so by the Old-Testament prophet aura of righteousness Kruger exuded. 'He reminded me more than anything else of the huge apes that I saw from time to time while I was pushing through the forests of Central Africa. His forehead was low, with great beetling brows. His eyes were little and half-shut, like a pig's; his huge jaw was hunched on to his shoulders, so that he appeared to have no neck, and a large briarwood pipe was clenched between his teeth . . . a rusty, old-fashioned frock-coat, old-fashioned even for the end of the nineteenth century, a crumpled stick in his hand and a little top-hat.'[47]

The interview went wrong as soon as Stanley raised the question of the rights of the Uitlanders in Johannesburg. Kruger became angry: 'his right hand went up and down like a sledgehammer, and from his eyes, small and dull as they were, flashed forth the most implacable resolve that surrender must be on their side, not his.'[48] This was the wrong tone to take with Stanley, for Kruger was in effect stealing his thunder; this was how *Stanley* liked to deal with those who disagreed with him. From this moment Stanley conceived the most violent detestation for Kruger and became an exponent of a forceful solution to the South African problem. After half an hour of Kruger's 'arrogance', 'vanity' and 'contempt' he came away convinced that Milner, Chamberlain, Salisbury and, indeed, any Englishmen who had not met Kruger were living in a fool's paradise if they thought a pacific solution was possible: 'I had seen enough, and heard more than enough, to convince me that this was an extreme case, which only force could remedy.'[49]

From Pretoria Stanley travelled through the Orange Free State and Natal, took ship from Durban to East London, then went back overland to Cape Town. On his last night there he was given a banquet, then on 15 December embarked on the SS *Moor* for England.[50] As the outline of Table Mountain merged with the horizon, Stanley watched wistfully from the deck. He told Hoffmann he had a strong premonition that this was his last glimpse of the 'Dark Continent'.[51]

He arrived back in London even more of an imperialist than when he left and began advocating a violent solution to the threat from the Boers. Indeed the story of Stanley's last six years of life can be encapsulated in three themes: his jingoism and passionate advocacy of the South African war; his devotion to his adopted son Denzil; and his increasingly frequent illnesses and ultimate physical decline.

The commitment to the British Empire and his implacable hostility to the Boers is amply documented from a variety of sources.[52] At the beginning of 1899 he felt reasonably confident about imperial prospects though concerned about the growing economic challenge from the USA and worried about American imperialistic tendencies as manifested in the Philippines: 'The year 1899 is starting so smoothly in England . . . we have long ago calmed down about the mad French attempt on the Upper Nile and we are so interested in the Czar's peace circular that we have relaxed our attention to Russian misdoing in China. With Germany we have no questions and America has civilly refrained from twisting our "lion's tail". Old Kruger is probably more concerned with his personal infirmities and the colonists are following their usual orderly habits.'[53] He even felt relaxed enough about British prospects in Africa in 1897-99 to engage in a friendly, though somewhat routine correspondence with the notable traveller in West Africa, Mary Kingsley.[54]

But the outbreak of the South African war in 1899 brought the old lion roaring back into the epistolary and speechmaking fray. He spoke out strongly on the necessity for the war and deplored the 'Stop the War' movement as misguided and unpatriotic.[55] He was tempted by an offer from Major Pond to tour the USA lecturing on the Transvaal and the war but decided that his parliamentary commitments precluded this. In private he lamented the incompetence that had led to the early British reversals in the war but hoped that Redvers Buller would bring the hated Kruger to his knees. Though the British must be degenerate to have allowed regulars to be chewed up by the raw Boer militia at Ladysmith, at least there was now a resolution of the 'evil humours' that had built up over the past nineteen years and action was being taken that should have been put in hand a decade before. 'No people on earth are so averse to war as we are and so prone to be guided by goody-goody sentiment

... if you have interests no amount of sentiment will protect them.' He believed in 'pray to God but keep your powder dry' and despised the beautiful phrase-mongering and impeccable logic of those who spoke 'Johnsonia-Gladstonese . . . direct simple English has no chance in these literate days.'[56]

He continued to lament British disasters in the field until the military tide turned in 1900: 'the Boers are first-class fighters in their way and deserve the utmost credit – but with different generalship they could have been sent flying.'[57] Correspondence from 1901 on the South African war also sees Stanley unwittingly pointing to the future. 'What is this I hear of your experiences with Winston Churchill? You must not be too hard upon him for remember he is very young. A little judicious talk with him would soon set the matter right I think, for excepting on this occasion, he has been distinguished for good sense.'[58]

In the autumn of 1898 Stanley decided to look for a country retreat within striking distance of London. No. 2 Richmond Terrace could hardly have been more convenient for the Commons, and the Welsh haven of Cadoxton Lodge, Neath in South Wales fitted the bill for extended stays away from London. But what he needed now was a medium-range establishment that Denzil could regard as his permanent home and where he could grow up serenely. After viewing twenty houses in Kent, Buckinghamshire, Berkshire and Sussex without finding anything suitable, the Stanleys located a mock-Tudor mansion at Furze Hill, Pirbright, Surrey. The house was set in its own grounds, complete with small lake, pine woods and meadows, but was in need of considerable renovation and redecoration.[59] Draft contracts were exchanged at Christmas 1898 in anticipation of vacant possession the following June. At last on 10 June 1899 the Stanleys moved in.[60] Stanley busied himself with the plans for building a new wing, for landscaping the gardens and installing electric lighting. He transformed one large room into a library and converted the vast entrance hall into a billiards room. In the autumn of 1899 the Stanleys moved in properly. From now on this was their true home, and Richmond Terrace (where Gertrude Tennant remained) was definitely second-best.

At last Stanley had a proper home for his beloved Denzil. His paternal affection for his adopted son shows the more attractive side of Stanley. The older the boy grew, the more attention the explorer paid him. His early jottings on his son show him almost in the vein of the Dickens of Little Nell vintage. 'Warmest greetings to darling Little Denzil, our own cherub! Possibly I think too much of him. If I were not busy with work and other things, I should undoubtedly dwell too much on him . . . look full into his angelic face, and deep down into those eyes so blue, as if two little orbs formed out of the bluest heaven were there, and bless him with your clean soul, untainted by any other thought than that which wishes him the best God can give him. At present, he is of such as are the beings of God's heaven, purity itself.'[61]

In an attempt to recall his beloved Africa, Stanley gave names to the different parts of the grounds on his Pirbright acreage. The lake was called Stanley Pool, the pine woods the Ituri forest, and so on. Stanley played games of 'Darkest Africa' with Denzil, or else they would trot round the grounds in a carriage and pretend they were in the USA. A letter from Stanley in 1899 gives a charming picture of domestic bliss at Furze Hill (and a hint of contemporary interest in the Dreyfuss case): 'Mrs Tennant if anything looks younger and Mrs Stanley is of such an amiable disposition that time is very partial to her. Baby is thriving. He is getting on to four now and has a predilection for politics. Every morning I take him a ride by train to some distant part of the States – Chicago to San Francisco or to New Orleans and he delights in playing the conductor's part – and calling out "Salt Lake City", "Sacramento" or "Atlanta" etc. He believes in Picquart and condemns Esterhazy.'[62]

Soon it was difficult for Stanley to write a personal letter at all without some reference to the 'beloved cherub'. From an early age the Stanleys seem to have encouraged the boy in the profession of arms he was eventually to adopt. The Wellcomes sent him a pistol when he was six at which his eyes opened wide but 'I cannot get his attention because of a new monkey called Mr Puff which he has just received from an admirer.'[63] They also dressed him in the uniform of a Horse Guard and inflamed his anger against the Boers. But Stanley, with his uneasy mixture of fire-eating bellicosity and Christian piety, got his comeuppance on one occasion when he reproached the boy for hating the Boers. 'If they are not wicked people, why do you fight them?' Denzil replied.[64]

William Hoffmann, who was a frequent visitor at Furze Hill after his successful outing to South Africa with Stanley, made the shrewd point that Stanley's adoption of Denzil was in a sense a re-enactment (this time successful) of the adoption of John Rowlands by the Stanleys in New Orleans forty years before. Certainly Stanley's empathy with Denzil seemed to bring out a childlike streak in his last years. Hoffmann would be ushered into the library where a disembodied Stanley voice would order 'Find Me!' After a lengthy and fruitless search a revolving bookcase would swing round to reveal the hidden explorer.[65] This behaviour was highly significant, since in psychological terms it embraced three different strands of the Stanley personality: the excessive secretiveness, the desire to 'have the drop' on other people and the wish to recapture an imaginary lost childhood.

Stanley spent the quiet years at Furze Hill working on his autobiography which, however, never progressed beyond the year 1862. In 1897 he revealed to Marston in effect that his unconscious was sabotaging his attempts to deal with his early years, though at the conscious level he rationalised this as pressure of time. 'It is just the most interesting part from my eighteenth to my twenty-fifty that wants the material which I only can supply. I have tried repeatedly to find an unbroken month or so to add to it, but so sure as I put pen to paper, so sure does a series of engagements interrupt me and compel me to lock it up.' Three years later he told Marston that the book had made no progress because of his political career.[66] Now not only did Stanley not have a political career worth mentioning, but this excuse is singularly feeble from a man who wrote the massive two-volume *In Darkest Africa* in fifty days. The truth is that, unconsciously, Stanley did not *want* to finish his autobiography. The years between his eighteenth and twenty-fifth birthdays were painful ones which reflected little credit on him, and he knew it.

In 1898 and 1899 Stanley was busy appealing for funds for the Livingstone monument to be built at Chitambo.[67] Perhaps not entirely coincidentally with his work on this appeal, in June 1899 Dorothy Stanley received the news she had long prayed for. Lord Salisbury wrote to offer Stanley the Grand Cross of the Bath, a higher grade of knighthood than he would have received in 1890 when his nationality was the impediment.[68] When Queen Victoria conferred the decoration a few weeks later she noted in her journal: 'He is grown very old and is rather altered in appearance.'[69]

This was not altogether surprising. Long bouts of illness had made Stanley's thoughts increasingly turn to death.[70] In particular he had the sort of superstitious feeling towards the Emin expedition that survivors of the 1922 Carnarvon expedition had towards the opening of the Tutankhamen tomb. He detected the old 'diablerie' at work that he had detected on arrival at Banalya in August 1888: 'Extraordinary as it may be, those connected with the Emin Relief Expedition steadily diminish in number, as if the very name of the Esau [sic] had a fatality. Fifteen young and old have already passed away.'[71] In 1902 he made out a death list of the principals which included the following: Mackay (1902), Vita Hassan (1892), Stairs (1892), Emin Pasha (1892), Grant (1892),

Mackinnon (1893), Sir Samuel Baker (1893), Parke (1893), Price (1893), Verney Cameron (1894), Joseph Thomson (1895), Charles Stokes (1895), Consul Holmwood (1895), Horace Waller, (1896), Bonny (1899) and Casati (1902).[72]

Memento mori was reinforced by Stanley's precarious and declining health. To have survived the rigours of four long expeditions in Africa when so many of his comrades dropped like flies indicated that Stanley's constitution was ox-like, and it is a reasonable inference that had he spent his career in England, he might have had a Gladstone-like span. But the hundreds of bouts of African fever had worn out even his doughty frame and aged him prematurely. Both his Continental trips in 1898 were visited with illness. First there was a nasty attack of 'flu in Monte Carlo in February. Then in August, in the Pyrenees, he was again stricken with the mysterious gastro-enteritis that had assailed him in Spain in 1896. He took to his bed in Biarritz, struggled up to Paris where he had a relapse, then staggered back home, where only a starvation diet and assiduous massaging restored him to health. For months he was so ill that he could not sit up in bed.[73]

The year 1900 saw a further sustained period of malady. Stanley was so ill that he could not even imbibe milk. He kept himself alive with white of egg and other spoon victuals. Dolly allayed the pains by injecting him with morphia. Yet in periods of normality he chafed at the strict diet imposed on him, as Dolly revealed to Henry Wellcome. 'How wearying illness is – and it seems such a waste of time – but Stanley is very patient and enduring. If only he were wiser – when I am not there to judge for him.'[74]

The strain of nursing an almost permanent invalid began to tell on Dolly. A decade of life had turned the ingenuous 'girl' into a somewhat grim *grande dame*. Stanley's granite-hard posture towards the world had affected her, so that her basically weak personality consented to be his creature and to do all in all as he did. The woman who had admired Gladstone's radicalism, fretted about the fate of miners and sympathised with the proletariat was by the turn of the century a neurotic dabbler in potions and astrology. Her weakness and unpopularity with servants comes through in the Wellcome correspondence where it is revealed that while Dolly was nursing Stanley at Richmond Terrace in 1903 'all sorts of robbery and wickedness . . . grew up when Stanley's strong hand was removed by that year of sickness.'[75] The hardness can be inferred from a number of sources. Dolly resented having guests visit Stanley at Furze Hill as it prevented her from taking a holiday. And she took the rather unwomanly stance of supporting vivisection and experiments on living animals; she even told Wellcome that she would like the law amended to make such experimentation easier.[76]

In her quest for potions, elixirs, nostrums and panaceas she had one unexpected ally. Mark Twain was a great believer in the 'Kellgren method' – a form of physiotherapy pioneered by the Swedish physician Dr Kellgren. In 1900 on a visit to London Twain found his old friend bedridden and in agony. He had given up on doctors, having tried sixteen of the best in seventeen years without success. The last one had predicted that the very next attack would kill him. Twain joined with Dolly's sister Eveleen Myers in urging that Kellgren (who had a practice in London) be called in. After some reluctance Dolly did so and the results were miraculous. Stanley sat up in bed, smoked a pipe and ate a hearty meal of bacon and eggs. Twain recorded that Dolly kissed him on both cheeks in gratitude. He laid all the credit at Kellgren's door. 'Today he [Stanley] resumes his seat in the House of Commons a well man. If he had had a doctor he would be under a slab in Westminster Abbey now.'[77]

But it was clear that Stanley was in no state to continue his career as politician. On 26 July 1900 he endured his last parliamentary sitting. His retirement from the House and his making the very last journal entry on 19 December 1901 indicate an awareness that death could not be long delayed, Kellgren notwithstanding. By this time he could not remain in London for more than four weeks at a time as he did not get enough sleep because of the noise.[78] In 1901 he made his last trip abroad to attend Frederick Myers's funeral. His final public appearance was on 9 August 1902 when he attended the coronation of Edward VII. Before the ceremony he wanted to cry off, especially as he had to rise from a sick-bed to attend. Even though he found the pageantry stunning, the uplift was momentary and he had to beat a hasty retreat to convalescence.[79]

By the spring of 1903 Stanley was complaining of giddiness and vertigo in addition to the malarial and gastritis attacks. Dolly went everywhere with him in case he had a fainting fit. But on 13 April he had a stroke, followed by an even more severe one four days later that completely paralysed him down the left side. Tended by four different doctors, he was dosed with ammonia and ether and given hypodermic injections of strychnine and digitalis. Dolly wrote to Wellcome in anguish: 'He cannot turn in bed or lift himself. The eyes do not form together so that when he closes one eye he sees double towards the right. Speech remains impaired by paralysis of left lip and jaw . . . owing to weakness and shock and grief he is highly emotional – I have no hopes of his precious life.'[80]

Throughout 1903 Stanley continued in this state, helpless as a baby, still, with his neurotic insistence on order, insisting that he shave himself with his good right hand.[81] His speech was laboured but – just – intelligible to his wife. Weakness and shock made him highly emotional. He was so debilitated that even when lifted from bed into a large armchair and swathed with blankets, he was so exhausted that he had to go back to bed after two hours. Soon there were complications. A bout of malaria led Dolly to cut out all sugar and to substitute Vichy water for champagne and whisky. In the summer his good non-paralysed leg started to swell; cardiac oedema affected the kidneys and caused dropsical swelling. But the great heart beat on and the explorer even seemed to mock death by taking to reading detective stories.[82] Yet the strain on Dolly was bringing her near breaking-point and she began to suffer from severe depression. 'It is difficult – *inwardly* – always to be cheerful and hopeful, but as long as I can *seem* so always that is the main thing – and I expect my occasional moods of depression are only because I have been a long time here and I haven't much outlet for energy.'[83]

In August they had a visit from Dr Allart, sometime medical officer at Vivi and Boma, now the Belgian consul in Tenerife. He thought that Stanley was not being moved, rubbed or manipulated enough. Dolly and the nurses accordingly arranged a daily schedule of massage. Additionally, Stanley underwent electric shock treatment but gave up when it seemed to exacerbate his symptoms.[84] Gradually Stanley made a partial recovery. He spent most of the day outside in a wheelchair and by September was able to take a few steps, supported. His speech had returned but fatigue followed any attempt at physical or mental effort or any real concentration of the mind.[85]

In the later autumn of 1903 the Stanleys went up to London and when they returned to Furze Hill for the Easter holidays of 1904 Stanley was able to walk, supported and with a stick, along the station platform – which was far more than he had been able to do the year before.[86] But in April he sustained a bad attack of pleurisy, so bad that Dolly barred the door to visitors.[87] As he recovered from this, he comforted himself with the thought that at death he would surely lie alongside Livingstone in Westminster Abbey. The doctors warned Dolly that his heart was now fading and he could not last long. As if in confirmation of this he said to her at the beginning of May: 'Goodbye, dear, I am going very soon, I have done.' The final death struggle began on 5 May. His mind wandered and his eyes had a faraway look but all was slow and painless.[88] In the last two days of life he murmured many valedictory messages. 'Oh! I want to be free – I want to go into the woods to be free.' 'I want to go home.' At 4 a.m. on 10 May he heard four o'clock striking and said: 'How strange! So that is time! Strange!' He died at 6 a.m. on Tuesday 10 May 1904.[89]

It was generally expected that Stanley would be buried in Westminster Abbey alongside Livingstone, but the Dean, Joseph Armitage Robinson, refused to allow this and declined to enter into reasons for his decision.[90] But correspondence in the Royal Archives reveals the reason. Predictably, Stanley's reputation as a man of blood had told against him, even though it was acknowledged that the idea of burial in the Abbey beside Livingstone had merit and would appeal to the Americans. Thus did the Revd Armitage Robinson explain his decision to the King's private secretary. 'There is not an unmixed feeling among good men whose counsel I have taken as to the claims of H. M. Stanley to be accorded one of the very few vacant spaces in the Abbey. One of our highest geographical authorities lays stress on the violence and even cruelty which marked some of his explorations, and contrasts this with the peaceful successes of other explorers. This chiefly weighed with me in giving my decision to restrict the honour done to him to what I may call *second* honours, i.e. burial refusal but the first part of the funeral service granted.'[91] This decision could only be overruled by direct intervention from Edward VII, which he declined to make. Dorothy Stanley was left with the clear impression that it was enmity from Sir Clements Markham that had tipped the scale but she braved out the rebuff by declaring that after his marriage Stanley had effectively renounced the world and all its pomp; therefore the rejection meant nothing.[92] Mark Twain's friend William D. Howells put it more forcibly. He said that Stanley was 'refused a grave in Westminster Abbey by a wretched, tyrannical parson'.[93]

Stanley's body was taken from Richmond Terrace to the Abbey for the service then to Pirbright for burial in the churchyard. The pall-bearers in the Abbey were Livingstone Bruce (Livingstone's grandson), Sir Alfred Lyall, Dr Scott Keltie, Sir George Tarban Goldie, the Duke of Abercorn, Mounteney Jephson, Henry Wellcome and Sir Harry Johnston.[94] Telegrams of condolence poured in: from Lord Kitchener, Lord Cromer, George Bernard Shaw, the polar explorer Peary, and many others. Perhaps the finest tribute came in a letter from Agnes Livingstone Bruce to Jephson: 'I have always felt that Stanley did so much for me personally in risking his life to find my father, and my children have grown up with the same feelings of affection and gratitude towards him.'[95]

Many of those whose lives Stanley had touched were dead already. Of the officers who had accompanied him across Africa on the Emin expedition, only Mounteney Jephson survived him. Jephson married the American Anna Head but could never entirely shake off the strains of fever he had picked up in Africa. After sustained ill health he died in 1908, aged forty-nine. Of the Rear Column veterans Ward survived until 1919 and served with distinction in the Great War. Hoffmann lived on until the late 1920s in increasingly desperate penury and destitution.

Stanley had outlived all the great African explorers. Of the great African proconsuls Lord Cromer (born in the same year) lived until 1917, Sir Harry Johnston until 1927 and Lugard to 1945. Leopold survived to see his Congo State taken over as a colony by Belgium (in 1908) in return for 50 million francs' blood money but not before the Congo had become a byword for savagery and atrocity that shocked and convulsed contemporary Europe.

The women in Stanley's life enjoyed mixed later fortunes. No trace is known to survive of Virginia Ambella, but Katie Gough-Roberts died soon after World War One. The most interesting sequel was that of Alice Pike Barney. She became a patroness of the arts and an amateur painter, and when her husband died she remarried a twenty-six-year-old millionaire artist, twenty-eight years her junior. A five-million-dollar heiress from her first marriage, Alice spoiled and pampered her daughter Natalie, who was later the lover of Colette and the friend of Proust. Alice herself grew bored with the marriage to her second husband Christian Hemmick, who divorced her in 1920 for desertion. Amazingly, the sexagenarian Alice then began a new career as a playwright, wrote eleven plays and won the Drama League of America award for *The Lighthouse* in 1927. She died in Hollywood, California, in 1931, aged seventy-five.

Yet the brightest torch for Stanley was always carried by Dolly. After his death she emulated Isabel Burton by building up the legend of Bula Matari. All evidence tending to work against the mythical picture she wanted for 'her' Stanley was ruthlessly suppressed. She tricked Katie Gough-Roberts into parting with Stanley's personal letters to her, bribed and browbeat Lewis Noe, dealt harshly and unsympathetically with Hoffmann's pleas for alms, and let it be known that she would go to law readily to defend Stanley's reputation. Her hopes for the heavily edited and doctored Stanley *Autobiography*, published in 1909, were that it would be a book that would live down the ages. It did not. By the end of Edward VII's reign interest in Stanley was minimal and the book fell still-born from the press.

In 1907 Dolly married again, a forty-year-old Harley Street surgeon called Henry Curtis, sixteen years her junior. But she insisted on retaining the name Lady Stanley, for she knew that her precarious niche in history rested entirely on the fame of her first husband. Looking around for a permanent memorial for Stanley, she instituted a search on Dartmoor for a granite monolith that would be his tombstone. At last she found what she was looking for: a stone 12 feet high by 4 feet wide. This was taken to Pirbright churchyard and erected over the grave. Below a cross cut deep in the top four feet of the monolith was carved the simple legend: HENRY MORTON STANLEY, BULA MATARI 1841-1904, AFRICA.

·CONCLUSION·

Henry Morton Stanley was far the greatest of the explorers of Africa. However critical one may be of aspects of his life, his achievements as an explorer are as unassailable as those of Marco Polo or Columbus. To deny this is as absurd as to deny the military skill of the man Stanley most liked to be compared to – Napoleon Bonaparte.[1] The expedition to find Livingstone was an astonishing achievement for a complete tiro in African exploration. The 1874-7 expedition was an even finer accomplishment, and the descent of the Congo in 1876-7 is one of those journeys that will live for ever in the annals of human discovery. Arguably, the foundation of the Congo Free State was, from the standpoint of history, the most solid memorial of all; Stanley himself cannot be blamed for the black hole into which Leopold and his bloody acolytes later plunged the territory. In the Emin Pasha relief expedition Stanley may well in a technical sense have effected the greatest feat of endurance in all land-based exploration. Certainly it is hard to think of anything that rivals the triple crossing of the Ituri forest or the achievement of the only 'double' in nineteenth-century exploration (the traverse of Africa east-west in 1874-7 and west-east in 1887-9).

This is not to say that Stanley was *overall* more significant than the explorers he outmatched. He did not have Burton's formidable intellect or literary skill, and still less did he have Livingstone's moral stature. As a genuine Africanist he was excelled not just by Livingstone but also by Emin and by lesser figures like Herbert Ward, who had a far more genuine feeling for the continent and its inhabitants as 'things in them-selves'. To paraphrase President Kennedy's famous phrase, we may say that whereas Livingstone, Emin and others were interested in what they could give Africa, Stanley was interested in what Africa could give him. Yet as an observer of Africa Stanley was shrewd and his perceptions of local societies much more acute than his facile critics give him credit

391

for.[2] He had none of the racial prejudice that disfigured the writings of Burton or Sir Samuel Baker; indeed, his white comrades frequently complained that he favoured Africans over them. The writing of African history from oral sources is still in its infancy, but it will be surprising if Stanley does not gain much stature when a proper inventory of tribal accounts is drawn up, especially considering the vast areas of Central Africa in which he was an active presence. Even at the Eurocentric level, if one sees Leopold as the true author of the 'scramble for Africa', one must legitimately concede that Stanley's role was crucial. And his niche in history is also secured by the 'Stanley craze' of the early 1890s, which was a powerful factor in the drive towards the full-blooded version of British imperialism.[3]

Stanley was a man of many and varied talents. He was highly intelligent, extremely well read and a great tribute to the power of autodidacticism. He was an outstanding journalist both in his ability to write fluent first drafts at will and in his 'feel' for a scoop. The Abyssinian triumph might have been enough for a lesser man, but Stanley went on to cap it with the 'finding' of Livingstone at Ujiji – a piece of journalistic opportunism and enterprise unmatched in the nineteenth century. He was also an administrative talent of a very high order, as his iron grip on the infant Congo State from 1879 to 1884 demonstrated. He had a powerful physical presence, was immensely physically courageous, was an inspired amateur military tactician and had the gift that most marks out the successful man of action – an unequalled capacity to improvise. Braconnier, his *bête noire* from the Congo who had no reason to respect him, left this judgement. 'He is a man of sudden resolution and irresolution. Ten minutes before he starts he hardly knows himself whether or where he is going. No one can admire Stanley's qualities more than I. He is a man of iron – easily discouraged indeed, but quick to regain courage; full of dogged will, which is his strength, but a splendid leader.'[4]

His Napoleonic achievements in Africa were complemented by a certain Bonapartism of physical demeanour or rather, given his rolling gait like that of a sailor on land, or a combined Nelson-Napoleon. Harry Johnston, meeting him on the Congo in 1883, spoke of the physical similarity to the French emperor: corpulent, short-legged, and with the same basilisk eye and sense of latent explosive energy that would make any man afraid to laugh at him. One always felt wary respect for Stanley, whether the deeper feelings were those of hero-worship or personal antipathy and detestation.[5]

Stanley, in short, had all the qualities of a great leader save one: he could never inspire his men by direct sympathy so that his aims became theirs automatically, as a Shackleton could. Not only was he unpredictable and unreliable and subject to frequent mood swings, but he was ruthless and inconsiderate to his comrades. When it suited his book, he abandoned his co-workers in Africa without a thought for their safety. In times of scarcity he always got more than his fair share of food and creature comforts, as Braconnier related: 'He treats his white companions as though he were a little king – lives apart, never chums with them, and at certain moments would think it justifiable to sacrifice any one of them for his own safety. I have watched him smoking under his tent, knowing all the time his officers had no tobacco, and it would never occur to him to offer them a pipe.'[6]

Additionally, Stanley doled out grudging praise for good work but produced stinging reproaches for jobs badly done. He had no sense of humour about himself, was hypersensitive to criticism, refused to take blame and always insisted that culpability be assigned elsewhere, declined to take the advice of others, and was a natural authoritarian, insisting on his own way even if all his officers had voted for an opposite course. Anger bubbled away never far from the surface and paranoia revealed itself in over-reaction to those who snubbed him or would not take him seriously. Obsessed with his image, he played down the achievements of other explorers or criticised the findings of those who had gone before him. He was not above claiming for himself discoveries that were in reality first made by his comrades (as in the case of Ruwenzori). He was convinced that he was an Ishmael, with every man's hand turned against him.[7]

This accounted for the blustering, disparaging tone he used with all who were not intimates. It was no accident that Stanley was considered 'no gentleman'; he did not stop at thinking the worst of others but uttered his suspicions in the coarsest possible terms. Thomas Barclay, who saw him at close quarters, said of him: 'Stanley was not a diplomatist. Uncompromising determination was stamped in his features. His angular form and hands were of a piece with truculent manner . . . as always we conversed à la Stanley, which meant that his words were final. He was unsympathetic yet fascinating, intensely in earnest and ruthless in his idea of duty yet when off his guard almost sentimentally tender.'[8] This chimed in with Hoffmann's assessment. 'He was on the whole a serious man, not given much to laughter: the hardships he had endured in childhood seemed to have dried up his natural capacity for gaiety. Yet there were times when his dry and witty remarks, his sky allusions to other members of the expedition, made me roar with laughter and convinced me that he was the most entertaining companion possible.'[9]

These contradictory facets of his personality go a long way to explaining the paradoxical aspects of the Stanley expeditions in Africa. The loss of life on his journeys was terrific. On the first two expeditions he lost all five white companions. The death toll during the Free State years (1879-84) excited international comment and worried even Leopold, no shrinking violet or 'bleeding heart' when it came to the expenditure of human life. On the Emin expedition, Jameson and Barttelot succumbed to the tenebrous forces of Africa. Additionally, hundreds of Africans died. Yet the *wangwana* were always ready to follow him into the unknown. A simple butcher or psychopath could not have inspired their loyalty.

It is the human cost of Stanley's great achievements in African exploration that fills up the debit side of the balance sheet and forces us to probe more deeply into the inner man. This was the sort of examination Stanley always feared and he did his defiant best to hold at bay anyone seeking to understand the demons that drove him. 'On purely personal matters I ought to be better informed than anyone else, and I claim to be able to report them accurately,' he declared with bravado. And again: 'The inner existence, the Me, what does anybody know of? Nay, you may well ask, what do I know? But, granted that I know little of my real self, still I am the best evidence for myself.'[10] But here Stanley protests too much. In psychological terms he was the classic 'resistant subject'. This was the true explanation for his notorious mendacity. Stanley doubtless began his career as a liar to conceal the 'shame' of his illegitimacy and workhouse origins, but in his later life he seems hardly to have been able to distinguish truth from falsehood. His lies had a traumatic origin; the cliché phrase about a 'pathological liar' has scarcely ever been more apt in the description of the life of a great man.

The 'heart of darkness' that was Stanley's psyche suggests a schizoid personality disorder, and the hypothesis hardens all the way along the line of inductive probability when we examine his sexual profile. The schizoid personality classically combines a desperate need for love with a desperate fear of intimacy – exactly the syndrome we observe in Stanley's relations with women. The origin of this malaise lies in the disastrous childhood – the perception of illegitimacy, the guilt about his mother's promiscuity which bred a mortal fear of sexuality, the horrors of casual dalliance and amateur prostitution he observed in St Asaph's workhouse. Typically, the schizoid personality has his true early bonding with an aged relative – in Stanley's case his grandfather Moses Parry – and adult sexual experience is deferred into the mid-twenties and beyond. Retreat into fantasy is the norm, and it is in the realm of fantasy that we should seek the aetiology of Stanley's notorious lies.

Schizoid personalities, though not psychotic, can become dangerous if their fantasy worlds break down. The abandonment of all hope of making loving relationships with real people can kindle the death instinct and fantasies of death. The genetic/environmental inheritance Stanley acquired could in certain other circumstances have turned him into a murderer. But his salvation was the strength of his will and the existence of Africa. Stanley could not make close emotional contacts because he feared that any love he would be given would be withdrawn from him. He pre-empted this possibility by unconsciously willing the destruction of his relationships with women and contriving his own rejection. Unwanted, humiliated, despised, unloved, with huge reservoirs of hostility towards others, Stanley found his salvation in Africa. African exploration provided a means of reconstituting an identity as well as, incidentally, permitting the exercise of homicidal impulses without incurring lethal social consequences.

Another sign of Stanley's basically schizoid personality was his failure to develop a true sense of conscience. Such a sense depends at root on the instilling of a moral sense by loved parents or mentors; strong ties of affectionate dependence then inculcate an 'altruistic' side, by which the individual learns the limits of the pleasure principle – no individual may do everything he or she desires to do. The absence of a father and the wretched inadequacy of his mother took Stanley perilously close to the dictum of Aleister Crowley: 'Do what thou wilt shall be the whole of the law.' Stanley's liking for dining alone and keeping his companions at arm's length denotes the classical schizoid 'lone wolf'. Such a man has decided that since nobody cares for him, he in turn will care for nobody; other people are then viewed merely as obstacles to desires or objects of gratification. The combination of powerful impulses linked to an absence of conscience leads to potentially lethal consequences.

Yet no man is purely a textbook case, and although the basic analysis of 'schizoid personality disorder' takes us some way into the psychic world of H.M. Stanley, it provides clues rather an an open-sesame master-key. For instance, the classical schizoid route to murder lies through abdication of the will. Stanley by contrast used his immense willpower to integrate the different strands of his personality. Yet the effort left him in a kind of emotional and psychic limbo. One aspect of this was a sort of repressed bisexuality. He was simultaneously attracted to and repelled by the sexuality of women and eventually 'solved' the conflict by a platonic marriage to Dorothy Tennant. The repressed homosexual side of his personality manifested itself in the long line of young males he needed always at his side: Edwin Balch, Edward King, Lewis Noe, Frank Pocock, Albert Christopherson, Mounteney Jephson, plus his servants Kalulu, Selim, Sali and William Hoffmann.

Yet another manifestation of his ambiguous profile and blunted sexuality was sado-masochism. The floggings, the excessive cruelties, the hangings and the abandonment of 'disobedient' men to the mercy of savage tribesmen bespeak something more than the autocratic disciplinarian. The almost willing embrace of hardship and the Grail-like acceptance of pain, especially in the Ituri forest, and the insistence on 'duty' as the supreme moral concept show the other side of the coin, and his own conclusion on his life is surely significant: 'I was not sent into the world to be happy, nor to search for happiness.'[11]

The role of religion in Stanley's inner life is peculiarly hard to pin down. Here is a hostile character-sketch from Frederick Jackson that encapsulates the link between many diverse strands: 'Where he excelled the other great African explorers was as a journalist, a professional journalist, trained in the forceful "take no denial" school of American journalism, with a studied insight into the psychology of his readers. He appears to have been a man with strong religious convictions and he understood the value of quotations from the Bible with a certain section of the public.'[12] The charge of religious humbug was frequently made against Stanley. In the Congo he jokingly told Coquilhat and Vangele that if you wanted to please the English public, you had to talk of God and quote the Bible.[13] But this apparent cynicism need not imply hypocrisy. Stanley's journalistic and entrepreneurial talents *were* sharp, but all the evidence suggests he was genuinely Christian in a formal Establishment way, with an added relish of Calvinism, and that he thought of God as his personal guardian. But he was neither the first nor last 'great man' to ally showmanship with a taste for the pious, the devout and the devotional.

What Stanley clearly did believe in was original sin. His sad childhood had made him profoundly sceptical of the innate goodness to be found in human nature, and the anomie of his meteoric rise from the gutter to knight of the realm left him with a worship of power that fed into these pessimistic convictions. In political and social matters Stanley was a rabid reactionary – a phenomenon often observed in those from an impoverished background who eventually climb the greasy pole.

Every individual has a unique psychological configuration, yet comparison can sometimes throw up the illuminating insight. If one sought for a twentieth-century Stanley, one would surely approach closest in the shape of T. E. Lawrence. The same basically schizoid personality is in evidence. Both men were born in illegitimacy in North Wales, both sought other names and identities (Shaw, Ross), both repressed their homosexuality and sought salvation in the open landscapes of an exotic terrain. The famous seduction/rape incident in Deraa finds a pre-echo by transference in Stanley's experience with Noe in Turkey in 1866. In Lawrence's case it was the masochistic side that was more highly developed, as in the floggings self-administered under orders from the 'old man'; in Stanley's it was the sadistic side, most notably evinced by the flogging of Lewis Noe in 1866. Both men were pathological liars, often genuinely unable to distinguish truth from falsehood.

Stanley, it seems, had the greater potential for contentment – he rejected happiness as an end in life – because he had angels of light to succour him, above all Livingstone. It was his tragedy that he chose to heed the Lucifer of the piece – Leopold. Stanley would have done well to follow the example of his great friend Mark Twain, who produced a satire on Leopold and his squalid 'red rubber' State and even promised Conan Doyle on his deathbed that he would give all assistance to the Congo Reform Campaign.[14] Stanley turned his back on the light and embraced the darkness. His marriage almost seems to have recapitulated the process, with Dorothy Tennant before and after the wedding reflecting the Janus face. Casati said of Stanley: 'Men like him are the great exception. A century has scarcely one such specimen.'[15] In a century that has witnessed a return to the Dark Ages, perhaps we may conclude that, for all his greatness, a Stanley is a luxury we can no longer afford.

· NOTES ·

Guide to abbreviations used in notes.

Add. MSS Additional Manuscripts, British Library
AECP Archives Etrangères, Correspondence Politique
AEMD Archives Etrangères, Mémoires et Documents, French Foreign
  Ministry, Quai d'Orsay
APR Archives du Palais Royal, Brussels
BL MSS RP Manuscripts in British Library
EIHC Essex Institute Historical Collections
HIFL *How I Found Livingstone in Central Africa* by H. M. Stanley (1872)
IDA *In Darkest Africa* by H. M. Stanley (1890)
JAH *Journal of African History*
JRGS *Journal of the Royal Geographical Society*
MP Mackinnon Papers
NLS National Library of Scotland
PRGS *Proceedings of the Royal Geographical Society*
RA Royal Archives, Windsor Castle
RCS Royal Commonwealth Society
RGS Royal Geographical Society Archives
SFA Stanley Family Archives
TDC *Through the Dark Continent* by H. M. Stanley (1878)
TNR *Tanzania (earlier Tanganyika) Notes and Records*
UJ *Uganda Journal*
ZA Zanzibar Archives

Chapter one

1. Ernesto de Vasconselos, 'Dos Autographos de H. M. Stanley', *Boletin da
   Sociedade de Geographia de Lisboa* (1904), pp. 217–20. For the Hatton and
   Cookson firm see Peschuel–Loesche, 'Das Kongobiet', *Deutsche Kolonial
   Zeitung* 1 (1884), pp. 257–64.
2. Olivier de Bouveignes, 'L'Arrivée de Stanley à Boma en 1877', *Revue
   Coloniale Belge* 36 (1947), pp. 200–4.
3. Alex Delcommune, *Vingt Années de Vie Africaine*, 2 vols (1922), ii,
   pp. 88–90.
4. TDC, ii, pp. 361–4.

5. Serpa Pinto, *How I Crossed Africa*, 2 vols (1881), i, pp. 25–9.
6. Luciano Cordeiro to Stanley, 22 May 1878, SFA.
7. TDC, ii, p. 366.
8. V. C. Malherbe, *Eminent Victorians in South Africa* (1972), pp. 99–100.
9. *Cape Times*, 23 October 1877.
10. *Cape Argus*, 23 October, 1 November 1877; *Cape Times*, 27 October 1877; *Cape Town Daily News*, 1 November 1877; *Cape Times Supplement*, 6 November 1877.
11. *Cape Argus*, 3 November 1877; *Cape Times Supplement*, 6 November 1877.
12. *Cape Times*, 3 November 1877; *Cape Argus*, 1 November 1877; *Cape Town Daily News*, 1 November 1877; *Cape Times Supplement*, 6 November 1877.
13. TDC, ii, pp. 367–8.
14. *The Standard and Mail, Cape Town*, 8 November 1877.
15. Kirk to Derby, 8 December 1877, ZA/RCS.
16. This issue had already been broached by Stanley ahead of his arrival in Zanzibar. See Kirk to Derby, 8 November 1877, F.O.84/1486.
17. Stanley to Kirk, 1 December 1877, ZA/RCS. Cf. also Kirk to Stanley, Stanley to Kirk, 2 December, ibid.
18. Kirk to Derby, 7 December 1877, ZA/RCS.
19. A. Maes, *Reisen naar Midden-Afrika* (1879), pp. 122–3; Stanley, *Congo*, i, p. 39, Cf. Norman Bennett, *From Zanzibar to Ujiji, The Journal of Arthur W. Dodgshun 1877–79* (1969) under 29 November 1877: 'In the afternoon we called on Dr Kirk and H. M. Stanley. The latter gave us a good deal of useful information and advised us to make for a populous district at the south end of the lake near the river Rufuva and avoid Ujiji altogether as he says it is overrun by wild young scamps of Arab descent and is also very unhealthy. H.M.S. looks older and worn from his late adventures.'
20. TDC, ii, pp. 370–73.
21. Journal, 3 January 1878, SFA.
22. E. E. Farnan, *Along the Nile with General Grant* (1904), pp. 7–29.
23. John Russell Young, *Around the World with General Grant*, 2 vols (1879), i, pp. 230–32. Ironically Stanley had been rather scathing about accounts in the *New York Herald* of Grant's second presidential levée (HIFL, pp. 108–9).
24. P. A. Roeykens, *Les débuts de l'oeuvre africaine de Leopold II, 1876–1879* (1955).
25. *Gazette du Midi*, 18 January 1878; *Le Sémaphore de Marseilles*, 19 January 1878.
26. Edward Marston, *After Work* (1904), p. 225.
27. Ibid., p. 226. For Stanley's time in Paris see also *New York Times*, 20 January, 3 February 1878.
28. B.L.Mss.R.P.1691.
29. See for example D. W. Malcolm, *Sukumaland* (1953), p. 105; Israel K.

Katoke, *The Karagwe Kingdom* (1975); Aylward Shorter, *Chiefship in Western Tanzania: a Political History of the Kimbu* (1972), pp. 282–3.

30. Gordon to Khairy Pasha, 21 November, 20 December 1875, 1 May 1876, in M. F. Shukry, ed., *Equatoria under Egyptian Rule: the Unpublished Correspondence of Colonel (later Major-General) C. G. Gordon with Ismail Khedive of Egypt and the Sudan 1874–76* (1953), pp. 318, 335, 433.

31. *The Times*, 14 July 1876.

32. Romolo Gessi, *Seven Years in the Sudan* (1892), p. 316.

33. Gordon to Khairy Pasha, 15 June, 30 August 1876, in Shukry, *Equatoria under Egyptian Rule*, pp. 340, 364.

34. For the Uganda mission see Holger Bent Hansen, *Mission, Church and State in a Colonial Setting* (1984), pp. 12–20. For the quick appreciation of the opportunities opened up in the Congo see Duparquet to Schnindhammer, 27 August, 3 September 1877; Cambroni to Franqui, 19 January 1878 in P. A. Roeykens, *La politique religieuse* (1965), pp. 71, 73–4, 99.

35. For the ambivalence see Stanley's many asides on the subject. 'Africans, however, would be less than men if they did not struggle, as the Ancient Romans did, against the advances of Christianity.' (*My African Travels*, p. 17). There is a longer reflection in the 1888 Emin Pasha diaries: 'I would as soon harm a woman or a child as a missionary. But all missionaries are not saints. There are many cranks among them. They are in the world but not of the world. They have a peculiar faculty of unconsciously violating the laws of good sense, more to act by impulse with an admirable disregard for consequences. Moral enough, perhaps, but they are singularly deficient in charity, of upright conduct doubtless, according to their code, but they are too purely narrow-minded and too unsympathetic to prevent them from serious errors of judgement, inhibited by their profession from employment of material instruments when thwarted or restrained, they generally resort to calumny – a powerful weapon, apt to prove a torrent even to the dullest mind but singularly efficacious against a sensitive man of honour and spirit, petulant as women when crossed, they have a peculiar similarity of expanding their feelings with the same vocabulary of epithet. The words such as "horrid", "monstrous", "awful" are special favourites of both missionaries and women.' (SFA)

36. G. Schweinfurth, *The Heart of Africa*, 2 vols (1874), ii, pp. 33–4.

37. Congo Diary, 2 December 1883, SFA.

38. R. W. Beachey, 'The East African Ivory Trade in the 19th Century', JAH 8 (1967), pp. 269–90.

39. Max Buchler, *Der Kongostaat Leopolds II*, 2 vols (1912), i, pp. 232–3.

40. See William Arens, *The Man Eating Myth* (1979).

41. See the similar arguments in E. E. Evans-Pritchard, 'Zaire Cannibalism', *Journal of the Royal Anthropological Institution* 90 (1960), pp. 238–58.

42. See Camille Coquilhat, *Sur le Haut Congo* (1888), pp. 270–74; John

Weeks, *Among Congo Cannibals* (1913), pp. 69–70, 226; Herbert Ward, *A Voice from the Congo* (1910), pp. 275–85; Jean Dybowski, *La route du Tchad* (1893), p. 102; John L. Brom, *Sur les traces de Stanley* (1958), p. 207.

43. See J. E. Mumbanza, 'Les Bangala et la première decennie du poste de Nouvelle-Anvers 1884–1894', *Lovanium* (U. of Kinshasa, Zaire, 1971), pp. 88–92.

44. *JRGS* 46 (1876), pp. 10, 17–23. For Stanley's confirmation of Speke see Franz Stuhlmann, *Mit Emin Pascha ins Herz von Afrika* (1894), p. 727.

45. *PRGS* 22 (1877–8), p. 408.

46. *PRGS* 20 (1875–6), p. 49. For Burton's intense interest in Stanley's achievements see 'Mr Stanley's last explorations', *Athenaeum* 2 (1877), pp. 568–9.

47. *PRGS* 4 N.S. (1882), p. 8.

48. Schweinfurth to Gessi, 24 May 1880 in Gessi, *Seven Years in the Sudan*, p. 438.

49. Wilhelm Blohm, *Die Nyamwezi: Land und Wirtschaft* (1931), p. 2.

50. A. M. Mackay, 'Boat voyage along the western shores of Lake Victoria', *PRGS* 6 (1884), pp. 273–83 (at pp. 282–3).

51. Robert I. Rotberg, *Joseph Thomson and the Exploration of Africa* (1971), pp. 90–91; H. H. Johnston, *The Nile Quest* (1903), pp. 224 *et seq.*

52. Stanley correctly located the ultimate source of the Nile in the Hagera river system (*New York Herald*, 27 March 1877). The principal exploration of the remote sources and tributaries (the River Luvironza feeds the Ruvunu, which feeds the Niavorondo, which flows into the Kagera) was by Richard Handt. See Handt, *Caput Nili*, 2 vols (1914), ii, pp. 52 *et seq.*

53. Kirk to RGS, 10 December 1877, *PRGS* 22 (1877–8), p. 454.

54. *PRGS* 20 (1875–6), pp. 10–14.

55. *PRGS* 21 (1876–7), pp. 465–8; Laurence Oliphant, 'African Explorers', *The North American Review* 24 (1877), pp. 383–403.

56. Stanley protested that the name 'Congo' was an etymological mistake ('a fraud' in Stanleyspeak) perpetrated by Diego Cao (*PRGS* 22 (1877–8), p. 410).

57. *New York Herald*, 27 March 1877. See also Stanley to Edward Levy, 13 August 1876: 'We have obtained a signal triumph over Cameron, the protégé of the RGS, whose attainments were said to be vastly superior to those of Burton, Speke, or Livingstone and Baker – if Markham was to be believed. At the Lukuga, he simply sounded the water at the end and then vanished from the scene, only taking the chief's word that the river went to Rua. Possibly he would have been more careful had he expected a "damn penny a liner" for a successor in that locality.' (Norman R. Bennett, *Stanley's Despatches to the New York Herald* (1970), pp. 463–5.)

58. See Robert Brown, *The Story of Africa and its Explorers*, 4 vols (1892–5). Stanley's animadversions on Cameron were responsible for much of the

coolness of the RGS towards him. Sir Henry Rawlinson, at an RGS meeting on 11 April 1876, produced a classic of damning by faint praise on the occasion of the reading of Cameron's report: 'We pay all possible honour to the old pioneers of African discovery; we can never forget the services which have been rendered by Captain Burton, by Speke and Grant, by Sir Samuel Baker, and I will say also by Mr Stanley.' (*PRGS* 20 (1875–6), p. 326.) Cameron, however, wrote a warm letter of congratulation when Stanley returned to England in January 1878 (SFA).

59. Stanley estimated that the Congo drained an area of 860,000 square miles (*New York Herald*, 14 November 1877). In fact the accepted figure is 1,445,000 square miles. On the other hand, he estimated the population of the Congo at 28 million, whereas it was only some 10 million in the early 1920s and 13 million in the 1940s (L. H. Gann & Peter Duignan, *The Rulers of Belgian Africa 1884–1914* (1979), p. 44). But his estimate of 750,000 souls for the Ganda state and 2,750,000 for Mutesa's extended empire is accepted as about right (see Lloyd A. Fallers, ed., *The King's Men* (1964)).

60. For the meeting see Richard Stanley & Alan Neame, eds, *The Exploration Diaries of H. M. Stanley* (1961), pp. 28, 119. For Broyon see Norman R. Bennett, 'Philippe Broyon: Pioneer Trader in East Africa', *African Affairs* 62 (1963), pp. 156–64.

61. *New York Herald*, 14 August 1876.

62. Stanley to Levy, 13 August 1975, in H. Depage, 'Notes au sujet de documents inédits à deux expéditions de H. M. Stanley', *Bulletin de l'Institut Royale Coloniale Belge* 25 (1954), pp. 130–52.

63. F.O. to Kirk, 21 September 1876, F.O.84.

64. Norman R. Bennett, 'Stanley and the American Consuls at Zanzibar', *EIHC* 100 (1964), pp. 41–58.

65. Kirk to Stanley, 11 December 1876, F.O.84.

66. See Hansard, 29 January 1878, 237, p. 623.

67. Burton to Kirk, 12 October 1876, quoted in Reginald Coupland, *The Exploitation of East Africa 1856–1890* (1939), p. 327.

68. *Pall Mall Gazette*, 28 December 1875.

69. Arnold to Bates, 24 October 1876; Hyndman to Bates, 28 October 1876, RGS.

70. *PRGS* 21 (1876–7), pp. 59–63; cf. also H. M. Hyndman, *The Record of an Adventurous Life* (1911), pp. 151–2.

71. H. Yule & H. M. Hyndman, *Mr Henry Morton Stanley and the Royal Geographical Society: Being the Record of a Protest* (1878), pp. 18–22.

72. *Pall Mall Gazette*, 29 November 1876.

73. Yule & Hyndman, *Mr Henry Morton Stanley and the RGS*, p. 24.

74. *New York Herald*, 19 August, 7, 25, 29 November 1876, 1 January, 14 March 1877.

75. *New York Herald*, 17 September 1877.
76. *Daily Telegraph*, 22 January 1878.
77. Hyndman and Yule later resigned and Waller wrote a letter to the RGS full of bile and hatred. See Hyndman to Bates, 1 March 1878; Waller to Bates, 2 March 1878, RGS.
78. *Pall Mall Gazette*, 30 January, 11 February 1878.
79. Kirk to Bates, 13 November 1877, RGS.
80. Kirk to Mackinnon, 13 December 1877, MP 22/87. Kirk also revealed his fury at the solicitude paid Stanley by the Royal Navy. 'It was exceedingly strange of the Commandant of the Cape to send him home in a British man of war, against the positive orders of the government.'
81. Kirk to Waller, 5 March 1880, Waller Papers, iii.f.45.
82. Kirk to F.O., 28 December 1877, F.O.84/1514.
83. Kirk to Derby, 1 May 1878, F.O.84/1514.
84. R. H. Mill, *The Record of the Royal Geographical Society 1830–1930* (1930), p. 119.
85. *PRGS* 22 (1877–8), p. 144–65.
86. 'It cannot be seriously contended that in judging an explorer's achievements in geographical discovery no account should be taken of his acts from a moral point of view. If a traveller were to secure a free passage through Central Africa by poisoning whole tribes of Turkomans by prussic acid, he would hardly expect a welcome in England.' (*The Standard*, 9 February 1878.)
87. Yule & Hyndman, *Mr Henry Morton Stanley and the RGS*, pp. 38–9.
88. *Pall Mall Gazette*, 11 February 1878.
89. 'With a larger military force than hitherto employed and making a determined use of it, Mr Stanley has conducted a geographical raid across the middle of Africa, which has led him into scenes of bloodshed and slaughter, beginning at the Victoria Nyanza, and not ending until he arrived in the neighbourhood of the West coast ... the question will no doubt be hotly discussed how far a private individual, travelling as a newspaper correspondent, has a right to pursue such a warlike attitude, and to force his way through native tribes, regardless of their rights, whatever those may be' (F. Galton, 'Letters of Henry Stanley from Equatorial Africa to the *Daily Telegraph*', *Edinburgh Review* 134 (1878), pp. 166–91).
90. Gordon to Burton, 19 October 1877 in W. H. Wilkins, *The Romance of Isabel Lady Burton*, 2 vols (1897), ii, p. 661.
91. Baker to Edwin Arnold, 20 January 1878, SFA.
92. W. R. Fox-Bourne, *The Other Side of the Emin Pasha Relief Expedition* (1891), p. 19.
93. Gerhardt Rohlfs, 'Cameron's Afrika-Reise', *Ausland* 50 (1877), pp. 918–19.
94. Fox-Bourne, *The Other Side of the Emin Pasha Relief Expedition*, p. 49.

95. For the 'blind hate' see *Autobiography*, p. 527. For a psychological interpretation of Bumbire see Gerben Hellinga, *Een Individualpsychologische Interpretatie* (1978), pp. 117–20.

96. 'Only the most insensitive of men could have failed to see that all this was going to cause an outcry in England. But then insensitiveness was part of Stanley's strength: he simply did not care' (Alan Moorehead, *The White Nile* (1964), p. 141).

97. *Saturday Review*, 16 February 1878.

98. *PRGS* 12 (1890), p. 329.

99. *New York Herald*, 14 November 1877.

100. RGS 1/4; *New York Times*, 18 January, 1 February, 29 June 1878.

101. Julian B. Arnold, *Giants in a Dressing Gown* (1942), pp. 76–7.

102. *New York Times*, 22 February 1878.

103. Stanley to Leopold, 30 January 1884, Congo letters, SFA.

104. *New York Times*, 4 November 1877. Nevertheless, Stanley consented to dine with Alice Pike's sister Hettie in London in 1878 (Journal, SFA). Another female voice from his past appeared in the form of two letters (with photograph) from Virginia Ambella in Athens, congratulating him on his Congo success (Virginia Ambella to Stanley, 15 March, 10 October 1877, SFA).

Chapter two

1. P. A. Roeykens, *Les débuts de l'oeuvre africaine de Leopold II, 1876–1879* (1955), p. 83.

2. Memo by Wylde, 20 January 1876, F.O.84/1447.

3. See Leopold to Queen Victoria, 26 May, 4 June 1876, RA/Q 4/155; RA/Y 160/33.

4. Jean Stengers, 'Textes Inédites d'Emile Banning', *Académie Royale des Sciences Coloniales* 1955, p. 14.

5. There is a considerable literature on the 1876 conference, most notably an extensive collection of essays: *La Conférence de Géographie en 1876: Recueil d'Etudes (Académie Royale des Sciences d'Outre Mer*, Brussels 1976). For Leopold's intentions see Count L. de Lichterwelde, *Leopold II* (1926), pp. 155–8.

6. G. Shepperson, *The Exploration of Africa in the Eighteenth and Nineteenth Centuries* (1971), p. 142.

7. APR, 55/1.

8. Barbara Emerson, *Leopold II of the Belgians: King of Colonialism* (1979), pp. 80–81.

9. Leopold to Queen Victoria, 14 January 1877, RA/Y 160/37; cf. also Knollys to Ponsonby, 27 December 1876, RA. Add.A 12/359.

10. Roeykens, *Les débuts*, pp. 165–8.

11. The theme of the outstanding study by Neal Ascherson, *The King Incorporated* (1963).

12. Roeykens, *Les débuts*, pp. 229–74. Cf. also Roeykens, *La période initiale de l'oeuvre africaine de Leopold II, 1875–1883* (1957), pp. 49–51.

13. Disraeli: 'I myself know nothing of Mr Stanley except from his public acts ... and it seems that our colonial authorities would not much care to assist Mr Stanley in making engagements of the kind suggested ... with men belonging to tribes subject to, and protected by, England.' (Beaconsfield to Leopold, 29 October 1878, APR, Fonds Congo 10/2.) Sanford wrote to Bennett on 7 October: 'With reference to Mr Stanley, have you been entirely satisfied with him, his economy, prudence, reliability, character, etc? I will esteem your reply to this quite confidential and I ask it solely with a view to future eventualities.' (François Bontinck, *Aux origines de l'Etat Indépendant du Congo* (1966), p. 23.)

14. Ironically, Sanford (born 1823) had in 1841 made the same crossing from Boston to Smyrna that Stanley made in 1866 in the *E. Y. Yarington*.

15. For French interest aroused by Stanley's 999-day epic see *Archives Etrangères, Mémoires et Documents, Afrique* 94, p. 80. As a 'catch' Stanley was a prize worth having: 'Stanley is surely the most capable of African explorers.' (Greindl to Solvyns, 7 November 1877, quoted in Roeykens *Les débuts*, p. 287.)

16. Leopold to Solvyns, 17 November 1877, APR, Fonds Congo, 100/1. Cf. also P. van Zuyler, *L'Echiquier Congolais ou le secret du roi* (1959), p. 43.

17. Roeykens, *Les débuts*, pp. 300–6.

18. Bontinck, *Aux origines*, pp. 25–9; R. S. Thomson, 'Leopold II et le Congo', *Congo* 12 (1931), pp. 168–70.

19. *L'Etoile Belge*, 16 January 1878; *L'Echo du Parlement*, 21 January 1878; *L'Indépendance Belge*, 22 January 1878.

20. Bontinck, *Aux origines*, p. 32.

21. Thomson, 'Leopold II et le Congo', p. 170.

22. Journal, 1 June 1878, SFA.

23. Journal, 10 June 1878, *Autobiography*, pp. 333–4.

24. Bontinck, *Aux origines*, pp. 34–5.

25. Leopold's shrewdness in 'reading' Stanley correctly is reinforced by this self-pitying passage from the *Autobiography*: 'What was my reward? Resolute devotion to a certain ideal of duty, framed after much self-exhortation to uprightness of conduct, and righteous dealing with my fellow creatures had terminated in my being proclaimed to all the world first as a forger, and then as a buccaneer, an adventurer, a fraud and an impostor. It seemed to reverse all order and sequence, to reverse all I had been taught to expect. Was this what awaited a man who had given up his life for his country and for Africa?' (*Autobiography*, p. 528).

26. Thomson, 'Leopold II et le Congo', p. 171.

27. For details of Stanley in Anvers and Brussels see 'Visite de Henry Stanley en Belgique', *Bulletin de la Société Belge Géographique* 2 (1878), pp. 277–81; 'Stanley à Anvers', *Bull. Soc. Géog d'Anvers* 2 (1878), pp. 388–400. For Leopold's overall favourable impressions of the explorer see Leopold to Queen Victoria, 9 June 1878, RA/Q 55/4.

28. Roeykens, *Les débuts*, pp. 319–34.

29. Journal, 15 July 1878, SFA.

30. Add. MSS. 43, 411 ff. 1–3; cf. also Stanley to Mackinnon, 18 August 1878, MP 55.

31. It was apparently during the Paris stay that Mark Twain tried to enlist Stanley as a companion on his journeys, for in Twain's diary under 2 August 1878 we read: 'Tried to get Stanley for a scout but too expensive.' (Frederick Anderson, Lin Salamo & Bernard L. Stein, eds, *Mark Twain's Notebooks and Journals*, ii (1877–83), (1984), p. 128.

32. A. J. Wauters, *Histoire Politique du Congo Belge* (1911), pp. 24–6.

33. Bontinck, *Aux origines*, pp. 39–42.

34. Thomson, '*Leopold II et le Congo*', pp. 174–5.

35. M. Luwel, 'Kapitein Ernest Cambier et Zanzibar 1882–1885', *Africa-Tervuren* 8 (1962), pp. 85–96; 9 (1963), pp. 11–31.

36. For these attempts see Kirk to Strauch, 23 August 1879; Carter to Strauch, 30 October 1879; Strauch to Lambermont, 10 July 1880; Strauch to Mackinnon, 23 September 1879; Carter to Mackinnon, 6 August 1879; Carter to Kirk, 18 December 1879, MP 56.

37. Adolph Burdo, *Les Belges dans l'Afrique Centrale. De Zanzibar au Lac Tanganika* (1886).

38. Congo notes, 1878, SFA.

39. Greindl to Stanley, 5 October 1878, SFA.

40. For Stanley's debt to Tuckey's maps see O. de Bouveignes, 'Tuckey et Stanley', *Zaire* 5 (1951), pp. 31–44.

41. *Manchester Guardian*, 23 October 1884.

42. Add. MSS. 43, 411 ff. 5–8.

43. Ibid., f.9. Stanley at this time was much preoccupied with both geographical questions and the Ancient Egyptians (ibid., ff. 9–11).

44. *Mark Twain's Notebooks and Journals*, ii, p. 304.

45. Stanley to Bruce, 25 November 1878, SFA.

46. A. J. Wauters, 'Le Comité d'Etudes du Haut Congo', *Le Mouvement Géographique* 28 (1911), p. 260.

47. MP 57/234.

48. Ascherson, *The King Incorporated*, p. 109.

49. MP 57/234; Bontinck, *Aux origines*, p. 49.

50. For Stanley's relations with Greindl see Greindl to Stanley, 19, 26 June, 26 September, 5, 7, 13 October, 18, 25 November 1878, SFA.

51. Congo Notes, 1878, SFA.
52. Congo Journal, 9 December 1878, SFA.
53. Strauch to Stanley, 9, 13 December 1878, SFA.
54. Congo Notes, December 1878.
55. Congo Journal, 2 January 1879.
56. For the Kruboys of Liberia and Sierra Leone see H. H. Johnston, *The River Congo* (1884), p. 26.
57. One of these was to proceed to Antwerp and was to be the senior assistant at $1500. The two others were to be paid $1000 each and were to proceed straight to the mouth of the Congo (Bontinck, *Aux origines*, pp. 51–3).
58. Congo Journal, 31 January 1879.
59. Congo Journal, 4 February 1879.
60. Congo Journal, 9 February 1879.
61. Strauch to Stanley, 5 February 1879, SFA.
62. Congo Journal, 13 February 1879.
63. Congo Journal, 20, 21 February 1879.
64. Congo Journal, 22–5 February.
65. Congo Journal, 27, 28 February; 8, 9, 18 March.
66. Sparhawk to Stanley, 4 July 1878, SFA.
67. Kirk to Salisbury, 4 July 1878, F.O.84/1515.
68. Rutherford Alkirk to Kirk, 16 February 1878, ZA/RCS. Kirk tried to stall. On 3 May he wrote to Derby that he had not yet been able to settle the claims 'owing to the time occupied in clearing up the many false statements gravely put forward by Mr Stanley as facts.' (ZA/RCS.) It took him most of 1878 to conclude the matter, which he did with bad grace on the grounds that many of the claims were fraudulent. He added pointedly: 'There remained a few others of the same band who, although they had not accompanied the special correspondent of the *Daily Telegraph* and the *New York Herald* on his recent journey, were equally entitled to consideration for their services to Dr Livingstone, to whom I . . . gave the same gratuity.' (Kirk to Salisbury, 4 July 1878, F.O.84/1515.)
69. Congo Journal, 19 March 1879. On the Uledi affair see also Stanley to Grefuls, 11 May 1879, SFA.
70. Kirk to Salisbury, 20 March 1879, F.O.84/1547 (containing Leopold to Barghash, 9 February 1879).
71. Kirk to Salisbury, 24 March 1879, F.O.84/1547 (containing Leopold to Kirk, 6 February 1879).
72. Kirk to Salisbury, 3 April 1879, F.O.84/1547.
73. Congo Journal, 20 March 1879.
74. Congo Journal, 1, 3, 10, 11, 13 April.
75. Kirk to Salisbury, 29 May 1879, F.O.84/1547.
76. The concession requested was for a road from the east coast to Lake Nyasa starting from Daar-es-Salaam (Mackinnon to Barghash, 7 March

1879, F.O.84/1547). For Kirk's attempts to discredit Stanley with Mackinnon see Kirk to Mackinnon, 3, 25 May, 1 June, 26 July 1879, MP 22/87. The Mackinnon papers in this file are full of Kirk's black propaganda against Stanley. See Kirk to Dawes, 28 April 1879, Kirk to Waller, 1 May 1879.

77. P. Masson, *Marseille et la colonisation française* (1905), pp. 457–8.

78. See the published volumes of the Foreign Office publication *Slave Trade* (1880), Nos. 307, 308, 324, 331, 337, 347, 352, 362.

79. Congo Journal, 26–29 April, 5, 7 May 1879.

80. *New York Herald*, 22 December 1871. For Sparhawk's service in the Congo see *Biographie Coloniale Belge*, 5 vols (Brussels 1948–58), i, pp. 859–60.

81. Stanley, *The Congo and the Founding of its Free State*, 2 vols (1895), i, p. 260.

82. Congo Journal, 30 May 1879.

83. Bontinck, *Aux origines*, pp. 94–7.

84. P. Ceulemans, 'Le séjour de Stanley à Zanzibar 18 Mars–fin Mai 1879', *Zaire* 11 (1957), pp. 675–85 (at p. 680).

85. Burdett-Coutts was an 'Africa buff'. In 1875 she tried to secure an invitation to the Geographical Conference (A. Roeykens, *Le dessein africain de Leopold II* (1956), pp. 96, 205). In 1885 she took Harry Johnston under her wing (Roland Oliver, *Sir Harry Johnston and the Scramble for Africa*, p. 84).

86. Congo Journal, 14 August 1879.

87. Congo Journal, 6 June 1879.

88. Leopold's brazen effrontery was further evinced by his treatment of Baroness Burdett-Coutts. On the liquidation of the CEHC, Burdett-Coutts withdrew her forward stake but offered Leopold 50,000 francs as a gift towards his humanitarian work. Leopold replied that he didn't need the money but was prepared to take it as a gesture of good faith! (P. Daye, *Leopold II* (1934), p. 170.)

89. Bontinck, *Aux origines*, pp. 90–91.

90. Congo Journal, 15 June 1879.

91. Roeykens, *Les débuts*, pp. 380–90.

92. Congo Journal, 8 July 1879.

93. Georg Schweinfurth, *The Heart of Africa*, 2 vols (1874).

94. Stanley to Strauch, 8 July 1879. Stanley at first said he would not be party to such 'madness' as the creation of a black state. But Strauch reassured him: 'There is no question of granting the slightest political power to negroes. That would be absurd.' (Stanley, *Congo*, i, p. 54; Albert Maurice, *H. M. Stanley: Unpublished Letters* (1957).)

95. Congo Journal, 14 August 1879.

96. Stanley to Strauch, 30 July 1879.

97. Congo Journal, 30 July 1879.
98. *Congo*, i, p. 61.
99. Congo Journal, 8 June, 15 August 1879.
100. *Biographie Coloniale Belge*, i, p. 402; ii, pp. 162–5, 640–46, 675–6; v, pp. 737–8.
101. Congo Journal, 14 August 1879.
102. Thomson, 'Leopold II et le Congo', p. 185.
103. See H. Brunschwig, *Brazza l'explorateur l'Ogooue, 1875–79* (1966).
104. P. Ceulemanns, 'Les tentatives de Leopold II pour engager le Col. Charles Gordon au service de l'AIA, 1880', *Zaire* 1958.
105. Congo Notes, 1879, SFA.

Chapter three

1. Journal, 16–21 August 1879.
2. *Congo*, i, pp. 68–70.
3. Stanley to Strauch, 20 August 1879, SFA.
4. *Congo*, i, pp. 141–2.
5. Ibid., p. 144–8.
6. Ibid., pp. 149–53. Alex Delcommune, *Vingt Années de la Vie Africaine*, i, p. 144, described it as an eagle's nest perched on a dominant spur.
7. Journal, 9 April 1880.
8. Journal, 31 March 1880.
9. *Document Notte Stanley au Congo, 1879–1884* (Ministère du Congo Belge et du Ruanda-Urundi Archives, 1960), p. 30.
10. *Congo*, i. p. 215.
11. Ibid., pp. 222–30.
12. *Doc. Notte*, pp. 15, 21, 45–6.
13. *Congo*, i. p. 159.
14. See H. Brunschwig, *Brazza l'explorateur.*
15. D. Neuville & C. Bréard, *Les voyages de Savorgnan de Brazza* (1884), p. 151.
16. Jean Stengers, 'Quelques observations sur le correspondence de Stanley', *Zaire* 1955, pp. 899–926.
17. E. Génin, *Les Explorations de Brazza* (1884).
18. Napoléon Ney, *Conférences et lettres de P. de Savorgnan de Brazza sur trois explorations effectués dans l'Ouest Africa 1876–1885* (1887), pp. 165–7.
19. H. Brunschwig, *French Colonialism 1871–1914: Myths and Realities* (1966), p. 47; Napoléon Ney, *Conférences*, pp. 165–7.
20. Although this judgement is contested by Delcommune, *Vingt Années*, on the grounds that Stanley's resources were superior.
21. Delcommune, *Vingt annés*, i, p. 142. Whereas Brazza was exuberant and

subtle, combining the 'intriguer' qualities of his native Italy with the sunny gaiety of his adopted France.

22. *Congo*, i, pp. 231–2.
23. Journal, 8 November 1880.
24. Miscellaneous Congo Notes, SFA.
25. Brunschwig, *Brazza l'explorateur*, pp. 142–3.
26. Journal, 8 November 1880.
27. *PRGS* N.S. 3 (1881), pp. 486–7. This was especially hypocritical since on 17 November Brazza wrote from Vivi: 'I admire the way you are accomplishing a task for giants with the resources of pygmies.' (*Doc. Notte*, p. 69.)
28. H. Brunschwig, 'La négociation du traité Makoko', *Cahiers d'Etudes Africaines* 17 (1965), pp. 5–56.
29. Mgr. Augouard, *Vingt-huit Années au Congo*, i (1905), p. 221.
30. Journal, 7 November 1880.
31. Stanley to Strauch (Ngoma, n.d.), SFA.
32. *Doc. Notte*, pp. 60–61, 63.
33. 'It is a marvel to me how quickly this name has come into general use. It was bestowed on me by Nsakala Bakki – subchief of De-de-de, a young man of 25 who is quite a native humourist. I had just received a consignment of sledgehammers and had passed them out to a party of Zanzibaris to break some rocks that were in our way when we first began roadmaking.' Stanley added that the Zanzibaris did not know how to use them and were pounding the tops of rocks into dust at such a rate that they would not have finished until 1890. 'Impatient at their dense understandings, I seized a sledgehammer and in a short time one of the rocks had been reduced to such portable fragments that it was carried away to the roadside. Nsakala, who was standing by, admiringly called out, "Ah, that is the way to break rocks," using the native term Bula Matari, a shaker or breaker of rocks.' (Journal, 8 December 1880.) Bula Matari also caught on because 'Stanley' was too difficult to say in local dialect.
34. *Doc. Notte*, pp. 81–3.
35. Ibid., p. 84.
36. Stanley to Strauch, 25 October 1880, SFA.
37. Stanley to Valcke, 1 January 1881, SFA.
38. For the African version of Stanley at Manyanga see L. Monnier & J. C. Williams, *Les Provinces du Congo. Structure et Fonctionnement, Vol. 2, Sud-Kasai, Hele, Kongo Central* (1964), p. 217.
39. *Congo*, i. pp. 266–70.
40. Journal, 27 January 1881.
41. Mrs W. H. Bentley, *The Life and Labours of a Congo Pioneer* (1907), pp. 73–80.
42. *Doc. Notte*, p. 88.

43. W. Holman Bentley, *Pioneering on the Congo* (1900), i, p. 365.
44. *Doc. Notte*, p. 99.
45. Ibid., pp. 100–1.
46. *Congo*, i, pp. 333–43. For a discussion of the fantasy nature of this story see Stengers, 'Quelques observations', p. 918.
47. *Congo*, i, pp. 377–81.
48. See Revd T. J. Comber, 'A Boat Journey round Stanley Pool', *PRGS* 6 N.S. (1884), pp. 71–5; Revd T. J. Comber & Revd George Grenfell, 'Explorations on the Congo', *PRGS* 7 (1885), pp. 353–73.
49. Stanley to Strauch, 6 January 1882, SFA.
50. Stanley to Strauch, 29 December 1881 in Albert Maurice, *H. M. Stanley, Unpublished Letters*, p. 94.
51. Journal, 30 March 1882.
52. Stanley to Strauch, 10 April 1882; Maurice, pp. 121–3.
53. Journal, 21 December 1881.
54. *Congo*, i, p. 375.
55. R. S. Thomson, *Fondation de l'Etat Indépendant du Congo* (1933), p. 115.
56. *Congo*, i, p. 395.
57. Ibid., pp. 399–401.
58. Ibid., pp. 443–6.

Chapter four

1. Journal, 3 October 1882.
2. Journal, 14 July 1882.
3. Leopold to Strauch, 14 January, 16 July 1882, Strauch Papers 93, 110.
4. Leopold to Strauch, 8 July 1882, Strauch Papers 107 bis.
5. Peschuel-Loesche, *Kongoland* (1887), pp. 2–3.
6. Ibid., pp. 18–19.
7. *Congo*, i, p. 449; *Doc. Notte*, pp. 112, 146–7.
8. Stanley to Marston, 3 July 1882, SFA.
9. Augouard, *Vingt-huit Années au Congo*, i, p. 278.
10. See the contrast between the BMS account of the rivalry between Stanley and Brazza (BMS to F.O., 25 June 1881, F.O. 84/1801; 23 March 1882, F.O. 84/1802) and the LIM account, which contrasted Stanley's commercial aims with Brazza's 'higher aims' (Fanny Guinness to Buxton, 21 February 1883, F.O. 84/1804).
11. Leopold to Strauch, 16 August, 16 November 1882, Strauch Papers 118, 142.
12. Journal, 17, 19 July 1882.
13. Journal, 15 October 1880.
14. Ibid.

15. Journal, 24 April 1880.
16. Stanley to Strauch, 15 September 1879.
17. 'Much as I have seen of the nude figure in Africa, it has as many charms for me now as it had when I was younger. The graces of it are infinite, every eye has a beauty of its own. Infancy excites the paternal interest, and its soft, satiny flesh, cool to touch and dimpling with the slightest pressure, is always a wonder to me. Youth is still more attractive, for its elastic and easy motions, rounded limbs, vivacious movements, and the elegant manner in which the firm but slender necks carry the head so lightly, nor must I forget the soft, limpid eyes. The adults call up ideas of fleetness, vigor, strength. There is never anything unsuitable or out of fashion in the nude, whatever its colour may be, nothing to provoke contempt or unkindly criticism. The skin may be more velvety than velvet, smoother than satin, or coarse as canvas, but it always fits better than a glove and its brown colour seems to suit the African atmosphere.' (Journal, October 1881)
18. Ibid.
19. Journal, 19 November 1881.
20. *Congo.* i, p. 458.
21. Ibid., p. 460.
22. Strauch to Mackinnon, 1 October 1882, MP 56/227.
23. *Doc. Notte*, pp. 147–8.
24. Congo Journal, 1882–4.
25. Ibid.
26. Journal, 1 October 1882.
27. Ibid.
28. Ibid.
29. Journal, 3 October 1882.
30. Journal, 4 October 1882.
31. Sanford to Mackinnon, 13 September 1882, MP 50/197.
32. Sanford to Mackinnon, 5 October 1882, MP 50/198. Paradoxically Sanford, an American himself, promoted with Leopold the idea that Stanley was an unreliable servant (Sanford to Mackinnon, 10 October 1882, MP 50/198). The truth is that Sanford strongly disliked Stanley (see Sanford to Mackinnon, 28 June, 30 July, August 1881, MP 49/193–94).
33. Kirk to Salisbury, 6 January 1880, F.O. 84/1574.
34. Kirk to Granville, 27 October 1883, F.O. 84/1645; same to same, 16 March, 31 July, 21 November 1885 (F.O.84/1679, 1724, 1727).
35. Solvyns to F.O., 5 October 1882, F.O.84/1802; Lumley to Villiers, 15 November 1882, F.O.84/1802.
36. Kirk to Granville, 27 October, 24 November 1883, F.O.84/1685; same to same, 8 December 1884, F.O.84/1679.
37. Leopold to Strauch, 7 April 1883, Strauch Papers 180.

38. Manchester Chamber of Commerce to F.O., F.O.84/1802.

39. Jean Stengers, 'L'impérialisme coloniale de la fin du XIXe siècle: mythe ou réalité?' *JAH* 3 (1962), pp. 469–91.

40. Leopold to Beyens (French Minister in Paris), 5 October 1882, Lambermont Papers 165, 175.

41. Jaureguiberry to Freycinet, 27 June, 19 July 1882; Jaureguiberry to Duclerc, 26 September 1882; Duclerc to Jaureguiberry, 10 October 1882; De Lesseps to Leopold, 12 October 1882, AEMD Afrique 59.

42. Kirk to Clement Hill, 18 February 1883, F.O.84/1803. Another anti-Stanley man, General Sanford, also poured scorn on their authenticity (Bontinck, *Aux Origines*, pp. 113–16). But Kirk's *personal* feud with Stanley did not abate: 'a self-seeking man without a spark of principle to guide him' (Kirk to Mackinnon, 10 November 1879, MP 23/89). Even stronger is the attack on Stanley during the 1882 European interlude (when Kirk was also on leave): 'I see Stanley has returned. All I can say is pity the poor king and I shall be very glad not to come in contact with Stanley. At the same time I wish the Congo scheme could be diverted into English hands.' (Kirk to Mackinnon, 30 September 1882, MP 23/91)

43. Leopold to Granville, 6 March 1884, Granville Papers, GD 29/156, PRO.

44. Leopold to Strauch, 16 October 1882, Strauch Papers 129. Leopold also suggested sending just one copy of the projected treaties to Stanley. If more were made, they could find their way into the wrong hands and cause great political difficulties (Leopold to Strauch, 27 October 1882, Strauch Papers 133).

45. Journal, 11, 15 October 1882.

46. Journal, 12 October 1882. For Brazza's use of this tactic see Ney, *Conférences*, p. 173. For a Belgian view on its essential falsity see Charles Liebrechts, *Leopold II: Fondateur d'Empire* (1932), pp. 47–8.

47. General de Chambrun, *Brazza* (1930), p. 120.

48. Journal, 19 October 1882.

49. *The Times*, 18, 20 October 1882. Stanley's speech was later published as a pamphlet by the London firm of J. M. Miles. See *Count Brazza and his pretensions* (1882).

50. Journal, 19 October 1882.

51. The twists and turns in nomenclature can be followed in R. S. Thomson, *Fondation de l'Etat Indépendant du Congo*, pp. 73–5, 79, 89, 93.

52. G. Valbert, 'M. Savorgnan de Brazza et M. Stanley', *Revue des Deux Mondes* 1, November 1882, pp. 205–16.

53. Journal, 19 October 1882.

54. Journal, 20 October 1882.

55. *The Times*, 30 November 1882.

56. Journal, 21 October 1882.

57. F. Latour da Veiga Pinto, *Le Portugal et le Congo au XIXe siècle*, p. 173. For the emotive nature of French fears see C. Coquery-Vidrovitch, *Brazza et la prise de possession du Congo* (1969), pp. 273, 347–9.

58. Documents diplomatiques français 1781–1914, 1st Series (1871–1900) (Paris 1933), v. No. 276.

59. There is a huge literature on the Stanley–Brazza rivalry and its international ramifications. See F. Carton de Tournai, *La rivalité de Brazza et de Stanley* (1963). See for contemporary views J. Reeves, *The International Beginnings of the Congo Free State* (1894); J. Scott-Keltie, *The Partition of Africa* (1893); H. H. Johnston, *History of the Colonisation of Africa by Alien Races* (1913); M. Koshitzky, *Deutsche Kolonialgeschichte*, 2 vols (1887–8).

60. Brazza to Ministry of Foreign Affairs, 27 December 1883, AEMD Afrique 88.

61. Brazza to Ministry of Foreign Affairs, 22 July 1884, AEMD Afrique 90. Jules Ferry, aware of Brazza's animus towards Stanley, advised him to keep away from him once he returned to Africa (Ferry to Brazza, 26 June 1883, AEMD Afrique 88).

62. Characteristically, Stanley could not see this: 'I am not conscious of having been "too hard" on de Brazza after fair warning' (Stanley to Keltie, 27 October 1882, RGS 2/1).

63. Journal, 22 October 1882.

64. Journal, 25 October 1882.

65. Stanley to Bruce, 6 November 1882, NLS 10705 f.27.

66. Journal, 5 November 1882.

67. Stanley to Marston, 3 November 1882, SFA.

68. Journal, 12 November 1882.

69. Ibid.

70. Devaux to Mackinnon, 24 November 1882, MP 1/1; Strauch to Mackinnon, November, December 1882, MP 56/228.

71. Journal, 12 November 1882.

Chapter five

1. Grant-Elliott, 'Exploration et organisation de la Province du Kwilou-Niari', *Bulletin Société Géographique Belgiques* 1886, pp. 106–12.

2. Van de Velde, 'La région du bas Congo et du Kwilou-Niari', *Bulletin Société Géographique Belgique* 1886, pp. 347–412.

3. *Congo*, i, pp. 471, 476–7; Stanley to Strauch, 18 July 1883, SFA.

4. *Doc. Notte*, pp. 151, 154, 165–73.

5. Leopold to Stanley, 27 May 1883; Stanley to Leopold, 18 July 1883, SFA.

6. Journal, 15–17 January 1883.

7. *Congo*, i, pp. 476–87.

8. Stanley to Strauch, 22 March 1883, SFA.
9. Journal, 26–7 February 1883.
10. *Doc. Notte*, pp. 156–8.
11. Stanley to Strauch, 31 March 1883, SFA.
12. Stanley to Leopold, 1 April 1883, SFA.
13. Journal, 7–8 April 1883.
14. Coquilhat, *Sur le Haut Congo*, pp. 60–63.
15. Jan Vansina, *The Tio Kingdom of the Middle Congo 1880–1892* (1973), p. 415.
16. Johnston, *The River Congo*, p. 210; Coquilhat, *Sur le Haut Congo*, p. 117.
17. Johnston, *The River Congo*, p. 298.
18. Vansina, *The Tio Kingdom*, p. 414.
19. Wyatt MacGaffey, *Custom and Government in the Lower Congo* (1970), p. 6.
20. Journal, 27 November 1883.
21. Journal, January 1884.
22. Stanley to Leopold, 30 January 1884, SFA.
23. *Congo*, ii, pp. 212–21; Journal, 21, 30 March, 5 April 1884.
24. Leopold to Stanley, 28 March 1884, SFA.
25. *The Times*, 24 February 1883.
26. Brazza to Minister of Foreign Affairs, 27 December 1883, AEMD Afrique 88.
27. Leopold to Mackinnon, 3 February 1883, APR Congo, 1/6; cf. also RA P 19/128A.
28. Stanley's Journal, 27 January 1884, contains a bitter attack on the 'stupid Portuguese' whose sole policy in the Congo would be to raise revenues by means of a 40 per cent tariff.
29. See Stanley's rebuke to Johnston on 23 July 1883 for his support of the Portuguese. 'It was Livingstone, an Englishman, who discovered this river; it was Anglo-American money which explored it and made it known. It was international money, part of which is English, which began the task of making it useful to the world. They are English goods, products, manufactures, which enable us to move on and win the love of the Congo nations. Will you still vote that we shall sacrifice all this in honour of Diego Cam, whose countrymen allowed the pearl of African rivers to lie idle for nearly four centuries? Bah, the very thought sickens me.' (Oliver, 'Six Unpublished Letters', pp. 354–6).
30. Granville to Cohen, 17 August 1883, F.O.84/1640.
31. Ascherson, *King Incorporated*, p. 122.
32. *Doc. Notte*, pp. 163–4.
33. Leopold to Prince of Wales, 13 March 1883, APR Congo 1/25.
34. Hansard 277, HC 1284–96, 3 April 1883.
35. Strauch to Mackinnon, 27, 29 April 1883, MP 57/231; cf. also Lord

Edward Fitzmaurice, *The Life of Granville George Leveson Gower, Second Earl Granville* (1905), ii, pp. 355–7.

36. H. H. Johnston, *The Story of My Life* (1923), pp. 117, 123; Roland Oliver, *Sir Harry Johnston and the Scramble for Africa* (1957), pp. 42–5.

37. Johnston to Fitzmaurice, 23 February 1884, F.O.84/1809.

38. Oliver, 'Six Unpublished Letters', pp. 352–6. The same sentiments were expressed in Stanley to Hutton, 11 July 1883, F.O.84/1407; cf. also CP 4865 (May–September 1883), F.O.403/15B.

39. *The Times*, 25 September 1883.

40. Stanley to Mackinnon, 10 May 1884, MP.

41. Leopold to Stanley, 30 September 1883.

42. Stanley to Johnston, 31 January 1884 in Oliver, 'Six Unpublished Letters', p. 356.

43. Strauch to Waters, 1 May 1911, Strauch Papers 769.

44. For a full discussion see Jean Stengers, 'Leopold II et l'Angleterre', *Le Flambeau* 4 (1954), pp. 378–86.

45. Sanford to Devaux, 27 May 1883, APR Congo, 2/14; cf. also Bontinck, *Aux Origines*, pp. 118–22, 124–8, 135.

46. *The Times*, 8 March 1884.

47. Anderson memo, 20 February 1884, F.O.30/29/198.

48. French ambassador, Brussels, to French Foreign Ministry, 8 March 1883, AECP, Belgique 75.

49. Strauch to Ferry, 23 April 1884, APR Congo, 136/2; Ferry to Strauch, 24 April 1884, APR Congo, 2/64.

50. Leopold to Granville, 22 May 1884, APR Congo, 61/3.

51. Ascherson, *King Incorporated*, p. 131.

52. For Stanley as 'marked man' with the Portuguese see CP Africa 1883, F.O.179/235. For Leopold's secret thoughts see Leopold to Strauch, 26, 28 September 1883, Musée de la Dynastie.

53. See the extensive analysis in M. Luwel, *Sir Francis de Winton* (1964).

54. Journal, 11 May 1884.

55. Journal, May 1884.

56. Journal, 10–27 June 1884; *Congo*, ii, pp. 228–33.

57. *Congo*, ii, p. 236.

58. Journal, 20 July 1884.

59. Journal, 23 July 1884.

60. Fred Puleston, *African Drums* (1930), p. 266.

61. Wilhelm Sievers, *Afrika: Eine allgemeine landeskunde* (1891), p. 431.

62. *Congo*, ii, pp. 352–77.

63. See the price lists in Norman R. Bennett, *Studies in East African History* (1963), p. 89.

64. *New York Herald*, 15 August 1872.

65. Stanley to de Winton, 10 September 1884, SFA. Stanley always had a

sentimental streak about animals, as one of his earliest letters to Mackinnon (from Paris, 26 August 1874) shows. 'Your hospitality is noble like yourself. Alas for grouse shooting! I do not believe in pigeon or grouse shooting. It is a sport for which I have no wish. I love to see the birds and I would not wantonly take their lives. Pigeons are beautiful things and I delight in hearing their melancholy woodland plaints and why should I harm ruthlessly things I admire for their beauty and song. And for the grouse they people the woods, they are an ornament to the forest tracks and I think we have enough of a variety of meat without disturbing the poor creatures.' (MP 55.)

66. *Autobiography*, pp. 351–2.

67. Maurice, *Unpublished Letters*, p. 160.

68. Coquery-Vidrovitch, *Brazza et la prise de possession du Congo*, pp. 115–16.

69. P. de Chavannes, *Avec Brazza: Souvenirs de la Mission de l'Ouest Africain* (1935), pp. 159–60; cf. also Ney, *Conférences*, pp. 231–2.

70. Vansina, *Tio Kingdom*, pp. 426–36.

71. Augouard to Nisard, 9 May 1884, AEMD Afrique 89 ff.359–61.

72. A. Thys, *Au Congo*, pp. 44–5; Bentley, *Pioneering*, ii, p. 36.

73. T. Masui, *D'Anvers à Bannyville* (1894), p. 61; Masui, *L'Etat Indépendant du Congo*, p. 411.

74. For full details of their careers see (for Coquilhat) *Biographie Coloniale Belge*, i, pp. 250–60; (for Vangele), ibid., ii, pp. 928–37. It was Lady Stanley who, in 1925, told Vangele that he and Coquilhat were Stanley's favourite lieutenants (Cuypers, *Vangele*, pp. 17–18).

75. Glave, *Six Years*, pp. 150, 165.

76. Obed-ben-Salim to Barghash, 16 May 1884, enclosed in Kirk to Salisbury, 31 July 1885, F.O.84/1727.

77. F. Bontinck, 'La station de Stanley Falls, 1 Dec. 1883–5 Juillet 1884', *Bulletin des Séances, Académie Royale des Sciences d'Outre Mer* 4 (1979), pp. 615–30.

78. Coquilhat, *Sur le haut Congo*, pp. 400–6; Cuypers, *Vangele*, pp. 25–6.

79. Cuypers, *Vangele*, pp. 26–32.

80. George Harker, *The Life of George Grenfell, Congo Missionary and Explorer* (1909), p. 215.

81. Stanley to Leopold, 30 January 1884, SFA.

Chapter six

1. *The Times*, 29, 30 July, 2 August 1884.

2. Journal, 27 July 1884.

3. Journal, August 1884.

4. Bontinck, *Aux Origines*, p. 215.

5. Dept of State Papers relating to the Foreign Relations of the USA, 1883 (Washington 1886), p. ix.

6. 'Report of the Secretary of State Relative to the Affairs of the Independent State of the Congo', Senate Executive Documents, 49th Congress, 1st session (1886) No. 196, p. 348. On the chain of stations see *New York Herald*, 25 June 1884.

7. Anderson Memo, 16 May 1884, F.O.30/29/128.

8. See R. T. Anstey, *Britain and the Congo in the Nineteenth Century* (1962), Chapters 5–7.

9. A. J. P. Taylor, *Germany's First Bid for Colonies* (1938), pp. 32–40. Cf. also Taylor, *The Struggle for Mastery in Europe* (1954), pp. 292–4.

10. Thomson, *Fondation de l'Etat*, p. 182.

11. Von Bleichroder to Leopold, 5 August 1884, APR, Congo, 117/12.

12. Stengers, 'Leopold II et la Fixation des Frontières du Congo', loc. cit.

13. French Ambassador to Quai d'Orsay, 30 August 1884, AECP, Allemagne, 58.

14. Bismarck to Leopold, 4 September 1884, APR, Fonds Congo, 116/5.

15. For Leopold's views on Johnston see Leopold to Strauch, 22 July 1883, 24 September, Musée de la Dynastie. For the accusation against Stanley in the *Journal des Débats* see APR Congo 2/30.

16. Stanley to Mackinnon, 10 May 1884, MP 55.

17. Stanley to Mackinnon, 7 August 1884, MP55.

18. *The Times*, 27 August 1884.

19. Bontinck, *Aux Origines*, pp. 216–17.

20. Memo by Granville, 29 August 1884, F.O.84/1812.

21. Leopold to Strauch, 5 August 1884, Strauch Papers 289.

22. *The Times*, 8 September 1884.

23. Stanley to Keltie, 12 September 1884 (RGS) accused *The Times* of suppressing his critical letter about Baker. Cf. Stanley to Keltie, 1884, n.d. (RGS). 'If Baker wants smashing, let him smash these arguments and I will go at him again.'

24. Borchgrave to Stanley, 8 September 1884, SFA.

25. Borchgrave to Stanley, 2 September 1884, SFA. Cf. also Bontinck, *Aux Origines*, p. 219.

26. Strauch to Stanley, 24 August 1884, SFA.

27. Lalaing to Stanley, 4, 10 September 1884.

28. Stanley to Leopold, 4 September 1884; Strauch to Stanley, 8, 18, 27 September 1884; Lalaing to Stanley, 13, 19 August, 10 October 1884; Stanley to de Winton, 1 July, 10 September 1884, SFA.

29. Ward, *Five Years with the Congo Cannibals* (1890), p. 26.

30. Ibid., p. 27. Ward took over Bangala station when Van Kerkhoven left it in 1886 (Coquilhat, *Sur le haut Congo*, p. 517).

31. *The Times*, 19 September 1884.

32. Stanley to Lalaing, 10 October; Lalaing to Stanley, 12 October 1884, SFA.
33. Stanley to Mackinnon, 5, 14 October, MP 55.
34. See *The Times*, 22, 23 October, 10 December 1884, 18 February 1885.
35. Manchester Chamber of Commerce to F.O., F.O.84/1814.
36. *Manchester Guardian*, 26, 27 September, 22 October, 4 November 1884.
37. Anstey, *Britain and the Congo*, p. 176.
38. Stanley to Bruce, NLS 10705 ff. 34, 40.
39. Leopold to Strauch, 4 September 1884, Strauch Papers 306.
40. Edward Younger, *John A. Kasson: Politics and Diplomacy from Lincoln to McKinley* (1955).
41. Dept of State, National Archives, Washington. Diplomatic Instructions, Germany 17 f.426.
42. 'Report of the Secretary of the State Relative to the Affairs of the Independent State of the Congo', Senate Executive Documents, 48th Congress, 1st session (1884), pp. 16–21.
43. Bontinck, *Aux Origines*, pp. 224–38.
44. Leopold memo, 8 November 1884, APR, Congo, 98/37.
45. Bontinck, *Aux Origines*, pp. 238–41.
46. Lalaing to Stanley, 1, 2 November 1884, SFA.
47. R. S. Thomson, 'Leopold II et la Conférence de Berlin', *Congo* 12 (1931), pp. 325–52.
48. Borchgrave to Stanley, 10 November 1884.
49. Bontinck, *Aux Origines*, pp. 242–4.
50. Ward, *A Voice from the Congo*, p. 163.
51. Hoffmann MSS, Wellcome Library 6670, p. 1.
52. Ibid., p. 2. For Hoffmann's experience during the Conference itself see Hoffmann, *With Stanley in Africa* (1938), pp. 20–24.
53. Journal, 15 November 1884.
54. Senate report, 48th Congress (1884), pp. 346–87.
55. A. Julien, *Les Constructeurs de la France d'Outre Mer* (1946), p. 298. See also Jules Ferry, *Discours et Opinions* (1897), *passim*.
56. G. de Courcel, *L'Influence de la Conférence de Berlin de 1885 sur le Droit Colonial International* (Paris 1935), p. 95.
57. A point made explicit by Sir Edward Grey in a speech in 1898 (*The Times*, 3 December 1898).
58. See the battle of Imperial Preference versus the 'Open Door' in W. R. Louis, *Imperialism at Bay 1941–45* (1977), Chapter One.
59. *Congo*, ii, pp. 394–5.
60. Malet to Granville, 22 November 1884, F.O.84/1815.
61. *PRGS* 6 N.S. (1884), p. 742.
62. Senate Report, 48th Congress (1884), p. 42.
63. Malet to Granville, 21, 22, 23 November 1884, F.O.84/1815. Cf. also

Bourgeois & Pages, eds, *Documents Diplomatiques Français 1871–1914*, Series I, Vol 5 (1933), Nos. 458–461.

64. Heinrich Ritter Puschinger, *Furst Bismarck und Seine Hamburger Freunde* (1903), p. 105.

65. Journal, 24 November 1884.

66. There is a huge literature on the Berlin Conference, much of it written in the bygone 'golden age' of diplomatic history. Among representative works are A. B. Keith, *The Belgian Congo and the Berlin Act* (1919); H. E. Yarnall, *The Great Powers and the Congo Conference 1884 and 1885* (1934); G. Konigk, *Die Berliner Congo Konferenz 1884–85* (1938). Material on the implications for the Congo and its future history can be found in E. Dupont, *Lettres sur le Congo* (1889); F. Masoin, *Histoire de l'Etat Indépendant du Congo* (1912); A. J. Wauters, *Histoire Politique du Congo Belge* (1911); Baron J. de Witte, *Les Deux Congo* (1913).

67. Emile Banning, *Mémoires Politiques et Diplomatiques* (1927), p. 26.

68. *Congo*, ii, p. 396.

69. Thomson, 'Leopold II et la Conférence de Berlin', pp. 336–7.

70. *The Times*, 4 December 1884.

71. For Thomson see Robert I. Rotberg, *Joseph Thomson and the Exploration of Africa* (1971). For his wit at Stanley's expense see ibid., p. 79. For his sardonic view of Stanley see Thomson, *To the Central African Lakes and Back* (1881), pp. 88–9.

72. J. B. Thomson, *Joseph Thomson, African Explorer* (1896), p. 132.

73. *The Scotsman*, 6 December 1884. This letter engendered a debate on Stanley in *The Scotsman*, 8 December 1884 and the *Glasgow Herald*, 19 December 1884.

74. Thomson to Bates, December 1884, RGS.

75. *The Times*, 8 December 1884. There are also traces of a controversy with Verney Cameron, as in Stanley's letter to Bruce: 'Poor Cameron! What on earth did he mean? Is he a Scotchman? Were the letters published – or were they merely private notifications because if published Cameron must have caused many people to think less of him than ever.' (NLS 10705 f.39)

76. Stanley to Bruce, 24 March 1885, SFA.

77. Stanley to Hutton, 10 December 1884, F.O.84/1817.

78. Journal 4 December 1884; Borchgrave to Stanley, 4 December, Strauch to Stanley, 8 December 1884, SFA.

79. Bontinck, *Aux Origines*, p. 259.

80. Thomson, 'Leopold II et le Congo'.

81. Stanley to Hutton, 10 December 1884, MP 17/66.

82. Journal 17–19, 24 December 1884; Stanley to Mackinnon, 15 December 1884, MP 55.

83. This was a long-standing French argument. See Cordier to Minister of

Marine and Colonies, 10 March 1884, AEMD Afrique 89; cf. also Stanley to Hutton, 13 December in *The Times*, 18 December 1885.

84. Stanley to Mackinnon, 17 December 1884, MP 55.
85. Stanley to Mackinnon, 30 December 1884, MP 55; Sanford to Mackinnon, 23 December 1884, MP 51/203. Cf. also *The Times*, 5 January 1885.
86. Borchgrave to Stanley, 1 January 1885.
87. P. Daye, *Stanley* (1936), p. 185; Bontinck, *Aux Origines*, p. 268.
88. *Congo*, ii, pp. 397–8.
89. Journal, 7–9 January 1885.
90. Journal, 19 January 1885.
91. Journal, 28 January 1885.
92. *Congo*, ii, pp. 350–51.
93. For Brazza's estimate see C. Coquery-Vidrovitch, *Brazza et la prise de possession du Congo*, p. 411. For the modern estimate of 12–13 millions see L. de St Moulin, *Panorama de l'histoire contemporaire* (1963). Stanley's population estimate has been criticised on the grounds that he tended to choose the highest possible figures and because he followed rivers or paths that inevitably passed through areas of abnormally high density. See T. C. Caldwell, 'The social repercussions of colonial rule: demographic impact', in A. Adu Boahen, ed., *General History of Africa, Vol. 7: Africa under Colonial Domination* (1985), pp. 458–507 (at p. 460).
94. *Congo*, ii, pp. 409–14.
95. Journal, 5 February 1885.
96. Journal 6, 10, 11, 15, 21, 23 February 1885; *Congo*, ii, pp. 400–3, 415–58.
97. Bontinck, *Aux Origines*, p. 291.
98. Borchgrave to Stanley, 23, 26 February, 2 March 1885, SFA. There is also evidence of Stanley's impatience with diplomacy in the Mackinnon Papers. See Sanford to Mackinnon, 17 February 1885: 'Stanley is impatient to get away and I think we'll let him off in a few days' (MP 52/205).
99. Sir J. Rennell Rodd, *Social and Diplomatic Memoirs 1884–1893* (1922), Chapter Two.
100. Emile Banning, *Mémoires politiques et diplomatiques*, pp. 19–21, 24, 39.
101. Oliver, 'Six Letters', pp. 357–8.
102. Borchgrave to Stanley, 16 March 1885, SFA.
103. Thomson, *Fondation de l'Etat*, pp. 293–5.
104. Peter Forbath, *The River Congo* (1978).

Chapter seven

1. Ward, *A Voice from the Congo*, p. 158.
2. Bernard Meyer, *Joseph Conrad, A Psychoanalytic Biography* (1967), p. 349

argues for the Congo as self-evident symbolism – the river shaped like an immense coiled snake which penetrates the body of the land.

3. Friedrich R. Karl, *Joseph Conrad. The Three Lives* (1979), pp. 286–7.

4. Robert I. Rotberg, *Africa and its Explorers* (1970), pp. 313–14.

5. For individual references see Richard Stanley and Alan Neame (eds), *The Exploration Diaries of H. M. Stanley* (1961), p. 201; *New York Herald*, 10 October 1877; Coquilhat, *Sur le haut Congo*, p. 226; Bennett, *Despatches*, pp. 309–10. For a general survey see Donald Simpson, *Dark Companions* (1975).

6. *Through the Dark Continent* (TDC), i, pp. 37–8.

7. Journal, 25 October 1883.

8. Liebrechts, *Souvenirs*, p. 255; W. Holman Bentley, *Pioneering on the Congo*, ii, p. 68.

9. *Congo*, ii, p. 41.

10. Thys confirmed this in an observation that would have particularly appealed to Stanley. He said that the difference between the red and black man was that the latter was a natural trader whereas the former was not. It was this which made it possible for Europeans to subject the black races without exterminating them (as in the USA). See A. Thys, *Au Congo et Kasai* (1888), p. 53.

11. Wyatt MacGaffey, 'Oral Tradition in Central Africa', *International Journal of African Historical Studies* 7 (1974), p. 426. Cf. also Jan Vansina, *Oral Tradition in History* (1985).

12. Bentley, *Pioneering*, ii, p. 115.

13. C. S. L. Bateman, *The First Ascent of the Kasai* (1889), p. 159.

14. H. H. Johnston, *The River Congo*, pp. 178–9.

15. Bentley, *Pioneering*, i, p. 178. Cf. also Ruth Slade, *King Leopold's Congo* (1962), pp. 54–5.

16. Bentley, i, pp. 81, 137, 313; Bateman, *Kasai*, pp. 135–7.

17. Wyatt MacGaffey, 'The West in Congolese Experience', in Philip Curtin, ed., *Africa and the West* (1972).

18. Robert W. Harms, *River of Wealth, River of Sorrow: the Central Zaire basin in the era of the slave and ivory trade 1500–1891* (1981), p. 210.

19. *Le Congo Illustré* 2 (1893), p. 83.

20. John Weeks, *Among the Primitive Bakongo* (1914), pp. 294–5.

21. Bateman, *Kasai*, pp. 150–51.

22. Stanley, *Tales from Africa*, pp. 79, 186–7.

23. L. Dieu, *Dans la brousse congolaise* (1946), pp. 76–7.

24. F. Guinness, *The New World of Central Africa* (1890), p. 272.

25. E. Dupont, *Lettres sur le Congo* (1889), p. 209.

26. Weeks, *Among the Primitive Bakongo* (1914), p. 30.

27. Bentley, *Pioneering*, ii, p. 115.

28. For Livingstone's reputation see Bridghal Pachai, ed., *Livingstone, Man of*

Africa (1972). For Baker's see Ruth F. Fisher, *Twilight Tales of the Black Baganda* (1912).

29. See H. H. Johnston, *The Nile Quest* (1903), p. 129; Livingstone Journal, 19 November 1868, NLS 10734; Bennett, *Despatches*, p. 476; C. T. Wilson & R. W. Felkin, *Uganda and the Egyptian Sudan* (1882), i, p. 133.

30. Andrew Roberts, ed., *Tanzania before 1900* (1968), p. 135.

31. For the peoples Stanley met in 1874–6 see Thomas Q. Reefe, 'The societies of the Eastern Savanna', in David Birmingham & Phyllis M. Martin, *History of Central Africa* (1983), i, pp. 160–204. For those he met on the 1876–7 journey see Jan Vansina, 'The Peoples of the Forest', ibid., i, pp. 75–117. Cf. also Vansina, 'L'Afrique Centrale vers 1875' in *La Conférence Géographique en 1876, Recueil d'Etudes* (Brussels 1976), pp. 1–31.

32. Joseph C. Miller, ed., *The African Past Speaks: Essays on Oral Tradition and History* (1980).

33. Miscellaneous Journals, SFA.

34. This was exactly the triad of attributes ascribed to him by the Bangala (Coquilhat, *Sur le haut Congo*, p. 199).

35. Ward, *A Voice from the Congo*, p. 166.

36. HIFL, p. 435.

37. See Emory Ross, *Out of Africa* (1936).

38. Fox-Bourne, *The Other Side of the Emin Pasha Expedition*, p. 68.

39. Colin M. Turnbull, *The Forest People* (1962), p. 175.

40. *New York Press*, 15 April 1890.

41. Lagergren, *Mission and State in the Congo*, p. 102.

42. Ruth Slade, *English-Speaking Missions in the Congo Independent State 1878–1908* (1959), pp. 68–9, 72–4.

43. Peters, *Die Deutsch Emin Pascha Expedition* (1910), pp. 414–23.

44. Zoe Marsh & G. W. Kingsworth, *An Introduction to the History of East Africa* (1957), p. 221.

45. Fox-Bourne, *The Other Side of the Emin Pasha Expedition*, pp. 13–14.

46. Ward, *Five Years Among the Congo Cannibals*, p. 239.

47. Johnston to Lady Stanley, 10 May 1904, SFA.

48. Coquilhat, *Sur le haut Congo*, pp. 133, 186.

49. *Congo*, ii, p. 28.

50. Stanley to Johnston, 9 July 1883, in Oliver, 'Six Unpublished Letters', p. 351.

51. H. W. von Wissmann, *In Inners Afrikas* (1891), pp. 20–21. For some further reflections on this aspect of the necessary evil of porterage see Liebrechts, *Souvenirs*, p. 202; F. Masoin, *Histoire de l'Etat Indépendant du Congo*, i, p. 361.

52. Thys, *Au Congo et Kasai*, p. 53; Bateman, *First Ascent*, p. 45. Weeks rebutted the 'gluttonous' canard by pointing out that Africans had only one meal a

day as against the Europeans' three (Weeks, *Among the Primitive Bakongo*, p. 90). There is, however, some truth in the taunt about African factionalism and disunity, for, as Johnston saw, it was this very fact that made Stanley's rapid progress on his expeditions possible in the first place (Johnston, *River Congo*, pp. 299–300).

53. For this aspect of Weeks see *Among the Primitive Bakongo*, pp. 28–30. Stanley's interest speaks for itself (*Tales from Africa*).

54. Delcommune, *Vingt Années*, i, pp. 233–4.

55. *Congo*, ii, p. 29.

56. Père Schynse, *A Travers l'Afrique avec Stanley et Emin-Pascha* (1890), p. 248.

57. Van Overberghe & de Jonghe, *Les Bangala* (1907), p. 367.

58. Liebrechts, *Souvenirs*, p. 250; Bentley, *Pioneering*, i, p. 379.

59. *Congo*, ii, p. 29.

60. D. Neuville & C. Bréard, *Les Voyages de Savorgnan de Brazza*, p. 211.

61. See Michel Colin, 'Quelques anecdotes sur Stanley', *La Voix du Congolais* 10 (1954) (Leopoldville), pp. 338–343.

62. Wyatt MacGaffey, *Custom and Government in the Lower Congo* (1970), p. 5.

63. Glave, *Six Years*, p. 44.

64. According to Ward, the correct spelling should be Bula Matadi (*ntadi*, a stone, *matadi*, plural, stones). The variant arose because in the interior of Africa and among the *wangwana*, 'r' was frequently substituted for 'd' (Ward, *A Voice*, p. 169).

65. George Mazenot, *La Likouala-Mossaka, Histoire de la Pénétration du Haut Congo 1878–1920* (1970), p. 43.

66. Alfred J. Swann, *Fighting the Slave Hunters in Central Africa* (1910, new edition 1969), p. 75.

67. F. Bontinck, 'Les deux Bula Matari', *Etudes Congolaises* 12 (1969), pp. 83–97. For further variants on the theme of Bula Matari see Vansina, *Tio Kingdom*, p. 88.

68. Leibrechts, *Souvenirs*, p. 255.

69. Patrice Lumumba, 'Un explorateur incomparable', *La Voix du Congolais* 10 (1954), pp. 516–22.

70. A good example of transitory impact is that of Emin on the Mangbetu kingdom in northern Zaire. When Emin withdrew in 1886 after a four-year presence from 1881 to 1885, during which the regulation of the slave and ivory trades was thought to have had a profound impact on the Mangbetu kingdom, the old Mangbetu order re-emerged comparatively unscathed (Curtis A. Keim, 'Long-Distance Trade and the Mangbetu', *JAH* 24 (1983), pp. 1–22).

71. Rotberg, *Africa and its Explorers*, pp. 9–10.

72. Thys, *Au Congo et Kasai*, p. 19.

73. Vansina, *Tio Kingdom*, pp. 281–8, 292–312. For price fluctuations in the Stanley Pool economy see ibid., pp. 288–92.

74. Harms, *River of Wealth*, pp. 223–5.

75. MacGaffey, *Custom and Government*, pp. 264–6.

76. Ibid., p. 243.

77. Gilles Sautter, *De l'Atlantique au fleuve Congo*, i, pp. 265–78.

78. Jerome Becker, *La Vie en Afrique* (1887), ii, p. 167.

79. Vansina, 'Long-Distance Trade Routes in Central Africa', *JAH* 3 (1962), pp. 375–90.

80. *St James's Gazette*, 26 March 1889.

81. *Morning Post*, 6 April 1889.

82. J. M. Schuffeleers, 'Livingstone and the Mang'Anja chiefs', in Pachai, *Livingstone, Man of Africa*, pp. 120–21. For the slave trade in general see Edward A. Alpers, *Ivory and Slaves . . .* (1975).

83. Thomas Q. Reefe, *The Rainbow and the Kings: A History of the Luba Empire to 1891* (1981), pp. 164–9.

84. Catherine Coquery-Vidrovich, 'Research on an African Mode of Production', in Martin Klein & G. Wesley Johnson, eds, *Perspectives on the African Past* (1972), pp. 33–51. Cf. Coquery-Vidrovich, 'The Political Economy of the African Peasantry and Modes of Production', in Peter Gutkind & Immanuel Wallerstein, eds, *The Political Economy of Contemporary Africa* (1976), pp. 90–111.

85. Samir Amin, *Unequal Development* (1976), p. 17.

86. The phrase 'scramble for Africa' was first popularised in an article in *The Times*, 15 September 1884.

87. Lenin regarded the period 1873–98 as one of *transition* to imperialism, characterised both by the growth of cartels and the completion of the territorial partition of the world. See Norman Etherington, *Theories of Imperialism: War, Conquest and Capital* (1984).

88. Lady Cecil, *Life of Robert, Marquis of Salisbury* (1932), iv, p. 310.

89. There is a huge literature on the economics of imperialism and its relationship to Africa. The leading titles are conveniently gathered together in Etherington, *Theories of Imperialism*. See also Wolfgang J. Mommsen & Jurgen Osterhammel, eds, *Imperialism and After* (1986). The standard starting point for any discussion of imperialism in Africa is Ronald Robinson & John Gallagher, *Africa and the Victorians: The Official Mind of Imperialism*, 2nd ed. (1981). There is a very lively popular overview of imperialism in East Africa in Charles Miller, *The Lunatic Express* (1971).

90. Ascherson, *King Incorporated*, p. 203.

91. W. R. Louis & Jean Stengers, *E. D. Morel's History of the Congo Reform Movement* (1968), p. 17.

92. J. S. Galbraith, *Mackinnon and East Africa 1878–1895* (Cambridge 1972).

93. Glave, *Six Years*, p. 231.

94. D. S. Landes, 'Some Thoughts on the Nature of Economic Imperialism', *Journal of Economic History* 21 (1961), pp. 496–512 (at p. 511). Interestingly, this seemingly unexceptionable proposition has been contested by Gavin White, 'Firearms in Africa: An Introduction', *JAH* 12 (1971), pp. 173–84. See also the other articles on guns in Africa in that issue.

95. Daniel R. Headrick, 'The Tools of Imperialism: technology and expansion of European colonial empires in the nineteenth century', *Journal of Modern History* 51 (1979), pp. 231–63.

96. R. W. Beachey, 'The Arms Trade in East Africa in the late Nineteenth Century', *JAH* 3 (1962), pp. 451–67.

97. Ibid., p. 467.

98. See John Ellis, *The Social History of the Machine Gun* (1975); G. S. Hutchinson, *Machine Guns: their history and technical employment* (1938).

99. Daniel Headrick, *The Tools of Empire* (1981), p. 100.

100. See Liebrechts, *Souvenirs*, p. 529; Coquilhat, *Sur le haut Congo*, p. 59; cf. also Sautter, *De l'Atlantique*, i, p. 372; A. J. Wauters, *Le Congo au point de vue économique* (1956), pp. 173–4.

101. The Arab issue is exhaustively discussed in P. Ceulemans, *La question Arabe et le Congo 1883–1892* (1959).

102. Becker, *La vie en Afrique* (1887), ii, pp. 45–7.

103. *Star*, 2 October 1888.

Chapter eight

1. Bontinck, *Aux Origines*, pp. 299–302.

2. P. Daye, *Stanley*, pp. 187–9.

3. Add. MSS. 43, 411 ff.12–20; cf. also M. Luwel, 'Stanley et son éditeur Marston', *La Revue Coloniale Belge* 228 (1955), pp. 220–21.

4. Stanley to Bruce, 1, 24 March 1885, NLS 10705 ff.44–7.

5. Stanley to Mackinnon, 17, 18 April 1885, MP 55.

6. Stanley to Bruce, 26 May 1885, NLS 10705 f.50.

7. Journal, May 1885.

8. Bontinck, *Aux Origines*, p. 308.

9. Borchgrave to Stanley, 31 May 1885, SFA.

10. Stanley to Borchgrave, 9 June 1885, SFA.

11. Stanley to Leopold 24 June; Borchgrave to Stanley, 28 June 1885, SFA.

12. Bontinck, *Aux Origines*, pp. 323–4.

13. Journal, June 1885.

14. Bontinck, *Aux Origines*, p. 327.

15. Stanley to Henry Wellcome, 14 June, 21 July 1885, RGS 3/1; Stanley to Mrs Sheldon, 25 June 1885, RGS 4/1.

16. Borchgrave to Stanley, 5 June 1885, SFA.

17. *The Times*, 29 May, 23 July 1885.

18. *PRGS* 7 N.S. (1885), pp. 481, 609–27.

19. Stanley to Cardinal Manning, 31 May 1885, B.L.MSS.R.P. 1899. Cf also R. Gray, *A History of the Southern Sudan 1839–1889* (1961), pp. 193–4.

20. For all his bitterness, Stanley defended Leopold publicly against charges that he was a fraud: 'A king who has given £1,000,000 and afterwards endows a state with £40,000 annually cannot be a swindler' (Stanley to Frederic, 24 July 1885, B.L.MSS.RP 1437).

21. R. J. Cornet, *La bataille du rail* (1953) p. 38.

22. For progress on the railway syndicate see Borchgrave to Stanley, 29 March 1885, SFA; Stanley to Mackinnon, 6 June 1885, MP 55; *The Times*, 28 December 1885.

23. Leopold to Strauch, 20 December 1885, Strauch Papers 510.

24. Stanley to Mackinnon, 16 September 1885, MP 55.

25. Strauch to Leopold, 6 December 1885; Leopold to Strauch, 24 December 1885, Strauch Papers 498, 512; Hutton to Mackinnon, 4, 10 December 1885, MP.

26. Stanley to Mackinnon, 21 May, 18 September 1886, MP 55.

27. Leopold's writings can be followed in *The Times*, 21 January, 6, 25 September, 6, 15, 29 October 1886; Borchgrave to Stanley, 13, 26 April 1886, SFA.

28. Cornet, *La bataille du rail*, p. 143.

29. P. Ceulemans, *La question arabe*, p. 194.

30. Stanley to Bruce, 30 December 1884, NLS 10705 ff. 42–3.

31. Quoted in Richard Hall, *Stanley* (1974), p. 274.

32. Marie von Bunsen, *The World I Used to Know 1860–1912* (1930), p. 149.

33. Ibid., pp. 150–53.

34. Stanley to unknown woman, 11 April 1885, National Library of Wales.

35. Bontinck, *Aux Origines*, p. 324.

36. Gertrude Tennant to Edward Arnold, 18 June 1885, SFA.

37. Dorothy Stanley Diary, SFA, 17, 25 June 1885.

38. Julian Arnold, *Giants in a Dressing Gown*, p. 79.

40. Arnold, *Giants*, p. 80.

41. Stanley to Arnold, 25 June 1885; Dolly Diary, 24 June 1885, SFA.

42. Dolly to Stanley, 1 July 1885.

43. Stanley to Bruce, 2, 28 July 1885, NLS 10705 ff. 52–5. Hearing of this Count Lalaing wrote to Mackinnon: 'The King has just heard that Stanley is to be with you for a week and he is extremely glad of it – Stanley has been thinking that we are neglecting him and that it was purposely that he was left for a little there without an answer to one of his letters . . . nothing is altered in our feelings towards M. Stanley and in our wish to employ him in Africa as soon as our interest commends it.' (Lalaing to Mackinnon, 5 July 1885, MP 27/105)

44. The first sitting was on 18 July (Dolly Diary).
45. Dolly Diary, 18 July 1885.
46. Stanley to Bruce, 18 July 1885, NLS 10705 ff. 54-5.
47. Dolly Diary, 18 July 1885.
48. Dolly Diary, 20 July 1885.
49. Journal, 1 August 1885.
50. Journal, 2 September 1885.
51. Stanley to Mackinnon, 16 September 1885, MP 55.
52. Lalaing to Stanley, 10 September 1885, SFA.
53. Bontinck, *Aux Origines*, p. 337.
54. Ibid., p. 340.
55. Stanley to Dolly, 6 September 1885, SFA.
56. Dolly to Stanley, 2 September, SFA.
57. *Autobiography*, p. 530. Stanley passed this view of socialism on to Ward, who accepted it uncritically (Ward, *A Voice*, pp. 201-2) and regarded it as a kind of 'Pol Pot' mania for equality, whatever the consequences.
58. R. J. Cornet, 'Mlle Jeanne Orianne et H. M. Stanley', *Revue Coloniale Belge* 199 (1954), pp. 43-5.
59. Dolly to Stanley, 2 October 1885, SFA.
60. Stanley to Mackinnon, 4 October 1885, MP 55/217.
61. Stanley to Mackinnon, 4 November 1885, MP 55/217.
62. Bontinck, *Aux Origines*, p. 342. For the routine tedium of Stanley's life at this time see Add. MSS. 42, 582 and 46, 345 f. 170.
63. Kirk to Mackinnon, 31 August 1885, MP 24/93.
64. Borchgrave to Stanley, 20, 27 November 1885.
65. *New York Herald*, 29 November 1885.
66. *New York Herald*, 16 December 1885. He gives some hints: 'The ridiculous pose of the commercial agent during his too brief stay at Stanley Pool . . . the big words he used . . . his disinclination to leave Berlin . . . his hurried departure from Stanley Pool.'
67. *New York Herald*, 24 January 1886.
68. Dolly Diary, 23 November 1885.
69. Stanley to Bruce, 27 July 1885, NLS 10705 f. 59. But on women of Gertrude Tennant's age Stanley remained consistent. Describing an old woman in Africa in the first volume of *In Darkest Africa*, under the date of 2 December 1887, he wrote: 'she, being vigorous and obstinate, like most of her sex just previous to dotage.'
70. Stanley to Baroness Van Dornop, Stanley letters, Wellcome Library.
71. Dolly Diary, January 1886.
72. 'I have succeeded for a wonder. *She* will come tomorrow Wednesday at 4 p.m. or up to 4.30 p.m.' (Stanley to Mackinnon, 29 December 1885, MP 55/217)
73. Dolly Diary, 7 January 1886.

74. Dolly Diary, 10 January 1886.
75. Stanley to Mackinnon, 14 January 1886, MP 55/217.
76. Bontinck, *Aux Origines*, p. 451.
77. Stanley to Mackinnon, 4 November 1885, MP 55/217.
78. Leopold to Strauch, 24 December 1885, Strauch Papers 512.
79. Stanley to Leopold, 16 January 1886, SFA.
80. Borchgrave to Stanley, 19 January 1886.
81. Journal, 16 January 1886.
82. Journal, January 1886.
83. Leopold to Strauch, 25 January 1886, Strauch Papers 539.
84. Stanley to Leopold, 23 January, 11 February 1886; Borchgrave to Stanley, 9 February 1886, SFA.
85. Devaux to Mackinnon, 18 February 1886, MP 2/7.
86. Dolly Diary, 12 February 1886.
87. Stanley to Borchgrave, 27 February 1886, SFA.
88. Journal, March 1886.
89. Stanley to Dolly, 16 March 1886.
90. Stanley to Mackinnon, 17 March 1886, MP 55/218.
91. Borchgrave to Stanley, 11 March 1886, SFA.
92. Stanley to Leopold, 18 March 1886, APR, Congo 170/1; cf. also Add. MSS. 44, 496 ff. 155-9.
93. Rosebery minute, 6 April 1886, Add. MSS. 44, 496 f. 161.
94. *Denbigh Free Press*, 9 February 1889. Details on the grave in Bodlewydden churchyard can be found in *Denbigh Free Press*, 23 January 1954.
95. B.L. MSS. RP 1691. Here Stanley was in clear contrast with his mentor Livingstone, for Livingstone had told his daughter Agnes: 'Avoid all nasty French novels. They are very injurious, and effect a lasting injury on the mind and heart.' (Oliver Ransford, *Livingstone: The Dark Interior* (1978), p. 234)
96. Stanley to Dolly, 29 March 1886. However, a letter to Mrs Sheldon tells a different story. Stanley complained of an attack of fever and being unable to walk a mile without fatigue (unknown correspondent to Sheldon, 24 March, RGS 4/1).
97. Journal, 3, 4 April 1886.
98. Stanley to Mackinnon, 6 April 1886, MP 55/218.
99. Journal, 7-10 April 1886.
100. Stanley to Dolly, 10 April 1886, SFA.
101. Dolly to Stanley, 3 April 1886, SFA.
102. Stanley to Mackinnon, 10 April 1886, MP 55/218; Stanley to Dolly, 10 April 1886, SFA.
103. Journal, 12-22 April 1886.
104. Stanley to Dolly, 19 April 1886, SFA.
105. Dolly to Stanley, 28 April 1886, SFA.

106. Stanley to Dolly, 2 May 1886, SFA. Cf. Stanley to Mackinnon, 4 May 1886, referring to a pro-Gladstone letter from 'Polly Hopkins', 'Yesterday I sent her as good as she gave me, reiterating in the most determined calligraphy my opinion that the GOM was an old goose.' (MP 55/218)

107. Stanley to Mackinnon, 29 April 1886, MP 55/218.

108. Ibid.

109. Stanley to Dolly, 2 May 1886, SFA.

110. Dolly Diary, 9, 18 May 1886.

111. Coquilhat, *Sur le haut Congo*, pp. 429–62.

112. Bontinck, *Aux Origines*, pp. 354–5.

113. Dolly Diary, 21 July 1886.

114. Journal, 14 August 1886.

115. Stanley to Dolly, 16 August 1886.

116. For the progress of Leopold's negotiations with the railway syndicate in 1886 see R. J. Cornet, *La bataille du rail*, pp. 53–78. Cf. also Leopold to Strauch, 15 July 1886, Strauch Papers 616. The final slamming of the door on the syndicate occurs in Borchgrave to Stanley, 12 September 1886, SFA.

117. Journal, September 1886.

118. Stanley to Mackinnon, 23 September 1886, MP 55/218.

119. *The Scotsman*, 28 December 1886. The lectures were to be in three parts dealing with (1) the Livingstone expedition, (2) the charting of the Congo 1876–7, (3) the foundation of the Congo Free State (Stanley to Hiram Ellis, 3 September 1886, B.L. MSS. RP 1032).

120. The full calendar of Stanley's British lecture tour was Harrogate (29 September), Nottingham (1 October), Leicester (2 October), Birkenhead (4 October), Keighley (5 October), London (6 October), Burnley (8 October), Southport (9 October), London (11 October), Harborne (12 October), Walsall (13 October), Moseley (14 October), Clifton College (15 October), Bath (16 October), Bristol (18 October), Aberdare (20 October), Swansea (21 October), Taunton (22 October), Torquay (25 October), Harrow (27 October), Wallasey (28 October), Rossall School (29 October), Acocksbreen (2 November), Tredegar (3 November), Ashton (4 November), Hull (5 October), Sunderland (6 October), Newcastle (7 October), Sutton Coldfield (8 November), London (9 November), Southampton (10 November), various public schools (11–13 November), London (15 November).

121. Stanley had often pressed the King on this idea (Stanley to Leopold, 3 September 1884, APR, Congo, 10/2).

122. Stanley to Mackinnon, 15 November 1886 (enclosed in Mackinnon to Fergusson, 15 November 1886, F.O. 84/1793).

123. Clemens to Howells, 12 December 1886, in Henry Nash Smith & William

M. Gibson, eds, *The Correspondence of Samuel L. Clemens and William Dean Howells 1872–1910* (1960), pp. 574–6.
124. F.O. 84/1795.

Chapter nine

1. G. Schweitzer, *Emin Pasha, his life and work* (1898). Emin's scientific curiosity is revealed in a series of letters to Felkin printed in *The Times*, 22 June 1888.
2. 'There is a great interest in the affairs of East Africa in these times. Germany today wants many colonies and in the neighbourhood of Zanzibar Bismarck has already ... seized two or three districts. England will also do something in East Africa, she only wants a good opportunity.' (Iain R. Smith, *The Emin Pasha Relief Expedition 1886–1890* (1972), p. 32).
3. Schweitzer, *Emin Pasha*, i, p. 45. For Emin's dislike of Leopold and the Congo State see Emin to Mackay, 1 October 1886, in Holmwood to Salisbury, 9 April 1887, F.O. 84/1852.
4. 'I am still waiting and hoping for help, and that from England' (Emin to Felkin, 22 July 1886, ZA/RCS). 'Is not England honour-bound?' (Emin to Mackay, 1 October 1886, in Holmwood to Salisbury, 9 April 1887, F.O. 84/1852).
5. *The Times*, 29 October, 1, 6 November, 2, 9, 11, 15, 18 December 1886, 14 January 1887.
6. Smith, *Emin Pasha Expedition*, p. 42.
7. *The Times*, 26 October 1886.
8. Salisbury minute, October 1886, F.O. 84/1775.
9. Memo by Anderson, 30 November 1886, F.O. 84/1794.
10. Anstey, *Britain and the Congo*, p. 207.
11. Smith, *Emin Pasha Expedition*, pp. 53, 58.
12. G. N. Sanderson, *England, Europe and the Upper Nile 1882–1899* (1965), p. 33.
13. Smith, *Emin Pasha Expedition*, pp. 54–61.
14. Thomson to Bates, 25 November 1886; Thomson to General Brackenbury, 26 November 1886, in *Correspondence Relating to the Relief of Emin Bey at Uganda*, C. 5433 (1886), p. 84.
15. Rotberg, *Joseph Thomson*, p. 237. Stanley's claim to have supported Thomson is in Stanley to Euan-Smith, 19 December 1889, in *Correspondence Respecting Mr Stanley's expedition for the relief of Emin Pasha* C 5906 (1890), p. 3. Further light is shed on Thomson's bid to serve on the EPRE by Stanley's journal entries for 16–17 January 1887; 'He would be an admirable assistant but I fear it is too late.' He suggested instead that the committee hire him on an independent mission to

bring stores to meet him when at Lake Victoria for the crossing to Bagamoyo. But on the 17th he recorded that the committee had turned Thomson down. 'It was the general opinion, that Thomson was of rather a cantankerous disposition and would somehow or other cause trouble.'

16. Mackay to Emin, 27 February, 14 March 1887, ZA/RCS.
17. *The Times*, 5 November 1886.
18. Stanley to Mackinnon, 15 November 1886, in Mackinnon to Fergusson, 15 November 1886, F.O.84/1793.
19. Anderson to Pauncefoote, 24 December 1886, F.O.84/1795.
20. Journal, 29 December 1886.
21. Stanley to Leopold, 27 December 1886, Van Eetvelde Papers, 63/1.
22. Leopold to Strauch, 17 December 1886, Strauch Papers 8694, 18 December 1886, ibid., 86102; Strauch to Leopold, 18 December 1886, ibid., 505.
23. *Le Mouvement Géographique* 5, 19 December 1886. Cf. Leopold to Lambermont, 15 December 1886, Lambermont Papers (Archives du Ministère des Affaires Etrangères) 240.
24. For this plan, first broached in 1884, as a seeming means of diverting the Mahdi's pressure from Gordon see Stanley to Leopold, 3 September 1884, APR 102/2.
25. Strauch to Leopold, 4 September 1884, 8 December 1886, Strauch Papers 505.
26. Journal, 30 December 1886.
27. Van Eetvelde Papers 63/2, 63/6; Leopold to Mackinnon, 30 December 1886, MP.
28. Borchgrave to Stanley, 7 January 1887, SFA.
29. Journal, 5 January 1887.
30. Journal, 1 January 1887. Over 4000 applications were received (*The Times*, 17 January 1887).
31. Journal, 6 January 1887.
32. Journal, 14 January 1887.
33. Journal, 10–13 January 1887.
34. Iddesleigh to Holmwood, 22, 25 December 1886, F.O.C.P.5433 pp. 102, 104.
35. Iddesleigh to Baring, 28 December 1886, F.O.C.P.5433 No. 76.
36. See MP 93 p. 9.
37. *In Darkest Africa* (1890), i, p. 37.
38. As Headrick has remarked: 'At no time in history has the distinction between tourists and conquerors been so blurred' (*Tools of Empire*, p. 117).
39. *Globe*, 19 January 1887; A. Bott, *Our Fathers 1870–1900* (1931), p. 122.
40. Journal, 4 January 1887.
41. MP 85/16.

42. Journal, 7 January 1887.
43. Journal, 8–9 January 1887.
44. Leopold to Lambermont, 15 January 1887, APR Congo, 72/14.
45. Borchgrave to EPRE, 11 January 1887, SFA.
46. Leopold to Strauch, 20 January 1887, Strauch Papers 635.
47. Journal, 12 January 1887; W. G. Barttelot, *The Life of Edmund Musgrave Barttelot* (1890), p. 51.
48. Journal, 13 January 1887; *The Times*, 14 January 1887.
49. Journal, 14 January 1887.
50. Journal, 15 January 1887.
51. Gosselin to Salisbury, 21 August 1887, F.O.C.P.5167, p. 49.
52. Journal, 17 January 1887.
53. Journal, 18 January 1887.
54. Journal, 19 January 1887.
55. *The Times*, 20 January 1887; *Morning Post*, 20 January 1887.
56. Journal, 20–21 January 1887.
57. Journal, 21 January 1887.
58. Journal, 24 January 1887.
59. IDA, i, p. 49.
60. Baring had already written to Salisbury along these lines (Baring to Salisbury, 23 January 1887, F.O.84/1878).
61. Journal, 27 January 1887. Among those Stanley cites against Schweinfurth is Kirk. Stanley and he in early 1887 finally composed their famous quarrel (see Stanley to Bruce, 7 January 1887, NLS 10705 ff.74–75; Kirk to Mackinnon, 26 January 1887, MP 24/94).
62. Documents diplomatiques français 1871–1914, 1st series (Paris 1929), vi, Nos. 416, 431.
63. W. Junker, *Travels in Africa 1882–86* (1892), iii, p. 59.
64. Journal, 28 January 1887.
65. Ibid.
66. Stanley to Borchgrave, 29 January 1887, APR Congo, 102/15. Cf. also *The Graphic*, 29 January 1887; *Globe*, 29 January 1887.
67. Journal, 29–30 January 1887.
68. Journal, 1 February 1887.
69. Salisbury to Baring, 24 January 1887, F.O.84/1878.
70. Baring to Salisbury, 2 February 1887, F.O.84/1878.
71. Journal, 1–2 February 1887.
72. Journal, 2 February 1887. For further material on Stanley's time in Cairo see MP 85/16; *The Times*, 9 February 1887.
73. Journal, 3 February 1887.
74. Strauch to Congo Executive Committee, 2 February 1887, MP 83/2.
75. Journal, 4–8 February 1887.
76. Journal, 12 February 1887.

77. Journal, 19–20 February 1887. For Lenz see Oscar Lenz, *Wanderung in Afrika* (Vienna 1895).
78. Journal, 21 February 1887.
79. Hoffmann, *With Stanley in Africa*, p. 39.
80. Reginald Coupland, *The Exploitation of East Africa* (1939), pp. 459–75.
81. Norman R. Bennett, *Arab versus European* (1986), pp. 222–3.
82. Holmwood to F.O., 24 December 1886, 8 January 1887, F.O.84/1777.
83. Jerome Becker, *La vie en Afrique* (1887), ii, pp. 45–7.
84. Ibid., pp. 36–7.
85. Holmwood to Salisbury, 3 March 1887, F.O.C.P., C 5617, pp. 33–4.
86. Borchgrave to Stanley, 18 January 1887, SFA.
87. Journal, 22 February 1887.
88. Bontinck, *Tippu Tip*, pp. 140–41.
89. Holmwood to Salisbury, 3 March 1887, F.O.C.P., C 5617, pp. 33–4.
90. A copy of this contract is at APR 62/9. For other accounts of the genesis of the contract see J. R. Werner, *A Visit to Stanley's Rearguard*, pp. 308–10; Rose Troup, *With Stanley's Rearguard*, pp. 355–6; Ceulemans, *La question arabe*, pp. 98–108; W. R. Fox-Bourne, *The Other Side of the Emin Pasha Relief Expedition*, pp. 38–9; W. G. Barttelot, *Life of Edmund Musgrave Barttelot*, pp. 402–3.
91. Lord Vivian to Salisbury, 9 April 1887, F.O.C.P. C 5617, No. 87; Ceulemans, *La question arabe*, pp. 104–7.
92. Mackinnon to F.O., 10 February 1887, F.O.C.P. 5167, No. 55.
93. *The Times*, 31 March 1887.
94. Journal, 23 February 1887.
95. Journal, 24 February 1887; Sultan of Zanzibar to Mackinnon, 22 February 1887; Holmwood to Salisbury, 25, 26 February 1887, F.O.84/1851; Holmwood to Salisbury, 14 March 1887, F.O.84/1852.
96. Journal, 24 February 1887.
97. Journal, 25 February 1887.
98. IDA, i, p. 74.
99. Ibid.
100. Journal, 7 March 1887.
101. Stanley to de Winton, 2 March 1887, MP 86/29; Journal, 7 March 1887.
102. Journal, 7 March 1887.
103. Ibid.
104. Hutton memo, 27 November 1886, MP 17/68.
105. Salisbury memo, 22 December 1887, F.O.84/1837.
106. RA P 19/149, 30 December 1886; Anderson memo, 30 November 1886, F.O.84/1794.
107. His rank was to be general and his salary £1500 p.a. (Euan-Smith to Salisbury, 14 March 1890, F.O.84/2060). For Leopold's ideas see Leopold to Stanley, 30 December 1886, SFA.

108. See Kirk's remarks to Mackinnon: 'Personally I am sorry the Congo route has been selected' (Kirk to Mackinnon, 14 January 1887, MP 24/94). Joseph Thomson argued that since the Masailand route was the only sensible one, the choice of the Congo itinerary either argued for Stanley's lamentable ignorance or showed that there was an ulterior motive behind the Emin expedition (*The Times*, 12 February 1887).

109. Leopold to Mackinnon, 30 December 1886, Van Eetvelde Papers, 63/6; Leopold to Strauch, 6 January 1888, Strauch Papers 8802.

110. Memo by Anderson, 5 January 1887, F.O.C.P. 5617, p. 4; Salisbury to Baring, 20 January 1887, F.O.84/1878; de Winton to F.O., 25 March 1887, F.O.84/1860.

111. Documents diplomatiques français, 1st series 1871–1900, vi, No. 416, and vii, No. 218.

112. Mackinnon to Iddesleigh, 27 November 1886; EPRE committee to F.O., 25 March, 1 April 1887, MP 85/23.

113. Journal, 26 February 1887.

114. Journal, 2 February 1887.

115. Journal, 28 February 1887.

116. Emin to Mackay, 15 April 1887, enclosed in MacDonald to Salisbury, 26 September 1887, F.O.C.P. 5617, p. 63–6.

117. Emin to Felkin, 17 April 1887 in G. Schweinfurth, F. Ratzel, R. W. Felkin & G. Hartland, eds, *Emin Pasha in Central Africa* (1888), pp. 508–11. Cf. Emin to Felkin, 15 August 1887: 'If Mr Stanley brings me ammunition, I shall only use it for the consolidation of our position.' (ZA/RCS)

118. For Emin's progress from the start of the expedition until his meeting with Stanley see Smith, *Emin Pasha Expedition*, pp. 141–54.

Chapter ten

1. Journal, 26 February, 4 March 1887.

2. Bontinck, *Tippu Tip*, p. 148; cf. also *The Times*, 31 December 1889.

3. IDA, i, pp. 70–71.

4. Ibid., pp. 71–2.

5. Dorothy Middleton, ed., *The Diaries of A. J. Mounteney-Jephson* (1969), p. 70 (hereinafter Jephson Diary).

6. Maurice Denham Jephson, *An Anglo-Irish Miscellany: some records of the Jephsons of Mallow* (1964), Chapter 16.

7. Jephson Diary, p. 75 (28 February 1887).

8. Parke, *My Personal Experiences in Equatorial Africa* (1891), p. 24.

9. *Cape Times*, 7 March 1887.

10. Hoffmann MSS, Wellcome Library, MS. 6670.

11. *Cape Times*, 9 March 1887; *Cape Argus*, 11 March 1887; cf. also *The Times*, 31 March 1887.
12. IDA, i, pp. 74–5.
13. Journal, 10 March 1887.
14. Journal, 14 March 1887.
15. Bontinck, Tippu Tip, p. 141.
16. Journal, 11 March 1887.
17. Jephson Diary, p. 80.
18. Journal, 18–19 March 1887.
19. Fred Puleston, *African Drums* (1930), pp. 264–6.
20. Journal, 20 March 1887.
21. Ibid.
22. Journal, 21 March 1887.
23. Puleston, *African Drums*, pp. 271–2.
24. Journal, 21 March 1887.
25. Hoffmann MSS, Wellcome Library 6670, pp. 7–8. For the peoples encountered on the march see J. Maes & O. Boone, *Les peuplades du Congo Belge* (1935), pp. 48–50, 176–85, 294–7; Marcel Soret, *Les Kongo Nord-Occidentaux* (1951); Jan Vansina, *Kingdoms of the Savanna* (1966), pp. 102–9, *Introduction à l'Ethnographie du Congo*, Chapter 9.
26. Barttelot, *Life*, pp. 55–6.
27. Journal, 26 March 1887.
28. Journal, 28 March 1887.
29. Journal, 31 March 1887; Parke, *My Personal Experiences*, p. 36.
30. Ward, *Five Years with the Congo Cannibals*, p. 33.
31. Journal, 3 April 1887; IDA, i, p. 86.
32. Journal, 2, 8 April 1887; IDA, i, p. 85.
33. Journal, 5 April 1887.
34. Barttelot, *Life*, p. 80.
35. Parke, *My Personal Experiences*, pp. 38–9.
36. James S. Jameson, *The Story of the Rear Column*, pp. 14, 17, 18.
37. Journal, 5 April 1887.
38. See Bonny Diary, 6, 7, 26 February, SFA. 'Stanley treats me with awful contempt in everything I do up to the present.' (23 April, Bonny Diary)
39. Journal, 7 April 1887.
40. Barttelot, *Life*, pp. 81–2; Parke, *My Personal Experiences*, p. 39.
41. Jameson, *Rear Column*, p. 19.
42. Journal, 13 April 1887.
43. Journal, 15 April 1887.
44. Journal, 18 April 1887.
45. Jameson, *Rear Column*, p. 20.
46. Jephson Diary, p. 90.
47. Jameson, *Rear Column*, p. 24.

48. Bonny Diary, 18 April 1887, SFA.

49. Journal, 20 April 1887.

50. Barttelot, *Life*, p. 83.

51. Journal, 15 April 1887. Casement also impressed Jephson (Jephson Diary, pp. 86–92).

52. Hoffmann MSS, Wellcome Library, 6670, pp. 9–10.

53. *The Times*, 10 May 1887.

54. Parliamentary Papers, C 5906, pp. 4–5; Jephson Diary, p. 94.

55. Troup, *With Stanley's Rearguard*, p. 85.

56. Stanley to Mackinnon, 26 April 1887, MP 55/218.

57. Bentley, *Pioneering*, ii, pp. 145–6.

58. Ruth M. Slade, *English-Speaking Missions*, pp. 87–9.

59. Journal, 22 April 1887.

60. Stanley to Mackinnon, 26 April 1887, MP 55/218.

61. Stanley to Mackinnon, RA P 19/149a. In the final version he omitted the words 'carnal' and 'cantankerous' and added 'some of' before 'these missionaries'. As another Englishman at Stanley Pool reported: 'This unfortunate outburst of passion on Mr Stanley's part at an announcement that would have exasperated anyone is the only fault that anyone finds in him in connection with the expedition, for Englishmen, Arabs, Zanzibari and Bantu all testify to his untiring patience with the natives of the country.' (Wilmot-Brooke to X, April 1888, MP 85/19.) Clearly Graham Wilmot-Brooke had not been on the trek from Matadi!

62. Liebrechts, *Souvenirs d'Afrique*, pp. 169–74.

63. Cuypers, *Vangele*, p. 42.

64. Jephson Diary, pp. 94–5.

65. Journal, 22 April 1887.

66. Journal, 23 April 1887.

67. Troup, *With Stanley's Rearguard*, p. 87.

68. Bentley to Newton, 15 July 1887, in Newton to F.O., 16 September 1887, F.O.84/1845.

69. Journal, 23 April 1887.

70. *The Times*, 17 July 1887. Cf. A. J. Wauters, *Stanley's Emin Pasha Expedition* (1890), pp. 198–204.

71. Lagergren, *Mission and State in the Congo*, p. 101. In the view of some, Billington destroyed his own case by accepting the financial deal (*Whitehall Review*, 1 December 1887).

72. James P. White, 'The Sanford Exploring Expedition', *JAH* 8 (1967), pp. 291–302.

73. *Philadelphia Times*, 2 March 1890.

74. *Philadelphia Press*, 9 March 1890.

75. IDA, i, p. 91. For Tippu Tip's relations with Ngalyema see F. Bontinck,

'Tippu et Ngaliema', *Ngonge, Carnet de Sciences Humaines Kongo* (1972), pp. 27–8.

76. Journal, 25 April 1887.
77. Journal, 26 April 1887.
78. Puleston, *African Drums*, p. 273.
79. IDA, i, pp. 98–100.
80. RA P 19/149a; MP 86/27.
81. See Stanley to Rose Troup, 30 April 1887; Rose Troup to de Winton, 27 June 1887, MP 85/16.
82. Glave, *Six Years*, pp. 208–9; Parke, *My Personal Experiences*, p. 56. For Glave's career see also Robert Howard Russell, 'Glave's Career', *Century Magazine* 28 No. 50 (1895), pp. 865–8; 'Cruelty in the Congo Free State. Extracts from the journals of the late E. J. Glave', *Century Magazine* 32 No. 54 (1897), pp. 699–706.
83. Jameson, *Rear Column*, p. 15.
84. Barttelot, *Life*, pp. 119–21; Jameson, *Rear Column*, p. 62.
85. Parke, *My Personal Experiences*, p. 127. Barttelot claimed Stanley actually preferred blacks (Barttelot, *Life*, p. 118). Parke's explanation was that Stanley liked justice to be seen to be done (Parke, p. 513).
86. Stanley to EPRE, 25 March 1890, MP; cf. also *Autobiography*, p. 385. The refusal to praise collaborators on the grounds that they are professionals, while castigating as 'amateurish' anyone who falls short of a putative standard, is *par excellence* the sign of personality disturbance.
87. Miscellaneous EPRE notes, SFA.
88. Ibid.
89. Journal, 5 May 1887.
90. *The Times*, 10 May 1887.
91. Journal, 12 May 1887.
92. Journal, 13 May 1887.
93. Barttelot, *Life*, p. 118.
94. Jameson, *Rear Column*, p. 44. This was the most serious, but by no means the only, outbreak of looting on the passage to Stanley Falls. The entire expedition left a bad taste in the mouths of both indigenous peoples and the Congo State authorities (see Lord Vivian to F.O., 25 November 1888, F.O.84/1895).
95. Journal, 20 May 1887.
96. Jameson, *Rear Column*, p. 47; Jephson Diary, pp. 96–9.
97. *Autobiography*, p. 380. For an analysis see Hellinga, *Individualpsychologische Interpretatie*, p. 68.
98. Barttelot, *Life*, p. 98.
99. Journal, 20 May 1887.
100. Typically, only Parke (p. 55) tried to play down the incident.
101. Jameson, *Rear Column*, p. 47.

102. Barttelot, *Life*, p. 97.
103. Journal, 25 May 1887.
104. *The Standard*, 20 August 1887; *The Times*, 6, 17 June, 20 August 1887.
105. *The Scotsman*, 21 January 1887.
106. Stanley to EPRE committee, 31 May 1887, MP 86/29.
107. Journal, 30 May–1 June 1887.
108. For which see Holmwood to Salisbury, 25 February 1887, F.O.84/1851.
109. Journal, 12 June 1887. See also *Glasgow Herald*, 9 April 1889. For the Soko at this juncture see Joseph Hallin, *Les Ababua* (Brussels 1910), p. 59.
110. Jephson Diary, pp. 107–8; Parke, *My Personal Experiences*, p. 65; Troup, *With Stanley's Rearguard*, p. 136; *The Standard*, 20 August 1887.
111. Stanley to de Winton, 19 June 1887, MP 86/29.
112. Journal, 21, 22 June 1887.
113. Barttelot to his father, 1, 18 June 1887, MP 85/16.
114. Bontinck, *Tippu Tip*, pp. 142–3.
115. Ibid., p. 167.
116. Jameson, *Rear Column*, p. 74.
117. Stanley to Euan-Smith, 19 December 1888, F.O.6039/86.
118. Tippu Tip to Holmwood, 21 July 1887 in Holmwood to F.O., 28 March 1888, F.O.84/1906.
119. Barttelot, *Life*, pp. 230, 240–6; Jameson, *Rear Column*, pp. 293–4, 301–5; Ward, *Five Years*, p. 167; Troup, *With Stanley's Rearguard*, pp. 253–63.
120. Barttelot, *Life*, p. 104.
121. Barttelot to his father, 23 June 1887, MP 85/16; cf. also *The Times*, 20 August, 23 September 1887.
122. Barttelot, *Life*, p. 119.
123. Journal, 23–25 June 1887.
124. F.O.C.P.5617, pp. 1–48.
125. Barttelot, *Life*, pp. 108–9, 113.
126. Ibid., pp. 134–9; *The Times*, 28 November 1887.
127. Journal, 24 June 1887.
128. Barttelot, *Life*, pp. 120, 124–5, 138; Jameson, *Rear Column*, pp. 70–1.
129. Barttelot, *Life*, p. 119; cf. also Barttelot to Mackinnon, 27 March 1888, MP 55/218. Stanley's later doctored account is at IDA, i, pp. 117–26.

Chapter eleven

1. IDA, i, p. 131.
2. Journal, 26 June 1887.
3. Jephson Diary, p. 114; Parke, *My Personal Experiences*, p. 73. For the geography of the Ituri forest see J. M. Meesen, *Ituri* (1951), pp. 22–55.

4. Journal, 28 June 1887.
5. Journal, 29 June–1 July 1887.
6. Journal, 2–3 July 1887.
7. Journal, 4 July 1887. For the people in this area see Daryll Forde, *Ethnographic Survey of Africa*, Part 3 (1957). On the hostility of the peoples, the case for their defence was well put in the *Globe*, 6 April 1887: 'As for the hostility of the natives, it has to be remembered that these unfortunate people have been accustomed to find ruthless enemies in every armed company moving through their territories. It is not given to them to differentiate between one party and another; for all they could tell, Mr Stanley might have been another and worse sort of man-hunter. That they are cannibals does not militate against their characters!'
8. Journal, 5–6 July 1887.
9. Journal, 7 July 1887.
10. Journal, 8–12 July 1887.
11. Journal, 19 October 1876.
12. Journal, 14 July 1887.
13. G. Sautter, *De l'Atlantique au fleuve Congo* (1966), ii, pp. 965–82, 996–9.
14. Journal, 15–17 July 1887.
15. IDA, i, pp. 142–7.
16. Journal, 17–20 July 1887.
17. Journal, 22–24 July 1887.
18. See H. van Geluwe, *Les Bira* (1956); van Geluwe, *The Bali* (1960).
19. Journal, 22 July 1887.
20. Journal, 25 July 1887; IDA, i, pp. 159–60; Jephson Diary, p. 128.
21. Journal, 26–27 July 1887.
22. Journal, 28–30 July 1887.
23. Journal, 1 August 1887.
24. Journal, 2–4 August 1887.
25. Journal, 5–7 August 1887.
26. Journal, 9–12 August 1887; IDA, i, pp. 165–9.
27. Stanley to Mackinnon, 28 August 1888, MP 86/29.
28. Journal, 13–14 August 1887.
29. Journal, 14–17 August 1887.
30. Journal, 17 August 1887; IDA, i, pp. 178–9.
31. IDA, i, p. 180.
32. Journal, 20 August 1887.
33. Jephson Diary, p. 140.
34. Journal, 21 August 1887.
35. Journal, 22, 26, 28, 29 August 1887.
36. Hoffmann, *With Stanley*, p. 47.
37. Journal, 31 August, 1 September 1887.
38. Jephson Diary, pp. 118, 124.

39. Journal, 1–3 September 1887.
40. Journal, 3 September 1887.
41. Journal, 4 September 1887.
42. Jephson Diary, p. 145.
43. Journal, 8, 12 September 1887.
44. Journal, 5, 12 September 1887; IDA, i, pp. 191–4.
45. Journal, 14 September 1887.
46. Journal, 16–18 September 1887; Jephson Diary, p. 150; IDA, i, p. 196.
47. IDA, i, pp. 198–9.
48. For the pygmies of the Ituri see R. P. Trilles, *Les Pygmées de la Forêt Equatoriale* (1932); P. Schébesta, *Les Pygmées du Congo Belge* (1952); C. Turnbull, 'The Mbuti Pygmies of the Congo', in J. L. Gibbs, ed., *Peoples of Africa* (1965), pp. 289–301.
49. IDA, i, pp. 202–5.
50. Journal, 19–20 September 1887.
51. Parke, *My Personal Experiences*, p. 111; Jephson Diary, p. 152.
52. Journal, 19, 27 September 1887.
53. Parke, *My Personal Experiences*, pp. 113–14.
54. Journal, 29 September 1887.
55. Journal, 4 October 1887.
56. IDA, i, pp. 209–19.
57. Jephson Diary, pp. 159–60; Parke, *My Personal Experiences*, p. 111.
58. Journal, 7–9 October 1887.
59. Journal, 10–12 October 1887. There are graphic descriptions of the horror of the October starvation march in both Hoffmann's accounts (the unpublished one in the Wellcome Library, MS. 6670, and his book *With Stanley in Africa*). Respectively: 'The month of October will never be forgotten by any of us.' 'Many a time, wracked with hunger and with scarcely enough strength left to stumble along, we would come upon a village clearing, only to find it abandoned and its store of food in ashes. And the long weary trek would begin again.' (p. 41)
60. Journal, 15–16 October 1887.
61. Journal, 18 October 1887; Jephson Diary, pp. 166–7.
62. IDA, i, pp. 227–8.
63. Stanley to Euan-Smith, 19 December 1889, C 5906 Africa No. 4 (1890).
64. Journal, 19–21 October 1887; Jephson Diary, p. 170. Jumah was found hiding in a cornfield. Stanley ordered him hanged by two men whose lives he had endangered. 'These two accordingly took him a few paces back from the camp, and strung him up until he was dead.' (Journal, 21 October)
65. Journal, 22 October 1887.
66. Journal, 22, 25 October 1887; IDA, i, p. 235.
67. Jephson Diary, p. 172.
68. Journal, 26–28 October 1887.

69. Parke, *My Personal Experiences*, p. 128.
70. Note the mendacious 'flowing board' Stanley describes in IDA, i, p. 237.
71. Jephson Diary, p. 173.
72. Journal, 28 October 1887.
73. IDA, i, p. 230.
74. Journal, 29 October, 2 November 1887.
75. For the Balese see H. van Geluwe, 'Les Manvu-Mangata et Balese Munba', in Daryll Forde, ed., *Ethnographic Survey*.
76. Journal, 10 November 1887.
77. Journal, 7, 10, 18 November 1887.
78. Journal, 12–16 November 1887.
79. Jephson Diary, p. 172.
80. Ibid., p. 175.
81. Parke, *My Personal Experiences*, p. 181; Jephson Diary, p. 177.
82. Jephson Diary, p. 181.
83. Nelson to Stanley, 6 November 1887, SFA.
84. Journal, 16 November 1887.
85. Journal, 17–18 November 1887.
86. Journal, 19–23 November 1887.
87. See IDA, i, pp. 254–5 for a rare example of Stanley sympathising with both sets of people, the Ibwiri and the *wangwana*. See also Journal, 11 November 1887: 'While we pity the natives most heartily, it behoves us to remind ourselves of their [the *wangwana*'s] fast in the wilderness, their patient obedience, their unfaltering trust and implicit faith in us, their kindness while starving in bestowing on us unasked the ripest and largest of the wild fruit they had discovered and their altogether . . . noble bearing during those terrible days of adversity.'
88. IDA, i, pp. 267–8.
89. Journal, 1, 2, 7 December 1887.
90. Stanley to Mackinnon, 28 August 1888, MP 86/29.
91. T. Alexander Barnes, *The Wonderland of the Eastern Congo* (1922), p. 154.
92. IDA, i, pp. 284–9.
93. Journal, 9–10 December 1887; IDA, i, pp. 288–9.
94. Jephson Diary, p. 205.
95. Stanley to Mackinnon, 28 August 1888, MP 86/29.
96. Jephson Diary, p. 212.
97. Journal, 14 December 1887.
98. IDA, i, pp. 311–13.
99. Jephson Diary, p. 213.
100. See Roger Jones, *The Rescue of Emin Pasha* (1972), p. 174.
101. Journal, 15 December 1887.
102. IDA, i, pp. 316–19.
103. Ibid., pp. 319–20.

104. Ibid., pp. 320–25. After these ferocious clashes with the Wahuma, it is disconcerting to find him calling them later 'a fine-featured, amiable, quiet and friendly people, with whom we have never exchanged words'(!) (IDA, i, p. 371) It was not just with reference to his personal life that Stanley rewrote history.

105. IDA, i, pp. 325–6.

106. Journal, 25 December 1887.

Chapter twelve

1. Journal, 6 January 1888; Parke, *My Personal Experiences*, p. 155.

2. Parke, *My Personal Experiences*, p. 187.

3. Puleston, *African Drums*, pp. 302–3.

4. Parke, *My Personal Experiences*, pp. 129–97.

5. Journal, 9 February 1888.

6. Journal, 12 February 1888; Jephson Diary, p. 227.

7. Journal, 16–19 February 1888.

8. Parke, *My Personal Experiences*, pp. 198–206.

9. Jephson Diary, pp. 228–9.

10. IDA, i, pp. 345–8.

11. Journal, 11 April 1888.

12. IDA, i, pp. 357–61.

13. Ibid., pp. 362–3.

14. Parke, *My Personal Experiences*, p. 216.

15. Franz Stuhlmann, ed., *Die Tagebücher von Dr Emin Pascha*, 6 vols (1916–27), iv, pp. 37, 47–8, 60–61, 66.

16. Jephson Diary, p. 240; Hoffmann, *With Stanley*, p. 65.

17. *Tagebücher*, iv, p. 97.

18. Jephson Diary, pp. 245, 248–50.

19. IDA, i, pp. 371–2.

20. Parke, *My Personal Experiences*, p. 218.

21. Journal, 27 April 1888.

22. Jephson Diary, p. 211.

23. Ibid., p. 211; *Tagebücher*, iv, p. 98.

24. Journal, 29 April 1888.

25. Ibid.

26. Parke, *My Personal Experiences*, pp. 223–4 (Jephson Diary, p. 211 records the champagne at Lake Albert).

27. *Tagebücher*, iv, p. 98.

28. Journal, 30 April 1888.

29. Jones, *The Rescue of Emin Pasha*, p. 202.

30. Journal, 29 April, 11 May 1888.

31. C. H. Stigand, *Equatoria, the Lado Enclave* (1923), p. 175.
32. IDA, i, pp. 375–7; Jephson Diary, p. 251.
33. *Tagebücher*, iv, p. 102; Jephson Diary, p. 254; Parke, *My Personal Experiences*, pp. 224–5; IDA, i, pp. 377–82.
34. Stanley to Euan-Smith, 19 December 1889, C 5906 Africa No. 4 (1890).
35. Gaetano Casati, *Ten Years in Equatoria with Emin Pasha* (1891), ii, p. 340.
36. The offer is mentioned, but not explicitly written down, in Borchgrave to Stanley, 26 February 1887, APR, Congo, 102/17.
37. *Tagebücher*, iv, p. 105; Euan-Smith to Salisbury, 14 March 1890, F.O.84/2060.
38. Stanley to Euan-Smith, 19 December 1889, Africa No. 4 (1890), C 5906 p. 8.
39. *Tagebücher*, iv, pp. 101, 107.
40. Stanley to Mackinnon, 3 September 1888, MP.
41. Jephson Diary, p. 253.
42. IDA, i, pp. 383–4.
43. Casati, *Ten Years*, ii, pp. 21–93.
44. *Tagebücher*, iv, pp. 103, 105, 108.
45. Journal, 4 May 1888.
46. *Tagebücher*, iv, p. 105.
47. Journal, 20 May 1888.
48. Journal, 14 May 1888.
49. Journal, 18 May 1888.
50. Journal, 2 May 1888.
51. IDA, i, p. 396.
52. IDA, i, pp. 398–403.
53. Ibid., pp. 395–7.
54. *Autobiography*, pp. 356–7; cf. also IDA, i, pp. 401–2.
55. Journal, 20, 24 May 1888.
56. *Tagebücher*, iv, p. 119.
57. IDA, i, p. 404.
58. *Tagebücher*, iv, pp. 120–23.
59. Stanley proposed to Emin that the renegades, when captured, should be kept roped together (Stanley to Emin, 24 May 1888, *Tagebücher*, iv, p. 120).
60. Ruwenzori was not finally climbed until the early twentieth century (see Filippo de Filippi, *Ruwenzori: an account of the expedition of HRH Prince Luigi Amadeo of Savoy* (1909)).
61. IDA, i, p. 405. 'It strikes me as singular that neither Baker, Gessi, Mason or Emin discovered it long ago.' (Ibid., p. 406)
62. Parke, *My Personal Experiences*, pp. 217, 220; Jephson Diary, pp. 255–6.
63. Journal, 25 May 1888.
64. Journal, 26 May 1888.

65. IDA, i, p. 409.
66. Jephson Diary, p. 255.
67. IDA, i, pp. 410–11.
68. Journal, 29 May 1888. The Russian Marxist Plekhanov cited Stanley's long description of this dance as demonstrating that primitive dance was a complete and complex art-form (G. Plekhanov, *Selected Philosophical Works* (1976), ii, p. 625; v, pp. 345, 347).
69. Parkes, *My Personal Experiences*, p. 237.
70. Jephson Diary, p. 207.
71. IDA, i, p. 428–33.
72. Ibid., p. 436–8.
73. Ibid., p. 439.
74. Casati, *Ten Years*, ii, p. 159.
75. Casati, *Ten Years*, ii, p. 161.
76. 'Who can say why the votaries of science, though eminently kindly in their social relations, are so angular of character? In my analysis of the scientific nature I am constrained to associate with it, as compared with that of men who are more Christians than scientists, a certain hardness, or rather indelicacy of feeling. They strike me as being somewhat unsympathetic, and capable of only cold friendship, coolly indifferent to the warmer human feelings. I may best express what I mean by saying that I think they are more apt to feel an affection for one's bleached skull and frame of unsightly bones, than for what is divine within a man. If one talks about the inner beauty, which to some of us is the only beauty worth having, they are apt to yawn and to return an apologetic and compassionate smile.' (IDA, ii, p. 147)
77. Journal, 16 June 1888.
78. Parke, *My Personal Experiences*, p. 244.
79. Ibid., p. 245.
80. Journal, 20 June 1888.
81. Journal, 22, 26, 28 June 1888; IDA, i, pp. 443–5.
82. Journal, 29 June 1888.
83. Journal, 6 July 1888; IDA, i, p. 447.
84. Journal, 8, 11, 13 July 1888; IDA, i, pp. 448–9.
85. IDA, i, pp. 450–51.
86. Journal, 21 July 1888.
87. IDA, i, pp. 453–5.
88. Journal, 26 July 1888.
89. IDA, i, pp. 455–6.
90. Ibid., pp. 457–9.
91. Hoffmann, *With Stanley*, p. 78.
92. Journal, 8 June 1888.
93. IDA, i, p. 468.

Chapter thirteen

1. *New York Tribune*, 4 December 1890; *Pall Mall Gazette*, 18 November 1890.
2. Barttelot, *Life*, pp. 112–15.
3. Ward, *My Life with Stanley's Rearguard*, pp. 30–31.
4. Troup, *With Stanley's Rearguard*, p. 145.
5. *Whitehall Review*, 1 December 1887.
6. Barttelot to Mackinnon, 15 August 1887 in *The Times*, 28 November 1887.
7. Bontinck, *Tippu Tip*, p. 143.
8. Quoted in Tony Gould, *In Limbo* (1978), p. 57.
9. Glave, *Six Years*.
10. Jameson, *Rear Column*, pp. 80, 207; Troup, *With Stanley's Rearguard*, p. 203; *The Times*, 14, 15 November 1889.
11. Barttelot, *Life*, pp. 228–31.
12. Journal, 18 August 1888.
13. Troup to de Winton, 18 October 1887, MP 85/17.
14. Barttelot to Sir Walter Barttelot, 19 March 1888, MP 85/17.
15. Parke, *My Personal Experiences*, p. 494.
16. Journal, 18 August 1888.
17. Jameson to Mackinnon, 10 April 1888; Barttelot to Mackinnon, 28 March 1888, MP 85/17.
18. Troup, *With Stanley's Rearguard*, p. 225.
19. Barttelot, *Life*, pp. 288–9.
20. Gould, *In Limbo*, pp. 100–4; see also Troup, *With Stanley's Rearguard*, pp. 246–7; *The Times*, 14, 15 November 1890.
21. IDA, i, p. 474. Barttelot did not miss a trick; he even sent soap and candles downriver (*The Times*, 14, 15 November 1890).
22. Journal, 18 August 1888.
23. Journal, 17 August 1888.
24. Journal, 18 August 1888.
25. Ward, *My Life*, pp. 30, 96, 119.
26. Ward to Mackinnon, 6, 17 May 1888, MP 85/18.
27. Ward, *My Life*, p. 125.
28. On the death of Barttelot, he journeyed to the coast again to cable for instructions. He was ordered by the committee to return to Stanley Falls, leave all Emin's goods there, sell the remainder to the Congo State, then bring Bonny and the Zanzibaris back to the coast. He arrived at Stanley Pool to learn that Stanley had arrived at Banalya and taken Bonny and the others on to Lake Albert. He then returned to England via the Canaries (Ward to Mackinnon, 17, 26 October, 3 November 1888, 20 April, 12 May 1889; Ward to EPRE committee, July 1889, MP 85/21–22).

29. For this dislike see Jameson, *Rear Column*, pp. 253–9; Barttelot, *Life*, p. 170; *The Times*, 15 November 1890.

30. For details of Jameson's voyage to Kasongo and sojourn there see Jameson, *Rear Column*, pp. 226–301; cf. also Bontinck, *Tippu Tip*, p. 143 and MP 88/36.

31. Jameson, *Rear Column*, p. 291.

32. Barttelot, *Life*, op. cit.

33. Ibid.

34. Alfred J. Swann, *Fighting the Slave Hunters in Central Africa* (1910), pp. 173–5.

35. A. J. Wauters, 'Les derniers événements du Haut Congo', *Le Mouvement Géographique* 5 (1888), p. 81–3.

36. Pierre Salomon, *Le Voyage de Van Kerkhoven aux Stanley Falls et au camp de Yambuya 1888* (1978).

37. Vivian to Salisbury, 25 August, 25 September 1888, F.O.123/244. For further evidence of the Belgian dislike of Tippu Tip see Barttelot, *Life*, p. 220; Ward, *My Life*, p. 119; Jameson, *Rear Column*, pp. 293–4.

38. Jameson, *Rear Column*, p. 306.

39. Cuypers, *Vangele*, p. 54.

40. J. R. Werner, *A Visit to Stanley's Rearguard*, p. 271.

41. Barttelot to Mackinnon, 4 June 1888, MP 85/17.

42. See *East Anglian Times*, 6 October 1888; *Cardiff Weekly Mail*, 29 September 1888; *Kentish Independent*, 29 September 1888.

43. *Daily Telegraph*, 16 October 1888.

44. *The Scotsman*, 16 October 1888.

45. *The Times*, 18 September 1888.

46. *Daily Telegraph*, 18 November, 17 December 1888; *The Times*, 15, 18 December 1888; *Nottingham Evening Post*, 19 December 1888; *Morning Post*, 17, 18 December 1888.

47. *Manchester Guardian*, 19 December 1888.

48. *Daily Telegraph*, 15 September 1888.

49. *The Times*, 20 December 1888.

50. *Le Voltaire*, 8 October 1888; *France Nouvelle*, 21 October 1888. The *York Evening Post*, 13 October 1888, commenting on Brazza's opinion, said that since Brazza was a great annexer 'he naturally thinks that Stanley, of whom he was at one time intensely jealous, will do the same.'

51. *Globe*, 23 October 1888; *Morning Post*, 19 October 1888; *Evening News*, 18 October 1888; *Morning Advertiser*, 19 October 1888.

52. *The Standard*, 19 September 1888.

53. Leopold to Queen Victoria, 28 August 1887, RA Y 161/26; same to same, 23 December 1888, RA Y 161/43; Leopold to Stanley, December 1888, MP 86/25; Ponsonby to Mackenzie, 21 December 1888, MP 83/8.

54. *The Times*, 19 October, 21 December 1888; *Daily News*, 17 September

1888; *Whitehall Review*, 29 November 1888; *Daily Telegraph*, 22 September 1888.

55. *Philadelphia Evening Telegraph*, 15 September 1888; Ceulemans, *La question arabe*, p. 138. Van Eetvelde told Lord Vivian that Leopold's commitment to Stanley's success was as strong as ever (Van Eetvelde to Vivian, 12 May 1888, MP 87/33). Leopold to Stanley, December 1888, MP 86/25 seems to bear this out. But Van Eetvelde also told Vivian that any further expedition sent out for Emin's relief would have to proceed via the east coast, since the Congo State had had nothing but trouble, anxiety and vexation with missionaries, tribesmen and Arabs ever since Stanley's expedition arrived (Vivian to Salisbury, 25 September 1888, MP 87/34).

56. *The Times*, 25 September 1888; *Glasgow Herald*, 29 September 1888; *Manchester Guardian*, 26 September 1888; *Whitehall Review*, 22 December 1887 had already raised this possibility.

57. *St James's Gazette*, 3, 16 April 1889; *Reynolds*, April 1889; *Truth*, 25 October 1888; *Bazaar*, 28 September 1888.

58. *The Times*, 1 October, 3, 5 November 1888.

59. 'On the threshold of the Dark Continent . . . stand the civilised races eyeing each other with all the hatred that jealousy and greed can inspire. The terra incognita is regarded principally as a treasury to be looted.' (*Cork Examiner*, 3 October 1888)

60. *St James's Gazette*, 26 January 1889; *Daily News*, 25 March 1889; *Evening Standard*, 25 March 1889; *Army and Navy Gazette*, 2 March 1889; *Leeds Mercury*, 29 January 1889.

61. *Echo*, 6 April 1889.

62. *John Bull*, 15 June 1889.

63. *Truth*, 11 April 1889.

64. *The Standard*, 19 September 1888.

65. *Daily News*, 28 September 1888.

66. *Daily News*, 11 October 1888.

67. *Daily News*, 28 September 1888; *Liverpool Echo*, 28 September 1888.

68. *Liverpool Echo*, 28, 29 September 1888.

69. *Star*, 2 October 1888.

70. *Pall Mall*, 28 September 1888.

71. Fox-Bourne, *The Other Side*, p. 130.

72. Barttelot, *Life*, p. 350.

73. Journal, 17 August 1888; *The Times*, 10 November 1890.

74. Barttelot, *Life*, pp. 350–51.

75. IDA, i, pp. 490–91.

76. Jameson, *Rear Column*, p. 359.

77. Jameson to Mackinnon, 3 August 1888, MP 85/19.

78. Bontinck, *Tippu Tip*, p. 145. See also the detailed transcript of the court martial at MP 88/35.

79. Ibid., p. 146.
80. Ward to Mackinnon, 19 August 1888, MP 85/19; cf. also MP 83/8.
81. IDA, i, p. 483.

Chapter fourteen

1. IDA, i, p. 489.
2. Jameson, *Rear Column*, pp. 365–6; cf. also Bonny to Jameson, August 1888, MP 85/20.
3. Stanley to Mackinnon, 3 September 1888, MP 85/20; cf. also Mackinnon to Leopold, 20 April 1889, APR Congo 82/78.
4. Journal, 18 August 1888.
5. Ibid.
6. Miscellaneous EPRE notes, SFA.
7. Stanley to Tippu Tip, 17 August 1888, enclosed in Stanley to Mackinnon, 7 December 1888, MP 85/22. Cf. also Ward, *My Life*, p. 139.
8. Tippu to Holmwood, 25 August 1888, F.O.84/1911; Euan-Smith to Salisbury, 21 December 1888, F.O.84/1913; Vivian to Salisbury, 19 January 1889, F.O.C.P. 5867 (1889) No. 89.
9. *The Times*, 3 April 1889, 15 November 1890. Traces of the Yambuya camp were still visible when Delcommune went up the Aruwimi in 1889 (Delcommune, *Vingt Années*, i, p. 319).
10. Stairs to Barttelot, 12 June 1888, SFA.
11. Bonny Diary, 25–26 August 1888, SFA.
12. IDA, ii, pp. 12–13.
13. Journal, 29 August 1888.
14. Journal, 4 September 1888; IDA, ii, pp. 17–19.
15. Ibid.
16. Journal, 6–7 September 1888, IDA, ii, pp. 20–22.
17. Journal, 11–13 September 1888.
18. Journal, 18–21 September 1888; IDA, ii, p. 24.
19. For an analysis of the arrows of the Ituri peoples and their poisons see Parke, *My Personal Experiences*, pp. 304–23. See also R. P. Trilles, *Les Pygmées de la Forêt Equatoriale*, pp. 449, 495. A long correspondence was engendered at the RGS about the exact nature of these poisons. Felkin thought that Stanley's men must have died a lingering death from tetanus rather than the Tikki arrows, as these killed within twenty minutes. German geographers also doubted Stanley's story that the poison for the arrows came from formic acid (see *PRGS* 11 N.S. (1889), pp. 261–72, 379–85).
20. Hoffmann, *With Stanley*, p. 94.
21. Journal, 16 September 1888.

22. IDA, ii, p. 27.
23. Journal, 26 September 1888.
24. Journal, 27 September 1888.
25. Journal, 1 October 1888.
26. Journal, 24 September 1888.
27. Journal, 27 September 1888.
28. Journal, 28 September 1888.
29. Journal, 16 September 1888.
30. Journal, 5 October 1888.
31. IDA, ii, p. 33.
32. Journal, 18 October 1888; IDA, ii, p. 34.
33. Bonny Diary, 13 October 1888, SFA.
34. Journal, 10 October 1888.
35. Bonny Diary, 9 October 1888, SFA.
36. Journal, 16 October 1888.
37. Ibid.
38. Journal, 19 October 1888.
39. Journal, 21–23 October 1888.
40. Journal, 25 October 1888; IDA, ii, pp. 38–9.
41. Journal, 6 March 1889; IDA, i, pp. 335–6.
42. Hoffmann, *With Stanley*, pp. 96–7.
43. Journal, 29 October 1888; IDA, ii, pp. 40–43.
44. IDA, ii, pp. 46–7.
45. Journal, 4 November 1888.
46. Bonny Diary, 29 October 1888.
47. Journal, 6–7 November 1888.
48. Journal, 8 November 1888.
49. Hoffmann, *With Stanley*, pp. 98–9.
50. Parke, *My Personal Experiences*, p. 345.
51. Hoffmann, *With Stanley*, pp. 101–2.
52. Journal, 10–13 November 1888; IDA, ii, pp. 49–50.
53. Journal, 14–19 November 1888.
54. Journal, 20–21 November 1888.
55. Bonny Diary, 16–17 November 1888.
56. Journal, 22 November 1888.
57. Journal, 24 November 1888; IDA, ii, pp. 55–8.
58. Journal, 1–4 December 1888.
59. Journal, 9 December 1888.
60. Journal, 14 December 1888.
61. Ibid.
62. Journal, 15–16 December 1888.
63. Journal, 20 December 1888.
64. Parke, *My Personal Experiences*, p. 335. Cf. Puleston, *African Drums*, pp.

310–11: 'Stanley went clean through this same infernal forest [Ituri] but if he lived till doomsday he could not give you one fragment of an idea of the daily torture he and all his men endured.'

65. Journal, 25–27 December 1888.
66. 'There is no doubt that William is a bad servant, being both a thief and a liar, in fact the most untrustworthy servant I ever met.' (Bonny Diary, 6 December 1888, SFA)
67. Memorandum dated 11 December 1888, Hoffmann Papers, SFA. Bonny recorded that Hoffmann had obtained goods dishonestly in Stanley's name all the way along the Congo, but that Stanley always forgave his servant provided he confessed. (Bonny Diary, 11 December 1888, SFA)
68. Bonny Diary, 28 November 1888.
69. Journal, 31 December 1888.
70. 'I was surprised, sorry, and ashamed to hear a man make such a remark when we are both on the verge of death by starvation.' (Bonny Diary, 16 December 1888)
71. Journal, 7 January 1889; Bonny Diary, 6 January 1889.
72. Journal, 10 January 1889.
73. IDA, ii, pp. 105–8.
74. *New York Herald*, 5 May 1890.
75. For Jephson's record of events from May 1888 to January 1889 see A. J. Mounteney Jephson, *Emin Pasha and the Rebellion at the Equator* (1890). Jones, *The Rescue of Emin Pasha*, pp. 274–7, largely recapitulates this. There is a more widely based account in Smith, *Emin Pasha Relief Expedition*, pp. 208–43.
76. *The Times*, 29 June 1888.
77. Jephson, *Emin Pasha*, pp. 388–400.
78. Jephson Diary, p. 329. For Jephson's disgust and anger on receipt of this letter see also *Tagebücher*, iv, pp. 208–9.
79. Stanley to Mackinnon, 5 August 1889, MP 86/29.
80. *Tagebücher*, 14 January 1889, iv, p. 202.
81. Journal, 8 April 1889.

Chapter fifteen

1. Bonny Diary, 11 January 1889.
2. Journal, 11 January 1889.
3. IDA, ii, p. 119.
4. Parke, *My Personal Experiences*, pp. 359–60. The other snag about the Maxim gun was that it could be thrown out of gear by becoming choked with sand. (Troup, *With Stanley's Rearguard*, p. 43)
5. Journal, 28 January 1889.

6. Bonny Diary, 2 December 1888.
7. *Tagebücher*, iv, pp. 206–7.
8. *Tagebücher*, iv, p. 191.
9. Casati, *Ten Years*, ii, pp. 216–17.
10. Journal, 6–11 February 1889.
11. IDA, ii, p. 131.
12. Stanley to Emin, 7 February 1889, *Tagebücher*, iv, pp. 218–20.
13. IDA, ii, p. 137.
13. Jephson Diary, p. 332.
15. *Tagebücher*, iv, pp. 214–18; Casati, *Ten Years*, ii, pp. 377–82.
16. *Tagebücher*, iv, p. 225. Stanley was sufficiently intrigued by Emin's second-in-command to leave a long description of him. 'He is six feet high, large of girth, about 50 years old, black as coal. I am rather inclined to like him. The malignant and deadly conspirator is always lean. I read in this man's face indolence, a tendency to pet his animalism. He is a man to be led, not to conspire. Feed him with good things to eat and plenty to drink, Selim would be faithful. Ah, the sleepy eye of the full-stomached man! This is a man to eat and sleep and snore, in the bed-chamber, to call for coffee fifty times a day, and native beer by the gallon: to sip and sip and smile, and then to sleep again; and so and so to his grave.' (IDA, ii, p. 138) Lugard dissented from this judgement: 'An enormous Sudanese – stout and of a giant's stature. Mr Stanley describes him as a man given up to good living and ease, but he struck me rather as a man of considerable character.' (Frederick Lugard, *The Rise of Our East African Empire*, ii, p. 209)
17. Journal, 17, 25 February 1889.
18. Journal, 26 February 1889.
19. IDA, ii, p. 143.
20. Parke, *My Personal Experiences*, pp. 374, 381.
21. IDA, ii, p. 144.
22. Journal, 22 February 1889.
23. Journal, 26 February 1889.
24. IDA, ii, p. 151.
25. Journal, 10 March 1889.
26. Journal, 23 February 1889.
27. Casati, *Ten Years*, ii, p. 237.
28. Journal, 28 February 1889.
29. Journal, 1 March 1889.
30. Journal, 5 March 1889.
31. Ibid.
32. Journal, 6 March 1889.
33. Journal, 21 March 1889.
34. Journal, 22 March 1889.

35. Journal, 6, 17 March 1889.
36. Journal, 13–14 March 1889.
37. Journal, 15 March 1889.
38. Journal, 20 March 1889; IDA, ii, p. 145.
39. Journal, 19 March 1889.
40. IDA, ii, p. 159.
41. *Tagebücher*, iv, pp. 237–45.
42. Journal, 26 March 1889.
43. Ibid.
44. IDA, ii, pp. 161–3.
45. Casati, *Ten Years*, ii, p. 239.
46. Parke, *My Personal Experiences*, p. 393.
47. *Tagebücher*, iv, p. 242.
48. Baring to F.O., 25 January 1890, F.O.84/2057.
49. Euan-Smith to Salisbury, 14 March 1890, F.O.84/2060.
50. Journal, 26 March 1889.
51. Journal, 29 March 1889.
52. Journal, 31 March 1889.
53. It is a sign of Parke's lack of perception (evident throughout in his naïve and uncritical evaluation of Stanley) that he identified Vita Hassan (a minor figure in Emin's counsels) rather than Casati as 'the Pasha's right-hand man' (Parke, *My Personal Experiences*, p. 374).
54. Casati, *Ten Years*, ii, pp. 239–40; IDA, ii, pp. 169–71.
55. Journal, 31 March 1889.
56. Ibid.
57. Ibid.
58. Journal, 3 April 1889.
59. Ibid.
60. Journal, 4 April 1889; cf. also Parke, *My Personal Experiences*, p. 379.
61. IDA, ii, pp. 181–4.
62. Journal, 5 April 1889.
63. *Tagebücher*, iv, pp. 247–8; Casati, *Ten Years*, ii, p. 249.
64. Casati, *Ten Years*, ii, p. 249.
65. Parke, *My Personal Experiences*, p. 402.
66. Journal, 5 April 1889.
67. Casati, *Ten Years*, ii, p. 250.
68. Journal, 5 April 1889.
69. Casati, *Ten Years*, ii, p. 249.
70. *Tagebücher*, iv, pp. 247–8.
71. Jephson Diary, p. 342.
72. Journal, 5 April 1889.
73. Journal, 6–7 April 1889.
74. Bonny Diary, 8 April 1889, SFA.

75. Journal, 8–9 April 1889; IDA, ii, pp. 190–91.
76. Journal, 10 April 1889.
77. Lugard, *The Rise*, ii, pp. 201–2; cf. also Margery Perham, ed., *The Diaries of Lord Lugard* (1959), ii, pp. 321–31.
78. Parke, *My Personal Experiences*, p. 406; Jephson Diary, p. 343.
79. *The Times*, 14 July 1892.

Chapter sixteen

1. Journal, 13 April 1889; Jephson Diary, pp. 345–6; Parke, *My Personal Experiences*, pp. 411–21.
2. Parke, *My Personal Experiences*, p. 416.
3. *Tagebücher*, iv, pp. 280–81.
4. Jephson Diary, pp. 347–8.
5. IDA, ii, pp. 195–8; Casati, *Ten Years*, ii, pp. 256–7.
6. Journal, 2 May 1889.
7. Parke, *My Personal Experiences*, pp. 419–20; Jephson Diary, p. 349.
8. 'Stairs went to Pasha this afternoon and asked when the affair to get carriers for him should be carried out. Pasha replied, "I do not care for it, my people do not deserve any help, but seeing that you want a slave, I don't care if I do help you." This is so characteristic of the Pasha. We have given the Pasha and Casati and Vita twenty-two of our carriers, we have about 25 supernumeraries without loads. Is it credible that Lt. Stairs should be in want of a carrier? On hearing this I sent Lt. Stairs to say decidedly that Emin Pasha should speak more positively.' (Journal, 3 May 1889)
9. Jephson Diary, pp. 350–51.
10. Journal, 4 May 1889.
11. For Vita Hassan see Vol. 2 of his book *Emin Pascha, die Aequatorial Provinz und der Mahdismus: Emin in Kampfe mit dem Mahdismus und seine ruckkehr mit Stanley's Expedition* (1895) esp. pp. 138–45, 157–61, 180–99.
12. IDA, ii, p. 201.
13. Journal, 5 May 1889.
14. Journal, 6 May 1889.
15. Journal, 8 May 1889; IDA, ii, p. 202.
16. Jephson Diary, p. 354; Parke, *My Personal Experiences*, pp. 424–33. Cf. also IDA, ii, p. 235.
17. Casati, *Ten Years*, ii, pp. 258–9.
18. Parl. Papers C.5906, p. 13.
19. IDA, ii, p. 203.
20. Ibid, pp. 231–2.
21. Journal, 11 May 1889.

22. Journal, 12–13 May 1889.
23. Journal, 13–15 May 1889.
24. Add. MSS. 43, 411 f.27. Emin had visited the Semliki before but not in this area (Schweinfurth, *Emin Pasha in Central Africa*, p. 507).
25. Stanley to RGS, 17 August 1889, RGS.
26. IDA, ii, pp. 235–9; Hoffmann, *With Stanley*, pp. 137–8.
27. IDA, ii, p. 239–41.
28. Journal, 20 May 1889.
29. Journal, 24 May 1889.
30. Journal, 26 May 1889.
31. Journal, 27 May 1889.
32. Hoffmann, *With Stanley*, p. 133.
33. Journal, 26 May 1889.
34. Journal, 25 May 1889.
35. IDA, ii, pp. 247–51; Casati, *Ten Years*, ii, p. 266.
36. Journal, 30 May 1889.
37. Jean-Pierre Halet, *Pygmy Kitabu* (1973), pp. 37–8, 40–43.
38. Journal, 3–5 June 1889.
39. Stairs to RGS, 8 June 1889, RGS.
40. IDA, ii, pp. 259–61.
41. Randall M. Packard, *Chiefship and Cosmology* (1981), pp. 59–60.
42. Casati, *Ten Years*, ii, p. 267.
43. Journal, 13 June 1889; *Tagebücher*, iv, p. 315.
44. Jephson Diary, pp. 361–2.
45. 'The Pasha knew that Stanley was going to make this arrangement weeks ago and had said it was just the thing, but when it came to the point he wanted Stanley to give all his boys Remington rifles but did not want to help us. This very naturally angered Stanley for the Pasha never will help him in any way and does all he can to oppose his plans. He never, too, seems to learn wisdom from experience and always says just the things calculated most to anger Stanley.' (Jephson, ibid.; cf. also Parke, *My Personal Experiences*, p. 439)
46. Journal, 16 June 1889.
47. Ibid.
48. Journal, 13–15 June 1889; *Tagebücher*, iv, p. 317.
49. IDA, ii, pp. 265–316.
50. Ibid., pp. 316–19.
51. Stanley to RGS, 17 August 1889, RGS.
52. IDA, ii, pp. 321–2.
53. Hoffmann, *With Stanley*, p. 147; Parke, *My Personal Experiences*, pp. 446–7.
54. Casati, *Ten Years*, ii, p. 270.
55. Parke, *My Personal Experiences*, pp. 449–50.
56. See Sir John Gray, 'Unpublished History of Ankole' (RCS), pp. 48–50.

For oral testimony from an African eyewitness concerning Stanley's journey through Ankole see RCS, MSS 45/146702. Cf. also *UJ* 29 (1965), pp. 185–92 and F. Lukyn Williams, 'Early Explorers in Ankole', *UJ* 2 (1934–5), p. 196.

57. Journal, 7 July 1889; IDA, ii, p. 337.
58. Journal, 10 July 1889; Casati, *Ten Years*, ii, p. 276. For the civil war in Uganda see *The Times*, 12 January 1889; *Daily News*, 14 January 1889.
59. Journal, 13 July 1889.
60. Journal, 15–16 July 1889.
61. Stanley to RGS, 17 August 1889, RGS.
62. Journal, 20–21 July 1889; IDA, ii, pp. 348–9.
63. Parke, *My Personal Experiences*, p. 458.
64. Jephson Diary, p. 383.
65. Jephson, *Emin Pasha and the Rebellion at the Equator*, p. 465.
66. Journal, 23 July 1889.
67. Parke, *My Personal Experiences*, p. 459.
68. IDA, ii, pp. 352–3.
69. Carl Peters, *New Light on Dark Africa* (1891), pp. 344–6.
70. Casati, *Ten Years*, ii, p. 281.
71. Hoffmann, *With Stanley*, p. 149.
72. Jephson Diary, p. 386; IDA, ii, pp. 374–5.
73. Jephson Diary, pp. 389–90.
74. Journal, 31 July 1889.
75. Journal, 8 August 1889.
76. Stanley to Euan-Smith, 19 December 1889, Africa No. 4 (1890), C 5906.
77. Journal, 7 August 1889.
78. Journal, 12 August 1889.
79. IDA, ii, p. 383.
80. Parke, *My Personal Experiences*, p. 469.
81. Jephson Diary, p. 393.
82. Casati, *Ten Years*, ii, p. 284.
83. Stanley to British Consul, 11 November 1889 in Smith to Salisbury, 28 November 1889, F.O.84/1981.
84. IDA, ii, pp. 383–5.
85. Journal, 16 August 1889.
86. For this meeting see J. W. Harrison (Mackay's sister), *The Story of the Life of Mackay of Uganda* (1898), p. 301. For his exploration see A. M. Mackay, 'Boat Voyage along the western shore of Lake Victoria', *PRGS* 6 (1884), pp. 273–83.
87. Journal, 28 August 1889.
88. Parke, *My Personal Experiences*, pp. 475–82.
89. Journal, 30 August 1889.
90. Stanley to Mackinnon, 31 August 1889, MP 55/218.

91. Frederick Jackson, *Early Days in Africa* (1930), p. 222. For further details on the Peters and Jackson expeditions see *Daily News*, 26 January 1889.

92. Mackay to Mackinnon, 2 September 1889, RA P 19/198.

93. *Tagebücher*, iv, pp. 417–20, 426–7, 438.

94. Casati, *Ten Years*, ii, p. 292.

95. Journal, 31 August 1889.

96. Stanley to British Consul, 29 August 1889 in Portal to Salisbury, 2 November 1889, F.O.84/1981; Emin to President of Council in Cairo, 28 August 1889, F.O.84/1982. For Stanley's dithyrambic attack on Emin see IDA, ii, pp. 208–9. Cf. also Journal, 24 August 1889: 'I knew quite half a dozen fellows on the Congo who could not have missed raising themselves very high in the world's opinion had they been in Emin's place – but Emin's conduct throughout I can only compare to that of a drunken captain of a ship of sots.'

97. Journal, 4 September 1889.

98. Peters, *New Light on Dark Africa*, p. 360. But Peters was hardly in a position to talk. When he visited Jackson's camp in his absence, he opened his personal letters and read them (Jackson, *Early Days*, p. 250).

99. Journal, 13–14 September 1889; cf. also Portal to Salisbury in F.O.84/1981.

100. Journal, 18 September 1889; IDA, ii, pp. 393–5.

101. Hoffmann, *With Stanley*, p. 155. For the toll inflation see IDA, ii, p. 403.

102. IDA, ii, pp. 397–8; Hoffmann, *With Stanley*, pp. 155–6.

103. Journal, 21 September 1889.

104. Journal, 22–23 September 1889; Jephson Diary, pp. 402–5.

105. Journal, 24 September 1889; Casati, *Ten Years*, ii, p. 295.

106. Journal, 29 September 1889.

107. Journal, 4, 10, 15 September 1889.

108. Journal, 18–19 October 1889; Casati, *Ten Years*, ii, p. 301. Schynse first met Stanley on the Lower Congo in March 1887. He returned to Algiers, Lisbon and Marseilles, thence to Zanzibar and Usambiro, where he met Stanley again at Mackay's mission (*The Times*, 19 April 1890).

109. Père Schynse, *A Travers l'Afrique*, pp. 144–6.

110. Journal, 21–24 October 1889.

111. Schynse, *A Travers l'Afrique*, pp. 160–74.

112. Casati, *Ten Years*, ii, p. 306.

113. Journal, 26–30 October 1889.

114. Schynse, *A Travers l'Afrique*, pp. 181–9.

115. Peters, *New Light*, pp. 522–3.

116. Schynse, *A Travers l'Afrique*, p. 194.

117. Ibid., p. 187.

118. Journal, 5 November 1889; Schynse, *A Travers l'Afrique*, pp. 201–8.

119. Journal, 9 November 1889; Casati, *Ten Years*, ii, p. 310.

120. Schynse, *A Travers l'Afrique*, pp. 221–2.

121. See *The Times*, 22, 25, 26 November, 4 December 1889. For Schmidt see R. Schmidt, *Geschichte des Araberaufstanden in Ost-Afrika*, pp. 121–40, 335–48.

122. Schynse, *A Travers l'Afrique*, pp. 236–56.

123. Journal, 18 November 1889.

124. *Tagebücher*, iv, p. 426. Emin found Stanley and his officers all suffering from a raging Germanophobia (*Tagebücher*, iv, pp. 428, 433).

125. Journal, 22 November 1889.

126. RGS 5/1; RGS 16/9; *St James's Gazette*, 18 January 1889. Vizetelly had been over-confident that he would be the first English-speaking journalist to interview Stanley (see *New York Herald*, 3, 4, 6 November 1889). Cf. also E. H. Vizetelly, *From Cyprus to Zanzibar by the Egyptian Delta*, pp. 428–53. For a German view see W. Langheld, *Zwanzig Jahre in deutschen Kolonien* (1909), pp. 21–101.

127. Thomas Stevens, *Scouting for Stanley in East Africa* (1890).

128. *Tagebücher*, iv, p. 437.

129. His attitude to Vizetelly is well conveyed in a journal entry on 2 December 1889: 'Mr Vizetelly gave way today to a habit which I fear is chronic with him and became madly abusive and beyond control. He threatened to shoot one of his boys and flourished a revolver in such an excitable state that when it was reported to me he had become dangerous, I ordered him to be disarmed and put under guard.'

130. Journal, 2–4 December 1889. For Wissmann's earlier movements see *The Times*, 19, 24 October 1889. Stanley recorded the following verdict at the Kingani when meeting Wissmann: 'As I saw Emin Pasha before the well-spread table, his face all aglow with pleasure, and bronzed Captain Casati bowing and nodding with a goblet of sparkling wine in hand . . . it became very clear to me that here my duty ended.' (Stanley's memo of 19 December 1889 in RCS/ZA)

Chapter seventeen

1. For the Wissmann–Peters rivalry see *The Times*, 19, 24 October 1889; *New York Herald*, 24 October 1889; cf. also *Daily News*, 31 October 1889; *York Evening Press*, 25 October 1889; *Dundee Advertiser*, 24 October 1889; *Leeds Mercury*, 25 October 1889; *Scottish Leader*, 24 October 1889; *Daily Telegraph*, 26 October 1889.

2. Journal, 4 December 1889; IDA, ii, pp. 416–17. For other accounts see G. Schweitzer, *Emin Pasha*, ii, p. 21; Hoffmann, *With Stanley*, pp. 162–4; Jephson, *Emin Pasha and the Rebellion at the Equator*, ii, pp. 473–4; Parke, *My Personal Experiences*, pp. 504–5.

3. Journal, 20 April 1890.
4. Ibid. Cf. also Journal, March 1890.
5. Journal, 6 December 1889.
6. Jephson, *Emin Pasha*, pp. 477–8.
7. See RA P 19/161–5; Victoria to Leopold, 10 May 1889, RA, Vic. Add. U/127.
8. RA P 19/188–94, 203–4.
9. The preparations for Stanley's coming are described in Euan-Smith to Salisbury, 2 December 1889, MP 88/37. Euan-Smith turned out every bit as autocratic as Kirk. One day a couple of Indian merchants passed him on the streets of Zanzibar without saluting. Euan-Smith sent for them and demanded an explanation. They said they had not recognised him. Euan-Smith then ordered that they should call on him every day for a month to pay their respects, after which they would surely know him well (MP 25/97).
10. Journal, 20, 23–26 December 1889.
11. Journal, 19–21 March 1890.
12. Euan-Smith to Salisbury, 24, 28 December, ZA/RCS.
13. Schweitzer, *Emin Pasha*, ii, pp. 5–28.
14. Jephson, Stairs, Nelson and Parke were 'certainly a splendid quartet of Englishmen, but there is no love lost between them and Stanley who, I fancy, though an unequalled leader of natives, does not understand how to treat Englishmen.' On Emin he recorded: 'It is easy to see that Stanley has neither liking nor admiration for him, and he openly expresses his opinion that the estimation in which Emin Pasha was held in England, as an heroic figure holding his post against overwhelming odds, is entirely false and misleading . . . in the meantime, the poor Pasha is something of a prisoner in the hands of the Germans, whose tender mercies are perhaps not without a tinge of unintentional cruelty.' (Euan-Smith to Sir Henry Ponsonby, December 1889, RA P 19/213).
15. Ibid.
16. Margery Perham, *Lugard*, p. 177.
17. Heinrich Brode, *Tippu Tip*, pp. 216–17.
18. APR, Congo, 53/11.
19. *Boston Commonwealth*, 15 November 1890.
20. Mackinnon to Euan-Smith, 10 July 1890, MP 84/14.
21. APR, Congo, 53/11.
22. J. A. Moloney, *With Captain Stairs to Katanga* (1893), p. 35.
23. Sir John Gray, 'Stanley versus Tippu Tip', *TNR* 18 (1944), pp. 12–27; MacDermott to Stanley, 8 September 1891, SFA.
24. Euan-Smith to Mackinnon, 30 December 1889, MP 4/13.
25. Journal, 1 January 1890; Currie to Secretary, EPRE committee, 2 January 1890, MP 88/37.

26. Stanley to Mackinnon, 14 February 1890, MP 55/218.

27. Journal, 26 December 1889, 1, 11, 25 January 1890.

28. RGS 16/5; E. M. Merrick, *With a Palette in Eastern Palaces* (1899), p. 55.

29. *The Times*, 27 January 1890; Journal, 14–16 January 1890; cf. also 'Stanley au Caire', *Bulletin de la Société Khediviale de Géographie*, Series 3, 5 (1890), pp. 329–56.

30. Journal, 1 February 1890.

31. Edmund Gosse, author of *Fathers and Sons*, wrote to Lord Wolseley on 9 April 1889 as a publisher's intermediary, offering an advance of £3000 for the copyright and a 15 per cent royalty on sales of more than 15,000 copies (MP 84/10). Marston also made a tempting offer to bring out Stanley's expeditionary correspondence at one shilling a copy but advised that it was not in Stanley's interest to agree to this (Marston to Mackinnon, 2 December 1889, MP 94/60).

32. Marston, *After Work* (1904), p. 238.

33. Marston, *How Stanley Wrote 'In Darkest Africa'* (1890), pp. 14–15.

34. *Glasgow Herald*, 28 June 1890.

35. *Bradford Observer*, 28 May 1889.

36. Jephson Diary, p. 207. Stanley adjusted the figures slightly in his own favour, respectively to 703 and 246 (Euan-Smith to F.O., 9 December 1889, F.O.84/1982).

37. *Africa* No. 4 (1890) C.5906, pp. 15–16.

38. Fox-Bourne, *Other Side*, p. 196.

39. Schynse, *A Travers l'Afrique*, pp. 200–201, 295; *Tagebücher*, iv, p. 430.

40. For ivory as the motive force of the expedition see Clarke to Salisbury, 29 November 1889, F.O.84/1972; Stanley to Mackinnon, 15 March 1890, MP 55/219. But the legend of Equatoria's ivory lived on. The Van Kerkhoven expedition of 1893 was designed to locate the hidden cache (Plunkett to Salisbury, 5 November 1893, F.O.10/597).

41. Stanley to Mackinnon, 14 February 1890, MP 55/218; cf. also Euan-Smith to Mackinnon, 2 February 1890, MP 4/14.

42. Marston, *How Stanley Wrote*, pp. 16–23.

43. E. M. Merrick, *With a Palette*, pp. 56–7.

44. Stanley to Mackinnon, 25 February 1890, MP 55/219.

45. Marston, *How Stanley Wrote*, pp. 27–48. Cf. also Add. MSS. 43, 411 f.33 for the maps.

46. RGS 16/8.

47. Journal, 1 January 1890. For Stairs's analysis of Stanley see his diary at Fort Bodo (April–December 1888) published as 'Shut up in the African Forest', *Nineteenth Century* 29 (1891), pp. 45–62 and the account of the march to the coast (which gives a favourable picture of Emin) in 'From the Albert Nyanza to the Indian Ocean', *Nineteenth Century* 29 (1891), pp. 953–68.

48. Stanley to Mackinnon, 25 March 1890, RA P 20/18. Jephson's opinion of Stanley was conveyed to Mackinnon on 20 January 1890: 'We all of us have the greatest admiration for our leader and one of the things which made our troubles in the expedition less hard to bear was the fact that in any crisis which arose we never for an instant doubted but that Mr Stanley would somehow or other get us out of it, though we often didn't quite see how.' (MP 19/75) For Parke's views see Parke, *My Personal Experiences*, pp. 512–13. Parke told Stevens of the *New York World* that Stanley, though a wonderful leader, was an enigma. He could steel his heart until there seemed no atom of pity or consideration for others left in him one day, yet be as tender as a woman the next. (Stevens, *Scouting for Stanley*, pp. 264–8)

49. As in the case of the acceptance of the honorary LL D conferred by Cambridge (see Marston to Macalister, 28 February 1890, B.L.MSS.RP 1576). Cf. also Marston, *How Stanley Wrote*, pp. 52–3.

50. For representative correspondence see Stanley to Sanford, 26 February 1890, MP 89; Stanley to Glave, 19 January 1890, B.L.MSS.RP 1468; Stanley to EPRE, 25 March 1890, MP 86/30; Stanley to Mackinnon, 4 February 1890, MP 55/218; Stanley to Bayer, 2 February 1890, MP 84/12. For the *Florida* affair see the huge file of correspondence in MP 88/38.

51. RA P 20/12,16; Jephson to Mackinnon, 7 April 1890, MP 19/75.

52. For details see special edition of *Le Soir*, Brussels, 20 April 1890; 'H. M. Stanley à la Société Royale Belge de Géographie de Bruxelles, 24 April 1890', *Soc. Royale Belge de Géographie* 14 (1890), pp. 187–217; 'Le retour triomphale de Stanley, 25 April 1890', *Antwerp Bulletin de la Soc. Royale de Géog* 14 (1889–90), pp. 197–261; G. Harry, 'Conversations avec Stanley, 25 April 1890', *Bulletin de la Soc. Royale de Géog* 14 (1889–90), pp. 262–99.

53. Journal, January 1890.

54. Stanley to Mackinnon, 6 February 1890, MP 55/218. Cf. also Perham, *Lugard*, pp. 258–9; W. R. Louis, *Ruanda-Urundi 1884–1919* (1963), pp. 11–15, 18–29; G. N. Sanderson, *England, Europe and the Upper Nile*, pp. 56–7.

55. F. F. Muller, *Deutschland–Zanzibar–Ostafrika* (1959), p. 475; *The Times*, 3 June 1890; Mackinnon to Stanley, 5 April 1889, F.O.84/2036.

56. *The Times*, 7 November 1889, 29, 30 May 1890; *New York Herald*, 7 November 1889; *Saturday Review*, 9 November 1889.

57. Mackinnon to Rawlinson, 14 April 1890, RA P 20/16.

58. Muller, *Deutschland–Zanzibar–Ostafrika*, p. 460.

59. Peters, *Die Deutsch Emin Pascha Expedition* (1899), p. 298; cf. also Muller, *Deutschland–Zanzibar–Ostafrika*, pp. 463–4.

60. *The Times*, 26, 27 May, 3 June 1890.

61. Salisbury to Malet, 25 June 1889, F.O.84/1954.

62. Queen Victoria to Salisbury, 3 June 1890, RA P 20/23. Salisbury replied that it would be impossible to get at the truth of Stanley's story 'without putting questions to the emperor which he would probably resent' (Salisbury to Queen Victoria, 4 June 1890, RA P 20/26). cf. the entry in Queen Victoria's journals for 6 May 1890 (RA, 1890 Journal, p. 113) in which she records that difficulties with Germany may impede the great projects Mr Stanley wants to carry out.

63. Lady Cecil, *Life of Robert, Marquis of Salisbury*, iv, pp. 284–6. For Salisbury's soundings with Leopold see Stanley to Leopold, 26 April 1890, APR Congo 357.

64. Anderson memo, 29 April 1890, F.O.403/142; Anderson to Currie, 19 May 1890; Malet to Salisbury, 10 May 1890, F.O.403/142.

65. Anderson to Malet, 9 May 1890, F.O.84/2031.

66. Anderson to Currie, 10 May 1890, F.O.84/2031.

67. Stanley to Mackinnon, 11 June 1890, MP 55/219.

68. Stevens, *Scouting for Stanley*, p. 260.

69. See Robert O. Collins, *King Leopold, England and the Upper Nile* (1968). For Stanley's 'Napoleonic' contempt for Emin see Journal, March 1890; *Saturday Review*, 30 November 1889. For Emin's fury and disdain at Stanley's criticisms see Emin to Schweitzer, 25 January 1890, ZA/RCS.

70. Euan-Smith to Mackinnon, 14 March 1890, MP 4/14; Euan-Smith to Salisbury, 14 March 1890, ZA/RCS.

71. Journal, 15 March 1890.

72. Kirk to Mackinnon, 1890, MP 24/99.

73. Euan-Smith to Salisbury, 21 May 1890, F.O.84/2061.

74. See MP 88/37 under 18 April and 3 June 1890.

75. Journal, 2 April 1890.

76. Journal, 4 April 1890.

77. *The Times*, 2, 3, 4 April 1890. Among Emin's few British supporters were Felkin and Horace Waller (*The Times*, 23 January, 8 February 1890).

78. Journal, 3 April 1890.

79. R. Cambier, 'Stanley et Emin Pasha', *Zaire* 3 (1949), pp. 533–48. But *The Times*, 23 September 1893 in its obituary pointed out that Stanley had not treated the Pasha as brutally in print as his erstwhile comrade Romolo Gessi had.

Chapter eighteen

1. *Pall Mall Gazette*, 28 April 1890.

2. De Winton to Stanley, 13 February 1890, SFA, about the eagerness of the Prince of Wales to meet him. Cf. also same to same, 25 February 1890, SFA, about the desire of the Queen for a personal interview. 'The

feeling is that you had best see her here rather than abroad, as it would please the general public better . . . you see I am taking a great deal upon myself, but I want your reception to be worthy of the work you have performed.'

3. See the correspondence between the monarchs on 26 April 1890 (RA P 20/19).
4. George V's journals, 27 April 1890 (RA, 1890 journal, p. 261).
5. RA P 20/33; *The Standard*, 3, 7 May 1890.
6. Queen Victoria's journals, 1890, p. 129; de Winton to Queen Victoria, 6 May 1890, RA P 20/21; Ponsonby to Stanley, 28 June 1890, RA PP Vic. 23818. Queen Victoria's journal for July–December 1890 (1 August, p. 42) comments on the completion of the Angeli head.
7. *The Times*, 3, 6, 14, 22, 26, 31 May, June 1890.
8. See Stanley to *New York Herald* in Wellcome MSS.
9. RGS; cf. also RGS 7/2–3; *PRGS* 12 N.S. (1890), pp. 313–28, 488–501.
10. *Saturday Review*, 10 May 1890.
11. *The Times*, 26 January, 16 May 1890; Marquess of Crewe, *Lord Rosebery*, i, pp. 336–7. John Bright's fiery rhetoric was especially noteworthy. 'Perhaps the Society of Friends cannot claim to any five-minute conversions of African kings, and may have the weakness of imagining that the Christian religion may possibly not be best introduced to savage nations under the patronage of an advertising newspaper and by armed expeditions which are bound to shoot many of those who oppose their exploring marches, and perhaps they have not advertised themselves and their deeds in books and on platforms so much as some might think profitable and appropriate, but the insolent sneers with which they are now rewarded will not meet with an echo from educated people in England.' (*The Times*, 17 May 1890)
12. Marston, *How Stanley Wrote*, pp. 63–71.
13. RGS 17/1; *The Times*, 10, 11, 12, 13, 16, 18, 23 June 1890.
14. See Dolly Diary, SFA, 25 July, 21 August 1887, 3 November, 21 December 1888, 10 December 1889, 6 April 1890.
15. Dolly to Stanley, 26 April 1890, SFA.
16. Stanley to Dolly, 4 May 1890.
17. Dolly to Stanley, 6 May 1890.
18. Stanley to Dolly, 7 May 1890.
19. Dolly Diary, 7 May 1890.
20. Stanley to Dolly, 8 May 1890.
21. Dolly to Stanley, 9 May 1890.
22. Dolly to Stanley, 13 May 1890.
23. *John Bull*, 22 November 1890.
24. *The Whirlwind*, 5 July 1890.
25. Or perhaps another Grail-seeker is the appropriate analogy, since Stanley,

writing of his experiences in the Ituri, said: 'A Sir Percival in search of the Holy Grail could not have met hotter opposition' (Stanley to Marston, 3 September 1889 in *The Standard*, 25 November 1889; cf. also Marston, *After Work*, p. 233).

26. *Sporting Truth*, 1 November 1890.
27. Norman Mackenzie, ed., *The Letters of Sidney and Beatrice Webb* (1978), i, p. 204.
28. Frank Harris, *My Life and Loves*, p. 561.
29. For F. W. Myers see A. C. Benson, *The Leaves of the Tree* (1911), pp. 163–86; Sir Oliver Lodge, *Convictions of Survival, Two discourses in memory of F. W. H. Myers* (1930).
30. Myers to Stanley, 16 May 1890, SFA.
31. Dolly to Stanley, May 1890, SFA.
32. Johnston to Stanley, 6 June 1890, SFA.
33. Johnston to Dolly, 26 June 1890.
34. Dolly to Johnston, 26 June 1890.
35. Stanley to Mackinnon, 2 July 1890, MP 55/219.
36. See the complete list of guests in the Wellcome archives; cf. also Merrick, *With a Palette*, p. 59.
37. *The Times*, 14 July 1890.
38. Dolly Diary, 12 July 1890, SFA.
39. 'They were all very nice, costly and well-chosen but there was very little of really useful' [*sic*]. Bruce gave him a complete edition of the *Encyclopaedia Britannica*. Stanley found another gift, the works of Ruskin, far more useful than the piles of mirrors, coffee pots and silver (Stanley to Mackinnon, 2 July 1890, MP 55/219).
40. Stanley to Knox, 18 July 1890, B.L.MSS.RP 1576; Dolly to Mackinnon, 20 July 1890, MP 55/221.
41. Stanley to Mackinnon, 23 July 1890, MP 55/219.
42. Jephson to Mackinnon, 2 August 1890, MP 19/75.
43. Stanley to Jephson, n.d., SFA.
44. Journal, 9 September 1890.
45. Stanley to Mackinnon, 7 September 1890, MP 55/219.
46. *Autobiography*, pp. 423–4.
47. Jephson to Mackinnon, 22 August 1890, MP 19/75.
48. Dolly to Mackinnon, 7 September 1890, MP 55/219.
49. Dolly to Mackinnon, 11 September 1890, MP 55/221; *Autobiography*, p. 424.
50. Stanley to Mrs Sheldon, 27, 29 September 1890, RGS 4/1.
51. Jephson to Mackinnon, 15 October 1890, MP 19/75.
52. Gertrude Tennant to Mrs Sheldon, n.d., RGS 4/1.
53. Journal, 27, 29 October 1890; *The Times*, 31 October 1890.
54. *New York Herald*, 7 November 1890. The journey over had not been

pleasant. 'Mrs Stanley said that their passage had been awful, and that they had had to stay below most of the time. On Saturday last the electric light wire had ignited the deck, and the woodwork had blazed up, but the fire had been soon quenched. The following day a fire had been discovered in the coal bunkers, which had burned until Tuesday.' (*Daily News*, 9 November 1890)

55. For a complete list of cities where Stanley lectured see Stanley MSS, Wellcome Library. For Stanley in Philadelphia on 15 November 1890 see RGS 16/24. For Stanley in Washington see *The Times*, 9 December 1890.

56. *Autobiography*, p. 425.

57. Stanley to Mrs Sheldon, 1 May 1891, RGS 4/1.

58. Stanley to Mackinnon, 25 December 1890, MP 55/219.

59. *Autobiography*, p. 426.

60. *The Standard*, 3 January 1891; Stanley to Mackinnon, 1 February 1891, MP 55/219; RGS 17/1. Stanley's choice of Sunday was all the more surprising in view of his own Christian scruple, as evinced in a revealing letter to Henry Wellcome in 1886: 'Young ladies! *Gott in himmel!* How provoking. Cannot you arrange some other way but this for me to gaze at young ladies and partake of the innocent delight civilized society offers? Boating on Sunday! Shocking! Beware of the accidents which generally befall Sabbath-breakers.' (Stanley to Wellcome, 16 July 1886, RGS 3/1)

61. Journal, 21 March 1891. See also his comments to Bruce, 26 March 1891, NLS 10705 f.90. 'California is the most wonderful state of all. At Fresno land that sold fifteen years ago for $2.50 an acre is now worth $1,000. One man cleared last year $80 per acre nett from 160 acres of fruit … another cleared $22,000 nett from an estate of 225 acres in 13 months.'

62. Journal, 29, 30 March, 4 April 1891.

63. Journal, 11, 15 April 1891.

64. *Autobiography*, p. 427.

65. Stanley to Mackinnon, 24 April 1891, MP 55/219.

66. Rhodes House, MSS. Afr. 1522 (5), ff.27–8.

67. Ibid., f.32.

68. Stanley to Smetham, 30 April 1891, ibid., ff.32–4.

69. Dolly to Mackinnon, 28 May 1891, MP 55/221; Stanley to Mackinnon, 9 May, 6 June 1891, MP 55/219; *Autobiography*, pp. 429–33.

70. Stanley to Mackinnon, 16 July 1891, MP 55/219; Dolly to Mackinnon, 24 July, MP 55/221.

71. Dolly to Mackinnon, 28 July 1891, MP 55/221; Stanley to Mackinnon, 17 August 1891, MP 55/219.

72. Aubrey Stanhope, *On the Track of the Great* (1914), p. 151.

73. Ibid., p. 152.

74. Ibid., pp. 153–4. Stanhope later told Leopold the story 'at which he laughed heartily, for it was well known that Stanley had often shown

marked irritability even before His Majesty' (ibid., p. 155). Seitz, *The James Gordon Bennetts*, p. 301, tells an even more melodramatic story. According to this, Stanhope lulled Stanley over a two-day period before springing this question on him on the third day: 'Do you beat your wife?' 'Now kill me,' he said to himself. He saw Stanley's fingers tighten at the end of his long arm and nerved himself for the worst. There was a silence. Then Stanley said sadly, 'God! I used to do that myself.'

75. Stanley to Mackinnon, September 1891, MP 55/219; Dolly to Mackinnon, 5 October 1891, MP 55/221.
76. *Autobiography*, p. 435.
77. Stanley to Mackinnon, 22 December 1891, MP 55/219.
78. Dolly to Wellcome, 17 December 1891, RGS 3/5.
79. Exhaustive Australian press coverage of the tour can be followed in *Melbourne Argus*, 10 October, 11, 13 November; *The Age* (Melbourne), 10, 13, 14 November; *The Leader* (Melbourne), 14 November; *Ballarat Courier*, 17–19 November; *Brisbane Boomerang*, 12, 19 December; *The Queenslander*, 26 December; *Geelong Advertiser*, 20, 21 November; *Sydney Morning Herald*, 1, 5, 10, 11 December; *The Bulletin*, 12 December 1891.
80. *Autobiography*, pp. 435–7. For Sir George Grey see J. Rutherford, *Sir George Grey* (1961).
81. *Launceston Examiner*, 10–13 February; *Hobart Mercury*, 15–19 February; *Melbourne Argus*, 23, 24, 25, 26, 29 February; *Adelaide Advertiser*, 11–15 March 1892.

Chapter nineteen

1. Jackson, *Early Days*, pp. 240–41.
2. Peters, *New Light*, pp. 419, 479, 548.
3. Cf. *Sporting Truth*, 1 November 1890, which describes the Stanley of *In Darkest Africa* thus: '[he] boomed with an unblushing effrontery that a quack doctor would scarcely dare, gives you the idea that he is the special care of a wise providence.'
4. *New York Herald*, 5 November 1890. The *Agnostic Journal*, 20 December 1890, described this as 'blasphemy' and 'hypocritical cant'. 'Stanley is today the direst enemy the African ever knew.'
5. *The Star*, 28 June 1890.
6. See *The Standard*, 15 July 1890; *The Whirlwind*, 19 July 1890; *St James's Gazette*, 28 June 1890. *The Referee*, 29 June 1890, suggested that *In Darkest Africa* should really be entitled, 'The Quest, Rescue and Retreat of Emin Pasha, together with a series of attacks upon him by his rescuer'.
7. Commenting on the extraordinary severity of the six-month clause, *Land and Water*, 1 November 1890, commented: 'Before all things, Stanley was

the pressman with an eye to business. We have, up till now, been anxious to demonstrate him no Yankee, but despite himself, a Welshman. I think, at present, we shall all be content to let America claim him.'

8. R. W. Beachey, *The Slave Trade of East Africa* (1976), p. 221.
9. RGS 16/27.
10. *Daily News*, 17, 26 September 1888.
11. *The Times*, 21 December 1889.
12. *St James's Gazette*, 26 March 1889.
13. *Morning Post*, 6 April 1889.
14. *Saturday Review*, 28 December 1889.
15. *Daily News*, 1 November 1890; *Man of the World*, 25 May 1889; cf. also *Birmingham Post*, 25 March 1889: '£800 per ton will pay a lot of expenses, doncher know.'
16. *Whitehall Review*, 21 September 1889; *Globe*, 12 September 1889. The American press argued that the excessive secrecy and disinformation surrounding the expedition, plus the British government's denial that it had anything to do with it, clinched the case (*New York World*, 20 January 1889).
17. *Truth*, 6 November 1890; *Pall Mall Gazette*, 30 October 1890.
18. Anon, 'Stanley's Expedition: A Retrospect', *Fortnightly Review* 277 (1890), p. 96.
19. *The Times*, 10 April 1890; *Illustrated London News*, 13 December 1890. A more non-committal position was taken in, e.g., *Newcastle Journal*, 8 December 1890, *Scottish Leader*, 4 December, *Daily Telegraph*, 1 December 1890.
20. *The Times*, 11 April 1890.
21. Casati, *Ten Years*, ii, pp. 162–3.
22. *Globe*, 27 October 1890; *The Times*, 27, 28 October 1890; *Daily Telegraph*, 23, 28 October 1890.
23. *Birmingham Post*, 28 October 1890.
24. *The Times*, 7 December 1889; *Whitehall Review*, 12 July 1890.
25. *St James's Gazette*, 28 October, 3 December 1890; *Yorkshire Pioneer*, 12 December 1890, *Inverness Courier*, 5 December 1890; *Evening Standard*, 6 December 1890; *Graphic*, 13 December 1890; *Birmingham Post*, 10 December 1890; *Morning Post*, 3 December 1890.
26. B.L.MSS.RP 1691.
27. *New York Herald*, 26 October 1890.
28. This story was later taken up by Wassermann to explain the fiasco of the Rear Column (Jakob Wassermann, *Bula Matari*, pp. 211–14).
29. *Globe*, 28 October 1890; *The Spectator*, 1 November 1890; *Scottish Observer*, 1 November 1890.
30. *Saturday Review*, 9 November 1890.
31. 'The Stanley–Barttelot controversy must have opened the eyes of a number

of silly people who feted and lionised this nickel-plated hero.' (*The Umpire*, 2 November 1890)

32. Queen Victoria's journals (July–December 1890), RA, 11, 21 November, pp. 138, 148.

33. *Débats*, 12 November 1890; *Le Temps*, 10 November 1890. This call was taken up by *St James's Gazette*, 11 November 1890 and *Pall Mall Gazette*, 11 November 1890.

34. *Le Figaro*, 1 November 1890.

35. *Leeds Mercury*, 22 November 1890.

36. *New York World*, 2 November 1890.

37. *New York Herald*, 28 October 1890; *The Pelican*, 8 November 1890.

38. *The Times*, 29 June 1889; *Whitehall Review*, 22 June 1889; *Newcastle Leader*, 1 July 1889; *St James's Gazette*, 2 July 1889; *Scottish Leader*, 3 July 1889; *Daily Graphic*, 22 May; *Morning Post*, 22 May 1890; *Scottish Leader*, 23 May 1890; *Pall Mall Gazette*, 24 May 1890.

39. *The Times, Morning Post, Daily Telegraph, Daily News, Daily Chronicle, Globe, Pall Mall Gazette, St James's Gazette* (all 7 November 1890); *Daily Graphic, Scotsman*, 10 November 1890; *Vanity Fair, St Stephen's Review*, 15 November 1890.

40. *New York Sun*, 28, 29, 31 October 1890.

41. Grant to RGS, 8 November 1890, RGS.

42. *The Times*, 8, 10 November 1890.

43. *New York Herald*, 1 November 1890.

44. *The Times*, 12 November 1890.

45. *Sunday Times*, 9 November 1890.

46. *The Times*, 15 November 1890.

47. Myers to Mackinnon, 14 December 1890, MP 94/60.

48. *The Times*, 14 November 1890.

49. *The Daily Telegraph*, 12 November 1890.

50. *The Times*, 14 November 1890.

51. *The Times*, 13, 14 November 1890; *Observer*, 9 November 1890; *Boston Post*, 15 November 1890.

52. *The Times*, 10 November 1890; *Western Morning News*, 8 November 1890; *Western Times*, 10 November 1890. *The Spectator*, 15 November 1890, took the extreme line: '*No* evidence is sufficient to prove such a charge against any educated European whatsoever.'

53. *The Times*, 14 November 1890; *Indépendance Belge*, 15 September 1888, 13 November 1890.

54. *Débats*, 9 November 1890.

55. *The Globe*, 8 November 1890.

56. *The Times*, 14 November 1890.

57. *The Times*, 15 November 1890.

58. *The Globe*, 15 November 1890.

59. *Pall Mall Gazette*, 15 November 1890.

60. Myers to Mackinnon, 16, 24 November 1890, MP 94/60.

61. Mrs Jameson to EPRE committee, 20 October, 11 November 1890, MP 84/15.

62. Euan-Smith to Salisbury, 2 February 1891, RA P 21/5.

63. Bontinck, *Tippu Tip*, pp. 148–9; Liebrechts, *Souvenirs*, p. 117.

64. *New York Herald*, 16 November 1890.

65. *Piccadilly*, 6 November 1890.

66. *The Speaker*, 15 November 1890.

67. Ibid.

68. Stanley to Mackinnon, 6 June 1891, MP 55/219.

69. Stanley to Mackinnon, 22 June, 2 July 1891, MP 55/219.

70. *Saturday Review*, 8 February 1891.

71. *Glasgow Herald*, 28 June 1890.

72. *Boston Globe*, 24 October 1890; *Boston Herald*, 1 October 1890. Troup's experience was similar to that of Lewis Noe twenty years earlier. See the interview with the reporter from the *New York Sun* in 1872. 'I notice,' said the reporter, 'that in many of these letters and in the diary he quotes scripture and talks more or less of piety.' 'He is excellent on that,' replied Noe. 'His pious talk was one of the things that gave my parents and brothers and sisters confidence in him. But he can swear and break the commandments as easy as he can quote the Bible – in fact a good deal better.' (*New York Sun*, 29 August 1872)

73. *Vanity Fair*, 1 November 1890; *The Lighthouse*, 1 November 1890.

74. *The Times*, 9 December 1890. The *Evening News* that very night ran a large item, 'Stanley as Pecksniff', in which it railed against the hypocrisy of talk of moral superiority by one who had blackened the reputation of the dead.

75. *The Star*, 28 June 1890. Cf. the *Sunday Chronicle*'s judgement on Stanley's 'Nietzschean' pretensions: 'I for one am at a loss to find anything in his heroic deeds to praise, or anything in his subsequent conduct to admire . . . the hero is simply someone who raises selfishness to an art form.'

76. *New York Herald*, 16 November 1890.

Chapter twenty

1. Leopold to Stanley, 9 July, 30 December 1888, SFA.

2. Miscellaneous EPRE notes, SFA.

3. Leopold to Mackinnon, 28 November 1889, APR Congo, 82/83.

4. Stanley to Mackinnon, 19 January 1890, MP 55/218.

5. Journal, January 1890.

6. Leopold to Lambermont, 8 December 1889, Lambermont Papers 942.

7. Leopold to Van Eetvelde, 12 March 1890, Van Eetvelde Papers 27.

8. Leopold to Stanley, 30 October 1889, SFA; Leopold to Lambermont, 12 December 1889, 9 March 1891, Lambermont Papers, 944, 1132.

9. Leopold to Stanley, 31 January 1890, SFA.

10. Journal, February 1890.

11. The value of exports from the Congo Free State in the second half of 1888 was £1,801,891, of which £527,030 was raised from the produce of the State (coconuts, palm oil, rubber and coffee) and £553,660 from the sale of ivory. (*The Times*, 17 January 1889)

12. Ferry to Borchgrave, 5 February 1885, APR Congo, 206/2; Beyers to Borchgrave, 19 May 1888, APR Congo 206/127.

13. Rothschild to Leopold, 9 January 1886, APR Congo 206/76; Leopold to Bernaert, 5 May 1889, APR Congo 12/24.

14. Cornet, *La Bataille du rail*, p. 143.

15. Van Zuyler, *L'Echiquier Congolais*, p. 197.

16. Emile Banning, *Mémoires politiques et diplomatiques*, p. 141; Liebrechts, *Leopold II, Fondateur d'Empire*, p. 50.

17. G. Harry, 'Conversations avec Stanley', loc.cit.

18. P. Daye, *Leopold II*, pp. 320–21.

19. Journal, 20 April 1890.

20. Journal, 21 April 1890.

21. Ibid.

22. Journal, 22 April 1890.

23. The idea may have been first planted in Leopold's mind by Lt. Baert. When he returned to Brussels in 1888, after a year on the Upper Congo, he reported that Stanley's aim, after linking up with Emin Pasha, was to conquer Khartoum. See *The Times*, 20 February 1889; *Leeds Mercury*, 23, 25 February 1889; *Globe, Evening Post, Morning Advertiser, Liverpool Daily Post*, 23 February 1889, *Western Press, York Evening Post*, 25 February 1889.

24. Journal, 23 April 1890.

25. Journal, 24 April 1890.

26. Stanley to Mackinnon, 19 January 1890, MP 55/218.

27. *Tagebücher*, iv, pp. 100–119; cf. also Euan-Smith to Salisbury, 14 March 1890, F.O.84/2060.

28. Ceulemans, *La question arabe*, pp. 145–6.

29. See Jerome Becker, *La troisième expédition belge* (1893).

30. Leopold to Queen Victoria, 29 June, 19 October 1890, RA P 20/37, P 20/60.

31. Leopold to Stanley, 22 October 1890, APR Congo, 102/19.

32. Leopold to Stanley, 17 November 1890, SFA.

33. Journal, November 1890.

34. *New York Gazette*, 9 June 1891; RGS 16/10–11.

35. Leopold to Stanley, 10 March 1891, SFA.
36. J. Stengers, 'Textes Inédites d'Emile Banning', p. 100.
37. A. J. Wauters, *Histoire Politique du Congo Belge* (1911), p. 203.
38. Ceulemans, *La question arabe*, pp. 218–19.
39. Liebrechts, *Leopold II*, p. 182.
40. For an examination of Leopold's motives see Daye, *Leopold II*; R. O. Collins, *The Southern Sudan 1883–1898: a struggle for control*; Collins, *King Leopold, England and the Upper Nile*; E. G. Langer, *The Diplomacy of Imperialism* (1972).
41. van Zuyler, *L'Echiquier Congolais*, p. 238.
42. See Salisbury's memo of 8 February 1893 (F.O.103/317).
43. See A. J. P. Taylor, 'Prelude to Fashoda: the Question of the Upper Nile 1894–95', *Essays in English History* (1976), pp. 129–69.
44. *The Times*, 4, 11 October, 2 November, 8 December 1892. Frederick Lugard thought this an exaggeration but considered that a figure not far short of this could be obtained if the population of the Nile area and all the lakes (including Lake Albert) were embraced (F. D. Lugard, *The Rise of our East African Empire*, i, p. 396).
45. *The Times*, 25 October 1892.
46. Harcourt attacked the Emin expedition as one of those 'filibustering expeditions in the mixed guise of commerce, religion, geography and imperialism, under which names any and every atrocity is regarded as permissible . . . an armed expedition like Stanley's claims and exercises the power of life and death and outrage upon all with whom they meet, powers which are exercised without remorse. They enlist men whom they call carriers, but who are really slaves, driven in by contract by the established slave drivers of the country. They work these men to death, and if they are recalcitrant flog or shoot them . . . what is really wanted is to concentrate public opinion upon the real nature of these transactions which are the worst form of piratical jingoism.' (A. G. Gardiner, *The Life of Sir William Harcourt* (1913), ii, p. 94)
47. Jephson to Mackinnon, 1 June 1892, MP 19/76.
48. Gardiner, *Life of Harcourt*, ii, pp. 194–5. Stanley was at the same time trying to become an MP so as to be able to answer Harcourt in the House of Commons. This is the import of the remark to Mackinnon on 4 June 1892: 'Sir William Harcourt will have his say – but I am sorry not to be in a position to answer him as he should be answered. The time will come I hope.' (MP 55/220)
49. Dolly to Mackinnon, 18 January 1893, MP 55/221.
50. See Stanley's account of a visit by Lugard in October 1892: 'I have taken a good look at him and have read him thoroughly. He is one of the most *cranky* men that I have seen, and I wonder more than ever that de Winton was so blind as not to see how he should have been managed . . . He is

the strangest mortal in temper, stubbornness and disposition you will have met for a long time ... he is a vastly clever man – but he can show a mulish temper and obstinacy such as I have rarely met.' (Stanley to Mackinnon, 8 October 1892, MP 55/220)

51. *The Times*, 16, 23 March 1893.

52. *Autobiography*, p. 457.

53. Roland Oliver, *Sir Harry Johnston and the Scramble for Africa* (1957), p. 194.

54. Leopold to Stanley, 9 March 1893, SFA.

55. Stanley to Leopold, 11 March 1893, SFA.

56. Leopold to Stanley, 14 March 1893, SFA.

57. Stanley to Rhodes, 17 March 1893, SFA.

58. *The Times*, 14 October 1893; *Autobiography*, pp. 454–5.

59. Borchgrave to Stanley, 19 March, 8 April, 4, 7 May, 20 October, 18 November 1893; Stanley to Borchgrave, 22 November 1893; Borchgrave to Stanley, 10, 18, 21, 29 June, 1, 13 July 1894; Stanley to Borchgrave, 11 June 1894, SFA.

60. For the Stokes affair see R. Cambier, 'L'affaire Stokes', *Revue Belge de Philologie et d'Histoire* 30 (1952), pp. 109–34; W. R. Louis, 'The Stokes affair and the origin of the anti-Congo campaign 1895–1896', *Revue Belge de Philologie et d'Histoire* 43 (1965), pp. 572–84. For the Stokes execution see also Jackson, *Early Days*, pp. 80–84. For Stokes's career in general see H. H. Johnston, *The Uganda Protectorate*, pp. 230–31; Anne Luck, *Charles Stokes in Africa* (1972); Nicholas Harman, *Bwana Stokesi and his African Conquests* (1986).

61. Stokes told him he was proud to be an Irishman and Stanley commented: 'What with the crossing of Africa by surgeon Parke, who is a perfect Irishman, and the exploits of Mr Stokes, the Irishmen are marching to the front very rapidly and I for one wish "more power to their elbows".' (Stanley to Mackinnon, 17 March 1890, MP 55/219)

62. Journal, 1 September 1895.

63. For this see A. J. P. Taylor, *Essays in English History*, pp. 129–69.

64. Stanley to Leibrechts, 2 September 1895, SFA. Nor was Stanley at all appeased by Leopold's defence of the execution (Leopold to Stanley, 1 September 1895).

65. Louis & Stengers, *Morel*, p. 55.

66. *African Review*, 23 November 1895. In fact there were just 223 missionaries on the Congo in 1897 (Lagergren, *Mission and State*, p. 153).

67. *The Times*, 16 September 1896; *Saturday Review* 82 (1896), p. 307. In *The Times*, 18 March 1895, Stanley even condoned the notorious corvée in the Congo as a means of habituating the Congolese to work discipline.

68. Leopold to Stanley, 2 September 1896, SFA.

69. See Hugh Reid Gilzean to Leopold, 19 September 1896, APR, Congo,

51/1; Stanley to Baron Whetnall, 28 September 1896, APR, Congo, 124/12.

70. Stanley to Leopold, 16 September 1896, APR, Congo, 102/100.

71. Leopold to Stanley, 20 September 1896, SFA.

72. Guy Burrows, *The Land of the Pygmies*; Brian Inglis, *Roger Casement*, pp. 48–9. But see Dolly to Sheldon, 9 February 1905, SFA, praising the Sheldons' purblind defence of Leopold's Congo: 'You are doing just the work Stanley wanted done: dispelling the lies and calumnies about the work on the Congo.' For a review of Stanley's views on the later Congo State see H. Wack, *The Story of the Congo Free State*, pp. 397–400.

73. Journal, 23 April 1897.

74. See Stanley's letter to the editor of *La Reforma* (Italy), 1896, SFA. For Leopold's desire for the lease of Abyssinia see L. Ravieri, *Relations entre l'Etat Indépendant du Congo et l'Italie* (1959), pp. 87, 104–5; cf. also P. Daye, *Leopold*, p. 412.

75. For later contacts see Borchgrave to Stanley, 10 May 1897; Leopold to Stanley, 3 June, 8 September 1897; Stanley to Edwin Arnold, 1 June 1897, B.L.MSS.RP 1153; Borchgrave to Stanley, 28 March 1898; Stanley to Borchgrave, 29 March 1898, SFA. The tailing off in the relationship can be observed at the personal level. The series of letters from Leopold to Dolly which began on 16 May 1890 ends on 24 June 1896, and Dolly's letters to Leopold on 21 June 1896 (APR, Congo, 101/17).

76. Leopold to Stanley, 18 May 1899, SFA.

Chapter twenty-one

1. Journal, 20 June 1892.

2. See the details in *Autobiography*, pp. 439–45.

3. RGS 16/13.

4. *Boston Globe*, 25 June 1892.

5. RGS 16/14–15.

6. *St James's Gazette*, 21 June 1892.

7. *Autobiography*, p. 439.

8. Dolly to Mackinnon, 6 October 1892, MP 55/221; Stanley to Mackinnon, 23 December 1892, MP 55/220.

9. Dolly to Mackinnon, 11 September 1892, MP 55/221.

10. Journal, 15 November 1893.

11. See 'The Legend of the Elephant and the Lion', *McClure's Magazine* 1 (1893), pp. 351–5; *H. M. Stanley and the Slave Trade in Africa* (1893) – an 86-page essay by Stanley. Introduction to Thomas H. Parke, *Guide to Health in Africa* and to E. J. Glave, *Six Years of Adventures in Congoland*. Stanley later became Associate Editor of *Illustrated Africa* and contributed

to 'How to Conquer the Continent' (No. 84, December 1895). He also wrote the preface to the autobiography, *The Adventures of Roger L'Estrange* (1896), to Lionel Decle's *Three Years in Savage Africa* and to Edward Oswell's *William Cotton Oswell, Hunter and Explorer*. For Stanley's uneasy relations with another famous hunter, Frederick Courtenay Selous, see Stephen Taylor, *The Mighty Nimrod* (1989).

12. *Autobiography*, pp. 450–65.
13. Ibid., pp. 446–9.
14. For Bruce's illness and death see Stanley to Mrs Bruce, 27 November 1893, 2, 5 February 1894, NLS 10705, ff.95–103. In 1895 there occurred the premature death of E. J. Glave. See Stanley to Mrs Glave, 21 June 1895, B.L.MSS.RP 1468.
15. Stanley to Mackinnon, 3 August 1892, 11 February 1893, MP 55/220.
16. Stanley to Mackinnon, 3 May 1893, MP 55/220.
17. Same to same, 25 May 1893, MP 55/220.
18. *The Standard*, 30, 31 October 1893.
19. See Stanley's Parliamentary diary, edited by Dolly from the original which contains much libellous material on his colleagues, in *Autobiography*, pp. 467–81.
20. Ibid., p. 476.
21. Hansard Parl. Debates, 4th Series, 1046, Vol. 36, 22 August 1895, C.505–6; 1047 Vol. 36, 22 August 1895, C.560.
22. Stanley to Mrs Sheldon, 13 September, 31 October, 8 November 1895, SFA.
23. See the journal of Stanley's tour of the USA covering the period 4 September–20 November 1895, SFA; cf. also Dolly to Keltie, 30 November 1895, RGS 2/8.
24. Her original diary ran from 10 March 1876 to 13 April 1890, with an entry religiously made for each day. After that there are merely occasional entries until 4 October 1891. Then, from 12 August to 11 September 1895, i.e. just before Stanley left for the USA, the daily entries recommence. For the Switzerland holiday see Stanley to Mrs Bruce, 18 July 1895, NLS 10705, ff.104–5.
25. Stanley to Mrs Bruce, 2 October 1896, NLS 10705, ff.106–9; Stanley to Leopold, 16 September 1896, SFA.
26. Hansard, 1048, Vol. 38, 3 March 1896, c.1522–6; 1050, Vol. 38, c.1549–50; 1051, Vol. 45, 5 February 1897–9, c.1487.
27. Hansard, 1053, Vol. 54, 3 March 1898, c.517–209; 1054, Vol. 70, 27 April 1899, c.700–701; 1055, Vol. 85, 3 July 1900, c.406–7.
28. Stanley to Johnston, 28 November 1895, quoted in Luwel, *H. M. Stanley et H. H. Johnston et le Congo* (1978), p. 91.
29. Journal, 1 January 1896; cf. also 'The Issue between Great Britain and America', *Nineteenth Century* 39 (1896), pp. 1–6.

30. *The Times*, 22 January, 6 March, 18 December 1894; 30 January, 24 February, 4 December 1896.

31. T. L. Garvin, *The Life of Joseph Chamberlain* (1933), iii, p. 641; ii, p. 18.

32. Marie von Bunsen noticed a physical similarity between Stanley and Schweinfurth: 'He [Schweinfurth] reminded me a little of Stanley, another square set, short figure, a yellowish brown face, in which the whites of the eyes stood out prominently; he, too, often gave one the impression of quiet reserves of strength. On the other hand, there is nothing moody or sombre about him; he is unaffectedly pleasant and cultured.' (von Bunsen, *The World I Used to Know*, p. 185)

33. Leon Edel, *Henry James, The Master 1901–1916* (1972), pp. 22–3, 233.

34. Leon Edel, ed., *Henry James Letters* (1984), iv, (1895–1916), p. 15.

35. Alphonse Daudet, *Quand vivait mon père* (1940), pp. 264–71. Daudet also recorded that Stanley spoke French with a heavy English accent and a slight pause at the beginning of words.

36. Von Bunsen, *The World I Used to Know*, p. 152.

37. Lewis Leary, ed., *Mark Twain's Correspondence with Henry Huttleston Rogers, 1893–1909* (1969), p. 138.

38. He suffered from malaria and Dolly nursed him with a potion brought from Madrid (Dolly to Wellcome, 14 June, 3 July, 1 August 1896, RGS 3/5).

39. Journal, April 1897.

40. Hoffmann, *With Stanley*, p. 247.

41. Journal, 13, 25 October 1897.

42. *African Review*, 16, 30 October 1897.

43. Hoffmann, *With Stanley*, pp. 248–9.

44. Ibid., pp. 249–50.

45. Quoted in Malherbe, *Eminent Victorians in South Africa*, pp. 162–3.

46. Stanley to Dolly, 20 November 1897, SFA.

47. Hoffmann, *With Stanley*, pp. 253–4.

48. *Autobiography*, p. 491.

49. Ibid., pp. 490–99.

50. *Cape Times*, 15 December 1897. But Stanley disliked the city. 'He is anything but pleased with Cape Town. A crude, noisy, uncomfortable place' (Dolly to Marston, 23 November 1897, SFA).

51. Hoffmann, *With Stanley*, p. 258.

52. See Stanley to Lucy, 23 January 1893, B.L.MSS.RP 1220 ('I think the Empire is doing fairly well, though it seems perilously near a convulsion at odd times.'); H. M. Stanley and others, *Africa, its partition and its future* (1898); 'British Foreign Policy', *Nineteenth Century* 43 (1898), pp. 869–78; 'The Origin of the Negro Race', *North American Quarterly* 170 (1900), pp. 656–65; 'Anglo-Saxon responsibility', *Outlook* 53 (1899), pp. 249–58. On hostility to the Boers and support of the Uitlanders see *The Times*, 8

January, 24 February 1898; 'South African Problems', speech delivered
at Lowestoft, 23 February 1898, SFA; 'South Africa', speeches delivered
on 11 and 19 May 1898, SFA.

53. Stanley to Pound, 6 February 1899, B.L.MSS.RP 1538.

54. The correspondence was more frequent on Mary Kingsley's side. See
Kingsley to Stanley, 7 July 1897, 7 February, 20, 23 March, 3 July 1898,
29 November 1899, SFA.

55. See speech at the Hercules Road School rooms, 30 November 1899, and
a speech of 15 March 1900 against the 'Stop the War' movement (SFA).

56. Stanley to Pond, 25 November 1899, B.L.MSS.RP 1594.

57. Same to same, 4 February 1900, ibid.

58. Same to same, 16 January 1902, RP 1268.

59. *Autobiography*, pp. 506–8.

60. Journal, 10 June 1899.

61. Journal, 21 December 1896.

62. Stanley to Pond, 6 February 1899, B.L.MSS.RP 1538.

63. Stanley to Wellcome, 4 September 1901, RGS 3/4.

64. Stanley to Pond, 25 November 1899, B.L.MSS.RP 1594.

65. Hoffmann, *With Stanley*, pp. 264–5.

66. Marston, *After Work*, p. 244.

67. See the RGS correspondence between Clements Markham and Stanley
dated 8 March 1898, 26, 27 May, 12 August, 29 November, 6, 12
December 1899, RGS; cf. also Stanley to Mrs Bruce, 21 August 1902,
NLS 10705, ff.111–12.

68. Stanley to Wellcome, 17 June 1899, RGS 3/4; Dolly to Wellcome, 18
June 1899, RGS 3/5.

69. Queen Victoria's Journals, RA, March–December 1899 (6 July), p. 121.

70. See 'My feelings towards death: answer to Addison Allen', 19 February
1903, SFA.

71. Stanley to Pond, 1 March 1894, SFA.

72. Miscellaneous notes, SFA.

73. *Autobiography*, pp. 484–5.

74. Dolly to Wellcome, 10 February 1900, RGS 3/5.

75. Winifred Coombe Tennant to Wellcome, 2 October 1904, RGS.

76. Dolly to Wellcome, 18 July, 4 August 1900, RGS 3/5.

77. Lewis Leary, ed., *Mark Twain's Correspondence*, pp. 433–5.

78. Stanley to Wellcome, 17 June 1899, RGS 3/1. Stanley's last letters to *The
Times*, on African subjects, also date from this period (*The Times*, 31 May
1901, 11 January 1902).

79. Stanley to Jephson, 11 August 1902, RGS 2/6.

80. Dolly to Wellcome, 29 April 1903, RGS 3/5.

81. *Autobiography*, p. 513.

82. Dolly to Wellcome, 3, 13, 22, 28, 31 May, 5, 7, 22 June 1903, RGS 3/5.

83. Dolly to Wellcome, 17 June 1903, RGS 3/5.
84. Same to same, 16, 29 August, 12 September 1903, ibid.
85. *Autobiography*, p. 514.
86. Stanley to Wellcome, 30 March 1904, RGS 3/5.
87. Hoffmann, *With Stanley*, p. 267.
88. Dolly to Wellcome, 1, 7 May 1904, RGS 3/5.
89. *Autobiography*, p. 515.
90. RGS 11/2.
91. J. Armitage Robinson to Sir Dighton Probyn, 11 May 1904, RA. ED. VII.B.4969.
92. Dolly to Wellcome, 1904 (n.d.), RGS 3/5.
93. Howells to Clemens, 11 February 1910 in Henry Nash Smith & William M. Gibson, eds, *Correspondence of Samuel L. Clemens and William Dean Howells 1872–1910*, p. 852.
94. RGS 16/16.
95. RGS 11/2.

Conclusion

1. Pieter Geyl in *Napoleon For and Against*, which is in sum a withering indictment of the emperor, makes a similar point. Whatever the ultimate verdict on Napoelon, denial of his military genius is utterly fatuous.
2. Harms, *River of Wealth*, op. cit. pp. 156, 177. The point is borne out by the Marxist social critic Plekhanov, who is not likely, on ideological grounds, to have been favourably disposed to Stanley. See G. Plekhanov, *Selected Philosophical Works*, 5 vols (Moscow 1976), ii, p. 625; iii, p. 145; v, pp. 145, 323, 331–32, 345, 347.
3. See E. Dicey, 'Is Central Africa Worth Having?', *The Nineteenth Century*, September 1890, pp. 489–96.
4. Quoted in Byron Farwell, *The Man Who Presumed* (1957), p. 179.
5. Daye, *Stanley*, pp. 181, 230.
6. Farwell, op. cit., p. 179.
7. Ward, *A Voice from the Congo*, p. 157.
8. Farwell, p. 189.
9. Hoffmann, *With Stanley*, p. 74.
10. Stanley to Dolly, 20 November 1893, SFA.
11. *Autobiography*, p. xvii.
12. Jackson, *Early Days*, p. 143.
13. Daye, p. 170.
14. Louis & Stenger, *Morel*, op. cit., p. 205.
15. *The Times*, 27 May 1890.

• BIBLIOGRAPHY •

1. Manuscript Sources
Stanley Family Archives (originals at Musée Royale Africaine, Tervuren, copies in British Library)
Royal Geographical Society Archives
Royal Archives, Windsor Castle
Mackinnon Papers, SOAS
Foreign Office Reports, Public Record Office
British Library, Add. MSS, RP etc.
Rhodes House, Oxford, African MSS
National Library of Scotland
Royal Commonwealth Society (copies from the Zanzibar Archives)
French Foreign Office Reports, Quai d'Orsay
Archives du Palais Royal, Brussels
Belgian Foreign Ministry Reports (Strauch Papers, Labermont Papers)
Archives de la Musée de la Dynastie, Brussels (Strauch Papers)
Archives générales du Royaume, Brussels (Van Eetvelde Papers)

2. Stanley's own writings
How I Found Livingstone in Central Africa (1872)
Through the Dark Continent, 2 vols (1878)
The Congo and the Founding of its Free State, 2 vols (1895)
In Darkest Africa, 2 vols (1890)
My African Travels (1886)
Autobiography, ed. Dorothy Stanley (1909)
Tales from Africa (1985) – new edition of original, published in 1893
H. M. Stanley and the Slave Trade in Africa (1893)
Africa, its Partitions and its Future (1898)

478

3. Published collections of primary sources, eyewitness reports, memoirs, correspondence, etc.

Anderson, Frederick, with Lin Salamo & Bernard L. Stein, eds, *Mark Twain's Notebooks and Journals* (1984)

Arnold, Julian B., *Giants in a Dressing Gown* (Chicago 1942)

Augouard, Mgr, *Vingt-huit Années au Congo*, 2 vols (Poitiers 1905)

Banning, Emile, *Mémoires politiques et diplomatiques* (Brussels 1927)

Barttelot, W. G., *The Life of Edmund Musgrave Barttelot* (1890)

Bateman, C. S. L., *The First Ascent of the Kasai* (1889)

Becker, Jerome, *La vie en Afrique*, 2 vols (Paris 1887)

Becker, Jerome, *La troisième expédition belge* (Brussels 1893)

Bennett, Norman R., *Stanley's Despatches to the New York Herald* (Boston 1970)

Bennett, Norman R., ed., *From Zanzibar to Ujiji. The Journal of Arthur W. Dodgshun 1877–79* (Boston 1969)

Bentley, W. Holman, *Pioneering on the Congo*, 2 vols (Oxford 1900)

Bentley, Mrs W. H., *The Life and Labours of a Congo Pioneer* (1907)

Bontinck, François, *L'Autobiographie de Hamed ben Mohammed el-Murjebi Tippu Tip* (Brussels 1974)

Brown, Robert, *The Story of Africa and its Explorers*, 4 vols (1892–5)

Bunsen, Marie von, *The World I Used to Know 1860–1912* (1930)

Burdo, Adolph, *Les Belges dans l'Afrique Centrale. De Zanzibar au Lac Tanganika* (Brussels 1886)

Burrows, Guy, *The Land of the Pygmies* (1895)

Casati, Gaetano, *Ten Years in Equatoria with Emin Pasha*, 2 vols (1891)

Cecil, Lady, *Life of Robert, Marquis of Salisbury*, 4 vols (1932)

Chavanne, Josef, *Reisen und Forschungen im Alten und Neuen Kongostaate in den Jahren 1884 und 1885* (Jena 1887)

Chavannes, P. de, *Avec Brazza: Souvenirs de la Mission de l'Ouest Africain* (Paris 1935)

Coquilhat, Camille, *Sur le haut Congo* (Paris 1888)

Daudet, Alphonse, *Quand vivait mon père* (Paris 1940)

Decle, Lionel, *Three Years in Savage Africa* (1898)

Delcommune, Alex, *Vingt Années de la Vie Africaine*, 2 vols (Brussels 1922)

Document Notte. Stanley au Congo, 1879–1884, Ministère du Congo Belge et du Ruanda Urundi Archives (1960)

Documents Diplomatiques Français 1871–1914, ed. by Bourgeois & Pages (Paris 1933)

Donos, Martin, *Les Belges en Afrique Centrale*, 3 vols (Brussels 1886)

Dupont, E., *Lettres sur le Congo* (Paris 1889)

Dybowski, Jean, *La route du Tchad* (Paris 1893)

Edel, Leon, ed., *Henry James Letters*, 4 vols (1984)

Farnan, E. E., *Along the Nile with General Grant* (N.Y. 1904)

Ferry, Jules, *Discours et Opinions* (Paris 1897)

Fitzmaurice, Lord Edward, *The Life of Granville George Leveson Gower, Second Earl Granville* (1905)

Fox-Bourne, W. R., *The Other Side of the Emin Pasha Relief Expedition* (1891)

Génin, E., *Les Explorations de Brazza* (Paris 1887)

Gessi, Romolo, *Seven Years in the Sudan* (1892)

Glave, E. J., *Six Years of Adventure in Congoland* (1893)

Guinness, F., *The New World of Central Africa* (1890)

Guiral, Leon, *Le Congo Français du Gabon à Brazzaville* (Paris 1889)

Handt, Richard, *Caput Nili*, 2 vols (Berlin 1914)

Harris, Frank, *My Life and Loves* (1964)

Harrison, J. W., *The Story of the Life of Mackay of Uganda* (1898)

Hassan, Vita, *Emin Pascha, die Aequatorial Provinz und der Mahdismus* (Berlin 1895)

Hoffmann, William, *With Stanley in Africa* (1938)

Hyndman, H. M., *The Record of an Adventurous Life* (N.Y. 1911)

Jackson, Frederick, *Early Days in Africa* (1930)

Jameson, James S., *The Story of the Rear Column* (1890)

Jephson, A. J. Mounteney, *Emin Pasha and the Rebellion at the Equator* (1890)

Johnston, Harry H., *The River Congo* (1884)

Johnston, Harry H., *The Nile Quest* (N.Y. 1903)

Johnston, Harry H., *History of the Colonisation of Africa by Alien Races* (Cambridge 1913)

Johnston, Harry H., *The Uganda Protectorate* (1914)

Johnston, Harry H., *The Story of My Life* (1923)

Junker, W., *Travels in Africa 1882–86*, trans. A. H. Keane, 3 vols (1892)

Koshitzky, M., *Deutsche Kolonialgeschichte*, 2 vols (1887–8)

Langheld, W., *Zwanzig Jahre in Deutschen Kolonien* (Berlin 1909)

Leary, Lewis, ed., *Mark Twain's Correspondence with Henry Huttleston Rogers, 1893–1909* (Berkeley 1969)

Lenz, Oscar, *Wanderung in Afrika* (Vienna 1895)

L'Estrange, Roger, *The Adventures of Roger L'Estrange* (1896)

Liebrechts, Charles, *Souvenirs d'Afrique: Congo, Leopoldville, Bolobo, Equateur* (Brussels, n.d.)

Liebrechts, Charles, *Leopold II: Fondateur d'Empire* (Brussels 1932)

Lugard, Frederick, *The Rise of Our East African Empire*, 2 vols (1893)

Maes, A., *Reisen naar Midden-Afrika* (Louvain 1879)

Marston, Edward, *How Stanley Wrote 'In Darkest Africa'* (1890)

Marston, Edward, *After Work* (1904)

Masui, T., *D'Anvers à Bannyville* (Brussels 1894)

Masui, T., *L'Etat Indépendant du Congo à l'Exposition Bruxelles–Tervuren* (Brussels 1897)

Maurice, Albert, *H. M. Stanley, Unpublished Letters* (1957)

Merrick, E. M., *With a Palette in Eastern Palaces* (1899)

Middleton, Dorothy, ed., *The Diaries of A. J. Mounteney-Jephson* (Cambridge 1969)

Moloney, J. A., *With Captain Stairs to Katanga* (1893)

Neuville, D. & Bréard, C., *Les Voyages de Savorgnan de Brazza: Ogooué et Congo 1875–1882* (Paris 1884)

Ney, Napoléon, *Conférences et lettres de P. de Savorgnan de Brazza sur trois explorations effectués dans l'Ouest Africa 1876–1885* (Paris 1887)

Oswell, Edward, *William Cotton Oswell, Hunter and Explorer*, 2 vols (1900)

Overberghe, Van & de Jonghe, *Les Bangala* (Brussels 1907)

Parke, Thomas H., *My Personal Experiences in Equatorial Africa* (1891)

Parke, Thomas H., *Guide to Health in Africa* (1893)

Perham, Margery, ed., *The Diaries of Lord Lugard*, 2 vols (1959)

Peschuel-Loesche, *Kongoland* (Jena 1886)

Peters, Carl, *New Light on Dark Africa* (1891)

Peters, Carl, *Die Deutsch Emin Pascha Expedition* (Berlin 1910)

Pinto, Serpa, *How I Crossed Africa*, 2 vols (1881)

Puleston, Fred, *African Drums* (1930)

Reeves, J., *The International Beginnings of the Congo Free State* (Baltimore 1894)

Rodd, Sir J. Rennell, *Social and Diplomatic Memoirs 1884–1893* (1922)

Ross, Emory, *Out of Africa* (N.Y. 1936)

Schendel, Theodore van, *Au Congo avec Stanley en 1879* (Brussels 1932)

Schmidt, R., *Geschichte des Araberaufstanden in Ost-Afrika* (Frankfurt, n.d.)

Schweinfurth, Georg, *The Heart of Africa*, 2 vols (N.Y. 1874)

Schweinfurth, Georg, with F. Ratzel, R. W. Felkin & G. Hartland, eds, *Emin Pasha in Central Africa* (1888)

Schweitzer, G., *Emin Pasha, his life and work*, 2 vols (1898)

Schynse, Père, *A Travers l'Afrique avec Stanley et Emin-Pascha* (Paris 1890)

Scott-Keltie, J., *The Partition of Africa* (1893)

Shukry, M. F., ed., *Equatoria under Egyptian Rule: the Unpublished Correspondence of Colonel (later Major-General) C. G. Gordon with Ismail Khedive of Egypt and the Sudan 1874–76* (1953)

Sievers, Wilhelm, *Afrika: eine allgemeine landeskunde* (Leipzig & Vienna 1891)

Smith, Henry Nash & Gibson, William M., eds, *Correspondence of Samuel L. Clemens and William Dean Howells 1872–1910* (Cambridge, Mass. 1960)

Stanhope, Aubrey, *On the Track of the Great* (1914)

Stanley, Richard & Neame, Alan, eds, *The Exploration Diaries of H. M. Stanley* (1961)

Stevens, Thomas, *Scouting for Stanley in East Africa* (1890)

Stuhlmann, Franz, *Mit Emin Pascha ins Herz von Afrika* (Berlin 1894)

Stuhlmann, Franz, ed, *Die Tagebücher von Dr Emin Pascha*, 6 vols (Hamburg 1916–27)

Swann, Alfred J., *Fighting the Slave Hunters in Central Africa* (1910)

Thomson, J. B., *Joseph Thomson, African Explorer* (1896)

Thomson, Joseph, *To the Central African Lakes and Back*, 2 vols (1881)

Thonner, Franz, *Dans la Grand Forêt de l'Afrique Centrale* (Brussels 1899)

Thys, A., *Au Congo et Kasai* (Brussels 1888)

Troup, Rose, *With Stanley's Rearguard* (1890)

Vizetelly, E. H., *From Cyprus to Zanzibar by the Egyptian Delta* (1901)

Wack, H., *The Story of the Congo Free State* (1905)

Ward, Herbert, *Five Years with the Congo Cannibals* (1890)

Ward, Herbert, *My Life with Stanley's Rearguard* (1891)

Ward, Herbert, *A Voice from the Congo* (N.Y. 1910)

Wauters, A. J., *Histoire Politique du Congo Belge* (Brussels 1911)

Wauters, A. J., *Stanley's Emin Pasha Expedition* (1890)

Weeks, John, *Among Congo Cannibals* (1913)

Weeks, John, *Among the Primitive Bakongo* (1914)

Werner, J. R., *A Visit to Stanley's Rearguard* (1890)

Wilkins, W. H., *The Romance of Isabel Lady Burton*, 2 vols (1897)

Wilson, C. T. & Felkin, R. W., *Uganda and the Egyptian Sudan*, 2 vols (1882)

Wissmann, H. W. von, *In Inners Afrikas* (Leipzig 1891)

Young, John Russell, *Around the World with General Grant*, 2 vols (N.Y. 1879)

Yule, H. & Hyndman, H. M., *Mr Henry Morton Stanley and the Royal Geographical Society: Being the Record of a Protest* (1878)

4. Secondary sources: books (articles in learned journals are cited in the notes)

Alpers, Edward A., *Ivory and Slaves: Changing Patterns of International Trade in East Central Africa to the late Nineteenth Century* (Berkeley 1975)

Amin, Samir, *Unequal Development* (N.Y. 1976)

Anstey, R. T., *Britain and the Congo in the Nineteenth Century* (Oxford 1962)

Arens, William, *The Man Eating Myth* (1979)

Ascherson, Neil, *The King Incorporated* (1963)

Bachelor, John & Julie, *In Stanley's Footsteps* (1990)

Barnes, T. Alexander, *The Wonderland of the Eastern Congo* (1922)

Beachey, R. W., *The Slave Trade of East Africa* (1976)

Bennett, Norman R., *Studies in East African History* (Boston 1963)

Bennett, Norman R., *Arab versus European, Diplomacy and War in Nineteenth Century East Central Africa* (N.Y. 1986)

Benson, A. C., *The Leaves of the Tree* (1911)

Birmingham, David & Martin, Phyllis M., *History of Central Africa*, 2 vols (1983)

Blohm, Wilhelm, *Die Nyamwezi: Land und Wirtschaft* (Hamburg 1931)

Boahen, A. Adu, ed., *General History of Africa, Vol 7: Africa under Colonial Domination* (1985)

Bontinck, François, *Aux origines de l'Etat Indépendant du Congo* (Paris 1966)

Bott, A., *Our Fathers 1870–1900* (1931)

Brode, Heinrich, *Tippu Tib* (1906)

Brom, John L., *Sur les traces de Stanley* (Paris 1958)

Brousseau, Georges, *Souvenirs de la mission Savorgnan de Brazza* (Paris 1925)

Brunschwig, H., *Brazza l'explorateur, L'Ogooue, 1875–79* (Paris 1966)

Brunschwig, H., *French Colonialism 1871–1914: Myths and Realities* (1966)

Buchler, Max., *Der Kongostaat Leopolds II*, 2 vols (Zurich 1912)

Ceulemans, P., *La question arabe et le Congo 1883–1892* (Brussels 1959)

Chambrun, General de, *Brazza* (Paris 1930)

Collins, Robert O., *The Southern Sudan 1883–1898, a struggle for control* (Yale 1962)

Collins, Robert O., *King Leopold, England and the Upper Nile* (Yale 1968)

Coquery-Vidrovitch, Catherine, *Brazza et la prise de possession du Congo* (Paris 1969)

Cornet, R. J., *La bataille du rail* (Brussels 1953)

Coupland, Reginald, *The Exploitation of East Africa 1856–1890* (1939)

Courcel, G. de, *L'Influence de la Conférence de Berlin de 1885 sur le Droit Colonial International* (1935)

Crewe, Marquess of, *Lord Rosebery*, 2 vols (1931)

Crummery, Donald, *Banditry, Rebellion and Social Protest in Africa* (1986)

Curtin, Philip, ed., *Africa and the West* (Madison 1972)

Cuypers, J. P., *Alphonse Vangele 1848–1939* (Brussels 1960)

Daye, P., *Leopold II* (Paris 1934)

Daye, P., *Stanley* (Paris 1936)

Dieu, L., *Dans la brousse congolaise* (Liège 1946)

Duignan, Peter & Gann, L. H., *The United States and Africa* (Cambridge 1984)

Edel, Leon, *Henry James, The Master 1901–1916* (1972)

Ellis, John, *The Social History of the Machine Gun* (N.Y. 1975)

Emerson, Barbara, *Leopold II of the Belgians: King of Colonialism* (1979)

Etherington, Norman, *Theories of Imperialism: War, Conquest and Capital* (1984)

Fallers, Lloyd E., ed., *The King's Men* (1964)

Filippi, Filippo de, *Ruwenzori: an account of the expedition of HRH Luigi Amadeo of Savoy* (1909)

Fisher, Ruth F., *Twilight Tales of the Black Baganda* (1912)

Forbath, Peter, *The River Congo* (1978)

Forde, Daryll, *Ethnographic Survey of Africa* (1957)

Galbraith, J. S., *Mackinnon and East Africa 1878–95* (1972)

Gann, L. H. & Duignan, Peter, *The Rulers of Belgian Africa 1884–1914* (Princeton 1979)

Gardiner, A. G., *The Life of Sir William Harcourt*, 2 vols (1913)

Garvin, T. L., *The Life of Joseph Chamberlain* (1933)

Geluwe, H. van, *Les Bira* (Tervuren 1956)

Geluwe, H. van, *The Bali* (1960)

Gibbs, J. L., ed., *Peoples of Africa* (1965)

Gould, Tony, *In Limbo* (1978)

Gray, R. A., *A History of the Southern Sudan 1839–1889* (1961)

Gutkind, Peter & Wallerstein, Immanuel, eds, *The Political Economy of Contemporary Africa* (Beverly Hills 1976)

Halet, Jean-Pierre, *Pygmy Kitabu* (N.Y. 1973)

Hallin, Joseph, *Les Ababua* (Brussels 1910)

Hansen, Holger Bent, *Mission, Church and State in a Colonial Setting* (1984)

Harker, George, *The Life of George Grenfell, Congo Missionary and Explorer* (1909)

Harman, Nicholas, *Bwana Stokesi and his African Conquests* (1986)

Harms, Robert W., *River of Wealth, River of Sorrow: the Central Zaire basin in the era of the slave and ivory trade 1500–1891* (Yale 1981)

Headrick, Daniel, *The Tools of Empire* (1981)

Healey, Edna, *Lady Unknown: the Life of Angela Burdett-Coutts* (1978)

Hellinga, Gerben, *Henry Morton Stanley. Een Individualpsychologische Interpretatie* (1978)

Holt, Peter M., *The Mahdist State in the Sudan 1881–1898. A Study of its Origins, Development and Overthrow* (Oxford 1970)

Hutchinson, G. S., *Machine Guns: their history and technical employment* (1938)

Inglis, Brian, *Roger Casement* (1973)

Jephson, Maurice Denham, *An Anglo-Irish Miscellany: some records of the Jephsons of Mallow* (Dublin 1964)

Jones, Emyr Wyn, *Sir Henry M. Stanley: the Enigma* (Denbigh 1989)

Jones, Roger, *The Rescue of Emin Pasha* (1972)

Julien, A., *Les Constructeurs de la France d'Outre Mer* (Paris 1946)

Karl, Friedrich R., *Joseph Conrad. The Three Lives* (N.Y. 1979)

Katoke, Israel K., *The Karagwe Kingdom* (Nairobi 1975)

Keith, A. B., *The Belgian Congo and the Berlin Act* (Oxford 1919)

Klein, Martin & Johnson, G. Wesley, eds, *Perspectives on the African Past* (Boston 1977)

Konigk, G., *Die Berliner Congo Konferenz 1884–85* (Essen 1938)

Lagergren, David, *Mission and State in the Congo* (Uppsala 1970)

Langer, E. G., *The Diplomacy of Imperialism* (N.Y. 1972)

Lederer, André, *Histoire de la navigation au Congo* (Tervuren 1965)

Lejeune, L., ed., *Le Vieux Congo* (Brussels 1930)

Lichterwelde, Count L. de, *Leopold II* (Brussels 1926)

Lodge, Sir Oliver, *Convictions of Survival. Two discourses in memory of F. W. H. Myers* (1930)

Louis, William Roger, *Ruanda-Urundi 1884–1919* (Oxford 1963)

Louis, William Roger, *Imperialism at Bay 1941–45* (Oxford 1977)

Louis, William Roger, ed., *Imperialism: the Robinson and Gallagher Controversy* (1976)

Louis, William Roger & Stengers, Jean, *E. D. Morel's History of the Congo Reform Movement* (Oxford 1968)

Luck, Anne, *Charles Stokes in Africa* (Nairobi 1972)

Luwel, M., *Sir Francis de Winton* (1964)

Luwel, M., *H. M. Stanley, H. H. Johnston et le Congo* (Tervuren 1978)

MacGaffey, Wyatt, *Custom and Government in the Lower Congo* (Berkeley 1970)

MacGaffey, Wyatt, *Religion and Society in Central Africa. The Bakongo of Lower Zaire* (Chicago 1986)

Mackenzie, Norman, ed., *The Letters of Sidney and Beatrice Webb*, 2 vols (1978)

Maes, J. & Boone, O., *Les peuplades du Congo Belge* (Brussels 1935)

Malcolm, D. W., *Sukumaland* (1953)

Malherbe, V. C., *Eminent Victorians in South Africa* (1972)

Marsh, Zoe & Kingsworth, G. W., *An Introduction to the History of East Africa* (Cambridge 1957)

Masoin, F., *Histoire de l'Etat Indépendant du Congo*, 2 vols (Namur 1912)

Masson, P., *Marseille et la colonisation française* (1905)

Mazenot, Georges, *La Likouala-Mossaka. Histoire de la Pénétration du Haut Congo 1878–1920* (Paris 1970)

Meesen, J. M., *Ituri* (Brussels 1951)

Meyer, Bernard, *Joseph Conrad. A Psychoanalytic Biography* (Princeton 1967)

Miers, Suzanne & Kopytoff, Igor, eds, *Slavery in Africa. Historical and Anthropological Perspectives* (Madison 1977)

Mill, R. H., *The Record of the Royal Geographical Society 1830–1930* (1930)

Miller, Charles, *The Lunatic Express* (1971)

Miller, Joseph C., ed., *The African Past Speaks: Essays on Oral Tradition and History* (Folkestone 1980)

Mommsen, Wolfgang J. & Osterhammel, Jurgen, eds., *Imperialism and After* (1986)

Monnier, L. & Williams, J. C., *Les Provinces du Congo. Structure et Fonctionnement. Vol. 2: Sud-Kasai, Hele, Kongo Central* (Leopoldville 1964)

Moorehead, Alan, *The White Nile* (1964)

Muller, F. F., *Deutschland–Zanzibar–Ostafrika* (Berlin 1959)

Oliver, Roland, *Sir Harry Johnston and the Scramble for Africa* (1957)

Oliver, Roland, *Six Unpublished Letters of H. M. Stanley to H. H. Johnston* (Brussels 1957)

Pachai, Bridghal, ed., *Livingstone, Man of Africa* (1972)

Packard, Randall M., *Chiefship and Cosmology* (Indiana 1981)

Perham, Margery, *Lugard: The Years of Adventure* (1956)

Pinto, F. Latour da Veiga, *Le Portugal et le Congo au XIXe siècle* (Paris 1972)

Plekhanov, G., *Selected Philosophical Works*, 5 vols (Moscow 1976)

Puschinger, Heinrich Ritter, *Furst Bismarck und Seine Hamburger Freunde* (Hamburg 1903)

Ransford, Oliver, *Livingstone: The Dark Interior* (1978)

Ravieri, L., *Relations entre l'Etat Indépendant du Congo et l'Italie* (Brussels 1959)

Reefe, Thomas Q., *The Rainbow and the Kings: A History of the Luba Empire to 1891* (Berkeley 1981)

Ricciardi, Lorenzo & Mirella, *African Rainbow* (1989)

Roberts, Andrew, ed., *Tanzania before 1900* (Nairobi 1968)

Robinson, Ronald & Gallagher, John, *Africa and the Victorians: The Official Mind of Imperialism*, 2nd ed. (1981)

Roeykens, P. A., *Les débuts de l'oeuvre africaine de Leopold II, 1876–1879* (Brussels 1955)

Roeykens, P. A., *Le dessein africain de Leopold II* (Brussels 1956)

Roeykens, P. A., *La période initiale de l'oeuvre africaine de Leopold II, 1875–1883* (Brussels 1957)

Roeykens, P. A., *La politique religieuse de l'Etat Indépendant du Congo* (Brussels 1965)

Rotberg, Robert I., *Africa and its Explorers* (Harvard 1970)

Rotberg, Robert I., *Joseph Thomson and the Exploration of Africa* (1971)

Rutherford, J., *Sir George Grey* (1961)

St Moulin, L. de, *Panorama de l'histoire contemporaine* (Leopoldville 1963)

Salomon, Pierre, *Le Voyage de van Kerkhoven aux Stanley Falls et au camp de Yambuya 1888* (Brussels 1978)

Sanderson, G. N., *England, Europe and the Upper Nile 1882–1899* (Edinburgh 1965)

Sautter, Gilles, *De l'Atlantique au fleuve Congo*, 2 vols (Paris 1966)

Schébesta, P., *Les Pygmées du Congo Belge* (Brussels 1952)

Seitz, Don C., *The James Gordon Bennetts* (Indianapolis 1928)

Shepperson, G., *The Exploration of Africa in the Eighteenth and Nineteenth Centuries* (Edinburgh 1971)

Sherry, Norman, *Conrad's Western World* (1971)

Shorter, Aylward, *Chiefship in Western Tanzania: a Political History of the Kimbu* (1972)

Simpson, Donald, *Dark Companions* (1975)

Slade, Ruth M., *English-Speaking Missions in the Congo Independent State 1878–1908* (Brussels 1959)

Slade, Ruth M., *King Leopold's Congo* (1962)

Smith, Henry Nash & Gibson, William, eds, *The Correspondence of Samuel L. Clemens and William D. Howells 1872–1910* (Cambridge, Mass. 1960)

Smith, Iain R., *The Emin Pasha Relief Expedition 1886–1890* (Oxford 1972)

Soret, Marcel, *Les Kongo Nord-Occidentaux* (Paris 1951)

Stigand, C. H., *Equatoria, the Lado Enclave* (1923)

Taylor, A. J. P., *Germany's First Bid for Colonies* (1938)

Taylor, A. J. P., *The Struggle for Mastery in Europe* (1954)

Taylor, A. J. P., *Essays in English History* (1976)

Taylor, Stephen, *The Mighty Nimrod. A Life of Frederick Courtenay Selous, African Hunter and Adventurer 1851–1917* (1989)

Thomson, R. S., *Fondation de l'Etat Indépendant du Congo* (Brussels 1933)

Tournai, F. C. de, *La rivalité de Brazza et de Stanley* (Louvain 1963)

Trilles, R. P., *Les Pygmées de la Forêt Equatoriale* (Paris 1932)

Turnbull, Colin M., *The Forest People* (N.Y. 1962)

Vansina, Jan, *Kingdoms of the Savanna* (Madison 1966)

Vansina, Jan, *Introduction à l'Ethnographie du Congo* (Brussels 1966)

Vansina, Jan, *The Tio Kingdom of the Middle Congo 1880–1892* (1973)

Vansina, Jan, *Oral Tradition in History* (Wisconsin 1985)

Wassermann, Jakob, *Bula Matari* (1932)

Wauters, A. J., *Le Congo au point de vue économique* (Brussels 1956)

Witte, Baron J. de, *Les Deux Congo* (Paris 1913)

Yarnall, H. E., *The Great Powers and the Congo Conference 1884 and 1885* (Gottingen 1934)

Younger, Edward, *John A Kasson: Politics and Diplomacy from Lincoln to McKinley* (Iowa 1955)

Zuyler, P. van, *L'Echiquier Congolais ou le secret du roi* (Brussels 1959)

· INDEX ·

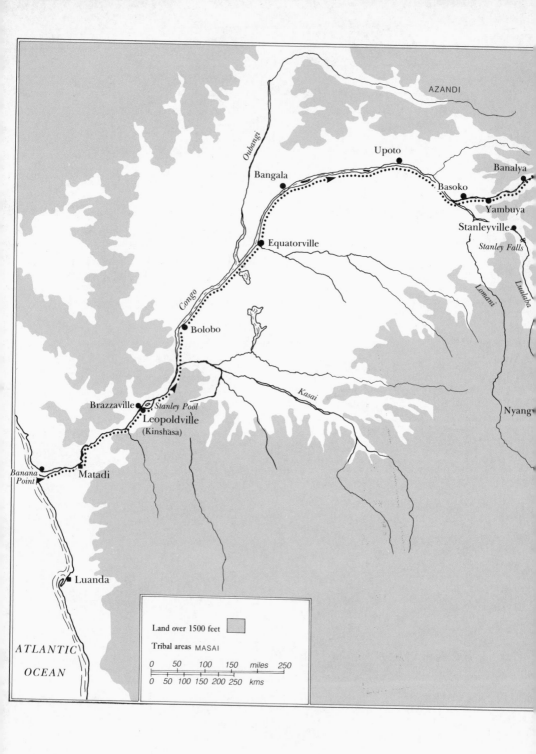

AZANDI

Upoto

Bangala

Banalya

Basoko

Yambuya

Stanleyville

Stanley Falls

Oubangi

Equatorville

Congo

Lomani

Lualaba

Bolobo

Nyang

Kasai

Brazzaville

Stanley Pool

Leopoldville
(Kinshasa)

*Banana
Point*

Matadi

Luanda

Land over 1500 feet

Tribal areas MASAI

| 0 | 50 | 100 | 150 | miles | 250 |

| 0 | 50 | 100 | 150 | 200 | 250 | kms |

*ATLANTIC
OCEAN*